A VOLUME IN THE CENSUS MONOGRAPH SERIES

THE FERTILITY
OF AMERICAN WOMEN

by

WILSON H. GRABILL
Bureau of the Census

CLYDE V. KISER
Milbank Memorial Fund

PASCAL K. WHELPTON
Scripps Foundation
Miami University

for the
SOCIAL SCIENCE RESEARCH COUNCIL
in cooperation with the
U. S. DEPARTMENT OF COMMERCE
BUREAU OF THE CENSUS

JOHN WILEY & SONS, INC., NEW YORK
CHAPMAN & HALL, LIMITED, LONDON

Copyright © 1958

BY

THE SOCIAL SCIENCE RESEARCH COUNCIL

———————

Library of Congress Catalog Card Number: 58–7899

PRINTED IN THE UNITED STATES OF AMERICA

FOREWORD

The statistical results compiled by the Bureau of the Census constitute a tremendous mass of detailed information about the population of the United States and its characteristics and economic activities. To meet the requirements of government agencies, business concerns, and investigators of social problems and to satisfy the needs of individual citizens, facts must be gathered and published, showing the distribution of the population in each large and small political unit with respect to age, sex, color, marital status, occupation, income, education, national origin, and other characteristics. This information provides the basis for apportionment of representatives in Congress, for answering many questions by direct reference, and for formulating many plans, at least in preliminary form.

It is the first business of the Bureau of the Census to put into print the census results that directly answer as many such questions as possible. Along with these results, similar data from one or two previous censuses are usually included. Limitations of time, space, and money prevent any extensive statement of the relations between particular results, the long-term trends of significant totals and subtotals, the shifting proportions of the people belonging to different categories, and various interesting and important relations such as those between income, occupation, and age. It is not that the Bureau of the Census fails in any sense to appreciate the value and need for such analyses, but rather that it must concentrate on its basic concern with the summary statistics that constitute its unique contribution to knowledge.

When plans for the 1950 Census were made, the need for more extensive analysis was recognized and a series of census monographs similar to those issued after the 1920 Census was proposed. Because of the pressures caused by the depression in the early 1930's and by defense and war in the early 1940's, plans for monographs based on those censuses could not be carried out. Late in the 1940's interested persons from business, research, and government agencies expressed the need for a series that would provide analyses of the most significant results of the 1950 Census. The Social Science Research Council, with the assistance of Russell Sage Foundation, took the lead in stimulating the formulation of suitable plans and in June 1950 appointed a Committee on Census Monographs to cooperate with the Bureau in organizing this project. The members of the Committee are:

Ralph G. Hurlin, Russell Sage Foundation (Chairman)

Robert W. Burgess, formerly Western Electric Company, since February 1953 Director of the Bureau of the Census

John D. Durand, United Nations

Ernest M. Fisher, Columbia University

F. F. Hill, Cornell University

Frederick F. Stephan, Princeton University

Conrad Taeuber, Bureau of the Census

Ralph J. Watkins, Dun & Bradstreet, Inc.

Paul Webbink, Social Science Research Council

J. Frederic Dewhurst, Twentieth Century Fund, and William F. Ogburn, University of Chicago, were members of the Committee during the first year and a half.

It is essential in any sound census monograph program to obtain the cooperation of authors with a broad understanding not only of the statistical information provided by the regular tabulations of the current census but also of the results of earlier censuses and other relevant knowledge and points of view from other sources and even from other countries. The preparation of a monograph should include broad exploration of new questions suggested by the new information, as well as narrowing the elements of doubt and controversy on old questions. The Social Science Research Council Committee early undertook, in consultation with leading figures in various professional fields, to develop a suggested list of monograph titles and authors and persuaded experts in the subject areas selected to undertake the preparation of memoranda outlining and discussing the topics proposed. Then, in 1951, arrangements were made for continuing cooperation between the Committee and the Bureau concerning the selection of topics, proposals of authors and consultants, and editorial supervision.

Throughout the conduct of the project there has been close collaboration with a number of interested Federal agencies and with universities and research organizations, which provided staff and facilities to help bring the project to completion. They and the Council, which also obtained necessary funds from the Rockefeller and Russell Sage Foundations, provided assistance without which the monographs could not have been prepared.

The task of preparing monographs is an essential part of the broad function of making the information secured by censuses fully available to satisfy the needs and interests of the community and to constitute a broad base for further studies in the social sciences. As Director of the Census and President of the Social Science Research Council, respectively, we wish to record our full approval of the monograph project. It is not implied, of course, that the views expressed in these reports are necessarily those of the Bureau of the Census, the Department of Commerce, or the

Social Science Research Council. The views are those of the individual authors, each of whom has been given the freedom to interpret available materials in the light of his technical knowledge and competence. This freedom of the individual authors is an essential element in making the most useful analyses and interpretations generally available to the community.

ROBERT W. BURGESS, DIRECTOR
BUREAU OF THE CENSUS

PENDLETON HERRING, PRESIDENT
SOCIAL SCIENCE RESEARCH COUNCIL

PREFACE

This book is about human fertility in the United States. It is concerned with trends in reproduction since Colonial times. It is also concerned with past and present variations in fertility rates by such factors as geographic and urban-rural residence, color, nativity, and age, and a variety of indicators of socio-economic status, such as occupation, education, income, and monthly rental value of the home.

Being a census monograph, this book is based mainly on census data, and more particularly on those of 1910, 1940, and 1950, concerning average number of children ever born and average number of children under 5 years old in relation to factors of the type listed above. However, the book is not restricted to census materials. Much use is made of the birth registration data (as, for example, in Chapter 9) and of special studies, such as those concerning the prevalence and effectiveness of contraceptive practice, the role of religion in family size, and the bearing of social and psychological factors on fertility.

Although the three authors did much team work in the preparation of this monograph, each one is responsible for certain chapters: Mr. Grabill is primarily responsible for Chapters 2 to 4, 8, and 10 and Appendix A, which include the description of historical trends in fertility, variations in fertility by residence, nativity, and ethnic groups, trends in marriage in relation to fertility, and the outlook for fertility; Dr. Kiser has chief responsibility for Chapters 1 and 5 to 7 on fertility differentials by occupation, education, and other socio-economic variables; and Professor Whelpton is responsible for Chapter 9 on cohort fertility and Appendix B. Chapter 11 was jointly prepared.

We are indebted, first of all, to the many people who have contributed to the collection and tabulation of the census data and other materials that have been utilized, to the Census Bureau and the Social Science Research Council for their planning of the census monograph series, and to the Population Council and the Milbank Memorial Fund for their grants which made it possible to secure the special fertility tabulations from the 1950 Census.

We wish to thank Dr. Conrad Taeuber for his constructive review of the entire manuscript and invaluable suggestions. Thanks are also due to Dr. Paul Webbink of the Social Science Research Council for reviewing the plans and the text, to Mrs. Mildred Russell of the Bureau of the Census for the editorial preparation of the manuscript and the tables for printing,

and to Miss Madeline R. Barry of the Milbank Memorial Fund for the final
tracing of most of the charts in the monograph.

For the great help that has been given at all stages of the project we
thank our colleagues in our respective offices. Any shortcomings in this
study are, of course, the authors' responsibility.

Mr. Grabill is indebted to Dr. Paul C. Glick and Dr. Henry S. Shryock,
Jr., for their invaluable advice on his part of the monograph and for ena-
bling him to devote the necessary time. He owes much to Mrs. Leah S.
Anderson for her many editorial contributions to the text and for her work
on the preparation of the tables. Thanks are also due to Mr. Calvin L.
Beale and Mrs. Helen R. White for their help some years ago in the collection of the historical materials.

Dr. Kiser is grateful to Dr. Frank G. Boudreau for his cooperation in
this project. He owes special thanks to Mrs. Adrienne Haine for her general statistical assistance and to Mrs. Sally Fettman and Miss Rose Schrei-
bersdorf for their help with the tables and manuscript.

Professor Whelpton's chapter is based on an intensive study of cohort
fertility by the Scripps Foundation for Research in Population Problems,
which study began in 1945 and is still in progress. The rates for native
white women in this chapter come from revised cohort fertility tables prepared by Mrs. Ruth W. Smith and Mrs. Evangelyn D. Minnis under the
direction of Professor Whelpton, with assistance from Dr. Norman B.
Ryder (formerly on the Foundation's staff). Their arduous and painstaking
work is deeply appreciated, as is the constructive review of the manuscript
of Chapter 9 by Mr. Arthur A. Campbell, Assistant Director of the Scripps
Foundation.

If this monograph is useful to future authors of census monographs, we
will feel that our debt to our predecessors will have been partially repaid.

WILSON H. GRABILL
CLYDE V. KISER
PASCAL K. WHELPTON

May 1958

C O N T E N T S

C H A P T E R   1

INTRODUCTION

The history of our country coincides in time with that of a tremendous upsurge in world population. According to the best estimates available, the population of the world was about one-half billion in 1650 and was still under one billion (836 million) in 1800—150 years later. Since then the curve of growth has risen sharply. The number of people reached about 1.6 billion in 1900—almost twice the 1800 figure—and is now about 2.7 billion. In short, world population has increased fivefold since 1650, and if the rate of the last 5 years is maintained, it will more than double between the years 1950 and 2000.

Even within the setting of large increases in world population, the population growth of the United States has been outstanding, because the process has been the peopling of a rich, empty country. It has been estimated that before the white settlers came, there were only about one million aborigines in the whole of what is now the United States and Canada.[1] Whatever the exact size of the Indian population may have been, the colonists initiated the great population growth. Since the first settlers were few in number, their *rates* of increase were frequently very high although the absolute increments were fairly small.

In this connection it may be recalled that one of the complaints lodged against the King of England in the Declaration of Independence was:

He has endeavored to prevent the population of these States; for that purpose obstructing the Laws of Naturalization of Foreigners; refusing to pass others to encourage their migration hither and raising the conditions of New Appropriations of Lands.

Since Thomas Jefferson, the chief author of the Declaration of Independence, was also an astute observer of population trends, it seems likely that the aforementioned complaint was directed against "obnoxious legislation" rather than any real "prevention of population." Benjamin Franklin had called attention earlier to the more rapid increase of population in the Colonies than in England.

Whatever may have been the attitudes of Jefferson and Franklin toward

---

[1] Carr-Saunders has stated, "The size of the aboriginal population [in North America] before the arrival of white men has often been exaggerated; but the figure of one million for the United States and Canada, adopted by Willcox, now meets with general acceptance." See A. M. Carr-Saunders, *World Population*, The Clarendon Press, Oxford, 1936, p. 32.

colonial population trends, the total population of the newly formed United States of America was a little less than 4 million at the time of our first census in 1790.   Growth thereafter was rapid indeed.   The population increased to 5.3 million in 1800, it was 23.2 million in 1850, 76 million in 1900, and is now about 170 million.[2]

The components of population change in any area are fertility, mortality, immigration, and emigration.   In the case of the United States, the area itself has increased from one restricted to the Atlantic Seaboard to one that stretches westward to the Pacific.

As for mortality we may simply note here that, despite the rigors of frontier life, the levels of living and the health conditions in early America were much better on the average than in Europe.   One reason is that the population here was predominantly rural and hence not so subject to contagious and infectious diseases as the more urban people of Europe. Partly for this reason and partly because of the youthfulness of the population, the mortality rates stayed well below fertility rates.

As in other countries of the Western Hemisphere, and in Australia and New Zealand, the population history of the United States has been heavily influenced by immigration.   Even within the setting of the "new world," the experience of our country has been unique with respect to both volume of immigration and ethnic diversity.   Warren S. Thompson has stated:

> . . . between 1820 . . . and 1950 about 39,325,000 immigrants entered the country. Of course, not all of these remained permanently, but probably not far from 32 million remained here and were incorporated into our national life.   This is the largest movement of immigrants into any country known to history, and considering the conditions now prevailing in the world, is not likely to be surpassed in the near future.[3]

The story of immigration to this country and of the resulting ethnic diversity is a fascinating one and is told in another census monograph.[4]

As indicated in the preface, this book is concerned with another component of population growth in this country, that of fertility.   The "new world" conditions that made this country attractive to immigrants also made it conducive to high fertility and large families.   The powerful impact of high fertility on population growth and composition by nativity may be appreciated when it is realized that the population of the American Colonies probably was predominantly native long before the Revolutionary War.   The "foreign-born" status of immigrants, of course, lasts only one generation; it is not cumulative from one generation to the next.   However, it may also be noted that even during the heavy immigration period pre-

---

[2] For a separate census monograph on this subject, see Conrad Taeuber and Irene B. Taeuber, *The Changing Population of the United States*, John Wiley and Sons, New York, 1958.

[3] Warren S. Thompson, *Population Problems* (Fourth Edition), McGraw-Hill Book Company, New York, 1953, p. 277.

[4] E. P. Hutchinson, *Immigrants and Their Children, 1850–1950*, John Wiley and Sons, New York, 1956.

ceding World War I (1910–13), the annual natural increase was one and a half to five times larger than the net immigration.[5]

In broad perspective the fertility history of the United States is one of a transition from large families to small families. From 1810 to 1940 there was a virtually uninterrupted decline in the ratio of young children to women. This decline often has been described as an accompaniment to the transition from rural and agricultural to urban and nonagricultural life and livelihood. In the new urban environment, the family was no longer an economic unit, and children tended to be regarded as increasing the family's expenses rather than its income. This does not mean that there has been no decline in rural fertility. A considerable part of the decline in the country as a whole is attributable to the decrease in the fertility of rural families.

Fundamentally the long decline in fertility during the nineteenth century and the early part of the twentieth century was prompted by desires for higher levels of living for self and for children and by the tangible evidence that levels of living could be further elevated. It was realized that there was a relation between size of family and level of living. The lowering of mortality levels, especially in the twentieth century, meant that it was no longer necessary to have a large number of babies in order to have a moderate number of them reach adulthood.

The prevalence of these new attitudes favoring reduced childbearing as a means of attaining a higher plane of living and the ability to implement them by family-planning presumably varied by urban-rural status and by various other characteristics including the socio-economic. In a sense, the timing and impact of the transition from high to low death and birth rates have differed not only by continent and country; they have varied within a given country. Geographic and cultural islands have served to shut off or postpone the currents of social change.

This book tells the story of the demographic impact of the economic depression. It describes the slump in both marriages and births during the 1930's and the pessimistic outlook at that time for population growth. It tells of the slow rise of the marriage and birth rates that accompanied the economic recovery and of the sharp increases during the period of defense preparation, the successive drafts, and the entrance of this country into the war. It recounts the unprecedented increases in marriages and births that followed demobilization and the evidence that the long downward trend in average size of completed families has at least been temporarily reversed.

The future course of population growth in this country probably will be determined mainly by the future trends in fertility. Yet, in modernized countries which have brought mortality under control and which have well-

---

[5] Warren S. Thompson and P. K. Whelpton, *Population Trends in the United States*, McGraw-Hill Book Company, New York, 1933, p. 301.

defined policies on immigration, the factor of fertility tends to be the least predictable of the three components of population growth.   Furthermore, with increases in the proportion of couples able to plan their families, it may be that fluctuations in the fertility rate will become more common than they have been in the past.   It is therefore highly important to learn as much as possible about the nature of the factors affecting trends and variations in human fertility.   It is hoped that this book will contribute toward that end and that it will help to illuminate the most promising next steps in research in this field.   The authors will consider that these purposes are at least partially served if the volume demonstrates the great value of collecting and tabulating adequate data on fertility in the decennial censuses.

CHAPTER 2

A LONG VIEW

A. The Colonial and early Federal periods

For more than two centuries, from the time of the first permanent settlements to the early decades of the nineteenth century, the fertility of the American people ranked among the world's highest. Estimates made by both contemporary and modern authorities, utilizing a variety of techniques and data, place the annual birth rate in the Colonial and early Federal periods at 50 to 57 births per 1,000 inhabitants. The women of completed fertility are variously estimated to have borne an average of eight children. According to Miller, the high American birth rate was sometimes cited for propaganda purposes before the Revolutionary War to indicate that it was only a question of time before the American population growth would shift the British Empire's balance of power westward.[1] Benjamin Franklin made this type of forecast himself.

Contemporary observations. The contemporary explanation for America's high fertility is illustrated by the following quotations.

In 1751, Benjamin Franklin wrote:

Tables of the proportion of Marriages to Births, of Deaths to Births, of Marriages to the number of inhabitants, &c., form'd on observations made upon the Bills of Mortality, Christenings, &c., of populous cities, will not suit countries; nor will tables form'd on observations made in full settled old countries, as *Europe*, suit new countries, as *America*.

2. For people increase in proportion to the number of marriages, and that is greater in proportion to the ease and convenience of supporting a family . . .

. . . which charges are greater in the cities, as Luxury is more common: many live single during life, and continue servants to families, journeymen to Trades, &c., hence cities do not by natural generation supply themselves with inhabitants; the deaths are more than the births.

4. In countries full settled, the case must be nearly the same; all Lands being occupied and improved to the heighth; those who cannot get land must labour for others that have it; when laborers are plenty, their wages will be low; by low wages a family is supported with difficulty; this difficulty deters many from marriage, who therefore long continue servants and single. Only as the Cities take supplies of people from the country, and thereby make a little more room in the country; Marriage is a little more encourag'd there, and the births exceed the deaths . . .

---

[1] John C. Miller, *Origins of the American Revolution,* Little, Brown and Company, Boston, 1943, pp. 433–435.

7. Hence, marriages in *America* are more general and more generally early, than in *Europe.* And if it is reckoned there, that there is but one marriage per annum among one hundred persons, perhaps we may here reckon two; and if in *Europe* they have but four Births to a marriage (many of their marriages being late) we may here reckon eight, of which one half grow up, and our marriages are made, reckoning one with another at twenty years of age our people must be at least doubled every twenty years.[2]

Thomas Jefferson in a letter to Count de Montmorin, dated July 1787, said:

A century's experience has shown that we double our numbers every twenty or twenty-five years. No circumstances can be foreseen, at this moment, which will lessen our rate of multiplication for centuries to come.

The Chevalier Félix de Beaujour, a former French consular official in the United States declared in 1814:

Every thing in the United States favours the progress of population; the emigrations from Europe, the disasters of the European colonies, but, above all, the abundance of the means of subsistence. Marriages are there easier than in Europe, births more multiplied, and deaths relatively less frequent. It is calculated that out of sixty individuals, two are married annually, that one is born out of every twenty, and that the proportion of deaths is only one in forty. This last report, founded on careful observations, seems incredible in a country so recently cleared and naturally not healthy; but it is nonetheless true, because it accords with the number of births, which there is greater than in Europe. In the United States, more children are necessarily born than among us, because the inhabitants, in such an extent of country, finding the means of subsistence more abundant, marry at an earlier age. No human consideration there operates as a hindrance to reproduction, and the children swarm on the rich land in the same manner as do insects.[3]

Beaujour's "observations" probably were based in part on estimates made by Samuel Blodget, which are reproduced in table 1 as an example of the work done in early times.[4]

Franklin's references to Europe seem to be based on an extensive investigation of parish records in several European countries by Süssmilch, a clergyman, who was much interested in population data and in the "laws"

---

[2] Benjamin Franklin, "Observations Concerning The Increase of Mankind, The Peopling of Countries, &c.," *The Magazine of History, with Notes and Quotes,* Extra Number, No. 63, 1755.

[3] Chevalier Félix de Beaujour, *Sketch of the United States of North America,* jointly published by several printing firms, London, 1814.

[4] Blodget probably made his estimates somewhat as follows: He began with data from the first two censuses of the United States (1790 and 1800) and figured the average annual percent increase in population (3 percent). This percent was then applied in a chain computation to obtain annual population estimates and annual amounts of numerical increase. From custom house and port records, Blodget secured data on "passengers arriving," and allowed for Americans returning from abroad, aliens in transit to Canada or here temporarily, etc. Subtraction of the (net) migration from annual population increase gave annual natural increase. From bills of mortality for a few communities and rural areas, Blodget estimated the national death rate to be "near 2½ percent." The estimated numbers of deaths are uniformly 2½ percent of the total population. The births seem to be a residual estimate, obtained by adding deaths to the estimated annual natural increase. The birth estimates are the only component of population growth shown to the last digit.

of population growth.[5] Franklin's remarks on urban and rural differences in marriages, etc., are evidently for Europe. Blodget's later data indicate that American cities around 1800 had about two births for every death (table 2). The population of America increased by about 35 percent in most decades from 1660 to 1790 (table 3). This corresponds to a doubling of population every 23 years.

TABLE 1.—ABSTRACT OF SAMUEL BLODGET'S ESTIMATES OF ANNUAL POPULATION INCREASE, BIRTHS, DEATHS, AND NET IMMIGRATION: 1790 TO 1805

[No correction has been made for errors in original table]

Year	Free persons	Slaves, increase yearly near 2 percent	Free blacks and persons of color	Annual migrations, free men and slaves	Births in each year, near 5 3/4 percent	Deaths in each year, near 2 1/2 percent	Total population, including Louisiana in the year 1804	Total increase each year, near 3 percent
1790	3,232,303	697,697	59,511	3,500	...	...	3,930,000	...
1791	3,333,761	714,139	63,500	4,000	215,900	101,000	4,047,900	117,900
1792	3,438,237	731,000	67,500	5,000	220,937	103,500	4,169,337	121,337
1793	3,446,417	748,000	71,600	3,600	227,680	107,100	4,294,417	125,180
1794	3,657,189	766,000	75,700	3,500	235,382	110,200	4,423,249	128,632
1795	3,771,946	784,000	79,800	3,900	242,197	113,400	4,555,946	132,697
1796	3,890,124	802,500	84,900	4,500	249,117	117,000	4,692,624	136,678
1797	4,012,902	820,500	89,900	3,500	257,516	120,300	4,833,402	140,776
1798	4,940,404	837,000	95,000	3,800	266,202	124,000	4,978,404	145,002
1799	4,273,756	854,000	100,600	4,000	273,334	128,000	5,127,756	149,352
1800	4,404,798	876,790	105,843	3,800	282,132	132,100	5,281,588	153,823
1801	4,544,300	898,300	110,800	4,000	290,712	136,200	5,440,100	158,512
1802	4,682,313	921,000	115,900	4,500	299,113	140,400	5,603,313	163,213
1803	4,727,412	944,000	121,900	3,900	308,749	144,550	5,771,412	168,099
1804	5,000,100	999,900	126,000	9,500	810,500	149,000	6,000,000	228,588
1805	5,156,000	1,024,900	131,000	...	321,000	153,000	6,180,000	180,000

Source: Samuel Blodget, *Economica, A Statistical Manual for the United States of America*, Washington, 1806, p. 58.

TABLE 2.—SAMUEL BLODGET'S VITAL RATES FOR VARIOUS LOCALITIES: CIRCA 1805

Area	Deaths per 100 births	Area	Population per death
Portsmouth, N. H.	50	Portsmouth, N. H.	48-49
Salem, Mass.	49-51	Salem, Mass.	48-49
Boston, Mass.	49-52	Boston, Mass.	47-49
Hartford, Conn.	48-49	Philadelphia, Pa.	44-50
Philadelphia, Pa.	51-54	Baltimore, Md.	43-49
Baltimore, Md.	51-53	Washington, D. C.	48-50
Washington, D. C.	50-51	Norfolk, Va.	40-47
Norfolk, Va.	52-54	Charleston, S. C.	35-40
Charleston, S. C.	55-60	Healthiest parts of Georgia	45-50
Healthiest parts of South Carolina and Georgia	45-49	New York State	44-50
New York City	51-53	Hartford, Conn.	50-55
		Rhode Island	50-56
Average for United States	49-51	Low grounds south of 38° N. latitude	34-39
		Average for United States	39-41

Source: Samuel Blodget, *Economica, A Statistical Manual for the United States of America*, Washington, 1806, pp. 75 and 76.

---

[5] Johann Peter Süssmilch, *Die göttliche Ordnung in den Veränderungen des menschlichen Geschlechts, aus der Geburt, dem Tode und der Fortpflanzung desselben erwiesen*, Berlin, 1741, and later editions. For an extended account in English, see Frederick S. Crum, "The Statistical Work of Süssmilch," *Quarterly Publications of the American Statistical Association*, Vol. VII, New Series, No. 55, September 1901.

TABLE **3.**—ESTIMATED POPULATION DURING COLONIAL AND CONTINENTAL PERIODS: 1610 TO 1790

Year	Number	Decennial increase, percent	Year	Number	Decennial increase, percent
1790	3,929,625	41.3	1690	213,500	37.2
1780	2,781,000	26.1	1680	155,600	35.9
1770	2,205,000	37.0	1670	114,500	35.0
1760	1,610,000	33.4	1660	84,800	64.0
1750	1,207,000	35.8	1650	51,700	85.0
1740	889,000	35.7	1640	27,947	390.3
1730	654,950	38.1	1630	5,700	128.1
1720	474,388	32.7	1620	2,499	1,090.0
1710	357,500	30.0	1610	210	...
1700	275,000	28.8			

Source: U. S. Bureau of the Census, *A Century of Population Growth in the United States, 1790-1900,* by W. S. Rossiter, pp. 9 and 10. Data based on estimates for separate Colonies made by a number of scholars who used tax lists, militia records, Colonial censuses, etc.

Fertility and migration. Although Franklin and some of his contemporaries spoke of the high rate of population growth in the American Colonies, they gave relatively little attention to the role played by migration of population from abroad. Bountiful natural increase was regarded as the main source of future growth. A birth rate of about 55 and a population of about 1,207,000 in 1750 meant about 66,000 births per year at that time, compared with annual net immigration amounting to perhaps 4,000. It is likely that annual births exceeded annual net immigration shortly after the initial settlements were made in the seventeenth century and that the proportion of the population that was native increased rapidly.[6] The steady rate of decennial population increase after 1660, in contrast to an irregular flow of immigration, suggests that natural increase predominated in population growth. Various Colonial censuses show a fair balance of males and females in the population, probably from natural increase, whereas seventeenth century European data on emigration to the New World indicate that males much outnumbered females. Some examples of sex ratios from Colonial censuses are shown in the accompanying table:

---

[6] Hypothetical computations can indicate something of the possibilities. One may assume, for illustrative purposes, (*a*) a constant flow of in-migration from year to year (the amount of immigration does not matter if one assumes an unchanging flow), (*b*) a sex ratio of 125 males per 100 females among the in-migrants, (*c*) an age distribution that places most of the immigrants within the young adult ages, (*d*) age-specific birth rates for women, of a level sufficient to yield a crude birth rate of 50 when applied to a population having an age-sex distribution similar to the one in the general population in 1800, and (*e*) mortality according to English life tables for 1838–1854.

The results of the computation indicate that within 10 years the annual number of births would be more than twice the annual number of immigrants. Within 20 years there would be more native- than European-born persons in the population. Thus, if the birth and death rates used were at all reasonable, there was a strong tendency for an early emergence of a large native population.

	Males per 100 females		Males per 100 females
New Hampshire:		Connecticut:	
1767	107.4	1774	93.2
1773	103.0	New York:	
		1698	108.3
Massachusetts:		1703	101.2
1754	104.5	1731	[1]136.5
1764	90.3	1737	103.8
		1771	106.8
Maine:		New Jersey:	
1764	103.3	1726	111.4
		1737	119.0
Rhode Island:		1745	102.8
1774	96.6		

[1] The high ratio in New York in 1731 reflected the presence of English soldiers and Indian braves in two towns; the ratios were much smaller in other parts of New York.

In 1790, if not at a much earlier date, the proportion of the population that was American born was over 90 percent as determined by computation. Further evidence of the existence of a largely native population appears in the 1820 Census which counted only 53,687 "foreigners not naturalized" in the population of 9,638,453. (Over half of these "foreigners" were in the State of New York.)

Lest what has just been said lead to an underevaluation of the very important role played by immigration, mention is made of the Beards' estimate that between 1600 and 1770 about 750,000 persons journeyed from Europe to America to seek a new way of life.[7] Others have estimated that migration to the New World prior to the Revolutionary War exceeded 2,000,000. There are several difficulties in using such data. Many of the out-migrants from Europe died enroute; others went to places such as Canada, the Caribbean, and South America. Many who came to North America found conditions not to their liking and returned to Europe. The numerous male immigrants sometimes died without progeny and in that sense proved to have been only temporary additions to the population. There were enough immigrants of the family type to account for the much larger population growth in America than in Canada or in the French and Spanish colonies.

One theory for the high fertility in Colonial times is that the women had little to say in such matters. According to Willison, it was a man's world.[8] Governor Bradford is quoted as indignantly denying a libel that women in New Plymouth had any new rights or privileges: "Touching our governemente, you are quite mistaken if you think we admite weomen . . .

---

[7] Charles A. and Mary R. Beard, *The Beards' Basic History of the United States,* Doubleday, Doran and Company, New York, 1944, p. 17.

[8] George F. Willison, *Saints and Strangers,* Reynal and Hitchcock, New York, 1945, p. 385.

to have to doe in the same, for they are excluded, as both reason and nature teacheth they should be." Willison says that more than one foreign
visitor noted that the women of New England were all "pittifully Tooth-
shaken" and apt to look much older than their years.

Fertility and household size. Although the women who reached
the end of the childbearing ages had an average of about eight children
ever born in Colonial and early Federal times, this did not necessarily
mean that the average household was very large. In 1790, the average
size of private households was 5.7 persons, or less than twice the size of
households in 1950, 3.4 persons (table 4). In 1790, there was an average
of 2.8 children (persons) under 16 years old per household, and in 1950
the average was 1.0 children of this age. The number of living children
per household was thus about three times as large in 1790 as in 1950.

TABLE 4.—PERCENT DISTRIBUTION OF HOUSEHOLDS, BY SIZE: 1790, 1900, AND 1950

Household size	Private households, 1790 (white and free colored)	Private households and quasi households, 1900	Occupied dwelling units, 1950	Household size	Private households, 1790 (white and free colored)	Private households and quasi households, 1900	Occupied dwelling units, 1950
Total........	100.0	100.0	100.0	7 persons..........	11.2	7.7	2.7
				8 persons..........	9.0	5.2	1.4
1 person...........	3.7	5.1	9.3	9 persons..........	6.5	3.2	0.8
2 persons..........	7.8	15.0	28.1	10 persons or more..	9.1	4.1	0.9
3 persons..........	11.7	17.6	22.8				
4 persons..........	13.8	16.9	18.4	Average number of persons............	5.7	4.6	3.4
5 persons..........	13.9	14.2	10.4				
6 persons..........	13.2	10.9	5.3				

Source: U. S. Bureau of the Census, *A Century of Population Growth in the United States, 1790-1900*, by W. S. Rossiter, p. 98; *1950 Census of Housing*, Vol. I, *General Characteristics*, Part 1, U. S. Summary, p. 8.

Infant mortality. What proportion of the high fertility in Colonial
and early Federal times was offset by high mortality among the children?
A very rough idea can be obtained thus: Tests indicate that a life table for
England and Wales in 1838–54 may fit fairly well the mortality conditions
in the United States around 1800.[9] According to this table, about 78 percent of the children born in a 5-year period would live to be enumerated
at the end of the period as children under 5 years old in a census, and
about 66 percent of newborn infants would live to the age of 20 years.
Applied to a rapidly growing population having an age-sex distribution
similar to the one existing in 1800, this mortality would result in as many

[9] Glover's life tables for white persons in the Original Death Registration Area in 1901 would yield
a crude death rate of about 16 if applied to a population having an age-sex distribution similar to that
of the white population in 1800. Obviously, this level of mortality is much too low if Blodget's estimate of about 25 for this time is correct. A similar computation, using Glover's life tables for Negroes
in the District of Columbia in 1901 as an example of very high mortality, would yield a crude death
rate of about 37. Interpolation between these two tables may be performed to obtain mortality rates
that would yield a crude death rate of about 25. The result is a life table with an expectation of life
of about 42 years for females and 39 years for males, or a table that closely resembles one for England and Wales in 1838–1854.

annual reports of deaths at ages under 20 years as at all later ages. This agrees with the little information on ages that was available in bills of mortality of the type seen by Franklin when he assumed that half of the children "grew up."

A discussion of mortality is incomplete without some mention of early American life tables such as the Wigglesworth life table of 1789 for Massachusetts and New Hampshire combined. These life tables were based on deaths alone, without adequate allowance for the age distribution of the population at risk of dying, and they underestimated the expectation of life if they included too many infant deaths in relation to adult deaths. The expectation of life at birth in the Wigglesworth table was 36 years. The earliest American life tables that take specific account of the population at risk of dying are the Kennedy life tables for Massachusetts and Maryland in 1850. The registration data used were of questionable reliability, however, and for this reason the life tables are of value mainly for checking on the applicability of the English life tables. The Massachusetts life tables yield an expectation of life at birth of 38.3 years for males and 40.5 years for females; for Maryland the corresponding figures are 41.8 for males and 44.9 for females. It is possible that the death rates really were larger in more urban Massachusetts than in less urban Maryland and thus did not necessarily reflect a more nearly complete registration in Massachusetts. Around 1850 Massachusetts was host to many thousands of immigrants who fled a serious potato famine in Ireland. These immigrants were crowded into slum areas with poor sanitation facilities.

Slaves. Early censuses obtained little detail on the characteristics of Negroes, many of whom were slaves. It may be inferred, nonetheless, that the Negroes were quite fertile. Despite high mortality and no appreciable immigration after 1790, the Negro population increased at an average rate of about 2.5 percent per year between 1790 and 1870. Fertility data for rural-farm Negro women 70 to 74 years old in the 1910 Census indicate an average of seven to eight births in a lifetime. Most of these women were slaves during a major part of their childbearing years. The early available ratios of young children to Negro women are not impressively large, probably because of the effect of heavy infant mortality and also because of a large undercount of children. Negro fertility is discussed more thoroughly in the section on trends in the nineteenth century.

Urban-rural differentials. The subject of urban-rural differentials in fertility is of interest but not of great numerical importance for America in the Colonial period because American cities were few and small. In 1750, the largest city in America (Boston) had only 15,731 inhabitants, Philadelphia and its suburbs had 13,400, New York had 13,300, and Newport had 6,000. As late as 1790 there were only 24 places in the United States with 2,500 inhabitants or more. Nationally, only 5 percent of the population resided in urban areas in 1790. The proportion ranged from none in a number of States to 13.1 percent in Massachusetts.

Table 5 presents a specially computed series of ratios of children under 16 to white women 16 years old and over, based on a series of early enumerations in the Colony of New York.   No other Colony had as extensive a series of censuses.   It may be noted from the figures in this table that the ratio of children to women declined appreciably as New York County (City) grew, but that between 1712 and 1786 the ratio remained nearly constant in the remainder of the Colony.   The population outside of New York County (City) was practically all rural.   The data in table 5 indicate, therefore, that differential urban-rural fertility began in the Colonies at a very early date.   It is possible, as Franklin suggests, that at least some of the difference came from relatively more unmarried adults and a later marriage age in cities than on farms.

TABLE 5.—TOTAL NUMBER OF INHABITANTS AND NUMBER OF CHILDREN UNDER 16 YEARS OLD PER 1,000 WHITE WOMEN 16 YEARS OLD AND OVER, FOR NEW YORK COUNTY AND THE REMAINDER OF THE COLONY OR STATE OF NEW YORK: 1703 TO 1786

[New York City, then at the southern tip of Manhattan Island, contained almost all of the population of New York County at each census]

Year	New York County		Remainder of the Colony or State of New York	
	Population	Children per 1,000 women	Population	Children per 1,000 women
1786	23,614	1,278	215,283	1,998
1771	21,863	1,279	146,154	1,886
1756	13,046	1,260	83,544	2,022
1749	13,294	1,441	60,054	2,025
1746	11,717	1,426	[1]49,872	2,179
1723	7,248	1,564	33,316	1,968
1712[2]	5,841	1,743	[3]13,563	2,057
1703	4,375	1,906	16,290	2,446

[1] Albany County was excluded from the enumeration "because of the enemy."

[2] The returns of this census are deemed imperfect, "the people being deterred by a simple superstition, and observation that sickness followed upon the last numbering of the people."

[3] Kings and Richmond Counties are excluded because no age detail is available.

Source: Computed from data on early Colonial enumerations presented in U. S. Bureau of the Census, *A Century of Population Growth in the United States, 1790-1900*, by W. S. Rossiter.

B. The nineteenth century

Birth statistics.   The New England States collected vital statistics long before the establishment of the Federal Government's Birth Registration Area in 1915.   Annual reports on births have been issued in each State since the date specified: Massachusetts (1842), Connecticut (1848), Rhode Island (1853), Vermont (1857), New Hampshire (1880), and Maine (1892).   Several States outside of New England, notably New York and Maryland, also have early data.   In 1930, Spengler made a study of the New England data and also made estimates of annual numbers of native white and foreign-born white women of childbearing age for use in birth rates.   His data, not corrected for underregistration (this was more serious in the early years), showed no consistent downward trend in the birth rate for native white women after about 1880.   In Massachusetts, for example, there were around 77 reported births per 1,000 native white women 15 to 49 years old in 1853–60, 66 in 1880–90, and 62 in 1910–20. In Maine there were increases from about 70 in 1891–1900 to about 76 in 1910–20. In New England as a whole, the uncorrected birth rate for native white women increased from about 65 in 1891–95 to 71 in 1921–25. The uncorrected birth rate for the foreign born declined from 138 to 102 in the same period.[10] (New England had a less fertile population than the Nation as a whole, as may be seen from data on ratios of young children to women in table 6.)

Ratios of children under 5 years old to women 20 to 44 years old. In the absence of national birth statistics until the twentieth century, it is fortunate that we have decennial census data since 1790 on the population classified by age and sex. Ratios of young children to women of childbearing age, computed from such data, are fully as useful as birth rates for many purposes, although they must be used with due regard for their limitations. (See Appendix A.)

Because many of the children under 5 years old are past the first year of life, when most infant mortality occurs, the ratios of young children to women are often described as measures of effective fertility. Those who wish to allow for the factor of mortality may recall the rough estimate given in the section on infant mortality to the effect that about 78 percent of white infants around 1800 survived from birth to about the midpoint of the "under 5 years" age group. A relatively good estimate for white infants in 1901, based on Glover's life tables for the United States Death Registration Area, is 84 percent, and an excellent one for 1950, based on National Office of Vital Statistics' life tables, is 97 percent. Corresponding estimates for Negro infants are 72 percent in 1901 and 95 percent in 1950.

Variations in the age distributions of women may have an important effect on ratios of young children to women for small areas, but they are not of much consequence on a national basis. As tested by computations, standardization for age of woman would change the ratios of children under 5 years old to white women 20 to 44 years old by only 4 percent nationally in the long swing between the population of young average age in 1800 and the population of much older average age in 1950.

Variations in the census undercount of young children are discussed in Appendix A. In general, it should be noted that the undercount was greater than usual in 1850, 1870, and 1890. The quality of the count of young children was improved in 1900 when a check question on date of birth was asked. In other censuses the estimated undercount amounted to about 5 to 7 percent of white children and 10 to 15 percent of nonwhite children under 5 years old.

[10] Joseph J. Spengler, "The Fecundity of Native and Foreign-Born Women in New England," *Brookings Institution Pamphlet Series*, Vol. II, No. 1, June 30, 1930.

Nineteenth century declines in current fertility. The data in table 6 show clearly that ratios of young children to white women, and by inference white birth rates, declined from a very early date. The national decline began at least as early as 1810. The patterns of variation and trends by geographic divisions are discussed at some length in the chapter on geographical variations. As stated there, ratios of 1,300 to 1,400 probably were normal for long-settled areas before the Revolutionary War. Higher values occurred in frontier areas, mainly from the selective migration of young married women. Selective migration had little or no effect on fertility ratios for the Nation as a whole in the first half of the nineteenth century because immigration was small in relation to the size of the total population.[11]

TABLE 6.—ADJUSTED NUMBER OF CHILDREN UNDER 5 YEARS OLD PER 1,000 WOMEN 20 TO 44 YEARS OLD BY RACE, BY DIVISIONS: 1800 TO 1950

[In an attempt to improve the comparability of white and Negro ratios, all ratios have been adjusted for underenumeration of children, and all except those for whites in 1800 to 1820 have been standardized indirectly to the age distribution of women in the United States in 1930. The number of enumerated white children under 5 has been increased by 5 percent, and of Negro children by 13 percent, these being factors obtained from a study of data for 1925 to 1930]

Year	White										Negro, total
	United States	New England	Middle Atlantic	East North Central	West North Central	South Atlantic	East South Central	West South Central	Mountain	Pacific	
1800	1,342	1,164	1,334	1,918	(¹)	1,402	1,875	(¹)	(¹)	(¹)	(¹)
1810	1,358	1,111	1,365	1,777	1,915	1,382	1,794	1,446	(¹)	(¹)	(¹)
1820	1,295	980	1,244	1,683	1,768	1,330	1,708	1,483	(¹)	(¹)	(¹)
1830	1,145	826	1,044	1,473	1,685	1,189	1,530	1,369	(¹)	(¹)	(¹)
1840	1,085	770	951	1,280	1,446	1,162	1,424	1,310	(¹)	(¹)	(¹)
1850	892	636	776	1,037	1,122	957	1,115	1,061	875	896	1,087
1860	905	639	784	1,016	1,118	940	1,056	1,103	1,054	1,035	1,072
1870	814	564	702	892	1,012	833	922	953	982	916	997
1880	780	520	648	781	930	879	952	1,066	892	808	1,090
1890	685	456	563	668	797	802	873	994	770	600	930
1900	666	497	567	620	731	802	855	942	742	532	845
1910	631	505	554	576	650	780	836	861	680	478	736
1920	604	543	562	570	605	720	760	706	686	447	608
1930	506	467	447	482	520	618	680	586	582	357	554
1940	419	365	337	407	452	480	556	492	546	358	513
1950	587	552	507	586	642	601	666	644	699	576	706

¹ Data not available.

Source: U. S. Bureau of the Census, *Forecasts of the Population of the United States, 1945-1975*, by P. K. Whelpton, p. 16, and computations from *1950 Census of Population*, Vol. II, *Characteristics of the Population*, Parts 2-50, table 15.

The ratio of children under 5 years old to 1,000 white women 20 to 44 years old declined 939 points between 1810 and 1940. About 29 percent of this decline occurred by 1840 and 74 percent occurred by 1900. The bulk of the decline in fertility as measured by ratios of young children to white women thus occurred in the nineteenth century, and a considerable amount occurred before the midcentury.

An important consideration is the extent to which fertility was adequate for maintenance of population. The ratios in table 6 may be compared with an intentionally too-large "replacement quota" for evidence that nine-

---

[11] U. S. Bureau of the Census, *Historical Statistics of the United States: 1789–1945*, p. 34.

teenth century fertility was far above replacement needs in most parts of
the country. A very high quota for permanent population replacement is
578 children under 5 years old per 1,000 women 20 to 44 years old.
This is based on life tables for Negroes in the District of Columbia in 1910
plus age standardization to match the ratios in table 6. The mortality
rates in the life tables that were used were high enough to yield a crude
death rate of about 35 deaths per 1,000 persons if applied to the white
population in 1800. (Blodget estimated a crude death rate of about 25
for around 1800.) A quota for 1940, based on United States life tables
for 1939–41 is 440. This is too low for use with prior years when mortality was higher. However, it helps to indicate that national fertility fell
below replacement needs by 1940. Low fertility did not pose a problem
of potential population decline until the 1930's and then only because of
a severe economic depression.

FIGURE 1.—RURAL AND URBAN POPULATION OF NEW ENGLAND: 1790 TO 1950

[Urban-rural classification by 1940 Census rules]

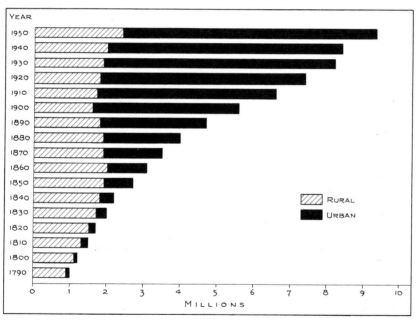

Source: *1950 Census of Population*, Vol. II, *Characteristics of the Population*, Part 1, U. S. Summary, p. 17.

The decline in ratios of young children to women reflected a genuine
demographic revolution, a growing disinclination of married couples to
have many children. The revolution was related to the same forces that
caused the development of modern society, the rapid advance in arts and
science and the adoption of a rational approach in individual and family
living. In America, fertility began to decline before there was any appre-

ciable proportion of the population residing in urban areas. In New England, an early stronghold of industrialization, there was little increase before 1830 in the proportion of the population residing in urban areas (figure 1). Because the urban population comprised a very small part of the total population in the early years, it could not have been chiefly responsible for the early declines in fertility. Although few people lived in urban areas, New England did have a considerable nonfarm economy. The Census of 1820 counted about 106,000 persons in New England as engaged in manufacturing and commerce, and 285,000 as engaged in agriculture.

Urban and rural declines in fertility. Some demographers have stated a theory that the trend toward birth control began in urban areas and subsequently spread to the surrounding rural areas. The reference here is not to the age-old urban and rural differentials in fertility but to the progressively greater family limitations which accompanied the evolution of modern civilization. If it occurred, the spread of family limitation practices from urban to rural areas must have begun very early in the United States. The data in table 7 indicate that after 1810 the declines in fertility ratios of the rural population more than kept pace with those of the urban population.[12] Ratios of young children to white women declined very early in the rural population, and were already low in New England in 1800 as compared with other geographic divisions. Between 1810 and 1840, on a national basis, both the urban and rural ratios of children under 5 years old declined by about 200 children per 1,000 women; between 1840 and 1910, the decline amounted to about 230 in the urban population and 350 in the rural population; and between 1910 and 1940 the decline amounted to about 160 in the urban population and 230 in the rural population. Thus, absolute differences in urban and rural fertility narrowed over the years, as measured by ratios of young children to women. A different picture is obtained when one compares changes in relative proportions. In 1810, the urban ratio (900) was 68 percent as large as the rural ratio (1,329) and in 1940 the urban ratio (311) was 56 percent as large as the rural ratio (551). The pattern of change is shown graphically in figure 2.

In the early part of the nineteenth century, the national ratio of young children to women was almost equal in size to the rural ratio (figure 2 and table 7). This was because about 91 percent of the white women 20 to 44 years old resided in rural areas in 1810. In 1940 and 1950, only 37 percent resided in rural areas, by the old definition of urban-rural residence. (According to the new definition adopted for use in the 1950

---

[12] Censuses from 1800 to 1840 presented separate data on the population by age, sex, and color for various small areas. By adding the data for specific places fertility ratios were derived for the urban population and the rural population. Urban-rural data were directly available in the reports of the 1910 and later censuses. The data in table 7 differ from those in table 6 in that they have neither been standardized for age of woman nor adjusted for an undercount of young children.

Census, only 32 percent of the women resided in rural areas.)   As the population became less rural, the national ratio of young children to women diverged in size from the rural ratio and approached the urban ratio.   The national ratio therefore declined more than either of the component urban and rural ratios.

TABLE 7.—NUMBER OF CHILDREN UNDER 5 YEARS OLD PER 1,000 WHITE WOMEN 20 TO 44 YEARS OLD, BY DIVISIONS, URBAN AND RURAL: 1800 TO 1840 AND 1910 TO 1950

[Ratios for 1800 to 1840 partly estimated from broad age groups.   Urban-rural classification by 1940 Census rules]

Area	1950	1940	1930	1920	1910	1840	1830	1820	1810	1800
United States........	551	400	485	581	609	1,070	1,134	1,236	1,290	1,281
Urban.....................	479	311	388	471	469	701	708	831	900	845
Rural.....................	673	551	658	744	782	1,134	1,189	1,276	1,329	1,319
New England............	516	347	441	518	482	752	812	930	1,052	1,098
Urban.....................	486	321	417	500	468	592	614	764	845	827
Rural.....................	612	443	541	602	566	800	851	952	1,079	1,126
Middle Atlantic........	471	320	424	539	533	940	1,036	1,183	1,289	1,279
Urban.....................	432	286	386	501	495	711	722	842	924	852
Rural.....................	596	457	590	680	650	1,006	1,100	1,235	1,344	1,339
East North Central.....	552	388	458	548	555	1,270	1,467	1,608	1,702	1,840
Urban.....................	491	326	400	485	470	841	910	1,059	1,256	...
Rural.....................	679	533	605	668	672	1,291	1,484	1,616	1,706	1,840
West North Central.....	600	431	495	584	630	1,445	1,678	1,685	1,810	...
Urban.....................	514	324	365	416	426	705	1,181	...	...	...
Rural.....................	702	538	614	711	760	1,481	1,703	1,685	1,810	...
South Atlantic.........	572	464	593	694	760	1,140	1,174	1,280	1,325	1,345
Urban.....................	450	305	401	458	485	770	767	881	936	861
Rural.....................	677	596	744	851	894	1,185	1,209	1,310	1,347	1,365
East South Central.....	631	539	655	734	817	1,408	1,519	1,631	1,700	1,799
Urban.....................	494	333	414	441	469	859	863	1,089	1,348	...
Rural.....................	720	648	781	846	922	1,424	1,529	1,635	1,701	1,799
West South Central.....	607	474	584	686	845	1,297	1,359	1,418	1,383	...
Urban.....................	542	342	410	445	504	846	877	866	727	...
Rural.....................	703	591	723	823	977	1,495	1,463	1,522	1,557	...
Mountain...............	663	526	582	664	661	...	...	...	...	...
Urban.....................	584	404	428	470	466	...	...	...	...	...
Rural.....................	754	643	712	807	810	...	...	...	...	...
Pacific...............	539	339	360	425	460	...	...	...	...	...
Urban.....................	478	283	306	344	360	...	...	...	...	...
Rural.....................	652	466	507	603	640	...	...	...	...	...

Source: Computed from reports of censuses from 1800 to 1950, with corrections for clerical and printing errors in Censuses of 1800 to 1820.

Some writers have speculated that the increase in the proportion of population residing in urban areas accounts for much of the decline in the Nation's fertility.   It is a fact that much of the population now resides in urban areas, where fertility normally is lower than in rural areas.   However, the Nation was so largely rural in much of the long period from 1810 to 1950 that declines in rural fertility had more effect on changes in national fertility than did the combined effects of (a) the increasing proportion of population residing in urban areas and (b) declines in urban fertility.   This fact can be demonstrated by an indirect standardization technique, with results as shown in table 8.[13]

---

[13] In standardization to determine the relative importance of components of change in a rate, one has a choice of several methods which are each logical but which give different, rough indications of the relative importance.   A direct method holds all components constant except the one being eval-

FIGURE **2.**—NUMBER OF CHILDREN UNDER 5 YEARS OLD PER 1,000 WHITE WOMEN 20 TO 44
YEARS OLD, URBAN AND RURAL: 1800 TO 1950

[Urban-rural classification by 1940 Census rules]

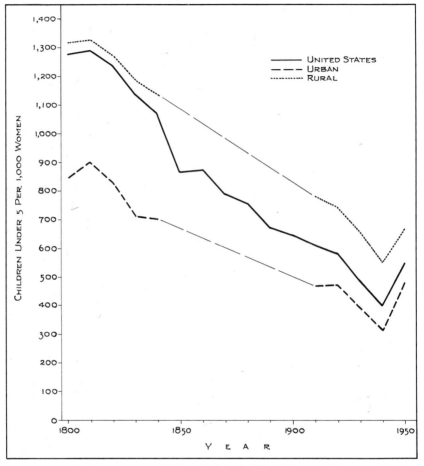

Source: Data for 1800 to 1840 and 1910 to 1950 from table 6; data for 1850 to 1900 computed from reports of pertinent population censuses.

Comparisons for different periods of time than 1810 to 1940 would give different results from those in table 8. A progressively later starting date than 1810 would give progressively more weight to declines in urban fertility and less weight to the other two factors shown. The changing

uated. An indirect or residual method holds constant only the component being evaluated. After all known components have been evaluated, both methods have left a small, unexplained residual which is often termed the "interaction component." In time series analysis involving only two dates like 1810 and 1940, the direct method works forward from 1810 and with the present data would emphasize the rural aspect, while the indirect method works backward from 1940 and would emphasize the urban aspect. The interaction component in the two methods turns out to be of identical magnitude but of opposite sign. An average of the two methods eliminates the interaction component, provides a centralized time reference, and avoids bias. Hence averages are shown in table 8.

proportion of population residing in urban areas, measured separately from trends in urban fertility and rural fertility, thus would account for less than 20 percent of the changes in national fertility if a later starting date than 1810 were used. Urban fertility became the most important component of national fertility after 1920.

TABLE **8.**—Urban-Rural Components of Decline in Number of Children Under 5 Years Old per 1,000 White Women 20 to 44 Years Old, by Divisions: 1810 to 1940

[Centralized averages]

Area	Absolute decline in children per 1,000 women	Percent distribution			
		Total	Decline due to--		
			Rural to urban shift of population	Decline in urban ratio	Decline in rural ratio
United States[1]...............	890	100.0	20.2	23.8	56.0
New England.....................	705	100.0	17.0	33.5	49.5
Middle Atlantic....................	969	100.0	20.4	30.7	48.9
East North Central.................	1,314	100.0	17.3	25.1	57.6
West North Central[2]...............	1,379	100.0	3.9	26.9	69.2
South Atlantic.....................	861	100.0	16.3	18.6	65.1
East South Central.................	1,161	100.0	9.9	15.3	74.9
West South Central.................	909	100.0	15.4	14.4	70.2

[1] Includes the Mountain and Pacific Divisions in 1940 but not in 1810 when they were nonexistent.

[2] There was a nonexistent urban population in the West North Central Division in 1810 which of course had an indeterminate 0/0 ratio of children to women. It was necessary to assign some value to the ratio. The rural ratio was assigned.

Source: Computed from table 7.

Negroes. Negroes have been enumerated by age in all censuses of the United States since 1820. The age intervals, such as 10 to 23 years, which were recorded for Negroes before 1850 obviously are not suitable for the computation of ratios of young children to women. However, it is possible to obtain some idea of trends in Negro fertility at early dates from other measures such as the proportion of young children in the population.

In 1820, 43.1 percent of the Negroes were children under 14 years old. Interpolation of other age detail results in an estimate that about 42.6 percent of the Negro population in 1850 were children under 14 years old. The nearly identical percentages under 14 in 1820 and 1850 indicate that little change probably occurred in the fertility of Negroes between 1820 and 1850. In 1830 and 1840, the age group "under 10" was listed in the census. More detailed data were obtained after 1840. This permits a comparison of the percentages that children under 10 years old comprised of the total nonwhite population:

1830... 34.2
1840... 33.2
1850... 31.3
1860... 30.5

These figures should be interpreted with caution because of a change in census procedures in 1850 which may have influenced the accuracy of age reporting. Comparisons between 1830 and 1840 and between 1850 and 1860 probably would not be affected, however. Both periods show declines of about 1 percentage point per decade in the proportion of young children in the population. It seems safe to say that there were no great changes in Negro fertility between 1830 and 1860 although a slight decline may have occurred.

Decennial rates of increase in the Negro population may also be used as indirect indicators of trends in Negro fertility but they are much rougher indicators than are data on the proportion of children in the population. They are of more value for showing that the fertility was ample for a considerable amount of population increase despite very high mortality. The intercensal increases were affected by varying degrees of completeness of the census enumerations. The first few enumerations probably were less complete than the later ones. It may be safe to assume that declines in rates of population increase among Negroes after 1810 did not come from any large increase in death rates. Importations of slaves were not an important factor, as these officially ceased in 1808.[14] The following data indicate some slowing down of the rate of population increase, and by inference a probable decline in fertility:

Period	Percent increase in Negro population
1790 to 1800	32.3
1800 to 1810	37.5
1810 to 1820	28.6
1820 to 1830	31.4
1830 to 1840	23.4
1840 to 1850	26.6
1850 to 1860	22.1

A series of ratios of children under 5 years old to women 20 to 44 years old was presented in table 6 and is repeated in the accompanying table for Negroes:

Year	Children under 5 per 1,000 Negro women 20 to 44 years old
1850	1,087
1860	1,072
1870	997
1880	1,090
1890	930
1900	845
1910	736
1920	608
1930	554
1940	513
1950	706

---

[14] For estimates of importations of slaves, see *Compendium of the Seventh Census, 1850*, page 83.

The series shows no large decline in the magnitudes of ratios of young children to women among Negroes before 1880. The 1870 ratio may be disregarded because the quality of enumeration was not as good as usual.[15] A decline of more than 50 percent occurred in the ratios between 1880 and 1940, despite the offsetting effect of very large declines in infant mortality. (The proportion of Negro infants dying in the first year of life declined from 20 percent in 1910 to 7 percent in the period from 1939 to 1941 and 5 percent in 1950.)

Declines in completed fertility. The 1910 Census probably provides the best data available in this country on the fertility of women during the latter part of the nineteenth century. The women 45 to 74 years old in 1910 had most of their children in the nineteenth century. Comparisons of data on the number of children ever born for women in successive age groups provide a rough indication of secular trends in fertility. The qualification "rough" is used because it is not entirely satisfactory to relate total fertility over a lifetime to secular trends. Bias may result from differential mortality between women who have had many children and women who have had few, and from any tendency for underreporting of children for old women. This bias may be negligible at ages up to 59 years and it may be as large as 10 percent or even more by age 70 to 74 years. (See Appendix A.) This should be kept in mind when data for aged women are compared. The bias means that, in general, the decline in fertility has been greater than is indicated by the data in tables 9 and 10.

Table 9 is for the total population of the United States. However, this table largely reflects white fertility because the white population comprises about nine-tenths of the total population. Other sections of this monograph show data for whites rather than for the total population, for reasons of convenience and precision of data. Separate data for the nonwhite population (97 percent Negro) are presented in table 10. The quality of census data and vital statistics for nonwhites has improved substantially since 1910 but is still below that for whites. Another reason for usually presenting separate data for whites is that there is more concern about fertility when it is low, and the whites thus far have more severely limited their fertility.

The data in table 9 for the Nation's total population show steady declines in completed fertility among the women in successive age cohorts, with the exception of the women 65 to 74 years old in rural-farm areas who were less fertile than the women in some of the subsequent cohorts. This exception can be traced to the South and it probably reflects adverse conditions during and after the War Between the States. The data for nonwhites in table 10 exhibit a similar pattern, except that at least three age cohorts of nonwhite women were adversely affected by conditions associated with the war and its aftermath. Perhaps the living conditions among the displaced ex-slaves were chaotic for many years.

---

[15] For evidence, see the reports of the 1880 Census.

TABLE **9.**—NUMBER OF CHILDREN EVER BORN PER 1,000 WOMEN 45 TO 74 YEARS OLD,
URBAN AND RURAL: 1910

Area and age of woman	Number of women	Percent ever married	Percent childless among ever married	Children ever born		
				Per 1,000 women	Per 1,000 women ever married	Per 1,000 mothers
UNITED STATES						
45 to 49 years..................	2,088,000	91.0	9.5	4,295	4,744	5,241
50 to 54 years..................	1,790,000	91.6	8.9	4,529	4,972	5,459
55 to 59 years..................	1,302,000	92.8	8.3	4,816	5,218	5,692
60 to 64 years..................	1,090,000	92.7	8.2	4,847	5,266	5,734
65 to 69 years..................	819,000	93.5	7.9	4,982	5,364	5,822
70 to 74 years..................	554,000	93.5	7.7	5,001	5,395	5,845
URBAN						
45 to 49 years..................	1,088,000	88.8	11.7	3,615	4,098	4,639
50 to 54 years..................	889,000	89.5	10.6	3,901	4,385	4,905
55 to 64 years..................	1,139,000	91.3	9.4	4,316	4,758	5,250
65 to 74 years..................	630,000	92.8	8.6	4,639	5,036	5,511
RURAL NONFARM						
45 to 49 years..................	402,000	91.3	9.2	4,270	4,704	5,178
50 to 54 years..................	365,000	91.5	9.4	4,367	4,808	5,308
55 to 64 years..................	549,000	92.7	8.8	4,724	5,129	5,625
65 to 74 years..................	367,000	93.6	8.5	4,953	5,333	5,831
RURAL FARM						
45 to 49 years..................	598,000	94.9	6.0	5,553	5,869	6,244
50 to 54 years..................	536,000	95.1	6.0	5,686	5,996	6,377
55 to 64 years..................	705,000	95.0	6.1	5,752	6,080	6,472
65 to 74 years..................	376,000	94.6	5.7	5,632	5,994	6,359

Source: *1940 Census of Population, Differential Fertility, 1940 and 1910,* Fertility for States and Large Cities, table 4.

The urban-rural classification in the tables reflects the residence of women in 1910 and may differ from the residence at the time most of the children were born. Only one-third of the Negro women lived on farms in 1910, although two-thirds lived in rural areas.

The white women 70 to 74 years old in the United States who had ever married had an average of 5.4 children ever born, compared with approximately 8 for Colonial times. This supports the preceding statement that a substantial amount of decline in fertility occurred prior to 1880. The Negro women probably had a much smaller decline, especially in rural-farm areas where the average in 1910 was still close to 8 children ever born. Nationally, the ever-married nonwhite women 70 to 74 years old in 1910 had an average of 6.9 children, compared with about 7.6 among nonwhite women in rural-farm areas. Although nonwhite women had more births, on the average, than the white women, this was nearly balanced by higher infant mortality; in consequence, the effective fertility of nonwhites was not much different from that of whites, as noted earlier in terms of ratios of young children to women (table 6).

Quite small percentages of the nonwhite women 70 to 74 years old in 1910 who had ever married had never borne a child. The percentage was less than 5 in rural-farm areas and it was about 9 in urban areas. The fact that at one time the incidence of involuntary childlessness was low among nonwhites should be kept in mind when examining more modern data. As noted in some later sections, Negroes in recent years have had very high proportions of childlessness and, because of studies which show that Negroes practice contraception infrequently and inefficiently, much of the childlessness has been assumed to reflect involuntary causes.

TABLE 10.—NUMBER OF CHILDREN EVER BORN PER 1,000 NONWHITE WOMEN 45 TO 74 YEARS OLD, URBAN AND RURAL: 1910

Area and age of woman	Number of women	Percent ever married	Percent childless among ever married	Children ever born		
				Per 1,000 women	Per 1,000 women ever married	Per 1,000 mothers
UNITED STATES						
45 to 49 years........................	194,000	95.2	8.7	5,864	6,183	6,771
50 to 54 years........................	154,000	95.3	7.8	6,281	6,626	7,186
55 to 59 years........................	99,000	96.2	7.0	6,586	6,874	7,390
60 to 64 years........................	92,000	95.9	6.5	6,529	6,852	7,327
65 to 69 years........................	59,000	96.8	6.8	6,762	7,021	7,537
70 to 74 years........................	41,000	95.7	5.6	6,576	6,935	7,347
URBAN						
45 to 49 years........................	69,000	93.3	13.4	4,174	4,503	5,200
50 to 54 years........................	51,000	93.2	11.6	4,680	5,059	5,726
55 to 64 years........................	61,000	94.5	9.9	5,218	5,558	6,166
65 to 74 years........................	30,000	95.4	8.7	5,916	6,237	6,834
RURAL NONFARM						
45 to 49 years........................	45,000	94.7	8.0	5,849	6,208	6,747
50 to 54 years........................	38,000	95.1	7.8	6,183	6,541	7,095
55 to 64 years........................	52,000	95.5	7.0	6,553	6,908	7,431
65 to 74 years........................	30,000	96.0	6.8	6,607	6,932	7,436
RURAL FARM						
45 to 49 years........................	80,000	97.2	5.2	7,308	7,534	7,948
50 to 54 years........................	64,000	97.0	4.9	7,605	7,860	8,262
55 to 64 years........................	79,000	97.6	4.3	7,598	7,809	8,156
65 to 74 years........................	40,000	97.2	4.2	7,356	7,608	7,941

Source: Same as table 9.

The low percentages of childless women in 1910, among whites and nonwhites alike, are also in sharp contrast to indications in some modern local studies and to judgments by many physicians and demographers that at least 10 percent of women are involuntarily sterile.[16] The increase in involuntary sterility after 1910 may reflect more present-day postponement in childbearing, coupled with reduced fecundity as the women age. Thus, the 1910 data are useful for assessing the meaning of some more modern figures.

The data in tables 9 and 10 indicate that, in general, the trend toward fewer births per woman in the nineteenth century did not involve any sudden large increase in childlessness. The increase that occurred was

---

[16] For a general discussion and citations to some of the lengthy literature on this topic, see P. K. Whelpton and Clyde V. Kiser, "The Comparative Influence on Fertility of Contraception and Impairments of Fertility," *Social and Psychological Factors Affecting Fertility*, Vol. Two, pp. 303–357, the Milbank Memorial Fund, New York, 1950.

gradual and accounted for only a part of the total decline in fertility.   It is probable that the "psychological availability of contraception" came about in a gradual fashion as attitudes changed.   That contraceptives and abortifacients were available is evident from newspaper advertisements between about 1820 and the passage of the Comstock Law in 1873.[17]

---

[17] For examples, see the January 1861 issues of the *Cleveland Plain Dealer*, the *Boston Herald*, and the *Louisville Democrat*.

CHAPTER 3

THE TWENTIETH CENTURY

A. Birth statistics

Although this monograph is intended to be mainly an analysis of census data on fertility, it would be incomplete without some use of the extensive and valuable birth registration data collected by the States and compiled on a national basis by the National Office of Vital Statistics. Most of the measures of fertility which have been developed thus far, including the relatively new field of cohort fertility, are derived from birth registration data.

A series of national estimates of annual births for the period from 1909 to 1934, prepared by P. K. Whelpton and published by the National Office of Vital Statistics, is used in some of the tables below. The series incorporates carefully prepared estimates for States not in the Birth Registration Area and also incorporates adjustments for underregistration. The Birth Registration Area was established in 1915, with ten States and the District of Columbia. Other States were admitted to the Area when their registration systems attained a required degree of reliability.[1] It attained nationwide coverage in 1933 with the admission of Texas. The tables make use of the National Office of Vital Statistics underregistration-corrected data for years from 1935. Attention is also called to the existence of other estimates of births and birth rates which various writers have prepared and published since at least 1806.[2] Thus, at least a rough idea can be obtained of the magnitude and trends of births and birth rates in the United States for many years before the completion of the Birth Registration Area.

Crude birth rates. At the beginning of the twentieth century, the United States had an estimated annual birth rate of 32 births per 1,000 inhabitants. The birth rate declined in irregular fashion, from about 30.0 in 1909 to 18.4 in 1933 (table 11). It dipped during World War I, recovered to a postwar high in 1921, and then declined fairly steadily. Monthly data indicate that the birth rate reached its lowest level in September 1933, about ten months after the presidential election in November 1932, which

---

[1] At least 90 percent of the births were supposed to be registered, although this condition was not always met. Only two States had less than 90 percent coverage in 1950 and both were close to that level. Nationally, 97.9 percent of births were registered in 1950, as compared with 92.5 percent in 1940.

[2] An example, Blodget's data, was given in Chapter 2, table 1.

THE FERTILITY OF AMERICAN WOMEN

was a time of uncertainty as to future economic conditions. This was only one of a number of occasions on which the birth rate reacted for a short while to political and economic events. Some other examples of short-run fluctuations were the sharp increases in birth rates about ten months after the passage of the Selective Service law in October 1940 and after the outbreak of war in December 1941. It seems quite certain that the birth rate became increasingly sensitive to social and economic conditions as a consequence of the spread of family limitation practices.

TABLE 11.—BIRTHS AND BIRTH RATES, BY COLOR: 1909 TO 1956

[Births adjusted for underregistration. Preliminary birth data for 1955 to 1956; data for 1909 to 1932 include estimates of births for States not in the Birth Registration Area]

Year	Number of births			Births per 1,000 population[1]		
	Total	White	Nonwhite	Total	White	Nonwhite
1956	4,203,000	3,583,000	619,000	25.1	24.0	34.0
1955	4,098,000	3,522,000	577,000	24.9	24.0	32.6
1954	4,078,000	3,475,000	603,000	25.3	24.1	34.9
1953	3,965,000	3,389,000	575,000	25.0	24.0	34.1
1952	3,913,000	3,358,000	555,000	25.1	24.1	33.6
1951	3,823,000	3,277,000	546,000	24.9	23.9	33.8
1950	3,632,000	3,108,000	524,000	24.1	23.0	33.3
1949	3,649,000	3,136,000	513,000	24.5	23.6	33.0
1948	3,637,000	3,141,000	495,000	24.9	24.0	32.4
1947	3,817,000	3,347,000	469,000	26.6	26.1	31.2
1946	3,411,000	2,990,000	420,000	24.1	23.6	28.4
1945	2,858,000	2,471,000	388,000	20.4	19.7	26.5
1944	2,939,000	2,545,000	394,000	21.2	20.5	27.4
1943	3,104,000	2,704,000	400,000	22.7	22.1	28.3
1942	2,989,000	2,605,000	384,000	22.2	21.5	27.7
1941	2,703,000	2,330,000	374,000	20.3	19.5	27.3
1940	2,559,000	2,199,000	360,000	19.4	18.6	26.7
1939	2,466,000	2,117,000	349,000	18.8	18.0	26.1
1938	2,496,000	2,148,000	348,000	19.2	18.4	26.3
1937	2,413,000	2,071,000	342,000	18.7	17.9	26.0
1936	2,355,000	2,027,000	328,000	18.4	17.6	25.1
1935	2,377,000	2,042,000	334,000	18.7	17.9	25.8
1934	2,396,000	2,058,000	338,000	19.0	18.1	26.3
1933	2,307,000	1,982,000	325,000	18.4	17.6	25.5
1932	2,440,000	2,099,000	341,000	19.5	18.7	26.9
1931	2,506,000	2,170,000	335,000	20.2	19.5	26.6
1930	2,618,000	2,274,000	344,000	21.3	20.6	27.5
1929	2,582,000	2,244,000	339,000	21.2	20.5	27.3
1928	2,674,000	2,325,000	349,000	22.2	21.5	28.5
1927	2,802,000	2,425,000	377,000	23.5	22.7	31.1
1926	2,839,000	2,441,000	398,000	24.2	23.1	33.4
1925	2,909,000	2,506,000	403,000	25.1	24.1	34.2
1924	2,979,000	2,577,000	401,000	26.1	25.1	34.6
1923	2,910,000	2,531,000	380,000	26.0	25.2	33.2
1922	2,882,000	2,507,000	375,000	26.2	25.4	33.2
1921	3,055,000	2,657,000	398,000	28.1	27.3	35.8
1920	2,950,000	2,566,000	383,000	27.7	26.9	35.0
1919	2,740,000	2,387,000	353,000	26.1	25.3	32.4
1918	2,948,000	2,588,000	360,000	28.2	27.6	33.0
1917	2,944,000	2,587,000	357,000	28.5	27.9	32.9
1916	2,964,000	2,599,000	(²)	29.1	28.5	(²)
1915	2,965,000	2,594,000	(²)	29.5	28.9	(²)
1914	2,966,000	2,588,000	(²)	29.9	29.3	(²)
1913	2,869,000	2,497,000	(²)	29.5	28.8	(²)
1912	2,840,000	2,467,000	(²)	29.8	29.0	(²)
1911	2,809,000	2,435,000	(²)	29.9	29.1	(²)
1910	2,777,000	2,401,000	(²)	30.1	29.2	(²)
1909	2,718,000	2,344,000	(²)	30.0	29.2	(²)

[1] For 1917 to 1919 and 1941 to 1946, based on population including Armed Forces overseas.
[2] Reliable estimates not available.

Source: Derived from National Office of Vital Statistics, *Vital Statistics—Special Reports*, Vol. 33, No. 8, table B-1, and Vol. 44, No. 8, table 8; *Vital Statistics of the United States, 1950*, Vol. I, table 6.02; and preliminary data supplied by the National Office of Vital Statistics. Population bases for birth rates in some years from U. S. Bureau of the Census, *Current Population Reports*, Series P-25, No. 146.

Instead of declining further as the economic depression lengthened and in contrast to the previous century-old downward trend, the birth rate fluctuated around a level of 18 or 19 from 1933 to 1940. It then rose to 20.3 in 1941, a year after the still prewar America became the "Arsenal of Democracy." Orders from abroad for war materials helped to end the economic depression. The birth rate increased further to 22.7 in 1943, reflecting war-induced prosperity and conceptions at a time (1942) when millions of men in the Armed Forces were still in training and not yet deployed overseas. On a monthly basis, the wartime peak in births occurred in October 1942, ten months after America became directly involved in World War II. During the war the liberal furloughs given to servicemen before embarkation, the allotments granted to their families, and other measures unintentionally helped to keep the birth rate at a high level. In June 1946, the recently discharged veterans of World War II had 3,120,000 own children under 5 years old living with them, or about a fourth of the Nation's children in this age group. During the war, jobs were plentiful, and many people married at younger ages than had formerly been customary. Older couples partly made up for births deferred during the economic depression of the 1930's. As the war period lengthened and couples were separated by overseas service of the husband, the birth rate declined to 20.4 in 1945, but it did not go as low as before the war. Within a few months after the end of World War II in the latter part of 1945, 12 million veterans returned to civilian life. One consequence was that the marriage rate reached an all-time high in 1946, and the crude birth rate increased to 26.6 in 1947, the highest rate since 1921. Subsequently the birth rate fluctuated around a level of 25 through 1956.

Absolute numbers of births. In terms of the impact on the Nation's economy, variations in the absolute numbers of births were of more importance than were variations in the crude birth rate. Because an increase in the number of women of childbearing age offset the effect of declining birth rates, the annual number of births increased considerably between Colonial times and 1921. The first sustained decline in the absolute number of annual births occurred between 1921 and 1933. Small increases occurred in the last half of the decade of the 1930's and large ones occurred in the 1940's, particularly after 1946. Although the crude birth rate was higher in 1947 than in any subsequent year through 1956, a new record for the largest annual number of births in the United States was set in each year from 1951 to 1956.

General fertility rates. Because the proportion of women of childbearing age in a population varies, it is more satisfactory to relate births to the women of childbearing age than to the total population. The number of births per 1,000 women of childbearing age is the "general fertility rate." Rates of this type are shown in table 12 and figure 3. These illustrate more forcefully than the crude birth rate the very large fluctuations in annual fertility which have occurred in the present century.

TABLE **12.**—BIRTHS PER 1,000 WOMEN 15 TO 44 YEARS OLD, BY COLOR: 1909 TO 1956

[Births adjusted for underregistration. Preliminary birth data for 1955 to 1956; data for 1909 to 1932 include estimates of births for States not in the Birth Registration Area]

Year	Total	White	Non-white	Year	Total	White	Non-white
1956	120.5	116.0	154.7	1932	81.7	79.0	104.0
1955	117.9	114.4	145.3	1931	84.6	82.4	102.7
1954	117.6	113.9	146.3	1930	89.2	87.1	106.0
1953	114.7	110.8	148.2	1929	89.3	87.3	106.1
1952	113.5	109.8	143.1	1928	93.8	91.7	111.0
1951	111.3	107.4	141.9	1927	99.8	97.1	121.7
				1926	102.6	99.2	130.3
1950	106.2	102.3	137.3	1925	106.6	103.3	134.0
1949	107.1	103.6	135.1	1924	110.9	107.8	135.6
1948	107.3	104.3	131.6	1923	110.5	108.0	130.5
1947	113.3	111.8	125.9	1922	111.2	108.8	130.8
1946	101.9	100.4	113.9	1921	119.8	117.2	140.8
1945	85.9	83.4	106.0	1920	117.9	115.4	137.6
1944	88.8	86.3	108.5	1919	111.2	109.0	129.2
1943	94.3	92.3	111.0	1918	119.8	118.3	131.5
1942	91.5	89.5	107.6	1917	121.0	119.7	131.6
1941	83.4	80.7	105.4	1916	123.4	121.8	(1)
1940	79.9	77.1	102.4	1915	125.0	123.2	(1)
1939	77.5	74.7	100.3	1914	126.6	124.6	(1)
1938	79.3	76.6	101.0	1913	124.7	122.4	(1)
1937	77.3	74.5	100.3	1912	125.8	123.3	(1)
1936	76.1	73.6	97.0	1911	126.3	123.6	(1)
1935	77.5	74.8	99.6	1910	126.8	123.8	(1)
1934	78.9	76.1	101.6	1909	126.8	123.6	(1)
1933	76.6	74.0	98.4				

¹ Reliable estimates not available.

Source: Derived from National Office of Vital Statistics, *Vital Statistics—Special Reports*, Vol. 42, No. 13, table 6; and preliminary data supplied by the National Office of Vital Statistics; population bases for birth rates in some years from U. S. Bureau of the Census, *Current Population Reports*, Series P–25, No. 114, tables 2 and 3, and No. 146, table 1.

Whites and nonwhites had essentially similar patterns of trend in the general fertility rate between 1917 and 1956. The nonwhites consistently had the higher rates. The excess of the nonwhite rate over the white rate widened and narrowed in erratic fashion in the period shown. The chart thus affords no evidence that whites and nonwhites were tending toward identical levels of annual birth rates, unlike findings from data on children under 5 years old (Chapter 2) and on children ever born (in a later section) which show that differentials in fertility by color narrowed considerably after 1910. A widening of color differentials in annual birth rates occurred after each World War and during the economic depression of the 1930's, interspersed with a narrowing of color differentials. The whites usually had larger fluctuations in annual birth rates than did the nonwhites, in large part no doubt, because the whites more effectively controlled their fertility and therefore reacted more readily to changes in social and economic conditions. This also stemmed in part, however, from the fact that in years before 1940 relatively large percentages of the nonwhites were low-income rural residents who were less affected by fluctuations in economic conditions than were urban residents. The situation has changed since 1940. In 1950, as large a proportion of nonwhite women as of white women lived in urban places and the rural population had adopted many urban ways of living. Despite a rising percentage of nonwhite population residing in urban areas where fertility is lower than in rural areas, the birth rate for nonwhites continued to increase after 1947. Perhaps it was the unprecedented high level of prosperity among nonwhites that indirectly caused a part of the increase in their birth rate despite the normally depressing effect of urban living conditions. The increased prosperity was accompanied by an increased proportion of women living with their husbands and a decreased proportion widowed, divorced, separated, or with husbands temporarily absent (discussed in Chapters 4 and 8). Some demographers think that much of the increase in the birth rate of nonwhites came about from improved health conditions.

FIGURE 3.—BIRTHS PER 1,000 WOMEN 15 TO 44 YEARS OLD, BY COLOR: 1909 TO 1956

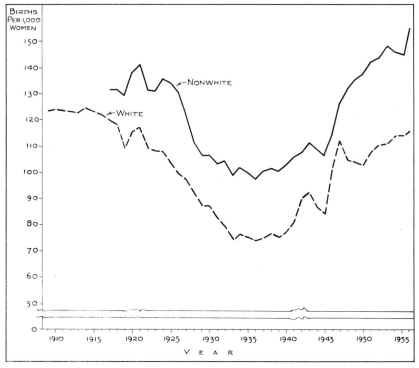

Note: Based on data in table 12.

Age-specific birth rates. The ages of women are highly correlated with factors that affect fertility, such as biological processes, marriage, and the attainment of a desired number of children. Puberty usually occurs at about the age of 13 years. Medical research indicates that the ability of groups of women to conceive is strongest between the ages of 18 and 24 years and then declines slowly, ending with the menopause at an average age of about 48 years.[3] The actual age-specific birth rates tend to

[3] Raymond Pearl, *The Natural History of Population*, Oxford University Press, Oxford, 1939.

follow this pattern but at magnitudes that are far below the biological possibilities. So few women give birth at other ages that the range from 15 to 44 years is cited as the childbearing period in most chapters of this monograph.

The characteristic bell-shaped distribution of age-specific birth rates is illustrated in figure 4, which shows data for the United States at a time when current fertility was severely limited (1938) and for Mexico at a time when there was little limitation (1939).[4] There was an essential similarity in the shape of the distribution in the two countries, although the magnitude of the birth rates differed widely.

FIGURE 4.—AGE-SPECIFIC BIRTH RATES FOR MEXICO, 1939, AND FOR THE UNITED STATES, 1938

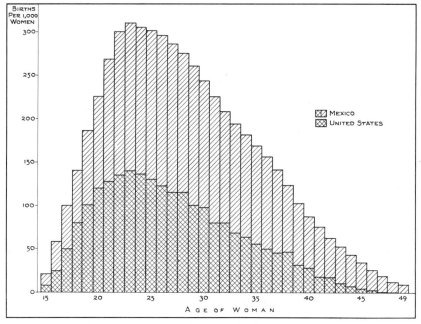

Source: Derived from Republic of Mexico, *Anuario Estadístico de Los Estados Mexicanos: 1940, and Resumen General del Sexto Censo de Población: 1940*; National Office of Vital Statistics, *Vital Statistics of the United States: 1938*, Part II; and unpublished population estimates for 1938 from the Bureau of the Census.

Trends in age-specific birth rates are shown for the United States in table 13. The effect of the wartime and postwar resurgence in fertility is strongly evident in the trend of birth rates for women at ages under 35 years.

---

[4] The data shown for the United States are based on births corrected for underregistration and those for Mexico are based on reported births. The rates shown would permit the women in Mexico who live to age 45 to have an average of about 5.5 births, which may be lower than the actual average. The Mexican birth rates were mathematically interpolated from rates for 5-year age groups, which accounts for their smoothness as compared with genuine single-year-of-age rates for the United States.

TABLE **13.**—AGE-SPECIFIC BIRTH RATES, BY COLOR: 1920 TO 1954

[Rates are live births per 1,000 women in specified age group. Births adjusted for underregistration. Data for 1920 to 1932 include estimates of births for States not in the Birth Registration Area]

Year and color	Total, 15 to 44 years[1]	Age of woman (years)					
		15 to 19[2]	20 to 24	25 to 29	30 to 34	35 to 39	40 to 44[3]
WHITE							
1954............................	113	79	229	186	114	57	16
1953............................	111	77	219	182	111	56	16
1952............................	110	75	213	179	112	55	16
1951............................	107	76	207	173	107	53	16
1950............................	102	70	190	165	103	51	16
1949............................	104	72	195	165	102	52	16
1948............................	104	72	196	164	104	54	16
1947............................	112	70	208	179	113	58	17
1946............................	100	51	180	164	110	58	17
1945............................	83	42	135	133	101	56	17
1944............................	86	46	148	138	98	54	17
1943............................	92	52	161	151	100	52	16
1942............................	90	52	163	146	92	47	15
1941............................	81	48	142	130	85	45	16
1940............................	77	46	131	124	83	45	17
NATIVE WHITE							
1940............................	78	46	131	122	83	46	17
1939............................	76	45	125	118	80	46	17
1938............................	78	47	128	119	81	47	18
1937............................	75	45	124	115	80	47	18
1936............................	74	44	121	114	79	49	20
1935............................	75	44	121	115	81	51	21
1934............................	76	43	122	117	85	52	22
1933............................	74	41	118	114	82	53	24
1932............................	79	44	126	120	86	57	25
1931............................	82	46	131	125	89	59	26
1930............................	86	50	139	130	93	62	27
1929............................	86	50	138	130	91	63	28
1928............................	90	52	143	133	97	68	29
1927............................	95	55	150	139	103	73	31
1926............................	96	55	151	142	106	75	33
1925............................	100	56	156	147	110	79	34
1924............................	104	57	163	151	114	82	35
1923............................	103	54	160	153	116	83	35
1922............................	104	54	158	154	116	83	36
1921............................	112	60	170	163	124	88	40
1920............................	109	55	167	160	122	86	40
NONWHITE							
1954............................	153	172	280	208	134	77	24
1953............................	147	168	264	199	128	72	24
1952............................	143	166	256	190	125	68	24
1951............................	142	171	253	182	120	67	25
1950............................	137	169	243	174	113	64	24
1949............................	135	168	241	167	107	64	24
1948............................	132	162	237	160	104	63	23
1947............................	126	151	224	151	102	63	25
1946............................	114	126	197	139	99	61	25
1945............................	106	121	172	125	97	61	26
1944............................	109	125	182	127	97	58	25
1943............................	111	137	187	125	94	57	25
1942............................	108	136	182	120	88	54	25
1941............................	105	132	175	118	86	54	26
1940............................	102	125	169	116	84	54	27
1939............................	100	124	161	115	81	55	23
1938............................	101	121	161	115	81	57	26
1937............................	99	116	161	113	80	58	27
1936............................	96	108	155	111	79	57	28
1935............................	99	109	159	113	84	59	29
1934............................	100	108	162	113	91	59	32
1933............................	97	103	153	111	89	59	32
1932............................	103	109	160	118	94	64	34
1931............................	102	108	157	116	94	64	33
1930............................	106	111	161	120	97	68	35

[1] Rate includes the relatively few births to females of other age than 15 to 44.
[2] Rate includes the relatively few births to females under 15 years old.
[3] Rate includes the relatively few births to females 45 years old and over.

Source: National Office of Vital Statistics, *Vital Statistics—Special Reports*, Vol. 44, No. 8, table 4; Vol. 40, No. 10, table 4; and Vol. 33, No. 8, table 3.

Between 1940 and 1954 the birth rate of women 35 to 39 years old increased by 10 to 12 births per 1,000 women, indicating that some of these older women made up for births postponed during the 1930's. The women 40 to 44 years old had no appreciable change in birth rates between 1940 and 1954. The small increase in birth rates for the women 35 to 39 years old and the stability in the rates for the women 40 to 44 years old in the period from 1940 to 1954 represented a change in trend from the sharp declines that occurred between 1920 and 1940. At these advanced ages the annual births occurred chiefly to mothers who had already borne an above-average number of children. Although the birth rates were low at these ages they tended to be of interest as rough indicators of the decline in large families. Between 1940 and 1954, however, the trend in annual age-specific birth rates no longer indicated the continued decline in large families. A more important, if temporary, determinant of the trend in the annual birth rate for women of advanced childbearing age was an increase in the minority of women who had a first, second, or third birth at an advanced age. Some of these women had postponed childbearing from an earlier date when economic conditions were unfavorable. Some were women who, because of changes in social and economic conditions, were able to marry or remarry at an advanced age. Examples of these were the schoolteachers who were required by some communities to be single as a condition of employment in the 1930's and the widowed and divorced women whose chances for remarriage improved considerably after the 1930's. More information on these matters will be found in Chapters 8 and 9.

The nonwhite women characteristically had higher birth rates than the white women at ages 15 to 19 years and 20 to 24 years. This situation reflected social conditions and an earlier average marriage age among nonwhites. Some writers have suggested that nonwhites may mature earlier than the whites but there is conflicting evidence on this possibility.

In many of the years shown, the nonwhite women had lower birth rates than the white women at ages 25 to 29 years and 30 to 34 years. (Materials presented later in this monograph indicate that when fertility data are limited to women living with their husbands, the nonwhites are more fertile than the whites at these ages. The nonwhites had a lower proportion of women living with their husbands and a larger proportion widowed, divorced, separated, and husband absent for reasons other than marital discord.) The proportion of nonwhite women living with a husband increased after 1940, and by 1949 the birth rates for all nonwhite women 25 to 29 years old and 30 to 34 years old became higher than those for all white women of these ages.

At ages 35 to 39 years and 40 to 44 years, the annual birth rate for nonwhite women was above that for white women in 1920 to 1954, regardless of economic conditions. This reflected characteristically the completion of more large families among nonwhites than whites and not just delayed childbearing or remarriage at an advanced age.

Birth rates by birth order. Much information of value on fertility characteristics can be derived from data on births by order of the birth, that is, by whether the birth is the mother's first live birth, second birth, or other specific number. Data of this type are especially useful for the computation of changes in cohort cumulative fertility in postcensal years.

Because the women are older at the time of each successive birth and because each birth order depends on the number of previous births, two characteristic features arise when age-specific birth rates are plotted by order of the birth (figure 5). The series of curves (one for each order) is centered at progressively older ages of women as the order increases and involves progressively smaller birth rates as the order increases.

It may be noted from figure 5 that in 1950 the peak of first-birth rates was reached among women at age 19. The peak of the second-birth rates was reached at about age 23, which also happened to be the peak age for total birth rates. The third-birth rates did not show a sharply defined peak, and the higher orders exhibited still less central tendency. The patterns of birth rates flattened out in progressive fashion after the first birth.

Trends in birth rates by birth order are shown for native white women in figure 6. These are plotted on the usual arithmetical scale in order to indicate the relative importance of each order. On such a scale, it appears that the largest fluctuations occurred in the first-birth rates and the magnitude of the fluctuations decreased as the order of birth increased. This is a correct impression, in terms of absolute amounts of change. The percents of change were of about equal magnitude in each order of birth, however, as would be seen if the data were plotted on a logarithmic scale.

The trends in first-birth rates suggest the possibility that there was some decline between 1920 and 1933 in the percentage of women with at least one child ever born and a corresponding increase in the percentage of women who had never borne a child, followed by a reversal of these changes after 1933. However, the trends in annual first-birth rates are not valid indications of trends in the final distribution of women by motherhood status, unless the first births are cumulated by cohorts. The annual first-birth rates reflect postponement or advancement of first births in addition to trends in the proportion of women who have at least one child.

The trend of the birth rate was U-shaped for most orders of birth in the period from 1920 to 1954 (figure 6). There was also a tendency for a progressive spread of fluctuations from one order of birth to another, that is, a change in the frequency of first births at one date tended to be followed in a year or two by a change in the frequency of second births, and so on. Thus, the low point in the depression was reached by first births in 1933, by second births in 1935, and by higher order births at progressively later dates. The first-birth rate had some recovery as early as 1934, whereas rates for other orders began to rise later and had a smaller degree of recovery. In the war years, a peak in first births occurred in 1942, a smaller peak for second births occurred in 1943, and a very small peak for third births occurred in 1943 and 1944.

FIGURE 5.—AGE-SPECIFIC BIRTH RATES BY ORDER OF THE BIRTH: 1950

[Figures above each curve refer to specific birth order. Tenth and higher orders not shown]

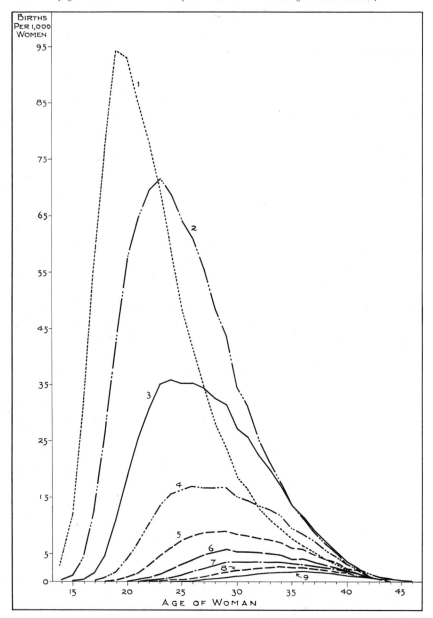

Source: Derived from National Office of Vital Statistics, *Vital Statistics of the United States, 1950*, Vol. II, table 23; *1950 Census of Population*, Vol. II, *Characteristics of the Population*, Part 1, U. S. Summary, table 94.

Age-parity-specific birth rates. One may make birth rates more specific by expressing them in terms of the number of women "at risk" to giving birth to a child of given order. Thus, only women who have never borne a child are "at risk" for a first birth, only women who have borne

FIGURE **6.**—BIRTHS PER 1,000 WOMEN 15 TO 44 YEARS OLD, BY ORDER OF THE BIRTH:
1920 TO 1954

[Births adjusted for underregistration. Rates for 1920 to 1932 include estimates of births for States not in
the Birth Registration Area. Rates not shown for eighth and higher orders of birth]

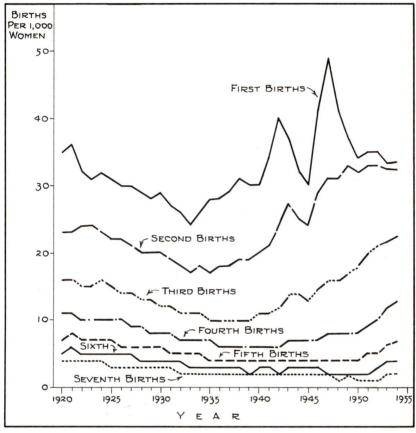

Source: National Office of Vital Statistics, *Vital Statistics—Special Reports*, Vol. 44, No. 8, table 9, and Vol. 40,
No. 10, table 7.

only one child are "at risk" for a second birth, and so on. The total number of live births a woman has had is her "parity" as the term is used
in demography. For example, the women with no children ever born have
zero parity.

The parity-specific birth rates require a special kind of population base
for their computation. The bases are available for some years from decennial census and Current Population Survey data on women by number
of children ever born, and they can be derived from cumulations of annual vital statistics as explained in Chapter 9.

Some age-parity-specific birth rates for native white women are shown
in figure 7. These were plotted from Whelpton's book, *Cohort Fertility*.[5]

---

[5] Pascal K. Whelpton, *Cohort Fertility: Native White Women in the United States*, Princeton University Press, Princeton, 1954.

The age-parity-specific birth rates for native white women exhibited U-shaped patterns of trend between 1920 and 1949, like the birth rates by order of the birth in figure 4, indirectly showing once again that variations in economic conditions affected the fertility of various segments of the population in a similar manner. However, the second and higher orders of births had a more noticeable downward trend between 1920 and 1935 on an age-parity-specific basis as shown in figure 7 than on a simple order basis as shown in figure 6, and they had less of a recovery in subsequent years. The rates in figure 6 were affected by the chain-action effect of a surge of births through progressively higher orders, whereas those in figure 7, being more nearly on an "at risk" basis, were not so affected.

FIGURE 7.—AGE-PARITY-SPECIFIC BIRTH RATES FOR NATIVE WHITE WOMEN OF ZERO TO THREE PARITY: 1920 TO 1949

[Preliminary data. Rates are annual number of births per 1,000 women of given age and parity and are adjusted for underregistration. Rates for 1920 to 1932 include estimates of births for States not in the Birth Registration Area]

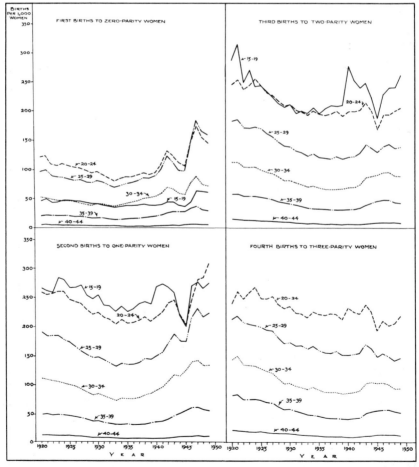

Source: Adapted from P. K. Whelpton, *Cohort Fertility: Native White Women in the United States*, Princeton University Press, Princeton, 1954, table F.

It may be deduced from an examination of figure 7 that although any postponement or making up of births may have been followed by some compensatory change, the counteraction was not immediate but was spread out over a period of time. It may also be deduced from the downward trend of third and higher parity-specific birth rates through 1949 that there was still an underlying tendency for declining fertility. The spread of the desire or ability to control fertility was not quite complete.

The measurement of reproduction. There are several possible methods for measuring reproduction; they meet different needs, and none of them is wholly free from criticism from all viewpoints. It is sometimes helpful to use crude measures of reproduction despite their limitations. Most of the measures of reproduction evaluate conditions in a particular year or 5-year period of time. These are a kind of average of more detailed data for the date and may or may not give some indication of what the growth of the population may be over a period of a generation or longer. A few measures make use of data for real cohorts of women and involve the 30-year period over which they bear children. The growth of the population depends on the experience of many cohorts of women, of course. None of the measures thus far available yields infallible indications of the inherent future growth tendencies of populations, although some of them measure past tendencies quite well. Because of the volatility of fertility trends in western countries during the past two decades, no measure of current reproduction, however refined, is completely satisfactory for all purposes.[6]

The simplest measure of population replacement consists of the difference between the crude birth rate and the crude death rate in a particular year. The difference is the crude rate of natural increase (or decrease, if deaths exceed births). It may give a misleading idea of current conditions because it ignores the composition of the population. The United States has never had a crude rate of natural increase of less than 0.7 percent per year (table 14).

Years ago, Lotka showed that with a long continuation of the age-specific birth and death rates of any date, and no migration, the population eventually would attain a fixed relative distribution by age and sex and thereafter would grow (or decrease) by a constant percentage each year.[7] The "stable population" that would result would have crude birth and death rates quite different from those in the current real population. Lotka called the resulting measures for the hypothetical stable population the intrinsic or "true" rates of birth, death, and natural increase. (Some rates of this type together with the crude rates are shown in table 14.) These

---

[6] For an extensive discussion of limitations of reproduction rates and for a guide to the literature and to methodology, see George J. Stolnitz and Norman B. Ryder, "Recent Discussion on the Net Reproduction Rate," *Population Index*, Vol. 15, No. 2, April 1949, pp. 114–128.

[7] F. Sharpe and A. J. Lotka, "A Problem in Age Distribution," *Philosophical Magazine*, Vol. 21, April 1911, pp. 435–438; Louis I. Dublin and A. J. Lotka, "On the True Rate of Natural Increase," *Journal of the American Statistical Association*, Vol. 20, No. 151, September 1925, pp. 305–399.

rates, as Lotka was careful to note, were not predictive of things to come but rather were an evaluation of the underlying or "true" conditions in a particular year or period, after the masking effect of the current age distribution had been removed.   Birth and death rates by age were known to change from year to year and hence were not regarded as likely to remain fixed long enough for the stable population to emerge.

Other measures, in more common use than the "intrinsic" rates, are the gross and net reproduction rates.   The gross reproduction rate in its conventional form shows the number of daughters a group of newborn female infants would have during their lifetime if the group were subject to the age-specific birth rates of a given date and if none of the infants died before reaching the end of the childbearing ages.   The gross reproduction rate is sometimes regarded as a measure of "pure" fertility.   (The gross reproduction rate may be multiplied by two for a rough approximation of the average number of children ever born to women reaching age 45.) The net reproduction rate is similar to the gross reproduction rate except that the group of infants is assumed to be subject not only to the age-specific birth rates of a particular date but also to the age-specific death rates.   For replacement in the next generation the group of female infants must produce an equal number of daughters during their lifetime.   The ratio of the two generations is the net reproduction rate.   Like the "intrinsic" measures, the gross and net reproduction rates are measures of conditions in a given year rather than predictions of things to come, because the age-specific birth and death rates are not expected to remain constant. The reproduction rates are easier to compute and to interpret than the "intrinsic" rates.   In fact, the net reproduction rate is an integral part of Lotka's methodology and must be computed before his "intrinsic" measures can be derived.   The net reproduction rate shows the potential increase (or decrease) of population per generation rather than per year. The mean length of a generation is defined as the average age of mothers at the time of birth of all their children, and it has been found to be fairly similar for many different populations the world over; it usually varies from 26 to 29 years.   Because of variations in the mean length of a generation, net reproduction rates are less comparable in a time sense for different populations than are intrinsic rates of natural increase.

It may be noted from table 14 that in the depression decade of the 1930's the net reproduction rates for the total population were slightly below replacement needs, for the first time in the Nation's history.   The rate was 980—2 percent below the replacement level of 1,000.   Subsequently there was a recovery to 1,560 in 1952, a value higher than any noted previously for the twentieth century.   But because the annual age-specific birth rates in the depression were below those any real cohort has experienced for more than a small part of their lifetime, and because those in 1952 included first births at too high a rate to persist indefinitely without an impossible result of more than one first child per woman, these rates were not indicative of true growth potentials.

TABLE **14.**—REPRODUCTION RATES, INTRINSIC RATES, AND CRUDE RATES OF BIRTH, DEATH, AND NATURAL INCREASE, BY COLOR: 1905–1910, 1930–1935, 1935–1940, AND ANNUALLY, 1940–1952

[Intrinsic rates per 1,000 female population not strictly comparable with crude rates per 1,000 total population. Intrinsic rates for 1946 to 1952 computed by approximate methods. Reproduction rates and intrinsic rates for 5-year periods computed from census data on women by own children under 5 years old and 5 to 9 years old. Minus sign (−) denotes decrease]

Year or period and color	Reproduction rate		Intrinsic rate			Crude rate		
	Gross	Net	Natural increase	Birth	Death	Natural increase	Birth	Death
TOTAL								
1952	1,640	1,560	16.2	24.1	7.9	15.5	25.1	9.6
1951	1,590	1,520	15.3	23.5	8.2	15.2	24.9	9.7
1950	1,510	1,440	13.2	22.1	8.9	14.5	24.1	9.6
1949	1,520	1,440	13.2	22.2	9.0	14.8	24.5	9.7
1948	1,510	1,440	13.2	22.3	9.1	15.0	24.9	9.9
1947	1,590	1,510	14.8	23.6	8.8	16.5	26.6	10.1
1946	1,430	1,340	10.6	20.8	10.2	14.1	24.1	10.0
1945	1,220	1,140	4.9	17.4	12.5	9.8	20.4	10.6
1944	1,260	1,170	5.8	18.1	12.3	10.6	21.2	10.6
1943	1,330	1,230	7.8	19.5	11.7	11.8	22.7	10.9
1942	1,280	1,190	6.5	18.6	12.1	11.9	22.2	10.3
1941	1,170	1,080	2.7	16.6	13.9	9.8	20.3	10.5
1940	1,120	1,020	0.9	15.7	14.8	8.6	19.4	10.8
April 1935 to 1940	1,100	980	-0.7	15.5	16.2	7.8	18.8	11.0
April 1930 to 1935	1,110	980	(^{1})	(^{1})	(^{1})	8.6	19.6	11.0
April 1905 to 1910	1,790	1,340	10.1	26.9	16.8	^{2}14.7	^{2}29.9	^{3}15.2
WHITE								
1952	1,580	1,510	15.1	23.1	8.0	14.7	24.1	9.4
1951	1,530	1,470	14.1	22.5	8.4	14.4	23.9	9.5
1950	1,450	1,390	12.0	21.0	9.0	13.5	23.0	9.5
1949	1,460	1,400	12.0	21.2	9.2	14.1	23.6	9.5
1948	1,470	1,400	12.5	21.7	9.2	14.3	24.0	9.7
1947	1,570	1,490	14.4	23.1	8.7	16.2	26.1	9.9
1946	1,410	1,330	10.2	20.3	10.1	13.8	23.6	9.8
1945	1,180	1,110	3.8	16.5	12.7	9.5	19.9	10.4
1944	1,220	1,140	4.8	17.3	12.5	10.1	20.5	10.4
1943	1,300	1,210	7.1	18.8	11.7	11.4	22.1	10.7
1942	1,250	1,170	5.9	18.0	12.1	10.4	21.5	10.1
1941	1,130	1,050	1.9	15.8	13.9	9.3	19.5	10.2
1940	1,080	1,000	0.0	14.9	14.9	8.2	18.6	10.4
April 1935 to 1940	1,060	960	-1.5	14.7	16.2	7.4	18.0	10.6
April 1930 to 1935	1,080	970	(^{1})	(^{1})	(^{1})	8.2	18.8	10.6
April 1905 to 1910	1,740	1,340	10.1	26.0	15.9	^{2}13.8	^{2}28.8	^{3}15.0
NONWHITE								
1952	2,060	1,890	23.3	31.2	7.9	22.6	33.6	11.0
1951	2,020	1,860	23.1	31.1	8.0	22.7	33.8	11.1
1950	1,940	1,780	21.3	29.8	8.5	22.1	33.3	11.2
1949	1,910	1,740	20.7	29.6	8.9	18.8	30.0	11.2
1948	1,850	1,680	19.4	28.7	9.3	21.0	32.4	11.4
1947	1,770	1,590	17.4	27.4	10.0	19.8	31.2	11.4
1946	1,600	1,440	13.3	24.8	11.5	17.3	28.4	11.1
1945	1,560	1,380	12.5	24.7	12.2	14.6	26.5	11.9
1944	1,580	1,380	12.7	25.2	12.5	15.0	27.4	12.4
1943	1,580	1,380	12.8	25.7	12.9	15.5	28.3	12.8
1942	1,510	1,320	10.8	24.2	13.4	15.0	27.7	12.7
1941	1,470	1,250	8.9	23.6	14.7	13.5	27.3	13.5
1940	1,410	1,200	7.3	22.7	15.4	12.9	26.7	13.8
April 1935 to 1940	1,410	1,140	4.4	22.1	17.7	11.6	26.0	14.4
April 1930 to 1935	1,340	1,070	(^{1})	(^{1})	(^{1})	11.6	26.5	14.9
April 1905 to 1910	2,240	1,330	10.1	34.6	24.5	^{2}14.7	^{2}38.1	^{3}23.4

^{1} Not available. ^{2} Estimated. ^{3} Death Registration Area.

Source: *Population Index*, Vol. 21, No. 2, April 1955, pp. 152 and 153; *1940 Census of Population, Differential Fertility, 1940 and 1910*, Standardized Fertility Rates and Reproduction Rates, tables 7 and 9; U. S. Bureau of the Census, *Statistical Abstract of the United States, 1955*, tables 58 and 69; National Office of Vital Statistics, *Vital Statistics—Special Reports*, Vol. 33, No. 8, table 1; *Vital Statistics of the United States: 1950*, Vol. I, table 8.40.

The "intrinsic" measures and the gross and net reproduction rates are usually based on data for females.   One reason is that the reproduction period is less well defined for males.   In a few cases they have been based on data for males, and joint computations occasionally have been made. The results for males and females usually differ, not only because the mean length of a generation is greater for males than for females, but also because males have higher mortality than females and because population data vary in quality by sex.   (For example, there may be a slightly less complete enumeration of transient young men than of young women, and studies of concentration on certain digits of age indicate that there may be slightly more misreporting of age by women.)   Various modifications of conventional gross and net reproduction rates have been made to take into account not only age-specific birth rates but also marriage rates, duration of marriage, parity of women, and other factors affecting fertility.   Many of the modified measures are superior to the conventional measures for some purposes.   Unfortunately, they often require data which are not widely available or else they are too complex for popular use.   Some of the modifications have been developed simply as logical extensions of the basic methodology.   Others have been developed in an effort to eliminate some of the temporary fluctuations in annual fertility that bias conventional reproduction rates.   For example, marriage-standardized reproduction rates are based upon observed age-specific birth rates for married women, weighted by assumed "normal" proportions of the married among all women at each age thereby eliminating the effect of temporary variations in proportions of the married.   This procedure has the limitation that it relies on the judgment of the analyst as to what constitutes "normal" proportions of the married.   Different analysts may therefore obtain different results from the same data.   However, the same may be said regarding the choice of any type of standard, and the procedure does tend to eliminate differences arising from time and space variations in proportions of the married.

In recent years, some who have searched for methods for accurately measuring reproduction have turned to the cohort fertility approach.[8]   A number of demographers have come to believe that reproduction rates embodying only the experience of a single year, or even the averages for a 5-year period, however refined, have too many elements of instability. They feel that the best approach involves real cohorts.   Thus, the childbearing experience of a group of women born in a particular year (an age cohort) or married in a particular year (a marriage cohort) is followed through life.   In 1947 Woofter published gross and net reproduction rates for cohorts of native white women in the United States, computed by "the

---

[8] One of the earliest uses of cohort reproduction rates appears in Pierre Depoid, *Reproduction nette en Europe depuis l'origine des statistiques de l'etat civil*, Statistique Generale de la France, Etudes Démographiques, No. 1, Paris, 1941, 42 pp.

generation method."[9] These reproduction rates made use of the actual birth rates of women in the past and they also made use of estimated future birth rates for those cohorts of women who had not yet attained age 45. In the absence of information on future patterns of marriage and on the childbearing intentions of married couples, the reproduction rate of a real cohort of women can be predicated with a high degree of accuracy only after the cohort has completed much of its childbearing, although rough estimates can be made at an earlier stage. Some of the information needed for improved estimates of future fertility may result from studies of the number of children young couples hope to have. Two research organizations have made such studies, but most of the results are not yet available and the data have not yet been tested in the crucible of time. (One study "Growth of American Families" is cited in Chapters 9 and 10. The other is "American Family Life," sponsored by the Milbank Fund and directed by the Office of Population Research (Princeton). See also H. V. Muhsam and Clyde V. Kiser, "XXXII. The Number of Children Desired at the Time of Marriage," *Social and Psychological Factors Affecting Fertility*, Vol. Five, pp. 1299–1324, Milbank Memorial Fund, New York, 1958.)

B. Children under 5 years old

Trends in ratios of children under 5 years old to women were discussed in Chapter 2 for the period from 1800 to 1950. It may be noted here that ratios of children under 5 years old to women can be computed not only from decennial census data but also from population estimates for intercensal and postcensal years. The Bureau of the Census has published annual estimates of the population of the United States by age, sex, and color, for years back to 1900. Only those for years since 1920 have been based on a balancing equation method (in which data from the last census are carried forward by the use of annual statistics of births, deaths, and net migration by age) and thus reflect annual fluctuations in fertility. Annual ratios of children to women are shown in table 15, for years between 1940 and 1955.

The secular trends in the ratios of children under 5 years old to women 15 to 49 years old are somewhat different from those of the crude birth rates examined earlier. The ratios of young children to women have increased each year since 1937 with the exception of 1952. The ratios have a much smoother secular trend than the annual crude birth rates. They exhibited neither a wartime peak in 1943 nor a postwar peak in 1947. A major reason for the smoother pattern of the ratios was that the annual data on children under 5 years old were a near equivalent to a 5-year moving total of birth rates to women 15 to 49 years old. Some short-run fluctuations in birth rates were thus smoothed over. In

---

[9] T. J. Woofter, "Completed Generation Rates," *Human Biology*, Vol. 19, No. 3, September 1947.

most years, reductions in infant mortality increased "effective fertility" in terms of surviving children over and above the effect of any rising birth rates. There was a somewhat greater widening between 1940 and 1955 of color differentials in ratios of children to women than in birth rates. This in part reflected a larger reduction in infant mortality among nonwhites than among whites. The number of white children under 5 years old in 1955, adjusted for a net undercount, was 97.4 percent of the number of white births in the previous 5 years, and the number of nonwhite children was 96.7 percent of the number of nonwhite births. The corresponding percentages in 1940 were 94.4 for whites and 90.6 for nonwhites.[10]

TABLE **15.**—ESTIMATED NUMBER OF CHILDREN UNDER 5 YEARS OLD PER 1,000 WOMEN 15 TO 49 YEARS OLD, BY COLOR: JULY 1, 1940 TO 1955

Year	Comparable to census			Adjusted for net undercount		
	Total	White	Nonwhite	Total	White	Nonwhite
1955.............................	459	448	548	479	465	595
1954.............................	450	438	537	470	455	585
1953.............................	443	432	527	463	449	575
1952.............................	437	428	513	458	445	562
1951.............................	441	434	502	462	451	551
1950.............................	421	415	469	441	432	518
1949.............................	404	399	446	425	416	496
1948.............................	389	384	423	410	402	475
1947.............................	378	374	408	399	392	460
1946.............................	349	344	390	371	362	443
1945.............................	345	340	388	367	358	442
1944.............................	335	330	379	357	348	435
1943.............................	323	318	369	346	337	426
1942.............................	307	300	358	330	319	416
1941.............................	297	291	346	320	310	406
1940.............................	292	287	340	316	306	401

Source: Derived from U. S. Bureau of the Census, *Current Population Reports*, Series P–25, Nos. 98 and 121.

Age-specific ratios of children to women. By age, the pattern of fertility ratios is similar to the bell-shaped arrangement of age-specific birth rates. Examples are given in figures 8 and 9. A major difference is that the mothers of the children under 5 years old are, on the average, somewhat older than at the time the children were born, so that the peak age of women for fertility ratios occurs at about age 27 for native white women instead of at age 23 as in annual births, and at age 23 or 24 among Negroes instead of at age 19. (Computation from annual age-specific birth rates indicate that these differences are explainable in terms of mathematical considerations, and hence they are typical.) Whereas the age range from 15 to 19 years is associated with an important proportion of annual births, it is associated with a small proportion of children under

---

[10] The term "undercount" is a fictitious term when applied to annual estimates of children under 5 years old "comparable to census." A census normally has a net undercount of young children, arising in part from misstatements of age and in part from underenumeration of children. The population estimates from births and deaths and net migration, however, are not subject to any such undercount. One is deliberately put in to meet the needs of some consumers for data comparable to what a census would show. The "adjusted" figures shown in table 15 are not depressed by the assumed undercount. (They are, however, subject to any errors of estimation, including any errors in adjusting for underregistration of births and deaths and in figuring net migration.)

5 years old. In terms of ratios of children under 5 years old to women, the age range of 45 to 49 years for women is sometimes more important than the range from 15 to 19 years, whereas in annual birth statistics the older ages are negligible.

FIGURE **8.**—NUMBER OF OWN CHILDREN UNDER 5 YEARS OLD PER 1,000 NATIVE WHITE WOMEN 15 TO 49 YEARS OLD, BY SINGLE YEARS OF AGE OF WOMAN: 1950, 1940, AND 1910

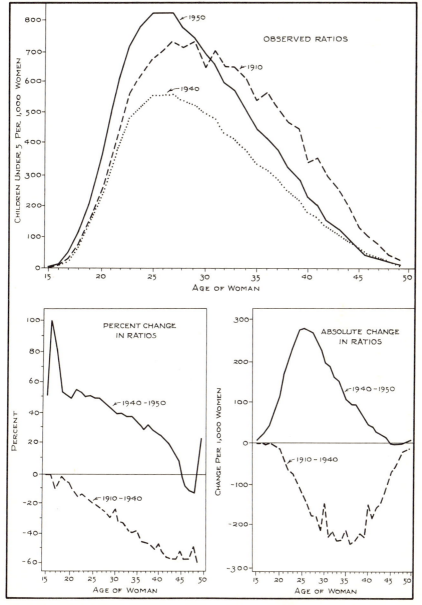

Source: Derived from *1940 Census of Population, Differential Fertility, 1940 and 1910,* Women by Number of Children Under 5 Years Old, tables 9 and 10, and unpublished tabulation detail for native white women from the 1950 Census of Population.

FIGURE **9.**—NUMBER OF OWN CHILDREN UNDER 5 YEARS OLD PER 1,000 NEGRO WOMEN 15
TO 49 YEARS OLD, BY SINGLE YEARS OF AGE OF WOMAN: 1950, 1940, AND 1910

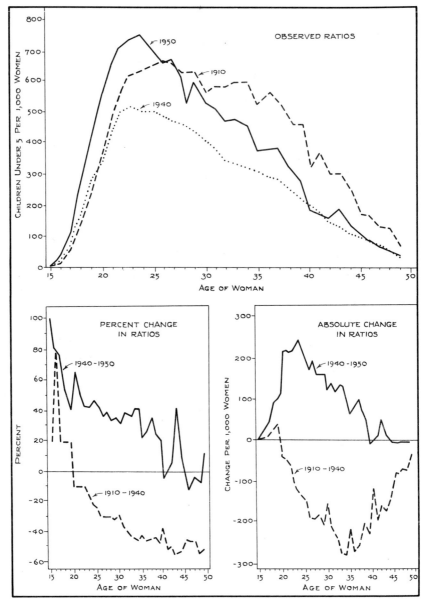

Source: Derived from *1940 Census of Population, Differential Fertility, 1940 and 1910,* Women by Number of Children Under 5 Years Old, tables 8 and 11, and unpublished tabulation detail for Negro women from the 1950 Census of
Population.

    The data in figures 8 and 9 are limited to own children of women, that
is, to those children living in the household who appeared to be the
woman's sons and daughters. The identification was made from collateral
information on the census schedules, such as the relationship of each per-

son to the household head, rather than from a direct question on own children of each woman. The identifiable adopted children and stepchildren were eliminated but most such children could not be distinguished from the woman's progeny and thus were counted. The restriction of the data to own children was desirable to permit a simultaneous classification of mother and children according to given characteristics of the mother. In 1950, own children comprised about 98.2 percent of enumerated white persons under 5 years old and 85.6 percent of enumerated nonwhite persons under 5 years old. According to life tables, fewer than 1 percent of the children, white or nonwhite, probably were maternal orphans. Some children lived with their grandmothers or other relatives while the mother worked, and there were also occasional problems of identification of children as own children when their surname differed from the mother's surname.

Native white women and Negro women had roughly similar patterns of change in age-specific fertility ratios between 1910 and 1950. Between 1910 and 1940, the ratios declined considerably at ages over 20 years. The relative decline increased with age and reflected an underlying trend toward smaller completed families. Absolute decreases in the fertility ratios were greatest among the women 30 to 39 years old. The women over 40 already had small fertility ratios in 1910 and hence did not have as large an absolute decrease as the women 30 to 39 years old.

Between 1940 and 1950 the ratios of children to native white women increased among women under 45 years old. The relative increase was largest among women under 20 years old and declined with age. The absolute increases had a bell-shaped pattern; the largest absolute increase occurred among native white women 25 years old.

The figures show numerous small fluctuations from one single year of age to another. These may reflect some reporting of approximate ages. A landlady, for example, may not have known the exact age of each lodger. The irregularities were less marked in 1950 and 1940 than in 1910. A spurious smoothness appears in the Negro data for 1940; for this group, age detail was estimated by mathematical interpolation of 5-year groups and this automatically resulted in a smooth pattern. It is evident from the fluctuations in the single-year-of-age data for Negroes in 1950 that some Negroes gave approximate ages rather than exact ages. The fluctuations were less marked in 1950 than in 1910, indicating that the quality of data on age had improved considerably.

C. Children ever born

Trends in completed fertility. It is possible to determine from census data the approximate lifetime fertility of women who completed the childbearing ages at any time during the first half of the twentieth century (table 16). (See also tables 9 and 10 of Chapter 2 which present census data for women who reached age 45 in the nineteenth century. Chapter 9 presents data derived from birth registration materials.) The data are approximate because, among other reasons, they are limited to the women living at the census date and hence to the survivors of the larger group of women who reached age 45 at dates before the census.[11]

TABLE **16.**—NUMBER OF CHILDREN EVER BORN PER 1,000 WOMEN OF COMPLETED FERTILITY, BY COLOR AND AGE: 1950, 1940, AND 1910

Year, color, and age of woman	Number of women	Percent ever married	Percent childless among ever married	Children ever born		
				Per 1,000 women	Per 1,000 women ever married	Per 1,000 mothers
WHITE						
1950:						
45 to 49 years	4,033,000	91.6	19.5	2,251	2,456	3,053
50 to 54 years	3,723,000	92.0	18.0	2,451	2,665	3,249
55 to 59 years	3,307,000	92.0	16.9	2,689	2,922	3,517
1940:						
45 to 49 years	3,651,000	91.1	[1]16.1	[1]2,704	[1]2,969	[1]3,539
50 to 54 years	3,203,000	90.9	[1]16.3	[1]2,821	[1]3,103	[1]3,709
55 to 59 years	2,631,000	91.0	[1]16.5	[1]2,962	[1]3,256	[1]3,899
60 to 64 years	2,165,000	90.5	15.0	3,047	3,413	4,015
65 to 69 years	1,749,000	90.0	14.0	3,218	3,630	4,220
70 to 74 years	1,204,000	90.0	12.5	3,383	3,821	4,365
1910:						
40 to 44 years	2,242,000	89.2	10.4	3,778	4,263	4,757
45 to 49 years	1,894,000	90.6	9.6	4,139	4,594	5,080
NONWHITE						
1950:						
45 to 49 years	447,000	95.0	28.1	2,663	2,803	3,897
50 to 54 years	354,000	95.8	25.1	2,981	3,112	4,154
55 to 59 years	260,000	96.1	24.1	3,214	3,344	4,403
1940:						
45 to 49 years	350,000	94.9	[1]23.4	[1]3,120	[1]3,288	[1]4,291
50 to 54 years	269,000	95.1	[1]19.4	[1]3,452	[1]3,629	[1]4,505
55 to 59 years	192,000	95.7	[1]19.1	[1]3,718	[1]3,886	[1]4,805
60 to 64 years	143,000	95.0	14.4	3,954	4,199	4,906
65 to 69 years	146,000	95.4	11.9	4,270	4,517	5,130
70 to 74 years	80,000	95.8	9.9	4,832	5,087	5,649
1910:						
40 to 44 years	233,000	93.9	10.4	5,160	5,527	6,170
45 to 49 years	195,000	95.2	8.7	5,864	6,183	6,771

[1] Revised figures as shown in the 1950 Census report. The revision incorporated estimates of children for women not reporting on children. The change increased the percent childless by about 1.3 points for whites and 2.1 points for nonwhites, and the rates of children per 1,000 women changed by less than 2 percent, as a rule. Comparisons with the unrevised figures shown for ages 60 and over in 1940 should be made with awareness of this change.

Source: Derived from *1950 Census of Population,* Vol. IV, *Special Reports,* Part 5, Chapter C, Fertility, tables 4 and 6; *1940 Census of Population, Differential Fertility, 1940 and 1910,* Fertility for States and Large Cities, tables 3 and 4.

Between 1910 and 1950, the average number of children ever born to white women 45 to 49 years old at the census date declined from 4.1 to 2.3 and that for nonwhite women in this age group declined from 5.9 to 2.7. This represented a decline of 54.6 percent in the average for nonwhites and of 45.6 percent for whites. This comparison of data for an identical age group at two censuses may be a more accurate indication of secular trends than is given by a comparison of data for women in successive age groups in a single census. Comparisons of data for women in successive age groups indicate that the decline in fertility progressed from one age-cohort of women to another in rather steady fashion in both color groups.

[11] For a more complete discussion of the quality of the data on children ever born, see Appendix A.

Between 1910 and 1950, the percentage of ever-married women 45 to 49 years old who had never borne a child more than doubled among whites and tripled among nonwhites. A smaller percentage of nonwhites than of whites in 1910 had never borne a child; in 1950 and in 1940 the relative situation was reversed.

The trend was not only toward increased childlessness among ever-married women but also toward fewer children per mother. There were sizable reductions among whites and nonwhites in the average number of children ever born per mother (table 16). The nonwhites had a larger absolute decline in number of children ever born per mother than did the whites. Between 1910 and 1950 there was a greater absolute decline in the average number of children ever born per nonwhite mother 45 to 49 years old than in the corresponding rate for white mothers. The nonwhites still had a higher average than the whites in 1950, however.

Trends in incomplete fertility. Data on children ever born for women still of childbearing age foreshadow trends in completed fertility. Methods of analysis of data for young women by number of children ever born have been developed, as in cohort analysis. Much research remains to be done before the full value of the data can be extracted.

As may be seen in table 17, there has been a considerable increase since 1940 in the average number of children ever born to women in 5-year age groups between 15 to 19 and 30 to 34. In contrast, there was little change between 1940 and 1954 in the rate of children ever born among women 35 to 39 years old, and there was a decline in the rate for women 40 to 44 years old.

There was a much larger percent increase between 1940 and 1954 in the rates of children ever born to all women under 35 years old than in rates limited to the women who had ever married. Thus, much of the increase in the cumulative total fertility of all women came about from more marriages at young ages rather than from an increase in marital fertility. Moreover, the large percent increases in cumulative fertility at young ages involved only the early stages of childbearing, and did not necessarily mean that the eventual size of completed families would be proportionately larger. Some women may have no increase in eventual family size as a result of early childbearing, but earlier childbearing may enable other women to have as many children as they desire and it increases the period during which an unplanned pregnancy may occur.

The census data on young women by number of children ever born are useful as a rough guide to the eventual completed fertility of these women, if assumptions are made as to the proportion of lifetime fertility already completed. In the United States, the women 25 to 29 years old have generally borne from 50 to 60 percent of their lifetime number of children; this range may indicate that the lifetime number can be predicted within a margin of error tolerable for some purposes. Women older than 25 to 29 years have generally completed larger proportions of their lifetime fertility and the range of variability is generally smaller than that just given for age group 25 to 29 years.   The percent of lifetime fertility completed by each age may be figured from census data or from vital statistics for various predecessor cohorts and used as a rough guide for current cohorts. (It would also be desirable to allow for changes in the timing of births as a result of changing social and economic conditions and for an increasing ability of women to have no more than a desired number of children.)   For example, according to census data the average number of children ever born for native white women 25 to 29 years old in 1910 was about 51 percent of the average for the surviving members of the cohort of women 30 years later, at age 55 to 59 years in 1940.   For nonwhites the corresponding figure was 60 percent.   For a more recent example, one may calculate from table 17 that the women of all races, 25 to 29 years old in 1940, probably had completed about 52 percent of their lifetime childbearing.[12]   Probably the women 25 to 29 years old in 1955 had completed more than 52 percent of their lifetime fertility because of an earlier start in marriage and childbearing than had been customary in the past. Thus, Whelpton predicted on the basis of preliminary findings from a study, "Growth of American Families," that the women of all races in the cohorts of 1926–30 who live to age 50 may have an average of about 2.9 children (see Chapter 10) as compared with an average of 1.9 on January 1, 1955, for the women in these cohorts who were then 25 to 29 years old. These figures imply that the women in 1955 had completed about 55 percent of their lifetime childbearing.   The 50-to-60 percent range cited earlier was based on other materials.

If the women 25 to 29 years old in the 1950's were about 55 percent of the way through childbearing, they may have an average of about 2.8 children by the time they reach age 45, in the 1970's.   This contrasts to the much lower averages shown in table 17 for women 45 to 49 years old in 1950, 1952, and 1954.   Other proportions may be applied to other age groups, for parallel anticipations of potential completed fertility.

Ages 20 to 29 are usually associated with maximum annual fertility.   The women 35 to 44 years old in 1950 had lived through some or all of these ages during the economic depression of the 1930's.   This may help to explain why these women showed no increase in fertility as compared with other women 35 to 44 years old in 1940.

Trends in childlessness and in the distribution of women by specific number of children ever born.   In 1940 (and also in 1910, not shown), the percent childless among the women who had ever married decreased with successively older ages of women.   In 1940 it decreased

---

[12] There were 1,132 children ever born per 1,000 women of all races, 25 to 29 years old, in 1940. The cumulative fertility of this cohort of women increased to 2,061 children per 1,000 women in 1950 and it was likely to increase further by less than 6 percent if one may judge from the data in table 17 for women 35 to 39 years old in 1940 and 45 to 49 years old in 1950.

from 19.9 among women 35 to 39 years old to 16.6 among women 50 to 54 years old. In 1950, 1952, and 1954, in contrast, there was no such regular pattern of decrease (table 18). Here, the smallest percent childless occurred among the women 30 to 34 years old, indicating that they had borne relatively more first children than had the women of older age. The percent childless was 17.3 among women 30 to 34 years old in 1950, about 14.7 in 1952, and about 13.4 in 1954. The women 25 to 29 years old in 1954 who had ever married had a smaller percent childless than the women 45 to 49 years old. The reductions since 1940 in the percentage of women who were childless were of course accompanied by corresponding increases in the percentage of women who had at least a first child. (See Chapter 9 for data on trends in percent childless among cohorts of native white women.)

TABLE **17.**—NUMBER OF CHILDREN EVER BORN PER 1,000 WOMEN 15 TO 49 YEARS OLD, BY AGE AND MARITAL STATUS OF WOMAN: APRIL 1910 TO 1954

Marital status and age of woman	1954	1952	1950	1940[1]	1910	Percent change, 1940 to 1954
ALL MARITAL CLASSES						
15 to 44 years......................	1,553	1,465	1,395	1,238	1,708	25.4
15 to 19 years....................	105	98	105	68	69	54.4
20 to 24 years....................	926	836	738	522	681	77.4
25 to 29 years....................	1,716	1,527	1,436	1,132	1,601	51.6
30 to 34 years....................	2,049	1,943	1,871	1,678	2,446	22.1
35 to 39 years....................	2,166	2,112	2,061	2,145	3,286	1.0
40 to 44 years....................	2,178	2,169	2,170	2,490	3,904	-12.5
45 to 49 years....................	2,267	2,172	2,292	2,740	4,295	-17.3
EVER MARRIED						
15 to 44 years......................	2,038	1,925	1,859	1,863	2,866	9.4
15 to 19 years....................	667	572	604	564	725	18.3
20 to 24 years....................	1,337	1,187	1,082	964	1,407	38.7
25 to 29 years....................	1,930	1,742	1,654	1,431	2,180	34.9
30 to 34 years....................	2,247	2,130	2,059	1,922	2,956	16.9
35 to 39 years....................	2,334	2,293	2,247	2,364	3,781	-1.3
40 to 44 years....................	2,335	2,346	2,364	2,690	4,383	-13.2
45 to 49 years....................	2,436	2,352	2,492	2,923	4,744	-16.7

[1] Revised figures from the 1950 Census report; these include estimates of children for women with no report on children.

Source: Derived from U. S. Bureau of the Census, *Current Population Reports*, Series P-20, No. 46, table A, and No. 65, table 1; *1950 Census of Population*, Vol. IV, *Special Reports*, Part 5, Chapter C, Fertility, tables 4 and 6; *1940 Census of Population, Differential Fertility, 1940 and 1910*, Fertility for States and Large Cities, table 4.

The small percent childless (15.9) among the women 50 years old and over in 1954 appears to reflect one of the infrequent large sampling fluctuations. It is below expectations from the 1952 survey and from the 1950 and 1940 Censuses.

Comparisons of data for women age 30 to 44 years old in 1940, 1950, 1952, and 1954 indicate some of the changes that are occurring in the distributions by number of children ever born. In 1954, only about 20.5 percent of the ever-married women 40 to 44 years old had four or more children ever born as compared with 21.7 percent in 1950 and 29.2 percent in 1940. A substantial increase occurred between 1940 and 1954 in the proportion of women 40 to 44 years old with two children ever born, and a smaller increase occurred in the proportion of women with one child ever born. The two-child completed families are the most common and usually are followed, in order of popularity, by one child, no children, and three children. It is evident from the low percentages of childlessness among today's young women that at some future date there will be relatively more women 45 years old and over with three children ever born than there will be women with no children.

TABLE **18.**—NUMBER OF WOMEN 15 TO 49 YEARS OLD BY MARITAL STATUS AND PERCENT DISTRIBUTION OF EVER-MARRIED WOMEN BY NUMBER OF CHILDREN EVER BORN, BY AGE OF WOMAN: APRIL 1940 TO 1954

[Number of women in thousands. Percent not shown where less than 0.1]

Year and age of woman	Total women	Single women	Women ever married							
			Number	Percent with specified number of children ever born						
				None	1	2	3	4	5 and 6	7 or more
1954										
15 to 44 years........	34,515	8,171	26,344	18.1	23.8	27.2	15.8	7.2	5.6	2.3
15 to 19 years......	5,362	4,515	847	47.0	42.4	7.5	3.1	...	...	...
20 to 24 years......	5,412	1,660	3,752	24.3	37.6	24.5	9.2	2.9	1.4	0.1
25 to 29 years......	6,045	665	5,380	16.9	24.5	28.7	17.1	7.7	4.5	0.6
30 to 34 years......	6,246	544	5,702	13.4	20.5	30.5	19.3	7.8	6.0	2.7
35 to 39 years......	5,842	415	5,427	15.9	18.0	28.6	17.4	9.5	7.3	3.3
40 to 44 years......	5,608	372	5,236	17.8	19.9	25.9	15.9	7.8	8.2	4.5
45 to 49 years........	4,996	343	4,653	19.0	20.8	23.7	13.3	8.8	7.8	6.6
50 years and over.....	18,899	1,397	17,502	15.9	16.2	19.3	13.3	10.7	12.3	12.3
1952										
15 to 44 years........	34,138	8,150	25,988	20.7	25.4	26.0	14.0	6.5	4.7	2.6
15 to 19 years......	5,228	4,330	898	54.3	35.4	8.9	1.3	...	...	...
20 to 24 years......	5,656	1,674	3,982	30.9	35.0	22.9	7.9	2.4	0.8	0.1
25 to 29 years......	6,188	764	5,424	18.5	29.2	27.9	14.3	6.1	3.5	0.4
30 to 34 years......	6,058	532	5,526	14.7	21.8	30.9	17.3	7.5	5.5	2.3
35 to 39 years......	5,730	452	5,278	16.7	20.0	27.1	16.8	8.6	6.3	4.4
40 to 44 years......	5,278	398	4,880	19.8	21.6	22.7	14.2	8.1	7.5	5.9
45 to 49 years........	4,796	368	4,428	19.4	21.9	23.2	14.7	7.5	7.3	6.1
50 years and over.....	17,948	1,402	16,546	17.1	17.6	19.8	13.6	9.7	11.6	10.6
1950										
15 to 44 years........	34,268	8,565	25,704	22.8	26.6	24.7	12.5	6.1	4.7	2.7
15 to 19 years......	5,343	4,418	925	52.8	36.4	8.9	1.4	0.3	0.1	...
20 to 24 years......	5,949	1,890	4,059	33.3	37.7	20.2	6.2	1.8	0.7	0.1
25 to 29 years......	6,329	832	5,497	21.1	30.3	27.4	12.3	5.0	3.1	0.8
30 to 34 years......	5,893	538	5,355	17.3	23.4	28.6	15.5	7.4	5.4	2.4
35 to 39 years......	5,672	470	5,201	19.1	20.9	25.4	15.1	8.2	7.0	4.3
40 to 44 years......	5,083	416	4,667	20.0	20.9	23.3	14.0	8.4	7.4	5.9
45 to 49 years........	4,480	360	4,120	20.4	19.8	21.7	13.8	8.7	8.4	7.2
50 to 54 years........	4,077	314	3,763	18.6	18.3	20.7	14.4	9.5	10.0	8.4
55 to 59 years........	3,567	274	3,293	17.5	16.5	19.7	14.4	10.3	11.0	10.7
1940[1]										
15 to 44 years........	31,884	11,145	20,739	26.5	25.4	20.3	11.4	6.5	6.1	3.7
15 to 19 years......	6,150	5,416	734	54.6	35.8	7.9	1.2	0.4	0.1	...
20 to 24 years......	5,885	2,769	3,116	39.9	34.5	16.8	6.1	1.9	0.7	0.1
25 to 29 years......	5,608	1,267	4,343	30.0	29.6	20.9	10.2	5.0	3.5	0.7
30 to 34 years......	5,145	749	4,396	23.3	24.5	22.7	12.7	7.2	6.7	2.9
35 to 39 years......	4,768	530	4,238	19.9	20.5	21.7	14.1	8.6	9.0	6.3
40 to 44 years......	4,328	414	3,914	17.5	18.1	20.7	14.6	9.8	10.6	8.8
45 to 49 years........	4,001	344	3,657	16.8	16.2	19.1	14.7	10.3	12.2	10.7
50 to 54 years........	3,472	304	3,168	16.6	15.2	17.8	14.4	10.7	13.1	12.2
55 to 59 years........	2,823	246	2,577	16.6	14.2	16.5	13.8	10.9	14.1	13.8

[1] Revised figures from the 1950 Census reports; these include estimates of children for women with no report on children.

Source: Derived from U. S. Bureau of the Census, *Current Population Reports*, Series P-20, No. 46, table 1, and No. 65, table 1; *1950 Census of Population*, Vol. IV, *Special Reports*, Part 5, Chapter C, Fertility, tables 1, 4, and 6.

CHAPTER   4

RESIDENCE, NATIVITY, AND ETHNIC GROUPS

A. Regions, divisions, and States

Ratios of young children to women.   Some information on trends since 1800 in ratios of children under 5 years old to white women 20 to 44 years old by geographic divisions was given in Chapter 2, table 6, with an analysis at the national level only.   The trends by geographic divisions are shown graphically in figure 10.

In 1800, the ratios of children under 5 years old to 1,000 white women 20 to 44 years old varied from 1,146 in the New England Division to 1,918 in the East North Central Division.   Values higher than 1,400 occurred only in the thinly populated newer areas of settlement and undoubtedly reflected migration that was selective of young women from the older areas, perhaps of women who already had some young children.[1] Such long-settled divisions as the Middle Atlantic, South Atlantic, and (in 1810) the West South Central,[2] had fertility ratios that were not far above or below a level of 1,400.   These long-settled areas probably had a larger proportion of single women and of married women who were not quite as fertile as the select group of women who migrated to frontier areas.

In the normal course of events, the fertility of women in the newer areas of settlement would have declined as the areas became more settled. It did decline, at a faster absolute pace between 1800 and 1850 in the two North Central Divisions and the East South Central Division than in the longer settled divisions.

It is possible that a ratio of about 1,400 children under 5 years old per 1,000 women 20 to 44 years old was the usual size for long-settled divisions, other than New England, for many years *before* 1800, and that by chance

---

[1] It is estimated that not more than 7 percent of the children under 5 years old had mothers 15 to 19 years old or 45 to 49 years old.   The ratios of children to women 20 to 44 years old include these additional children.   For ratios as large as 1,918 to exist, there must have been very low infant mortality and most of the women must have been less than 35 years old.   In 1910 Census data for the supposedly quite fertile ever-married white and Negro women in rural-farm areas of the South, the ratio did not exceed 1,374 own children under 5 years old per 1,000 ever-married women at any single year of age and the ratio was much smaller among women in the broad age range of 20 to 44 years. Perhaps the frontier women had an average of about 11 births in a lifetime, compared with a national average of about 8.

[2] The West South Central Division was a "long settled" area in 1810 in the sense that the bulk of the people enumerated was in the then 92-year old city of New Orleans, in long-established small villages along the lower Mississippi, and in the nearby populated rural territory.

FIGURE **10.**—ADJUSTED NUMBER OF CHILDREN UNDER 5 YEARS OLD PER 1,000 WOMEN
20 TO 44 YEARS OLD

[Adjusted as explained in headnote of table 6]

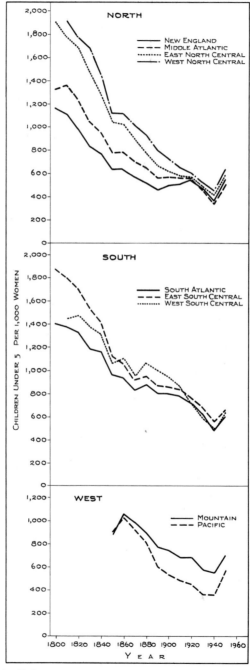

Note: Based on data in table 6.

the first few Federal censuses were taken about the time when declines in fertility began in earnest. These Federal censuses began in 1790 and a decline was evident in ratio of children to women *after* 1810. Comparisons (not shown) of ratios of children under 16 years old to white women 16 years old and over from Colonial censuses before 1776 in Massachusetts, Rhode Island, New York, New Jersey, and Maryland with corresponding ratios from the Federal Census of 1800 suggest that effective fertility in these areas was at about the same level *before the Revolutionary War* as in 1800. That is, New England may have had a less fertile population than the other geographic divisions as early as 1774. The populations of the individual colonies were small, however, and the ratios of children to women fluctuated somewhat. It is doubtful that higher infant mortality was a cause of New England's relatively low ratio of children to women; fragmentary data suggest that New England areas had relatively favorable mortality.

New England's women probably were less fertile than the women in other geographic divisions because of later marriage, a smaller percentage of women who ever married, and perhaps a greater resort to family limitation. A Colonial census of Connecticut in 1774 showed that only 74 percent of 38,503 women 20 to 69 years old were married. Connecticut had a young population, so it is likely that many of the remaining 26 percent were single women 20 to 24 years old. If there was much truth in the saying that in the old days an unmarried woman of 18 was regarded as an old maid, New England in 1774 apparently had many spinsters. The legend of marriage by age 18 may fit the very early stages of colonization when there were relatively few women and many men. Colonial and early Federal censuses frequently showed more women than men in the New England population, in contrast to slightly fewer women than men in many areas outside New England. Some of the New England men may have been temporarily absent, in whaling, maritime commerce, and fishing, and some may have gone to other parts of the country in search of new land. Under the common practice of primogeniture in New England, the oldest son was expected to remain with the parents, take care of them in their old age, and eventually inherit the family farm. The younger children often had no prospects except to migrate. History records that people from New England settled parts of New Jersey before 1728 and parts of western New York, Pennsylvania, and the Ohio River Basin at an early date. Other parts of America also had considerable in-and-out movement of American-born persons. New England apparently was harder hit by out-movement of its young men than most other areas.

Figure 10 shows that all geographic divisions had early declines in ratios of young children to women. If one assumes that there were normal differences among divisions with respect to variations in the proportion of women who were married, the degree of settlement, etc., and if one allows for a few chance fluctuations, it would seem that fertility declined on a nationwide basis rather than by any pattern of progressive spread from one area (New England) to another. It may be noted that the Mountain and Pacific Divisions around 1850 or 1860 began with a level of fertility that was not greatly different from the level in the two North Central Divisions or the three Southern divisions at the same date. The Mountain Division is not a fair example, however. In 1850, the bulk of its white population consisted of quite fertile Mexicans, and the fertile Mormons of Utah were an important minority. Very high infant mortality among the Mexicans, amounting to about a fourth of infants in the first year of life, kept the ratios of young children to women at a relatively low level. After 1860, an influx of population from other geographic divisions to Colorado and other Mountain States gradually reduced to a minority level the proportion of the Mountain Division's population residing in New Mexico and Utah. However, fertility declined slowly in New Mexico and Utah, and this retarded the decline in the division as a whole, despite larger declines in fertility in the other Mountain States.

On a geographic division basis, the ratios of young children to women tended to converge over the years. The Nation became much more homogeneous with respect to fertility.

In examining figure 10, the reader should allow somewhat for a heavier than usual undercount of young children in 1850, for both an undercount and depressed fertility in the South in 1870, and for another heavier than usual undercount in 1890. Allowances should be made for the effect of very heavy immigration of fertile white women from Europe in the period from about 1880 to 1920. This immigration caused a rise or leveling-off of ratios of young children to white women in the New England and Middle Atlantic Divisions. Within the South, there was a slower decline in fertility ratios after the War Between the States than before it, with the exception of a temporary dip in 1870. The pattern of decline of fertility in the South suggests that the war perhaps indirectly slowed the progress of the demographic revolution in the South for a generation.

For a long time after 1800, the two North Central Divisions and the two South Central Divisions comprised the most fertile part of the country in terms of ratios of young children to women. These divisions were then frontier areas, and their settlers were chiefly engaged in the establishment and development of family farms or homesteads. (In their formative years, the Mountain and Pacific Divisions had considerable nonfarm populations in mining camps and trading centers, and there may have been a lesser need for large families than existed in other "new" areas.) By 1890, more rapid declines brought the ratios in the two North Central Divisions down to a point below that of any Southern division. The South, by a process of slower decline, thus became the most fertile part of the country. Hence, the South was not always the Nation's most fertile area.

Sharp declines in fertility ratios, reminiscent of those before 1850, occurred in all geographic divisions after World War I or after 1920. It is now known that the low levels reached by the ratios of young children to women in all geographic divisions in 1940 were partly a consequence of the severe economic depression of the 1930's. No one in the 1930's regarded the trend as other than a continuation of the long-time downward trend, however, and the outlook at that time was for an eventual decline in population if fertility should continue to drop. In 1940, the fertility ratios were below the level needed for the permanent maintenance of the population through births. Only the South and the Mountain Division in 1940 had fertility ratios above permanent replacement needs.[3] With the outbreak of World War II and the return of prosperous conditions, the birth rate rose, and a further surge after the end of the war in 1945 caused ratios of children under 5 years old to women 20 to 44 years old to increase considerably in all geographic divisions by 1950. In the North and in the Pacific Division, the fertility ratios increased to a level about as high as that prevailing 50 years earlier. (Birth rates were higher in 1900 than in 1950 but were offset at the earlier date by high infant mortality.) In the South and in the Mountain Division, the increase by 1950 was to a level barely above that prevailing in 1930, or just before the economic depression.

Children ever born to white women 70 to 74 years old in 1910. The oldest group of women for whom data on children ever born are available from tabulations of the 1910 Census consists of the women who were 70 to 74 years old. This group, therefore, represents the furthest point in time for which data on children ever born have been tabulated for all States (table 19).[4] These women were 20 to 24 years old in 1860 and 40 to 44 years old in 1880. Caution must be used in interpreting the data because the surviving women 70 to 74 years old may not be strictly representative of their generation (Appendix A).

In 1910, there were wide differences among the States with respect to the lifetime fertility of white women 70 to 74 years old. The levels of fertility were lowest in the largely rural New England States of Maine, New Hampshire, and Vermont. In these three States, the women (including childless single women) had an average of 3.3 to 3.5 children ever born. This was less than half as many as in Utah where the white women had an average of 7.4 children per woman. In Maine, New Hampshire, and Vermont, the then relatively low proportion of 5 or 6 percent of women ever married had 10 or more children ever born and 17 to 18 percent had 7

[3] A replacement quota computed from United States life tables for white women in 1939–41 is 440.
[4] Information on children ever born appears on the still-extant 1900 Census schedules. The schedules for 1890 also had such information but were destroyed in a warehouse fire. Massachusetts obtained data on children ever born, in 1875 and 1885, as did at least two other New England States about this time, and New York obtained data in 1865. For a recent analysis of data for one county in the State of New York in 1865, see Wendell H. Bash, "Differential Fertility in Madison County, New York, 1865," the *Milbank Memorial Fund Quarterly*, April 1955, Vol. XXXIII, No. 2, pp. 161–186.

or more children. In Utah the corresponding figures were 33 percent with
10 or more children and 65 percent with 7 or more children. From 11
to 16 percent of the ever-married women in Maine, New Hampshire, and
Vermont were childless as compared with about 2 percent in Utah. (Two
younger age groups had 4 percent childless in Utah; the 2-percent figure
among the women 70 to 74 years old may be a chance fluctuation arising
either from the small population or from sampling variability.)

TABLE **19.**—DISTRIBUTION OF WHITE WOMEN 70 TO 74 YEARS OLD BY NUMBER OF CHILDREN
EVER BORN, BY STATES: 1910

[States not shown where there are fewer than 1,200 white women 70 to 74 years old]

State	Children ever born		Percent of women ever married with specified number of children ever born							
	Per 1,000 women	Per 1,000 women ever married	None	1	2	3	4	5 and 6	7 to 9	10 or more
United States........	4,885	5,278	7.9	7.8	9.7	10.2	10.2	19.1	21.7	13.4
New England:										
Maine..................	3,464	3,784	11.1	12.3	13.1	18.2	11.8	15.1	13.8	4.5
New Hampshire..........	3,297	3,680	16.2	13.2	15.0	13.8	11.6	12.5	11.4	6.3
Vermont...............	3,412	3,719	12.2	13.6	15.0	8.0	19.2	5.1
Massachusetts.........	3,592	4,064	12.5	12.2	14.4	13.6	9.6	16.0	13.9	7.8
Rhode Island..........	3,963	4,532	10.0	12.4	12.4	10.8	8.4	20.8	16.0	9.1
Connecticut...........	3,794	4,279	11.6	12.8	12.5	9.9	11.2	17.8	15.6	8.5
Middle Atlantic:										
New York..............	4,033	4,438	10.6	10.6	12.4	12.4	11.2	17.6	15.7	9.4
New Jersey............	4,141	4,590	10.0	9.3	12.9	11.4	11.3	18.6	17.2	9.4
Pennsylvania..........	4,870	5,410	6.8	7.6	10.0	9.5	10.7	19.2	21.4	15.0
East North Central:										
Ohio..................	4,864	5,234	7.4	7.3	10.0	10.4	9.9	20.4	22.1	12.6
Indiana...............	5,197	5,408	7.4	6.0	7.9	9.0	11.1	23.1	22.2	13.2
Illinois..............	5,414	5,694	6.4	6.4	7.8	9.7	9.7	20.2	25.0	14.9
Michigan..............	4,867	5,064	7.1	8.8	10.4	10.8	10.4	20.3	20.6	11.6
Wisconsin.............	5,793	6,056	4.8	5.8	6.8	7.0	9.8	22.4	26.2	17.2
West North Central:										
Minnesota.............	5,670	5,879	5.9	5.3	8.1	7.7	11.2	21.0	24.6	16.2
Iowa..................	5,833	6,001	5.7	4.6	7.5	9.7	11.1	17.3	26.6	17.4
Missouri..............	5,830	6,074	5.8	5.0	7.5	8.4	9.1	18.8	27.2	18.2
South Dakota..........	5,954	6,116	3.4	6.1	8.2	9.6	5.5	23.8	25.9	17.5
Nebraska..............	5,925	6,024	5.9	4.2	6.6	8.7	9.7	21.4	26.2	17.1
Kansas................	5,779	5,965	5.4	4.6	6.9	8.5	9.4	22.2	27.2	16.0
South Atlantic:										
Maryland..............	4,853	5,465	10.0	6.5	7.9	9.3	9.7	16.6	24.9	15.3
District of Columbia...	4,153	4,703	7.8	9.4	15.6	11.7	7.1	18.0	23.5	6.9
Virginia..............	4,742	5,581	9.5	6.3	7.6	8.5	8.9	19.4	25.7	14.2
West Virginia.........	5,916	6,363	4.1	5.3	7.3	8.1	7.6	19.7	27.0	20.9
North Carolina........	4,943	5,831	6.2	7.1	6.9	6.5	11.3	22.5	23.8	15.7
South Carolina........	4,653	5,675	6.6	8.8	6.6	8.8	8.8	21.4	23.7	15.3
Georgia...............	4,939	5,444	6.7	8.2	8.7	9.8	6.9	22.1	25.2	12.5
Florida...............	4,398	5,107	7.7	14.4	5.1	11.1	8.5	19.5	21.2	12.6
East South Central:										
Kentucky..............	5,557	6,012	5.6	6.5	5.7	9.4	9.0	18.6	29.0	16.4
Tennessee.............	5,250	5,761	8.2	6.4	7.4	7.7	8.9	18.9	27.0	15.4
Alabama...............	5,230	5,865	7.9	5.9	8.6	9.5	8.1	16.8	24.1	19.1
Mississippi...........	5,349	5,820	7.4	5.6	11.1	8.3	8.8	13.9	29.6	15.1
West South Central:										
Arkansas..............	5,932	6,341	5.9	3.8	5.2	7.6	11.4	18.6	27.8	19.8
Louisiana.............	5,426	5,923	7.6	6.5	5.3	8.1	12.2	15.3	27.1	17.9
Oklahoma..............	6,404	6,553	5.1	1.6	5.9	7.9	8.7	19.8	28.3	22.7
Texas.................	6,036	6,293	4.4	5.9	6.5	7.6	9.9	18.2	26.6	21.0
Mountain:										
Colorado..............	4,972	5,197	6.2	10.7	8.5	10.2	11.6	18.9	20.6	13.3
Utah..................	7,444	7,521	1.6	5.7	7.3	3.3	4.0	13.7	31.2	33.3
Pacific:										
Washington............	5,444	5,563	6.5	4.6	8.0	12.3	12.6	17.5	24.7	13.6
Oregon................	5,992	6,168	2.6	5.8	6.8	9.7	7.8	24.2	25.9	17.2
California............	4,546	4,776	9.3	8.6	12.2	9.7	11.5	19.3	20.2	9.2

Source: Derived from unpublished tabulation detail from the 1910 Census of Population.

In 1910, the largely urban New England States of Massachusetts, Rhode Island, and Connecticut had higher rates of children ever born among women 70 to 74 years old than the largely rural States of Maine, New Hampshire, and Vermont. This situation was traceable to the presence of many fertile foreign-born white women in the first three States just cited. The fertile foreign-born women resided largely in cities and more than offset existing urban-rural fertility differentials among native white women in New England. Rhode Island had the largest average number of children ever born for all women 70 to 74 years old in New England, 4.0 children, and also the highest percentage of women of this age residing in urban areas, 88 percent. In urban areas of Rhode Island in 1910, the women 50 to 74 years old had an average of 3.9 children ever born as compared with a corresponding average of 3.2 in rural-nonfarm areas and 3.0 in rural-farm areas. (The broad age group 50 to 74 is used in this example because separate data for age 70 to 74 years are not available by residence.) Rural fertility was also lower than urban fertility in Massachusetts, Connecticut, New Hampshire, New York, and New Jersey. Here, also, fertile foreign-born women comprised a large proportion of white women 70 to 74 years old in urban areas. Elsewhere, the traditional pattern of higher rural than urban fertility occurred.

The white women 70 to 74 years old in New York in 1910 had about the same average number of children ever born as the women in Rhode Island, the most fertile New England State. New Jersey ranked next to New York with respect to a relatively low observed lifetime fertility among white women 70 to 74 years old in 1910 residing outside the New England States and was followed in turn by the District of Columbia, Florida, and California.

Pennsylvania, with an average of 5.4 children ever born per woman ever married, 70 to 74 years old in 1910, had a more fertile group of women than Ohio and Michigan among the East North Central States. Pennsylvania's moderate fertility may have reflected the presence of Quakers, Mennonites, and other sects which probably were slow to depart from a tradition of fairly large families. This State, despite heavy industrialization, has usually had fertility not far from the national average. The high fertility of immigrants from Poland and other countries of southern and eastern Europe has helped to bolster the birth rate of Pennsylvania. Many other factors also helped, such as the tendency for coal miners to have large families.

The women in the District of Columbia had an average of 4.7 children per white women ever married, 70 to 74 years old in 1910. This was a low average by 1910 standards but a high one by present standards. Only 8 percent of the ever-married women 70 to 74 years old in the District of Columbia were childless, compared with about 10 percent in the adjacent States of Maryland and Virginia and with 4 to 8 percent in most other Southern States. The District of Columbia, it may be noted, had the Nation's least fertile urban women 45 to 49 years old in 1910, with an average of only 3.3 children ever born per white woman ever married. The qualification "urban" is essential here. In Massachusetts and New Hampshire, rural women 45 to 49 years old had an average of 2.7 children and 3.2 children, respectively, or fewer children than the women in the urban part of any State or the District of Columbia.

The women who were 70 to 74 years old in 1910 bore most of their children between 1851 and 1885, in a period when many of the central and western States were being settled. In those central and western States which were settled largely by farmers, the women 70 to 74 years old in 1910 generally had a higher average number of children ever born than may be noted for most of the largely rural but longer settled South Atlantic States. Utah, settled largely by the Mormons, was the only State in which the average, 7.4 children, approached the average of about 8 children previously noted for Colonial America. California and Colorado had averages of 4.5 and 5.0, respectively, which were below those of other "young" States but above those of some of the "old" States. California and Colorado were settled in part by people who did not farm the land— by people who were attracted by the commercial opportunities associated with the discovery of gold and silver. California, in particular, attracted many women who sailed from New England and the Middle Atlantic seaports, and who may have had some knowledge of methods of birth control; this State had a very rapid decline in birth rates and soon had one of the least fertile State populations.

Children ever born to white women 45 to 49 years old in 1910, 1940, and 1950. The ranking of the States by fertility varies considerably according to the data used, the measure, and the date. In this sense, more than one State could be said to contain the Nation's most fertile population. The State with the most fertile white population usually is one of several southern States, Utah, New Mexico, or North Dakota. The State with the least fertile white population usually is one of several northeastern States, California, Nevada, or, when shown with the States, the District of Columbia. Figure 11 shows how the States ranked in 1950 in respect to the number of children ever born per 1,000 white women 45 to 49 years old. It also shows the considerable declines in completed fertility among women in this age group between 1910 and 1950.

Southern and Mountain States predominated among the twelve States with the most fertile women in 1950, 1940, and 1910. Most of the States with relatively fertile women were largely rural and most of those with relatively infertile women were largely urban. Because of its Mormons, Utah was an interesting exception in that two-thirds of its people lived in urban areas in 1950, and yet the State ranked high with respect to fertility. In 1910 the New England States ranked very low with respect to the fertility of their women 45 to 49 years old. By 1950, Vermont, Maine, and New Hampshire occupied positions that were more in keeping with their large proportions of rural population.

FIGURE 11.—NUMBER OF CHILDREN EVER BORN PER 1,000 WHITE WOMEN 45 TO 49 YEARS OLD, FOR STATES: 1950, 1940, AND 1910

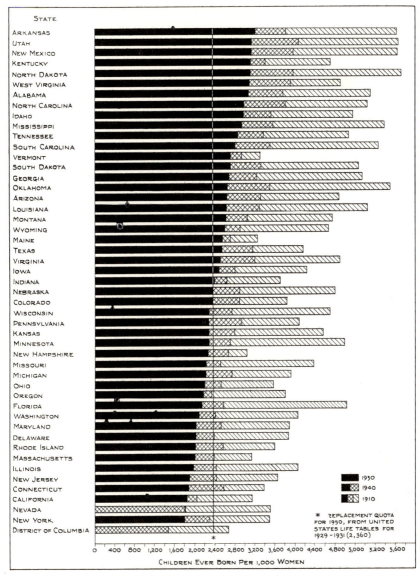

Source: *1950 Census of Population*, Vol. IV, *Special Reports*, Part 5, Chapter C, Fertility, table 32; *1940 Census of Population, Differential Fertility, 1940 and 1910*, Fertility for States and Large Cities, tables 31 and 32.

On the basis of United States life tables for 1929–31, the white women 45 to 49 years old in 1950 should have had an average of about 2,360 children ever born per 1,000 women for population replacement purposes.[5]

[5] Replacement quotas may be computed as follows: For replacement, a net reproduction rate of 1,000 is needed. If this rate of 1,000 is divided by a life table survival proportion from birth to age 28, the

The actual rates for white women 45 to 49 years old in 1950 were below 2,360 in 21 States and in the District of Columbia (figure 11). These women were 25 to 29 years old in 1930, or old enough to be well started on family life before the economic depression of the 1930's. They were not the least fertile cohort in the Nation's history, although they came close. Other data indicate that the women 45 to 49 years old in 1954 were less fertile than the women just discussed.

Children ever born to white women 25 to 29 years old in 1940 and 1950. In contrast to the decline in lifetime fertility among older women between 1940 and 1950, young white women had a considerable increase in number of children ever born, as illustrated by the data in figure 12 for women 25 to 29 years old. The prospects were bright for a substantial future increase in lifetime fertility among these women. The likelihood of such an increase depends on many things, such as the extent to which earlier than usual marriage and childbearing are associated with economic and psychological conditions that also influence some couples to have larger families than they otherwise would have.

In several States, the white women 25 to 29 years old had a rate of children ever born which indicated that these women might not be replaced by at least an equal number of daughters at the same age in the next generation. This improbability was determined by a comparison of the rate of children ever born to women 25 to 29 years old with a replacement quota. Three replacement quotas were computed on the basis of a United States life table for 1950 and on the respective assumptions that the women 25 to 29 years old were 50, 55, and 60 percent through childbearing.[6] The States with women of cumulative fertility below one or more of the three replacement quotas were Maryland, Illinois, Pennsylvania, Delaware, Rhode Island, Connecticut, New York, and New Jersey. The wholly urban District of Columbia had a lower rate than any State.

The low rates of children ever born to women 25 to 29 years old in the States just cited may in part reflect heavy in-migration to these States of young unmarried women from other States in search of employment. Evidence of the heavy in-migration of young women to these States exists in comparisons of the larger number of women enumerated in 1950 at ages 20 to 24 years and 25 to 29 years with the smaller number enumerated

result is a close approximation of the corresponding gross reproduction rate. The gross reproduction rate is then multiplied by the ratio of births of both sexes to female births (or by 2,060 for whites) and the result is the desired replacement quota. It is best to use a life table for about the time when the women were 28 years old or were near the mean age of childbearing (table 27, page 77).

[6] The States vary considerably in respect to the proportion of lifetime fertility already achieved by the women 25 to 29 years old. This proportion is estimated from age-specific birth rates in 1950 to range from about 50 percent in Massachusetts and Connecticut, where marriages are "late," to about 60 percent in South Carolina, where marriages are "early." Corresponding proportions estimated from age-specific birth rates in 1940 are only 2 to 4 percentage points less than those cited for 1950, indicating that the proportions may be fairly stable. See also the cohort materials given in footnote 12 of Chapter 3, page 48.

FIGURE **12.**—NUMBER OF CHILDREN EVER BORN PER 1,000 WHITE WOMEN 25 TO 29 YEARS OLD, FOR STATES: 1950 AND 1940

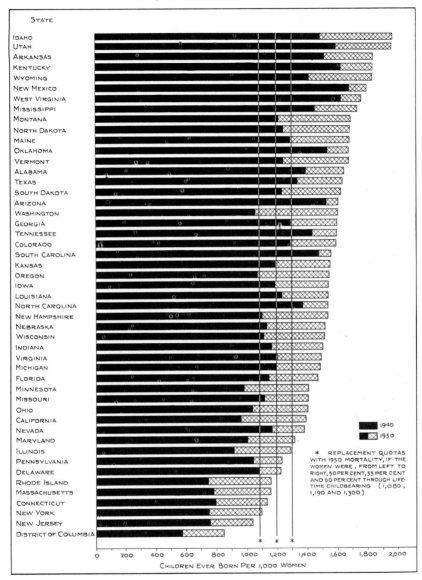

Source: *1950 Census of Population*, Vol. IV, *Special Reports*, Part 5, Chapter C, Fertility, table 32; *1940 Census of Population, Differential Fertility, 1940 and 1910*, Fertility for States and Large Cities, table 31.

in 1940 at ages 10 to 14 years and 15 to 19 years. Although the rates of children ever born to women were low, there were enough young women to produce many births. Year in and year out these States with inadequate fertility on a cohort basis have had between two and three births per death in the population. If in-migration of young women were to cease, the other young women might have a larger proportion married and the birth rate per woman might increase, but the total annual number of births in the States might decrease. Thus, it is difficult to evaluate the true level of fertility in States which are much affected by migration of population.

Nonwhites. Before many Negroes moved North and West, fertility trends among Negroes in the South largely determined the trends among nonwhites in the Nation. It was noted in earlier chapters that on a national basis, Negroes had little decline in fertility until long after the War Between the States. Figure 13 illustrates the formerly great concentration of nonwhites in the Southern States and the increase in Negro population in the North and in California after 1910. A large-scale movement of Negroes to the North and the West occurred after World War I and particularly during and after World War II.

The movement of the Negroes to the North and West was symptomatic of the gradual changes in ways of living that indirectly caused the fertility of the Negroes to decline by a considerable amount. Some other indications of the changes in ways of living may also be noted. In 1910, 64.9 percent of the nonwhite women 45 to 49 years old lived in rural areas as compared with only 29.9 percent among nonwhite women of this age in 1950. Until some years after World War I, most Negro men were farm laborers and sharecroppers, and the minority in urban areas were mostly poorly paid laborers and service workers. Most of them had relatively little education. Between 1930 and 1940, the educational opportunities for Negro children improved considerably, and this trend accelerated after 1940. Between 1940 and 1950, Negroes achieved proportionate representation in the major occupation group "operatives and kindred workers," reflecting gains in education and other improvements. The Negro's qualifications and opportunities for advancing above the unskilled labor level were much improved but in 1950 they were still far behind those of the average white person.[7] In view of the social and economic history of Negroes, the fact that they have been slower than the whites to control fertility is understandable.

The 1910 Census data indicate that it was usual for nonwhite women of completed fertility in rural-farm areas of the South to have an average of 7 to 8 children ever born (table 20). Such a high level of fertility suggests that little previous decline had occurred. In contrast, the nonwhite women 45 to 49 years old in the rural-nonfarm parts of the Southern States in 1910 had an average of 5 to 6 children ever born and those in the urban parts had 4 to 5 children. Because the bulk of the nonwhite women resided in rural areas where the fertility of women was high, the sizable differences in fertility by residence had little effect on national levels of nonwhite fertility in 1910. On a national basis, three-tenths of

[7] John Hope II, "The Employment of Negroes in the United States by Major Occupation Group and Industry," *The Journal of Negro Education*, Vol. XXII, No. 3, Summer 1953, pp. 307–321.

the ever-married nonwhite women 70 to 74 years old and one-fourth of those 45 to 49 years old in 1910 had borne at least 10 children (table 21). The average number of children ever born per nonwhite woman 45 to 49 years old declined greatly in all areas between 1910 and 1950.

FIGURE 13.—NONWHITE POPULATION, BY STATES: 1950, 1940, AND 1910

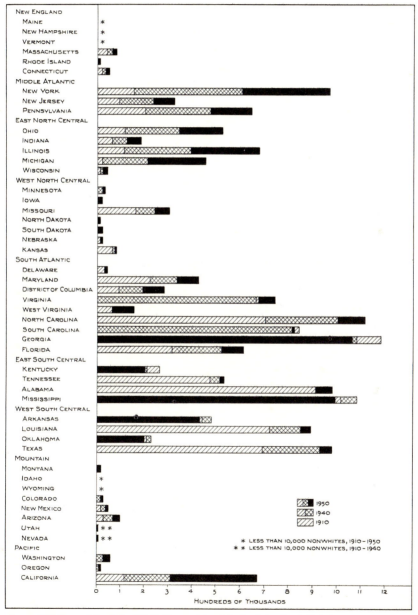

Source: *1950 Census of Population*, Vol. II, *Characteristics of the Population*, Part 1, U. S. Summary, table 59; *1940 Census of Population*, Vol. II, *Characteristics of the Population*, Parts 1-7, State table 4.

TABLE 20.—NUMBER OF CHILDREN EVER BORN PER 1,000 NONWHITE WOMEN 45 TO 49 YEARS OLD IN SELECTED STATES, URBAN AND RURAL: 1950, 1940, AND 1910

[Rate not shown for areas where there are fewer than 4,000 women 45 to 49 years old in 1950, 3,000 in 1940, and 1,200 in 1910]

State	1950				1940				1910			
	Total	Urban	Rural non-farm	Rural farm	Total	Urban	Rural non-farm	Rural farm	Total	Urban	Rural non-farm	Rural farm
United States.....	2,663	2,128	2,920	4,696	3,185	2,316	3,520	4,853	5,830	4,174	5,702	7,308
Middle Atlantic:												
New York............	1,672	1,636	...	...	1,750	1,739	...	...	3,264	3,261	...	...
New Jersey..........	2,399	2,351	...	...	2,164	2,159	...	...	3,624	3,144	...	...
Pennsylvania........	2,438	2,376	...	...	2,175	2,013	...	...	3,716	3,475	...	...
East North Central:												
Ohio................	2,251	2,139	...	...	2,160	2,126	...	...	3,791	3,581	...	...
Indiana.............	2,093	2,081	...	...	2,354	2,342	...	...	3,858	3,740	...	...
Illinois............	2,060	2,091	...	...	1,958	1,786	...	...	3,904	3,316	...	...
Michigan............	1,866	1,866	...	...	2,120	2,120	...	...	...	...	...	...
West North Central:												
Missouri............	2,137	1,940	...	...	2,039	1,894	...	...	4,390	4,034	...	...
South Atlantic:												
Maryland............	2,481	2,390	...	...	2,490	1,887	...	...	5,458	4,175	...	...
Dist. of Columbia...	1,683	1,683	...	...	1,903	1,903	...	...	3,794	3,794	...	...
Virginia............	2,786	2,221	2,865	...	3,416	2,347	3,751	4,741	6,221	4,670	6,073	7,607
West Virginia.......	2,623	...	...	...	...	...	...	...	...	...	...	...
North Carolina......	3,615	2,543	2,934	5,557	4,309	3,170	3,522	5,707	6,547	5,088	5,843	7,560
South Carolina......	3,646	2,594	...	4,987	4,895	2,645	3,949	6,002	6,956	4,841	6,135	7,880
Georgia.............	3,098	2,392	3,464	4,584	3,281	2,515	3,232	4,308	6,486	4,683	5,619	7,726
Florida.............	2,538	2,253	...	...	3,504	3,015	...	...	5,856	4,242	5,585	...
East South Central:												
Kentucky............	1,993	1,763	...	...	2,676	1,826	...	...	4,605	3,576	...	...
Tennessee...........	2,765	2,115	...	...	3,107	2,562	...	4,293	5,605	4,389	...	6,828
Alabama.............	2,930	2,419	2,607	4,290	3,587	2,850	3,750	4,268	5,831	4,443	5,027	6,704
Mississippi.........	3,528	2,189	2,811	4,424	3,843	2,488	...	4,422	6,388	4,420	5,116	6,977
West South Central:												
Arkansas............	3,281	2,237	...	4,529	3,507	2,417	...	4,110	6,950	5,245	6,005	7,642
Louisiana...........	3,086	2,443	3,096	4,761	3,706	2,781	3,860	5,105	6,357	4,587	6,640	7,589
Oklahoma............	2,803	...	...	...	3,982	...	...	...	6,458	...	...	...
Texas...............	2,503	2,112	...	...	3,342	2,452	3,486	4,817	6,500	4,937	5,971	7,760
Pacific:												
California..........	2,159	2,127	...	...	3,003	2,315	...	...	...	...	...	...

Source: *1950 Census of Population*, Vol. IV, *Special Reports*, Part 5, Chapter C, Fertility, tables 1 and 32; *1940 Census of Population*, *Differential Fertility, 1940 and 1910*, Fertility for States and Large Cities, tables 3, 4, 31, and 32; and corrections of records.

The nonwhite women 45 to 49 years old in 1950 should have had about 2,600 children ever born per 1,000 women 45 to 49 years old so that 1,000 daughters would survive to about age 28 in the next generation.[8] By this standard, the nonwhite women in the rural parts of all States shown in table 20 had a fertility rate in 1950 that was more than ample for replacement of their generation. The nonwhite women in the urban parts of most States had a level of fertility that was inadequate for replacement of their numbers in the next generation even if a far larger allowance were made for possible underreporting of children ever born than would be indicated by the data in Appendix A, table A–1. In the country as a whole, the nonwhite women 45 to 49 years old in 1950 had an average of 2,663 children ever born per 1,000 women, a rate slightly above replacement needs.

[8] The method of obtaining the quota was similar to that explained in footnote 5, page 59.

The declines in rates of children ever born were, of course, accompanied by declines in the proportion of women who had borne at least 10 children (table 21). Comparisons of data for nonwhite women 70 to 74 years old in 1910 with those 45 to 49 years old suggest that a small decline occurred in the nineteenth century. The rates for the older nonwhite women may be too low to be representative of their generation. Nonetheless, there is little doubt that declines in fertility of nonwhite women before 1910 were small as compared with the large declines that occurred after 1910. Despite the large declines after 1910, a few of the Southern States in 1950 still had an important percentage of nonwhite women with at least 10 children. In North Carolina, one-ninth of the nonwhite women ever married, 45 to 49 years old, were in this category in 1950.

TABLE 21.—PERCENT OF EVER-MARRIED NONWHITE WOMEN IN SELECTED AGE GROUPS WITH FEWER THAN THREE CHILDREN EVER BORN AND PERCENT WITH TEN CHILDREN OR MORE, FOR SELECTED STATES: 1950, 1940, AND 1910

[State or percent not shown where there are fewer than 4,000 nonwhite women 45 to 49 years old in 1950, 3,000 in 1940, and 1,200 in 1910]

State	0 to 2 children ever born				10 children or more			
	Women 45 to 49 years old			Women 70 to 74	Women 45 to 49 years old			Women 70 to 74
	1950	1940	1910	1910	1950	1940	1910	1910
United States..........	59.7	49.8	26.5	20.7	4.9	6.4	25.4	30.8
Middle Atlantic:								
New York................	71.9	70.3	49.7	...	1.9	1.1	7.5	...
New Jersey..............	62.0	62.4	41.9	...	3.4	4.0	12.5	...
Pennsylvania............	63.0	67.5	43.1	...	4.7	4.0	10.8	...
East North Central:								
Ohio....................	65.7	66.4	38.9	...	2.5	2.1	8.6	...
Indiana.................	70.5	61.0	45.3	...	2.9	3.8	9.2	...
Illinois................	71.9	71.2	42.0	...	3.0	2.3	11.0	...
Michigan................	72.8	72.2	...	...	1.0	1.8	...	...
West North Central:								
Missouri................	61.8	66.9	31.1	...	2.0	1.3	10.2	...
South Atlantic:								
Maryland................	61.2	58.9	28.2	...	4.2	6.4	21.7	...
District of Columbia.....	73.2	67.0	36.4	...	2.1	2.2	11.4	...
Virginia................	57.5	45.6	23.7	20.3	5.3	7.9	29.3	29.5
West Virginia...........	62.1	...	...	...	4.8	...	...	...
North Carolina..........	46.6	34.3	18.9	16.7	10.8	11.4	33.7	32.2
South Carolina..........	45.1	30.4	18.5	18.2	8.1	13.6	32.9	38.8
Georgia.................	54.1	46.5	21.8	20.5	6.6	7.0	30.6	35.9
Florida.................	61.3	46.5	28.2	...	4.2	7.0	24.9	...
East South Central:								
Kentucky................	69.1	54.1	34.0	17.1	2.6	3.0	15.3	33.7
Tennessee...............	58.9	48.4	29.4	18.6	5.9	4.8	21.1	34.1
Alabama.................	57.7	43.3	27.2	19.0	7.4	9.0	26.5	33.7
Mississippi.............	49.0	39.3	22.5	17.2	6.8	8.4	29.0	32.2
West South Central:								
Arkansas................	52.4	43.7	20.1	...	7.6	6.4	31.2	...
Louisiana...............	50.8	41.6	24.5	20.5	5.6	7.0	30.8	33.5
Oklahoma................	58.3	37.7	21.9	...	4.2	9.6	27.9	...
Texas...................	63.2	47.7	22.1	23.3	3.4	6.6	29.2	35.7
Pacific:								
California..............	64.5	46.8	...	...	2.9	4.0	...	...

Source: *1950 Census of Population*, Vol. IV, *Special Reports*, Part 5, Chapter C, Fertility, tables 2 and 32; *1940 Census of Population, Differential Fertility, 1940 and 1910*, Fertility for States and Large Cities, tables 1, 2, 29, and 30; and unpublished tabulation detail from the 1910 Census of Population.

Figure 14 presents data for 1940 and 1950 on the number of children ever born for nonwhite women 25 to 29 years old, for States containing at least 4,000 such women in 1950. Negroes comprised virtually all of the nonwhite population in the States shown, with the exceptions of California and Oklahoma where Orientals and Indians comprised up to a third of the nonwhite group.

FIGURE 14.—NUMBER OF CHILDREN EVER BORN PER 1,000 NONWHITE WOMEN 25 TO 29 YEARS OLD, FOR SELECTED STATES: 1950 AND 1940

[Data shown for States having at least 4,000 nonwhite women 25 to 29 years old in 1950]

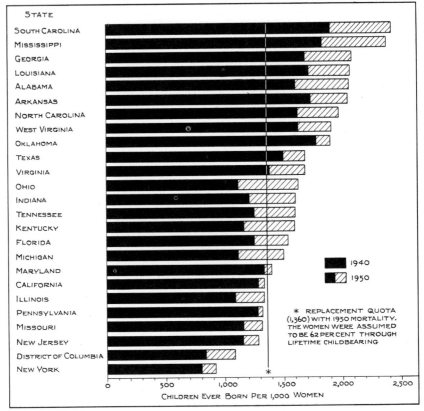

Source: *1950 Census of Population*, Vol. IV, *Special Reports*, Part 5, Chapter C, Fertility, table 32; *1940 Census of Population, Differential Fertility, 1940 and 1910*, Fertility for States and Large Cities, table 31.

In most States of the Deep South in 1950, the nonwhite women 25 to 29 years old had a fertility rate that was ample for a very considerable amount of population growth. The top eleven States in figure 14, all Southern, had rates of children ever born which ranged from 24 to 75 percent above replacement needs.[9] In 1940, the corresponding range for

[9] The women 25 to 29 years old should have had about 1,360 births of both sexes per 1,000 women in order to be a proper stage toward a goal of 1,000 daughters surviving to age 27 years in the next generation. This estimate is based on United States life tables for nonwhites in 1950 and on

these same eleven States was from a deficit of about 8 percent below the replacement quota (about 1,500 in 1940) in Virginia to an excess of about 27 percent in South Carolina.

In addition to Virginia, seven States had rates which were below replacement needs in 1940 and a little above replacement needs in 1950: Ohio, Indiana, Tennessee, Kentucky, Florida, Michigan, and Maryland. The rates were below replacement needs in 1950 as well as in 1940 in California, Illinois, Pennsylvania, Missouri, New Jersey, and particularly in the District of Columbia and New York. All the States listed below Virginia in figure 14 had substantial urban concentrations of nonwhites in 1940 as well as in 1950.

Women living with husband. In most investigations of the current fertility of the population, account is taken of the proportion of the women who have married. This is done on a national basis in the present report. It may be more pertinent to measure the proportion of women who are living with a husband. These do not account for all State variations in fertility, however, as may be seen from the following data for women of all races, white and nonwhite.

According to a presence-of-husband measure, women could expect to spend about 66.3 percent of the childbearing age range in a married-and-husband-present status on the basis of age-specific percentages in 1950.[10] In 1940, the corresponding figure was 60.0 percent. By States, the percentage in 1950 ranged from 58.6 in Massachusetts to 75.7 percent in Idaho (table 22). The percent with husband present was relatively high in the Mountain States and among whites in the more rural of the Southern States, where fertility also was relatively high. The percent was relatively low in highly urban Massachusetts, Rhode Island, Connecticut, and New York, where fertility was relatively low. In New York the percent with husband present was only 44.6 percent among nonwhites. Connecticut, Pennsylvania, and the District of Columbia also had presence-of-husband percentages of less than 50 for nonwhites.

The lower presence-of-husband proportions for nonwhites than for whites in most States are a reflection of economic and social problems such as desertion by husbands unable or unwilling to support a wife and children. Other data indicate that relatively more nonwhite than white women have been married.

---

an assumption that the nonwhite women 25 to 29 years old had completed about 62 percent of their eventual lifetime fertility. A corresponding quota for 1940 is about 1,500 children ever born per 1,000 nonwhite women 25 to 29 years old.

[10] The presence-of-husband measure is computed as follows: The percent married and husband present is noted for women in 5-year age groups from 15–19 years through 40–44 years. The percentages for the six 5-year age groups are added together. The sum is expressed as a percentage of 600.0 and the result is the presence-of-husband measure. The measure may be said to show the proportion of time a hypothetical cohort would live with husbands as it passed through the childbearing ages, if the cohort were to experience the given age-specific percents living with husbands. Real cohorts of women, of course, experience age-specific percents living with husbands as they pass through life that differ somewhat from those noted for the population at a given instant in time.

TABLE 22.—Presence-of-Spouse Measure per 1,000 Women During Childbearing Ages,
by States, 1950 and 1940, with Color for Selected States, 1950

[Color shown for States containing 50,000 nonwhite inhabitants or more. See text for explanation of measure]

State	1950			1940, total
	Total	White	Nonwhite	
United States..........................	66.3	67.7	55.4	60.0
New England:				
Maine................................	66.9	...	...	60.0
New Hampshire........................	65.3	...	...	57.1
Vermont..............................	65.7	...	...	60.0
Massachusetts........................	58.6	58.8	50.0	50.4
Rhode Island.........................	61.1	...	...	52.6
Connecticut..........................	61.2	61.5	49.3	54.4
Middle Atlantic:				
New York.............................	60.1	61.4	44.6	53.7
New Jersey...........................	62.6	63.4	51.2	55.5
Pennsylvania.........................	62.6	63.6	48.5	56.7
East North Central:				
Ohio.................................	67.4	68.4	55.7	60.7
Indiana..............................	70.2	70.9	57.0	64.4
Illinois.............................	65.1	66.4	52.2	58.2
Michigan.............................	68.6	69.4	58.5	63.7
Wisconsin............................	67.5	...	...	60.4
West North Central:				
Minnesota............................	66.3	...	...	57.6
Iowa.................................	70.7	...	...	62.8
Missouri.............................	67.8	69.1	53.4	61.4
North Dakota.........................	70.3	...	...	60.3
South Dakota.........................	71.5	...	...	62.0
Nebraska.............................	69.9	...	...	61.7
Kansas...............................	71.7	72.4	57.7	63.0
South Atlantic:				
Delaware.............................	65.2	...	...	57.9
Maryland.............................	65.2	68.0	51.5	58.6
District of Columbia.................	50.9	51.5	49.9	48.5
Virginia.............................	66.1	69.3	54.2	59.7
West Virginia........................	68.6	69.2	57.4	63.8
North Carolina.......................	66.5	70.1	56.2	61.0
South Carolina.......................	66.1	70.4	58.6	61.5
Georgia..............................	67.4	71.8	57.3	61.4
Florida..............................	66.2	70.0	53.7	61.0
East South Central:				
Kentucky.............................	70.0	71.2	54.3	65.1
Tennessee............................	68.5	70.6	57.9	62.4
Alabama..............................	67.6	72.4	56.8	62.7
Mississippi..........................	68.6	73.0	62.9	64.7
West South Central:				
Arkansas.............................	71.7	74.2	62.6	67.3
Louisiana............................	67.4	71.5	58.4	62.3
Oklahoma.............................	72.3	73.8	56.8	66.1
Texas................................	71.0	72.7	59.7	64.4
Mountain:				
Montana..............................	72.2	...	...	64.5
Idaho................................	75.7	...	...	69.7
Wyoming..............................	75.5	...	...	68.4
Colorado.............................	69.4	...	...	63.2
New Mexico...........................	71.2	71.9	62.2	66.8
Arizona..............................	69.1	69.8	64.1	65.7
Utah.................................	73.7	...	...	66.8
Nevada...............................	71.3	...	...	67.6
Pacific:				
Washington...........................	71.1	71.4	59.4	62.8
Oregon...............................	72.6	...	...	64.3
California...........................	67.6	68.3	57.9	61.2

Source: Derived from *1950 Census of Population*, Vol. II, *Characteristics of the Population*, Part 1, U. S. Summary, table 104, and Parts 2-50, table 57; *1940 Census of Population*, Vol. IV, *Characteristics by Age*, Part 1, U. S. Summary, tables 6 and 9, and Parts 2-4, tables 7 and 11.

Trends between 1940 and 1950 in ratios of children under 5 years old to women 15 to 49 years old. Ratios of children under 5 years old to women 15 to 49 years old can be computed for every State, urban and rural, from "complete count" census data on the population by age and sex. These particular ratios are not subject to sampling variability but they are subject to other kinds of error, and ratios based on small numbers of women may vary in erratic fashion over time. Ratios are shown for all races in 1950 and 1940 in table 23. The ratios are for areas classified as urban or rural by the 1940 Census rules of classification and have been indirectly standardized for age of woman. They have not been adjusted for a net undercount of children under 5 years old in the census (Appendix A). Nationally, an increase of about 3 percent in the ratios of children to women came from a more complete count of young children under 5 years old in 1950 than in 1940 (see Appendix A), 2 percent came from reductions in child mortality, and 35 percent came from higher birth rates.

There was a tendency for the largest percent increases in fertility to occur in areas where fertility was low in 1940. Thus, the percent increase between 1940 and 1950 generally was higher in the Far Western States and in the Northern States than in the Southern or Mountain States. There were a number of exceptions to this general tendency, however. For example, Utah had the second highest statewide fertility ratio in 1940 but this did not prevent the State from having a considerable further gain over its previous high level and a percent increase that exceeded that of eleven other States. In terms of absolute increases in fertility ratios in 1940 to 1950, there was no clear pattern of association of amount of the change with the 1940 level of fertility. Nationally, the fertility ratios increased in size by 130 children per 1,000 women in urban areas, by 130 in rural-nonfarm areas, and by 110 in rural-farm areas. The majority of the States had absolute increases in fertility ratios of about these magnitudes in urban and rural areas, regardless of the level of fertility in 1940.

Nonwhite ratios for 1950. Ratios of children under 5 years old to nonwhite women 15 to 49 years old are shown in table 24 for a complete listing of States, urban and rural. The rates have not been corrected for a net undercount of nonwhite children under 5 years old in the census. This undercount was estimated to be about 9.7 percent of the true number nationally in 1950, 10.5 percent in the South and 7.5 to 7.8 percent in the other three regions of the country.

In examining the ratios in table 24, it is helpful to have a rough notion of replacement needs. A conventional "replacement quota" computed from United States life tables for nonwhites in 1950, with age standardization to match the ratios in table 24, is 323 children under 5 years old per 1,000 nonwhite women 15 to 49 years old. This quota assumes that all the children were counted. The quota may be reduced by 10 percent, or to 290 for rough comparability with the ratios in table 24. (Of course, the national life tables have only an approximate applicability to the various local areas since mortality varies considerably.) On this basis it appears that all States, urban and rural, with the exception of New York had ratios in 1950 that were substantially above replacement needs.

TABLE **23.**—NUMBER OF CHILDREN UNDER 5 YEARS OLD PER 1,000 WOMEN OF ALL RACES 15 to 49 YEARS OLD, STANDARDIZED FOR AGE OF WOMAN, BY STATES, URBAN AND RURAL: 1950 AND 1940

[Urban-rural by 1940 Census rules of classification. Data standardized by indirect method to the age distribution of white women in the United States in 1950]

State	Total			Urban		Rural nonfarm		Rural farm	
	1950	1940	Percent increase, 1940 to 1950	1950	1940	1950	1940	1950	1940
United States........	422	300	40.7	363	230	495	361	584	473
New England:									
Maine.................	474	354	33.9	415	285	507	394	576	452
New Hampshire.........	438	300	46.0	410	269	470	345	534	363
Vermont...............	488	364	34.1	401	277	521	391	610	473
Massachusetts.........	380	247	53.8	370	242	456	299	450	295
Rhode Island..........	374	242	54.5	363	238	465	292	451	291
Connecticut...........	367	231	58.9	344	219	412	260	408	260
Middle Atlantic:									
New York..............	348	218	59.6	322	203	454	292	540	383
New Jersey............	355	220	61.4	341	209	414	274	428	280
Pennsylvania..........	373	275	35.6	338	235	435	357	502	415
East North Central:									
Ohio..................	413	279	48.0	375	238	495	368	524	410
Indiana...............	430	309	39.2	386	261	488	363	515	410
Illinois..............	376	251	49.8	346	220	470	337	506	401
Michigan..............	427	314	36.0	381	267	518	403	555	472
Wisconsin.............	459	324	41.7	393	259	522	378	607	462
West North Central:									
Minnesota.............	477	324	47.2	404	244	547	357	628	481
Iowa..................	465	335	38.8	400	267	493	346	566	430
Missouri..............	403	285	41.4	349	210	468	333	535	438
North Dakota..........	550	401	37.2	429	267	554	376	651	501
South Dakota..........	525	378	38.9	442	272	533	356	609	471
Nebraska..............	457	322	41.9	391	251	494	333	557	410
Kansas................	444	311	42.8	394	256	482	315	531	403
South Atlantic:									
Delaware..............	396	271	46.1	334	227	442	305	512	388
Maryland..............	405	278	45.7	356	231	459	334	534	427
District of Columbia...	278	180	54.4	278	180	...	...	...	...
Virginia..............	438	347	26.2	345	220	496	394	557	488
West Virginia.........	482	404	19.3	345	237	551	464	599	539
North Carolina........	473	385	22.9	352	235	493	373	607	528
South Carolina........	518	412	25.7	385	249	525	377	682	564
Georgia...............	476	359	32.6	380	230	506	345	643	520
Florida...............	403	281	43.4	336	208	486	358	593	479
East South Central:									
Kentucky..............	498	408	22.1	377	247	558	443	596	534
Tennessee.............	449	351	27.9	359	227	490	392	560	469
Alabama...............	494	387	27.6	392	236	542	385	636	530
Mississippi...........	551	404	36.4	397	215	515	330	706	514
West South Central:									
Arkansas..............	521	393	32.6	393	222	540	365	648	501
Louisiana.............	491	351	39.9	404	230	567	385	674	522
Oklahoma..............	453	362	25.1	390	250	507	383	570	502
Texas.................	454	324	40.1	409	246	530	350	563	454
Mountain:									
Montana...............	503	354	42.1	427	263	542	383	614	481
Idaho.................	528	406	30.0	465	315	550	428	611	497
Wyoming...............	486	360	35.0	432	288	532	363	587	483
Colorado..............	449	338	32.8	390	256	528	415	572	488
New Mexico............	556	476	16.8	480	340	620	525	667	606
Arizona...............	495	415	19.3	409	303	534	435	630	597
Utah..................	555	425	30.6	503	355	639	512	670	564
Nevada................	409	322	27.0	348	245	489	371	514	432
Pacific:									
Washington............	453	277	63.5	401	222	514	340	544	383
Oregon................	444	276	60.9	381	205	507	340	515	385
California............	397	247	60.7	358	214	481	332	497	375

Source: Derived from *1950 Census of Population*, Vol. II, *Characteristics of the Population*, Part 1, U. S. Summary, table 38, and Parts 2–50, table 15.

TABLE **24.**—NUMBER OF CHILDREN UNDER 5 YEARS OLD PER 1,000 NONWHITE WOMEN 15 TO 49 YEARS OLD, STANDARDIZED FOR AGE OF WOMAN, BY STATES, URBAN AND RURAL: 1950

[Urban-rural by 1940 Census rules of classification. Data standardized by indirect method to the age distribution of nonwhite women in the United States in 1950. Rate not shown where base is less than 100 women]

State	Total	Urban	Rural nonfarm	Rural farm
United States..........................	460	364	568	751
New England:				
Maine................................	579	477	625	...
New Hampshire........................	398	...	...	...
Vermont..............................	...	...	...	...
Massachusetts........................	374	368	494	...
Rhode Island.........................	448	440	548	...
Connecticut..........................	375	381	330	...
Middle Atlantic:				
New York.............................	283	282	278	503
New Jersey...........................	349	337	426	485
Pennsylvania.........................	361	351	492	497
East North Central:				
Ohio.................................	365	357	467	564
Indiana..............................	383	382	407	399
Illinois.............................	338	333	469	670
Michigan.............................	371	359	517	624
Wisconsin............................	471	387	752	763
West North Central:				
Minnesota............................	568	412	891	748
Iowa.................................	454	446	553	...
Missouri.............................	372	345	509	736
North Dakota.........................	844	614	863	887
South Dakota.........................	717	617	729	743
Nebraska.............................	460	421	681	741
Kansas...............................	420	407	480	655
South Atlantic:				
Delaware.............................	414	350	459	625
Maryland.............................	428	386	503	651
District of Columbia.................	312	312	...	...
Virginia.............................	472	359	534	660
West Virginia........................	466	361	525	597
North Carolina.......................	555	383	578	735
South Carolina.......................	620	420	640	764
Georgia..............................	533	396	589	770
Florida..............................	427	365	521	687
East South Central:				
Kentucky.............................	412	365	475	578
Tennessee............................	453	380	499	702
Alabama..............................	561	430	610	776
Mississippi..........................	655	437	585	802
West South Central:				
Arkansas.............................	610	441	623	768
Louisiana............................	570	448	641	811
Oklahoma.............................	552	455	629	741
Texas................................	453	369	565	710
Mountain:				
Montana..............................	804	606	826	840
Idaho................................	624	446	709	672
Wyoming..............................	582	374	660	816
Colorado.............................	391	368	540	527
New Mexico...........................	662	436	739	710
Arizona..............................	658	421	704	719
Utah.................................	507	371	701	632
Nevada...............................	503	390	594	690
Pacific:				
Washington...........................	484	417	660	746
Oregon...............................	459	408	561	610
California...........................	386	355	512	572

Source: Same as table 23.

The nonwhite ratios on a statewide basis were below 400 (uncorrected) in thirteen States and in the District of Columbia, all of which had large concentrations of nonwhites in urban areas. They were above 600 in nine States which had large concentrations of nonwhites in rural areas. The highest statewide ratios were noted in North and South Dakota and Montana, where most of the nonwhites were Indians. Ratios of 700 to 800 were common in the rural-farm areas of many States, regardless of whether Negroes or Indians predominated in the nonwhite population. Ratios at the 700 to 800 level may not necessarily be typical of groups with little family limitation. It will be recalled that national data for ever-married rural-farm nonwhite women indicated that the women 45 to 49 years old in 1950 had an average of only 4.9 children ever born, compared with 5.1 for women in this age group in 1940 and 7.5 in 1910. The urban-rural spread in nonwhite ratios of young children to women was impressively large in most States. Nationally in 1950, the rural-farm ratio was more than twice as large as the urban ratio.

The ratios of children to nonwhite women in 1950 were lower in Colorado than the other Mountain States. Colorado's Japanese population was responsible for these small ratios.

New York State contained the Nation's least fertile nonwhite population in 1950, in terms of ratios of young children to women. The District of Columbia was next lowest with a ratio of young children to nonwhite women that was about 10 percent higher than New York's 283. No other State had a ratio nearly as low as that for New York. Generalizations made for New York State also fit New York City since the city contained most of the State's nonwhite population in 1950. The State (and city) was an area of fairly heavy net in-migration of nonwhites from the South. In 1950, it contained many more nonwhite women than nonwhite men, age for age.

Miscellaneous measures of fertility computed from data on own children under 5 years old by age of mother, for regions, urban and rural. Tabulations were made for regions and States in 1940 and 1910 of the number of own children under 5 years old among women classified by age. A similar tabulation was not made in 1950. Although not recent, the data for 1940 and 1910 have value for various purposes and merit much more analysis and discussion than can be given here. They show age patterns in current fertility by geographic areas in 1910, two decades before the completion of the Birth Registration Area in 1933. They show the age patterns at a time (1940) when current fertility was abnormally low and at a time (1910) when there were still some population groups of quite high fertility. They show age patterns by urban-rural residence, which information is not easily obtained from registration data because of residence classification problems and lack of a "farm" category. The age patterns permit fuller and more complete comparisons of current fertility than are possible when ratios of young children to women are for the whole childbearing age range.

Data on own children under 5 years old by age of mother may be used in their own right (table 25), or they may be used in conjunction with life tables to estimate age-specific birth rates (table 26) and gross and net reproduction rates, Lotka's measures of the mean length of a generation and "intrinsic" or "true" rates of births, deaths, and natural increase (table 27).   These measures help one to understand the general level of current fertility at past dates although the fertility was changing so much over time that it is somewhat academic to relate the data to a hypothetical cohort of women (as in gross and net reproduction rates) or to a hypothetical stable population (as in Lotka's "intrinsic" measures).   The derived measures are analogous to the speedometer on a car in that they measure the approximate speed or force of reproduction at a given time but not necessarily the actual distance being covered or the actual time required to reach the destination.   The "speed" fluctuates too much for reliable measures of distance.   Nevertheless, we like to know what the "speed" is at specific times.

TABLE **25.**—NUMBER OF OWN CHILDREN UNDER 5 YEARS OLD PER 1,000 WHITE WOMEN 15 TO 49 YEARS OLD, BY AGE OF WOMAN, FOR REGIONS (WITH NONWHITE FOR THE SOUTH), URBAN AND RURAL: 1940 AND 1910

Year and area	Total, 15 to 49 years	Age of woman (years)						
		15 to 19	20 to 24	25 to 29	30 to 34	35 to 39	40 to 44	45 to 49
1940								
Northeast...................	228	24	265	464	406	249	112	31
Urban........................	208	17	228	426	383	228	98	27
Rural nonfarm................	295	44	406	601	465	300	147	40
Rural farm...................	317	48	401	667	599	436	231	64
North Central..............	278	43	379	561	454	287	140	39
Urban........................	230	37	309	467	378	223	100	25
Rural nonfarm................	341	67	515	660	517	319	151	37
Rural farm...................	372	41	489	800	661	463	254	80
South, total..............	338	83	502	614	478	336	182	59
Urban........................	234	62	350	440	331	197	88	28
Rural nonfarm................	383	104	591	682	512	340	170	47
Rural farm...................	434	88	630	810	667	524	319	104
South, nonwhite..........	324	123	494	521	412	321	179	88
Urban........................	192	108	328	292	218	155	86	36
Rural nonfarm................	326	122	495	548	400	298	153	63
Rural farm...................	472	133	660	813	698	574	316	163
West........................	275	61	437	540	412	248	112	31
Urban........................	220	44	337	448	343	193	77	17
Rural nonfarm................	362	98	613	654	493	301	147	41
Rural farm...................	375	64	586	807	622	435	220	78
1910								
Northeast...................	367	33	374	662	617	468	252	70
Urban........................	347	27	340	626	591	439	233	63
Rural nonfarm................	459	64	550	815	703	546	286	84
Rural farm...................	369	29	346	701	683	565	333	91
North Central..............	407	40	414	729	680	534	322	97
Urban........................	328	32	331	591	541	405	231	66
Rural nonfarm................	456	65	519	809	724	547	307	81
Rural farm...................	503	35	488	931	898	737	476	154
South, total..............	551	93	635	930	874	711	434	124
Urban........................	349	52	388	611	560	403	217	56
Rural nonfarm................	591	130	730	974	860	666	373	109
Rural farm...................	647	95	724	1,114	1,081	924	596	171
South, nonwhite..........	447	93	567	708	637	559	344	161
Urban........................	233	66	316	351	298	249	125	53
Rural nonfarm................	471	143	638	703	604	498	296	143
Rural farm...................	559	80	676	974	897	794	505	235
West........................	380	49	424	647	593	458	264	82
Urban........................	283	36	299	493	446	334	178	48
Rural nonfarm................	495	82	605	814	726	550	316	101
Rural farm...................	515	44	563	920	870	719	448	153

Source: *1940 Census of Population, Differential Fertility, 1940 and 1910,* Fertility for States and Large Cities, tables 21 and 22.

At all dates, the ratios of own children under 5 years old tend to be maximal when the women are 25 to 29 years old, or about 7 years after the usual age at marriage. The relative importance of fertility at the older ages has decreased over the years. Birth control practices probably increase in intensity after the family has attained a desired size. In 1910, and by inference for prior years when fertility was higher still, the women 35 to 39 years old frequently had more children under 5 years old than did the women 20 to 24 years old and those 45 to 49 years old had two to three times as many young children as did the women 15 to 19 years old. By 1940, the women 35 to 39 years old in the urban and rural parts of regions frequently had fewer young children than did the women 20 to 24 years old, despite the fact that a much larger proportion of the older women were married. By 1940, the women 45 to 49 years old had as few or fewer young children, on the average, as the women 15 to 19 years old.

Some regional variations in patterns of current fertility by age may be noted. Partly because of late marriages, the women 20 to 24 years old in the Northeast Region in 1940 had fewer children under 5 years old than did those 30 to 34 years old. The highest fertility ratios at young ages of women were found in the South. Women over 30 in the urban areas of the Northeast had higher ratios of young children than the women over 30 in the urban areas of other regions, but the differences were not large. With the exception of the Northeast, rural-nonfarm areas have the largest fertility ratios for women 15 to 19 years old and in most regions the women 20 to 24 years old in rural-nonfarm areas also have a higher fertility ratio than do those in urban and rural-farm areas. The 1910 data for the Northeast Region yield relatively low fertility ratios for women at most ages in rural-farm areas as compared with either rural-farm areas in other regions or with rural-nonfarm areas in the Northeast. Perhaps the farmers in the Northeast in 1910 were more inclined to practice family limitation than were those in other regions. Immigration of fertile foreign-born white women caused the fertility ratios of women of several age groups in urban areas in the Northeast in 1910 to exceed those for the corresponding groups in the urban areas of other regions and probably also inflated the rural-nonfarm ratios in the Northeast.

The ratios of children under 5 years old to women by age do not reflect the age patterns of the women at the time the children were born. The women are up to 5 years older at the time of the census than at the time their young children were born. The differences in patterns may be seen by comparing table 25 with table 26. It will be noted, for example, that age group 15 to 19 years is relatively important in data on annual births but is much less so in data on children under 5 years old. Age group 45 to 49 years usually is negligible in data on births but assumes greatly increased importance in data on own children under 5 years old.

TABLE **26.**—ESTIMATED AVERAGE ANNUAL NUMBER OF BIRTHS PER 1,000 WHITE WOMEN 15 TO 49 YEARS OLD, BY AGE, FOR REGIONS (WITH NONWHITE FOR THE SOUTH), URBAN AND RURAL: 1935 TO 1940 AND 1905 TO 1910

[Asterisks denote estimates having coefficients of variation of 2.5 to 4.9 percent (*) and of 5 percent or more (**). Rates derived from data on women by number of own children under 5 years old]

Period and area	Total, 15 to 49 years	Age of woman (years)						
		15 to 19	20 to 24	25 to 29	30 to 34	35 to 39	40 to 44	45 to 49
1935 TO 1940								
Northeast..............	55	27	95	111	77	40	*14	**2
Urban..................	49	21	83	103	71	35	*12	**2
Rural nonfarm..........	72	*46	135	133	87	*51	**19	**2
Rural farm.............	*88	**49	*156	*178	*137	*88	**34	**4
North Central..........	66	42	121	123	83	47	18	**2
Urban..................	52	33	97	100	65	33	*12	**1
Rural nonfarm..........	81	62	153	140	94	*51	**18	**2
Rural farm.............	94	*52	173	185	131	85	*36	**5
South, total..........	84	67	150	132	94	61	26	**4
Urban..................	54	45	102	91	58	30	*11	**2
Rural nonfarm..........	92	78	166	139	95	57	*22	**2
Rural farm.............	117	84	203	187	146	107	*49	**6
South, nonwhite.......	100	94	169	136	108	73	*37	**10
Urban..................	55	*69	101	*71	*53	*34	**16	**4
Rural nonfarm..........	*95	*87	*166	*132	*95	**63	**27	**6
Rural farm.............	159	119	253	233	197	*136	*69	**20
West..................	66	55	130	115	75	40	*14	**2
Urban..................	51	40	101	95	59	*28	**8	**1
Rural nonfarm..........	86	82	167	133	90	*49	*19	**2
Rural farm.............	102	*74	201	188	*130	*82	*34	**6
1905 TO 1910								
Northeast..............	95	42	136	169	136	89	*36	**5
Urban..................	91	38	127	162	130	83	**33	**4
Rural nonfarm..........	115	*65	177	193	150	*101	**40	**6
Rural farm.............	*102	**41	*147	*200	*171	*124	**54	**6
North Central..........	103	46	144	179	147	103	48	**7
Urban..................	81	36	114	142	112	74	*33	**4
Rural nonfarm..........	114	61	168	192	152	*102	**43	**5
Rural farm.............	133	*53	183	241	204	152	*76	**12
South, total..........	153	85	217	243	206	149	68	**8
Urban..................	95	51	138	160	126	79	*32	**3
Rural nonfarm..........	153	96	222	230	185	126	*54	**7
Rural farm.............	187	96	260	304	269	205	*99	**12
South, nonwhite.......	161	102	231	229	197	152	*80	**23
Urban..................	86	*66	132	*118	*96	*67	**28	**8
Rural nonfarm..........	*155	*115	*225	*203	*168	*123	**64	**20
Rural farm.............	212	114	302	331	286	*225	*122	**35
West..................	94	49	137	155	126	86	*39	**6
Urban..................	68	34	98	116	91	*59	**24	**3
Rural nonfarm..........	120	72	178	185	149	*100	**45	**7
Rural farm.............	139	*65	200	239	*204	*151	**74	**13

Source: *1940 Census of Population, Differential Fertility, 1940 and 1910,* Standardized Fertility Rates and Reproduction Rates, table 8.

The age-specific birth rates in table 26 were derived from data on own children under 5 years old plus allowances for children not living with their mothers, for a net undercount of young children in the census, and for deaths since the birth dates of the children. The data were interpolated by Sprague's fifth difference formula. The results were affected by any errors in the basic data. The very high birth rates estimated for nonwhite women 45 to 49 years old in rural-farm areas in 1940 and 1910 may in part reflect an incorrect enumeration of some Negro grandchildren under 5 years old as children instead of as grandchildren. The estimates for whites compare well on a national basis with birth rates from vital statistics and probably are satisfactory on a regional and urban-rural basis. Those for nonwhites are of poor quality.[11]

In most of the tables presented thus far for regions and States, data have been shown for nonwhites only where they are numerous. Where the nonwhites are a small minority of the population, data for whites alone are usually informative of conditions in the total population. The close agreement between fertility values for the total population and those for whites in regions other than the South is illustrated in table 27.

The data in table 27 are descriptive of the approximate force of current age-specific birth rates in the periods 1935 to 1940 and 1905 to 1910 and death rates in 1930 to 1939 and 1909 to 1911 without taking into account whether these rates were normal or biased for any reason. The period 1935 to 1940 was one of an economic depression and the age-specific birth rates were abnormally low. It may be noted that in this period, the South was the only region with fertility above replacement needs. The derived measures for urban areas may present an unrealistic picture if the age-specific birth rates in urban areas are lowered by the perennial in-migration of single women in search of jobs.[12] Conversely, the measures for rural-farm areas may reflect birth rates increased by the residual effect of out-movement of single women.

Region of residence by region of birth of women. The census reports on fertility present data on region of birth of women for 1940 but not for 1950. The data for 1940 are useful for a general indication of what happens to the fertility of women when they move from one region to another.

---

[11] *1940 Census of Population, Differential Fertility, 1940 and 1910,* Standardized Fertility Rates and Reproduction Rates, text table 3.

AVERAGE ANNUAL NUMBER OF BIRTHS PER 1,000 WOMEN 15 TO 49 YEARS OLD, BY AGE AND COLOR OF WOMAN, BASED ON REGISTERED BIRTHS, AND BASED ON CHILDREN UNDER 5 YEARS OLD, FOR THE UNITED STATES: 1935 TO 1940
[Rates based on registered births are adjusted for underregistration. Rates based on own children under 5 were derived from a 3.3-percent sample adjusted for underenumeration of children and for children not represented in the sample because they were not living with the mother]

Age of woman	All classes		White		Nonwhite	
	Based on registered births	Based on children under 5	Based on registered births	Based on children under 5	Based on registered births	Based on children under 5
Total, 15 to 49 years	69	70	66	67	89	90
15 to 19 years	52	50	44	46	118	90
20 to 24 years	130	126	126	122	158	159
25 to 29 years	119	122	119	121	113	122
30 to 34 years	80	85	80	83	80	94
35 to 39 years	47	49	46	47	54	64
40 to 44 years	17	19	17	18	20	32
45 to 49 years	2	3	2	2	3	8

[12] The biased nature of the birth rates is suggested by the following computation and comparison. A rough approximation to an expected number of children ever born is obtained by multiplying the gross reproduction rate by two. This yields an estimate of about 1,600 children ever born per 1,000 women for urban areas in 1935–1939. In contrast, the lowest real rate of children ever born on record for women of completed fertility in urban areas nationally was about 1,900 for white women 45 to 49 years old in 1950, and for nonwhite women it was 2,100.

TABLE **27.**—REPRODUCTION RATES AND INTRINSIC RATES OF BIRTH, DEATH, AND NATURAL INCREASE, AND MEAN LENGTH OF A GENERATION, BY COLOR, FOR REGIONS, URBAN AND RURAL: 1935 TO 1940 AND 1905 TO 1910

[Rates derived from data on women by number of own children under 5 years old, adjusted for children not living with their mothers and for net undercount. Minus sign (−) denotes decrease]

Area and color	Reproduction rate				Intrinsic rate						Mean length of generation (years)	
	Gross		Net		Natural increase		Birth		Death			
	1935 to 1940	1905 to 1910	1935 to 1940	1905 to 1910	1935 to 1940	1905 to 1910	1935 to 1940	1905 to 1910	1935 to 1940	1905 to 1910	1935 to 1940	1905 to 1910
Northeast	881	1,476	794	1,120	-7.9	3.8	11.7	21.9	19.6	18.1	28.3	28.9
White	881	1,488	797	1,134	-7.7	4.4	11.7	22.1	19.4	17.7	28.3	28.9
Urban	791	1,386	715	1,033	-11.7	1.0	10.1	20.5	21.8	19.5	28.4	29.0
White	788	1,400	715	1,048	-11.5	1.7	10.1	20.8	21.6	19.1	28.5	29.0
Rural nonfarm	1,147	1,784	1,035	1,426	1.5	12.5	16.4	26.5	14.9	14.0	27.6	28.2
White	1,143	1,784	1,035	1,435	1.4	12.7	16.2	26.5	14.8	13.8	27.6	28.2
Rural farm	1,563	1,810	1,406	1,439	12.1	12.3	23.3	26.3	11.2	14.0	28.4	29.5
White	1,562	1,804	1,410	1,441	12.2	12.4	23.2	26.3	11.0	13.9	28.5	29.5
North Central	1,045	1,626	944	1,308	-2.0	9.2	14.5	24.1	16.5	14.9	27.7	29.1
White	1,047	1,637	952	1,324	-1.4	9.6	14.5	24.2	15.9	14.6	27.8	29.1
Urban	831	1,236	753	963	-10.2	-1.5	10.5	18.0	20.7	19.5	27.7	29.0
White	827	1,251	753	981	-10.2	-0.7	10.3	18.3	20.5	19.0	27.7	29.1
Rural nonfarm	1,266	1,756	1,146	1,451	5.3	13.1	18.4	26.0	13.1	12.9	27.1	28.4
White	1,256	1,753	1,140	1,454	5.1	13.3	18.2	26.0	13.1	12.7	27.1	28.4
Rural farm	1,609	2,233	1,452	1,834	13.6	20.7	24.0	32.1	10.4	11.4	28.2	29.4
White	1,603	2,227	1,451	1,836	13.6	20.8	23.9	32.1	10.3	11.3	28.2	29.4
South	1,363	2,343	1,182	1,614	6.0	17.1	20.2	36.0	14.2	18.9	27.4	28.3
White	1,296	2,358	1,154	1,687	5.2	18.6	18.7	35.3	13.5	16.7	27.5	28.3
Nonwhite	1,558	2,491	1,253	1,476	8.0	13.9	24.5	38.0	16.5	24.1	27.1	28.0
Urban	836	1,368	712	764	-12.8	-9.5	10.6	20.8	23.4	30.3	27.0	28.1
White	827	1,425	726	874	-12.0	-4.6	10.1	21.6	22.1	26.2	27.1	28.3
Nonwhite	872	1,269	679	568	-15.3	-20.8	12.2	19.6	27.5	40.4	26.5	27.4
Rural nonfarm	1,375	2,234	1,211	1,591	7.2	16.9	20.4	34.1	13.2	17.2	26.8	27.7
White	1,358	2,229	1,222	1,668	7.5	18.5	19.9	33.7	12.4	15.2	26.8	27.8
Nonwhite	1,439	2,269	1,189	1,456	6.0	13.4	22.0	35.1	16.0	21.7	26.8	27.4
Rural farm	2,071	3,131	1,812	2,199	21.4	27.8	31.0	44.0	9.6	16.2	27.8	28.5
White	1,894	3,003	1,696	2,222	19.1	28.1	28.3	42.4	9.2	14.3	27.9	28.6
Nonwhite	2,539	3,465	2,076	2,173	26.3	27.6	38.0	48.1	11.7	20.5	27.6	28.3
West	1,057	1,479	941	1,166	-1.9	5.3	14.5	21.9	16.4	16.6	27.0	28.7
White	1,041	1,453	933	1,162	-2.4	5.2	14.1	21.5	16.5	16.3	27.0	28.8
Urban	806	1,033	726	807	-11.5	-7.5	9.8	14.6	21.3	22.1	27.1	28.8
White	804	1,032	726	812	-11.7	-7.2	9.7	14.6	21.4	21.8	27.0	28.8
Rural nonfarm	1,331	1,832	1,174	1,459	6.3	13.3	19.5	27.2	13.2	13.9	26.6	28.2
White	1,311	1,789	1,166	1,457	6.0	13.3	19.1	26.6	13.1	13.3	26.5	28.2
Rural farm	1,773	2,335	1,559	1,848	16.4	21.2	26.8	33.8	10.4	12.6	27.5	29.0
White	1,719	2,289	1,524	1,852	15.7	21.3	26.0	33.1	10.3	11.8	27.5	29.0

Source: *1940 Census of Population, Differential Fertility, 1940 and 1910,* Standardized Fertility Rates and Reproduction Rates, tables 7 and 9.

Data on children ever born for native white women 45 to 49 years old in 1940 indicate that both the in-migrants and the out-migrants for any region tend to be less fertile than the women who remain in their region of birth (table 28). This situation arises in part because the interregional migration often involves an urban destination. The "long distance" migrants may move from rural areas and small towns but they, like in-migrants from abroad, often go to large cities where jobs for themselves or their husbands are relatively plentiful. The selection of an urban destination is most important in the South where 64.3 percent urban residents among the in-migrant native white women and 64.1 percent urban among the out-migrant native white women contrast sharply with only 39.7 percent urban among the native white women born and still living in the South in 1940.

TABLE **28.**—REGION OF RESIDENCE BY REGION OF BIRTH OF NATIVE WHITE AND NEGRO WOMEN 45 TO 49 YEARS OLD, BY NUMBER OF CHILDREN EVER BORN: 1940

Region of residence and region of birth	Number of women[1]	Children ever born per 1,000 women	Percent of women residing in urban areas in 1940
NATIVE WHITE			
Northeast:			
Born and living in Northeast......................	707,020	2,183	74.1
Born elsewhere, living in Northeast...............	49,640	1,850	76.7
Born in Northeast, living elsewhere..............	83,860	1,921	77.2
Birthplace not reported[2]......................	15,260	2,442	80.6
North Central:			
Born and living in North Central.................	944,060	2,496	57.8
Born elsewhere, living in North Central...........	96,680	2,651	70.6
Born in North Central, living elsewhere...........	236,980	2,213	64.6
Birthplace not reported[2]......................	8,520	2,645	69.5
South:			
Born and living in South.........................	717,880	3,400	39.7
Born elsewhere, living in South..................	86,180	2,222	64.3
Born in South, living elsewhere..................	114,140	2,697	64.1
Birthplace not reported[2]......................	4,260	2,873	68.1
West:			
Born and living in West..........................	135,680	2,426	63.0
Born elsewhere, living in West...................	214,500	2,236	64.1
Born in West, living elsewhere...................	12,020	2,193	66.9
Birthplace not reported[2]......................	5,900	2,723	67.5
NEGRO			
North and West:			
Born in South, living in North and West...........	68,100	2,062	[3]
Other, living in North and West[4]..................	28,820	2,005	[3]
South:			
Born and living in South.........................	241,060	3,589	44.9
Other, living in South[4].........................	1,800	[5]2,279	[5]72.2

[1] Includes women with no report on children ever born.
[2] Includes the small number of native women born abroad.
[3] Not available by birthplace; percent urban for total living in North and West is about 90.
[4] Comprises women born in North and West, women with birthplace not reported, and the small number born abroad.
[5] Rate or percent based on about 70 observations in the uninflated sample.

Source: Derived from *1940 Census of Population, Differential Fertility, 1940 and 1910*, Women by Number of Children Ever Born, tables 39 and 101.

In-migrants to the North Central Region and to the Northeast Region came largely from the South. Those who went to the North Central Region were the most fertile interregional migrant group whereas those who went to the Northeast Region were the least fertile migrant group. Different conditions in the host regions undoubtedly explain why it was that the two movements had very different effects on the fertility of out-migrants from the South. The pattern also indicates that there is no simple answer to the question of whether the region of birth or the region of residence has the greater effect on the fertility of migrants. The answer varies.

The interregional migrants were characterized by fertility rates too low for permanent replacement, perhaps partly because a sizable proportion of the migrants went to urban areas. They had fewer than the 2,450 children ever born per 1,000 white women 45 to 49 years old required for permanent replacement on the basis of life tables for whites in 1919–21. The data in table 28 are for women who bore most of their children before the onset of the economic depression of the 1930's. The women

45 to 49 years old in 1940 lived in an era when the spread of the small-family system had not yet run its full course. It seems likely that later cohorts of women will have fewer children ever born, on the average, and the interregional migrants in later cohorts will continue to have a below-replacement average number of children ever born.

Data on region of birth were also obtained for Negro women in 1940 (table 28). It may be noted that the movement of Negroes from the South either had the effect of reducing their fertility or the migration was selective of infertile women. The reverse movement may have increased the fertility of women from the North and West. The majority of the Negro women living in the North and West in 1940 were born in the South.

B. Counties

Net reproduction rates for the white population by counties are shown for 1945–50 and 1935–40 in figures 15 and 16. These rates were computed from census data on children under 5 years old and on women by age.[13] The net reproduction rates are shown in preference to ratios of young children to women, because they are easier to interpret for analytical purposes and are as easy to compute as fertility ratios standardized for age of women and adjusted for an undercount of young children. Standardization for age and adjustment for an undercount would be necessary in any event for a fair comparison of ratios of young children to women in areas as small as counties. The net reproduction rate automatically standardizes for age. Allowances have been made for an undercount of young children. The distribution of population by counties should be kept in mind when examining the maps.

Figure 15, for 1945–50, is for a period in which most parts of the United States had substantial net reproduction rates, a period in which birth rates were high as a result of prosperous economic conditions, a postwar surge in marriages, etc. Figure 16, for 1935–40, is for a period in which a severe economic depression caused birth rates to be at a low level.[14] A "normal" picture of county variations in fertility may lie between the low rates of 1935–40 and the higher rates of 1945–50. Figure 15, and figure 16 in lesser degree, indicate some longstanding geographical patterns of variation in current fertility. It will be noted that the areas of highest fertility are found along the northern and southern borders of the United States

---

[13] The procedure used was derived from and was mathematically identical with the method conventionally used with vital statistics. (Wilson H. Grabill, "A Method for Calculating Gross and Net Reproduction Rates from Census Data," unpublished M.A. thesis, American University, Washington, D.C., 1942.) Although the methods are mathematically identical, differences in the data used have some effect. Thus, only an approximate adjustment can be made for a net undercount of young children in the census (or if vital statistics were used, for underregistration of births). A single United States life table for white persons in 1950 was used throughout for the rates in 1945–50; geographic division life tables for white persons in 1930 to 1939 were used for the rates in 1935–40. The life tables, of course, can only approximate mortality conditions on a county basis.

[14] The net reproduction rate of the Nation's white population in 1935–40 was 978.

FIGURE 15.—ESTIMATED NET REPRODUCTION RATE OF THE WHITE POPULATION, BY COUNTIES: 1945 TO 1950

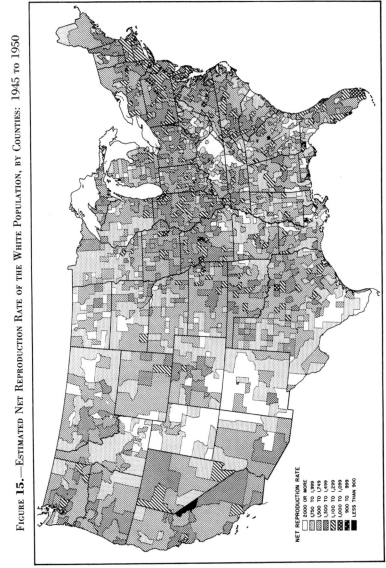

NET REPRODUCTION RATE

☐ 2,000 OR MORE
1,750 TO 1,999
1,500 TO 1,749
1,300 TO 1,499
1,100 TO 1,299
1,000 TO 1,099
900 TO 999
■ LESS THAN 900

Source: Computed from *1950 Census of Population,* Vol. II, *Characteristics of the Population,* Parts 2–50, table 41; from estimates of the completeness of enumeration of children under 5 years old by counties, and from lifetable allowances for mortality among children and women since the birthdate of the children under 5 years old in 1950.

FIGURE 16.—ESTIMATED NET REPRODUCTION RATE OF THE WHITE POPULATION, BY COUNTIES: 1935 TO 1940

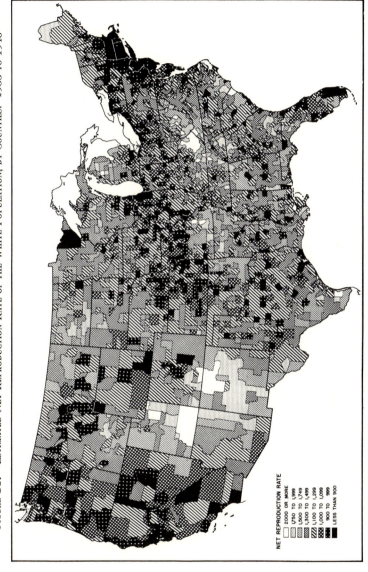

NET REPRODUCTION RATE

2,000 OR MORE
1,750 TO 1,999
1,500 TO 1,749
1,300 TO 1,499
1,100 TO 1,299
1,000 TO 1,099
900 TO 999
LESS THAN 900

Source: U. S. Bureau of the Census, *Current Population Reports*, Series P-20, No. 29.

and connect in the West to form a huge horseshoe pattern. Areas of low fertility are found in the interior of this area and on the Pacific coast. This picture was noted earlier from 1930 Census data by the National Resources Committee, which used an index of population reproduction that differed from the present net reproduction rate although also based on children under 5 years old and on life tables.[15]

The Appalachian area is one of the more fertile parts of the country.[16] This is the mountain area in the southern part of West Virginia, the western part of North Carolina, the eastern part of Kentucky, and the eastern part of Tennessee. Kentucky had 38 counties, mostly in the Appalachian area, where the net reproduction rate for the white population was above 2,000 in 1945–50. It had 20 counties with net reproduction rates this large in 1935–40. Other States also had some counties with rates above 2,000 in 1945–50. Texas had 24 counties of this type in 1945–50, Georgia had 18, New Mexico had 15, and Tennessee and Utah were tied at 13 each. The Nation had 247 counties with net reproduction rates above 2,000 in 1945–50. Kennedy County and Loving County, both in Texas, tied for the highest net reproduction rate, 2,989, but these two counties contained very few people and their birth rates were subject to large fluctuations. People with little education, of Mexican descent, predominated in the two counties; most of them worked on cattle ranches.

Areas with low fertility usually are urban in character or are in the vicinity of large cities. Fertility conditions were unusual in 1945–50 in that most of the large cities had net reproduction rates above 1,000. Philadelphia, Chicago, Los Angeles, and three of the five boroughs of New York City are examples of large cities with net reproduction rates above 1,000. In 1935–40, most such places had net reproduction rates of around 700, and as early as 1920 their reproduction ratios figured from current fertility also were below 1,000.[17]

In 1945–50, only 24 counties and independent cities in the United States had net reproduction rates below 1,000 in their white populations (table 29). (An independent city is one that is legally not a part of any county.) Sometimes special local circumstances affect the reproduction rates. For example, in the independent city of Williamsburg, Virginia, the net reproduction rate was low because of the presence of the College of William and Mary and a large State mental hospital, both of which con-

[15] National Resources Committee, *The Problems of a Changing Population*, United States Government Printing Office, Washington, D.C., 1938, pp. 122–123.

[16] The Appalachian area was noted until the present century as an isolated area in which the mountain folk maintained many of the traditions of early America, including folk songs and Elizabethan speech. An unpublished tabulation from the 1910 Census schedules for women in rural-farm parts of many Appalachian counties indicated that the women 50 to 54 years old, married once and husband present, had an average of 6.9 children ever born per woman and 7.4 per mother. Those who had been married 35 years and over, and hence had married quite young, reported an average of 8.9 children ever born per woman and 9.2 per mother.

[17] Warren S. Thompson, *Ratios of Children to Women: 1920, op. cit.*

tained many unmarried women. The presence of a large mental hospital also explained why Baldwin County, Georgia, had one of the Nation's lowest net reproduction rates, in both 1945–50 and 1935–40.

TABLE **29.**—DISTRIBUTION OF COUNTIES BY SIZE OF NET REPRODUCTION RATE OF THE WHITE POPULATION, AND PERCENT OF THE WHITE POPULATION LIVING IN THESE COUNTIES: 1950 AND 1940

[Counties and independent cities as constituted in 1950 and in 1940. Reproduction rate for 5-year period ending on census date; computed from data on children under 5 years old in lieu of births]

Net reproduction rate	Number of counties		Percent distribution of white population		Counties which gained or lost white population between 1940 and 1950[1]	
	1950	1940	1950	1940	Gained	Lost
Total......................	3,103	3,098	100.0	100.0	1,661	1,442
2,000 and over..................	248	49	2.4	0.7	89	159
1,900 to 1,999..................	182	34	1.6	0.3	54	128
1,800 to 1,899..................	303	64	2.9	0.7	106	197
1,700 to 1,799..................	417	91	4.8	1.2	178	239
1,600 to 1,699..................	501	145	6.9	1.8	242	259
1,500 to 1,599..................	492	197	9.6	2.5	261	231
1,400 to 1,499..................	418	274	12.0	3.3	286	132
1,300 to 1,399..................	253	409	12.0	5.5	200	53
1,200 to 1,299..................	149	450	15.4	6.6	124	25
1,100 to 1,199..................	84	463	17.0	8.9	77	7
1,000 to 1,099..................	32	388	12.1	10.4	25	7
900 to 999.....................	12	239	1.7	8.9	11	1
800 to 899.....................	5	156	0.5	11.5	4	1
700 to 799.....................	2	95	1.2	20.2	1	1
Less than 700..................	5	44	0.1	17.5	3	2

[1] By size of net reproduction rate in April 1945 to 1950.

Source: Derived from *1950 Census of Population*, Vol. II, *Characteristics of the Population*, Parts 2–50, table 41; *1940 Census of Population*, Vol. II, *Characteristics of the Population*, Parts 1–7, table 22; U. S. Bureau of the Census, *Current Population Reports*, Series P–20, No. 29; life tables for 1945 to 1950; and materials on the completeness of the enumeration of young children.

C. Urban-rural

General. Urban-rural differentials in fertility have been discussed at several places in this monograph in conjunction with various other characteristics of the population. A brief summary is given here. The urban-rural differentials in fertility are among the oldest and best known of demographic phenomenon. Over the years, they have narrowed considerably in the United States but they are not likely to disappear completely within the foreseeable future.[18] They arise from many causes. The main cause probably is the greater money cost and inconvenience of raising children in an urban area than on a farm.[19] Some other causes are the migration of unmarried women from rural to urban areas, later marriage and more education in urban areas, and more incentive to practice birth control in urban areas. It is true that the factors are differences in degree. It is doubtful that the tendency to limit family size spread from urban areas to

[18] The narrowing is in terms of absolute differences; the relative differences widened as was shown in Chapter 2, figure 2.

[19] For an extensive discussion of this point, see Warren S. Thompson, *Ratios of Children to Women: 1920, op. cit.*

rural areas only as the latter became more "urban minded." It was noted in Chapter 2 that large declines occurred in fertility ratios in rural areas of the United States at an early date, before any large proportion of the population became urban and that declines in rural fertility more than kept pace with those in urban areas between 1810 and 1950. Despite the greater absolute decline in rural fertility ratios, the rural areas continued to have much higher fertility than the urban areas.

Old and new definitions of urban-rural. Since a change of definition of "urban" was introduced in the 1950 Census it is of interest to ascertain the extent to which this change of definition influenced the urban-rural differentials in fertility. Approximately 7.6 million people were added to the urban population in 1950 because of the change in definition of "urban" from that used in previous censuses. About four-fifths of these were the inhabitants of the populous areas adjacent to cities of 50,000 or more that were given urban status in 1950; the remaining fifth were residents of unincorporated places of 2,500 population or more, which also received "urban" status under the new definition. Some data on fertility by the old definition of urban were tabulated for 1950, for purposes of comparison.

The 1950 Census tabulations of data on fertility were limited to data for women 15 to 59 years old. A total of nearly 2 million (1,961,600) women 15 to 59 years old who had ever been married were involved in the group that achieved urban status in 1950 under the new definition. More precisely, this is a *net* figure after deduction of a very small group, mostly in New England townships, that lost urban status as a result of the dropping of a category that was no longer needed, "Urban by special rule." Almost all of these (1,954,040) would have been classified as "rural non-farm" under the old definition of urban. However, about 7,560 would have been classified as "rural farm."

The approximately 2 million ever-married women 15 to 59 years old who were added to the urban group as a result of the change in definition had a fertility rate (1,963 children ever born per 1,000 women) that was relatively high by urban standards and relatively low by rural-nonfarm standards. The fertility rate for the urban group under the old definition would have been 1,858 and that for the rural-nonfarm group under the old definition would have been 2,264. This intermediate position is not surprising since the group is of marginal urban-rural status. Therefore, the effect of the transfer was to raise the fertility rate slightly within both urban and rural-nonfarm areas. The very slight change induced by the transfer of 7,560 women from rural-farm to urban status was also in the direction of an increase.

Under the new definition of urban, the fertility rate for ever-married women 15 to 59 years old was 1,866 in urban areas and 2,346 in rural-nonfarm areas. Thus, although the change of definition of urban could have no bearing on the total fertility rate, it actually increased the fertility within each type of area considered separately. Although this may appear at first glance to be a statistically freak result, it simply arises from the fact that the group transferred to urban status under the new definition, was of high fertility in comparison with the urban group and of low fertility in comparison with the rural-nonfarm and rural-farm group. The actual impact of the transfer on the fertility of the urban group was negligible because the group that was added to urban under the new definition comprised only 8 percent of the total urban group under the new definition. The impact of the change in definition was somewhat larger on the rural-nonfarm group because those transferred from "rural nonfarm" to "urban" under the definition comprised about 21 percent of the "rural nonfarm" under the old definition and because the group transferred had lesser fertility than the 79 percent not transferred. The number of rural-farm women affected by the new definition of "urban" was too small to have appreciable impact on the fertility rate of this group.

The above statements hold in principle for the whites and nonwhites considered separately.

Figure 17 presents age-specific cumulative fertility rates for whites in urban and rural-nonfarm areas. Again, it is seen that although the group transferred to urban was characterized by relatively high fertility in comparison with the total urban group, the change caused imperceptible increases in the fertility rate. The group transferred was characterized by relatively low fertility in comparison with the rural-nonfarm group. The removal of this group from the rural-nonfarm category resulted in higher average levels of fertility among those remaining in the rural-nonfarm category under the new definition.

Finally, as indicated in figure 17, the institution of the new definition of urban caused little perceptible change in urban-rural differentials in fertility. Although the fertility of each group was raised by the nature of the change, only the rural-nonfarm group had an appreciable change.

Size of place. When data for many cities are grouped by size of place, a tendency may be noted for fertility to be lower in the larger places, on the average, than in the smaller places. As will be noted a little later, there are wide differences in fertility among places of similar size and it may often happen that a particular small place has a less fertile population than does a large place, and conversely. The differences among places grouped by size reflect relative job opportunities and migration of women, relative costs of living, the existence or nonexistence of many large apartment buildings with restrictions against children, and a host of similar factors. In recent years, city planners have attempted to make some large cities healthier and more attractive places in which to live, to eliminate slums and delinquency, and this may have some effect on fertility. It seems doubtful that large cities always were consumers rather than producers of people, despite European data on more deaths than births in the eighteenth century. In America, inadequate fertility seems to be a development of the twentieth century in terms of children ever born per

FIGURE **17.**—EFFECT OF NEW DEFINITION AND OLD DEFINITION OF URBAN-RURAL RESIDENCE ON NUMBER OF CHILDREN EVER BORN PER 1,000 EVER-MARRIED WHITE WOMEN 15 TO 59 YEARS OLD, BY AGE: 1950

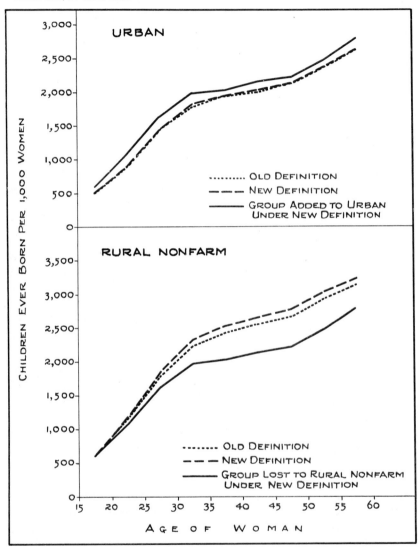

Source: Derived from *1950 Census of Population*, Vol. IV, *Special Reports*, Part 5, Chapter C, Fertility, tables 1 and 4.

woman of completed fertility. Thus, in 1910, the native white women 45 to 49 years old in American cities of 100,000 inhabitants or more reported an average of 2.8 children ever born per woman, despite the fact that only 85 percent of the women had ever been married.[20] About 2.7 children were required for replacement of the women in the next generation

---

[20] *1940 Census of Population, Differential Fertility, 1940 and 1910*, Women by Number of Children Ever Born, table 10.

on the basis of Glover's life tables for 1910 which involved quite high mortality. Women over 50 in 1910 had considerably more children than did those 45 to 49 years old. The women 65 to 74 years in cities of 100,000 or more in 1910 had an average of 3.8 children ever born. Some allowance must be made for the effect of rural-to-urban migration of widows.

Table 30 shows some of the variations in number of children ever born for native white women in places of different sizes in 1940. More recent data for all races from the Current Population Survey are presented in table 31. The urbanized areas shown in table 31 are much better as units of measure than are the city size groups shown in table 30 because the former include the contiguous suburban districts where many young families reside. However, the data in table 31 are subject to much greater sampling variability than are those from the 1940 Census. Similar tabulations by size of place were not made in 1950.

A replacement quota for use with the data for women 45 to 49 years old in 1940 in table 30 is 2,480 children per 1,000 women, based on United States life tables for 1919–21. Older women would need more than 2,480 as their children were subject to higher mortality, and younger women would need fewer children. The women 45 to 49 years old in cities of 250,000 inhabitants or more had only 1,802 children and even those in the smallest urban-size group shown had too few, 2,398 children, for replacement of their generation. Only the rural areas had rates above replacement needs. In cities of 250,000 or more in 1940, 34 percent of the native white women 45 to 49 years old had never borne a child; the corresponding proportion was 25 percent in the smallest urban-size group shown and 14 percent in rural-farm areas. These percentages include single women. The proportions of women who had married were larger in the smaller urban areas and in rural areas than in large cities as may be noted from the top section of table 30. Perhaps it is more significant to compare the proportions of women reported as married once and husband present, or in unbroken first marriages. This proportion usually was highest among the women 30 to 34 years old. In 1940, the proportion of women 30 to 34 years old who were married once and living with husband ranged from 59 percent in large cities to 72 percent in rural-farm areas. These percentages indicate once again that fertility variations by residence reflect other differences as well as family limitation practices.

The data in table 31 are for women of all races and are not strictly comparable with those for native white women in table 30. Replacement quotas for use with table 31 are not easily figured because of the broad age groups necessarily used on account of limitations of the sample. A minimum quota for women 45 years old and over would be 2,060 plus an allowance for mortality. Any reasonable allowance for mortality would result in a quota above the actual rates for urbanized areas of 1,000,000 inhabitants or more but perhaps not for areas of 250,000 to 1,000,000 inhabitants. The data for women 15 to 44 years old indicate that the urban-size differentials in fertility probably will persist for some time.

TABLE **30.**—MARITAL STATUS, PERCENT CHILDLESS, AND NUMBER OF CHILDREN EVER BORN, BY AGE OF WOMAN, FOR NATIVE WHITE WOMEN, URBAN (BY SIZE OF PLACE) AND RURAL: 1940

Subject and age of woman	United States	Urban				Rural nonfarm	Rural farm
		Total	Cities of 250,000 or more	Places of 25,000 to 250,000	Places of 2,500 to 25,000		
PERCENT EVER MARRIED							
Total, 15 to 44 years.....	63.3	60.9	58.7	61.3	63.4	69.1	64.4
15 to 19 years...............	11.1	8.5	6.3	9.8	9.9	15.1	13.6
20 to 24 years...............	51.9	46.4	42.6	48.3	49.5	62.6	58.6
25 to 29 years...............	77.1	73.1	70.0	74.1	76.5	84.2	82.9
30 to 34 years...............	85.1	82.4	80.4	82.8	84.7	90.7	89.1
35 to 39 years...............	88.2	85.8	84.0	86.4	87.5	91.5	92.2
40 to 44 years...............	89.5	87.0	85.1	87.7	89.0	92.3	94.0
PERCENT MARRIED ONCE AND HUSBAND PRESENT							
Total, 15 to 44 years.....	47.8	44.7	42.9	44.7	47.6	53.3	51.4
15 to 19 years...............	8.6	6.5	4.8	7.5	7.6	12.0	10.5
20 to 24 years...............	41.5	36.5	33.8	37.8	39.0	51.1	47.8
25 to 29 years...............	60.8	39.4	41.7	56.9	59.7	67.5	67.7
30 to 34 years...............	64.8	61.0	59.1	60.5	64.4	69.8	71.8
35 to 39 years...............	63.9	60.0	58.1	60.0	62.8	67.4	72.7
40 to 44 years...............	62.2	58.0	55.2	58.4	62.1	64.9	72.4
PERCENT CHILDLESS, INCLUDING SINGLE WOMEN							
Total, 15 to 44 years.....	54.3	58.7	61.8	58.3	54.7	47.4	47.9
15 to 19 years...............	95.6	96.9	97.7	96.5	96.4	93.4	94.5
20 to 24 years...............	69.9	76.3	79.8	74.9	72.6	59.1	59.3
25 to 29 years...............	45.8	52.9	56.9	52.3	47.7	35.8	31.2
30 to 34 years...............	33.8	39.7	43.5	39.1	34.7	26.6	21.5
35 to 39 years...............	28.2	33.5	37.9	32.1	28.9	22.8	17.2
40 to 44 years...............	25.5	30.4	34.7	29.2	25.4	21.1	14.8
45 to 49 years...............	24.9	29.8	34.4	28.8	24.5	21.2	14.3
50 to 54 years...............	25.5	30.4	35.1	28.9	26.1	22.5	14.8
55 to 64 years...............	25.8	31.0	35.4	29.9	26.6	22.8	15.4
65 to 74 years...............	25.1	29.9	34.6	28.2	26.7	21.9	15.0
CHILDREN EVER BORN PER 1,000 WOMEN, INCLUDING SINGLE WOMEN							
Total, 15 to 44 years.....	1,138	903	790	925	1,043	1,364	1,641
15 to 19 years...............	54	37	28	43	43	82	68
20 to 24 years...............	475	348	285	369	419	669	704
25 to 29 years...............	1,090	836	730	859	971	1,394	1,669
30 to 34 years...............	1,643	1,303	1,153	1,320	1,498	1,959	2,483
35 to 39 years...............	2,107	1,667	1,453	1,733	1,894	2,405	3,197
40 to 44 years...............	2,417	1,917	1,682	1,973	2,204	2,704	3,667
45 to 49 years...............	2,602	2,067	1,802	2,111	2,398	2,880	3,850
50 to 54 years...............	2,684	2,140	1,854	2,209	2,441	2,938	3,913
55 to 64 years...............	2,850	2,286	1,972	2,355	2,606	3,122	4,054
65 to 74 years...............	3,100	2,556	2,219	2,639	2,846	3,412	4,301

Source: Derived from *1940 Census of Population, Differential Fertility, 1940 and 1910,* Women by Number of Children Ever Born, tables 7, 17, and 21.

In their 1950 Census monograph on the social characteristics of urban and rural communities,[21] Duncan and Reiss present three tables of fertility ratios which are here reproduced as tables 32, 33, and 34. The Duncan and Reiss ratios show the number of children under 5 years old per 1,000 women 20 to 44 years old, computed from "complete count" census data on the population by age and sex, using some unpublished detail. The

[21] Otis Dudley Duncan and Albert J. Reiss, Jr., *Social Characteristics of Urban and Rural Communities, 1950,* John Wiley and Sons, New York, 1956.

data in table 32 indicate that the inverse relation between size of place and fertility ratios existed in all regions of the country in 1950. (Because of varying degrees of completeness of the count of young children, varying age distributions of women, and other factors, interregional comparisons and color comparisons should be made with some caution.)

TABLE 31.—NUMBER OF CHILDREN EVER BORN PER 1,000 WOMEN, BY AGE AND MARITAL STATUS, URBAN (BY SIZE OF PLACE) AND RURAL: APRIL 1952

Area	Women 15 to 44 years old, standardized for age[1]		Women 45 years old and over	
	All marital classes	Ever married	All marital classes	Ever married
United States......................	1,465	1,925	2,594	2,813
Urban..............................	1,285	1,713	2,343	2,571
In urbanized areas...............	1,211	1,642	2,251	2,460
Areas of 3,000,000 or more..........	1,091	1,547	2,070	2,248
Areas of 1,000,000 to 3,000,000.......	1,110	1,539	2,125	2,391
Areas of 250,000 to 1,000,000........	1,277	1,685	2,395	2,616
Areas of less than 250,000..........	1,400	1,824	2,442	2,614
Other urban areas.................	1,451	1,873	2,539	2,812
Places of 25,000 or more...........	1,438	1,836	2,603	2,878
Places of 2,500 to 25,000..........	1,459	1,897	2,507	2,778
Rural nonfarm........................	1,689	2,128	2,899	3,089
Rural farm...........................	2,126	2,742	3,489	3,645

[1] The standard is the distribution by age of women of the given marital status in the entire United States.

Source: U. S. Bureau of the Census, *Current Population Reports*, Series P-20, No. 46, table 3.

TABLE 32.—NUMBER OF CHILDREN UNDER 5 YEARS OLD PER 1,000 WOMEN 20 TO 44 YEARS OLD BY SIZE OF PLACE, BY REGIONS (WITH COLOR FOR THE SOUTH): 1950

Size of place	United States	North-east	North Central	South		West
				White	Nonwhite	
Urbanized areas:						
3,000,000 or more................	433	419	443	...	...	464
1,000,000 to 3,000,000...........	478	461	491	455	449	527
250,000 to 1,000,000.............	503	477	510	498	514	526
Under 250,000....................	510	481	531	494	526	563
Places outside urbanized areas:						
25,000 or more...................	522	482	519	519	550	567
10,000 to 25,000.................	525	490	535	516	552	558
2,500 to 10,000..................	570	512	578	550	637	643
1,000 to 2,500...................	609	557	626	595	690	644
Under 1,000 (incorporated).......	629	575	640	582	747	692
Other rural:						
Nonfarm..........................	717	625	719	746	861	713
Farm.............................	766	687	722	725	1,067	723

Source: Otis Dudley Duncan and Albert J. Reiss, Jr., *Social Characteristics of Urban and Rural Communities, 1950*, Census Monograph Series, John Wiley and Sons, Inc., New York, 1956, table 6.

TABLE 33.—NUMBER OF CHILDREN UNDER 5 YEARS OLD PER 1,000 WOMEN 20 TO 44 YEARS OLD, FOR CENTRAL CITIES AND SUBURBS OF URBANIZED AREAS, BY SIZE OF AREA: 1950

Size of urbanized area	Total area	Central cities	Suburbs and urban fringe
All urbanized areas.................	476	452	534
3,000,000 or more.......................	433	404	495
1,000,000 to 3,000,000..................	478	444	531
250,000 to 1,000,000....................	503	480	569
Under 250,000...........................	510	490	586

Source: Otis Dudley Duncan and Albert J. Reiss, Jr., *Social Characteristics of Urban and Rural Communities, 1950*, Census Monograph Series, John Wiley and Sons, Inc., New York, 1956, table 50.

TABLE **34.**—NUMBER OF CHILDREN UNDER 5 YEARS OLD PER 1,000 WOMEN 20 TO 44 YEARS OLD, BY FARM RESIDENCE AND TYPE OF COUNTY, BY DIVISIONS: 1950

Division and residence	All counties	Type of county			
		Metropolitan, by size of largest place in standard metropolitan area		Nonmetropolitan, by size of largest place in county	
		250,000 or more	Under 250,000	25,000 or more	Under 25,000
RURAL NONFARM					
United States.................	681	618	670	671	704
New England..........................	621	594	574	658	670
Middle Atlantic......................	592	559	602	575	626
East North Central..................	671	642	682	673	679
West North Central..................	669	691	694	721	661
South Atlantic......................	710	648	687	661	731
East South Central..................	743	666	708	737	757
West South Central..................	720	677	729	736	722
Mountain............................	771	747	788	695	782
Pacific.............................	676	664	686	690	675
RURAL FARM					
United States.................	762	613	700	741	778
New England..........................	670	553	571	684	739
Middle Atlantic......................	671	583	681	688	703
East North Central..................	699	609	684	705	709
West North Central..................	742	671	697	780	744
South Atlantic......................	815	673	716	764	830
East South Central..................	824	701	768	799	830
West South Central..................	777	609	768	779	781
Mountain............................	811	621	789	775	820
Pacific.............................	651	596	645	690	658

Source: Otis Dudley Duncan and Albert J. Reiss, Jr., *Social Characteristics of Urban and Rural Communities, 1950,* Census Monograph Series, John Wiley and Sons, Inc., New York, 1956, table B-5.

The data in table 33 indicate the relative importance of current fertility in the central cities of the urbanized areas and that of the "suburbs and urban fringe."[22] It illustrates very well the markedly higher fertility of women who live in the areas outside the central cities.

In table 34, Duncan and Reiss demonstrate anew the fact that the influence of large cities probably does not stop at their boundaries but may also extend to the rural population in the surrounding area. That is, the rural people in the vicinity of large cities tend to be less fertile than those farther removed. There undoubtedly are many "causes" of this situation.

Individual large cities. Cities, like people, have individual characteristics of their own, which are known only in part by their most serious students and which often escape the casual observer. Attempts to account for the considerable differences in fertility levels are at best only partly successful.[23]

---

[22] The proportion of women residing in the "suburbs" is sufficiently high so that their fertility should be considered in any discussion of whether large cities are self-sustaining. The proportion of women 20 to 44 years old residing in the central city can be figured by the simple algebraic formula

$$x = \frac{\text{Total area ratio} - \text{"suburbs" ratio}}{\text{"Central cities" ratio} - \text{"suburbs" ratio}}$$

For all areas, $x = \frac{476-534}{452-534} = .71$

In other words, 71 percent of the women resided in the "central cities" and 29 percent in the "suburbs."

[23] Warren S. Thompson, *Ratios of Children to Women: 1920, op. cit.,* pp. 40–71.

Data on children ever born for women in individual large cities were tabulated in the 1940 Census but not in the 1950 Census. In 1940, the rate of children ever born per 1,000 white women 45 to 49 years old ranged from 1,441 in San Francisco to 2,669 in Pittsburgh (table 35). Of the 37 cities in 1940 with 250,000 inhabitants or more, 17 had rates below replacement needs under an assumption of zero mortality below age 28, and 14 others had rates that were inadequate on the basis of appropriate life tables.[24] Only Pittsburgh, Buffalo, Newark, Jersey City, Cleveland, and San Antonio had rates above replacement needs.

As indicated in table 35, there was no tendency for fertility to vary in a consistent way with the size-ranking of individual large cities. New York, Chicago, and Philadelphia, the three largest cities, had an intermediate ranking among the cities with respect to fertility, and Los Angeles, then the fifth largest city, ranked low in fertility. A geographical pattern of variation may be discerned, however. In general, the rates were highest in the Northeast and lowest in the West. This geographical pattern arose in part from past heavy immigration, which concentrated in the Northeast and in the North Central cities of Chicago, Detroit, and Cleveland.

As may be seen from table 36, large proportions of the white women in the northeastern large cities were foreign born. Past immigration was heavy from countries of eastern and southern Europe, where educational standards formerly were rather low and many of the women were of rural origin and of Roman Catholic faith. The church membership proportions for 1936 shown in table 36 for large cities partly reflect the past immigration and are not representative of recent conditions in the entire United States.[25]

Declines in fertility were rapid in most cities despite any religious objection to some forms of family limitation. Cities with large percentages of Roman Catholics usually had as much decline in fertility as other cities, in terms of comparisons of the 1940 Census rate of children ever born for women 45 to 49 years old who had ever married with that for similar women 65 to 74 years old. For example, according to the 1936 Census of Religious Bodies, more than two-thirds of the church members in San Francisco were Roman Catholics. Yet this city had only 1,669 children ever born per 1,000 white women ever married and 45 to 49 years old in 1940 as compared with 2,540 for similar women 65 to 74 years old. New Orleans, 73 percent Catholic, also had a very large decline in fertility. The factors shown in table 36—religion, nativity, labor force participation of women, and education of women—may not explain all of the inter-city variations in fertility, but they certainly illustrate the complex nature of the causes.

---

[24] A rate of 2,060 would yield 1,000 daughters (and 1,060 sons) to replace 1,000 women at age 28 in the next generation if all children survived. The quota is 2,480 on the basis of United States life tables for 1919–21.

[25] According to the 1954 Yearbook of American Churches, published by the National Council of Churches of Christ in the U.S.A., among the more than 97 million persons with religious affiliation, 57 million were Protestant, 32 million were Roman Catholic, and 5½ million were Jewish.

Table **35.**—Percent Distribution of White Women 45 to 49 Years Old by Number of Children Ever Born, and Number of Children Ever Born per 1,000 Women 45 to 49 Years Old and 65 to 74 Years Old, for Cities of 250,000 or More: 1940

[Cities ranked by size of total population in 1940]

Rank	City	Number of women, including single women	Percent of women ever married with specified number of children ever born						Children ever born		
			None	1	2	3	4	5 or more	Per 1,000 women	Per 1,000 women ever married	
										45 to 49 years old	65 to 74 years old
	NORTHEAST										
1	New York, N. Y..........	243,720	16.3	16.0	24.8	18.9	10.5	13.6	2,221	2,535	3,505
3	Philadelphia, Pa........	61,740	15.8	18.1	21.0	16.1	10.7	18.2	2,324	2,729	3,329
9	Boston, Mass............	27,280	18.7	13.1	19.3	14.5	12.7	21.7	2,341	2,914	3,064
10	Pittsburgh, Pa..........	20,940	14.7	15.0	19.7	14.8	11.1	24.7	2,669	3,071	3,457
14	Buffalo, N. Y...........	20,620	16.3	16.3	19.1	16.8	9.6	21.8	2,499	2,935	3,353
18	Newark, N. J............	12,520	13.6	15.2	21.7	17.9	12.5	19.0	2,614	2,936	3,807
23	Rochester, N. Y.........	12,200	17.6	16.2	23.4	16.4	9.0	17.2	2,131	2,620	2,838
30	Jersey City, N. J.......	9,740	15.5	18.4	16.5	14.4	15.2	20.0	2,532	2,951	3,690
37	Providence, R. I........	8,320	18.8	16.4	20.1	11.7	10.1	22.7	2,375	2,901	3,375
	NORTH CENTRAL										
2	Chicago, Ill............	114,820	18.2	17.4	23.1	16.4	9.7	15.2	2,215	2,473	3,220
4	Detroit, Mich...........	49,140	18.1	17.5	21.0	14.9	10.0	18.5	2,458	2,642	3,491
6	Cleveland, Ohio.........	29,300	14.3	17.5	20.1	17.7	11.9	18.4	2,570	2,800	3,576
8	St. Louis, Mo...........	27,600	22.0	21.7	22.1	15.8	7.1	11.4	1,822	2,148	3,056
13	Milwaukee, Wis..........	20,080	15.6	19.9	22.7	16.1	11.0	14.7	2,284	2,594	3,713
16	Minneapolis, Minn.......	18,260	18.1	22.1	22.3	16.6	9.5	11.3	1,989	2,281	3,306
17	Cincinnati, Ohio........	14,520	23.1	23.5	21.6	10.7	8.3	13.0	1,799	2,221	3,111
19	Kansas City, Mo.........	13,240	24.4	23.8	22.7	13.8	5.8	9.3	1,687	1,947	2,702
20	Indianapolis, Ind.......	11,920	25.6	20.6	20.6	16.0	6.9	10.5	1,845	2,050	2,740
26	Columbus, Ohio..........	10,000	24.9	21.4	20.3	11.2	7.7	14.5	1,955	2,293	2,965
33	St. Paul, Minn..........	10,500	17.7	18.5	23.3	14.2	10.1	16.2	2,062	2,511	3,368
34	Toledo, Ohio............	9,960	24.6	18.4	21.7	13.3	8.2	13.8	1,969	2,221	2,947
	SOUTH										
7	Baltimore, Md...........	23,200	16.6	20.4	20.5	16.6	10.6	15.3	2,211	2,576	3,177
11	Washington, D. C........	18,860	26.8	22.4	24.3	11.9	7.1	7.4	1,473	1,849	2,590
15	New Orleans, La.........	11,660	18.1	18.1	19.2	15.7	9.4	19.6	2,247	2,653	3,961
21	Houston, Texas..........	9,080	21.3	19.7	23.3	12.3	9.0	14.3	2,202	2,332	3,721
25	Louisville, Ky..........	8,780	20.3	24.6	19.7	17.1	6.6	11.7	1,909	2,214	2,778
28	Atlanta, Ga.............	7,320	18.6	20.6	16.6	17.6	10.5	16.2	2,196	2,493	3,555
31	Dallas, Texas...........	7,880	24.0	20.5	21.7	13.6	9.5	10.8	1,961	2,130	3,316
32	Memphis, Tenn...........	5,580	19.8	22.9	22.9	13.2	7.9	13.1	2,001	2,256	3,458
35	Birmingham, Ala.........	5,160	15.9	(1)	(1)	(1)	(1)	(1)	2,228	2,420	(1)
36	San Antonio, Texas......	7,400	15.2	21.8	20.9	13.6	9.2	19.3	2,504	2,710	3,690
	WEST										
5	Los Angeles, Calif......	52,740	27.5	24.7	21.3	11.9	6.5	8.0	1,613	1,820	2,714
12	San Francisco, Calif....	23,060	28.1	25.9	22.8	12.6	4.2	6.3	1,441	1,669	2,540
22	Seattle, Wash...........	13,180	21.1	26.0	22.4	16.0	5.8	8.6	1,738	1,928	2,705
24	Denver, Colo............	10,800	21.9	23.1	22.1	15.8	8.0	9.2	1,863	2,046	2,717
27	Portland, Oreg..........	12,640	24.0	25.4	25.6	11.8	7.2	6.1	1,608	1,802	2,989
29	Oakland, Calif..........	10,880	23.5	22.0	23.3	14.5	7.1	9.3	1,806	1,990	2,672

[1] Data not available.

Source: *1940 Census of Population, Differential Fertility, 1940 and 1910*, Fertility for States and Large Cities, table 41, and unpublished data.

Fertility ratios for individual large cities in 1950 and 1940 are shown in table 37. These, of course, reflect the effective fertility of only 5 years' time, ending on the census date, and are subject to varying degrees of incompleteness in the count of young children. Most of the differential undercount probably would be taken care of, if the reader would allow for

TABLE **36.**—SELECTED CHARACTERISTICS OF WHITE WOMEN 45 TO 49 YEARS OLD, 1940, AND OF THE TOTAL MEMBERSHIP OF CHURCHES, 1936, FOR CITIES OF 250,000 OF MORE

[Cities ranked by size of total population in 1940]

Rank	City	White women 45 to 49 years old			Percent distribution of church membership by type		
		Percent foreign born	Percent in labor force	Median years of school completed	Protestant	Roman Catholic	Jewish
	NORTHEAST						
1	New York, N. Y...............	53.2	25.2	8.4	15.6	36.5	47.9
3	Philadelphia, Pa.............	33.2	26.6	8.4	31.8	43.9	24.3
9	Boston, Mass.................	46.6	28.6	8.7	18.1	59.2	22.7
10	Pittsburgh, Pa...............	26.8	21.2	8.4	35.6	52.9	11.5
14	Buffalo, N. Y................	28.4	22.7	8.5	28.5	65.7	5.8
18	Newark, N. J.................	48.4	23.2	8.2	17.4	60.0	22.6
23	Rochester, N. Y..............	32.0	[1]31.2	[1]8.5	34.1	53.9	12.0
30	Jersey City, N. J............	38.8	23.3	8.3	14.9	77.0	8.1
37	Providence, R. I.............	40.5	[1]30.9	[1]8.4	21.0	67.0	12.0
	NORTH CENTRAL						
2	Chicago, Ill.................	38.5	26.2	8.5	29.9	49.9	20.2
4	Detroit, Mich................	40.8	20.8	8.5	35.1	51.2	13.7
6	Cleveland, Ohio..............	45.6	23.1	8.1	28.2	54.4	17.4
8	St. Louis, Mo................	12.2	28.2	8.4	38.1	49.6	12.3
13	Milwaukee, Wis...............	21.6	[1]25.5	[1]8.4	35.9	54.8	9.3
16	Minneapolis, Minn............	16.8	[1]29.9	[1]8.9	59.6	30.4	10.0
17	Cincinnati, Ohio.............	8.3	27.5	8.6	43.8	45.4	10.8
19	Kansas City, Mo..............	7.5	32.6	10.1	59.1	25.9	15.0
20	Indianapolis, Ind...........	4.6	27.7	9.4	70.8	23.0	6.2
26	Columbus, Ohio...............	6.0	27.1	9.0	62.1	31.3	6.6
33	St. Paul, Minn...............	14.0	[1]26.5	[1]8.8	39.2	52.3	8.5
34	Toledo, Ohio.................	14.7	25.8	8.7	44.8	48.1	7.1
	SOUTH						
7	Baltimore, Md................	15.8	25.3	8.2	39.6	43.6	16.8
11	Washington, D. C.............	11.2	43.0	11.8	63.5	29.7	6.8
15	New Orleans, La..............	5.7	26.0	8.3	24.1	72.6	3.3
21	Houston, Texas...............	8.4	26.0	10.1	72.1	19.1	8.8
25	Louisville, Ky...............	3.0	27.4	8.8	52.0	40.6	7.4
28	Atlanta, Ga..................	3.3	33.6	9.9	86.6	5.5	7.9
31	Dallas, Texas................	4.5	34.6	10.8	79.2	12.1	8.7
32	Memphis, Tenn................	4.1	28.5	8.4	79.1	11.2	9.7
35	Birmingham, Ala..............	4.5	24.0	10.3	87.5	7.7	4.8
36	San Antonio, Texas..........	22.8	28.0	8.5	40.0	54.9	5.1
	WEST						
5	Los Angeles, Calif..........	22.7	34.3	10.3	41.2	39.6	19.2
12	San Francisco, Calif........	28.7	35.0	9.0	17.3	67.1	15.6
22	Seattle, Wash................	21.3	31.5	10.1	58.6	27.4	14.0
24	Denver, Colo.................	9.4	[1]30.8	[1]10.1	49.9	34.7	15.4
27	Portland, Oreg...............	15.2	[1]32.0	[1]10.0	57.8	31.3	10.9
29	Oakland, Calif...............	19.9	28.5	9.4	32.3	60.6	7.1

[1] For women of all races; data not available by color.

Source: Derived from *1940 Census of Population*, Vol. II, *Characteristics of the Population*, Parts 1-7, State table 35, and Vol. IV, *Characteristics by Age*, Parts 2-4, tables 19 and 24; U. S. Bureau of the Census, *Religious Bodies: 1936*, Vol. I, table 31.

a 5 percent greater undercount among nonwhites than among whites, and for a 2 percent greater undercount in 1940 as compared with 1950.

All large cities had substantial increases in fertility ratios between 1940 and 1950. The increases tended to be least in the northeastern cities and greatest in the western cities. Replacement quotas computed from United States life tables for 1950, with standardization for age and reduced to match census undercounts of white and nonwhite children, are 305 for whites and 290 for nonwhites. In 1950, the fertility ratios for whites were above the replacement quota of 305 in all large cities except Washington, D.C., and San Francisco, and those for nonwhites were above 290 in all except New York. In 1940, most cities had ratios that were far below replacement needs.

TABLE 37.—NUMBER OF CHILDREN UNDER 5 YEARS OLD PER 1,000 WOMEN 15 TO 49 YEARS OLD, STANDARDIZED FOR AGE, BY COLOR, FOR CITIES OF 250,000 OR MORE: 1950 AND 1940

[Data are indirectly standardized to the age distribution of the white population of the United States in 1950. Cities ranked by size in 1950]

Rank	City	1950			1940, total	Percent increase, 1940 to 1950
		Total	White	Nonwhite		
	NORTHEAST					
1	New York, N. Y.	304	308	276	190	60.0
3	Philadelphia, Pa.	323	320	328	220	46.8
10	Boston, Mass.	338	337	349	232	45.7
12	Pittsburgh, Pa.	330	325	363	225	46.7
15	Buffalo, N. Y.	335	335	339	233	43.8
21	Newark, N. J.	310	308	317	203	52.7
32	Rochester, N. Y.	343	343	358	198	73.2
37	Jersey City, N. J.	329	326	364	205	60.5
	NORTH CENTRAL					
2	Chicago, Ill.	325	326	320	207	57.0
5	Detroit, Mich.	349	352	337	245	42.4
7	Cleveland, Ohio.	348	351	337	213	63.3
8	St. Louis, Mo.	328	323	347	198	65.7
13	Milwaukee, Wis.	355	354	385	231	53.7
17	Minneapolis, Minn.	338	338	383	208	62.5
18	Cincinnati, Ohio.	357	365	321	217	64.5
20	Kansas City, Mo.	316	319	296	189	67.2
23	Indianapolis, Ind.	362	364	348	231	56.7
28	Columbus, Ohio.	346	345	353	221	56.6
35	St. Paul, Minn.	402	401	445	238	68.9
36	Toledo, Ohio.	373	372	378	237	57.4
39	Akron, Ohio.	400	397	432	232	72.4
40	Omaha, Nebr.	377	374	415	239	57.7
	SOUTH					
6	Baltimore, Md.	346	335	379	226	53.1
9	Washington, D. C.	278	258	312	180	54.4
14	Houston, Texas.	352	358	329	201	75.1
16	New Orleans, La.	373	345	425	216	72.7
22	Dallas, Texas.	336	340	311	188	78.7
25	San Antonio, Texas.	468	479	336	286	63.6
26	Memphis, Tenn.	364	340	404	200	82.0
30	Louisville, Ky.	378	383	350	232	62.9
33	Atlanta, Ga.	318	307	332	195	63.1
34	Birmingham, Ala.	374	334	432	216	73.1
38	Fort Worth, Texas.	356	358	344	209	70.3
	WEST					
4	Los Angeles, Calif.	322	324	305	194	66.0
11	San Francisco, Calif.	302	293	365	169	78.7
19	Seattle, Wash.	350	346	403	191	83.2
24	Denver, Colo.	367	368	351	230	59.6
27	Oakland, Calif.	337	335	346	207	62.8
29	Portland, Oreg.	362	359	421	186	94.6
31	San Diego, Calif.	390	388	431	243	60.5
41	Long Beach, Calif.	352	350	416	209	68.4

Source: Derived from *1950 Census of Population*, Vol. II, *Characteristics of the Population*, Parts 2–48, table 33 for each State; *1940 Census of Population*, Vol. II, *Characteristics of the Population*, Parts 1–7, table 35 for each city.

Variations within cities. Cities have business districts and residential areas, apartment-house areas and single-family areas, slum areas and well-to-do areas. Fertility patterns within cities vary considerably by these types of areas, in a manner that may be generalized for many cities.

In large cities, the central business area typically contains few residents, some of whom live in hotels and in janitors' quarters. The birth rate per woman of reproductive age tends to be low in the business area.

Adjacent to the central business area, one often finds densely populated "slum" areas, containing mostly run-down older houses or apartments inhabited by people of low income, who may "double up," several families to a house if the local laws permit this. The birth rate per woman of childbearing age tends to be relatively high in the slum areas. The extent of the slum or blighted district varies from city to city in accordance with measures taken to arrest the blight, the enforcement of strict housing codes, redevelopment plans, and the speed of growth of the encroaching business district. Slums in American urban areas normally contain only a minor fraction of the total population of the city.

Beyond the slums, away from the center of the city, one usually finds residential areas inhabited mainly by people of moderate income, and comprising the bulk of the inhabitants of the city. These people, many of whom may live in apartments, frequently have a low birth rate per woman of reproductive age.

Beyond the older middle-class area, one often finds areas containing newer houses and more apartment buildings. These newer areas often contain relatively young women than do the older middle-class areas. They may have a higher birth rate than the older middle-class areas. Perhaps the highest birth rates of all are found in some of the suburbs, especially in new areas containing many young married women.

The inter-area variations in birth rates per 1,000 women of reproductive age are illustrated by the data presented for the city of Chicago in figures 18 and 19. (Figure 19 helps to locate the blighted, middle class, and wealthy areas.) The birth rate tended to be highest, over 100, in the low-income areas near the center of the city, along Lake Michigan. Areas of fairly low fertility, 70 to 79 births per 1,000 women of childbearing age, occurred in areas adjacent to the low-income areas. Beyond the areas of low fertility, there were areas with birth rates of 80 to 89, and toward the outskirts were some areas of relatively high fertility and also some wealthy districts with low fertility. The inter-area variations in birth rates were inversely but not strongly correlated with variations in average family income in Chicago ($r = -.46$). Some of the exceptions to the correlation of areas by birth rates and average family income may be traced to concentrations of the foreign born and their descendants. Thus, the South Side of Chicago (at bottom of chart) contains some areas whose inhabitants are almost entirely of Polish origin and who have a high birth rate per woman of childbearing age (over 100) as well as an average family income of $4,000 to $4,499.

Another indication of why fertility varies from one part of a city to another is given by data on type of dwelling unit. The number of dwelling units in the structure is a crude index of intensity of urban congestion. Apartment buildings are very common in large cities and less common in

FIGURE **18.**—BIRTHS PER 1,000 WOMEN 15 TO 44 YEARS OLD, FOR 75 COMMUNITY AREAS IN CHICAGO, ILLINOIS: 1950

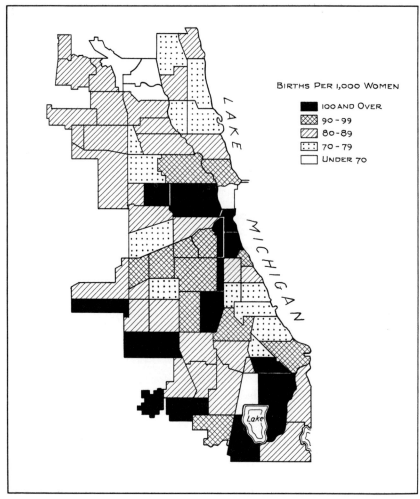

Source: Philip M. Hauser and Evelyn Kitagawa (Editors), *Local Community Fact Book for Chicago, 1950*, Chicago Community Inventory, University of Chicago, Chicago, 1953, table G.

smaller places. In 1947, about 44 percent of the wives 15 to 49 years old in urban areas lived in structures containing either two or more dwelling units or a business and one or more dwelling units (table 38). The other 56 percent of the women lived in single-dwelling unit structures. The number of own children under 5 years old living in the household per 1,000 wives 15 to 49 years old was largest among women in single-dwelling unit structures. The fertility ratio decreased as the number of dwelling units in the structure increased. Wives living in structures containing a business had the smallest ratio.

Variations within metropolitan areas. For the purpose of this section, the term "metropolitan area" is used loosely to mean an area con-

FIGURE **19.**—MEDIAN MONEY INCOME OF FAMILIES IN 1949, FOR 75 COMMUNITY AREAS IN
CHICAGO, ILLINOIS: 1950

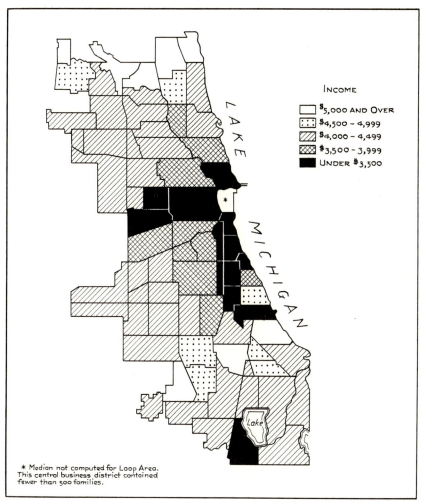

INCOME

☐ $5,000 AND OVER
▦ $4,500 – 4,999
▨ $4,000 – 4,499
▩ $3,500 – 3,999
■ UNDER $3,500

* Median not computed for Loop Area.
This central business district contained
fewer than 500 families.

Source: Same as figure 18.

taining a large city and the thickly populated, territory adjacent to the city.
Several kinds of metropolitan areas have been used in census reports.

In table 33, from the Duncan and Reiss monograph, fertility ratios are
shown for urbanized areas subdivided by "central cities" and "suburbs
and urban fringe." [26]   It may be noted that fertility ratios were considerably larger in the area beyond the central cities than in the central cities

---

[26] In general, urbanized areas as established by the Bureau of the Census for use in 1950 comprise
at least one city of 50,000 inhabitants or more plus the adjacent "urban fringe" or contiguous area
containing at least 500 dwelling units per square mile.   In some areas, places of 50,000 inhabitants
or more are adjacent to much larger cities and have such a small portion of the total population that
they are not classified as central cities but as part of the balance of the urbanized area.

and that the population outside the central cities materially increased the ratio for the total urbanized area. The fertility ratio for the "suburbs and urban fringe" part of all urbanized areas in 1950 was 18.1 percent larger than that of the central cities and the ratio for the total urbanized areas was 5.3 percent larger than that of the central cities. The excess of the fertility ratio in total urbanized areas over that in central cities was larger in the giant urban areas than in the smaller ones:

Size of urbanized area	Percent by which the fertility ratio in the total urbanized area exceeded the ratio in the central city	Percent by which the fertility ratio in the balance of the urbanized area exceeded the ratio in the central city
Total	5.3	18.1
3,000,000 or more	7.2	22.5
1,000,000 to 3,000,000	7.7	19.6
250,000 to 1,000,000	4.8	18.5
Under 250,000	4.1	19.6

The smaller urbanized areas, as a group, had a smaller proportion of their population living outside the central city than did the larger ones and hence they had a smaller percent excess of area-wide fertility ratios over the central cities ratios.

TABLE **38.**—NUMBER OF OWN CHILDREN UNDER 5 YEARS OLD PER 1,000 WOMEN 15 TO 49 YEARS OLD MARRIED AND HUSBAND PRESENT, BY TYPE OF HOUSING, FOR URBAN AREAS: CIVILIAN POPULATION, APRIL 1947

[Fertility ratios standardized to the age distribution of all women married and husband present in the United States]

Type of housing	Number of women 15 to 49 years old	Own children under 5 years per 1,000 women, standardized for age
Total	14,848,000	479
Structures without business	13,864,000	483
1 dwelling unit	8,333,000	510
2 dwelling unit	2,356,000	474
3 dwelling unit or more	3,175,000	435
Structures with business	984,000	420

Source: U. S. Bureau of the Census, *Current Population Reports*, Series P-20, No. 18, table 13.

The 1940 Census reports presented data on women by number of children ever born for the five largest metropolitan districts, subdivided by urban-rural components.[27] A summary of the data is shown in table 39.

The data in table 39 are subject to considerable sampling variability, especially those for the thinly populated "rural" parts of the metropolitan districts. In only two of the five districts do the data exhibit a consistent

[27] In general, metropolitan districts as used in 1940 comprise a city or cities of 50,000 inhabitants or more, together with all contiguous minor civil divisions or incorporated places having a population of 150 or more per square mile.

pattern in which fertility is least in the central city and greatest in the rural parts. Also, they show that the usually higher fertility of the women in the outlying parts of metropolitan districts is not simply a result of differences in marital status from movement of married women to the suburbs. The pattern persists when the comparisons are limited to women who have ever married.

TABLE **39.**—NUMBER OF CHILDREN EVER BORN PER 1,000 WHITE AND NONWHITE WOMEN 45 TO 49 YEARS OLD, FOR THE FIVE LARGEST METROPOLITAN DISTRICTS, URBAN AND RURAL: 1940

[Rate and percent not shown where there are fewer than 3,000 women]

Area and color	Number of women	Percent childless		Children ever born	
		Total	Ever married	Per 1,000 women	Per 1,000 women ever married
CHICAGO					
White..........................	151,240	25.8	17.5	2,256	2,508
Central city....................	114,820	26.7	18.2	2,215	2,473
Other urban.....................	32,100	22.6	15.0	2,346	2,574
Rural nonfarm...................	3,640	27.8	...	2,625	...
Rural farm......................	680	...	...	...	...
Nonwhite........................	11,520	38.3	34.2	1,823	1,944
Central city....................	9,880	38.6	34.8	1,703	1,809
DETROIT					
White..........................	69,700	22.4	16.7	2,497	2,679
Central city....................	49,140	23.8	18.1	2,458	2,642
Other urban.....................	16,640	17.8	11.7	2,625	2,818
Rural nonfarm...................	3,560	26.3	22.4	2,480	2,611
Rural farm......................	360	...	...	...	...
Nonwhite........................	5,400	33.3	29.8	1,998	2,104
Central city....................	4,600	34.3	30.2	1,949	2,071
LOS ANGELES					
White..........................	100,520	30.7	23.1	1,861	2,064
Central city....................	52,740	35.8	27.5	1,613	1,820
Other urban.....................	33,980	26.3	18.8	2,014	2,220
Rural nonfarm...................	12,800	23.3	18.9	2,365	2,498
Rural farm......................	1,000	...	...	...	...
Nonwhite........................	3,120	44.0	...	2,243	...
Central city....................	2,320	...	...	...	...
NEW YORK-NORTHEASTERN NEW JERSEY					
White..........................	384,180	25.9	15.8	2,252	2,558
Central city....................	243,720	26.6	16.3	2,221	2,535
Other urban.....................	119,060	24.1	14.7	2,320	2,608
Rural nonfarm...................	20,520	26.8	16.8	2,194	2,494
Rural farm......................	880	...	...	...	...
Nonwhite........................	21,700	39.6	31.9	1,800	2,028
Central city....................	15,600	39.3	32.2	1,727	1,928
Other urban.....................	5,300	39.7	31.4	2,042	2,324
PHILADELPHIA					
White..........................	93,180	27.2	15.5	2,362	2,743
Central city....................	61,740	28.3	15.8	2,324	2,729
Other urban.....................	22,340	25.3	14.8	2,258	2,575
Rural nonfarm...................	8,300	23.7	14.5	2,884	3,232
Rural farm......................	800	...	...	...	...
Nonwhite........................	10,180	37.2	33.2	2,226	2,369
Central city....................	7,980	37.8	35.4	2,075	2,153

Source: Derived from *1940 Census of Population, Differential Fertility, 1940 and 1910,* Fertility for States and Large Cities, table 41.

In four of the five giant metropolitan districts, rates of children ever
born were much less among the Negro women than among the white women
45 to 49 years old.   This contrasts with table 37, where it was noted that
in 1950 nonwhites in a majority of the large cities had higher fertility ratios
of children under 5 years old than the whites.   The data for nonwhite
women 45 to 49 years old in 1940 in table 39 reflect the effect of a considerable in-migration in the previous 20 years, and the Negroes may have
had difficulty in becoming acclimated to an urban environment.   The data
in table 37 may reflect a superior adjustment of young Negroes in recent
years.   Certainly, the data for 1950 in table 37 do not present a picture
of potential "racial suicide" through inadequate fertility, unlike the picture which may be drawn from fertility ratios for earlier censuses and from
the 1940 Census data on children ever born for nonwhites in cities.   A
more conclusive evaluation of whether a permanent adjustment to urban
life has been made will be possible when the 1960 Census data on children
ever born become available.

Duncan and Reiss made some use of fertility ratios for "metropolitan"
and "nonmetropolitan" counties, as shown in table 34.   Their "metropolitan" counties were counties which form parts of the official "standard
metropolitan areas" (SMA's), extensively used in the 1950 Census reports.
These SMA's usually cover a much wider territory than do the urbanized
areas.   The rural-farm and rural-nonfarm parts of metropolitan areas had
lower fertility ratios than did the corresponding parts of nonmetropolitan
counties.   This again suggests that proximity to a large city adversely
affects fertility ratios in rural areas.

Urban-rural migration in relation to current fertility.   The
American people have always been a very mobile group.   In each year
since 1947, about a fifth of the population moved from one house to another.[28]   In 1952, it was found that among persons 25 to 34 years old, 29
percent had moved at least once within the previous year, about 83 percent within the previous 5 years, and 99 percent within their lifetime.[29]
Typically, about two-thirds of the annual moves involved people who moved
within the same county and one-third involved migrants between counties
or States.   Exact data are not available but perhaps a third of the moves
involved a change in urban-rural type of residence, as from rural-nonfarm
areas to urban areas.   Many of the local moves were a result of a marriage
or of the changing housing needs of families, rather than a movement in
search of economic opportunity.   In contrast, much of the inter-area movement is related to economic opportunities.

The urban-rural differences in fertility may be explained in small part
by a movement of single women from rural areas to urban areas and sometimes by a movement of married women from cities to the nearby suburbs.

---

[28] U. S. Bureau of the Census, *Current Population Reports*, Series P–20, No. 57, table 1.

[29] U. S. Bureau of the Census, *Current Population Reports*, Series P–20, No. 47, table 6.

According to data from the 1940 Census for native white women 15 to 49 years old, urban areas attracted thousands of single women from rural areas between 1935 and 1940, but they also gave up other thousands of women to rural areas (table 40). The urban-rural movement was not determined for 3,641,000 single women who moved within a county but only for the 1,187,000 single women who moved between counties. Among the single intercounty movers, 45.1 percent changed type of residence, but there was a net gain to urban areas of only 7.0 percent from an excess of in-movement to urban areas over out-movement to rural areas. These figures exclude women who were single at the time of migration but married by 1940. The figures were biased by a sizable number of migrants who

TABLE **40.**—Urban-Rural Movement Between 1935 and 1940 of Native White Women 15 to 49 Years Old, by Marital Status and Number of Own Children Under 5 Years Old in 1940

[Data reflect heavy overreporting of urban residence in 1935; see text. Fertility ratios standardized to the age distribution of all native white women of pertinent marital status in the United States]

Area and mobility status	Women 15 to 49 years old		Own children under 5	
	Single	Ever married	Per 1,000 women standardized for age	Per 1,000 women ever married standardized for age
SAME HOUSE, 1935 AND 1940				
Urban in 1940..............................	3,021,000	3,205,000	141	334
Rural nonfarm in 1940......................	877,000	1,368,000	252	457
Rural farm in 1940.........................	1,164,000	1,677,000	329	587
INTRACOUNTY MOVERS[1]				
Urban in 1940..............................	2,579,000	6,026,000	258	369
Rural nonfarm in 1940......................	574,000	1,958,000	408	501
Rural farm in 1940.........................	488,000	1,583,000	523	643
MIGRANTS BETWEEN COUNTIES				
Urban to urban.............................	481,000	1,358,000	225	314
Rural nonfarm to rural nonfarm.............	78,000	273,000	371	464
Rural farm to rural farm...................	93,000	294,000	538	659
Urban Interchange				
Rural nonfarm to urban.....................	170,000	345,000	238	344
Rural farm to urban........................	104,000	152,000	272	407
Urban to rural nonfarm.....................	147,000	553,000	314	400
Urban to rural farm........................	44,000	165,000	378	470
Net change................................	+83,000	-222,000	...	...
Rural-Nonfarm Interchange				
Urban to rural nonfarm.....................	147,000	553,000	314	400
Rural farm to rural nonfarm................	48,000	131,000	409	520
Rural nonfarm to urban.....................	170,000	345,000	238	344
Rural nonfarm to rural farm................	22,000	80,000	452	548
Net change................................	+3,000	+259,000	...	...
Rural-Farm Interchange				
Urban to rural farm........................	44,000	165,000	378	470
Rural nonfarm to rural farm................	22,000	80,000	452	548
Rural farm to urban........................	104,000	152,000	272	407
Rural farm to rural nonfarm................	48,000	131,000	409	520
Net change................................	-86,000	-38,000	...	...

[1] Urban-rural residence in 1935 not tabulated for intracounty movers.

Source: *1940 Census of Population, Differential Fertility, 1940 and 1910,* Women by Number of Children Under 5 Years Old, table 35.

failed to distinguish a suburban address from a nearby urban place as their residence in 1935.   According to table 40, urban areas had a (probably fictitious) net "loss" of 222,000 ever-married women to rural areas.   A net gain probably would result if proper correction could be made for mis-reporting of urban-rural residence in 1935.   There is no doubt, however, that in the interchange of movement between urban and rural areas, cities tend to gain many more single persons than married persons.   The migra-tion does tend to reduce the proportion married in the city population as compared with the rural population.

Among migrant native white women 15 to 49 years old, those who moved from one urban area to another urban area had the lowest ratio of own children under 5 years old to women and those who moved from one rural-farm area to another rural-farm area had the highest ratio, both among women ever married and among women of all marital classes.   The rural-farm migrants had larger ratios than the rural-farm nonmigrants, prob-ably because the farm-to-farm migrants included many very fertile wives of tenant farmers and farm laborers.

Rural women who moved to urban areas had lower fertility than the urban women who moved to rural areas.   For example, the ever-married women who moved from rural-farm areas to urban areas after 1935 had a fertility ratio of 407 per 1,000 in 1940 as compared with a ratio of 470 among the women who moved from urban areas to rural-farm areas.   In general, among ever-married women the fertility ratios of migrants tended to be intermediate between the fertility ratios of nonmovers in the host area and the origin area.   Thus, the out-migrants from urban areas to rural areas had fertility ratios (400 rural nonfarm, 470 rural farm) that were not as high as those of the nonmovers in rural areas (457 rural nonfarm, 587 rural farm), but they had much higher ratios than did the nonmovers in urban areas (334).

District of Columbia birthplace and residence.   The District of Columbia (Washington, D.C.) is the only urban place which can be identi-fied from answers to the census question on State of birth.   It was possi-ble to tabulate 1950 Census data on children ever born by whether or not the women were born in the District of Columbia.   The data are not strictly representative of all urban places.   Washington, as the seat of gov-ernment, has a large "floating" population which comes from, and often returns to, other areas.   Thus, about three-fourths of the women of child-bearing age in the District of Columbia in 1950 were born elsewhere. Washington has the Nation's least fertile large-city population, with the possible exception of San Francisco.   It appears that there was not a great deal of difference between the completed fertility of the natives of Wash-ington and that of the in-migrants (table 41).   Because of sampling vari-ability it cannot be said that either group had the higher completed fertility. There was a tendency for the average number of children ever born to be higher for young native women than for young in-migrant women.

TABLE **41.**—District of Columbia Birthplace and Residence for Women 15 to 59 Years
Old, by Number of Children Ever Born: 1950

Age and birthplace of woman	Women			Children ever born	
	Total	Single	Ever married	Per 1,000 total women	Per 1,000 women ever married
15 to 44 years.....................	216,000	66,000	150,000	928	1,338
Born in Washington, D. C..............	53,000	20,000	33,000	[1]1,113	[1]1,580
Born elsewhere........................	163,000	46,000	117,000	[1]883	[1]1,277
45 to 59 years.....................	75,000	10,000	64,000	1,669	1,936
Born in Washington, D. C..............	14,000	2,000	12,000	1,670	1,904
Born elsewhere........................	61,000	9,000	52,000	1,668	1,944

[1] Standardized for age distribution of all women of pertinent marital status in the District.

Source: *1950 Census of Population*, Vol. IV, *Special Reports*, Part 5, Chapter C, Fertility, table 33.

D. Race, nativity, and ethnic groups

Race and nativity. Age-specific rates of children ever born are shown in figure 20 by urban-rural residence, race, and nativity. It may come as a surprise to some that in the United States as a whole, in 1950, the fertility rates for the foreign-born white women who had ever married fall below those for native whites at all ages of the 20-to-44 span. This arises in part from the fact that the foreign-born whites are more heavily concentrated in urban areas (and particularly in large cities) and in part it reflects immigration quotas that are somewhat selective of women from countries of western Europe, where birth rates are now low. It may be noticed that among ever-married women 25 to 34 years old the fertility rates of the foreign-born whites fall in lowest position in each type of residence. The situation in 1950 represents a marked change from the one-time high fertility of the foreign born which is discussed more fully in the next section.

The relative positions of the Negro and other nonwhite women are also of interest. In the country as a whole the fertility rates of the Negro and other nonwhite ever-married women are virtually the same at ages 20 to 34. At later ages, however, the fertility rates of the other nonwhites are higher than those of Negro women. At these ages the fertility rate of the other nonwhite women surpasses that of the Negro women in urban and rural-nonfarm areas considered separately. However, it scarcely equals the conspicuously high fertility of Negroes in the rural-farm areas.

In 1950, the age-specific fertility rates of the ever-married Negro women surpassed those of the native whites at all ages in the country as a whole and within the rural-nonfarm and rural-farm areas. Within the urban areas, the fertility rate of the Negroes surpassed that of the native whites at ages under 35; at later ages there was little difference between Negro and native white ever-married women with respect to fertility.

Immigration, nativity, and parentage. The kinds and amount of immigration may have influenced the shaping of the Nation's fertility patterns, at least indirectly. Sixty years ago, General Walker noted that the birth rates of natives were relatively low in areas where there were many immigrants.[30] He concluded that immigration was not a net gain to the population; it was rather a substitution of the immigrant and his children for the children of natives. He argued that in order to reduce expenses and compete with the foreigners in a cheap labor market, the natives had smaller families than they otherwise would have had.

FIGURE **20.**—NUMBER OF CHILDREN EVER BORN PER 1,000 EVER-MARRIED WOMEN 15 TO 44 YEARS OLD, BY RACE AND AGE OF WOMAN, URBAN AND RURAL: 1950

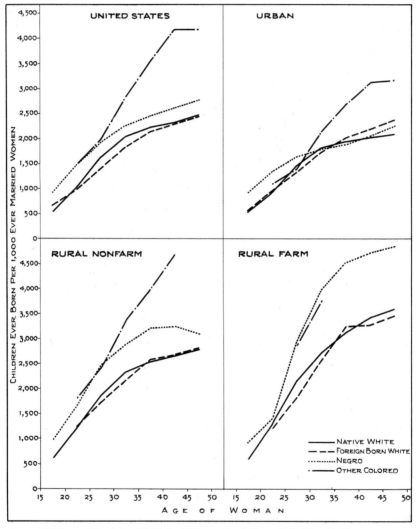

Source: *1950 Census of Population,* Vol. IV, *Special Reports,* Part 5, Chapter C, Fertility, table 12.

---

[30] Francis A. Walker, "Restriction of Immigration," *Atlantic Monthly,* Vol. 77, 1896, pp. 822–829.

Because there is no way of measuring the size of families which would have occurred in the absence of immigration, the Walker theory cannot be definitely proved or disproved. However, the problem has been investigated indirectly by many writers. In large part, they have concluded that immigration probably was not a main cause of decline in birth rates and that it produced more population gain than loss. This monograph shows that some areas with few foreign-born people also had low fertility, indicating that influences other than migration were at work. Thus, rural-farm areas in New England in 1910 contained the Nation's least fertile old white women in terms of children ever born but they contained relatively few foreign-born people. (See the first section of this chapter.) It was noted previously that national ratios of young children to women declined sharply before 1850, before there was large-scale immigration. Although the immigrants settled largely in urban areas, where fertility normally is low, they had such high fertility that they caused a leveling-off or increase in ratios of young children to white women in the Middle Atlantic States between 1880 and 1920, and thus caused a net gain in current fertility, whether or not the natives had depressed fertility as a consequence of this heavy immigration.

Opinions differ as to whether the immigrants were an elite group, superior in some respects to those in the homeland, or were mainly people who were unsuccessful at home. Both types migrated, in varying proportions at different times. Probably most people who migrated in search of economic opportunity were poor. As will be noted later, they were much more fertile than American-born women in the nineteenth century.

Annual immigration occurred in important amounts from about the middle of the nineteenth century. It rose from about 10,000 in 1825 to 114,000 in 1850. At later dates there were large "waves" of immigrants from various countries. Peak numbers of 428,000 immigrants arrived in 1854, 460,000 in 1873, 789,000 in 1882, and an average of about a million a year arrived between 1905 and the outbreak of World War I in 1914. Legislation in 1921 and 1924 drastically curtailed immigration and the new quota system coincidentally favored countries where the birth rate was low.

In 1910, about one-fourth of the Nation's white women 15 to 74 years old were foreign born. In addition, one-fifth were natives of foreign or mixed parentage. By 1940, the foreign-born women comprised only one-seventh of the white women 15 to 74 years old and a smaller proportion of the women of childbearing age. By 1950, less than 5 percent of the white women 15 to 44 years old were foreign born.

Table 42 shows how the foreign-born and native women compared with respect to the average number of children ever born, in 1940 and 1910. Standardization for urban-rural residence would further emphasize the higher fertility of the foreign-born women as compared with that of the native women in 1940 and 1910.

The data in table 42 indicate that the immigrants less severely limited their childbearing than the native Americans before 1910. This was true despite the fact that many of the foreign-born women had lived in the United States for some years before the census date or long enough to become partly assimilated or to have adopted American ways of living. The high rates of children ever born among the foreign-born women in 1910 indicate that in that era the old-country values and ways of living were not easily put aside. They are also in accord with what is known about the lack of a trend toward fewer children per woman in most parts of Europe until about 1875. Comparisons of census data indicate that the foreign-born women in 1940 had a much smaller average number of children ever born than the foreign-born women in 1910.

TABLE **42.**—NATIVITY AND PARENTAGE OF EVER-MARRIED WHITE WOMEN BY NUMBER OF CHILDREN EVER BORN: 1940 AND 1910

Nativity and age of woman	1940		1910	
	Number of women ever married	Children ever born per 1,000 women ever married	Number of women ever married	Children ever born per 1,000 women ever married
NATIVE				
Native Parentage				
Total, 15 to 74 years.............	21,230,000	2,409	10,436,000	3,396
15 to 19 years........................	541,000	601	337,000	717
20 to 24 years........................	2,176,000	1,028	1,237,000	1,388
25 to 29 years........................	2,872,000	1,515	1,514,000	2,138
30 to 34 years........................	2,811,000	2,016	1,397,000	2,905
35 to 39 years........................	2,563,000	2,475	1,287,000	3,669
40 to 44 years........................	2,276,000	2,795	1,051,000	4,166
45 to 49 years........................	2,065,000	2,965	889,000	4,406
50 to 54 years........................	1,764,000	3,065	822,000	4,591
55 to 64 years........................	2,607,000	3,275	1,188,000	4,765
65 to 74 years........................	1,554,000	3,596	715,000	4,822
Foreign or Mixed Parentage				
Total, 15 to 74 years.............	5,976,000	2,287	3,460,000	3,147
15 to 19 years........................	57,000	650	59,000	626
20 to 24 years........................	478,000	854	360,000	1,180
25 to 29 years........................	801,000	1,280	521,000	1,835
30 to 34 years........................	810,000	1,809	531,000	2,514
35 to 39 years........................	732,000	2,255	532,000	3,223
40 to 44 years........................	695,000	2,560	439,000	3,774
45 to 49 years........................	629,000	2,781	364,000	4,177
50 to 54 years........................	527,000	2,886	296,000	4,561
55 to 64 years........................	757,000	3,045	267,000	4,984
65 to 74 years........................	489,000	3,387	92,000	5,172
FOREIGN BORN				
Total, 15 to 74 years.............	4,377,000	3,297	4,282,000	4,275
15 to 19 years........................	6,000	728	46,000	660
20 to 24 years........................	44,000	969	331,000	1,355
25 to 29 years........................	163,000	1,452	518,000	2,245
30 to 34 years........................	307,000	1,912	536,000	3,171
35 to 39 years........................	455,000	2,396	543,000	4,161
40 to 44 years........................	549,000	2,905	510,000	4,877
45 to 49 years........................	632,000	3,447	462,000	5,278
50 to 54 years........................	621,000	3,679	375,000	5,506
55 to 64 years........................	987,000	3,870	580,000	5,836
65 to 74 years........................	613,000	4,255	382,000	6,073

Source: Derived from *1940 Census of Population, Differential Fertility, 1940 and 1910,* Women by Number of Children Ever Born, tables III, 7, 10, 31, and 32, and Fertility for States and Large Cities, tables 3 and 4.

In 1940 and 1910 alike, the native white women of foreign or mixed parentage had fewer children on the average than did the women of native parentage. If the comparisons were limited to women in urban areas, not shown separately in table 42, it would be seen that in urban areas the native white women of foreign or mixed parentage had slightly more children on the average than the women of native parentage.

At least some of the foreign-born women in 1910 were not much affected in respect to children ever born by the length of their stay in the United States. Whether they migrated long ago or recently, their fertility was much the same, indicating that in their case the old-country customs may have been more important than the changed environment (table 43).

TABLE **43.**—YEARS IN THE UNITED STATES BY NUMBER OF CHILDREN EVER BORN, FOR EVER-MARRIED FOREIGN-BORN WHITE WOMEN 45 TO 54 YEARS OLD: 1910

Years in the United States	Women ever married	Children ever born per 1,000 women ever married	Years in the United States	Women ever married	Children ever born per 1,000 women ever married
Total..................	837,000	5,380	20 to 24..................	122,000	5,315
			25 to 29..................	169,000	5,498
Less than 5..............	37,000	5,861	30 to 34..................	93,000	5,364
5 to 9...................	41,000	5,572	35 to 44..................	126,000	5,345
10 to 14.................	36,000	5,377	45 and over..............	40,000	5,071
15 to 19.................	66,000	5,481	Not reported.............	108,000	5,124

Source: *1940 Census of Population, Differential Fertility, 1940 and 1910*, Women by Number of Children Ever Born, table 46.

In 1940 and 1910, the women from northern and western Europe had fewer children on the average than women from eastern and southern Europe (table 44). In 1910, the women from most foreign countries had more children than did the native population. The women from Canada, with English as their mother tongue, were an exception. They had an average of 4,366 children ever born per 1,000 women ever married as compared with 4,633 among natives in the entire United States. The 1910 rate for immigrant women from England and Wales (5,107) can be roughly compared with the rate (5,014) in the 1911 Census of England and Wales for all marriages of completed fertility, wife 45 years old and over.[31] Because the data in the English Census were limited to women living with their husbands, the rate of 5,014 may be a little too large for strict comparability with the American data, although a partly compensating shortage arose from the English count of children in the present marriage only. It is estimated that in 1910 the immigrant women 45 to 74 years old in the United States from England and Wales were about 4 percent more fertile than the women 45 years and over who remained in England and Wales, which is a negligible difference. Standardization for urban-

---

[31] General Register Office, *Census of England and Wales, 1911*, Vol. XIII, *Fertility of Marriage*, Part I, page 337, His Majesty's Stationery Office, London, 1917.

rural residence might increase the difference. The reader is reminded that American women were one of the most fertile groups in the world in the early part of the nineteenth century and that birth rates declined rapidly after 1810. Data from the 1910 Census indicate that ever-married native white women 65 to 74 years old had an average of 4.9 children ever born per woman as compared with 5.6 for women of this age and marital status who were born in England and Wales (and with 5.1 for wives 70 to 74 years old living with their husbands in the 1911 Census of England and Wales). These women were of childbearing age in the period from 1851 to 1890. Although the data indicate that for some years before 1910 the American women were less fertile than women from England and Wales, the latter subsequently became a group of lesser fertility. By 1940, the women 45 to 74 years old in the United States who were born in England and Wales had an average of 2,689 children per 1,000 women ever married as compared with 3,161 for native white women in the entire United States and with 2,308 for native white women in cities of 250,000 or more.

TABLE 44.—COUNTRY OF BIRTH OF FOREIGN-BORN WHITE WOMEN BY NUMBER OF CHILDREN EVER BORN, FOR EVER-MARRIED WOMEN 45 TO 74 YEARS OLD: 1940 AND 1910

Country of birth and census year	Women ever married	Children ever born per 1,000 women ever married	Country of birth and census year	Women ever married	Children ever born per 1,000 women ever married
Total:			Czechoslovakia, 1940.......	97,000	4,476
1940......................	2,853,000	3,815	Austria, 1940..............	142,000	4,041
1910......................	1,799,000	5,669	Hungary, 1940.............	87,000	3,682
England and Wales:			Austria-Hungary, 1910[1].....	85,000	6,044
1940......................	170,000	2,689	Russia (U.S.S.R.):		
1910......................	171,000	5,107	1940....................	280,000	3,777
Scotland:			1910[1]....................	74,000	7,156
1940......................	62,000	2,756	Italy:		
1910......................	41,000	5,452	1940....................	370,000	4,984
Irish Free State, 1940.....	165,000	3,332	1910....................	74,000	5,942
Ireland, 1910..............	283,000	5,428	Canada--French:		
Norway, Sweden, Denmark,			1940....................	65,000	4,352
and Iceland:			1910....................	54,000	7,382
1940......................	222,000	3,181	Canada--Other:		
1910......................	195,000	5,306	1940....................	161,000	2,627
Germany:			1910....................	141,000	4,366
1940......................	305,000	3,342	Mexico:		
1910[1]....................	515,000	5,785	1940....................	57,000	5,664
Poland:			1910....................	16,000	6,507
1940......................	287,000	4,689	All other and not reported:		
1910[2]....................	57,000	7,422	1940....................	381,000	3,627
			1910....................	92,000	5,610

[1] Exclusive of those who reported Polish mother tongue.

[2] Poland was not a political entity in 1910. The category "Poland" comprises persons who nonetheless reported Poland as their birthplace and those who reported that they were born in Germany, Austria-Hungary, and Russia, but who reported Polish mother tongue.

Source: Derived from *1940 Census of Population, Differential Fertility, 1940 and 1910*, Women by Number of Children Ever Born, tables 8, 11, 40, and 43.

Indians, persons of Spanish surname, and other small ethnic groups. In using census data on Indians, one should keep in mind that the race classification is based on popular concepts, including culture, rather than solely on physical anthropology. The number of persons with an appreciable percentage of Indian blood is far greater than the number classified as Indian. Thus, the Mexicans and Spanish-Americans of the Southwest have been classified as white, unless they were obviously Indian, in all censuses of the United States except in 1930, when persons born in Mexico or who were of Mexican parentage were classified as "Mexican" in an effort to learn more about these people, many of whom speak Spanish exclusively. The classification of persons by race is based not on a direct question but on observation by the enumerator of persons present at the interview, a question being asked only when there is doubt. A few enumerators probably regarded Indians in areas far from a reservation as just dark-complexioned white persons. The bulk of the Indians classified as such in the census live on reservations or in areas with high concentrations of Indians. In 1950, 72 percent of the enumerated Indians were in major Indian Agency areas, or areas with at least 2,500 Indians.

According to the census, there were 343,310 Indians in 1950, 333,936 in 1940, and 332,397 in 1930. This nearly constant number may reflect some misclassification of race or out-migration of nomads to Mexico and Canada rather than any near balance of births and deaths. According to vital statistics, there were 61,194 more registered births than deaths of Indians in the decade from 1940 to 1949. Allowance for incomplete registration might increase this figure, if births were less completely registered than deaths. (Birth registration tests indicated that 85.1 percent of Indian births were reported in 1950 and 68.3 percent in 1940. Tribal midwives and medicine men help to report these events.) Published birth rates of 33.1 per 1,000 Indian population in 1950 and of 26.5 in 1940, obtained by dividing corrected births by the census counts of Indians, may be too high if there was a stronger tendency to report "Indian" on birth records (which were sometimes checked by the parents) than on census records.[32]

Ratios of young children to women computed from census data on the Indian population classified by age and sex are not affected by the problem of comparability of vital statistics and census data. These ratios also indicate that the Indians have a quite high level of effective fertility by modern standards (table 45). Ratios of children under 5 years old to Indian women 15 to 49 years old, indirectly standardized for age, were among the highest in the United States in 1950. They were of about the same magnitude as for the fertile women of Spanish surname in five southwestern States and for Negroes in rural-farm areas of the United States.

The data on children under 5 years old indicate that Indians, nationally, had a level of "effective fertility" in 1945 to 1950 that was at least 68 percent higher than that of the total population of the United States. If one allows for a possibly greater undercount of children under 5 years old relative to adults among Indians than among the general population, from a poorer reporting of age, and also if allowance is made for higher infant

---

[32] National Office of Vital Statistics, *Vital Statistics of the United States: 1950*, Vol. I, pp. 79–80.

mortality, it may be said that the Indian birth rate per woman of child-bearing age probably was over 80 percent larger than that of the general population.

TABLE **45.**—NUMBER OF CHILDREN UNDER 5 YEARS OLD PER 1,000 WOMEN 15 TO 49 YEARS OLD, STANDARDIZED FOR AGE, FOR SELECTED POPULATION GROUPS: 1950

[Data standardized by indirect method to age distribution of women of all races in the United States as a whole]

Area and group	Children per 1,000 women	Area and group	Children per 1,000 women
All races......................	416	Spanish surname..................	683
Urban.................................	369	Urban.................................	640
Rural nonfarm........................	504	Rural nonfarm........................	807
Rural farm...........................	576	Rural farm...........................	820
Indian...........................	748		
Urban.................................	531	Negro, rural farm................	769
Rural nonfarm........................	817		
Rural farm...........................	771	White, Utah rural farm...........	608

Source: Derived from *1950 Census of Population*, Vol. II, *Characteristics of the Population*, Part 1, table 38; and Part 44, table 15; Vol. IV, *Special Reports*, Part 3, Chapter B, Nonwhite Population by Race, tables 2 and 3, and Chapter C, Persons of Spanish Surname, table 3.

Census data on number of children ever born for women of "other races" in rural parts of the United States can be used for rough inferences as to the lifetime fertility of the Indians. Some background qualifications should be noted first, which are also of interest in their own right.

According to complete-count census data, Indians comprised 75 percent of the 81,812 women of "other races" 15 to 49 years old in rural areas of the United States in 1950. (The category "other races" comprises non-white persons not classified as Negro.) Another 9 percent consisted of women of mixed white, Negro, and Indian blood. These lived in locally recognized, long-existing ethnic communities or "racial islands" in eastern parts of the United States, and the groups were known by such names as "Croatan," "Tunica," "Wesort," etc. The majority were Croatans in North Carolina, who were largely of Indian blood and practiced quasi-tribal ways of life. The remaining 16 percent of women of "other races" in rural areas were Japanese, Filipinos, Chinese, and other minor races. The Indian women in rural areas of the United States in 1950 had 771 enumerated children under 5 years old per 1,000 women 15 to 49 years old. Those of mixed stock had a corresponding ratio of 803 while the Japanese and Chinese had 487 and 549, respectively. The few (1,723) Filipino women in rural areas had the remarkable ratio of 1,475—a level reminiscent of whites in Colonial times. (The 7,171 Filipino women in urban areas had a ratio of 643.) The Indian ratios were affected by a high infant mortality. This mortality amounts to more than 10 percent in the first year of life according to inferences from vital statistics for "other races" in 1950.

Data on children ever born are available for a sample of the women of "other races" in rural areas of the United States in 1950 and for another sample of such women in rural areas of the South in 1910. The southern group in 1910 was almost completely Indian in composition, but comprised only about a fourth of the Nation's Indian women. The Indians in the rural areas of the South in 1910 were less isolated geographically from the white man's civilization and had more of a farming economy than the more numerous Indians in the West. It is not known whether differences in ways of living caused the Indians in the South to differ from those in the West in respect to fertility.

According to data presented in table 46, the women of "other races" 45 to 59 years old in rural areas in 1950 had 4,629 children ever born per 1,000 women, and those who were 15 to 44 years old had 2,083 children per 1,000 women. The rural women of "other races" who were 25 to 29 years old in 1950, not shown separately, had 2,184 children ever born per 1,000 women, and should have been about halfway through childbearing at that age.

TABLE **46.**—WOMEN OF OTHER RACES (LARGELY INDIAN) BY NUMBER OF CHILDREN EVER BORN, FOR RURAL AREAS OF THE UNITED STATES, 1950, AND OF THE SOUTH, 1910

Subject	15 to 44 years old		45 to 59 years old, 1950	45 to 74 years old, 1910
	1950	1910[1]		
MARITAL STATUS				
Number of women.........................	76,830	17,676	17,910	4,325
Single....................................	25,620	5,443	690	223
Ever married..............................	51,210	12,233	17,220	4,102
CHILDREN EVER BORN				
Per 1,000 women...........................	2,083	2,545	4,629	5,568
Per 1,000 women ever married..............	3,125	3,744	4,814	5,935
PERCENT OF WOMEN EVER MARRIED WITH SPECIFIED NUMBER OF CHILDREN EVER BORN				
Total.................................	100.0	100.0	100.0	100.0
None......................................	13.9	11.0	15.3	7.9
1 child...................................	19.3	14.1	7.1	6.3
2 children................................	16.7	14.9	8.9	7.2
3 children................................	12.9	14.9	8.9	7.7
4 children................................	11.9	9.6	9.6	9.6
5 and 6 children..........................	13.5	18.8	17.2	18.6
7 to 9 children...........................	9.5	12.7	23.2	21.8
10 or more children.......................	2.3	4.0	9.8	21.0

[1] Rates and percentages standardized to the age distribution of women of "other races" in rural areas of the United States in 1950.

Source: Derived from *1950 Census of Population*, Vol. IV, *Special Reports*, Part 5, Chapter C, Fertility, table 12; *1940 Census of Population, Differential Fertility, 1940 and 1910*, Fertility for States and Large Cities, table 18, and Women by Number of Children Ever Born, table 74.

The data for rural areas of the United States in 1950 and for the South in 1910 suggest that Indians have had some decline in fertility. The 1950 and 1910 comparisons suggest that appreciable reductions have occurred in the proportion of Indian women having five children or more. Such a trend would be expected on the basis of education. Other census data, not shown, indicate that the Nation's Indian women 25 to 44 years old in

1950 had completed an average (median) of 8.2 years of grade school whereas those 45 years old and over had completed only 4.8 years. The Indian women in rural areas still are a relatively fertile group, however. They had about as many children ever born at most ages in 1950 as the Negroes in rural-farm areas.

Data for women of "other races" in the rural areas of the South in 1940 indicate that many Indian women marry at a young age. Thus, among 5,820 reporting women 30 to 74 years old, married once and husband present, 1,460 married before age 18, 1,680 married at age 18 and 19, 920 married at age 20 and 21, and 1,760 married at age 22 and over.[33]

---

[33] Figures derived from U. S. Bureau of the Census, *1940 Census of Population, Differential Fertility, 1940 and 1910*, Fertility for States and Large Cities, table 47, and *Differential Fertility, 1940 and 1910*, Women by Number of Children Ever Born, table 86.

C H A P T E R   5

TRENDS AND DIFFERENTIALS IN FERTILITY
BY OCCUPATION

The question of differential reproduction according to socio-economic status has long been a matter of scientific and public interest. Eugenists traditionally have been much concerned about the tendency for the so-called "upper" classes to have fewer children on the average than the so-called "lower" classes. They have emphasized the possible genetic implications of differential fertility. Although there are marked differences of opinion regarding their meaning and significance, various studies have indicated that intelligence test scores (I.Q.) of school children tend to be correlated directly with occupational status of the father and inversely with number of children in the family.[1] Some students believe that continuation of the inverse relation of fertility to socio-economic status may bring a lowering of the average intelligence of a population.[2] Recent studies in Scotland yielded "no evidence of a fall in average intelligence" in 1947 as compared with 1932, but the authors also emphasized the complexity of the problem and the need for more intensive investigations.[3]

Other students have stressed the economic, social, and public health implications of differential fertility. Various studies carried out before World War II indicated, for instance, that a disproportionate part of our annual births was coming from the so-called rural problem areas where levels of living were lowest, where schools were poorest, and where facilities for child health were least developed. Within cities, the unskilled laboring class tended to be the only occupational group that was having enough children for purposes of self-replacement. There doubtless are complex and deep-seated reasons why some groups of families have more children than others. Whatever these may be, it is well known that group differences in the prevalence and effectiveness of contraceptive practice constitute the immediate reasons for the differentials. Studies have in-

---

[1] National Resources Committee, *The Problems of a Changing Population*, Government Printing Office, Washington, 1938, pp. 146 and 147.

[2] Cyril Burt, "Intelligence and Fertility—The Effect of the Differential Birth Rate on Inborn Mental Characteristics," *Occasional Papers on Eugenics*, No. 2, The Eugenics Society, Cassell and Company, London, 1952.

[3] James Maxwell, "Intelligence, Fertility and the Future: A report on the 1947 Scottish Mental Survey," *Eugenics Quarterly*, Vol. 1, No. 4, December 1954, p. 247.

dicated beyond much doubt that the laborers have more children, on the average, than professional people, not because there are occupational differences in fecundity or the physiological ability to reproduce, but because there are group differences in age at marriage and in the prevalence and effectiveness of deliberate family limitation.

The above does not mean that social and economic group differences in fertility did not exist before the modern methods of contraception came into widespread use. Using available indices of the two variables, Jaffe found a rather consistent and marked inverse relation of fertility to "plane of living" among white populations in selected urban and rural areas of the United States during 1800 to 1840.[4] On the basis of his analysis (in 1940), Jaffe expressed the opinion that "it is likely that fertility differentials were as large at the beginning of the nineteenth century as they are today. Consequently, it may well be assumed that they had been in existence since the beginning of the eighteenth century, if not earlier, for a culture would take some time—at least three or four generations—to develop such differentials."[5]

It seems to us that in the last sentence Jaffe goes somewhat beyond his data. Nevertheless, his study does suggest the existence of differential fertility at the beginning of the nineteenth century. It seems likely that these differentials were implemented by differences in age at marriage, in proportions remaining in unbroken first marriages, and in the use of simple and untutored methods of contraception.

A. Census data on differential fertility according to major occupation group of the husband

Census data on children ever born in relation to occupational class of the father provided the bases for some comprehensive studies of differential fertility in this country. The question regarding the total number of children ever born was asked of all ever-married women in the Censuses of 1890, 1900, and 1910. It was asked of a 5-percent sample of ever-married women in 1940 and of a 3 1/3-percent sample in 1950. Since questions regarding occupation of the husband also were asked in all the above-mentioned censuses, basic data for studies of differential fertility according to occupational class became available in this country as early as 1890.[6]

---

[4] A. J. Jaffe, "Differential Fertility in the White Population in Early America," *Journal of Heredity*, Vol. 31, No. 9, September 1940, pp. 407–411.

[5] *Ibid.*, p. 411.

[6] Several of the State censuses antedated the Federal census by several decades in inserting a question on number of children ever born. These may have provided the incentive. In a letter dated November 23, 1955, Clyde V. Kiser asked Dr. W. F. Willcox the following: "I wonder whether you would happen to know who was chiefly responsible for inclusion of the question regarding total number of children ever born in the U. S. Census enumeration schedules of 1890, 1900, and 1910." In a reply scribbled at the bottom of the letter of inquiry, Dr. Willcox stated: "I can only guess that it was W. A. King or John Shaw Billings, with the chance, perhaps, in favor of the latter." These two

Although the question on total number of children ever born first appeared in the 1890 Census, the replies to the question in that census were never tabulated and, as previously stated, most of the enumeration schedules for that census eventually were lost in a fire. Dr. Joseph A. Hill of the Bureau of the Census utilized some of the data on children ever born as reported in the 1900 Census for a study of the fertility of immigrant women of different nationalities which he carried out for the Immigration Commission.[7] However, it was not until the late 1920's that some of the data from the 1900 and 1910 schedules were transcribed for studies of differential fertility by occupation. In 1928, a sample of records was extracted from the 1910 Census for about 100,000 urban and rural native white married women living in northern and western States. This was done through a cooperative arrangement of the Census Bureau and the Milbank Memorial Fund and it resulted in the study by Sydenstricker and Notestein "Differential Fertility According to Social Class," published in the March 1930 issue of the *Journal of the American Statistical Association.* Somewhat later, analogous materials were secured from the 1900 Census for selected samples of married women living in the East North Central States.[8] This was done largely through the stimulus of Professor W. F. Ogburn who was then director of the President's (Hoover's) Research Committee on Recent Social Trends. During the 1940's the Bureau of the Census tabulated the data for a much larger and more comprehensive sample from the 1910 Census for comparison with 1940 and published a series of reports on various aspects of differential fertility in 1940 and 1910.

Occupation as an index of socio-economic status. There is a longer history of census inquiry regarding occupation than of any other criterion of socio-economic status. Questions on occupation have been asked in censuses of the United States since the Census of 1820. Their association with data on fertility has been much more recent. Occupational group of the husband was used in Stevenson's studies of differential fertility based upon 1911 Census materials for England and Wales.[9] This variable afforded the basis for classification in the analyses of differential fertility based upon the 1900 and 1910 Censuses of the United States. In

---

men were noted census demographers who began work with the Census Office about 1880. Billings was in charge of vital statistics in the Census of 1880 and in charge of vital and social statistics in the 1890 Census.

[7] J. Hill, "Fecundity of Immigrant Women," *U. S. Immigration Commission Reports,* Vol. 28, *Occupations of the First and Second Generations of Immigrants in the United States,* Government Printing Office, Washington, 1911, pp. 731–824.

[8] Clyde V. Kiser, "Fertility of Social Classes in Various Types of Communities of the East North Central States in 1900," *Journal of the American Statistical Association,* Vol. 27, No. 180, December 1932, pp. 371–382; also "Trends in the Fertility of Social Classes from 1900 to 1910," *Human Biology,* Vol. 5, No. 2, May 1933, pp. 256–273.

[9] General Register Office, *Census of England and Wales, 1911,* Vol. XIII, *Fertility of Marriage,* Part I, His Majesty's Stationery Office, London, 1917.

his recent study of differential fertility in Madison County, New York, in 1865, Bash was able to present fertility rates by occupational group of the husband.[10]

Like other indices of socio-economic status, occupational group of the husband has certain weaknesses and strengths. As for weakness, recent studies have suggested that a small proportion of wives do not describe their husbands' occupations with sufficient accuracy to have it placed in the correct broad class.[11] It is also commonly recognized that the conventional broad occupational groups contain a wide variety of specific occupations and a wide range of social and economic gradation. Unlike educational attainment (but like rental and income status), occupation is subject to change. This subjection to change is advantageous for purposes of studies of intragenerational social mobility; it is disadvantageous for application in measures of fertility like the net or gross reproduction rate. It should also be noted that whereas educational, income, and rental classifications are quantitative and continuous, the occupational classifications usually are more qualitative and discrete. Finally, it should be pointed out that whereas educational attainment is equally applicable to single and married women, occupational group of the husband, by definition, cannot be applied to single women. Since it is an attribute of husbands enumerated in the census, occupation of the husband is not obtainable from the census data for women classified as widowed, divorced, or separated. Hence, the data by occupational group are available only for women described as "married and husband present." The data are further limited in the fertility tabulations to women who have been married only once.

Despite the above-described limitation of occupational classifications, there are manifest advantages. Also despite the heterogeneous composition of certain broad occupational groups, there are sociologists who maintain that occupation delineates style of life more sharply than does education or income.

That there were early studies of fertility differences by occupation attests to the value of this attribute for studies of group differences in fertility. That those early studies, for the United States and other countries,[12] were entitled and contemporaneously referred to as studies of differential fertility according to "social class" is an indication of the early significance attached to occupation as a criterion of socio-economic status.

---

[10] Wendell H. Bash, "Differential Fertility in Madison County, New York," *The Milbank Memorial Fund Quarterly*, Vol. 33, No. 2, April 1955, pp. 161–186.

[11] *1950 Census of Population*, Vol. II, *Characteristics of the Population*, Part I, U. S. Summary, p. 63.

[12] See for example E. Sydenstricker and F. W. Notestein, "Differential Fertility According to Social Class," *Journal of the American Statistical Association*, Vol. 25, No. 169, March 1930, pp. 9–32; C. V. Kiser, "Fertility of Social Classes in Various Types of Communities in the East North Central States in 1900," *op. cit.*; J. W. Innes, *Class Fertility Trends in England and Wales, 1876–1934*, Princeton University Press, Princeton, 1938; K. A. Edin, "Fertility in Marriage and Infantile Mortality in the Different Social Classes in Stockholm from 1919–1922," *Proceedings of the World Population Conference*, Edward Arnold and Co., London, 1927, pp. 205–207.

B. Percent distribution of women by occupation group of the husband in 1940 and 1950

The distribution of women (married once and husband present) according to occupation group of the husband differs by a variety of factors such as age, color, and urban-rural residence (tables 47–48 and figures 21–22). The age of wife is relevant because it is closely correlated with age of husband, and there are certain occupations that are statistically related to age. To be a proprietor, for instance, requires some capital, and time is usually required to accumulate it. Hence, the proportion of proprietors increases with age; among white women married once and husband present the percentage with husbands listed as proprietors in the 1950 Census extended from 3.1 percent for wives 15 to 19 years old to 17.2 percent for those 45 to 49 years old.

TABLE 47.—PERCENT DISTRIBUTION BY MAJOR OCCUPATION GROUP OF HUSBAND, FOR WHITE WOMEN 15 TO 49 YEARS OLD MARRIED ONCE AND HUSBAND PRESENT, BY AGE OF WOMAN: 1950 AND 1940

[Data for white women in 1950 and native white women in 1940]

Year and major occupation group of husband	15 to 19 years	20 to 24 years	25 to 29 years	30 to 34 years	35 to 39 years	40 to 44 years	45 to 49 years
1950							
Number of women, occupation of husband reported....................	596,850	2,785,200	3,793,800	3,712,170	3,454,440	2,972,730	2,460,480
Percent......................	100.0	100.0	100.0	100.0	100.0	100.0	100.0
Profess'l, techn'l, & kindred wkrs...	2.4	7.1	9.9	9.3	9.2	9.0	8.0
Mgrs., offs., & propr's, exc. farm...	3.1	6.3	9.5	13.0	15.7	17.3	17.2
Clerical, sales, & kindred workers...	10.5	15.3	14.9	13.4	12.4	12.2	12.7
Craftsmen, foremen, & kindred wkrs...	17.2	20.1	22.1	22.7	22.5	22.6	22.3
Operatives and kindred workers.......	33.7	28.1	23.8	21.9	19.7	17.4	16.0
Service workers, incl. priv. hshld...	2.7	3.2	3.3	3.5	3.7	4.1	4.9
Laborers, except farm and mine.......	12.6	7.9	5.9	5.2	4.9	4.7	4.9
Farmers and farm managers...........	10.0	8.4	8.5	9.3	10.4	11.3	12.5
Farm laborers and foremen...........	8.0	3.5	2.2	1.7	1.6	1.4	1.5
1940							
Number of women, occupation of husband reported....................	364,940	1,806,040	2,558,800	2,445,240	2,106,440	1,802,940	1,533,200
Percent......................	100.0	100.0	100.0	100.0	100.0	100.0	100.0
Profess'l, techn'l, & kindred wkrs...	1.9	4.5	7.0	8.0	7.5	6.8	6.6
Mgrs., offs., & propr's, exc. farm...	3.2	6.4	9.8	12.6	14.7	15.9	16.3
Clerical, sales, & kindred workers...	8.8	13.7	15.1	15.0	14.5	14.3	13.2
Craftsmen, foremen, & kindred wkrs...	12.0	14.7	16.2	17.6	18.1	18.8	18.6
Operatives and kindred workers.......	29.1	28.9	24.8	20.8	17.3	14.3	12.2
Service workers, incl. priv. hshld...	3.4	3.7	4.0	4.1	4.3	4.6	4.5
Laborers, except farm and mine.......	13.5	9.8	7.4	5.9	4.9	4.4	4.4
Farmers and farm managers...........	15.0	12.3	12.3	13.7	16.8	19.2	22.5
Farm laborers and foremen...........	13.2	6.0	3.5	2.3	1.9	1.7	1.6

Source: Derived from *1950 Census of Population*, Vol. IV, *Special Reports*, Part 5, Chapter C, Fertility, table 28; *1940 Census of Population, Differential Fertility, 1940 and 1910*, Fertility by Duration of Marriage, table 11.

The tendency for people to climb the occupational ladder is also reflected in the *decrease* with age in the proportionate importance of such occupations as operatives and laborers. However, secular changes in manufacturing processes, in technologies, and in education are also reflected in some of the relationships of age to the occupational composition of a population. Thus, in 1950, 33.7 percent of the white wives 15 to 19 years old had husbands who were "operatives" as compared with 16.0 percent for those 45 to 49 years old.

FIGURE **21.**—PERCENT DISTRIBUTION BY MAJOR OCCUPATION GROUP OF HUSBAND, FOR WHITE WOMEN 15 TO 49 YEARS OLD MARRIED ONCE AND HUSBAND PRESENT, BY AGE OF WOMAN: 1950 AND 1940

[Data for white women in 1950 and native white women in 1940]

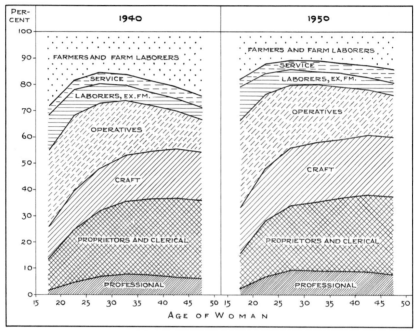

Note: Based on data in table 47.

The differences by color in occupational composition reflect at once differences in educational attainment and in occupational opportunity. Thus, among women 30 to 34 years old in 1950 the proportion with husbands of "white collar" status (professional, proprietary, and clerical) was 35.7 percent for whites and 10.1 for nonwhites. Craftsmen were represented to the extent of 22.7 percent for the whites and 10.3 percent for the nonwhites. Operatives formed 21.9 percent of the whites and 23.9 percent of the nonwhites. Service workers represented 3.5 percent of the whites and 12.2 percent of the nonwhites. Unskilled laborers formed 5.2 percent of the whites and 23.9 percent of the nonwhites. Farmers and farm laborers accounted for 11.0 percent of the whites and 19.7 percent of the nonwhites.

Marked changes took place during 1940 to 1950 in the distribution of women of childbearing age according to major occupation group of the husband. Most conspicuous in this connection has been the reduction in the proportion of farmers and farm managers. In 1940, among native white women of childbearing age, married once and husband present, the proportion classified as wives of farmers and farm managers extended from about 12 percent at ages 20 to 24 and 25 to 29 to 22.5 percent at ages 45 to 49. In 1950, the range for total whites was from 8 percent at ages 20 to 24 to 12.5 percent at ages 45 to 49.

TABLE **48.**—PERCENT DISTRIBUTION BY MAJOR OCCUPATION GROUP OF HUSBAND, FOR NON-WHITE WOMEN 15 TO 49 YEARS OLD MARRIED ONCE AND HUSBAND PRESENT, BY AGE OF WOMAN: 1950 AND 1940

[Data for nonwhite women in 1950 and Negro women in 1940]

Year and major occupation group of husband	15 to 19 years	20 to 24 years	25 to 29 years	30 to 34 years	35 to 39 years	40 to 44 years	45 to 49 years
1950							
Number of women, occupation of husband reported...................	91,110	293,070	337,440	296,850	278,670	207,630	155,160
Percent........................	100.0	100.0	100.0	100.0	100.0	100.0	100.0
Profess'l, techn'l, & kindred wkrs...	0.5	1.5	2.7	3.1	2.8	3.1	1.9
Mgrs., offs., & propr's, exc. farm...	0.8	1.3	1.8	2.8	3.0	3.2	3.6
Clerical, sales, and kindred workers.	3.0	4.7	5.4	4.2	3.9	3.8	3.4
Craftsmen, foremen, & kindred wkrs..	6.9	8.6	9.4	10.3	9.5	9.9	9.3
Operatives and kindred workers.......	24.8	26.6	26.2	23.9	22.2	20.0	17.4
Service workers, incl. priv. hshld...	8.8	10.7	11.6	12.2	12.2	13.5	14.0
Laborers, except farm and mine.......	26.3	26.0	24.5	23.9	24.8	23.4	23.4
Farmers and farm managers............	14.6	12.9	12.2	14.2	17.2	18.7	21.6
Farm laborers and foremen............	14.5	7.6	6.2	5.5	4.5	4.5	5.5
1940							
Number of women, occupation of husband reported...................	69,840	219,680	235,660	195,360	178,660	127,140	99,440
Percent........................	100.0	100.0	100.0	100.0	100.0	100.0	100.0
Profess'l, techn'l, & kindred wkrs...	0.6	0.9	1.7	2.5	2.5	2.7	3.2
Mgrs., offs., & propr's, exc. farm...	0.5	0.7	1.0	1.6	1.6	2.0	1.8
Clerical, sales, & kindred workers...	0.7	1.8	1.9	2.4	2.5	2.3	2.6
Craftsmen, foremen, & kindred wkrs...	2.5	3.7	4.9	5.4	6.3	6.2	6.3
Operatives and kindred workers.......	11.0	14.5	15.0	15.3	14.3	13.3	9.4
Service workers, incl. priv. hshld...	10.5	12.3	14.6	14.6	13.2	13.1	13.4
Laborers, except farm and mine.......	22.4	24.3	24.0	23.8	22.6	19.9	17.2
Farmers and farm managers............	24.5	23.4	24.0	25.6	29.1	32.9	38.2
Farm laborers and foremen............	27.3	18.5	13.0	8.9	8.0	7.7	7.9

Source: Derived from *1950 Census of Population,* Vol. IV, *Special Reports,* Part 5, Chapter C, Fertility, table 29; *1940 Census of Population, Differential Fertility, 1940 and 1910,* Fertility by Duration of Marriage, table 12.

A decline in the proportion of women whose husbands were farm laborers is also found for the United States as a whole. Thus, among native white married women, the proportion classified as wives of farm laborers extended from 13.2 percent for wives 15 to 19 years old to 1.6 percent for wives 45 to 49 years old. In 1950, the comparable figures for white wives were 8.0 and 1.5 percent.

The diminishing proportion of wives of farm owners and farm laborers in the United States, of course, reflects the marked drop in the farm population. This reduction, in turn, reflects the mechanization of agriculture and the urbanward shift of the population. However, another factor in the decline in the proportion of married women of childbearing age who are wives of agricultural workers may be that in 1940 the rural-farm women had a greater advantage over the urban women with respect to early marriage than they did in 1950. This factor may be of fairly substantial importance in the declining representation of agricultural work among the husbands of young married women.

Figure **22.**—Percent Distribution by Major Occupation Group of Husband, for Nonwhite Women 15 to 49 Years Old Married Once and Husband Present, by Age of Woman: 1950 and 1940

[Data for nonwhite women in 1950 and Negro women in 1940]

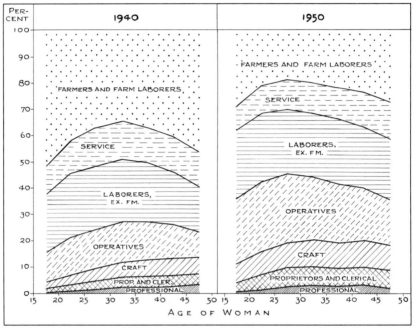

Note: Based on data in table 48.

Unskilled labor also declined in relative importance at all ages and the proportion of women with husbands classified as "operatives" was smaller in 1950 than in 1940 for white women 20 to 29 years old. There were also very slight declines in the small proportion of wives of service workers at most ages. All other occupation groups of husbands, that is, the craftsmen, clerical workers, proprietors, and professional men gained in representation during 1940 to 1950 among the white women married once and husband present. The increase in representation of the professional group was particularly noticeable. Thus, in 1940 the proportions in this group were 1.9 percent for husbands of women 15 to 19 years old and 6.6 for husbands of women 45 to 49 years old. In 1950 the comparable proportions were 2.4 percent for wives 15 to 19 years old and 8.0 percent for wives 45 to 49 years old. The increases were especially sharp for the wives of professional and technical workers who were in the middle ages of the childbearing period and reflect the increases in proportions married in the upper socio-economic groups as well as some general upward shift of occupational composition inherent in the increasing popularity of college education and the evolution of a technical economy.   As expected, the urban areas contained the largest and the rural-farm areas the smallest proportions of "white collar" workers (professional, proprietary, and clerical).   Among urban white women married once and husband present the proportion with husband classified as "white collar" workers in 1950 extended from 22 percent for wives 15 to 19 years old to about 47 percent for wives 45 to 49 years old.   The corresponding range was 13 to 33 percent within rural-nonfarm areas and 3 to 8 percent within rural-farm areas.

The relative importance of "craftsmen" was a little lower in urban than in rural-nonfarm areas, except among the wives under 25 years of age. However, at no age was the difference wide.   Among white wives of various ages within the childbearing span, 18 to 28 percent were classified as wives of craftsmen on the basis of 1950 occupation returns.   The proportionate importance of "operatives" was a little higher in rural-nonfarm than in rural-farm areas at all ages.

As expected, the nonwhites are much more concentrated in the unskilled, semiskilled, and service jobs than are the whites.   These three occupational groups included 55 to 63 percent of the nonwhite husbands' occupations in 1950.   However, the 1940–50 comparisons reveal a shift from agricultural to nonagricultural occupations.   There were modest increases in the proportions in "white collar" and skilled occupations.

The 1940–50 changes in occupational composition that were previously described for the country as a whole also apply in general within urban, rural-nonfarm, and rural-farm populations.   Thus, among the whites there were, for both urban and rural-nonfarm areas, slight increases within most ages in the proportionate importance of wives of professional men, craftsmen, and operatives.   There were slight decreases in the proportionate importance of wives of proprietors, clerical workers, service workers, and unskilled laborers.   Within rural-farm areas there was a marked decrease in the proportion of wives 35 to 44 years old whose husbands were farmers.   In rural-farm areas in 1940 about three-fourths of the native white wives 35 to 44 years old had husbands who were farmers.   The proportion was only about two-thirds for the white women in 1950.   The proportion of wives of farm laborers declined at all ages under 45; the decline was most conspicuous at youngest ages.

C. Percent changes in cumulative fertility rates and fertility ratios, 1910–40 and 1940–50, by occupation group of husband

Percent changes in fertility rates.   The trend of cumulative fertility rates during 1910 to 1940 was generally downward.   The percent declines in total number of children ever born during 1910 to 1940 are shown in table 49 for native white women married once and husband present, by age of wife, urban-rural residence, and major occupation group of husband.

TABLE **49.**—PERCENT CHANGE, 1910 TO 1940, IN NUMBER OF CHILDREN EVER BORN PER 1,000 NATIVE WHITE WOMEN 15 TO 49 YEARS OLD MARRIED ONCE AND HUSBAND PRESENT, BY AGE OF WOMAN AND MAJOR OCCUPATION GROUP OF HUSBAND, URBAN AND RURAL

[Percent change not shown where there are fewer than 3,000 women in 1940 or 1,200 in 1910]

Area and major occupation group of husband	15 to 19 years	20 to 24 years	25 to 29 years	30 to 34 years	35 to 39 years	40 to 44 years	45 to 49 years
URBAN							
Professional, technical, and kindred wkrs...	-27.6	-28.8	-25.2	-19.3	-22.1	-23.7	-28.8
Managers, officials, and propr's, exc. farm.	-32.0	-30.8	-28.1	-27.0	-30.3	-32.3	-34.7
Clerical, sales, and kindred workers........	1.4	-28.5	-26.5	-25.8	-28.0	-30.2	-35.4
Craftsmen, foremen, and kindred workers.....	-21.5	-28.4	-26.7	-25.8	-29.1	-33.0	-34.4
Operatives and kindred workers..............	-16.4	-26.8	-27.2	-25.7	-27.7	-31.0	-35.0
Service workers, incl. private household....	-22.9	-28.0	-27.1	-26.5	-28.8	-30.5	-35.4
Laborers, except farm and mine..............	-18.8	-30.1	-33.6	-27.9	-29.5	-32.9	-32.6
RURAL NONFARM							
Professional, technical, and kindred wkrs...	...	-33.7	-30.0	-33.9	-35.0	-33.8	-34.9
Managers, officials, and propr's, exc. farm.	-33.7	-25.0	-32.5	-32.9	-36.0	-36.0	-34.3
Clerical, sales, and kindred workers........	-30.8	-27.1	-32.1	-33.4	-34.9	-31.5	-32.6
Craftsmen, foremen, and kindred workers.....	-16.0	-24.2	-29.7	-28.6	-30.8	-30.3	-30.8
Operatives and kindred workers..............	-18.7	-26.0	-25.9	-26.9	-32.2	-31.9	-32.5
Service workers, incl. private household....	...	-25.5	-32.9	-28.4	-30.9	-29.8	-23.6
Laborers, except farm and mine..............	-18.2	-24.3	-24.9	-24.6	-24.8	-23.9	-20.2
Farmers and farm managers...................	...	-25.0	-30.9	-23.7	-29.1	-30.7	-30.8
Farm laborers and foremen...................	-11.9	-27.7	-25.0	-29.0	-27.8	-23.3	-18.4
RURAL FARM							
Professional, technical, and kindred wkrs...	...	...	-25.0	-44.2	-40.9	-39.1	-32.1
Managers, officials, and propr's, exc. farm.	...	-25.6	-31.2	-38.4	-35.1	-35.2	-27.8
Clerical, sales, and kindred workers........	...	-24.5	-22.8	-21.3	-31.7	-31.5	-36.3
Craftsmen, foremen, and kindred workers.....	...	-13.8	-13.7	-24.0	-24.9	-18.4	-23.3
Operatives and kindred workers..............	...	-19.6	-21.4	-22.3	-19.5	-21.0	-21.7
Service workers, incl. private household....	...	...	...	...	...	...	...
Laborers, except farm and mine..............	-5.0	-16.8	-14.5	-22.2	-19.9	-15.2	-19.9
Farmers and farm managers...................	-15.9	-19.4	-22.4	-24.4	-25.4	-25.9	-26.0
Farm laborers and foremen...................	16.9	4.0	-3.1	-8.4	-3.7	-6.4	-14.5

Source: Derived from table 54.

With three minor exceptions, every percent change shown in table 49 is a decrease. Decreases of the order of 25 to 35 percent occurred within urban and rural-nonfarm areas. Those in rural-farm areas generally were a little lower, 15 to 35 percent.

The percent declines in fertility of native whites during 1910 to 1940 were relatively low for the women 15 to 19 years old but there was not additional relation of age to percent change in fertility rates during 1910 to 1940. The percent declines tended to be relatively large for the three "white collar" groups (wives of professional, proprietary, and clerical workers). They were conspicuously low for the wives of farm laborers. Otherwise, there was little relation of husband's occupation to magnitude of decline in fertility rates during 1910 to 1940.

As with the whites, the fertility of nonwhites within each occupational group was lower in 1940 than in 1910. The percent decreases tended to be relatively large for the wives of professional men but otherwise the decreases were not very systematic (table 50).

TABLE **50.**—PERCENT CHANGE, 1910 TO 1940, IN NUMBER OF CHILDREN EVER BORN PER 1,000 NEGRO WOMEN 20 TO 49 YEARS OLD MARRIED ONCE AND HUSBAND PRESENT, BY AGE OF WOMAN AND MAJOR OCCUPATION GROUP OF HUSBAND

[Percent change not shown where there are fewer than 3,000 women in 1940 or 1,200 in 1910]

Major occupation group of husband	20 to 24 years	25 to 29 years	30 to 34 years	35 to 39 years	40 to 44 years	45 to 49 years
Professional, technical, and kindred workers...	...	-44.9	-52.6	-54.1	-42.0	-58.3
Managers, officials, and propr's, exc. farm....	...	...	...	...	...	...
Clerical, sales, and kindred workers...........	-36.2	-27.1	-48.1	-40.3	...	...
Craftsmen, foremen, and kindred workers........	-22.2	-30.5	-25.5	-32.3	-42.7	-46.0
Operatives and kindred workers.................	-26.9	-26.3	-34.2	-34.6	-39.5	-42.7
Service workers, including private household...	-18.0	-25.1	-16.9	-26.6	-31.5	-36.8
Laborers, except farm and mine.................	-23.4	-24.5	-28.2	-27.6	-41.6	-42.9
Farmers and farm managers......................	-14.4	-16.1	-16.7	-22.4	-31.9	-35.0
Farm laborers and foremen......................	-13.8	-17.8	-22.2	-26.0	-35.7	-27.3

Source: Derived from table 55.

It is somewhat unfortunate that the lack of data prevents a subdivision of the 1910–40 period. The comparisons of the 1910 and 1940 data alone suggest little net change of occupational differences in fertility over this period. Other data, however, suggest that there may have been some enlargement of fertility differentials by occupation until about the middle of the 1920's and some narrowing during the next 15 years, that is, approximately 1925 to 1940. The percent declines in the fertility of the groups of topmost socio-economic status appeared to be smaller than that of certain other groups. The emergence of the now-familiar exceptions to the straight inverse association of fertility to socio-economic status suggested some narrowing of the fertility differentials.[13]

Whatever may have been the situation over the 1910–40 period, there is no doubt about the existence of differential changes in fertility over the 1940–50 period. In table 51, the 1940–50 percent changes in total number of children ever born are shown for white women (native white in 1940), by age, urban-rural residence and major occupation group of the husband.

Among urban white women under 35 years old (married once and husband present) the fertility rates for all occupation groups increased over the 1940–50 decade (figure 23). Among those 20 to 34 years old, the increases tended to be directly related to occupation group of the husband. At these ages, the percentage increases tended to be highest for wives of professional men and lowest for wives of unskilled laborers. Among women 40 to 44 and 45 to 49 years old the fertility rates were consistently lower in 1950 than in 1940. Among those 35 to 39 years old, 1940–50 increases in fertility were exhibited by wives of "white collar" workers and decreases by wives of manual workers.

[13] J. W. Innes, "Class Birth Rates in England and Wales, 1921–1931," *The Milbank Memorial Fund Quarterly*, Vol. XIX, No. 1, January 1941, pp. 72–96; F. W. Notestein, "Differential Fertility in the East North Central States," *The Milbank Memorial Fund Quarterly*, Vol. XVI, No. 2, April 1938, pp. 173–191; C. V. Kiser, *Group Differences in Urban Fertility*, The Williams and Wilkins Company, Baltimore, 1942; P. K. Whelpton and C. V. Kiser (Editors), *Social and Psychological Factors Affecting Fertility*, Vol. 1, *The Household Survey*, The Milbank Memorial Fund, New York, 1946, pp. 1–60.

TABLE **51.**—PERCENT CHANGE, 1940 TO 1950, IN NUMBER OF CHILDREN EVER BORN PER 1,000 WHITE WOMEN 15 TO 49 YEARS OLD MARRIED ONCE AND HUSBAND PRESENT, BY AGE OF WOMAN AND MAJOR OCCUPATION GROUP OF HUSBAND, URBAN AND RURAL

[Data for white women in 1950 and native white women in 1940. Percent change not shown where there are fewer than 4,000 women in 1950 or 3,000 in 1940]

Area and major occupation group of husband	15 to 19 years	20 to 24 years	25 to 29 years	30 to 34 years	35 to 39 years	40 to 44 years	45 to 49 years
URBAN							
Professional, technical, and kindred wkrs...	32.9	30.6	53.3	35.6	11.9	-6.0	-14.6
Managers, officials, and propr's, exc. farm.	21.5	32.5	37.6	27.2	7.8	-7.4	-10.9
Clerical, sales, and kindred workers........	2.6	31.2	38.2	26.0	7.0	-4.6	-6.7
Craftsmen, foremen, and kindred workers.....	1.3	21.7	21.1	9.8	-5.2	-9.6	-11.8
Operatives and kindred workers..............	10.7	20.2	22.4	9.7	-6.0	-10.2	-6.2
Service workers, incl. private household....	7.4	25.0	31.1	13.8	-3.6	-13.8	-8.9
Laborers, except farm and mine..............	14.1	12.5	18.7	2.0	-5.6	-4.0	-3.2
RURAL NONFARM							
Professional, technical, and kindred wkrs...	...	38.3	40.6	36.6	8.9	-6.4	-19.5
Managers, officials, and propr's, exc. farm.	14.2	12.6	28.9	18.3	3.1	-8.7	-11.5
Clerical, sales, and kindred workers........	19.9	17.8	29.9	19.7	-0.5	-9.4	-14.9
Craftsmen, foremen, and kindred workers.....	-0.3	10.5	16.2	8.9	-4.1	-6.5	-12.2
Operatives and kindred workers..............	7.7	10.1	9.7	2.0	-2.0	-8.4	-12.2
Service workers, incl. private household....	...	29.8	29.2	6.6	-1.3	-13.0	-15.4
Laborers, except farm and mine..............	-12.5	11.7	9.2	5.1	-2.4	-9.7	-10.4
Farmers and farm managers...................	...	-2.6	10.9	-6.9	-13.8	-19.1	-18.9
Farm laborers and foremen...................	-8.0	19.5	18.5	18.2	9.6	3.5	2.9
RURAL FARM							
Professional, technical, and kindred wkrs...	...	...	25.7	53.4	-0.2	3.5	3.0
Managers, officials, and propr's, exc. farm.	...	...	19.2	19.4	2.8	-13.0	-20.9
Clerical, sales, and kindred workers........	...	1.1	3.6	13.3	-9.6	-0.1	-7.0
Craftsmen, foremen, and kindred workers.....	...	3.5	9.1	7.9	-4.6	-12.0	-13.0
Operatives and kindred workers..............	12.8	7.4	13.0	1.7	-3.9	-8.9	-5.5
Service workers, incl. private household....	...	...	...	...	...	...	...
Laborers, except farm and mine..............	-8.8	10.7	9.5	-0.6	-3.7	-2.4	-0.4
Farmers and farm managers...................	-11.0	0.9	3.5	-3.4	-11.5	-14.2	-13.9
Farm laborers and foremen...................	-5.9	6.6	11.0	-2.3	1.9	-10.3	-3.4

Source: Derived from table 54.

As previously noted, the maximum percent increases in cumulative fertility rates during 1940 to 1950 came at ages 25 to 29. Among urban white women this held true for all occupational classes represented in figure 23 with the exception of craftsmen. The increases at ages 25 to 29 were especially prominent for the wives of men in the three white-collar groups (professional, proprietary, and clerical).

By age, the percent increase in cumulative fertility rates for the wives of professional men ranged from 12 to 53 percent for age groups under 40; the corresponding range for the wives of laborers, except farm and mine, was from a decrease of 6 percent at ages 35 to 39 to an increase of 19 percent at ages 25 to 29. At ages of 40 and over, decreases rather than increases in fertility were the rule.[14]

[14] It should be noted, however, that although there were declines during 1940–50 in the average number of children ever born among women 40 to 49 years old, there were increases in the ratios of children under 5 years old to women 40 to 49 years old. This means that the women of those ages in 1950 participated to some extent in the 1940–50 baby boom, but not sufficiently to counteract the long-time decline in total size of family among women of completed fertility.

FIGURE **23.**—PERCENT CHANGE, 1940 TO 1950, IN NUMBER OF CHILDREN EVER BORN PER
1,000 WHITE WOMEN 15 TO 49 YEARS OLD MARRIED ONCE AND HUSBAND PRESENT, BY
AGE OF WOMAN AND MAJOR OCCUPATION GROUP OF HUSBAND, FOR URBAN AREAS

[Data for white women in 1950 and native white women in 1940]

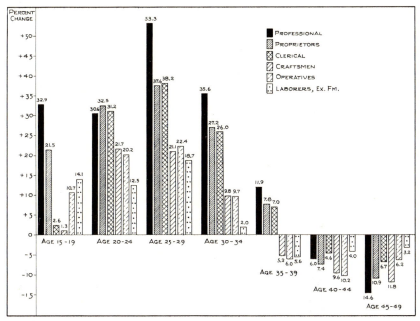

Note: Based on data in table 51.

The tendency for percent increases in fertility to be largest for urban
groups and smallest for rural-farm groups persists in reduced form when
occupation group is held constant. Thus, at ages 25 to 29 the percent increases in the cumulative fertility rate for wives of professional men were
53 percent for the urban group, 41 percent for the rural-nonfarm group,
and 26 percent for the rural-farm group. However, an opposite type of
relationship is found for the professional group at ages 30 to 34.

The patterns of increase in the fertility of whites by occupational group
of the husband were about the same in rural-nonfarm as in urban areas.
That is, among rural-nonfarm women under 35 years old the percent increases in fertility tended to be largest for wives of professional men and
smallest for wives of operatives and unskilled laborers. At ages above
35, decreases rather than increases in fertility were the rule (figure 24).

The pattern of *decreases* in fertility rates by age, occupation, and type
of residence is also of interest. Thus, among urban wives 35 to 39 years
old, 1940–50 decreases were found for all wives of nonfarm manual
workers. At ages 40 to 44 and 45 to 49, there were decreases for all except the very few wives of farmers in the urban areas. The somewhat
anomalous groups, such as the farmers and farm laborers in urban areas

and professional and other white-collar groups in rural-farm areas, were few in number and the data are subject to large sampling variability.

Among the wives of farmers and farm laborers in rural-farm areas, 1940–50 decreases rather than increases in fertility rates were found in most cases. Exceptions were found for the wives of farmers and farm laborers at ages 20 to 29 and those of farm laborers at ages 35 to 39.

FIGURE 24.—PERCENT CHANGE, 1940 TO 1950, IN NUMBER OF CHILDREN EVER BORN PER 1,000 WHITE WOMEN 15 TO 49 YEARS OLD MARRIED ONCE AND HUSBAND PRESENT, BY AGE OF WOMAN AND MAJOR OCCUPATION GROUP OF HUSBAND FOR RURAL-NONFARM AREAS

[Data for white women in 1950 and native white women in 1940]

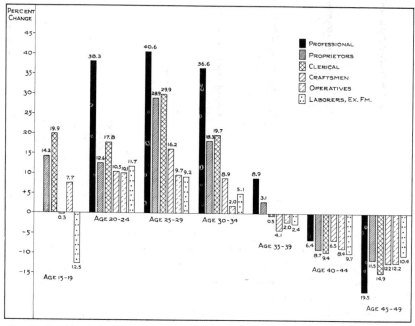

Note: Based on data in table 51.

The conspicuous increases during 1940 to 1950 in the fertility rates among young women with husbands of various occupational groups arise in considerable measure from decreases in proportions childless. The increases in the fertility of "mothers" during this decade were relatively slight. For instance, among urban white women 20 to 24 years old who were wives of professional men, the fertility rate increased by 31 percent during the 1940–50 decade, but the fertility rate for "mothers" was virtually the same in 1950 as in 1940. The proportion of childless women at ages 20 to 24 decreased by 19 percent. Among women 25 to 29 years old, the increase in average fertility rate per 1,000 wives was 53 percent; the increase was only 15 percent for "mothers." In the 30-to-34 age group the respective increases were 36 and 16 percent.

In summary, the 1910–40 percent changes in cumulative fertility rates were fairly uniform or at least not systematically different by occupational group. The 1940–50 changes, in contrast, differed by occupational group in such a manner as to bring reductions of occupational differences in fertility.

Percent changes in fertility ratios. Table 52 exhibits the 1940–50 percent changes in the number of own children under 5 years old per 1,000 women, by age of woman, urban-rural residence, and major occupation group of the husband. For both 1940 and 1950, the data relate to women described as "married once and husband present." As before, there are differences between the 1940 and 1950 data with respect to nativity, color, and residence that are available from the tabulations of occupation and education in relation to fertility. Thus, the 1940 data relate to native whites, and the 1950 data relate to whites regardless of nativity. By residence, the 1940 data are based upon 1940 Census definitions of urban and rural whereas the 1950 data are based upon the new census definitions.

TABLE **52.**—PERCENT CHANGE, 1940 TO 1950, IN NUMBER OF OWN CHILDREN UNDER 5 YEARS OLD PER 1,000 WHITE WOMEN 15 TO 44 YEARS OLD MARRIED ONCE AND HUSBAND PRESENT, BY AGE OF WOMAN AND MAJOR OCCUPATION GROUP OF HUSBAND, URBAN AND RURAL

[Data for white women in 1950 and native white women in 1940. Percent change not shown where there are fewer than 4,000 women in 1950 or 3,000 in 1940]

Area and major occupation group of husband	15 to 19 years	20 to 24 years	25 to 29 years	30 to 34 years	35 to 39 years	40 to 44 years
URBAN						
Professional, technical, and kindred workers.....	31.9	51.1	63.9	50.8	54.2	86.5
Managers, officials, and proprietors, exc. farm..	39.0	45.4	48.6	50.4	63.3	78.7
Clerical, sales, and kindred workers.............	12.2	39.4	54.9	53.1	65.2	57.0
Craftsmen, foremen, and kindred workers.........	12.8	27.9	36.8	37.0	34.7	18.9
Operatives and kindred workers...................	21.2	26.1	35.7	37.4	25.9	18.6
Laborers, except farm and mine..................	5.0	3.7	20.1	15.5	19.3	2.7
RURAL NONFARM						
Professional, technical, and kindred workers.....	...	50.8	52.4	47.0	40.8	34.2
Managers, officials, and proprietors, exc. farm..	23.4	30.2	41.8	33.4	49.1	74.0
Clerical, sales, and kindred workers.............	25.3	21.5	39.5	34.8	47.9	31.9
Craftsmen, foremen, and kindred workers.........	11.3	20.6	24.6	29.2	17.2	11.6
Operatives and kindred workers...................	18.8	20.0	22.2	13.8	21.3	6.4
Laborers, except farm and mine..................	-12.6	11.7	4.6	4.9	4.6	-25.9
Farmers and farm managers.......................	...	4.3	16.3	5.8	24.9	32.4
Farm laborers and foremen.......................	6.6	25.2	23.2	10.9	8.8	46.2
RURAL FARM						
Professional, technical, and kindred workers.....	...	...	28.1	49.4	-20.8	-21.6
Managers, officials, and proprietors, exc. farm..	...	...	36.5	32.1	27.3	8.9
Clerical, sales, and kindred workers.............	...	10.1	22.5	32.1	20.7	68.4
Craftsmen, foremen, and kindred workers.........	25.3	11.5	22.2	6.8	-0.6	12.1
Operatives and kindred workers...................	-11.0	15.4	17.8	7.3	0.4	-8.6
Laborers, except farm and mine..................	-7.9	5.6	-1.5	-25.3	-15.4	4.3
Farmers and farm managers.......................	4.1	15.4	16.4	6.1	-2.0	-4.9
Farm laborers and foremen.......................	7.8	14.5	20.9	8.4	10.0	32.4

Source: Derived from table 60.

Fertility ratios, the number of own children under 5 years old per 1,000 women of given age, have certain weaknesses and strengths as measures of fertility. As previously stated, some weaknesses, as compared with rates based upon all children, are that the fertility ratios are affected by child mortality, by some children living apart from the mother, and by the timing of births. Quantitative information on the first two items is given in Appendix A. As indicated there, the two items of mortality and nonresident children may be especially important among the nonwhites. The timing of births has direct influence on the fertility ratios at given ages and does not necessarily reflect the eventual family size. For instance, population groups that are characterized by relatively late age at marriage may exhibit relatively high fertility ratios at advanced ages and yet these groups may have relatively few children in their lifetimes.

Despite the weaknesses of the fertility ratio, an outstanding strength or advantage is that the ratio represents current fertility or, more accurately, fertility during the preceding 5 years.

Whereas, the 1940–50 percent increases in the average number of children ever born were restricted to women under 40 years old, the percent increases in ratios of young children occurred among women as old as 45 to 49 years, within the urban and rural-nonfarm groups. In fact, among the urban white wives of professional men and proprietors there was a virtually direct relation of age to 1940–50 percent increases in fertility ratios. The percent increases in fertility ratios were higher at ages 40 to 44 than at any younger age for these two occupational groups. It is true that at this late age the fertility ratios were low. For instance, although the 1940–50 increase in the fertility ratio for urban white wives of professional men was 87 percent at ages 40 to 44, the actual ratios were only 104 and 194 per 1,000 women in 1940 and 1950, respectively.

The 1940–50 percent increases in fertility ratios (table 52) are not only more pervasive by age than are the increases in cumulative fertility rates (table 51), they are also found more frequently in the various cross classifications by occupation group and type of community.

The 1940–50 percent increases in fertility ratios tend to be higher, as well as more prevalent, than the increases in fertility rates. This arises from the fact that whereas cumulative fertility rates are influenced by conditions *since marriage* regardless of age, the fertility ratios reflect current fertility or, more precisely, the fertility over the preceding 5 years.

Table 53 presents 1910–50 percent changes in fertility ratios of the nonwhites by age and occupational class. These bring out the rather astonishing fact that at virtually all occupational levels of husbands, the age-specific fertility ratios of nonwhite women under 35 years old in 1950 were higher than those of Negro women of comparable age and occupation group of husband in 1910. Some of the ratios for ages 20 to 24 and 25

to 29 were 25 to 75 percent higher in 1950 than in 1910. Reductions
in infant mortality explain some of the increases in fertility ratios. Also,
nonwhite children probably were somewhat less completely enumerated
in 1910 than in 1950 (Appendix A). On the other hand, the considerably
higher proportion of the population that was rural in 1910 than in 1950
makes the contrast more striking.[15]

TABLE 53.—PERCENT CHANGE, 1910 TO 1950, IN NUMBER OF OWN CHILDREN UNDER 5 YEARS
OLD PER 1,000 NONWHITE WOMEN 20 TO 44 YEARS OLD MARRIED ONCE AND HUSBAND
PRESENT, BY AGE OF WOMAN AND MAJOR OCCUPATION GROUP OF HUSBAND

[Data for nonwhite women in 1950 and Negro women in 1910. Percent change not shown where there are fewer than 4,000
women in 1950 or 1,200 in 1910]

Major occupation group of husband	20 to 24 years	25 to 29 years	30 to 34 years	35 to 39 years	40 to 44 years	45 to 49 years
Professional, technical, and kindred workers.....	24.9	7.9	-9.0	-1.3	27.7	...
Managers, officials, and proprietors, exc. farm..	...	-17.7	28.6	-20.5	-54.6	86.4
Clerical, sales, and kindred workers............	27.3	18.8	-0.6	-23.2	...	...
Craftsmen, foremen, and kindred workers.........	50.9	5.0	4.7	-11.9	-38.1	62.3
Operatives and kindred workers..................	34.8	23.8	6.5	-15.9	-33.9	-52.3
Service workers, including private household.....	76.4	40.8	18.7	-7.2	-6.8	-20.3
Laborers, except farm and mine..................	54.4	25.5	-6.1	-5.4	-22.7	-11.1
Farmers and farm managers.......................	27.8	9.3	7.2	-10.1	-17.0	-42.9
Farm laborers and foremen.......................	30.0	11.2	-7.8	-15.1	-48.1	-28.9

Source: Derived from table 61.

D. Children ever born, by major occupation group of the husband

Standardized fertility rates by occupational group of the husband are
shown for 1940 and 1950 in figure 25. The 1950 data relate to white
women and the 1940 data to native white women, 15 to 49 years old, married once and husband present. The urban-rural classification is by the
somewhat different definitions used in 1950 and 1940.

It will be noted that in the standardized rates the excesses of the 1950
over the 1940 rates that do occur are generally of small magnitude. This
small magnitude results from the fact that in the rates for women 15 to
49 years old combined the 1940–50 *increases* in cumulative fertility rates
for women under 35 tend to be cancelled by the *decreases* in similar rates
for women 35 and over. Thus, although the fertility rates standardized
for age do not exhibit much change in the pattern of differential fertility
by occupation, it is obviously necessary to consider the data for specific
age groups.

The data for 1910, 1940, and 1950 are shown in age-specific form for
white women by urban-rural residence in table 54 and figures 26, 27, and

---

[15] The increases in fertility ratios between 1910 and 1950 (tables 53 and 61) contrast sharply with
the large decreases in cumulative fertility between 1910 and 1940 (table 50) that were only partly offset by increases between 1940 and 1950 (tables 55 and 59).

28. The data for 1910 and 1940 pertain to native whites and those for 1950 to whites.   However, in 1950 among ever-married white women 15 to 49 years old, the proportions that were *native white* were

           94 percent for the United States
           93 percent for urban areas
           97 percent for rural-nonfarm areas
           98 percent for rural-farm areas

FIGURE **25.**—STANDARDIZED NUMBER OF CHILDREN EVER BORN PER 1,000 WHITE WOMEN 15 TO 49 YEARS OLD MARRIED ONCE AND HUSBAND PRESENT, BY MAJOR OCCUPATION GROUP OF HUSBAND, URBAN AND RURAL: 1950 AND 1940

[Data for white women in 1950 and native white women in 1940. The standard is the distribution by age of all women 15 to 49 years old married once and husband present, in the United States in 1950]

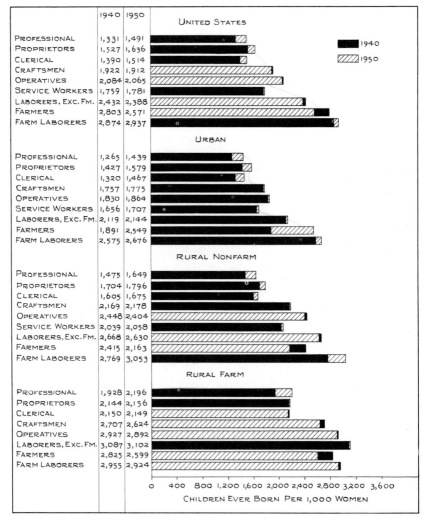

	1940	1950
UNITED STATES		
PROFESSIONAL	1,331	1,491
PROPRIETORS	1,527	1,636
CLERICAL	1,390	1,514
CRAFTSMEN	1,922	1,912
OPERATIVES	2,084	2,065
SERVICE WORKERS	1,759	1,781
LABORERS, EXC. FM.	2,432	2,388
FARMERS	2,803	2,571
FARM LABORERS	2,874	2,937
URBAN		
PROFESSIONAL	1,265	1,439
PROPRIETORS	1,427	1,579
CLERICAL	1,320	1,467
CRAFTSMEN	1,757	1,775
OPERATIVES	1,830	1,864
SERVICE WORKERS	1,656	1,707
LABORERS, EXC. FM.	2,119	2,144
FARMERS	1,891	2,549
FARM LABORERS	2,575	2,676
RURAL NONFARM		
PROFESSIONAL	1,475	1,649
PROPRIETORS	1,704	1,796
CLERICAL	1,605	1,675
CRAFTSMEN	2,169	2,178
OPERATIVES	2,448	2,404
SERVICE WORKERS	2,039	2,058
LABORERS, EXC. FM.	2,668	2,630
FARMERS	2,415	2,163
FARM LABORERS	2,769	3,053
RURAL FARM		
PROFESSIONAL	1,928	2,196
PROPRIETORS	2,144	2,156
CLERICAL	2,150	2,149
CRAFTSMEN	2,707	2,624
OPERATIVES	2,927	2,892
LABORERS, EXC. FM.	3,087	3,102
FARMERS	2,825	2,599
FARM LABORERS	2,955	2,924

■ 1940
▨ 1950

CHILDREN EVER BORN PER 1,000 WOMEN

Source: Derived from age-specific rates in table 54 and from standard distribution computed from *1950 Census of Population*, Vol. IV, *Special Reports*, Part 5, Chapter C, Fertility, table 1.

TABLE 54.—NUMBER OF CHILDREN EVER BORN PER 1,000 WHITE WOMEN 15 TO 49 YEARS OLD MARRIED ONCE AND HUSBAND PRESENT, BY AGE OF WOMAN AND MAJOR OCCUPATION GROUP OF HUSBAND, URBAN AND RURAL: 1950, 1940, AND 1910

[Data for white women in 1950 and native white women in 1940 and 1910. Rate not shown where there are fewer than 4,000 women in 1950, 3,000 in 1940, or 1,200 in 1910]

Age of woman and major occupation group of husband	United States			Urban			Rural nonfarm			Rural farm		
	1950	1940	1910	1950	1940	1910	1950	1940	1910	1950	1940	1910
WOMEN 15 TO 19 YEARS OLD												
Professional, technical, and kindred workers	459	326	501	436	328	453	...	...	552	...	...	...
Managers, officials, and proprietors, exc. farm	454	401	585	440	362	532	492	431	650	...	...	...
Clerical, sales, and kindred workers	439	415	456	434	423	417	439	366	529	...	...	...
Craftsmen, foremen, and kindred workers	518	521	634	465	459	585	609	611	727	663	625	...
Operatives and kindred workers	584	551	669	548	495	592	657	610	750	545	...	...
Service workers, including private household	517	452	595	464	432	560	...	...	677	...	...	...
Laborers, except farm and mine	599	609	734	608	533	656	570	651	796	660	724	762
Farmers and farm managers	589	672	797	...	...	...	552	...	703	600	674	801
Farm laborers and foremen	580	610	683	552	...	...	625	679	771	559	594	508
WOMEN 20 TO 24 YEARS OLD												
Professional, technical, and kindred workers	714	567	838	670	513	721	913	660	996	...	...	1,204
Managers, officials, and proprietors, exc. farm	882	720	1,035	832	628	907	1,020	906	1,208	...	1,004	1,349
Clerical, sales, and kindred workers	793	625	886	766	584	817	914	776	1,064	929	919	1,218
Craftsmen, foremen, and kindred workers	1,041	898	1,218	972	799	1,116	1,199	1,085	1,432	1,277	1,234	1,432
Operatives and kindred workers	1,112	968	1,316	1,019	848	1,159	1,275	1,158	1,565	1,342	1,249	1,554
Service workers, including private household	1,010	809	1,121	959	767	1,066	1,225	944	1,267	...	...	...
Laborers, except farm and mine	1,195	1,093	1,491	1,070	951	1,360	1,363	1,220	1,612	1,505	1,360	1,634
Farmers and farm managers	1,294	1,306	1,629	689	...	1,284	1,070	1,099	1,465	1,331	1,319	1,636
Farm laborers and foremen	1,346	1,233	1,516	1,164	1,188	1,276	1,420	1,188	1,644	1,333	1,250	1,202
WOMEN 25 TO 29 YEARS OLD												
Professional, technical, and kindred workers	1,280	880	1,232	1,234	805	1,076	1,436	1,021	1,459	1,803	1,434	1,913
Managers, officials, and proprietors, exc. farm	1,462	1,101	1,607	1,410	1,025	1,426	1,615	1,253	1,855	1,853	1,554	2,259
Clerical, sales, and kindred workers	1,307	967	1,365	1,262	913	1,242	1,519	1,169	1,721	1,706	1,646	2,132
Craftsmen, foremen, and kindred workers	1,650	1,400	1,917	1,543	1,274	1,738	1,875	1,614	2,295	2,195	2,012	2,332
Operatives and kindred workers	1,736	1,500	2,017	1,589	1,298	1,782	1,986	1,811	2,444	2,363	2,091	2,660
Service workers, including private household	1,565	1,209	1,707	1,518	1,158	1,589	1,773	1,372	2,046	...	...	...
Laborers, except farm and mine	1,917	1,720	2,400	1,717	1,446	2,177	2,157	1,976	2,457	2,438	2,227	2,606
Farmers and farm managers	2,132	2,056	2,661	2,228	...	2,191	1,884	1,699	2,457	2,146	2,074	2,672
Farm laborers and foremen	2,298	2,004	2,518	2,280	1,815	2,019	2,379	2,007	2,675	2,245	2,022	2,087
WOMEN 30 TO 34 YEARS OLD												
Professional, technical, and kindred workers	1,777	1,321	1,820	1,724	1,271	1,575	1,956	1,432	2,166	2,494	1,626	2,916
Managers, officials, and proprietors, exc. farm	1,876	1,526	2,206	1,824	1,434	1,965	2,019	1,706	2,543	2,383	1,995	3,241
Clerical, sales, and kindred workers	1,689	1,365	1,906	1,638	1,300	1,752	1,868	1,560	2,344	2,532	2,235	2,840
Craftsmen, foremen, and kindred workers	2,075	1,920	2,605	1,931	1,759	2,370	2,358	2,165	3,032	2,822	2,615	3,441
Operatives and kindred workers	2,193	2,084	2,775	2,000	1,823	2,452	2,511	2,461	3,367	2,968	2,919	3,757
Service workers, including private household	1,880	1,690	2,325	1,817	1,597	2,173	2,137	2,004	2,798	...	...	...

TABLE 54.— NUMBER OF CHILDREN EVER BORN PER 1,000 WHITE WOMEN 15 TO 49 YEARS OLD MARRIED ONCE AND HUSBAND PRESENT, BY AGE OF WOMAN AND MAJOR OCCUPATION GROUP OF HUSBAND, URBAN AND RURAL: 1950, 1940, AND 1910—Cont.

Age of woman and major occupation group of husband	United States			Urban			Rural nonfarm			Rural farm		
	1950	1940	1910	1950	1940	1910	1950	1940	1910	1950	1940	1910
WOMEN 30 TO 34 YEARS OLD—Cont.												
Laborers, except farm and mine	2,457	2,448	3,248	2,168	2,125	2,946	2,810	2,674	3,547	3,114	3,132	4,025
Farmers and farm managers	2,713	2,805	3,706	3,138	...	2,817	2,402	2,581	3,381	2,721	2,817	3,726
Farm laborers and foremen	2,969	2,800	3,565	2,988	2,418	2,865	3,134	2,651	3,733	2,829	2,898	3,159
WOMEN 35 TO 39 YEARS OLD												
Professional, technical, and kindred workers	1,836	1,673	2,364	1,794	1,603	2,058	1,971	1,810	2,786	2,285	2,289	3,872
Managers, officials, and proprietors, exc. farm	1,956	1,861	2,788	1,898	1,761	2,526	2,091	2,028	3,169	2,654	2,582	3,976
Clerical, sales, and kindred workers	1,807	1,730	2,483	1,760	1,645	2,285	1,959	1,969	3,026	2,434	2,692	3,940
Craftsmen, foremen, and kindred workers	2,239	2,377	3,614	2,064	2,178	3,070	2,539	2,646	3,824	3,168	3,319	4,419
Operatives and kindred workers	2,456	2,604	2,982	2,161	2,299	3,178	2,951	3,010	4,439	3,554	3,698	4,595
Service workers, including private household	2,048	2,141	...	1,956	2,028	2,849	2,353	2,384	3,448	...	3,297	...
Laborers, except farm and mine	2,871	3,049	4,074	2,514	2,663	3,775	3,224	3,303	4,395	3,802	3,946	4,925
Farmers and farm managers	3,072	3,475	4,663	3,265	2,384	3,627	2,580	2,993	4,219	3,098	3,501	4,694
Farm laborers and foremen	3,652	3,596	4,432	3,114	...	3,647	3,681	3,358	4,649	3,790	3,720	3,863
WOMEN 40 TO 44 YEARS OLD												
Professional, technical, and kindred workers	1,812	1,926	2,749	1,747	1,858	2,435	1,934	2,065	3,119	2,900	2,801	4,598
Managers, officials, and proprietors, exc. farm	1,942	2,144	3,259	1,871	2,021	2,987	2,143	2,348	3,668	2,573	2,957	4,565
Clerical, sales, and kindred workers	1,853	1,978	2,858	1,794	1,881	2,694	2,020	2,229	3,255	2,977	2,981	4,349
Craftsmen, foremen, and kindred workers	2,399	2,666	3,854	2,204	2,437	3,635	2,763	2,956	4,242	3,417	3,884	4,759
Operatives and kindred workers	2,612	2,931	4,157	2,321	2,583	3,746	3,139	3,427	5,034	3,768	4,135	5,232
Service workers, including private household	2,164	2,564	3,596	2,087	2,420	3,482	2,460	2,826	4,025	...	4,012	...
Laborers, except farm and mine	3,162	3,403	4,633	2,858	2,978	4,441	3,350	3,709	4,876	4,224	4,329	5,107
Farmers and farm managers	3,344	3,914	5,292	3,344	2,610	4,121	2,652	3,278	4,729	3,388	3,950	5,332
Farm laborers and foremen	3,980	4,281	4,976	3,532	...	3,838	4,140	3,999	5,212	3,980	4,435	4,738
WOMEN 45 TO 49 YEARS OLD												
Professional, technical, and kindred workers	1,751	2,069	3,079	1,678	1,964	2,759	1,873	2,325	3,569	2,994	2,906	4,282
Managers, officials, and proprietors, exc. farm	1,978	2,283	3,493	1,897	2,128	3,261	2,215	2,502	3,810	2,726	3,444	4,772
Clerical, sales, and kindred workers	1,928	2,108	3,242	1,866	1,999	3,094	2,079	2,443	3,627	2,781	2,991	4,699
Craftsmen, foremen, and kindred workers	2,480	2,847	4,224	2,320	2,630	4,008	2,793	3,182	4,600	3,461	3,976	5,182
Operatives and kindred workers	2,753	3,037	4,496	2,514	2,679	4,121	3,107	3,538	5,243	3,482	4,399	5,621
Service workers, including private household	2,416	2,737	4,027	2,283	2,507	3,883	2,915	3,445	4,512	4,158	...	...
Laborers, except farm and mine	3,356	3,627	4,869	3,127	3,230	4,794	3,515	3,922	4,916	4,414	4,431	5,531
Farmers and farm managers	3,510	4,104	5,551	3,100	2,701	4,176	2,843	3,506	5,068	3,568	4,144	5,603
Farm laborers and foremen	4,222	4,270	5,176	3,607	...	4,424	4,456	4,332	5,311	4,235	4,385	5,130

Source: *1950 Census of Population,* Vol. IV, *Special Reports,* Part 5, Chapter C, Fertility, table 28; *1940 Census of Population, Differential Fertility, 1940 and 1910, Fertility by Duration of Marriage,* tables 11 and 13.

FIGURE **26.**—NUMBER OF CHILDREN EVER BORN PER 1,000 WHITE WOMEN 15 TO 49 YEARS OLD MARRIED ONCE AND HUSBAND PRESENT, BY AGE OF WOMAN AND MAJOR OCCUPATION GROUP OF HUSBAND, FOR URBAN AREAS: 1950, 1940, AND 1910

[Data for white women in 1950 and native white women in 1940 and 1910]

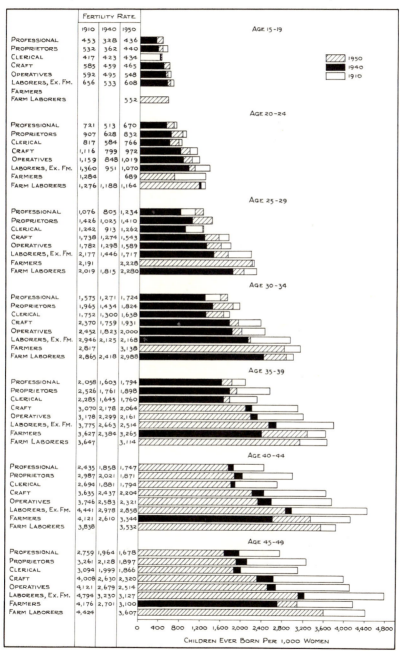

	FERTILITY RATE		
	1910	1940	1950
AGE 15-19			
PROFESSIONAL	453	328	436
PROPRIETORS	532	362	440
CLERICAL	417	423	434
CRAFT	585	459	465
OPERATIVES	592	495	548
LABORERS, Ex. Fm.	656	533	608
FARMERS			
FARM LABORERS			552
AGE 20-24			
PROFESSIONAL	721	513	670
PROPRIETORS	907	628	832
CLERICAL	817	584	766
CRAFT	1,116	799	972
OPERATIVES	1,159	848	1,019
LABORERS, Ex. Fm.	1,360	951	1,070
FARMERS	1,284		689
FARM LABORERS	1,276	1,188	1,164
AGE 25-29			
PROFESSIONAL	1,076	805	1,234
PROPRIETORS	1,426	1,025	1,410
CLERICAL	1,242	913	1,262
CRAFT	1,738	1,274	1,543
OPERATIVES	1,782	1,298	1,589
LABORERS, Ex. Fm.	2,177	1,446	1,717
FARMERS	2,191		2,228
FARM LABORERS	2,019	1,815	2,280
AGE 30-34			
PROFESSIONAL	1,575	1,271	1,724
PROPRIETORS	1,965	1,434	1,824
CLERICAL	1,752	1,300	1,638
CRAFT	2,370	1,759	1,931
OPERATIVES	2,452	1,823	2,000
LABORERS, Ex. Fm.	2,946	2,125	2,168
FARMERS	2,817		3,138
FARM LABORERS	2,865	2,418	2,988
AGE 35-39			
PROFESSIONAL	2,058	1,603	1,794
PROPRIETORS	2,526	1,761	1,898
CLERICAL	2,285	1,645	1,760
CRAFT	3,070	2,178	2,064
OPERATIVES	3,178	2,299	2,161
LABORERS, Ex. Fm.	3,775	2,663	2,514
FARMERS	3,627	2,384	3,265
FARM LABORERS	3,647		3,114
AGE 40-44			
PROFESSIONAL	2,435	1,858	1,747
PROPRIETORS	2,987	2,021	1,871
CLERICAL	2,694	1,881	1,794
CRAFT	3,635	2,437	2,204
OPERATIVES	3,746	2,583	2,321
LABORERS, Ex. Fm.	4,441	2,978	2,858
FARMERS	4,121	2,610	3,344
FARM LABORERS	3,838		3,532
AGE 45-49			
PROFESSIONAL	2,759	1,964	1,678
PROPRIETORS	3,261	2,128	1,897
CLERICAL	3,094	1,999	1,866
CRAFT	4,008	2,630	2,320
OPERATIVES	4,121	2,679	2,514
LABORERS, Ex. Fm.	4,794	3,230	3,127
FARMERS	4,176	2,701	3,100
FARM LABORERS	4,424		3,607

Legend: ▨ 1950 ■ 1940 ☐ 1910

CHILDREN EVER BORN PER 1,000 WOMEN
0 400 800 1,200 1,600 2,000 2,400 2,800 3,200 3,600 4,000 4,400 4,800

Note: Based on data in table 54.

FIGURE **27.**—NUMBER OF CHILDREN EVER BORN PER 1,000 WHITE WOMEN 15 TO 49 YEARS OLD MARRIED ONCE AND HUSBAND PRESENT, BY AGE OF WOMAN AND MAJOR OCCUPATION GROUP OF HUSBAND, FOR RURAL-NONFARM AREAS: 1950, 1940, AND 1910

[Data for white women in 1950 and native white women in 1940 and 1910]

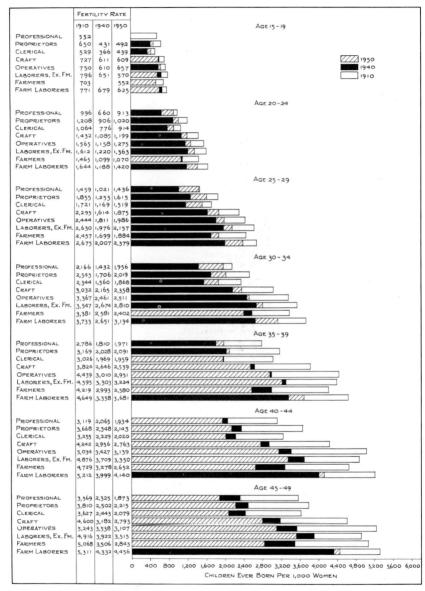

Note: Based on data in table 54.

FIGURE **28.**—NUMBER OF CHILDREN EVER BORN PER 1,000 WHITE WOMEN 15 TO 49 YEARS OLD MARRIED ONCE AND HUSBAND PRESENT, BY AGE OF WOMAN AND MAJOR OCCUPATION GROUP OF HUSBAND, FOR RURAL-FARM AREAS: 1950, 1940, AND 1910

[Data for white women in 1950 and native white women in 1940 and 1910]

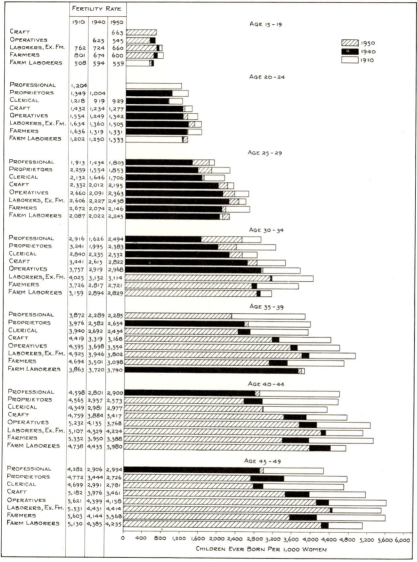

Note: Based on data in table 54.

As expected, in each type of community and within each age and occupational group, the fertility rates tend to be highest in 1910. Below age 35 the rates for urban whites for 1950 tend to surpass those for 1940. At ages 35 and over the rates for all except the white-collar and agricultural classes show a continuous decline from 1910 to 1950.

Despite the relatively high percentage increase in the fertility of wives of professional men at ages under 35, the 1950 fertility levels of the wives of professional men at these ages still tended to be lowest. Again it is emphasized that we are here referring to cumulative fertility rates; the 1950 pattern of fertility ratios relating to children under 5 years old shows a relatively high position for the wives of professional men at ages 30 to 39.

The pattern of differentials in fertility by occupational group is much the same in rural-nonfarm as in urban areas. Within rural-farm areas, too, the familiar inverse relation of fertility to occupational group is found. Also as expected, the 1950 rates for farm laborers tend to surpass those for farmers (owners and tenants) within rural-farm areas. It may be somewhat surprising, however, to find that the fertility rates for both farmers and farm laborers tend to be a little lower than those for residents of rural-farm areas classified as "operatives" and "laborers, except farm and mine." It may be that the semiskilled and unskilled workers living in rural-farm areas are a select group with respect to high fertility. Some may live on farms *because* of high fertility. More specifically, a large family may cause some to live on a subsistence farm because of lower housing and living costs although the husband may have a nonfarm job.

Figures 29, 30, and 31 afford another method of depicting time changes in the fertility of each occupational class. Figure 30 points up the marked increase in the fertility of young women of upper socio-economic status during the 1940–50 decade. Thus, at ages 20 to 34, the fertility rates for urban white wives of professional men actually were higher in 1950 than in 1910. Among urban white wives of professional men in 1950, those 30 to 34 years old already had as many children on the average as did those 45 to 49 years old.

Occupational differentials in the fertility of nonwhites. As with the whites, the age-standardized cumulative fertility rates for nonwhite wives 15 to 49 years old were slightly higher in 1950 than in 1940 within most of the occupation groups (figure 32). Like the whites, the nonwhites tended to exhibit increases in cumulative fertility rates during 1940 to 1950 at ages under 35 and, in most cases, decreases at older ages (figures 33 and 34). The tendency for the 1950 fertility of urban nonwhites to surpass that of urban whites at young ages and to fall below at older ages was most sharply exhibited by the wives of "laborers, except farm and mine," but it was also found for the wives of service workers and clerical workers (figure 35).

FIGURE **29.**—COMPARISON OF THE AGE-SPECIFIC CUMULATIVE FERTILITY RATES OF NATIVE WHITE WOMEN IN 1910 AND 1940 WITH THOSE OF WHITE WOMEN IN 1950, FOR WOMEN 15 TO 49 YEARS OLD MARRIED ONCE AND HUSBAND PRESENT, BY MAJOR OCCUPATION GROUP OF HUSBAND, FOR URBAN AREAS

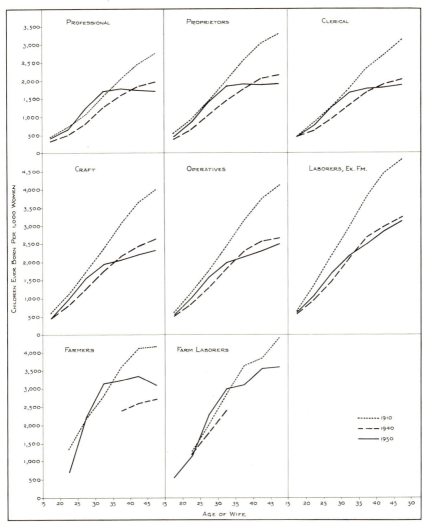

Note: Based on data in table 54.

The 1940–50 percent increases in the fertility of women under 30 years old and married to "laborers, except farm or mine" were much more pronounced for urban nonwhites than for urban whites. This probably reflects relatively greater improvement in economic and health conditions among nonwhites than among whites during this period. The economic changes may have reduced the frequency of husbands seeking work away from

FIGURE **30.**—COMPARISON OF THE AGE-SPECIFIC CUMULATIVE FERTILITY RATES OF NATIVE WHITE WOMEN IN 1910, AND 1940 WITH THOSE OF WHITE WOMEN IN 1950, FOR WOMEN 15 TO 49 YEARS OLD MARRIED ONCE AND HUSBAND PRESENT, BY MAJOR OCCUPATION GROUP OF HUSBAND, FOR RURAL-NONFARM AREAS

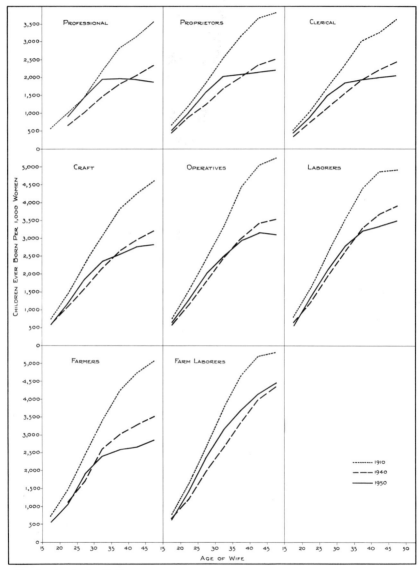

Note: Based on data in table 54.

home, especially for nonwhites.   The improvements in health conditions may have reduced the incidence of sterility.

In 1950, the pattern of fertility differentials by occupation among the nonwhites was much like that of the whites (table 55 and figure 36).   The

FIGURE **31.**—COMPARISON OF THE AGE-SPECIFIC CUMULATIVE FERTILITY RATES OF NATIVE WHITE WOMEN IN 1910 AND 1940 WITH THOSE OF WHITE WOMEN IN 1950, FOR WOMEN 15 TO 49 YEARS OLD MARRIED ONCE AND HUSBAND PRESENT, BY MAJOR OCCUPATION GROUP OF HUSBAND, FOR RURAL-FARM AREAS

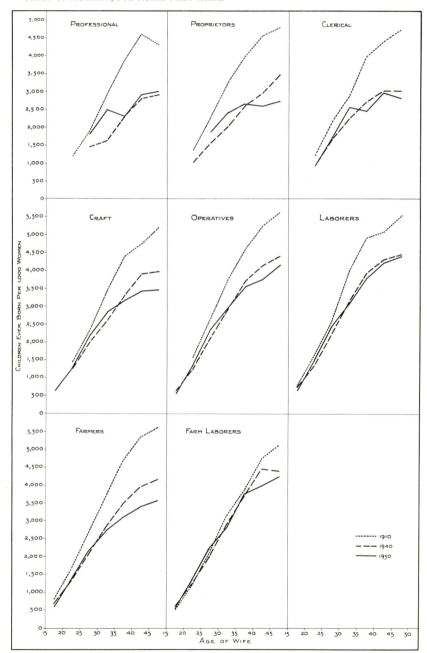

Note: Based on data in table 54.

nonwhite wives of men in white-collar occupations were less fertile than wives of men in manual and farm occupations. However, only 9 percent of the nonwhite wives 15 to 49 years old had husbands in white-collar occupations.

FIGURE 32.—STANDARDIZED NUMBER OF CHILDREN EVER BORN PER 1,000 NONWHITE WOMEN 15 TO 49 YEARS OLD MARRIED ONCE AND HUSBAND PRESENT, BY MAJOR OCCUPATION GROUP OF HUSBAND: 1950 AND 1940

[Data for nonwhite women in 1950 and Negro women in 1940. The standard is the distribution by age of all women 15 to 49 years old married once and husband present, in the United States in 1950]

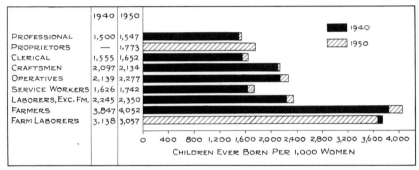

	1940	1950
PROFESSIONAL	1,500	1,547
PROPRIETORS	—	1,773
CLERICAL	1,555	1,652
CRAFTSMEN	2,097	2,134
OPERATIVES	2,139	2,277
SERVICE WORKERS	1,626	1,742
LABORERS, EXC. FM.	2,245	2,350
FARMERS	3,847	4,052
FARM LABORERS	3,138	3,057

Source: Derived from age-specific birth rates in table 55 and from standard distribution computed from *1950 Census of Population,* Vol. IV, *Special Reports,* Part 5, Chapter C, Fertility, table 1.

Fertility rates by occupation and duration of marriage. Special tabulations of number of children ever born by *age of wife and duration of marriage,* by occupation group of the husband, and number of years of school completed by the wife were made for a 1-percent sample of the white women married once and husband present in the United States as a whole in 1950. The basic data appeared in a census release[16] and were discussed in a paper by Tietze and Grabill.[17]

As expected, the patterns of variation in fertility by occupation group and *duration of marriage* are much like those by occupation of husband and *age of wife.* Also as expected, duration of marriage varies for wives of men in different occupations, even within given 5-year age groups. Hence, part of the occupational variations in age-specific fertility rates accrues from occupational differences in duration of marriage.

In figure 37, age-specific fertility rates by occupation group of the husband are presented with and without standardization for duration of marriage. It will be noted that standardization for duration of marriage tends to reduce the range of variation of the age-specific fertility rates, especially in the 25-to-34 and 35-to-39 age groups.

---

[16] *1950 Census of Population,* Series PC–14, No. 22.

[17] Christopher Tietze and Wilson H. Grabill, "Differential Fertility by Duration of Marriage," *Eugenics Quarterly,* Vol. 4, No. 1, March 1957, pp. 3–7.

FIGURE **33.**—NUMBER OF CHILDREN EVER BORN PER 1,000 NONWHITE WOMEN 15 TO 49 YEARS OLD MARRIED ONCE AND HUSBAND PRESENT, BY AGE OF WOMAN AND MAJOR OCCUPATION GROUP OF HUSBAND: 1950, 1940, AND 1910

[Data for nonwhite women in 1950 and Negro women in 1940 and 1910]

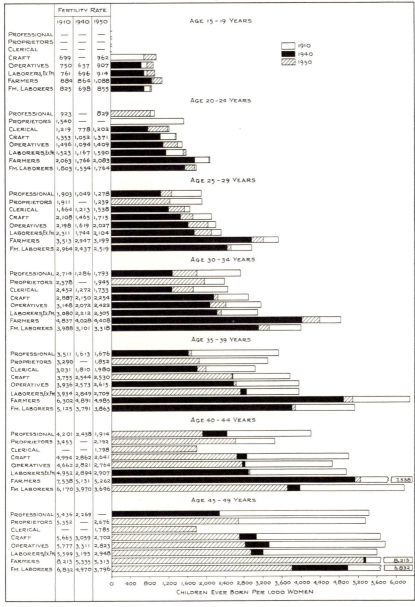

Note: Based on data in table 55.

FIGURE **34.**—COMPARISON OF THE AGE-SPECIFIC CUMULATIVE FERTILITY RATES OF NEGRO WOMEN IN 1940 AND 1910 WITH THOSE OF NONWHITE WOMEN IN 1950, FOR WOMEN 15 TO 49 YEARS OLD MARRIED ONCE AND HUSBAND PRESENT, BY MAJOR OCCUPATION GROUP OF HUSBAND

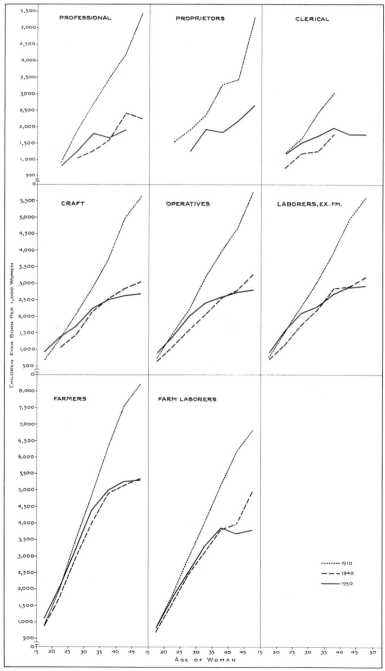

Note: Based on data in table 55.

FIGURE **35.**—COMPARISON OF THE AGE-SPECIFIC CUMULATIVE FERTILITY RATES OF WHITE WOMEN WITH THOSE OF NONWHITE WOMEN 15 TO 49 YEARS OLD MARRIED ONCE AND HUSBAND PRESENT, BY MAJOR OCCUPATION GROUP OF HUSBAND, FOR URBAN AREAS: 1950

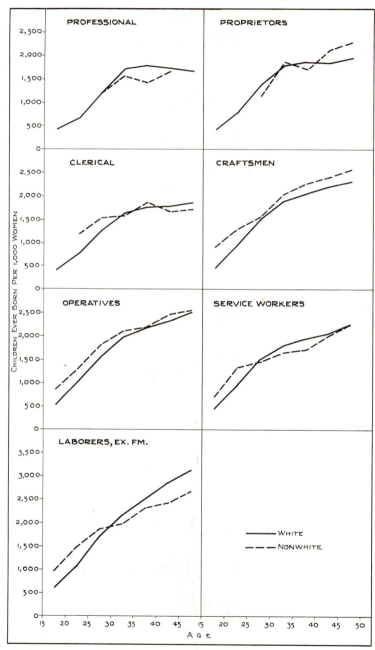

Note: Based on data in tables 54 and 55.

FIGURE **36.**—NUMBER OF CHILDREN EVER BORN PER 1,000 WOMEN 15 TO 49 YEARS OLD MARRIED ONCE AND HUSBAND PRESENT, BY COLOR AND AGE OF WOMAN AND MAJOR OCCUPATION GROUP OF HUSBAND, FOR URBAN AREAS: 1950

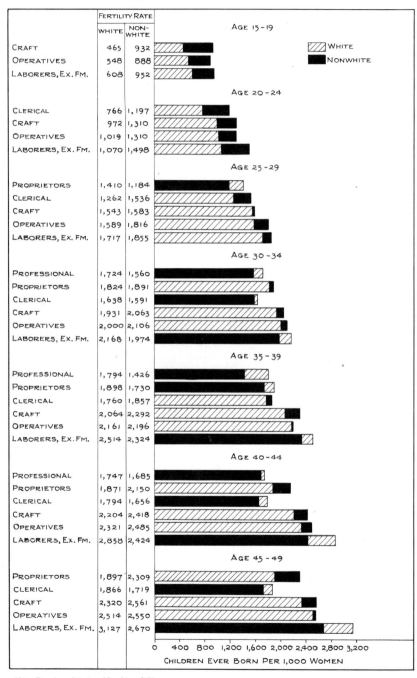

Note: Based on data in tables 54 and 55.

TABLE **55.**—NUMBER OF CHILDREN EVER BORN PER 1,000 NONWHITE WOMEN 15 TO 49 YEARS OLD MARRIED ONCE AND HUSBAND PRESENT, BY AGE OF WOMAN AND MAJOR OCCUPATION GROUP OF HUSBAND: 1950 (WITH URBAN AND RURAL), 1940, AND 1910

[Data for nonwhite women in 1950 and Negro women in 1940 and 1910. Rate not shown where there are fewer than 4,000 women in 1950, 3,000 in 1940, or 1,200 in 1910]

Age of woman and major occupation group of husband	United States			Urban, 1950	Rural nonfarm, 1950	Rural farm, 1950
	1950	1940	1910			
WOMEN 15 TO 19 YEARS OLD						
Professional, technical, and kindred workers.....	...	...	...	...	...	...
Managers, officials, and proprietors, exc. farm..	...	...	...	...	...	...
Clerical, sales, and kindred workers.............	...	...	...	...	...	...
Craftsmen, foremen, and kindred workers..........	962	...	699	932	...	...
Operatives and kindred workers...................	907	637	750	888	951	...
Service workers, including private household.....	763	637	557	738	...	...
Laborers, except farm and mine...................	914	696	761	952	910	...
Farmers and farm managers........................	1,088	864	884	...	...	1,090
Farm laborers and foremen........................	855	698	825	...	883	838
WOMEN 20 TO 24 YEARS OLD						
Professional, technical, and kindred workers.....	829	...	923	...	...	...
Managers, officials, and proprietors, exc. farm..	...	...	1,540	...	...	...
Clerical, sales, and kindred workers.............	1,202	778	1,219	1,197	...	...
Craftsmen, foremen, and kindred workers..........	1,371	1,052	1,353	1,310	...	...
Operatives and kindred workers...................	1,409	1,094	1,496	1,310	1,641	...
Service workers, including private household.....	1,362	875	1,067	1,350	...	...
Laborers, except farm and mine...................	1,590	1,167	1,523	1,498	1,853	...
Farmers and farm managers........................	2,083	1,766	2,063	...	...	2,080
Farm laborers and foremen........................	1,764	1,554	1,803	...	1,849	1,786
WOMEN 25 TO 29 YEARS OLD						
Professional, technical, and kindred workers.....	1,278	1,049	1,903	1,242	...	...
Managers, officials, and proprietors, exc. farm..	1,239	...	1,911	1,184	...	...
Clerical, sales, and kindred workers.............	1,538	1,213	1,664	1,536	...	...
Craftsmen, foremen, and kindred workers..........	1,715	1,465	2,108	1,583	...	...
Operatives and kindred workers...................	2,027	1,619	2,198	1,816	2,735	...
Service workers, including private household.....	1,506	1,151	1,536	1,464	...	...
Laborers, except farm and mine...................	2,104	1,744	2,311	1,855	2,851	...
Farmers and farm managers........................	3,199	2,947	3,513	...	...	3,237
Farm laborers and foremen........................	2,519	2,437	2,964	...	2,446	2,740
WOMEN 30 TO 34 YEARS OLD						
Professional, technical, and kindred workers.....	1,793	1,286	2,714	1,560	...	...
Managers, officials, and proprietors, exc. farm..	1,945	...	2,378	1,891	...	...
Clerical, sales, and kindred workers.............	1,733	1,272	2,452	1,591	...	...
Craftsmen, foremen, and kindred workers..........	2,254	2,150	2,887	2,063	2,987	...
Operatives and kindred workers...................	2,422	2,072	3,148	2,106	3,317	...
Service workers, including private household.....	1,746	1,586	1,909	1,658	...	...
Laborers, except farm and mine...................	2,305	2,212	3,080	1,974	3,210	...
Farmers and farm managers........................	4,408	4,028	4,837	...	...	4,464
Farm laborers and foremen........................	3,318	3,101	3,988	...	3,829	3,286
WOMEN 35 TO 39 YEARS OLD						
Professional, technical, and kindred workers.....	1,676	1,613	3,511	1,426	...	...
Managers, officials, and proprietors, exc. farm..	1,852	...	3,290	1,730	...	...
Clerical, sales, and kindred workers.............	1,980	1,810	3,031	1,857	...	...
Craftsmen, foremen, and kindred workers..........	2,530	2,544	3,755	2,292	...	...
Operatives and kindred workers...................	2,615	2,573	3,936	2,196	3,844	...
Service workers, including private household.....	1,830	1,926	2,625	1,716	...	...
Laborers, except farm and mine...................	2,709	2,849	3,934	2,324	3,742	...
Farmers and farm managers........................	4,985	4,891	6,302	...	...	5,070
Farm laborers and foremen........................	3,863	3,791	5,125	...	4,174	4,074
WOMEN 40 TO 44 YEARS OLD						
Professional, technical, and kindred workers.....	1,914	2,438	4,201	1,685	...	...
Managers, officials, and proprietors, exc. farm..	2,192	...	3,453	2,150	...	...
Clerical, sales, and kindred workers.............	1,798	...	...	1,656	...	...
Craftsmen, foremen, and kindred workers..........	2,641	2,862	4,994	2,418	...	...
Operatives and kindred workers...................	2,764	2,821	4,662	2,485	3,290	...
Service workers, including private household.....	2,066	2,305	3,365	2,015	...	...
Laborers, except farm and mine...................	2,907	2,894	4,952	2,424	4,131	...
Farmers and farm managers........................	5,262	5,131	7,538	...	...	5,382
Farm laborers and foremen........................	3,696	3,970	6,170	...	3,649	...

TABLE **55.**—NUMBER OF CHILDREN EVER BORN PER 1,000 NONWHITE WOMEN 15 TO 49 YEARS
OLD MARRIED ONCE AND HUSBAND PRESENT, BY AGE OF WOMAN AND MAJOR OCCUPATION
GROUP OF HUSBAND: 1950 (WITH URBAN AND RURAL), 1940, AND 1910—Cont.

Age of woman and major occupation group of husband	United States			Urban, 1950	Rural nonfarm, 1950	Rural farm, 1950
	1950	1940	1910			
WOMEN 45 TO 49 YEARS OLD						
Professional, technical, and kindred workers.....	...	2,269	5,436	...	...	...
Managers, officials, and proprietors, exc. farm..	2,676	...	5,352	2,309	...	...
Clerical, sales, and kindred workers.............	1,785	...	...	1,719	...	...
Craftsmen, foremen, and kindred workers..........	2,702	3,059	5,663	2,561	...	...
Operatives and kindred workers...................	2,823	3,311	5,777	2,550	3,557	...
Service workers, including private household.....	2,324	2,379	3,762	2,266	...	...
Laborers, except farm and mine...................	2,948	3,195	5,599	2,670	3,833	...
Farmers and farm managers........................	5,313	5,335	8,213	...	...	5,413
Farm laborers and foremen........................	3,796	4,970	6,832	...	3,759	...

Source: *1950 Census of Population*, Vol. IV, *Special Reports*, Part 5, Chapter C, Fertility, table 29; *1940 Census of Population, Differential Fertility, 1940 and 1910*, Fertility by Duration of Marriage, tables 12 and 14.

FIGURE **37.**—STANDARDIZED AND UNSTANDARDIZED NUMBERS OF CHILDREN EVER BORN PER
1,000 WHITE WOMEN 15 TO 44 YEARS OLD MARRIED ONCE AND HUSBAND PRESENT, BY
AGE OF WOMAN AND MAJOR OCCUPATION GROUP OF HUSBAND: 1950

[The standard is the distribution by duration of marriage of white women 15 to 44 years old married once and husband present, in the United States in 1950]

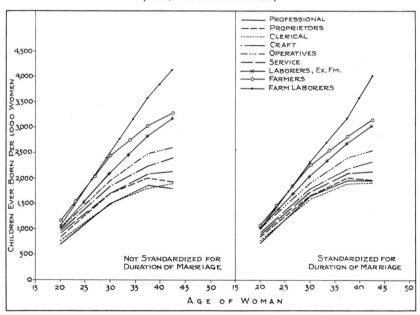

Source: Derived from *1950 Census of Population*, Series PC-14, No. 22, pp. 11–16.

E. Distribution of women by number of children ever born, by age and color of the wife and occupation of the husband

Tables 56, 57, and 58 present 1950 Census data on the distribution of women married once and husband present by number of children ever born, according to urban-rural residence, color and age of the wife, and major occupation group of the husband.   (See also figure 38.)

TABLE **56.**—PERCENT DISTRIBUTION BY NUMBER OF CHILDREN EVER BORN, FOR WOMEN IN SPECIFIED AGE GROUPS MARRIED ONCE AND HUSBAND PRESENT, BY COLOR OF WOMAN AND MAJOR OCCUPATION GROUP OF HUSBAND, FOR URBAN AREAS: 1950

[Occupation of husband not shown for either white or nonwhite women when reported by fewer than 4,000 nonwhite women]

Color and age of woman and major occupation group of husband	Number of women	Percent with specified number of children ever born						Children ever born per 1,000 women
		None	1	2	3	4	5 or more	
WOMEN 25 TO 29 YEARS OLD								
White								
Professional, technical, and kindred wkrs....	306,450	26.3	35.7	28.8	7.5	1.4	0.3	1,234
Managers, officials, and propr's, exc. farm..	276,870	20.4	35.3	31.8	9.2	2.5	0.8	1,410
Clerical, sales, and kindred workers.........	472,860	24.9	37.3	27.7	8.0	1.7	0.5	1,262
Craftsmen, foremen, and kindred workers......	597,900	18.9	33.0	31.1	11.9	3.4	1.7	1,543
Operatives and kindred workers...............	610,800	19.4	32.1	29.7	11.9	4.4	2.5	1,589
Service workers, incl. private household.....	103,800	19.6	34.8	29.1	11.4	3.2	1.9	1,518
Laborers, except farm and mine...............	132,630	19.4	29.7	28.1	13.3	5.4	4.1	1,717
Nonwhite								
Professional, technical, and kindred wkrs....	7,710	38.9	28.4	16.3	5.4	8.6	2.3	1,242
Managers, officials, and propr's, exc. farm..	5,430	37.0	34.3	11.0	12.2	3.9	1.7	1,184
Clerical, sales, and kindred workers.........	17,430	31.7	25.0	19.4	11.5	8.3	4.1	1,536
Craftsmen, foremen, and kindred workers......	26,850	37.9	21.7	14.5	10.9	7.0	7.9	1,583
Operatives and kindred workers...............	70,080	30.1	22.4	17.8	11.1	8.9	9.6	1,816
Service workers, incl. private household.....	36,360	36.6	24.6	16.5	10.7	5.6	5.9	1,464
Laborers, except farm and mine...............	62,520	31.2	20.8	17.4	11.0	9.6	10.0	1,855
WOMEN 35 TO 39 YEARS OLD								
White								
Professional, technical, and kindred wkrs....	256,050	18.0	22.4	35.2	16.6	5.0	2.9	1,794
Managers, officials, and propr's, exc. farm..	425,940	15.7	22.5	35.3	16.6	6.2	3.6	1,898
Clerical, sales, and kindred workers.........	356,370	20.1	24.6	31.4	14.2	5.8	3.9	1,760
Craftsmen, foremen, and kindred workers......	550,410	15.9	22.4	30.2	16.8	7.9	6.8	2,064
Operatives and kindred workers...............	463,050	16.8	20.9	28.3	16.9	8.5	8.6	2,161
Service workers, incl. private household.....	106,890	21.1	20.9	27.3	16.7	7.7	6.2	1,956
Laborers, except farm and mine...............	98,340	15.1	19.0	26.4	14.9	10.3	14.3	2,514
Nonwhite								
Professional, technical, and kindred wkrs....	6,600	40.9	15.5	20.5	14.1	4.5	4.6	1,426
Managers, officials, and propr's, exc. farm..	7,560	29.8	27.4	17.5	8.7	7.1	9.5	1,730
Clerical, sales, and kindred workers.........	9,960	35.8	20.8	12.0	10.2	9.9	11.1	1,857
Craftsmen, foremen, and kindred workers......	22,740	30.5	20.3	16.6	7.3	7.7	17.7	2,292
Operatives and kindred workers...............	48,030	35.7	14.7	15.2	10.2	7.5	16.7	2,196
Service workers, incl. private household.....	31,470	40.6	19.7	13.3	8.3	6.7	11.3	1,716
Laborers, except farm and mine...............	52,440	33.1	18.4	12.8	10.2	7.0	18.5	2,324
WOMEN 45 TO 49 YEARS OLD								
White								
Managers, officials, and propr's, exc. farm..	334,890	19.8	24.5	28.6	14.8	6.3	5.9	1,897
Clerical, sales, and kindred workers.........	260,430	22.4	23.9	27.3	13.6	6.1	6.7	1,866
Craftsmen, foremen, and kindred workers......	404,580	17.6	20.5	24.5	15.9	9.3	12.1	2,320
Operatives and kindred workers...............	280,620	17.3	19.4	23.3	14.8	10.0	15.3	2,514
Service workers, incl. private household.....	98,730	21.1	21.6	22.5	12.9	9.4	12.6	2,283
Laborers, except farm and mine...............	75,510	13.2	14.7	21.7	15.4	11.7	23.4	3,127
Nonwhite								
Managers, officials, and propr's, exc. farm..	4,680	37.8	14.7	14.7	10.9	5.8	16.1	2,309
Clerical, sales, and kindred workers.........	4,710	40.8	17.2	14.0	10.8	7.0	10.1	1,719
Craftsmen, foremen, and kindred workers......	12,210	28.0	18.2	12.3	13.5	8.4	19.7	2,561
Operatives and kindred workers...............	21,480	29.3	20.3	14.8	10.6	5.7	19.3	2,550
Service workers, incl. private household.....	20,010	34.0	21.4	11.7	9.3	6.9	16.6	2,266
Laborers, except farm and mine...............	29,220	31.1	13.2	16.2	11.6	6.2	21.7	2,670

Source: Derived from *1950 Census of Population*, Vol. IV, *Special Reports*, Part 5, Chapter C, Fertility, tables 28 and 29.

Family size by color. At all age and occupational levels considered, the proportions of childless women were higher among the nonwhites in 1950 than among the whites. However, the difference by color was small among wives of farmers and farm managers in rural-farm areas.

TABLE **57.**—PERCENT DISTRIBUTION BY NUMBER OF CHILDREN EVER BORN, FOR WOMEN IN SPECIFIED AGE GROUPS MARRIED ONCE AND HUSBAND PRESENT, BY COLOR OF WOMAN AND MAJOR OCCUPATION GROUP OF HUSBAND, FOR RURAL-NONFARM AREAS: 1950

[Occupation of husband not shown for either white or nonwhite women when reported by fewer than 4,000 nonwhite women]

Color and age of woman and major occupation group of husband	Number of women	Percent with specified number of children ever born						Children ever born per 1,000 women
		None	1	2	3	4	5 or more	
WOMEN 25 TO 29 YEARS OLD								
White								
Operatives and kindred workers.......	246,030	13.9	26.0	30.1	17.0	7.2	5.8	1,986
Laborers, except farm and mine.......	74,190	15.3	22.4	26.5	19.3	8.0	8.5	2,157
Farm laborers and foremen............	29,610	12.4	18.8	25.7	21.5	11.7	9.9	2,379
Nonwhite								
Operatives and kindred workers.......	15,150	17.6	18.2	13.5	18.0	10.1	22.5	2,735
Laborers, except farm and mine.......	17,160	19.1	14.0	15.7	15.2	14.0	22.0	2,851
Farm laborers and foremen............	9,660	23.0	14.6	18.3	14.9	10.9	18.3	2,446
WOMEN 35 TO 39 YEARS OLD								
White								
Operatives and kindred workers.......	166,620	11.4	16.3	23.0	16.6	12.3	20.3	2,951
Laborers, except farm and mine.......	51,630	10.5	14.0	22.6	14.3	13.4	25.2	3,224
Farm laborers and foremen............	21,630	12.5	15.0	12.2	15.7	12.3	32.4	3,681
Nonwhite								
Operatives and kindred workers.......	10,980	22.4	13.1	12.3	7.1	7.9	37.2	3,844
Laborers, except farm and mine.......	13,110	22.2	11.9	10.1	9.2	7.1	39.6	3,742
Farm laborers and foremen............	4,920	22.6	11.6	6.1	9.1	9.1	41.5	4,174
WOMEN 45 TO 49 YEARS OLD								
White								
Operatives and kindred workers.......	87,780	14.1	16.7	19.6	15.0	11.1	23.5	3,107
Laborers, except farm and mine.......	34,620	12.8	12.0	17.6	16.3	12.5	28.7	3,515
Farm laborers and foremen............	15,570	11.6	10.2	13.9	10.8	9.2	44.3	4,456
Nonwhite								
Operatives and kindred workers.......	4,740	19.0	16.5	12.7	15.2	8.9	27.9	3,557
Laborers, except farm and mine.......	5,370	21.8	10.6	14.0	10.6	7.8	35.1	3,833
Farm laborers and foremen............	4,170	27.3	5.8	15.8	7.9	7.2	36.0	3,759

Source: Same as table 56.

It will be noted that the higher percent childless for nonwhites than for whites persisted even among groups in which the average fertility rate was higher for nonwhites. This, in fact, is the usual situation within the rural-nonfarm and rural-farm populations. This means that in rural populations the proportions with large families tend to be higher among the nonwhites than among the whites despite the usually higher proportions childless among the former. Thus, among wives of "operatives" in rural-nonfarm areas the cumulative fertility rate at age 35 to 39 was 2,951 children ever born per 1,000 white women in 1950 and 3,844 per 1,000 nonwhite women. Yet, the percent childless was 22.4 percent for the nonwhites and 11.4 percent for the whites. The proportions with one, two, three, and four children were lower for nonwhites than for whites (collectively 40.4 percent as compared with 68.2 percent). The proportion with five or more children was 37.2 percent for nonwhites as compared with 20.3 percent for whites.

TABLE **58.**—PERCENT DISTRIBUTION BY NUMBER OF CHILDREN EVER BORN, FOR WOMEN IN
SPECIFIED AGE GROUPS MARRIED ONCE AND HUSBAND PRESENT, BY COLOR OF WOMAN AND
MAJOR OCCUPATION GROUP OF HUSBAND, FOR RURAL-FARM AREAS: 1950

[Occupation of husband not shown for either white or nonwhite women when reported by fewer than
4,000 nonwhite women]

Color and age of woman and major occupation group of husband	Number of women	Percent with specified number of children ever born						Children ever born per 1,000 women
		None	1	2	3	4	5 or more	
WOMEN 25 TO 29 YEARS OLD								
White:								
Farmers and farm managers........	293,520	11.6	22.4	31.6	18.8	9.5	6.2	2,146
Farm laborers and foremen........	41,430	14.0	22.2	23.9	19.6	11.0	9.3	2,245
Nonwhite:								
Farmers and farm managers........	38,280	13.8	12.9	15.4	14.0	14.2	29.7	3,237
Farm laborers and foremen........	8,640	20.8	14.9	13.2	18.1	9.0	23.9	2,740
WOMEN 35 TO 39 YEARS OLD								
White:								
Farmers and farm managers........	328,980	10.3	14.0	21.5	18.8	13.0	22.3	3,098
Farm laborers and foremen........	25,260	6.9	11.9	15.8	19.8	12.9	32.6	3,790
Nonwhite:								
Farmers and farm managers........	45,150	11.4	9.6	6.6	9.2	9.0	54.1	5,070
Farm laborers and foremen........	5,820	20.1	10.8	9.3	12.9	8.8	38.1	4,074
WOMEN 45 TO 49 YEARS OLD								
White: Farmers and farm managers.....	280,650	12.0	12.3	18.8	16.1	11.5	29.4	3,568
Nonwhite: Farmers and farm managers..	31,740	13.2	7.5	8.1	8.6	8.3	54.3	5,413

Source: Same as table 56.

Similarly, among certain urban occupational groups in which the average fertility rate of nonwhites was below that of whites by virtue of an especially high proportion childless, the proportion with large families was higher among nonwhites than among whites. Thus, among urban women 35 to 39 years old who were wives of proprietors, the cumulative fertility rate in 1950 was 1,898 among the whites and 1,730 among the nonwhites. The proportions childless were, respectively, 15.7 percent and 29.8 percent. However, the proportion with five or more children was 3.6 percent for the whites and 9.5 percent for the nonwhites.

Among the nonwhite women there appears to be little in the way of systematic differences in proportions childless by occupation of the husband. The women whose husbands were farmers and farm laborers had the smallest percent of childlessness in 1950; those whose husbands were professional and technical workers tended to have the highest percentage of childlessness. However, the variations in proportions childless among the remaining occupational groups were not systematic insofar as nonwhite women were concerned. The women whose husbands were service workers sometimes had a higher percent childless than the women whose husbands were clerical workers or proprietors. Many of the nonwhite service workers were janitors, sextons, and porters. Some of these occupations probably are selective of couples without children. Thus, in some cases only childless couples are hired as caretakers of apartment buildings and as domestic servants. This type of selection may be

FIGURE **38.**—PERCENT DISTRIBUTION BY NUMBER OF CHILDREN EVER BORN FOR WOMEN IN SPECIFIED AGE GROUPS MARRIED ONCE AND HUSBAND PRESENT, BY COLOR OF WOMAN AND MAJOR OCCUPATION GROUP OF HUSBAND, FOR URBAN AREAS: 1950

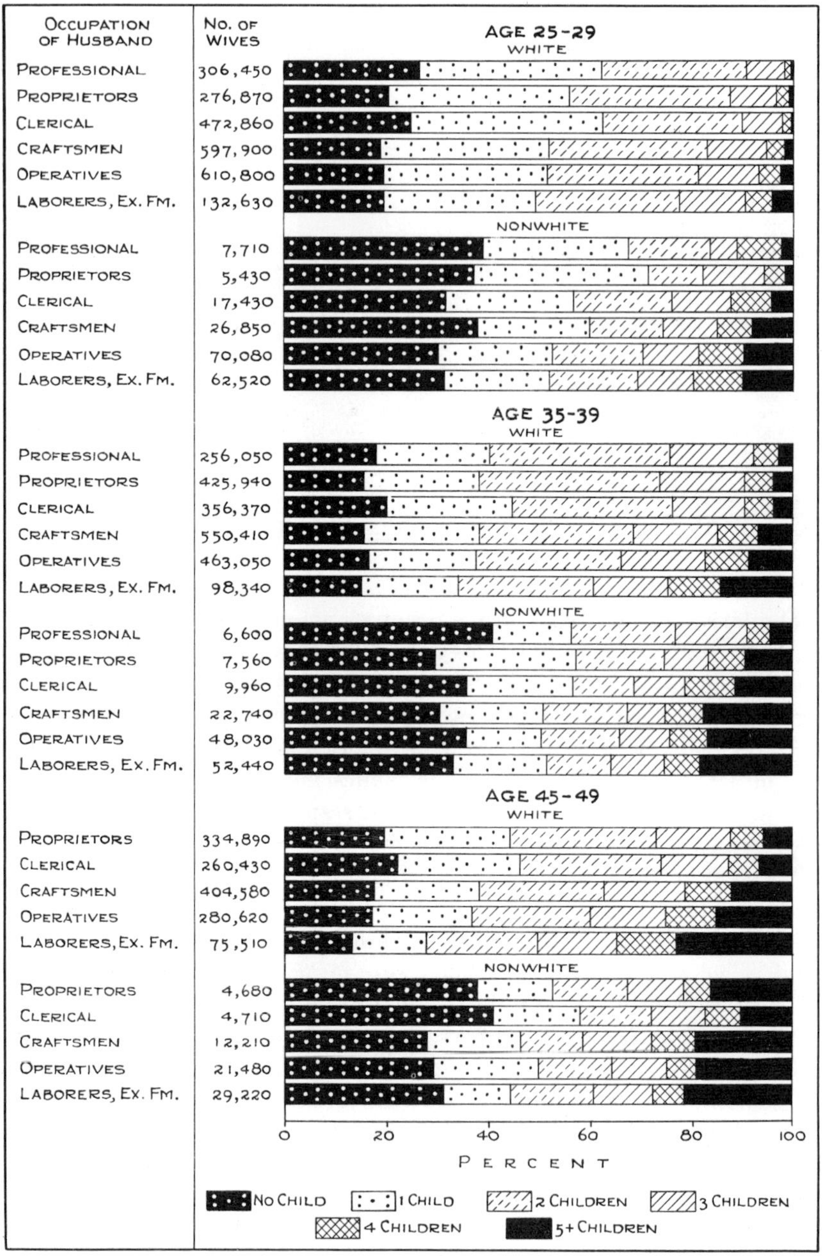

Note: Based on data in table 56.

stronger among nonwhites than among white service workers joining the households of employers. Among nonwhites, the quite high percentage of childlessness among the wives of professional workers and among the wives who have a college education (shown later) reflects to some extent a "late" average age at marriage and some voluntary childlessness. Some of the variation in percent childless by occupation of the husband doubtless reflects the small number of nonwhites in certain occupations and the variability or instability that is associated with small numbers.

Childlessness by occupation. Among urban white wives 45 to 49 years old in 1950, the proportion childless extended from 13 percent for wives of unskilled laborers to 25 percent for wives of professional men. The percent childless was a little higher (22 percent) for wives of clerical workers than for wives of proprietors (20 percent). The proportions with one and two children were also directly related to occupational group. The proportions with four or more live births were inversely associated with occupational status of the husband.

Among urban nonwhite wives 45 to 49 years old, the proportions childless were lowest for wives of skilled workers and semiskilled operatives (28 and 29 percent, respectively) and highest for wives of clerical workers (41 percent) and proprietors (38 percent). The percent childless was 31 for wives of laborers.

The declines in proportions childless among both whites and nonwhites may be seen by internal comparisons of the 1950 data as well as by comparisons of the 1940 and 1950 Census data for women of the same age. Ordinarily, of course, one would expect considerably higher proportions not yet having a child among married women 25 to 29 years old than among those 45 to 49 years old. Actually, however, in 1950 the proportion childless tended to be only a little higher among the urban white married women 25 to 29 years old than among those 45 to 49 years old with husbands of similar occupational status. Similar situations prevailed in rural-nonfarm and rural-farm areas. Likewise, among the nonwhites, the proportions childless frequently were about the same among women 25 to 29 years old as among those 45 to 49 years old with husbands of similar occupational status. Thus the percent childless among urban nonwhite wives of unskilled laborers was 31 at ages 25 to 29 and 31 at ages 45 to 49. Among wives of semiskilled operatives the respective percentages were 30 and 29; among nonwhite wives of skilled craftsmen they were 38 and 28. Among urban nonwhite wives of white-collar workers the percent childless was actually lower at ages 25 to 29 than at ages 45 to 49 (34 and 41 percent, respectively).

Among both whites and nonwhites, the proportion childless decreases and the proportion with four or more children increases as one passes from urban to rural-nonfarm to rural-farm areas. This tends to hold within each occupational group. Thus, among the white wives 25 to 29 years old whose husbands were "laborers, except farm and mine," the proportion childless was 19 percent in urban areas, 15 percent in rural-nonfarm areas and 13 percent in rural-farm areas. The proportions with four or more children were 10 percent, 17 percent, and 24 percent, respectively.

Trends in childlessness among nonwhites during 1940-50. In a previous section, trends in childlessness among whites and nonwhites were analyzed according to residence. The 1940 data on childlessness of nonwhites by occupation group of the husband were not published by residence. However, it is possible from data for the country as a whole to note the 1940-50 trends in childlessness among the nonwhites by occupational class. It is also possible to note the bearing of trends in childlessness on trends in fertility during the decade under consideration.

Table 59 presents for Negro wives in 1940 and for nonwhite wives in 1950 (of similar age and occupation group) the following three sets of data: percent childless and 1940-50 percent change; children ever born per 1,000 wives and 1940-50 percent change; and children ever born per 1,000 mothers and 1940-50 percent change.

It should be emphasized again that 1940-50 comparisons in proportions childless are subject to special limitations inherent in the nonreports on children ever born in 1940 (Appendix A). Suffice it to say here that because childless women formed more than their proportionate share of the group "not reporting on children ever born," the proportions childless among those "reporting on children" were disproportionately low. Hence, if the data indicate a lower percent childless in 1950 than in 1940, it may be assumed that the decrease would be even higher if corrected figures for 1940 were available. Likewise, if the percent childless are higher in 1950 than in 1940, it may be assumed that the increase would be lowered if corrected figures were available. It is likely that some of the 1940-50 "increases" in proportions childless that are of small magnitude would be changed to small "decreases" if corrected figures were available.

Another limitation is one inherent in combining the data for the country as a whole. In both 1940 and 1950 the percent childless among non-white women tended to be considerably higher in urban than in rural areas and the contrast between the urban and rural-farm populations was especially marked. However, although the subdivision by residence is lost in any treatment of the country as a whole, the subdivision by major occupation group yields at least a separation of the farmers and farm laborers from the other occupational groups.

Finally, it should be emphasized again that whereas the 1940 data relate to Negroes, those for 1950 relate to all nonwhites. However, the Negroes comprised about 98 percent of the total nonwhite population in 1950. The percent childless is higher among Negroes than among other nonwhites.

In general, it may be noted that 1940-50 *decreases* generally occurred in the percent childless among nonwhite wives under 40 and *increases* generally occurred among those 40 years old and over.

TABLE **59.**—PERCENT CHILDLESS, NUMBER OF CHILDREN EVER BORN PER 1,000 WOMEN, AND NUMBER OF CHILDREN EVER BORN PER 1,000 MOTHERS, FOR NONWHITE WOMEN 20 TO 49 YEARS OLD MARRIED ONCE AND HUSBAND PRESENT, BY AGE OF WOMAN AND MAJOR OCCUPATION GROUP OF HUSBAND: 1950 AND 1940

[Data for nonwhite women in 1950 and Negro women in 1940. Percent and rate not shown where there are fewer than 4,000 women in 1950 or 3,000 in 1940]

Age of woman and major occupation group of husband	Percent childless			Children ever born per 1,000 women			Children ever born per 1,000 mothers		
	1950	1940	Per-cent change, 1940 to 1950	1950	1940	Per-cent change, 1940 to 1950	1950	1940	Per-cent change, 1940 to 1950
WOMEN 20 TO 24 YEARS OLD									
Profess'l, techn'l, & kindred wkrs..	42.5	...	...	829	...	...	...	...	...
Mgrs., offs., & propr's, exc. farm..	...	...	...	...	...	...	...	...	...
Clerical, sales, & kindred workers..	28.4	56.2	-49.5	1,202	778	54.5	1,678	...	...
Craftsmen, foremen, & kindred wkrs..	30.9	43.1	-28.3	1,371	1,052	30.3	1,983	1,848	7.3
Operatives and kindred workers......	28.8	44.4	-35.1	1,409	1,094	28.8	1,978	1,968	0.5
Service workers, incl. priv. hshld..	30.9	51.9	-40.5	1,362	875	55.7	1,970	1,819	8.3
Laborers, except farm and mine......	24.2	41.7	-42.0	1,590	1,167	36.2	2,098	2,000	4.9
Farmers and farm managers...........	16.9	22.8	-25.9	2,083	1,766	18.0	2,505	2,286	9.6
Farm laborers and foremen...........	21.6	28.9	-25.3	1,764	1,554	13.5	2,249	2,186	2.9
WOMEN 25 TO 29 YEARS OLD									
Profess'l, techn'l, & kindred wkrs..	34.3	55.9	-38.7	1,278	1,049	21.8	1,947	...	...
Mgrs., offs., & propr's, exc. farm..	36.6	...	...	1,239	...	...	...	...	...
Clerical, sales, & kindred workers..	31.8	45.9	-30.7	1,538	1,213	26.8	2,257	...	...
Craftsmen, foremen, & kindred wkrs..	34.8	40.2	-13.4	1,715	1,465	17.1	2,629	2,451	7.3
Operatives and kindred workers......	27.5	40.0	-31.3	2,027	1,619	25.2	2,795	2,697	3.6
Service workers, incl. priv. hshld..	35.7	47.4	-24.7	1,506	1,151	30.8	2,343	2,187	7.1
Laborers, except farm and mine......	28.1	35.8	-21.5	2,104	1,744	20.6	2,924	2,718	7.6
Farmers and farm managers...........	14.1	16.2	-13.0	3,199	2,947	8.6	3,724	3,516	5.9
Farm laborers and foremen...........	23.6	24.0	-1.7	2,519	2,437	3.4	3,296	3,209	2.7
WOMEN 30 TO 34 YEARS OLD									
Profess'l, techn'l, & kindred wkrs..	33.0	45.6	-27.6	1,793	1,286	39.4	2,676	...	...
Mgrs., offs., & propr's, exc. farm..	27.8	...	...	1,945	...	...	2,696	...	...
Clerical, sales, & kindred workers..	34.1	48.4	-29.6	1,733	1,272	36.2	2,631	...	...
Craftsmen, foremen, & kindred wkrs..	30.7	33.5	-8.4	2,254	2,150	4.8	3,254	3,231	0.7
Operatives and kindred workers......	28.8	35.3	-18.4	2,422	2,072	16.9	3,402	3,203	6.2
Service workers, incl. priv. hshld..	38.6	45.5	-15.2	1,746	1,586	10.1	2,845	2,912	-2.3
Laborers, except farm and mine......	30.4	34.2	-11.1	2,305	2,212	4.2	3,312	3,359	-1.4
Farmers and farm managers...........	12.4	13.1	-5.4	4,408	4,028	9.4	5,030	4,634	8.5
Farm laborers and foremen...........	18.5	19.0	-2.6	3,318	3,101	7.0	4,073	3,826	6.5
WOMEN 35 TO 39 YEARS OLD									
Profess'l, techn'l, & kindred wkrs..	37.5	39.6	-5.3	1,676	1,613	3.9	2,683	...	...
Mgrs., offs., & propr's, exc. farm..	28.4	...	...	1,852	...	...	2,587	...	...
Clerical, sales, & kindred workers..	33.8	36.4	-7.2	1,980	1,810	9.4	2,990	...	...
Craftsmen, foremen, & kindred wkrs..	29.2	33.3	-12.3	2,530	2,544	-0.6	3,572	3,812	-6.3
Operatives and kindred workers......	32.5	31.9	1.9	2,615	2,573	1.6	3,876	3,779	2.6
Service workers, incl. priv. hshld..	39.9	41.8	-4.6	1,830	1,926	-5.0	3,044	3,307	-8.0
Laborers, except farm and mine......	30.3	26.9	12.6	2,709	2,849	-4.9	3,884	3,897	-0.3
Farmers and farm managers...........	11.6	13.4	-13.4	4,985	4,891	1.9	5,638	5,649	-0.2
Farm laborers and foremen...........	24.4	18.4	32.6	3,863	3,791	1.9	5,109	4,645	10.0
WOMEN 40 TO 44 YEARS OLD									
Profess'l, techn'l, & kindred wkrs..	42.9	29.7	44.4	1,914	2,438	-21.5	...	...	...
Mgrs., offs., & propr's, exc. farm..	30.5	...	...	2,192	...	...	3,154	...	...
Clerical, sales, & kindred workers..	37.7	...	...	1,798	...	...	2,885	...	...
Craftsmen, foremen, & kindred wkrs..	30.6	26.3	16.3	2,641	2,862	-7.7	3,806	3,883	-2.0
Operatives and kindred workers......	30.3	29.8	1.7	2,764	2,821	-2.0	3,967	4,021	-1.4
Service workers, incl. priv. hshld..	34.8	35.0	-0.6	2,066	2,305	-10.4	3,166	3,544	-10.7
Laborers, except farm and mine......	30.5	29.9	2.0	2,907	2,894	0.4	4,184	4,131	1.3
Farmers and farm managers...........	15.1	12.0	25.8	5,262	5,131	2.6	6,195	5,830	6.3
Farm laborers and foremen...........	22.4	17.1	31.0	3,696	3,970	-6.9	4,763	4,786	-0.5

TABLE **59.**—PERCENT CHILDLESS, NUMBER OF CHILDREN EVER BORN PER 1,000 WOMEN, AND NUMBER OF CHILDREN EVER BORN PER 1,000 MOTHERS, FOR NONWHITE WOMEN 20 TO 49 YEARS OLD MARRIED ONCE AND HUSBAND PRESENT, BY AGE OF WOMAN AND MAJOR OCCUPATION GROUP OF HUSBAND: 1950 AND 1940—Cont.

Age of woman and major occupation group of husband	Percent childless			Children ever born per 1,000 women			Children ever born per 1,000 mothers		
	1950	1940	Percent change, 1940 to 1950	1950	1940	Percent change, 1940 to 1950	1950	1940	Percent change, 1940 to 1950
WOMEN 45 TO 49 YEARS OLD									
Profess'l, techn'l, & kindred wkrs..	...	29.6	...	...	2,269	...	...	...	...
Mgrs., offs., & propr's, exc. farm..	34.4	...	...	2,676	...	...	...	...	...
Clerical, sales, & kindred workers..	39.4	...	...	1,785	...	...	...	...	...
Craftsmen, foremen, & kindred wkrs..	27.3	27.8	-1.8	2,702	3,059	-11.7	3,719	4,237	-12.2
Operatives and kindred workers......	26.7	25.7	3.9	2,823	3,311	-14.7	3,852	4,457	-13.6
Service workers, incl. priv. hshld..	33.0	34.6	-4.6	2,324	2,379	-2.3	3,467	3,636	-4.7
Laborers, except farm and mine......	28.7	22.8	25.9	2,948	3,195	-7.7	4,134	4,140	-0.2
Farmers and farm managers...........	13.8	11.7	17.9	5,313	5,335	-0.4	6,161	6,042	2.0
Farm laborers and foremen...........	22.3	12.4	79.8	3,796	4,970	-23.6	4,888	5,672	-13.8

Source: Derived from *1950 Census of Population*, Vol. IV, *Special Reports*, Part 5, Chapter C, Fertility, table 29; *1940 Census of Population, Differential Fertility, 1940 and 1910*, Fertility by Duration of Marriage, table 12.

By occupation group, the decreases in proportion childless during 1940 to 1950 were relatively small among the two agricultural classes, farmers and farm laborers. This arises from the fact that among the nonwhites in rural-farm areas, the proportion childless was already small in 1940, so that there was not much chance for a substantial decrease. For example, among nonwhite wives of farmers, the proportion childless at 30 to 34 years old was 13.1 percent in 1940 and 12.4 percent in 1950, a decrease of only 5.4 percent. Among comparable wives of farm laborers, the percents were 19.0 in 1940 and 18.5 in 1950, a decline of only 2.6 percent. Among nonwhite wives of professional men, in contrast, the percents were 45.6 in 1940 and 33.0 in 1950, a decline of 27.6 percent.

Other classes exhibiting relatively high proportions childless in 1940 and relatively sharp decreases during 1940 to 1950 were the clerical workers, service workers, operatives, and laborers, except farm and mine.

It will be noted that much of the 1940–50 increase in fertility among nonwhites was due to decreases in proportions childless. The 1940–50 changes in the fertility of nonwhite "mothers," that is, women who had at least one live birth, were relatively small. For instance, among nonwhite wives of "operatives" (semiskilled workers) the cumulative fertility rate at age 25 to 29 was 1,619 children ever born per 1,000 wives in 1940 and 2,027 in 1950, an increase of 25 percent. Among the "mothers" the fertility rate increased from 2,697 to 2,795, or by less than 4 percent. The explanation is that childlessness declined from a level of 40 percent of the couples in 1940 to 28 percent in 1950.

Among women 45 to 49 years old, the higher proportion childless in 1950 as compared to 1940 is part and parcel of the previously described declines in completed fertility rates. It has been noted previously that whereas women who were nearing the end of their childbearing periods during 1940 to 1950 did exhibit somewhat higher *current fertility* rates than did their counterparts during the 1930–40 decade, their participation in the "baby boom" was not sufficient to prevent lower completed fertility rates in 1950 than in 1940.   There appears to be little systematic difference by occupation in the 1940–50 increases in childlessness among nonwhites 40 years old and over.   It is possible that a substantial part of the decrease in childlessness among nonwhites at ages under 40 years during the 1940–50 decade has been due to an improvement in health conditions.   In 1950, the percents childless among ever-married women under 25 years old were generally lower among nonwhites than whites, even in urban areas.

F. Fertility ratios by occupation group of the husband, 1910, 1940, and 1950

Fertility ratios standardized for age of women are presented in figure 39 by major occupation group of the husband for the years 1940 and 1950. These relate to native white women in 1940 and to white women in 1950, 15 to 49 years old married once and husband present.   Figure 40 presents the data for Negroes in 1910 and for nonwhites in 1950.   Also as before, the 1950 classification by urban-rural residence is based upon the "new" definition of urban, whereas those for 1910 and 1940 are based upon the "old" definition.

The age-standardized fertility ratios for 1950 were higher than those for 1940 among whites at nearly all occupational levels.   Furthermore, the 1950 ratios were higher than those for 1910 among nonwhites in nearly all occupational groups.   This reflects the conspicuously high fertility during the 5 years preceding 1950—a period of demobilization, early marriages, and high employment levels.

The 1940–50 change in the pattern of standardized fertility ratios was less conspicuous by occupation of the husband than by education of the wife (considered in the next chapter).   However, the increases in fertility ratios over the decade were definitely higher in the white-collar groups than in the others, and there was a definite reduction in the range of variations in fertility ratios by occupation group.

Age-specific fertility ratios by occupational class of the husband are shown for whites in table 60 and for nonwhites in table 61 for the years 1910, 1940, and 1950.   Figure 41 points up the relatively low levels of fertility ratios in 1940 as compared with 1910 and 1950.   As brought out better in figures 42, 43, and 44, the fertility ratios for 1950 are frequently higher than those for 1910 among women of comparable age, residence, and occupation group of the husband.   The excess of the 1950 over the 1910 ratios is especially striking among urban white women 20 to 34 years old who were wives of white-collar workers.

TABLE 60.—NUMBER OF OWN CHILDREN UNDER 5 YEARS OLD PER 1,000 WHITE WOMEN 15 TO 49 YEARS OLD MARRIED ONCE AND HUSBAND PRESENT, BY AGE OF WOMAN AND MAJOR OCCUPATION GROUP OF HUSBAND, URBAN AND RURAL: 1950, 1940, AND 1910

[Data for white women in 1950 and native white women in 1940 and 1910. Ratio not shown where there are fewer than 4,000 women in 1950, 3,000 in 1940, or 1,200 in 1910]

Age of woman and major occupation group of husband	United States			Urban			Rural nonfarm			Rural farm		
	1950	1940	1910	1950	1940	1910	1950	1940	1910	1950	1940	1910
WOMEN 15 TO 19 YEARS OLD												
Professional, technical, and kindred workers	397	295	340	376	285	316	...	...	343	...	...	...
Managers, officials, and proprietors, exc. farm	436	340	427	424	305	405	464	376	451	...	...	...
Clerical, sales, and kindred workers	390	343	327	386	344	312	396	316	356	...	...	...
Craftsmen, foremen, and kindred workers	495	442	460	442	392	431	581	522	512	663	529	...
Operatives and kindred workers	551	475	485	525	433	437	614	517	537	479	538	...
Service workers, including private household	487	401	445	438	374	431	...	500	487	...	...	...
Laborers, except farm and mine	560	593	515	...	541	480	539	617	546	605	657	474
Farmers and farm managers	527	514	552	...	...	...	455	...	440	539	518	556
Farm laborers and foremen	516	466	444	493	439	...	578	542	517	484	449	312
WOMEN 20 TO 24 YEARS OLD												
Professional, technical, and kindred workers	648	450	598	615	407	519	802	532	706	...	693	817
Managers, officials, and proprietors, exc. farm	780	566	750	743	511	677	883	678	843	...	709	949
Clerical, sales, and kindred workers	723	540	655	704	505	612	820	675	761	777	706	867
Craftsmen, foremen, and kindred workers	912	740	873	861	673	807	1,038	861	1,010	1,038	931	1,016
Operatives and kindred workers	957	783	936	889	705	848	1,079	899	1,075	1,109	961	1,082
Service workers, including private household	884	668	789	847	625	764	1,055	813	858	...	...	...
Laborers, except farm and mine	1,014	983	1,020	914	881	944	1,153	1,032	1,093	1,240	1,174	1,055
Farmers and farm managers	1,102	969	1,128	816	...	940	919	881	987	1,126	976	1,134
Farm laborers and foremen	1,092	936	1,013	924	882	870	1,157	924	1,116	1,083	946	781
WOMEN 25 TO 29 YEARS OLD												
Professional, technical, and kindred workers	947	601	730	931	568	654	1,021	670	838	985	769	1,057
Managers, officials, and proprietors, exc. farm	924	633	844	914	615	772	943	665	943	1,054	772	1,103
Clerical, sales, and kindred workers	896	594	759	883	570	701	957	686	928	1,028	839	1,059
Craftsmen, foremen, and kindred workers	945	718	954	926	677	896	978	785	1,078	1,094	895	1,061
Operatives and kindred workers	965	749	985	928	684	901	1,030	843	1,142	1,110	942	1,177
Service workers, including private household	941	645	802	939	623	765	934	714	902	...	800	...
Laborers, except farm and mine	1,010	935	1,098	972	809	1,014	1,051	1,005	1,187	1,129	1,146	1,146
Farmers and farm managers	1,150	994	1,275	941	772	1,088	1,034	889	1,144	1,163	999	1,281
Farm laborers and foremen	1,160	963	1,116	1,091	952	962	1,173	952	1,232	1,172	969	994
WOMEN 30 TO 34 YEARS OLD												
Professional, technical, and kindred workers	855	571	677	852	565	619	866	589	754	874	585	970
Managers, officials, and proprietors, exc. farm	714	490	670	722	480	603	675	506	762	740	560	962
Clerical, sales, and kindred workers	709	476	620	709	463	588	697	517	702	831	629	892
Craftsmen, foremen, and kindred workers	663	504	759	652	476	699	685	530	870	724	678	958
Operatives and kindred workers	667	530	799	646	470	719	693	609	946	794	740	1,042
Service workers, including private household	640	461	659	635	447	625	663	510	771	...	...	...

TABLE 60.—NUMBER OF OWN CHILDREN UNDER 5 YEARS OLD PER 1,000 WHITE WOMEN 15 TO 49 YEARS OLD MARRIED ONCE AND HUSBAND PRESENT, BY AGE OF WOMAN AND MAJOR OCCUPATION GROUP OF HUSBAND, URBAN AND RURAL: 1950, 1940, AND 1910—Cont.

Age of woman and major occupation group of husband	United States			Urban			Rural nonfarm			Rural farm		
	1950	1940	1910	1950	1940	1910	1950	1940	1910	1950	1940	1910
WOMEN 30 TO 34 YEARS OLD—Cont.												
Laborers, except farm and mine	726	715	884	700	606	799	777	741	970	716	959	1,097
Farmers and farm managers	812	764	1,099	946	673	839	748	707	958	813	766	1,106
Farm laborers and foremen	862	772	1,034	944	716	856	857	773	1,071	843	778	959
WOMEN 35 TO 39 YEARS OLD												
Professional, technical, and kindred workers	499	339	487	498	323	428	521	370	574	369	466	752
Managers, officials, and proprietors, exc. farm	409	261	481	405	248	425	413	277	563	475	373	715
Clerical, sales, and kindred workers	418	261	432	413	250	396	429	290	524	490	406	738
Craftsmen, foremen, and kindred workers	392	316	566	373	277	506	422	360	667	502	505	808
Operatives and kindred workers	420	351	626	379	301	538	490	404	788	572	570	867
Service workers, including private household	402	267	459	386	249	424	448	291	589	552	552	...
Laborers, except farm and mine	501	499	693	451	378	623	550	526	766	639	755	906
Farmers and farm managers	525	532	879	476	322	655	512	410	733	527	538	887
Farm laborers and foremen	617	566	804	577	469	618	595	547	840	648	589	728
WOMEN 40 TO 44 YEARS OLD												
Professional, technical, and kindred workers	194	116	244	194	104	204	196	146	285	174	222	496
Managers, officials, and proprietors, exc. farm	164	97	253	159	89	213	181	104	313	196	180	439
Clerical, sales, and kindred workers	164	109	208	157	100	185	178	135	265	315	187	413
Craftsmen, foremen, and kindred workers	175	154	312	157	132	277	193	173	372	333	297	470
Operatives and kindred workers	197	181	363	172	145	305	233	219	480	317	347	579
Service workers, including private household	154	143	251	139	133	239	217	150	299	...	301	...
Laborers, except farm and mine	249	284	391	228	222	351	232	313	444	415	398	454
Farmers and farm managers	294	305	543	308	179	332	298	225	431	294	309	550
Farm laborers and foremen	418	325	489	318	340	316	424	290	514	449	339	499
WOMEN 45 TO 49 YEARS OLD												
Professional, technical, and kindred workers	32	22	56	31	19	39	33	28	79	42	41	132
Managers, officials, and proprietors, exc. farm	22	20	63	20	16	50	29	20	85	46	69	112
Clerical, sales, and kindred workers	31	24	50	27	21	48	44	34	57	72	48	72
Craftsmen, foremen, and kindred workers	37	38	84	32	31	71	50	46	107	60	75	154
Operatives and kindred workers	44	50	101	34	37	81	54	69	141	117	98	156
Service workers, including private household	26	37	69	23	29	61	34	61	100	67	58	...
Laborers, except farm and mine	58	94	107	44	68	96	76	97	119	93	163	175
Farmers and farm managers	83	91	158	208	37	111	88	57	117	78	93	160
Farm laborers and foremen	96	90	136	38	78	107	133	53	144	83	114	124

Source: Derived from 1950 Census of Population, Vol. IV, Special Reports, Part 5, Chapter C, Fertility, table 48; 1940 Census of Population, Differential Fertility, 1940 and 1910, Women by Number of Children Under 5 Years Old, tables 41 and 42.

THE FERTILITY OF AMERICAN WOMEN

TABLE 61.—NUMBER OF OWN CHILDREN UNDER 5 YEARS OLD PER 1,000 NONWHITE WOMEN 15 TO 49 YEARS OLD MARRIED ONCE AND HUSBAND PRESENT, BY AGE OF WOMAN AND MAJOR OCCUPATION GROUP OF HUSBAND: 1950 (WITH URBAN AND RURAL) AND 1910

[Data for nonwhite women in 1950 and Negro Women in 1910. Ratio not shown where there are fewer than 4,000 women in 1950 or 1,200 in 1910]

Age of woman and major occupation group of husband	United States 1950	United States 1910	Urban, 1950	Rural nonfarm, 1950	Rural farm, 1950
WOMEN 15 TO 19 YEARS OLD					
Professional, technical, and kindred workers........	...	...	...	...	...
Managers, officials, and proprietors, except farm...	...	...	...	...	...
Clerical, sales, and kindred workers................	...	...	...	...	...
Craftsmen, foremen, and kindred workers.............	914	463	888	...	...
Operatives and kindred workers......................	811	446	815	834	...
Service workers, including private household........	718	342	691	...	...
Laborers, except farm and mine......................	781	468	798	807	...
Farmers and farm managers...........................	982	567	...	...	988
Farm laborers and foremen...........................	736	496	...	773	704
WOMEN 20 TO 24 YEARS OLD					
Professional, technical, and kindred workers........	747	598	...	...	...
Managers, officials, and proprietors, except farm...	...	800	...	...	...
Clerical, sales, and kindred workers................	965	758	962	...	...
Craftsmen, foremen, and kindred workers.............	1,044	692	993	...	...
Operatives and kindred workers......................	1,046	776	968	1,226	...
Service workers, including private household........	1,023	580	1,009	...	...
Laborers, except farm and mine......................	1,169	757	1,122	1,310	...
Farmers and farm managers...........................	1,462	1,144	...	...	1,455
Farm laborers and foremen...........................	1,251	962	...	1,305	1,294
WOMEN 25 TO 29 YEARS OLD					
Professional, technical, and kindred workers........	783	726	755	...	...
Managers, officials, and proprietors, except farm...	510	620	530	...	...
Clerical, sales, and kindred workers................	766	645	771	...	...
Craftsmen, foremen, and kindred workers.............	751	715	687	...	...
Operatives and kindred workers......................	883	713	808	1,103	...
Service workers, including private household........	708	503	685	...	...
Laborers, except farm and mine......................	891	710	793	1,191	...
Farmers and farm managers...........................	1,386	1,268	...	...	1,417
Farm laborers and foremen...........................	1,145	1,030	...	1,025	1,309
WOMEN 30 TO 34 YEARS OLD					
Professional, technical, and kindred workers........	566	622	576	...	...
Managers, officials, and proprietors, except farm...	634	493	610	...	...
Clerical, sales, and kindred workers................	530	533	515	...	...
Craftsmen, foremen, and kindred workers.............	580	554	544	739	...
Operatives and kindred workers......................	636	579	549	894	...
Service workers, including private household........	464	391	438	...	...
Laborers, except farm and mine......................	571	608	470	872	...
Farmers and farm managers...........................	1,177	1,098	...	...	1,193
Farm laborers and foremen...........................	806	874	...	900	826
WOMEN 35 TO 39 YEARS OLD					
Professional, technical, and kindred workers........	448	454	386	...	...
Managers, officials, and proprietors, except farm...	356	448	357	...	...
Clerical, sales, and kindred workers................	360	469	331	...	...
Craftsmen, foremen, and kindred workers.............	386	438	340	...	...
Operatives and kindred workers......................	428	509	342	661	...
Service workers, including private household........	282	304	264	...	...
Laborers, except farm and mine......................	474	501	412	664	...
Farmers and farm managers...........................	873	971	...	...	889
Farm laborers and foremen...........................	645	760	...	793	588
WOMEN 40 TO 44 YEARS OLD					
Professional, technical, and kindred workers........	244	191	160	...	...
Managers, officials, and proprietors, except farm...	94	207	96	...	...
Clerical, sales, and kindred workers................	150	...	143	...	...
Craftsmen, foremen, and kindred workers.............	195	315	148	...	...
Operatives and kindred workers......................	199	301	158	272	...
Service workers, including private household........	165	177	165	...	...
Laborers, except farm and mine......................	232	300	156	422	...
Farmers and farm managers...........................	526	634	...	...	533
Farm laborers and foremen...........................	256	493	...	224	...

TABLE **61**.—Number of Own Children Under 5 Years Old per 1,000 Nonwhite Women 15 to 49 Years Old Married Once and Husband Present, by Age of Woman and Major Occupation Group of Husband: 1950 (with Urban and Rural) and 1910—Cont.

Age of woman and major occupation group of husband	United States		Urban, 1950	Rural nonfarm, 1950	Rural farm, 1950
	1950	1910			
WOMEN 45 TO 49 YEARS OLD					
Professional, technical, and kindred workers........	...	68	...	...	...
Managers, officials, and proprietors, except farm...	151	81	90	...	...
Clerical, sales, and kindred workers.................	51	...	45	...	...
Craftsmen, foremen, and kindred workers.............	211	130	214	...	...
Operatives and kindred workers......................	61	128	61	44	...
Service workers, including private household........	59	74	54	...	...
Laborers, except farm and mine......................	112	126	85	212	...
Farmers and farm managers...........................	173	303	...	...	173
Farm laborers and foremen...........................	170	239	...	144	...

Source: *1950 Census of Population*, Vol. IV, *Special Reports*, Part 5, Chapter C, Fertility, table 49; *1940 Census of Population, Differential Fertility, 1940 and 1910*, Women by Number of Children Under 5 Years Old, table 43.

Figure 41 does not yield precisely the same types of results as those brought out in the next chapter in a similar chart by educational attainment. It is noted in the next chapter that in both 1940 and 1950 there was a marked reversal with age in the direction of the education-fertility ratio relationship. More specifically, at ages under 25, the inverse relation was found and at ages 30 to 34 and 35 to 39 a rather marked direct relation was found. This is described as arising from differences by education in age at marriage and spacing of children. Figure 41 does not afford any comparable instance of direct relation of occupation group to fertility ratio. It will be noted, however, that among urban white wives 30 to 34 and 35 to 39 years old the highest fertility ratios in 1950 are those for wives of professional men. A similar situation is found with respect to the rural-nonfarm group of wives 30 to 34 years of age.

The inverse relation of occupation group to fertility ratio is clear-cut among young women. This inverse relation persisted to later ages in the data for 1910 and 1940 than in those for 1950. In 1950, the total range of variation in fertility ratios at ages 25 to 29 was narrow and, except for relatively high ratios for wives of professional men at ages 30 to 34, the ratios were much the same in magnitude. It is, of course, in the nature of the case that all fertility ratios approach zero by about age 50.

G. Proportionate contribution of children by specific occupation groups

Table 62 indicates the extent to which the wives of men in white-collar occupations (professional, proprietary, and clerical) had contributed their proportionate share of children ever born and children under 5 years old in 1950. The data are shown by age, color, and urban-rural residence. The proportion of women of given age group with husbands of white-collar status provides the "expected" proportion. For instance, among white

FIGURE **39.**—STANDARDIZED NUMBER OF OWN CHILDREN UNDER 5 YEARS OLD PER 1,000 WHITE WOMEN 15 TO 49 YEARS OLD MARRIED ONCE AND HUSBAND PRESENT, BY MAJOR OCCUPATION GROUP OF HUSBAND, URBAN AND RURAL: 1950 AND 1940

[Data for white women in 1950 and native white women in 1940. The standard is the distribution by age of all women 15 to 49 years old married once and husband present, in the United States in 1950]

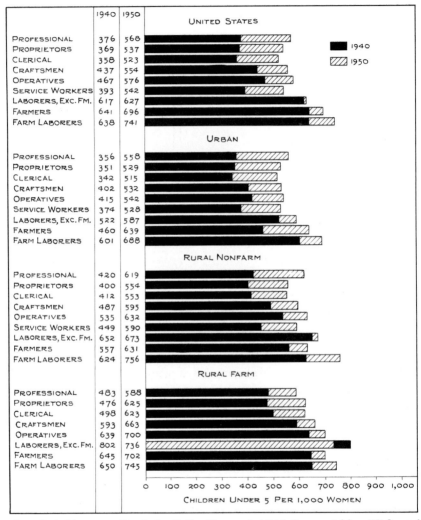

Source: Derived from age-specific ratios in table 60 and from standard distribution computed from *1950 Census of Population*, Vol. IV, *Special Reports*, Part 5, Chapter C, Fertility, table 1.

women 25 to 29 years old, 34.3 percent were wives of white-collar workers. These women contributed a little less than their expected quota; they contributed 28.2 percent of the children ever born and 32.5 percent of the children under 5 years old born to white women 25 to 29 years of age in 1950.

FIGURE **40.**—STANDARDIZED NUMBER OF OWN CHILDREN UNDER 5 YEARS OLD PER 1,000 NONWHITE WOMEN 15 TO 49 YEARS OLD MARRIED ONCE AND HUSBAND PRESENT, BY MAJOR OCCUPATION OF HUSBAND: 1950 AND 1910

[Data for nonwhite women in 1950 and Negro women in 1910. The standard is the distribution by age of all women 15 to 49 years old married once and husband present, in the United States in 1950]

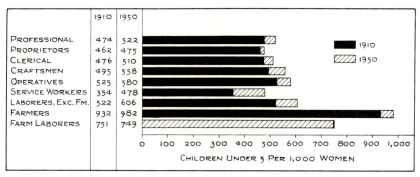

Source: Derived from age-specific ratios in table 61 and from standard distribution computed from *1950 Census of Population*, Vol. IV, *Special Reports*, Part 5, Chapter C, Fertility, table 1.

Whereas table 62 is restricted to the white-collar class, figure 45 depicts for three age groups of women the complete distributions of the women, children ever born, and children under 5 years old, with respect to occupation group of the husbands of the women concerned.

From both types of data it is clear that in the United States in 1950 the whites in the white-collar classes had failed to contribute their proportionate share of *children ever born* despite the notable increase in fertility rates in these classes. The margin of this failure tends to become wider after age 35 because at these ages the number of children ever born is influenced by current fertility only to a minor extent. Also, among the nonwhites in the United States, the white-collar workers failed to contribute their proportionate share of children ever born or children under 5 years old except at youngest ages (table 62).

Their past history of low fertility accounts for much of the failure of the wives of white-collar workers to contribute their proportionate share of children ever born. The wives of the white-collar workers make a much better showing with respect to children under 5 years old. At ages 30 to 34 this group contributed a little more than its proportionate share of children of this age. At ages 35 to 39 it contributed almost exactly its proportionate share, and at ages 25 to 29 the deficit of children under 5 years old was very slight. Within the urban areas the wives of white-collar workers contributed substantially more than their proportionate share of children at ages 30 to 39 and their approximate share at ages 25 to 29 and 40 to 44.

As already indicated, the data regarding children under 5 years old provide better criteria of current fertility than do data on children ever

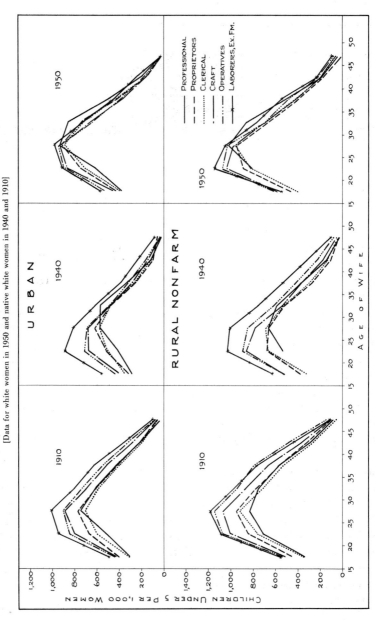

FIGURE 41.—NUMBER OF OWN CHILDREN UNDER 5 YEARS OLD PER 1,000 WHITE WOMEN 15 TO 49 YEARS OLD MARRIED ONCE AND HUSBAND PRESENT, BY AGE OF WOMAN AND MAJOR OCCUPATION GROUP OF HUSBAND, FOR URBAN AND RURAL-NONFARM AREAS: 1950, 1940, AND 1910

[Data for white women in 1950 and native white women in 1940 and 1910]

Note: Based on data in table 60.

FIGURE **42.**—COMPARISON OF THE AGE-SPECIFIC FERTILITY RATIOS OF NATIVE WHITE WOMEN IN 1910 AND 1940 WITH THOSE OF WHITE WOMEN IN 1950, FOR WOMEN 15 TO 49 YEARS OLD MARRIED ONCE AND HUSBAND PRESENT, BY MAJOR OCCUPATION GROUP OF HUSBAND, FOR URBAN AREAS

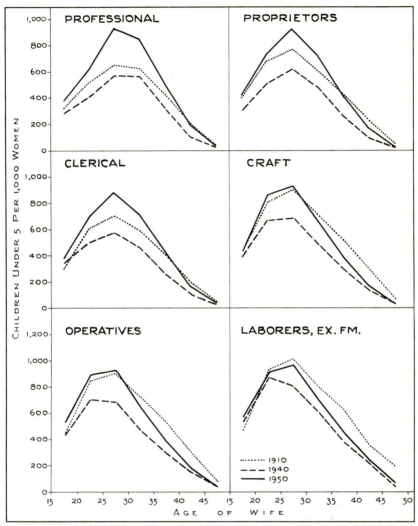

Note: Based on data in table 60.

born. As also indicated, however, the high fertility ratios of wives of white-collar workers at ages 30 to 39 arise, in part, from late age at marriage and delay in starting a family.

Within the rural-farm areas, the wives of farmers and farm managers predominated, and they contributed their proportionate share of children within these areas. Thus, in 1950, they formed 60 to 70 percent of all women of specified age and they had about this same proportion of chil-

FIGURE **43.**—COMPARISON OF THE AGE-SPECIFIC FERTILITY RATIOS OF NATIVE WHITE WOMEN
IN 1910 AND 1940 WITH THOSE OF WHITE WOMEN IN 1950, FOR WOMEN 15 TO 49 YEARS
OLD, BY MAJOR OCCUPATON GROUP OF HUSBAND, FOR RURAL-NONFARM AREAS

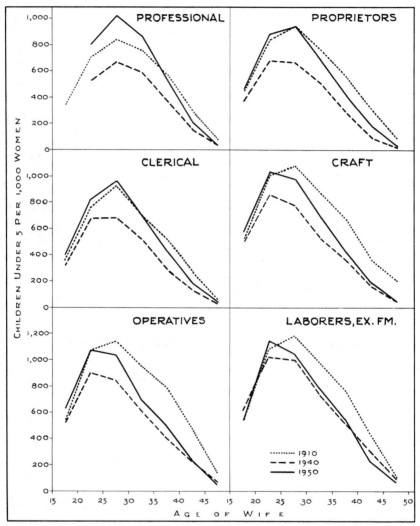

Note: Based on data in table 60.

dren ever born. The wives of farm laborers contributed only slightly
more than their share of births.

Finally, it should be emphasized that although agricultural workers contribute but slightly more children than their proportionate share within
the rural-farm areas, they contribute substantially more children than their
proportionate share within the country as a whole. Thus, among white
women married once and husband present in the United States, the wives

of agricultural workers constituted about 12 percent at ages 20 to 24 and about 14 percent at ages 45 to 49 in 1950. The wives of agricultural workers contributed 15 percent of the children ever born to women 20 to 24 and 20 percent of those ever born to women 45 to 49. They contributed 15 percent of the children under 5 years old born to women 20 to 24 years old and 28 percent of those born to women 45 to 49 years old.

FIGURE **44.**—COMPARISON OF THE AGE-SPECIFIC FERTILITY RATIOS OF NATIVE WHITE WOMEN IN 1910 AND 1940 WITH THOSE OF WHITE WOMEN IN 1950, FOR WOMEN 15 TO 49 YEARS OLD MARRIED ONCE AND HUSBAND PRESENT, BY MAJOR AGRICULTURAL OCCUPATION GROUP OF HUSBAND, FOR RURAL-FARM AREAS

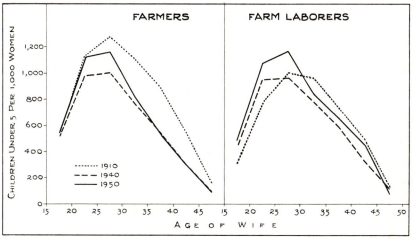

Note: Based on data in table 60.

H. Parity progression ratios

As the term implies, the parity progression ratio indicates the extent to which women have progressed from one parity to the next. The distributions of women by number of children ever born provide the basic data. From these it is possible to ascertain for women of given age and other characteristics (*a*) the total number ever having been of parity N and (*b*) the total number ever having been of parity N + 1. The parity progression ratio is the percent of *the number of women of parity N that have progressed to parity* N + 1. A woman is considered as "at risk" of parity N + 1 status only if she was of parity N status. It should be emphasized that the parity progression ratios are not "birth probabilities" of the conventional type in that no specific time period, such as 1 year, is imposed. The indicated ages of women as of 1950 may serve as rough indirect indications of the duration of marriage, however, because the average age at marriage is about 22 years.

FIGURE **45.**—PERCENT DISTRIBUTION OF WOMEN, CHILDREN EVER BORN, AND OWN CHILDREN UNDER 5 YEARS OLD, BY MAJOR OCCUPATION OF HUSBAND, FOR WHITE WOMEN IN SPECIFIED AGE GROUPS MARRIED ONCE AND HUSBAND PRESENT, URBAN AND RURAL: 1950

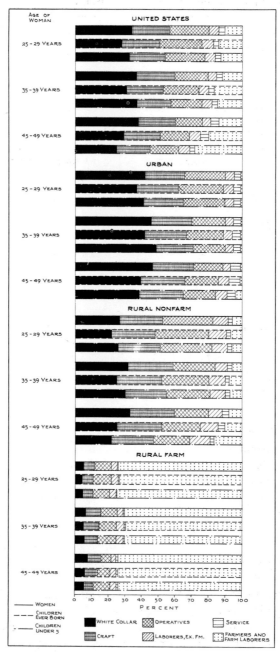

Note: Part of the legend has reference to the border of the bar, and indicates that the sets of distributions relate respectively to women, children ever born, and children under 5.

Source: Derived from *1950 Census of Population*, Vol. IV, *Special Reports*, Part 5, Chapter C, Fertility, tables 28 and 48.

TABLE **62.**—PERCENT OF "WHITE COLLAR" WORKERS AMONG HUSBANDS OF WOMEN 15 TO 49 YEARS OLD MARRIED ONCE AND HUSBAND PRESENT, AND PERCENT OF CHILDREN EVER BORN AND OF OWN CHILDREN UNDER 5 YEARS OLD WHOSE FATHERS ARE "WHITE COLLAR" WORKERS, BY COLOR AND AGE OF WOMAN, URBAN AND RURAL: 1950

[White-collar workers include professional and technical workers; managers, officials, and proprietors, except farm; and clerical and sales workers]

Area and age of woman	White			Nonwhite		
	Women	Children ever born	Children under 5	Women	Children ever born	Children under 5
UNITED STATES						
15 to 19 years	16.0	12.9	12.6	4.3	5.1	5.3
20 to 24 years	28.7	22.1	23.0	7.5	5.4	5.9
25 to 29 years	34.3	28.2	32.5	9.9	6.7	7.8
30 to 34 years	35.7	30.5	37.4	10.1	7.2	8.5
35 to 39 years	37.3	30.7	37.1	9.7	6.1	7.4
40 to 44 years	38.5	30.2	33.4	10.1	6.4	6.3
45 to 49 years	37.9	29.0	24.8	8.9	5.9	7.7
URBAN						
15 to 19 years	22.1	18.8	18.0	7.4	9.6	9.6
20 to 24 years	36.4	30.1	30.9	10.6	8.6	9.3
25 to 29 years	41.9	37.1	41.2	13.4	11.1	12.6
30 to 34 years	43.5	40.1	47.0	13.4	11.5	14.6
35 to 39 years	45.7	41.7	48.5	13.3	10.8	13.4
40 to 44 years	47.1	41.2	46.9	14.0	11.2	11.8
45 to 49 years	46.5	39.4	38.4	12.3	10.0	10.4
RURAL NONFARM						
15 to 19 years	13.1	10.3	9.9	1.6	1.4	1.6
20 to 24 years	21.1	16.6	17.2	3.0	2.0	2.3
25 to 29 years	26.7	22.0	25.9	3.9	2.1	2.7
30 to 34 years	28.9	24.3	29.6	6.8	6.1	5.8
35 to 39 years	31.7	25.0	30.2	6.0	4.5	6.2
40 to 44 years	33.2	25.3	28.5	7.2	5.6	7.2
45 to 49 years	33.0	25.3	21.7	7.6	5.6	13.7
RURAL FARM						
15 to 19 years	2.6	2.2	2.2	0.4	0.4	0.4
20 to 24 years	4.5	3.2	3.3	1.5	0.7	0.8
25 to 29 years	5.4	4.5	4.9	0.9	0.7	0.4
30 to 34 years	6.0	5.3	6.0	1.3	0.8	0.4
35 to 39 years	7.0	5.6	6.0	1.0	0.9	0.4
40 to 44 years	7.5	6.1	5.5	1.1	0.7	1.0
45 to 49 years	7.9	6.3	5.6	1.1	1.4	1.3

Source: Derived from *1950 Census of Population*, Vol. IV, *Special Reports*, Part 5, Chapter C, Fertility, tables 28, 29, 48, and 49.

Parity progression ratios are presented by age of wife and major occupation group of the husband for urban white wives (table 63) and for rural-nonfarm white wives (table 64). To illustrate, among urban white women 20 to 24 years old the 2-to-3 parity progression ratios (number ever having third births per 100 women ever having second births) ranged from 13.1 for the wives of professional men to 31.5 for wives of laborers, except farm and mine.

The data for urban white women are charted in three forms in figures 46 to 48. In figure 46 a separate panel is devoted to each age group and this chart points up the relatively small amount of occupational differentials in the 0-to-1 and 1-to-2 progression ratios. The occupational differentials are much more pronounced in the 2-to-3, 3-to-4, and 4-to-5 parity progression ratios. This same type of contrast is pointed up in a different way in figure 48 which devotes separate panels to specific parities of birth.

TABLE **63.**—PARITY PROGRESSION RATIOS—PERCENT OF WOMEN EVER OF GIVEN PARITY (N) WHO EVER PROGRESSED TO THE NEXT PARITY (N + l), FOR WHITE WOMEN 20 TO 49 YEARS OLD MARRIED ONCE AND HUSBAND PRESENT, BY AGE OF WOMAN AND MAJOR OCCUPATION GROUP OF HUSBAND, FOR URBAN AREAS: 1950

[Ratio not shown where there are fewer than 4,000 women]

Age of woman and parity progression	Total	Professional, techn'l, and kindred workers	Managers, officials, and proprietors, exc. farm	Clerical, sales, and kindred workers	Craftsmen, foremen, and kindred workers	Operatives and kindred workers	Service workers, incl. private household	Laborers, except farm and mine
20 TO 24 YEARS								
0 to 1 parity	61.1	51.2	58.5	56.4	64.9	67.4	65.7	66.9
1 to 2 parity	35.9	26.7	35.7	30.2	38.9	38.6	37.1	42.1
2 to 3 parity	22.5	13.1	15.4	15.7	22.5	24.9	19.2	31.5
3 to 4 parity	21.0	...	14.8	16.0	18.8	23.4	...	25.0
4 to 5 parity	27.5	...	...	...	23.4	26.1	...	...
25 TO 29 YEARS								
0 to 1 parity	78.1	73.7	79.6	75.1	81.1	80.6	80.4	80.6
1 to 2 parity	56.7	51.6	55.7	50.4	59.3	60.1	56.7	63.1
2 to 3 parity	34.1	24.4	28.1	26.8	35.4	38.7	36.2	44.8
3 to 4 parity	31.9	18.7	26.5	21.4	30.0	36.5	30.8	41.8
4 to 5 parity	35.6	20.3	24.3	23.9	34.0	35.4	38.1	43.5
30 TO 34 YEARS								
0 to 1 parity	83.9	84.1	85.8	81.5	85.1	85.4	82.0	83.0
1 to 2 parity	70.2	69.3	71.9	65.5	71.4	71.6	69.1	73.8
2 to 3 parity	43.6	36.1	38.4	36.3	45.9	49.2	44.4	55.8
3 to 4 parity	39.6	26.7	32.3	31.5	41.2	43.7	41.9	53.2
4 to 5 parity	39.0	28.8	28.3	33.1	36.5	41.2	38.7	52.1
35 TO 39 YEARS								
0 to 1 parity	82.3	82.0	84.3	79.9	84.1	83.2	78.9	84.9
1 to 2 parity	73.2	72.8	73.3	69.2	73.4	74.8	73.5	77.7
2 to 3 parity	48.9	41.0	42.9	43.3	51.1	54.6	52.9	59.9
3 to 4 parity	45.4	32.1	37.4	40.6	46.9	50.1	45.6	62.4
4 to 5 parity	46.7	35.9	37.1	40.3	46.5	49.9	44.6	58.0
40 TO 44 YEARS								
0 to 1 parity	80.8	78.2	81.6	78.4	83.0	82.0	80.4	83.9
1 to 2 parity	72.6	70.3	71.5	69.1	74.0	74.1	71.5	80.2
2 to 3 parity	53.1	44.4	45.2	44.6	56.1	60.3	57.2	68.8
3 to 4 parity	51.6	38.9	42.7	45.2	52.9	57.5	53.0	67.1
4 to 5 parity	51.9	37.8	38.3	46.9	52.1	57.6	48.4	60.5
45 TO 49 YEARS								
0 to 1 parity	80.1	75.0	80.2	77.6	82.4	82.7	78.9	86.8
1 to 2 parity	73.3	68.7	69.4	69.2	75.1	76.6	72.6	83.1
2 to 3 parity	56.7	45.2	48.6	49.2	60.3	63.2	60.7	70.0
3 to 4 parity	56.1	40.0	45.3	48.5	57.4	63.2	63.1	69.5
4 to 5 parity	57.0	40.8	48.5	52.2	56.6	60.4	57.4	66.7

Source: Derived from *1950 Census of Population*, Vol. IV, *Special Reports*, Part 5, Chapter C, Fertility, table 28.

Within each occupational group, the 0-to-1 progression ratios tend to level off after about age 30. This simply means that regardless of occupation group, some 80 to 85 percent had first births by age 30 (figure 47).

The seven occupational groups fall into three divisions insofar as third births to women at risk are concerned. Thus, throughout all ages of the childbearing span the three white-collar groups exhibit equally low 2-to-3 progression ratios. The craftsmen, operatives, and service workers form an intermediate group, and the laborers, except farm and mine, form the highest group (figure 48).

The data may seem to suggest that when parity is held constant, the differentials by occupational class remain much the same by age. On this

TABLE **64.**—PARITY PROGRESSION RATIOS—PERCENT OF WOMEN EVER OF GIVEN PARITY (N) WHO EVER PROGRESSED TO THE NEXT PARITY (N + 1), FOR WHITE WOMEN 20 TO 49 YEARS OLD MARRIED ONCE AND HUSBAND PRESENT, BY AGE OF WOMAN AND MAJOR OCCUPATION GROUP OF HUSBAND, FOR RURAL-NONFARM AREAS: 1950

[Ratio not shown where there are fewer than 4,000 women]

Age of woman and parity progression	Total	Profes- sional, techn'l, and kindred workers	Managers, offi- cials, and pro- prietors, exc. farm	Clerical, sales, and kindred workers	Crafts- men, foremen, and kindred workers	Opera- tives and kindred workers	Service workers, incl. private house- hold	Labor- ers, except farm and mine
20 TO 24 YEARS								
0 to 1 parity.........	73.5	63.1	68.2	64.1	75.0	76.3	76.4	78.4
1 to 2 parity.........	46.7	38.4	38.4	35.4	44.8	48.2	48.3	52.9
2 to 3 parity.........	27.1	14.7	20.4	17.2	26.0	28.8	21.2	28.6
3 to 4 parity.........	26.1	...	...	...	21.9	26.0	...	28.6
4 to 5 parity.........	25.3	...	...	...	...	25.6	...	...
25 TO 29 YEARS								
0 to 1 parity.........	84.1	80.4	82.4	80.2	84.7	86.1	82.5	84.7
1 to 2 parity.........	67.4	56.5	61.6	60.5	68.9	69.8	65.0	73.5
2 to 3 parity.........	46.2	28.4	37.8	31.0	45.6	49.9	46.3	57.5
3 to 4 parity.........	42.0	25.2	33.5	27.6	41.4	43.4	38.0	46.0
4 to 5 parity.........	43.3	...	...	...	39.2	44.4	...	51.1
30 TO 34 YEARS								
0 to 1 parity.........	87.9	86.8	87.4	86.0	88.3	89.5	87.3	89.7
1 to 2 parity.........	75.9	74.6	72.2	66.9	76.9	77.6	72.1	81.8
2 to 3 parity.........	57.1	44.6	48.4	45.3	56.9	61.2	48.4	67.4
3 to 4 parity.........	52.0	33.5	39.7	35.9	51.7	55.2	52.8	61.6
4 to 5 parity.........	52.4	33.5	38.2	41.3	52.5	53.7	...	56.3
35 TO 39 YEARS								
0 to 1 parity.........	86.1	84.5	84.3	82.5	86.9	88.6	83.5	89.5
1 to 2 parity.........	78.9	75.2	75.8	72.8	79.8	81.6	75.0	84.4
2 to 3 parity.........	61.6	47.4	50.3	51.6	60.7	68.1	57.0	70.1
3 to 4 parity.........	59.9	36.2	46.2	40.5	58.9	66.3	61.8	73.0
4 to 5 parity.........	58.4	31.7	43.4	42.7	54.0	62.4	...	65.2
40 TO 44 YEARS								
0 to 1 parity.........	83.7	78.9	81.5	80.8	85.9	86.8	80.4	87.6
1 to 2 parity.........	78.9	69.1	74.3	70.0	81.1	82.2	75.6	83.8
2 to 3 parity.........	66.2	53.8	57.9	54.3	65.7	71.5	61.8	71.6
3 to 4 parity.........	64.3	50.8	52.8	52.2	61.8	69.1	60.5	70.6
4 to 5 parity.........	61.9	41.3	51.9	46.2	60.1	65.9	...	70.5
45 TO 49 YEARS								
0 to 1 parity.........	82.5	76.7	80.0	77.1	84.2	85.9	87.8	87.2
1 to 2 parity.........	80.0	70.7	76.9	75.3	79.6	80.5	82.2	86.2
2 to 3 parity.........	66.8	51.7	57.9	53.5	67.4	71.7	69.2	76.6
3 to 4 parity.........	66.4	52.7	54.1	56.1	67.0	69.8	64.5	71.7
4 to 5 parity.........	64.6	...	52.6	58.5	62.0	67.8	54.4	69.7

Source: Same as table 63.

point, it should be remembered that the actual birth of the order considered could have occurred long before the census age indicated on the chart.

Finally, it may be noted that the tendency for probabilities of third and higher orders of births to increase with age simply arises from the fact that time is not rigidly controlled. For instance, although the data regarding third births relate to women ever "at risk" to a birth of this order, those 40 to 44 years old had a longer period of opportunity to have the third birth than those of younger ages. If the data related to probability of having a birth of a given order during a specific period of time, one would expect the probabilities to decrease rather than to increase with age.

FIGURE **46.**—PARITY PROGRESSION RATIOS—PERCENT OF WOMEN EVER OF GIVEN PARITY (N)
WHO PROGRESSED TO THE NEXT PARITY (N + 1), FOR WHITE WOMEN 20 TO 49 YEARS OLD
MARRIED ONCE AND HUSBAND PRESENT, BY AGE OF WOMAN AND MAJOR OCCUPATION GROUP
OF HUSBAND, FOR URBAN AREAS: 1950

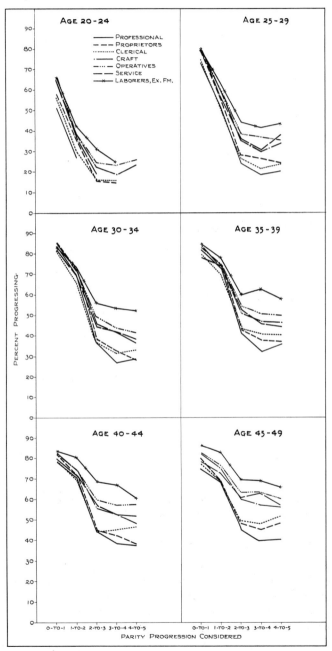

Note: Based on data in table 63.

FIGURE **47.**—PARITY PROGRESSION RATIOS—PERCENT OF WOMEN EVER OF GIVEN PARITY (N)
WHO PROGRESSED TO THE NEXT PARITY (N + 1), FOR WHITE WOMEN 20 TO 49 YEARS OLD
MARRIED ONCE AND HUSBAND PRESENT, BY MAJOR OCCUPATION GROUP OF HUSBAND AND
AGE OF WOMAN, FOR URBAN AREAS: 1950

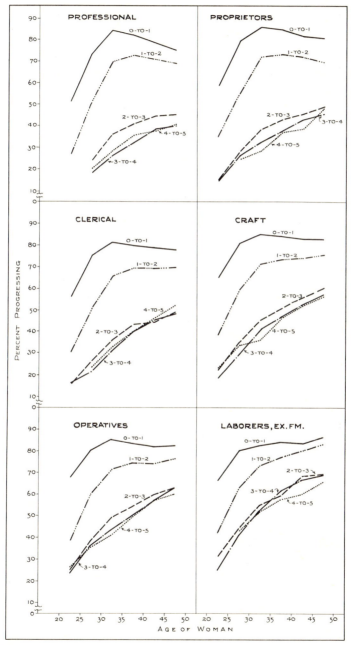

Note: Based on data in table 63.

FIGURE **48.**—PERCENT OF WOMEN EVER OF GIVEN PARITY (N) WHO PROGRESSED TO THE
NEXT PARITY (N + 1), FOR WHITE WOMEN 20 TO 49 YEARS OLD MARRIED ONCE AND
HUSBAND PRESENT, BY AGE OF WOMAN AND MAJOR OCCUPATION GROUP OF HUSBAND, FOR
URBAN AREAS: 1950

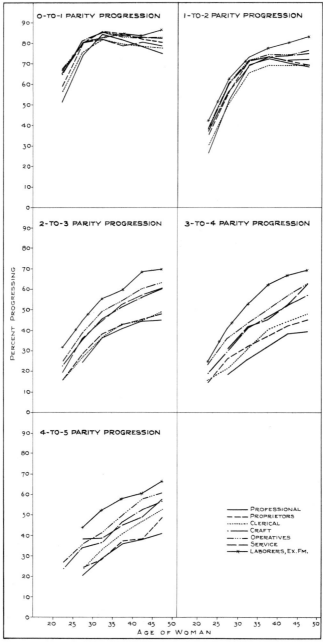

Note: Based on data in table 63.

The parity progression ratios by occupation group of the husband are not shown for years earlier than 1950. However, those by educational attainment of the wife are shown in a later section for 1940 and 1950. Parity progression ratios for several cohorts of women are presented in Chapter 9.

I. Indices of the trend of fertility differentials by occupation in 1910, 1940, and 1950

Figure 26 presented age-specific fertility rates by occupation for 1910, 1940, and 1950. From this chart one can ascertain only in general terms whether the differentials have been diminishing, enlarging, or remaining about the same. This is particularly true insofar as 1910–40 comparisons are concerned. The average levels of the fertility rates become so different that it is difficult to tell at a glance whether the interclass differences in the fertility rates underwent a change during this period. Even with respect to the 1940–50 period, the fertility rates themselves afford no quantitative indication of the extent of the expansion or contraction of fertility differentials.

Two methods have been used for more precise indications of trends in differentials in fertility by occupation of the husband since 1910. Briefly stated, the two methods are (a) the average of the percent deviations of the fertility rates of the seven nonagricultural occupational classes within an age group from the base rate for the total age group, regardless of the direction of that deviation and (b) the relative spread of the fertility rates by occupational class obtained by expressing the fertility rate of each occupational class within an age group as a percent of the base rate for the total age group.

As for comparative merits, indices have the advantages and disadvantages of averages in general. They are single-figure quantitative indicators, but they tell nothing about the total range or pattern of the variations in fertility rates.

The relative variations are not single-figure indicators of the extent of variations in fertility. They afford comparability of the pattern of differential fertility on two separate dates in which absolute levels of fertility have changed.[18] They show explicitly which classes are below and which classes are above the averages represented by base rates.

---

[18] Some changes in the pattern of fertility differentials may arise from changes in occupation groups. These may be due to changes in the classification of specific occupations and to changes in the relative importance or even existence of specific occupations within the broad group. It is interesting to note, however, that after his recent intensive research with U. S. Census materials on occupational classification for each census since that of 1870, Hutchinson observed: "Comparison over time is . . . impeded by the change in the classification of occupation from a predominantly industrial basis in 1870 to 1900 inclusive to a more fully occupational basis thereafter . . . Fortunately, the occupational data from 1910 onward constitute a more uniform series, and permit classification of workers according to their position or occupational status." See E. P. Hutchinson, *Immigrants and Their Children, 1850–1950*, Census Monograph Series, John Wiley and Sons, New York, 1956, pp. 75 and 76.

For each type of measure the base rate is simply the average fertility rate for the total age group, standardized for occupational composition. Because of the nature of occupation in relation to residence, the indices are restricted to urban and rural-nonfarm populations. For each of these types of residence in 1910, 1940, and 1950, the "base rates" were derived by weighting the fertility rates for seven nonagricultural classes according to the proportionate importance of these groups in 1950.[19] The weights were the percentage distribution by major occupation group of the husband for white women married once and husband present, computed separately for each 5-year age group of women in the 15-to-49-year span.

Index of average deviation. The indices indicate in general a very small average net contraction of class difference in fertility by occupation from 1910 to 1940 and marked contractions from 1940 to 1950 for white wives under 35 years old, and especially for those at ages 25 to 39 (table 65). For example, at ages 25 to 29 the average percent deviation of the rates of the seven occupational groups from the "base rate" was about 18 percent in 1910, 16 percent in 1940, and 10 percent in 1950. For ages 30 to 34, the average percent differences were 16 percent for 1910, 15 percent for 1940, and 7 percent for 1950. For ages 35 to 39, the three respective figures are 16, 15, and 10.

TABLE 65.—MEASURE OF AVERAGE INTERCLASS DIFFERENCES IN CUMULATIVE FERTILITY RATES BY MAJOR OCCUPATION GROUP OF HUSBAND, FOR WHITE WOMEN 15 TO 49 YEARS OLD MARRIED ONCE AND HUSBAND PRESENT, BY AGE OF WOMAN, URBAN AND RURAL NONFARM: 1950, 1940, AND 1910

[Data for white women in 1950 and native white women in 1940 and 1910. An operational definition of the measure is as follows: First, for each area and age group, fertility rates for each of seven nonagricultural major occupation groups were listed for 1950, 1940, and 1910. Second, "base rates" or standardized average rates for the seven occupational groups combined were computed. (The rates for 1940 and 1910 were standardized to the 1950 occupational distribution.) Third, for each census year, the percent difference (regardless of direction) of the fertility rate for each of the seven occupational groups from the base rate was computed. Fourth, the simple averages of these seven percentage differences were obtained and these are the figures given in the table]

Area and age	1950	1940	1910	Area and age	1950	1940	1910
URBAN				RURAL NONFARM			
15 to 19 years	12.8	13.3	11.1	15 to 19 years	11.3	18.8	11.6
20 to 24 years	12.7	16.8	16.3	20 to 24 years	13.1	16.8	15.0
25 to 29 years	9.6	16.0	17.7	25 to 29 years	11.7	19.9	16.2
30 to 34 years	7.4	15.2	16.3	30 to 34 years	12.4	18.5	14.7
35 to 39 years	9.5	15.2	16.2	35 to 39 years	16.3	18.8	15.2
40 to 44 years	13.5	15.0	16.7	40 to 44 years	18.2	18.1	14.6
45 to 49 years	17.1	15.1	15.7	45 to 49 years	19.7	18.4	13.0

Source: Derived from *1950 Census of Population*, Vol. IV, *Special Reports*, Part 5, Chapter C, Fertility, table 28; *1940 Census of Population, Differential Fertility, 1940 and 1910*, Fertility by Duration of Marriage, tables 11 and 13.

It should be pointed out that the comparatively small change in the occupational differentials in fertility from 1910 to 1940 may arise from opposite types of trends during the early and latter part of this 30-year span.

---

[19] The seven nonagricultural occupation groups are professional, proprietary, clerical, craft, operatives, service workers, and laborers (except farm).

It is possible that occupational differentials in fertility tended to become larger during the early part of this period and smaller during the latter part. There is no doubt about a diminution of occupational differences in fertility from 1940 to 1950 within the age groups 25 to 39 (table 65).

The age patterns of the average deviations are somewhat like those described later with reference to educational groups. However, the average deviations by occupation run lower than those by education. The magnitude of average deviations, of course, is partly a function of number and type of subgroups. For several reasons, however, fertility may vary more sharply by education of the wife than by occupation group of the husband. The number of years of school completed is more readily placed on a scale than is the occupation group. The data on education relate to the wife and those on occupation relate to the husband. Furthermore, whereas number of years of school completed usually is a stable characteristic after a given age, the occupation group of the husband may change over time. The significance of this is that frequently the husband was in another occupational group when some of his children were born.

Another possible reason that the fertility rates vary more widely by education than by occupation is that the relatively small (but also relatively fertile) group of farmers and farm laborers in the urban and rural-nonfarm areas, were removed from consideration in the data by occupation. They were not removed in the analysis by education. The farmers and farm laborers probably tend to be unduly concentrated in the lower educational categories and hence may tend to enhance the average differentials in fertility by education of the wife. Whatever the reasons, the average deviations by occupation run a little lower than those by education, and this holds true for the 1940 and 1950 data—urban and rural nonfarm.

It will also be noted that the age pattern of the indices in 1950 is much different from that of 1910 or 1940. Thus, whereas the indices for the earlier dates fall within a narrow band of variation throughout ages 20 to 49, the indices for 1950 are relatively high at ages 20 to 24, dip to a low at ages 30 to 34, and then increase with age. This means that at ages 30 to 34 the urban white women married once and husband present exhibited the lowest degree of variation in fertility by occupation group of the husband; they exhibited highest variability at ages 40 to 44 and 45 to 49 in 1950.

Relative variations. In table 66 and figure 49 the relative variations in the fertility rates by occupational class of the husband are presented for urban white women of specific age, married once and husband present.

The device of expressing the age-specific fertility rate for each occupation group as a percent of the average (base) rate for all women of that age facilitates comparison of the interclass differences and relative spread of the rates by occupation at the three dates considered. This method eliminates the effect of changes in general levels of fertility.

TABLE **66.**—RELATIVE VARIATION OF CUMULATIVE FERTILITY RATES BY MAJOR OCCUPATION GROUP OF HUSBAND, FOR WHITE WOMEN 15 TO 49 YEARS OLD, BY AGE OF WOMAN, URBAN AND RURAL NONFARM: 1950, 1940, AND 1910

[Data for white women in 1950 and native white women in 1940 and 1910. An operational definition of the relative variation of fertility rates is as follows: First, "base rates" are computed as in table 65. These are standardized fertility rates for women of given age in the United States; the standard is the distribution by major nonagricultural occupation groups of the husbands of white women of given age in the United States in 1950. Second, the observed cumulative fertility rate of women of given age, occupation of husband, urban-rural area, and year, is expressed as a percent of the corresponding "base rate." Relative variation not shown where there are fewer than 4,000 women in 1950 or 3,000 in 1940]

Age of woman and major occupation group of husband	Urban			Rural nonfarm		
	1950	1940	1910	1950	1940	1910
WOMEN 15 TO 19 YEARS OLD						
Base rate.........................	514	471	570	594	569	711
Relative variation, total (base rate)......	100	100	100	100	100	100
Professional, technical, and kindred workers...	85	70	80	...	...	78
Managers, officials, and propr's, exc. farm....	86	77	93	83	76	91
Clerical, sales, and kindred workers..........	84	90	73	74	64	74
Craftsmen, foremen, and kindred workers.......	90	97	103	102	107	102
Operatives and kindred workers...............	107	105	104	111	107	106
Service workers, including private household...	90	92	98	...	...	95
Laborers, except farm and mine................	118	113	115	96	114	112
WOMEN 20 TO 24 YEARS OLD						
Base rate.........................	925	755	1,051	1,154	1,015	1,370
Relative variation, total (base rate)......	100	100	100	100	100	100
Professional, technical, and kindred workers...	72	68	69	79	65	73
Managers, officials, and propr's, exc. farm....	90	83	86	88	89	88
Clerical, sales, and kindred workers..........	83	77	78	79	76	78
Craftsmen, foremen, and kindred workers.......	105	106	106	104	107	105
Operatives and kindred workers...............	110	112	110	110	114	114
Service workers, including private household...	104	102	101	106	93	92
Laborers, except farm and mine................	116	126	129	118	120	118
WOMEN 25 TO 29 YEARS OLD						
Base rate.........................	1,470	1,149	1,584	1,784	1,503	2,112
Relative variation, total (base rate)......	100	100	100	100	100	100
Professional, technical, and kindred workers...	84	70	68	81	68	69
Managers, officials, and propr's, exc. farm....	96	89	90	91	83	88
Clerical, sales, and kindred workers..........	86	79	78	85	78	81
Craftsmen, foremen, and kindred workers.......	105	111	110	105	107	109
Operatives and kindred workers...............	108	113	113	111	121	116
Service workers, including private household...	103	101	100	99	91	97
Laborers, except farm and mine................	117	126	137	121	131	125
WOMEN 30 TO 34 YEARS OLD						
Base rate.........................	1,874	1,620	2,178	2,246	2,024	2,867
Relative variation, total (base rate)......	100	100	100	100	100	100
Professional, technical, and kindred workers...	92	78	72	87	71	76
Managers, officials, and propr's, exc. farm....	97	88	90	90	84	89
Clerical, sales, and kindred workers..........	87	80	80	83	77	82
Craftsmen, foremen, and kindred workers.......	103	109	109	105	107	106
Operatives and kindred workers...............	107	112	113	112	122	117
Service workers, including private household...	97	99	100	95	99	98
Laborers, except farm and mine................	116	131	135	125	132	124
WOMEN 35 TO 39 YEARS OLD						
Base rate.........................	2,003	2,014	2,808	2,438	2,457	3,636
Relative variation, total (base rate)......	100	100	100	100	100	100
Professional, technical, and kindred workers...	90	80	73	81	74	77
Managers, officials, and propr's, exc. farm....	95	87	90	86	83	87
Clerical, sales, and kindred workers..........	88	82	81	80	80	83
Craftsmen, foremen, and kindred workers.......	103	108	109	104	108	105
Operatives and kindred workers...............	108	114	113	121	123	122
Service workers, including private household...	98	101	101	97	97	95
Laborers, except farm and mine................	125	132	134	132	134	121

TABLE **66.**—RELATIVE VARIATION OF CUMULATIVE FERTILITY RATES BY MAJOR OCCUPATION GROUP OF HUSBAND, FOR WHITE WOMEN 15 TO 49 YEARS OLD, BY AGE OF WOMAN, URBAN AND RURAL NONFARM: 1950, 1940, AND 1910—Cont.

Age of woman and major occupation group of husband	Urban			Rural nonfarm		
	1950	1940	1910	1950	1940	1910
WOMEN 40 TO 44 YEARS OLD						
Base rate.....................................	2,087	2,275	3,310	2,543	2,770	4,056
Relative variation, total (base rate)......	100	100	100	100	100	100
Professional, technical, and kindred workers...	84	82	74	76	75	77
Managers, officials, and propr's, exc. farm....	90	89	90	84	85	90
Clerical, sales, and kindred workers...........	86	83	81	79	80	80
Craftsmen, foremen, and kindred workers........	106	107	110	109	107	105
Operatives and kindred workers.................	111	114	113	123	124	124
Service workers, including private household...	100	106	105	97	102	99
Laborers, except farm and mine.................	137	131	134	132	134	120
WOMEN 45 TO 49 YEARS OLD						
Base rate.....................................	2,188	2,411	3,666	2,592	2,980	4,335
Relative variation, total (base rate)......	100	100	100	100	100	100
Professional, technical, and kindred workers...	77	81	75	72	78	82
Managers, officials, and propr's, exc. farm....	87	88	89	85	84	88
Clerical, sales, and kindred workers...........	85	83	84	80	82	84
Craftsmen, foremen, and kindred workers........	106	109	109	108	107	106
Operatives and kindred workers.................	115	111	112	120	119	121
Service workers, including private household...	104	104	106	112	116	104
Laborers, except farm and mine.................	143	134	131	136	132	113

Source: Same as table 65.

Like the indices of average deviation, the data regarding relative spread point up the lack of substantial change in pattern of occupational differentials in fertility in 1940 as compared with 1910. Thus, for 1910, if the rate for the urban white married women 25 to 29 years old is expressed as 100, the rate for the professional group is about 68 and that for the unskilled laborers is about 137. This is a range of 69 points. In 1940, the corresponding rates are 70 and 126, a range of 56 points.

The great reduction in the spread of the rates in 1950 is indicated by the comparable figures of 84 for the professional group and 117 for the unskilled laborers, a range of 33 points.

Substantial reductions in the relative spread of the fertility rates by occupational class were found in all age groups under 40. For age groups 40–44 and 45–49 there appeared to be little in the way of change in relative spread of fertility rates by occupational class.

The data for the rural-nonfarm white women differ from those for urban white women in one important respect (table 66 and figure 50). Among the rural-nonfarm women, the relative spread of the fertility rates by occupation group tended to be a little wider in 1940 than in 1910. Among the urban women the reverse was the case. In fact, among the rural-nonfarm women the relative range of the rates was lower in 1910 than in 1950 insofar as age groups 35–39, 40–44, and 45–49 are concerned. However, for urban and rural-nonfarm white women under 40 years old the variations in fertility by occupation were of smaller range in 1950 than in 1940. The maximum ranges appeared in 1910 for the urban whites and in 1940 for the rural-nonfarm whites.

FIGURE **49.**—RELATIVE SPREAD OF CUMULATIVE FERTILITY RATES BY MAJOR OCCUPATION GROUP OF HUSBAND, FOR WHITE WOMEN 15 TO 49 YEARS OLD MARRIED ONCE AND HUSBAND PRESENT, BY AGE OF WOMAN, FOR URBAN AREAS: 1950, 1940, AND 1910

[Data for white women in 1950 and native white women in 1940 and 1910. See source table for definition of relative spread of rates]

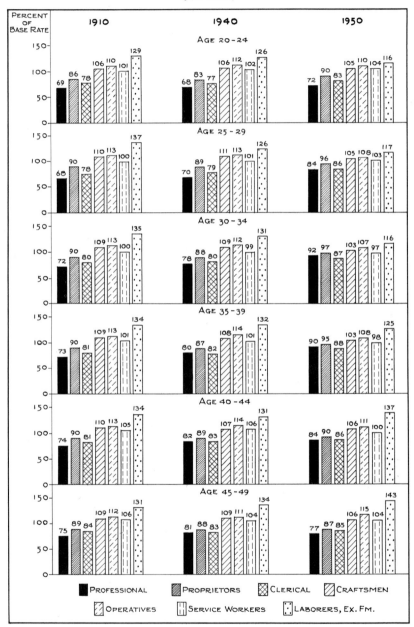

Note: Based on data in table 66.

FIGURE **50.**—RELATIVE SPREAD OF CUMULATIVE FERTILITY RATES BY MAJOR OCCUPATION GROUP OF HUSBAND, FOR WHITE WOMEN 15 TO 49 YEARS OLD MARRIED ONCE AND HUSBAND PRESENT, BY AGE OF WOMAN, FOR RURAL-NONFARM AREAS: 1950, 1940, AND 1910

[Data for white women in 1950 and native white women in 1940 and 1910. See source table for definition of relative spread of rates]

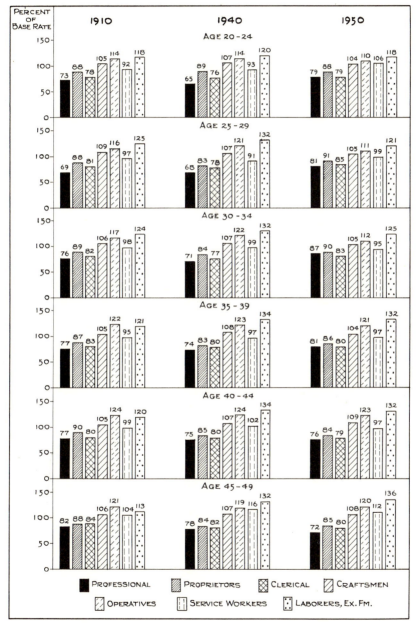

Note: Based on data in table 66.

J. General

The phenomenon of differential fertility according to occupational or socio-economic status has sometimes been described as a transitional phase of declining fertility. The theory is that the declines begin in the so-called "upper" occupational classes in urban areas. Later, the declines affect the so-called "middle" classes and finally the so-called "lower" occupational classes. In the meantime the declines spread outward to the rural areas and presumably the process runs the same type of course there.

If fertility declines do proceed according to the pattern described above, one would expect them to bring at first an enlargement and later a contraction of group differences in fertility. This type of process has been experienced at least in part in England and Wales. There was a distinct widening of occupational differentials in fertility there during the last part of the nineteenth century.[20] Innes reported a contraction of class differences in fertility in England and Wales during 1921 to 1931 owing to more rapid declines in fertility of the lower than of the upper classes during this decade.[21] In this regard his finding was not fully corroborated by subsequent studies made for the Royal Commission on Population, but these later studies did indicate that at least the manual-nonmanual differential in fertility had narrowed.[22]

It is still more difficult to document a clear-cut pattern of initial enlargement and subsequent diminution of group differences in fertility within the United States. It is not certain that the United States experienced an "initial widening" of group differences in fertility. As already indicated, Jaffe found suggestions of differentials in fertility along socio-economic lines in early America.[23] On the basis of their analysis of age-specific fertility rates by occupational group of the husband among a sample of northern native white married couples of completed fertility, Sallume and Notestein reported that "from whatever causes, the decline in fertility of the northern native white population prior to 1910 was general and of long standing, although it was more rapid in the city than in the country, and probably somewhat more rapid in the 'upper' than in the 'lower' classes."[24] (See also Chapter 2 where it was noted that rural areas had greater *absolute* declines but lesser *relative* declines in fertility than urban areas had after 1810.)

---

[20] See John W. Innes, "Class Fertility Trends in England and Wales, 1876–1934," *op. cit.*, p. 69; F. W. Notestein, "Class Differences in Fertility," *The Annals of the American Academy of Political and Social Science*, Vol. 188, November 1936, p. 27.

[21] J. W. Innes, "Class Birth Rates in England and Wales, 1921–1931," *op. cit.*, p. 79.

[22] Royal Commission on Population, *Report*, His Majesty's Stationery Office, London, 1949, p. 152.

[23] A. Jaffe, *op. cit.*

[24] X. Sallume and F. W. Notestein, "Trends in the Size of Families Completed Prior to 1910 in Various Social Classes," *The American Journal of Sociology*, Vol. 38, No. 3, November 1932, pp. 398–408.

Comparisons of samples of fertility data from the 1900 and 1910 Censuses for the East North Central States indicate that some expansion of occupational differentials in fertility may have occurred in that area during the first decade of the century.[25]   However, as indicated in Chapters 2 and 3, there are somewhat conflicting indications that certain types of differentials in fertility were becoming smaller rather than larger prior to 1910.   Thus, the similarity in the trend of fertility ratios in urban and rural areas suggested that farmers kept pace with other occupational groups in respect to absolute declines in fertility.   Also the tendency for different States to become more nearly alike after 1810 with respect to magnitude of fertility ratios would seem to argue against substantial enhancement of occupational or socio-economic differentials in fertility.

As for trends in occupational differentials in fertility since 1910, the net change during 1910 to 1940 appears to have been a minor amount of convergence for urban whites but not for rural-nonfarm whites.   There was a considerable diminution of such differentials in fertility at certain ages during the 1940–50 decade.   There is some uncertainty, however, regarding the nature of the trends during the 30 years 1910–40.   Did the small net contraction of occupational differentials observed for urban whites represent a gradual trend in this direction throughout the whole period or did it represent the result of opposite types of trends during the early and later parts of the period?   There is some basis for the hypothesis that during 1910 to 1940 a period of widening was followed by an onset of narrowing of occupational differentials in fertility in this country. Some suggestions of enlargement of such differentials during 1900 to 1910 have already been mentioned.   Also, according to Ogburn's comparison of family size in 1930 with that in 1900, the changes in family size varied sharply by occupation group of the heads.   The decline in size was 10 percent for the professional group, 6 percent for the proprietary group, 5 percent for the clerical group, 3 percent for the skilled and semiskilled group, and 1 percent for the unskilled group.   There was also a decrease of 1 percent in the size of farm-owner families, but an increase of 5 percent in the size of farm-renter families and 13 percent in the size of farm-laborer families.[26]

If there was an initial widening and subsequent contraction of occupational differentials in fertility during 1910 to 1940 it is impossible to ascertain the precise date of the turning point from expansion to contraction of class differences in fertility in this country.   In an article based

---

[25] C. V. Kiser, "Trends in the Fertility of Social Classes from 1900 to 1910." *Human Biology*, Vol. 5, No. 2, May 1933, pp. 256–273.

[26] W. F. Ogburn (with the assistance of Clark Tibbitts), "The Family and Its Functions," *Recent Social Trends in the United States*, Vol. 1, McGraw-Hill Book Company, New York, 1933, p. 686.   Note: It is possible that the data reflect changes in family composition as well as changes in fertility.

upon data for the East North Central States regarding children under 10 years old in homes of couples married 5 to 9 years in the 1930 Census, by rental value of the home, Notestein found the now-familiar exceptions to the inverse relation of fertility to socio-economic status. This was the failure of the group of highest rental-value status to exhibit the lowest fertility ratios.[27]

Similar exceptions to the inverse relation of fertility to socio-economic status were noted in the data from the National Health Survey of 1935–1936.[28] Reversals of this type were documented on a comprehensive basis in the fertility data collected in the 1940 Census.[29]

At all events, although the fertility rates for 1940 are considerably lower than those for comparable groups in 1910, there appears to be little difference between the two sets of data with respect to average deviation of the fertility rate for the various occupational groups from the mean fertility rate for the age group considered.[30] As explained, this similarity could mask opposite types of trends during the 30 years under consideration.

Whatever may have been the situation prior to 1940 there is no doubt about the existence of marked contractions in fertility differentials by occupation since 1950 among urban white couples with wives under 35 years old. In this instance, the diminution of social and economic group differences in fertility arose from group differences in *increases* in fertility rather than from *declines* in fertility. The increases in fertility were considerably higher among the "upper" than among the "lower" occupational and educational groups. The recent lessening of fertility differentials, of course, gives no assurance that similar changes will continue during coming years.

---

[27] F. W. Notes*ein, "Differential Fertility in the East North Central States," *op. cit.*, pp. 186–187.

[28] C. V. Kiser, *Group Differences in Urban Fertility*, The Williams and Wilkins Company, Baltimore, 1942, pp. 244–247.

[29] See the bibliography for a listing of the special reports from the United States Bureau of the Census bearing the general title *Population: Differential Fertility, 1940 and 1910*.

[30] Charles F. Westoff, "Differential Fertility in the United States: 1900 to 1952," *American Sociological Review*, Vol. 19, No. 5, October 1954, pp. 549–561.

CHAPTER 6

TRENDS AND DIFFERENTIALS IN FERTILITY BY EDUCATION OF THE WOMAN

A. Type of data available

For some decades prior to 1940, the United States Census contained questions regarding ability to read and write. In the 1940 and 1950 Censuses these questions on literacy were replaced by those regarding highest grade of school completed. This chapter presents the analysis of fertility rates and ratios in 1940 and 1950 in relation to educational attainment of the woman.[1]

The educational attainment of the woman has certain advantages over occupation group of the husband as a variable for use in studies of differential fertility. In the first place, classifications based upon occupation group of the husband are, in the nature of the case, restricted to married women. Those presented in the preceding chapter actually relate only to women described as married once and husband present. The classifications by educational attainment of the woman, in contrast, were available for all women and ever-married women as well as for those described as married once and husband present. This made it possible to compute general as well as marital fertility rates and ratios. It also permitted the computation of (a) proportions of women ever married among all women, by educational attainment, (b) proportions of those married once and husband present (unbroken first marriages) among the ever-married women, by educational attainment, and (c) period gross and net reproduction rates by educational attainment.

In the second place, unlike occupation which is subject to change in time, the "highest grade of school completed" is a fairly stable attribute after a certain age is reached. It does not decrease at all, and very rarely increases after certain ages, perhaps especially among women. Thus, with reference to number of children ever born to women of a given educational attainment, one can be fairly sure that in most cases all of the woman's children were born while she was of the stated educational class.

---

[1] As in previous instances the fertility rates for the whites in 1950 are compared with those for native whites of comparable ages, residence, and education in 1940. Likewise the 1950 data relate to nonwhites and the 1940 data to Negroes. These types of comparison were forced by the character of tabulations available.

The characteristic of stability also has definite advantages insofar as interpretation of reproduction rates by educational attainment is concerned.

Except for the additions mentioned above, the materials presented in this chapter parallel those in the preceding chapter. The topics, all in relation to educational attainment, include the percent ever married, stability of marriage, percent changes and levels of cumulative fertility rates and fertility ratios, 1940 and 1950 distribution of women by number of children ever born, proportionate contribution of children, parity progression ratios, period gross and net reproduction rates, and index of trends in fertility differentials.

B. Percent ever married by educational attainment

Since information regarding highest grade of school completed was collected in the 1940 and 1950 Censuses for single women as well as ever-married women, it is possible to present data on the proportion of women who had ever married by educational attainment. The data for 1940 relate to native whites and Negroes and those for 1950 relate to whites and nonwhites. The 1940 and 1950 definitions of urban were used respectively for the classification of the 1940 and 1950 data according to residence of the woman.

Certain limitations of the data inherent in the age-grade relationships should be noted for the 15-to-19 and 20-to-24 age groups. In the first place, it is readily apparent that since very few women as young as 15 to 19 years have completed 4 or more years of college, women of that educational level are virtually ruled out of the 15-to-19 age group by definition. Also, in both 1940 and 1950 the percentage ever married within the 15-to-19 age group was higher for the women who had completed 4 years of high school than for those who had completed 1 to 3 years of high school. This is a spurious deviation from the usual inverse relation of proportions married to educational attainment. The explanation is that within the 15-to-19 group the women who had finished high school were about 2 years older, on the average, than those who started but did not finish high school. Also, within the 15-to-19 age group the women reporting only 1 to 3 years of high school were more likely to be still in school than those reporting 4 years of high school. For both these reasons the proportion ever married was likely to be higher among the "high school: 4 years" women 15 to 19 years of age than among the "high school: 1 to 3 years" women of this age group. A census report on education indicates that among women 18 and 19 years old, the percent ever married was about 39 for those who had completed 1 to 3 years of high school and 22 for those who had finished 4 years of high school.

The above specific forms of bias do not apply to any appreciable extent at higher age groups, and in the older ages the inverse relation of educational attainment to percentage ever married is, with one type of exception, fairly regular.

TABLE **67.**—PERCENT EVER MARRIED AMONG WOMEN 15 TO 49 YEARS OLD, BY AGE, COLOR, AND YEARS OF SCHOOL COMPLETED, URBAN AND RURAL: 1950 AND 1940

[Percent not shown where there are fewer than 4,000 women in 1950 or 3,000 in 1940]

Age and years of school completed	1950 White				1950 Nonwhite				1940 Native white				Negro total
	United States	Urban	Rural nonfarm	Rural farm	United States	Urban	Rural nonfarm	Rural farm	United States	Urban	Rural nonfarm	Rural farm	
15 TO 19 YEARS OLD													
College: 4 yrs. or more	14.6	13.5	...	...	...	...	...	...	5.4	...	...	...	...
1 to 3 years	7.5	6.6	12.9	10.1	8.0	9.2	...	...	4.5	4.6	5.9	2.8	4.9
High school: 4 years	20.5	17.2	30.3	27.7	19.4	18.6	27.9	13.9	10.5	8.6	15.2	12.7	13.7
1 to 3 years	13.8	12.9	18.0	11.6	19.1	20.5	19.6	13.8	8.4	7.0	11.5	9.3	14.0
None or elementary	21.8	20.3	25.9	20.2	24.1	24.6	27.8	21.5	17.8	13.9	21.8	19.3	22.2
20 TO 24 YEARS OLD													
College: 4 yrs. or more	45.2	44.3	49.8	48.6	37.0	38.4	...	...	24.1	24.9	22.9	19.6	25.5
1 to 3 years	45.1	41.9	57.6	57.9	44.0	46.2	31.6	...	28.4	28.4	33.7	21.6	29.1
High school: 4 years	67.3	63.5	78.4	74.1	61.7	63.2	60.4	46.0	44.2	40.1	55.6	49.0	47.7
1 to 3 years	81.6	78.9	88.3	83.9	74.5	76.1	75.9	63.6	64.2	58.8	76.6	70.0	62.9
None or elementary	77.8	75.7	83.4	75.4	74.2	74.7	75.8	72.0	64.5	58.1	73.6	67.3	69.2
25 TO 29 YEARS OLD													
College: 4 yrs. or more	72.6	70.8	80.4	78.4	69.3	70.3	...	...	52.9	52.4	56.0	47.2	52.7
1 to 3 years	82.7	80.5	89.7	89.1	75.7	76.5	...	...	68.7	66.9	74.6	67.2	62.5
High school: 4 years	87.0	85.0	92.9	91.4	83.9	84.4	77.3	81.5	72.5	68.6	82.1	79.2	72.8
1 to 3 years	92.1	90.6	95.9	94.5	88.0	88.0	89.1	86.0	84.0	80.4	91.5	89.0	80.7
None or elementary	89.0	87.3	91.6	89.9	87.5	87.0	88.3	88.2	83.0	79.2	88.2	85.7	83.8
30 TO 34 YEARS OLD													
College: 4 yrs. or more	80.3	78.4	87.2	86.6	81.9	81.1	...	...	66.7	65.3	71.4	67.1	69.9
1 to 3 years	88.6	87.1	93.2	92.3	89.2	89.4	...	...	.80.0	77.6	84.2	83.5	78.6
High school: 4 years	90.9	89.4	95.2	94.2	89.7	90.0	88.6	...	81.7	78.8	88.8	87.9	83.5
1 to 3 years	94.1	92.9	96.9	96.0	92.6	92.6	92.6	92.6	89.3	87.0	94.0	92.2	86.2
None or elementary	91.8	90.4	93.8	93.0	92.5	91.8	92.8	94.5	89.2	87.2	92.3	90.4	89.1
35 TO 39 YEARS OLD													
College: 4 yrs. or more	78.8	76.7	86.0	85.5	86.2	87.0	...	...	69.3	67.1	76.1	71.2	75.8
1 to 3 years	89.9	88.4	93.6	94.1	92.7	93.2	...	...	83.6	81.5	87.7	86.5	83.7
High school: 4 years	91.1	89.8	94.6	95.0	92.4	92.4	...	...	85.0	82.5	90.8	91.3	88.1
1 to 3 years	94.6	93.6	96.8	96.7	93.9	93.5	94.2	97.0	90.7	88.9	94.1	93.7	91.0
None or elementary	93.1	92.1	94.5	94.8	93.7	93.5	92.6	95.3	91.8	90.2	93.6	93.4	92.5
40 TO 44 YEARS OLD													
College: 4 yrs. or more	78.3	76.3	84.0	87.6	89.0	88.5	...	...	69.3	66.9	76.5	76.4	87.1
1 to 3 years	89.8	88.4	93.2	92.9	91.2	91.9	...	...	85.1	82.1	89.7	91.8	89.4
High school: 4 years	90.6	89.2	94.4	96.0	94.5	94.6	...	...	86.5	84.1	91.4	94.7	92.0
1 to 3 years	94.7	93.8	96.5	96.7	95.6	95.7	94.8	96.4	91.2	89.1	94.2	95.0	94.4
None or elementary	93.7	92.9	94.5	95.4	94.5	94.3	94.0	96.0	92.6	91.1	93.9	94.4	93.9
45 TO 49 YEARS OLD													
College: 4 yrs. or more	75.1	73.2	79.6	88.0	86.2	86.0	...	...	69.9	66.4	78.8	83.2	82.7
1 to 3 years	89.1	87.2	92.1	95.3	94.1	94.9	...	...	84.2	81.7	87.8	90.4	83.8
High school: 4 years	90.4	89.1	94.5	95.3	93.6	94.1	...	...	87.5	85.6	90.8	94.7	92.4
1 to 3 years	93.8	93.0	95.5	95.8	94.2	94.4	91.0	95.6	91.8	89.8	94.3	96.0	95.7
None or elementary	94.3	93.6	95.1	95.5	95.7	95.6	94.6	96.8	93.0	91.5	93.8	95.3	95.1

Source: Derived from *1950 Census of Population*, Vol. IV, *Special Reports*, Part 5, Chapter C, Fertility, tables 20 and 22; *1940 Census of Population, Differential Fertility, 1940 and 1910*, Women by Number of Children Ever Born, tables 49 and 50.

The exception is the rather consistent tendency for the proportion ever married to be a little higher for the women who started but did not finish high school than for those of lower educational attainment. The group of lowest educational attainment includes those with no formal schooling;

therefore it contains many of the mental defectives. These mental defectives constitute a small proportion of the total population, but since they are mainly unmarried, they could easily account for the smaller percent ever married in the "none or elementary" group than in the group of women who started but did not finish high school. Also, the group of women who started but did not complete high school may be a select group in that many may have stopped school in order to be married.

Figure 51 presents data on the percent ever married among urban native white women in 1940 and urban white women in 1950, by age and educational attainment of the woman. By age, the most pronounced increases during 1940 to 1950 in proportion ever married were those for women aged 20 to 24. By education, the 1940–50 increases in proportions ever married were especially conspicuous for the college graduates. Thus, among urban white women 20 to 24 years old who had completed 4 or more years of college, the percent ever married was 25 for 1940 and 44 for 1950. Among urban white women 25 to 29 years old who had completed 4 or more years of college, the percent ever married was 52 for 1940 and 71 for 1950. Among the women 30 to 34 years old who were college graduates, about two-thirds were married in 1940 and over three-fourths in 1950. In 1940, the maximum percent ever married for *any* age group was 67 percent (ages 35 to 39 and 40 to 44). The recent increase in marriage among college graduates is also seen by internal comparisons of the 1950 data. Among urban white women who finished college the percent ever married was higher for the women 30 to 34 years old than for the women of any older age (table 67).

Using a slight modification of a method recently described by Hajnal for ascertaining mean age at marriage from census data on marital status, Tietze and Lauriat estimated that among white women in the United States in 1940 and 1950 who had completed at least 4 years of college, the mean ages at marriage were 25.4 and 23.2, respectively.[2] Among white male college graduates the corresponding figures were 27.7 for 1940 and 25.7 for 1950. In their study, Tietze and Lauriat attempted to estimate the "ultimate" educational status of persons under 25 years of age.

Increases in proportions married among young women during 1940 to 1950 occurred at all educational levels. However, the 1940–50 changes tended to become less striking with lowering of educational level. Thus, among urban white women 20 to 24 years old who did not go beyond the eighth grade, the proportion ever married was 58 percent in 1940 and 76 percent in 1950. Among those 25 to 29 years old, the corresponding figures were 79 percent for 1940 and 87 percent for 1950. At ages 30 to 34, the proportion ever married among urban white women of elemen-

[2] John Hajnal, "Age at Marriage and Proportions Marrying," *Population Studies*, Vol. 7, No. 2, November 1953, pp. 111–136. Christopher Tietze and Patience Lauriat, "Age at Marriage by Educational Attainment," *Population Studies*, Vol. 9, No. 2, November 1955, pp. 159–166.

FIGURE **51.**—PERCENT EVER MARRIED AMONG WHITE WOMEN 15 TO 49 YEARS OLD, BY AGE
AND YEARS OF SCHOOL COMPLETED, FOR URBAN AREAS: 1950 AND 1940

[Data for white women in 1950 and native white women in 1940. Percent not shown where there are fewer than 3,000
women in 1940]

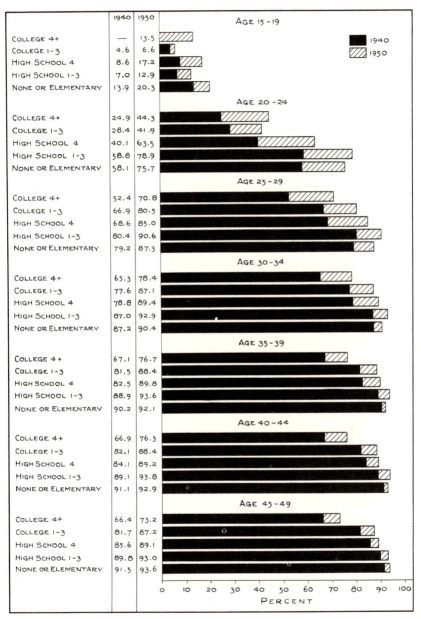

Note: Based on data in table 67.

tary school status was about as high in 1940 as in 1950, 87 percent as compared with 90 percent. The changes between 1940 and 1950 in proportions ever married were of essentially the same pattern in the rural-nonfarm and rural-farm areas as in the urban areas.

At ages under 35, the percent ever married among the white women was lowest in urban areas, intermediate in the rural-farm areas, and highest in the rural-nonfarm areas. At ages 35 and over, the proportions ever married were lowest in the urban areas and tended to be highest in the rural-farm areas. The urban-rural differences in proportion ever married may have arisen in part from out-migration of some unmarried women from rural to urban areas.

Nonwhites. The nonwhites also exhibited sharp increases in proportions ever married among each education group of women under 35 years of age during the 1940–50 decade. The published 1940 data of this type did not distinguish urban-rural residence. For the country as a whole, however, the nonwhites resembled the whites in that the increases in proportions ever married were especially conspicuous for women who had some college training (figure 52).

Within urban areas the proportion ever married in 1950 tended to be about the same among nonwhites as among whites of similar age and education. Within rural-nonfarm and rural-farm areas, however, the proportions tended to be a little lower for the nonwhites than for the whites. It will also be noticed that for the whites, but not for the nonwhites, the proportions ever married tended to be a little higher in rural-nonfarm than in urban areas.

C. Stability of marriage by educational attainment

Some indication of the stability of marriage by educational attainment may be secured from the materials by relating the data for women who are married once and husband present to data for women who have ever been married. The 1950 data are available by age, color, and residence (table 68). As expected, the percent representing the married-once-and-husband-present group of the ever-married group declines with age because it is with the passage of time that marriages are broken through death, separation, and divorce. However, one exception to the above is the frequently encountered relatively low proportion of ever-married women 15 to 19 years old classified as married once and husband present. This may reflect some misreporting of marital status by women with an illegitimate child. In the 1950 data, the important factor is that many of the wives under 20 years old had husbands who were away from home in military service.

The proportion of ever-married women who were married once and husband present in 1950 was much higher among whites than among nonwhites of similar age, education, and residence. Among both whites and

FIGURE **52.**—PERCENT EVER MARRIED AMONG NONWHITE WOMEN 15 TO 49 YEARS OLD, BY
AGE AND YEARS OF SCHOOL COMPLETED: 1950 AND 1940

[Data for nonwhite women in 1950 and Negro women in 1940]

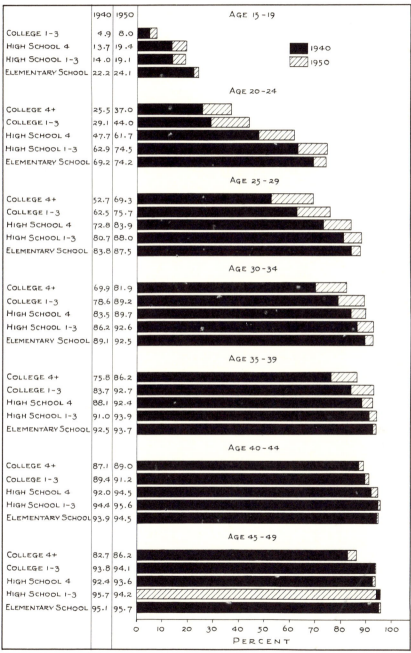

Note: Based on data in table 67.

TABLE **68.**—PERCENT MARRIED ONCE AND HUSBAND PRESENT AMONG EVER-MARRIED WOMEN 15 TO 49 YEARS OLD, BY AGE, COLOR, AND YEARS OF SCHOOL COMPLETED, URBAN AND RURAL: 1950

[Percent not shown where there are fewer than 4,000 women]

Age and years of school completed by woman	White			Nonwhite		
	Urban	Rural nonfarm	Rural farm	Urban	Rural nonfarm	Rural farm
15 TO 19 YEARS OLD						
College: 4 years or more.......	...	...	...	...	...	...
1 to 3 years..........	85.8	...	...	...	...	...
High school: 4 years...............	90.0	92.6	93.2	75.3	...	...
1 to 3 years..........	83.5	88.6	85.5	71.2	81.9	74.1
None or elementary.................	80.6	86.6	85.6	66.8	78.3	77.0
20 TO 24 YEARS OLD						
College: 4 years or more.......	92.7	91.5	91.6	73.1	...	...
1 to 3 years..........	90.6	91.6	90.9	74.8	...	...
High school: 4 years...............	88.9	90.7	90.7	71.3	79.9	80.8
1 to 3 years..........	81.0	84.8	86.7	64.3	74.2	73.6
None or elementary.................	79.5	83.7	86.0	62.4	70.2	74.3
25 TO 29 YEARS OLD						
College: 4 years or more.......	90.0	88.5	88.1	76.5	...	...
1 to 3 years..........	86.3	88.1	88.9	66.1	...	...
High school: 4 years...............	85.2	87.8	89.8	65.6	71.6	84.7
1 to 3 years..........	78.6	81.1	86.4	59.5	69.9	71.4
None or elementary.................	77.0	81.0	86.4	56.1	66.0	70.0
30 TO 34 YEARS OLD						
College: 4 years or more.......	87.0	88.6	89.5	68.2	...	...
1 to 3 years..........	83.3	84.9	88.2	68.1	...	...
High school: 4 years...............	83.1	84.5	88.3	58.3	...	...
1 to 3 years..........	77.4	79.4	86.5	54.7	64.4	73.6
None or elementary.................	76.5	80.5	86.4	51.6	61.7	70.7
35 TO 39 YEARS OLD						
College: 4 years or more.......	84.1	85.6	87.6	62.7	...	...
1 to 3 years..........	80.5	83.8	87.3	52.1	...	...
High school: 4 years...............	79.4	81.3	89.2	55.5	...	...
1 to 3 years..........	73.8	78.0	85.7	48.2	57.0	77.8
None or elementary.................	74.3	77.0	84.9	47.4	53.7	67.8
40 TO 44 YEARS OLD						
College: 4 years or more.......	79.3	84.2	82.1	61.8	...	...
1 to 3 years..........	77.1	80.8	88.1	52.6	...	...
High school: 4 years...............	76.1	77.7	84.7	48.1	...	...
1 to 3 years..........	72.2	73.9	84.3	46.2	52.5	65.6
None or elementary.................	71.2	73.0	83.1	39.4	52.0	63.3
45 TO 49 YEARS OLD						
College: 4 years or more.......	75.5	79.9	87.2	55.8	...	...
1 to 3 years..........	73.8	76.6	84.2	49.4	...	...
High school: 4 years...............	72.7	75.5	85.4	45.6	...	...
1 to 3 years..........	69.6	71.1	83.4	41.7	...	...
None or elementary.................	68.3	70.3	81.5	34.4	43.1	60.8

Source: Derived from *1950 Census of Population*, Vol. IV, *Special Reports*, Part 5, Chapter C, Fertility, tables 20-23.

nonwhites of given age and educational attainment, the proportion of unbroken first marriages tended to increase slightly from urban to rural-nonfarm to rural-farm areas.

The proportion of ever-married women classified as married once and husband present tended to be positively correlated with educational attainment. This type of relation was generally more clear-cut for the whites than for nonwhites. It was sharpest and most consistent for the urban whites. By residence it was sharpest for the urban areas and least in evidence for the rural-farm areas.

Although all analyses are made by age, the past duration of marriage is shorter, on the average, for the well-educated women than for others.[3] This would be expected on the basis of relatively late age at marriage of the women of high educational attainment.[4] This type of bias doubtless helps to account for the somewhat higher proportions classified as married once and husband present among the ever-married women of college status than among those of lower educational attainment.

D. Percent distribution of women by years of school completed, 1940 and 1950

The trends and differentials in the distribution of women by educational attainment are shown in tables 69 and 70 and figures 53 and 54.

TABLE 69.—PERCENT DISTRIBUTION BY YEARS OF SCHOOL COMPLETED, FOR EVER-MARRIED WHITE WOMEN 15 TO 49 YEARS OLD, BY AGE: 1950 AND 1940

[Data for white women in 1950 and native white women in 1940]

Year and years of school completed	15 to 19 years	20 to 24 years	25 to 29 years	30 to 34 years	35 to 39 years	40 to 44 years	45 to 49 years
1950							
Number, education reported.....	771,840	3,520,020	4,829,130	4,724,610	4,558,890	4,114,710	3,630,930
Percent...................	100.0	100.0	100.0	100.0	100.0	100.0	100.0
College: 4 years or more...	0.2	3.1	5.2	5.4	5.4	5.9	5.0
1 to 3 years......	1.9	8.4	9.2	8.9	8.9	9.5	8.6
High school: 4 years..........	25.2	42.4	42.3	36.6	29.2	23.5	19.5
1 to 3 years......	43.0	26.7	23.0	23.1	23.0	21.2	18.9
None or elementary............	29.7	19.4	20.4	26.0	33.5	39.8	48.1
1940							
Number, education reported.....	595,560	2,639,840	3,654,480	3,598,640	3,270,740	2,947,260	2,672,100
Percent...................	100.0	100.0	100.0	100.0	100.0	100.0	100.0
College: 4 years or more...	...	1.6	3.7	4.6	4.2	3.6	3.2
1 to 3 years......	1.5	5.2	7.7	8.9	8.4	7.2	6.4
High school: 4 years..........	17.3	32.3	28.4	23.1	19.0	17.2	15.0
1 to 3 years......	38.6	29.2	25.5	23.3	21.0	18.8	17.4
None or elementary............	42.6	31.8	34.7	40.1	47.5	53.2	58.0

Source: Derived from *1950 Census of Population*, Vol. IV, *Special Reports*, Part 5, Chapter C, Fertility, table 20; *1940 Census of Population, Differential Fertility, 1940 and 1910*, Women by Number of Children Ever Born, table 49.

The data for both white and nonwhite ever-married women in 1940 and 1950 reflect the secular improvements in education in that the proportions classified as "none or elementary" increase with age, after age 20

---

[3] *1940 Census of Population, Differential Fertility, 1940 and 1910*, Fertility by Duration of Marriage, p. 3.

[4] *1950 Census of Population*, Vol. IV, *Special Reports*, Part 2, Chapter E, Duration of Current Marital Status, table 5.

TABLE **70.**—PERCENT DISTRIBUTION BY YEARS OF SCHOOL COMPLETED, FOR EVER-MARRIED
NONWHITE WOMEN 15 TO 49 YEARS OLD, BY AGE: 1950 AND 1940

[Data for nonwhite women in 1950 and Negro women in 1940]

Year and years of school completed	15 to 19 years	20 to 24 years	25 to 29 years	30 to 34 years	35 to 39 years	40 to 44 years	45 to 49 years
1950							
Number, education reported....	138,300	481,950	589,230	551,880	564,810	474,330	415,320
Percent...................	100.0	100.0	100.0	100.0	100.0	100.0	100.0
College: 4 years or more..	0.1	1.2	2.8	2.8	2.5	2.9	1.7
1 to 3 years.....	0.9	4.4	4.1	3.6	3.7	3.0	2.6
High school: 4 years..........	7.9	17.8	17.5	12.9	9.8	7.1	6.0
1 to 3 years.....	36.5	30.5	24.3	20.6	17.0	14.3	10.8
None or elementary...........	54.6	46.1	51.4	60.1	67.0	72.7	79.0
1940							
Number, education reported....	125,500	401,400	486,320	449,340	469,740	376,300	317,500
Percent...................	100.0	100.0	100.0	100.0	100.0	100.0	100.0
College: 4 years or more..	...	0.5	1.1	1.4	1.0	1.0	0.9
1 to 3 years.....	0.4	1.7	2.4	2.6	2.1	1.7	2.0
High school: 4 years..........	4.1	8.8	7.4	6.4	4.8	4.5	3.6
1 to 3 years.....	22.0	19.7	16.8	13.2	10.8	9.2	7.5
None or elementary...........	73.5	69.2	72.3	76.4	81.4	83.6	86.0

Source: Derived from *1950 Census of Population*, Vol. IV, *Special Reports*, Part 5, Chapter C, Fertility, table 22; *1940 Census of Population, Differential Fertility, 1940 and 1910*, Women by Number of Children Ever Born, table 50.

FIGURE **53.**—PERCENT DISTRIBUTION OF EVER-MARRIED WHITE WOMEN 15 TO 49 YEARS OLD
BY YEARS OF SCHOOL COMPLETED, BY AGE: 1950 AND 1940

[Data for white women in 1950 and native white women in 1940]

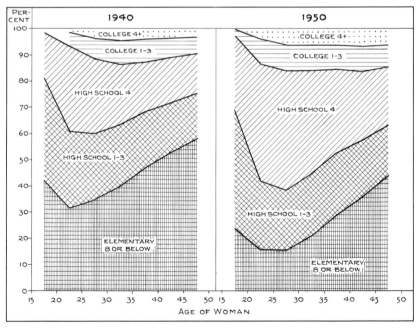

Note: Based on data in table 69.

to 24. The upgrading of the educational status of women during the 1940–50 decade may also be seen by comparing the data for specific age groups. Thus, in 1940, the proportion of native white ever-married women who reported not more than 8 completed years of elementary school extended from about 32 percent for those 20 to 24 years old to 58 percent for those 45 to 49 years old. In 1950, the corresponding figures were 19 and 48 percent. There were some increases in the relative importance of all higher educational groups, but the most conspicuous increase among the whites was found for the group that reported 4 years of high school. Thus, in 1940, about 32 percent of the native white women 20 to 24 years old and 15 percent of those 45 to 49 years old were of "high school: 4 years" status. In 1950 the corresponding percentages were about 42 and 19.

As expected, the educational attainment of whites was considerably higher than that of nonwhites within each type of community, and for both whites and nonwhites the educational status tended to be highest in urban areas, intermediate in rural-nonfarm areas, and lowest in rural-farm areas.

FIGURE 54.—PERCENT DISTRIBUTION OF EVER-MARRIED NONWHITE WOMEN 15 TO 49 YEARS OLD BY YEARS OF SCHOOL COMPLETED, BY AGE: 1950 AND 1940

[Data for nonwhite women in 1950 and Negro women in 1940]

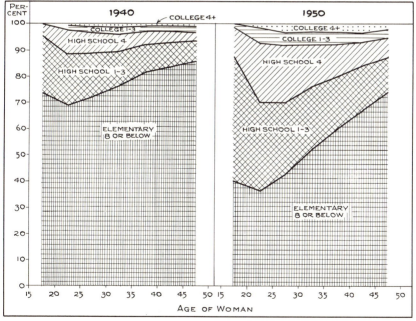

Note: Based on data in table 70.

Among white ever-married women 20 to 24 years old the proportions classified as "none or elementary" in 1950 were 15 percent in
urban areas, 25 percent in rural-nonfarm areas, and 31 percent in rural-
farm areas. The corresponding percents for the nonwhites were 36, 61,
and 72.

E. Percent changes in cumulative fertility rates and fertility ratios by educational attainment

Percent changes in cumulative fertility rates.   The central point
of importance revealed by table 71 is the direct relation of educational attainment to percent increase in cumulative fertility rates in *age groups exhibiting increases,* that is, generally in age groups 20 to 39.   This is illustrated in the data for urban ever-married white women, shown in
figure 55.   For example, among the women of this category, 25 to 29
years old, the 1940–50 increases in cumulative fertility rates extended
from 19 percent for those of "none or elementary" status to 70 percent
for those of "college: 4 years or more" status.

As noted in table 71, the 1940–50 percent increases in the general
cumulative fertility rates exceed those of the marital cumulative fertility
rates at each educational level because of the increase in marriage rates.
The direct relation of education to percent increase in cumulative fertility
rates is more pronounced in the general cumulative fertility rates than in
the marital cumulative rates, especially within the young age groups.   For
instance, among urban white women 20 to 24 years old, the 1940–50 increase in marital cumulative fertility rates extended from 14 percent for
those of "none or elementary" status to 30 percent for those of "college:
4 years or more" status.   The corresponding increase in general cumulative fertility rates extended from 59 percent to 171 percent.   As indicated in previous chapters, the 1940–50 percent increases in fertility
tended generally to be lowest in rural-farm areas and highest in urban
areas.   It is known that the education of women tends to be higher in
urban than in rural areas.   When the analysis is made by educational attainment, as in table 71, there is still some tendency for the 1940–50 percent increases in general and marital cumulative fertility rates to be
highest in urban groups and lowest in rural-farm groups.   Among women
of all marital classes, 30 to 34 years old, who had completed 1 to 3 years
of college, the percent increases in fertility rates were 57, 45, and 34 for
the urban, rural-nonfarm, and rural-farm groups, respectively.   However,
there were conspicuous exceptions among women 20 to 24 years old, reporting 1 to 3 years of college.   The percent increases in general cumulative fertility rates were 141 for the urban group, 194 for the rural-nonfarm group, and 254 for the rural-farm group.   (See also figures 56 and 57.)

TABLE **71.**—PERCENT CHANGE, 1940 TO 1950, IN NUMBER OF CHILDREN EVER BORN PER 1,000 WHITE WOMEN 15 TO 49 YEARS OLD, BY AGE, MARITAL STATUS, AND YEARS OF SCHOOL COMPLETED, URBAN AND RURAL

[Data for white women in 1950 and native white women in 1940. Totals include the relatively few women for whom school years was not reported. Percent not shown where there are fewer than 4,000 women in 1950 or 3,000 in 1940 or where percent is less than 0.1]

Age and years of school completed	United States		Urban		Rural nonfarm		Rural farm	
	All marital classes	Ever married	All marital classes	Ever married	All marital classes	Ever married	All marital classes	Ever married
15 to 19 years old............	70.4	-9.6	102.7	-5.3	64.6	-6.7	44.1	-12.9
College: 4 years or more......	...	...	...	...	...	...	...	...
1 to 3 years.........	111.1	-8.9	77.8	-10.3	583.3	...	110.0	...
High school: 4 years..............	124.1	-8.6	136.4	-2.0	116.3	-12.7	166.7	-14.6
1 to 3 years.........	102.5	-0.8	125.0	1.4	79.4	-3.5	72.5	-0.2
None or elementary.................	45.3	-3.4	70.5	-1.4	42.1	0.5	27.0	-5.7
20 to 24 years old............	47.6	3.2	67.2	11.0	43.8	6.7	39.2	-0.8
College: 4 years or more......	193.8	32.3	170.5	30.2	324.3	64.1	352.6	...
1 to 3 years.........	149.2	36.9	140.7	43.5	193.5	49.1	253.9	8.9
High school: 4 years..............	104.6	21.9	124.0	28.3	84.6	21.3	95.8	14.4
1 to 3 years.........	52.2	13.0	69.6	18.8	31.5	9.9	39.4	9.4
None or elementary.................	37.4	7.0	58.5	13.5	29.1	8.9	25.5	4.8
25 to 29 years old............	29.3	10.8	47.6	22.3	22.7	9.6	18.2	4.6
College: 4 years or more......	144.7	64.3	148.6	70.0	137.8	52.9	198.3	58.6
1 to 3 years.........	72.3	36.6	82.3	44.8	74.0	39.3	72.1	21.5
High school: 4 years..............	62.6	30.3	84.6	42.7	42.1	22.4	41.1	17.9
1 to 3 years.........	34.8	20.1	49.4	29.3	25.2	18.1	16.8	8.1
None or elementary.................	21.8	10.7	34.9	18.8	13.5	7.5	15.0	7.2
30 to 34 years old............	12.4	3.4	29.7	12.5	11.9	5.2	3.1	-3.4
College: 4 years or more......	82.5	44.2	84.0	45.7	87.0	46.5	86.9	37.3
1 to 3 years.........	44.6	27.2	57.3	36.4	45.1	28.5	34.0	18.0
High school: 4 years..............	40.4	23.5	52.7	31.1	33.1	22.5	18.0	8.3
1 to 3 years.........	17.4	10.0	28.0	17.9	13.2	9.0	8.6	3.2
None or elementary.................	4.0	-0.4	9.9	4.3	4.6	1.9	-0.6	-4.5
35 to 39 years old............	-3.7	-8.5	5.1	-1.8	-0.5	-4.3	-6.9	-10.4
College: 4 years or more......	45.3	22.6	51.6	27.0	35.6	15.9	35.8	7.7
1 to 3 years.........	20.0	9.4	27.0	14.5	17.2	8.2	20.6	8.7
High school: 4 years..............	15.4	5.7	20.6	8.5	15.2	9.4	4.1	-1.0
1 to 3 years.........	2.8	-2.4	11.3	4.2	0.5	-2.9	-3.8	-7.6
None or elementary.................	-5.2	-7.7	-0.9	-4.2	...	-1.8	-4.1	-6.3
40 to 44 years old............	-11.8	-14.9	-4.8	-9.7	-7.9	-10.0	-11.6	-13.5
College: 4 years or more......	17.3	-0.2	21.9	2.4	14.2	0.9	0.9	-14.9
1 to 3 years.........	1.9	-5.1	6.6	-3.0	6.6	1.5	-7.5	-9.6
High school: 4 years..............	-0.8	-6.8	3.1	-4.7	0.6	-3.6	-7.6	-9.5
1 to 3 years.........	-3.9	-8.4	2.4	-4.0	-0.8	-3.8	-6.8	-9.0
None or elementary.................	-9.1	-11.1	-4.3	-7.2	-4.9	-6.2	-6.5	-8.2
45 to 49 years old............	-13.5	-15.9	-6.3	-10.3	-9.8	-12.0	-11.3	-12.4
College: 4 years or more......	-12.4	-21.5	-9.8	-21.4	-18.2	-21.1	-9.9	-17.4
1 to 3 years.........	-11.4	-17.9	-8.6	-16.1	-10.1	-15.6	-14.6	-20.1
High school: 4 years..............	-6.0	-10.3	-3.2	-8.5	-5.3	-10.0	-5.4	-6.6
1 to 3 years.........	-7.4	-12.2	-2.0	-6.5	-13.0	-14.7	-8.6	-8.8
None or elementary.................	-9.0	-11.0	-2.2	-5.5	-4.0	-6.1	-7.1	-7.9

Source: Derived from *1950 Census of Population*, Vol. IV, *Special Reports*, Part 5, Chapter C, Fertility, table 20; *1940 Census of Population, Differential Fertility, 1940 and 1910*, Women by Number of Children Ever Born, tables 7 and 49.

Percent changes in fertility ratios.

The 1940–50 percent changes in fertility ratios among whites are presented in table 72 by age and educational attainment. They are given for all women, ever-married women, and for women married once and husband present.

The 1940–50 percent increases in fertility ratios not only tended to be greater than the percent increases in cumulative fertility rates, but the increases were also much more pervasive by age, education, and type of community. Thus, whereas increases in cumulative fertility rates were virtually confined to women under 40 years old and whereas there were decreases in the fertility of younger women in rural-farm areas and in lower educational groups within urban areas, the 1940–50 changes in fertility ratios represented in table 72 were increases in nearly all cases.

Figure 55.—Percent Change, 1940 to 1950, in Number of Children Ever Born per 1,000 Ever-Married White Women 15 to 49 Years Old, by Age and Years of School Completed, for Urban Areas

[Data for white women in 1950 and native white women in 1940]

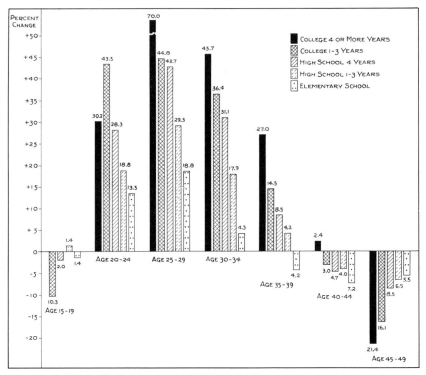

Note: Based on data in table 71.

The fact that 1940–50 increases in fertility ratios extended throughout the childbearing period meant that the women of all ages participated to some exent in the "baby boom." Actually, in many instances the percent increases in fertility ratios were considerably higher at ages 40 to 44 and 45 to 49 than at younger ages. However, at these late ages the number of own children under 5 years old tends to be very small, so that even a moderate absolute increase yields an impressive percentage increase. The 1940–50 increases at these ages apparently were "too little and too late" to have any substantial effect on the cumulative fertility rate for women of virtually completed fertility. The women near the end of the childbearing period exhibited higher fertility ratios but lower cumulative fertility rates in 1950 than in 1940.

FIGURE 56.—PERCENT CHANGE, 1940 TO 1950, IN NUMBER OF CHILDREN EVER BORN PER 1,000 EVER-MARRIED WHITE WOMEN 15 TO 49 YEARS OLD, BY AGE AND YEARS OF SCHOOL COMPLETED, FOR RURAL-NONFARM AREAS

[Data for white women in 1950 and native white women in 1940]

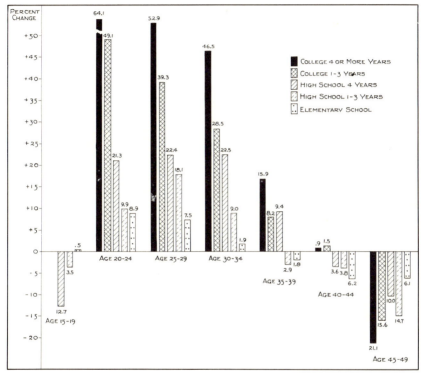

Note: Based on data in table 71.

Like the increases in fertility rates, the 1940–50 percent increases in fertility ratios were directly related to educational attainment. This held true within each age and residence group. There was a consistent tendency for the percent increases in fertility ratios to be highest for women of all marital classes, intermediate for ever-married women, and lowest for women married once and husband present.

Nonwhites. In the main, the 1940–50 percent changes in cumulative fertility rates and ratios among the nonwhites were similar in pattern to those of the whites (tables 73 and 74). As among the whites, the cumulative fertility rates for nonwhites under 35 years old were higher in 1950 than in 1940 at all educational levels. However, whereas the maximum percent increases tended to come at ages 25 to 29 for whites, they tended to come at ages 20 to 24 for nonwhites. At ages 20 to 24 the percent increases for the nonwhites tended to exceed those for the whites, especially among women who had completed 1 to 3 years of high school or less.

FIGURE 57.—PERCENT CHANGE, 1940 TO 1950, IN NUMBER OF CHILDREN EVER BORN PER 1,000 EVER-MARRIED WHITE WOMEN 15 TO 49 YEARS OLD, BY AGE AND YEARS OF SCHOOL COMPLETED, FOR RURAL-FARM AREAS

[Data for white women in 1950 and native white women in 1940]

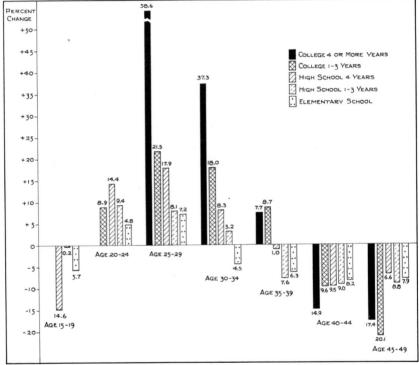

Note: Based on data in table 71.

As among the whites, the 1940–50 percent increases in fertility ratios exceeded the percent increases in cumulative fertility rates. The percent increases in cumulative fertility rates and fertility ratios tended to be directly related to educational attainment of the women.

F. Children ever born, by education of the woman

Despite the relatively large 1940–50 increases in the fertility of young women who had attended college, the cumulative fertility rates based upon children ever born were inversely related to education of the woman in

1950. Figure 58 presents age-standardized fertility rates by residence and educational attainment for ever-married white women 15 to 49 years old in 1940 and 1950. Similar materials are shown for nonwhites in the United States as a whole in figure 59.

The differences between the standardized rates for 1940 and those for 1950 were small because *increases* in the cumulative fertility rates for the younger women were largely offset by the *decreases* in the corresponding rates for the older women.

TABLE **72.**—PERCENT CHANGE, 1940 TO 1950, IN NUMBER OF OWN CHILDREN UNDER 5 YEARS OLD PER 1,000 WHITE WOMEN 20 TO 49 YEARS OLD, BY AGE, MARITAL STATUS, AND YEARS OF SCHOOL COMPLETED, URBAN AND RURAL

[Data for white women in 1950 and native white women in 1940. Percent not shown where there are fewer than 4,000 women in 1950 or 3,000 in 1910 or where percent is less than 0.1]

Age and years of school completed	Urban			Rural nonfarm			Rural farm		
	All marital classes	Ever married	Married once, husband present	All marital classes	Ever married	Married once, husband present	All marital classes	Ever married	Married once, husband present
20 TO 24 YEARS OLD									
College: 4 yrs. or more..	192.2	64.4	61.7	292.4	79.3	76.4	494.1	...	...
1 to 3 years....	140.0	62.3	57.6	179.4	63.4	62.9	261.3	35.0	33.8
High school: 4 years........	131.1	45.5	41.0	89.9	34.8	30.6	100.3	32.2	32.3
1 to 3 years....	71.4	27.7	26.2	39.1	20.5	18.3	39.2	16.2	14.2
None or elementary..........	58.2	21.6	20.5	34.5	18.8	18.6	28.6	14.8	15.7
25 TO 29 YEARS OLD									
College: 4 yrs. or more..	147.3	83.3	80.2	147.1	71.9	70.6	189.5	74.5	70.8
1 to 3 years....	91.7	59.9	55.3	80.4	50.2	47.9	84.9	39.4	35.4
High school: 4 years........	91.0	54.2	50.2	52.8	34.9	32.4	43.0	23.8	24.7
1 to 3 years....	57.3	39.6	37.3	32.7	26.6	23.9	17.5	10.8	9.9
None or elementary..........	41.9	28.9	27.3	20.2	15.8	12.5	21.1	15.5	13.8
30 TO 34 YEARS OLD									
College: 4 yrs. or more..	86.5	55.1	51.3	96.0	60.2	55.5	92.7	49.3	46.0
1 to 3 years....	76.4	57.0	52.5	56.2	41.3	39.8	47.8	33.6	33.4
High school: 4 years........	75.7	54.7	48.0	47.0	37.3	34.9	22.2	14.2	11.5
1 to 3 years....	50.0	40.5	35.6	21.0	17.4	13.5	11.2	6.9	4.6
None or elementary..........	37.4	32.4	29.5	17.3	15.3	12.8	4.4	1.6	0.4
35 TO 39 YEARS OLD									
College: 4 yrs. or more..	78.0	55.5	49.2	60.5	42.3	40.4	85.2	54.1	52.4
1 to 3 years....	84.1	69.0	58.7	66.5	56.3	50.6	29.8	19.3	14.3
High school: 4 years........	84.9	69.6	58.1	66.2	59.8	53.7	17.1	12.7	7.3
1 to 3 years....	57.6	49.3	42.1	19.2	15.7	13.6	-2.4	-5.5	-9.5
None or elementary..........	36.5	33.7	29.0	23.3	22.1	17.6	4.1	2.6	1.7
40 TO 44 YEARS OLD									
College: 4 yrs. or more..	114.3	87.8	85.3	95.8	79.2	51.3	75.8	53.3	48.0
1 to 3 years....	77.6	63.4	48.2	67.0	60.7	47.2	11.0	9.7	2.0
High school: 4 years........	94.0	84.8	73.1	54.7	50.0	44.6	7.5	6.1	4.4
1 to 3 years....	53.6	46.8	34.2	51.3	47.5	43.6	9.1	6.9	7.4
None or elementary..........	31.5	28.6	15.4	16.0	15.0	7.8	4.5	3.7	0.6
45 TO 49 YEARS OLD									
College: 4 yrs. or more..	66.7	50.0	50.0	100.0	94.4	95.5	28.9	21.7	31.9
1 to 3 years....	100.0	92.3	121.4	47.8	42.3	31.3	22.2	15.0	19.0
High school: 4 years........	57.1	56.3	42.1	89.5	81.0	62.5	4.3	2.0	...
1 to 3 years....	16.7	15.0	8.3	27.6	26.7	8.1	-4.7	-4.5	-15.8
None or elementary..........	...	-3.2	-2.7	9.8	9.3	6.3	-6.4	-6.1	-8.5

Source: Derived from *1950 Census of Population*, Vol. IV, *Special Reports*, Part 5, Chapter C, Fertility, table 44; *1940 Census of Population, Differential Fertility, 1940 and 1910*, Women by Number of Children Under 5 Years Old, table 25.

TABLE **73.**—PERCENT CHANGE, 1940 TO 1950, IN NUMBER OF CHILDREN EVER BORN PER 1,000 EVER-MARRIED NONWHITE WOMEN 15 TO 49 YEARS OLD, BY AGE AND YEARS OF SCHOOL COMPLETED

[Data for nonwhite women in 1950 and Negro women in 1940. Percent not shown where there are fewer than 4,000 women in 1950 or 3,000 in 1940]

Years of school completed	15 to 19 years	20 to 24 years	25 to 29 years	30 to 34 years	35 to 39 years	40 to 44 years	45 to 49 years
College: 4 years or more	...	...	48.1	30.4	6.5	-2.3	...
1 to 3 years	...	39.6	30.0	7.4	-12.8	-14.6	-3.3
High school: 4 years	9.1	26.3	17.9	10.9	-8.3	-17.4	-11.3
1 to 3 years	24.8	22.9	19.5	12.3	2.3	-4.9	-10.3
None or elementary	18.0	21.4	13.0	3.4	-3.8	-10.3	-14.8

Source: *1950 Census of Population*, Vol. IV, *Special Reports*, Part 5, Chapter C, Fertility, table 22; *1940 Census of Population, Differential Fertility, 1940 and 1910*, Women by Number of Children Ever Born, table 50.

TABLE **74.**—PERCENT CHANGE, 1940 TO 1950, IN NUMBER OF OWN CHILDREN UNDER 5 YEARS OLD PER 1,000 NONWHITE WOMEN 20 TO 44 YEARS OLD, BY AGE, MARITAL STATUS, AND YEARS OF SCHOOL COMPLETED

[Data for nonwhite women in 1950 and Negro women in 1940. Percent not shown where there are fewer than 4,000 women in 1950 or 3,000 in 1940]

Age and years of school completed	All marital classes	Ever married	Married once, husband present
20 TO 24 YEARS OLD			
College: 4 years or more	72.2	...	...
1 to 3 years	216.2	108.1	101.6
High school: 4 years	93.0	49.0	44.9
1 to 3 years	65.0	39.4	41.4
None or elementary	51.1	40.9	42.2
25 TO 29 YEARS OLD			
College: 4 years or more	130.0	74.9	46.8
1 to 3 years	69.6	39.9	49.5
High school: 4 years	82.6	58.6	53.7
1 to 3 years	45.8	33.7	24.0
None or elementary	43.7	37.8	33.6
30 TO 34 YEARS OLD			
College: 4 years or more	172.2	133.2	125.4
1 to 3 years	90.3	67.5	49.7
High school: 4 years	70.6	58.5	51.2
1 to 3 years	42.4	32.8	17.0
None or elementary	42.1	36.9	28.0
35 TO 39 YEARS OLD			
College: 4 years or more	218.1	178.9	...
1 to 3 years	232.5	201.0	240.9
High school: 4 years	54.9	48.0	57.4
1 to 3 years	50.0	45.6	41.5
None or elementary	28.0	25.8	15.8
40 TO 44 YEARS OLD			
College: 4 years or more	165.4	158.3	...
1 to 3 years	47.6	44.7	68.6
High school: 4 years	-30.7	-32.3	-38.4
1 to 3 years	47.7	45.8	47.2
None or elementary	16.5	15.4	11.4

Source: Derived from *1950 Census of Population*, Vol. IV, *Special Reports*, Part 5, Chapter C, Fertility, table 45; *1940 Census of Population, Differential Fertility, 1940 and 1910*, Women by Number of Children Under 5 Years Old, table 26.

FIGURE **58.**—STANDARDIZED NUMBER OF CHILDREN EVER BORN PER 1,000 EVER-MARRIED WHITE WOMEN 15 TO 49 YEARS OLD BY YEARS OF SCHOOL COMPLETED, URBAN AND RURAL: 1950 AND 1940

[Data for white women in 1950 and native white women in 1940. The standard is the distribution by age of all ever-married women 15 to 49 years old in the United States in 1950]

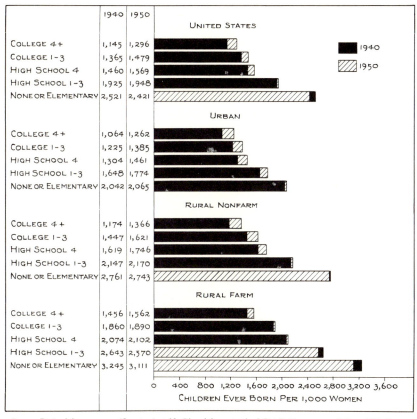

Source: Derived from age-specific rates in table 76 and from standard distribution computed from *1950 Census of Population*, Vol. IV, *Special Reports*, Part 5, Chapter C, Fertility, table 1.

FIGURE **59.**—STANDARDIZED NUMBER OF CHILDREN EVER BORN PER 1,000 EVER-MARRIED NONWHITE WOMEN 15 TO 49 YEARS OLD BY YEARS OF SCHOOL COMPLETED: 1950 AND 1940

[Data for nonwhite women in 1950 and Negro women in 1940. The standard is the distribution by age of all ever-married women 15 to 49 years old in the United States in 1950]

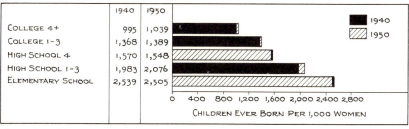

Source: Derived from age-specific rates in table 77 and from standard distribution computed from *1950 Census of Population*, Vol. IV, *Special Reports*, Part 5, Chapter C, Fertility, table 1.

Figures 60, 61, and 62 present the age-specific cumulative fertility rates by education and residence. Over the decade of 1940 to 1950, the range of differentials in cumulative fertility rates by education of the woman tended to become smaller. Among urban ever-married white women the

FIGURE **60.**—NUMBER OF CHILDREN EVER BORN PER 1,000 EVER-MARRIED WHITE WOMEN 15 TO 49 YEARS OLD, BY AGE AND YEARS OF SCHOOL COMPLETED, FOR URBAN AREAS: 1950 AND 1940

[Data for white women in 1950 and native white women in 1940]

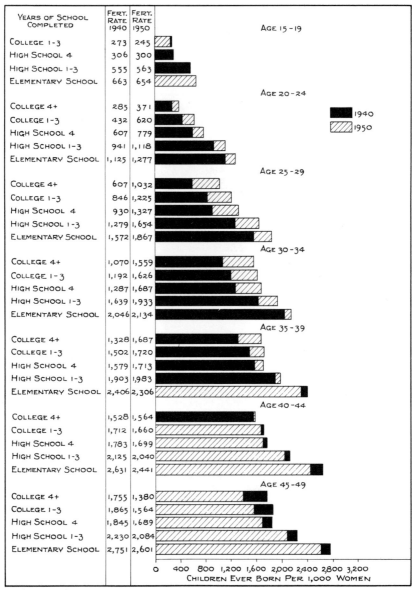

Note: Based on data in table 76.

contractions were especially marked at ages 25 to 39. The explanation is that at these ages the absolute increases tended to be largest among couples characterized by lowest fertility in 1940. The magnitude of the differentials in fertility by education among women 40 and over was about the same in 1950 as in 1940.

FIGURE **61.**—NUMBER OF CHILDREN EVER BORN PER 1,000 EVER-MARRIED WHITE WOMEN 15 TO 49 YEARS OLD, BY AGE AND YEARS OF SCHOOL COMPLETED, FOR RURAL-NONFARM AREAS: 1950 AND 1940

[Data for white women in 1950 and native white women in 1940]

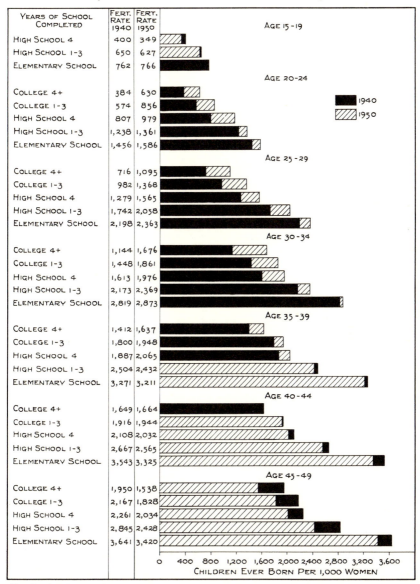

Note: Based on data in table 76.

TABLE **75.**—NUMBER OF CHILDREN EVER BORN PER 1,000 WHITE WOMEN 15 TO 49 YEARS
OLD, BY AGE AND YEARS OF SCHOOL COMPLETED, URBAN AND RURAL: 1950 AND 1940

[Data for white women in 1950 and native white women in 1940. Rate not shown where there are fewer than 4,000
women in 1950 or 3,000 in 1940]

Age and years of school completed	1950				1940			
	United States	Urban	Rural non-farm	Rural farm	United States	Urban	Rural non-farm	Rural farm
15 TO 19 YEARS OLD								
College: 4 years or more......	89	98	...	...	...	...	...	...
1 to 3 years..........	19	16	41	21	9	9	6	10
High School: 4 years..............	65	52	106	96	29	22	49	36
1 to 3 years..........	81	72	113	69	40	32	63	40
None or elementary..................	154	133	199	146	106	78	140	115
20 TO 24 YEARS OLD								
College: 4 years or more......	191	165	314	344	65	61	74	76
1 to 3 years..........	304	260	493	453	122	108	168	128
High school: 4 years..............	573	495	768	787	280	221	416	402
1 to 3 years..........	989	882	1,202	1,199	650	520	914	860
None or elementary..................	1,113	967	1,322	1,209	810	610	1,024	963
25 TO 29 YEARS OLD								
College: 4 years or more......	766	731	880	1,032	313	294	370	346
1 to 3 years..........	1,056	986	1,227	1,387	613	541	705	806
High school: 4 years..............	1,231	1,128	1,455	1,675	757	611	1,024	1,187
1 to 3 years..........	1,663	1,498	1,973	2,098	1,234	1,003	1,576	1,796
None or elementary..................	1,913	1,629	2,164	2,314	1,571	1,208	1,907	2,012
30 TO 34 YEARS OLD								
College: 4 years or more......	1,285	1,222	1,462	1,667	704	664	782	892
1 to 3 years..........	1,518	1,416	1,734	1,958	1,050	900	1,195	1,461
High school: 4 years..............	1,634	1,509	1,882	2,188	1,164	988	1,414	1,855
1 to 3 years..........	1,986	1,797	2,297	2,639	1,692	1,404	2,030	2,431
None or elementary..................	2,311	1,929	2,694	2,910	2,223	1,755	2,576	2,925
35 TO 39 YEARS OLD								
College: 4 years or more......	1,334	1,295	1,408	1,655	918	854	1,038	1,219
1 to 3 years..........	1,639	1,521	1,823	2,169	1,366	1,198	1,556	1,799
High school: 4 years..............	1,687	1,538	1,954	2,367	1,462	1,275	1,696	2,274
1 to 3 years..........	2,066	1,857	2,354	2,822	2,009	1,669	2,342	2,933
None or elementary..................	2,582	2,124	3,035	3,517	2,725	2,143	3,036	3,666
40 TO 44 YEARS OLD								
College: 4 years or more......	1,249	1,193	1,397	1,524	1,065	979	1,223	1,511
1 to 3 years..........	1,628	1,467	1,811	2,290	1,598	1,376	1,699	2,476
High school: 4 years..............	1,657	1,516	1,919	2,439	1,671	1,471	1,907	2,640
1 to 3 years..........	2,153	1,914	2,476	3,063	2,240	1,870	2,496	3,288
None or elementary..................	2,724	2,269	3,143	3,798	2,998	2,372	3,304	4,063
45 TO 49 YEARS OLD								
College: 4 years or more......	1,079	1,009	1,224	1,591	1,231	1,119	1,496	1,766
1 to 3 years..........	1,513	1,364	1,683	2,126	1,707	1,492	1,873	2,488
High school: 4 years..............	1,643	1,505	1,922	2,482	1,747	1,554	2,030	2,624
1 to 3 years..........	2,148	1,939	2,319	3,119	2,370	1,978	2,667	3,411
None or elementary..................	2,852	2,436	3,253	3,905	3,134	2,490	3,388	4,203

Source: Derived from *1950 Census of Population*, Vol. IV, *Special Reports*, Part 5, Chapter C, Fertility, table 20; *1940 Census of Population, Differential Fertility, 1940 and 1910*, Women by Number of Children Ever Born, table 49.

It has been noted that among young women with college training there were especially marked increases in proportions married as well as increases in marital fertility. Nevertheless, the inverse relation of education to general cumulative fertility rates as well as to marital cumulative fertility rates still existed in 1950 (tables 75 and 76). It is true that there was considerable reduction in the range of general cumulative fertility rates by education. Thus, among urban native white women 25 to 29 years old in 1940, the general cumulative fertility rate for women reporting 4 or more years of college was only about one-fourth that of women of "none or elementary" status. In 1950, the comparable rate for white women of "college: 4 years or more" status was almost half that of women of "none or elementary" status.

TABLE 76.—NUMBER OF CHILDREN EVER BORN PER 1,000 EVER-MARRIED WHITE WOMEN 15 TO 49 YEARS OLD, BY AGE AND YEARS OF SCHOOL COMPLETED, URBAN AND RURAL: 1950 AND 1940

[Data for white women in 1950 and native white women in 1940. Rate not shown where there are fewer than 4,000 women in 1950 or 3,000 in 1940]

Age and years of school completed	1950				1940			
	United States	Urban	Rural non-farm	Rural farm	United States	Urban	Rural non-farm	Rural farm
15 TO 19 YEARS OLD								
College: 4 years or more	...	...	...	...	...	...	...	...
1 to 3 years	256	245	...	...	281	273	...	...
High school: 4 years	319	300	349	346	349	306	400	405
1 to 3 years	586	563	627	598	591	555	650	599
None or elementary	707	654	766	723	732	663	762	767
20 TO 24 YEARS OLD								
College: 4 years or more	422	371	630	706	319	285	384	...
1 to 3 years	675	620	856	783	493	432	574	719
High school: 4 years	851	779	979	1,062	698	607	807	928
1 to 3 years	1,212	1,118	1,361	1,429	1,073	941	1,238	1,306
None or elementary	1,431	1,277	1,586	1,604	1,338	1,125	1,456	1,531
25 TO 29 YEARS OLD								
College: 4 years or more	1,055	1,032	1,095	1,316	642	607	716	830
1 to 3 years	1,277	1,225	1,368	1,557	935	846	982	1,281
High school: 4 years	1,415	1,327	1,565	1,832	1,086	930	1,279	1,554
1 to 3 years	1,805	1,654	2,058	2,220	1,503	1,279	1,742	2,054
None or elementary	2,150	1,867	2,363	2,574	1,942	1,572	2,198	2,402
30 TO 34 YEARS OLD								
College: 4 years or more	1,601	1,559	1,676	1,925	1,110	1,070	1,144	1,402
1 to 3 years	1,713	1,626	1,861	2,121	1,347	1,192	1,448	1,797
High school: 4 years	1,798	1,687	1,976	2,324	1,456	1,287	1,613	2,145
1 to 3 years	2,112	1,933	2,369	2,750	1,920	1,639	2,173	2,665
None or elementary	2,519	2,134	2,873	3,129	2,529	2,046	2,819	3,277
35 TO 39 YEARS OLD								
College: 4 years or more	1,693	1,687	1,637	1,936	1,381	1,328	1,412	1,797
1 to 3 years	1,822	1,720	1,948	2,306	1,665	1,502	1,800	2,121
High school: 4 years	1,851	1,713	2,065	2,491	1,751	1,579	1,887	2,517
1 to 3 years	2,184	1,983	2,432	2,917	2,238	1,903	2,504	3,158
None or elementary	2,772	2,306	3,211	3,710	3,002	2,406	3,271	3,959
40 TO 44 YEARS OLD								
College: 4 years or more	1,595	1,564	1,664	1,740	1,598	1,528	1,649	2,045
1 to 3 years	1,813	1,660	1,944	2,465	1,911	1,712	1,916	2,727
High school: 4 years	1,829	1,699	2,032	2,540	1,962	1,783	2,108	2,806
1 to 3 years	2,274	2,040	2,565	3,168	2,482	2,125	2,667	3,483
None or elementary	2,906	2,441	3,325	3,981	3,269	2,631	3,543	4,337
45 TO 49 YEARS OLD								
College: 4 years or more	1,437	1,380	1,538	1,809	1,831	1,755	1,950	2,189
1 to 3 years	1,698	1,564	1,828	2,230	2,067	1,865	2,167	2,790
High school: 4 years	1,818	1,689	2,034	2,606	2,026	1,845	2,261	2,790
1 to 3 years	2,290	2,084	2,428	3,257	2,607	2,230	2,845	3,573
None or elementary	3,025	2,601	3,420	4,088	3,400	2,751	3,641	4,437

Source: Same as table 75.

FIGURE **62.**—NUMBER OF CHILDREN EVER BORN PER 1,000 EVER-MARRIED WHITE WOMEN 15 TO 49 YEARS OLD, BY AGE AND YEARS OF SCHOOL COMPLETED, FOR RURAL-FARM AREAS: 1950 AND 1940

[Data for white women in 1950 and native white women in 1940]

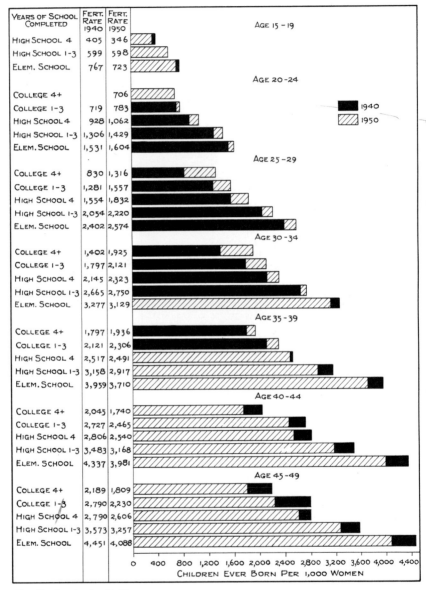

Note: Based on data in table 76.

Quantitative indices of the fertility differentials by education in 1940 and 1950 are presented in the last section of this chapter. It may simply be noted here that there was a greater reduction during 1940 to 1950 in the relative spread of general cumulative fertility rates by education than in the relative spread of marital cumulative fertility. Nevertheless, in 1950 the relative spread of general cumulative fertility rates by education was still greater than that of marital cumulative fertility rates.

Figures 63, 64, and 65 point up the tendency for the 1950 rates to exceed those for 1940 at young ages and to fall below those for 1940 at older ages. Of special interest is the fact that for urban white ever-married women who finished college, the cumulative fertility rate became lower for successively older cohorts of women in the 35-to-49 age span. Women who completed college in more recent years had more children than their predecessors. To a somewhat smaller extent the same may be said regarding women who attended college 1 to 3 years and those who completed high school.

FIGURE **63.**—COMPARISON OF THE AGE-SPECIFIC FERTILITY RATES OF WHITE WOMEN IN 1950 WITH THOSE OF NATIVE WHITE WOMEN IN 1940, FOR EVER-MARRIED WOMEN 15 TO 49 YEARS OLD, BY YEARS OF SCHOOL COMPLETED, FOR URBAN AREAS: 1950 AND 1940

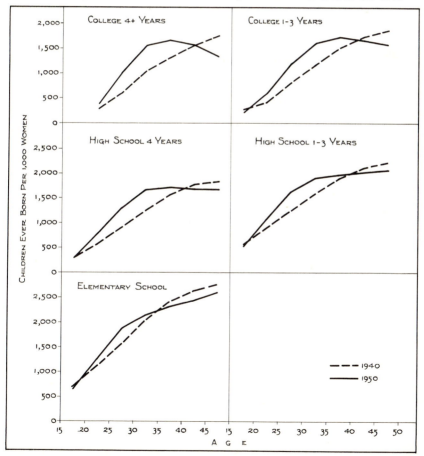

Note: Based on data in table 76.

FIGURE **64.**—COMPARISON OF THE AGE-SPECIFIC FERTILITY RATES OF WHITE WOMEN IN 1950 WITH THOSE OF NATIVE WHITE WOMEN IN 1940, FOR EVER-MARRIED WOMEN 15 TO 49 YEARS OLD, BY YEARS OF SCHOOL COMPLETED, FOR RURAL-NONFARM AREAS

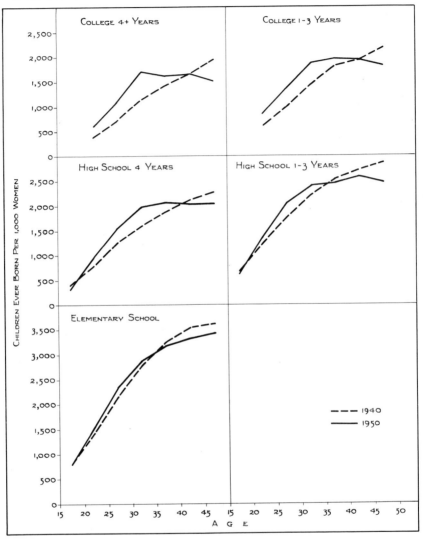

Note: Based on data in table 76.

Marital status. It will be noted that the cumulative fertility rates are considerably higher for women in unbroken first marriages than for other ever-married women. This type of differential was especially prominent among the nonwhites. Within each type of marital status group, however, the regular differential by education was maintained (see figures 66 and 67).

FIGURE **65.**—COMPARISON OF THE AGE-SPECIFIC FERTILITY RATES OF WHITE WOMEN IN 1950
WITH THOSE OF NATIVE WHITE WOMEN IN 1940, FOR EVER-MARRIED WOMEN 15 TO
49 YEARS OLD, BY YEARS OF SCHOOL COMPLETED, FOR RURAL-FARM AREAS

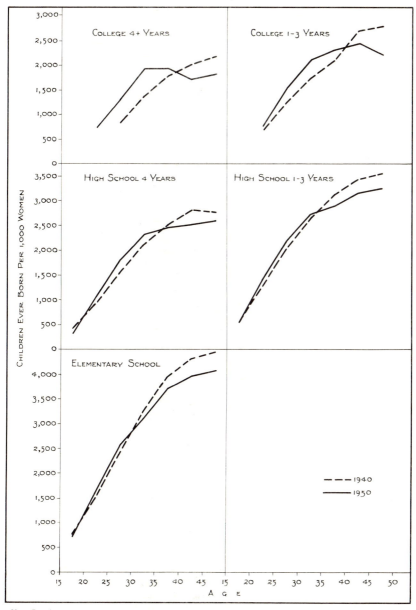

Note: Based on data in table 76.

FIGURE **66.**—NUMBER OF CHILDREN EVER BORN PER 1,000 EVER-MARRIED WHITE WOMEN 15 TO 49 YEARS OLD, BY MARITAL STATUS, BY AGE AND YEARS OF SCHOOL COMPLETED BY WOMAN, FOR URBAN AREAS: 1950

[Rate not shown where there are fewer than 4,000 women]

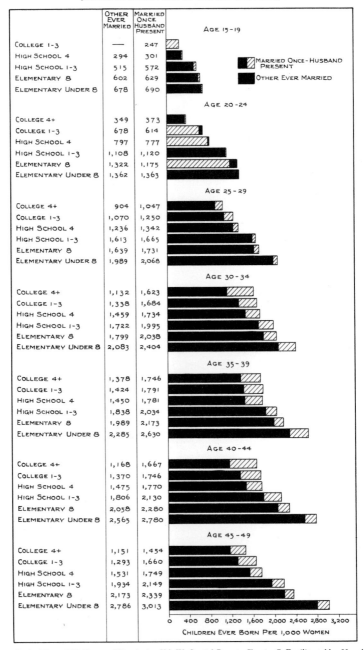

	OTHER EVER MARRIED	MARRIED ONCE HUSBAND PRESENT
AGE 15-19		
COLLEGE 1-3	—	247
HIGH SCHOOL 4	294	301
HIGH SCHOOL 1-3	515	572
ELEMENTARY 8	602	629
ELEMENTARY UNDER 8	678	690
AGE 20-24		
COLLEGE 4+	349	373
COLLEGE 1-3	678	614
HIGH SCHOOL 4	797	777
HIGH SCHOOL 1-3	1,108	1,120
ELEMENTARY 8	1,322	1,175
ELEMENTARY UNDER 8	1,362	1,363
AGE 25-29		
COLLEGE 4+	904	1,047
COLLEGE 1-3	1,070	1,250
HIGH SCHOOL 4	1,236	1,342
HIGH SCHOOL 1-3	1,613	1,665
ELEMENTARY 8	1,639	1,731
ELEMENTARY UNDER 8	1,989	2,068
AGE 30-34		
COLLEGE 4+	1,132	1,623
COLLEGE 1-3	1,338	1,684
HIGH SCHOOL 4	1,459	1,734
HIGH SCHOOL 1-3	1,722	1,995
ELEMENTARY 8	1,799	2,038
ELEMENTARY UNDER 8	2,083	2,404
AGE 35-39		
COLLEGE 4+	1,378	1,746
COLLEGE 1-3	1,424	1,791
HIGH SCHOOL 4	1,450	1,781
HIGH SCHOOL 1-3	1,838	2,034
ELEMENTARY 8	1,989	2,173
ELEMENTARY UNDER 8	2,285	2,630
AGE 40-44		
COLLEGE 4+	1,168	1,667
COLLEGE 1-3	1,370	1,746
HIGH SCHOOL 4	1,475	1,770
HIGH SCHOOL 1-3	1,806	2,130
ELEMENTARY 8	2,058	2,280
ELEMENTARY UNDER 8	2,565	2,780
AGE 45-49		
COLLEGE 4+	1,151	1,454
COLLEGE 1-3	1,293	1,660
HIGH SCHOOL 4	1,531	1,749
HIGH SCHOOL 1-3	1,934	2,149
ELEMENTARY 8	2,173	2,339
ELEMENTARY UNDER 8	2,786	3,013

MARRIED ONCE-HUSBAND PRESENT

OTHER EVER MARRIED

0   400   800   1,200   1,600   2,000   2,400   2,800   3,200
CHILDREN EVER BORN PER 1,000 WOMEN

Source: Derived from *1950 Census of Population*, Vol. IV, *Special Reports*, Chapter C, Fertility, tables 20 and 21.

FIGURE **67.**—NUMBER OF CHILDREN EVER BORN PER 1,000 EVER-MARRIED NONWHITE WOMEN 15 TO 49 YEARS OLD BY MARITAL STATUS, BY AGE AND YEARS OF SCHOOL COMPLETED BY WOMAN, FOR URBAN AREAS: 1950

[Rate not shown where there are fewer than 4,000 women]

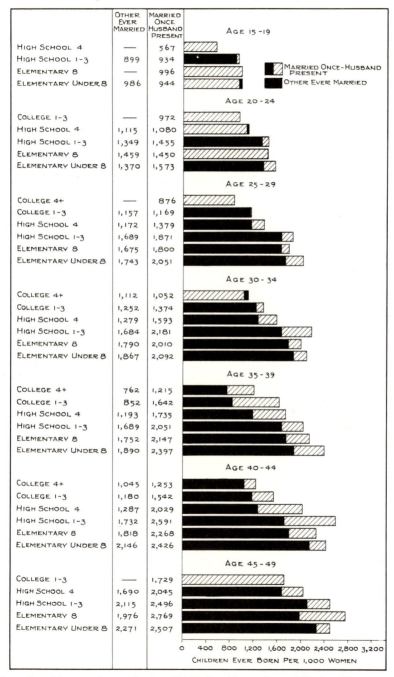

	Other Ever Married	Married Once Husband Present
AGE 15-19		
HIGH SCHOOL 4	—	567
HIGH SCHOOL 1-3	899	934
ELEMENTARY 8	—	996
ELEMENTARY UNDER 8	986	944
AGE 20-24		
COLLEGE 1-3	—	972
HIGH SCHOOL 4	1,115	1,080
HIGH SCHOOL 1-3	1,349	1,455
ELEMENTARY 8	1,459	1,450
ELEMENTARY UNDER 8	1,370	1,573
AGE 25-29		
COLLEGE 4+	—	876
COLLEGE 1-3	1,157	1,169
HIGH SCHOOL 4	1,172	1,379
HIGH SCHOOL 1-3	1,689	1,871
ELEMENTARY 8	1,675	1,800
ELEMENTARY UNDER 8	1,743	2,051
AGE 30-34		
COLLEGE 4+	1,112	1,052
COLLEGE 1-3	1,252	1,374
HIGH SCHOOL 4	1,279	1,593
HIGH SCHOOL 1-3	1,684	2,181
ELEMENTARY 8	1,790	2,010
ELEMENTARY UNDER 8	1,867	2,092
AGE 35-39		
COLLEGE 4+	762	1,215
COLLEGE 1-3	852	1,642
HIGH SCHOOL 4	1,193	1,735
HIGH SCHOOL 1-3	1,689	2,051
ELEMENTARY 8	1,752	2,147
ELEMENTARY UNDER 8	1,890	2,397
AGE 40-44		
COLLEGE 4+	1,045	1,253
COLLEGE 1-3	1,180	1,542
HIGH SCHOOL 4	1,287	2,029
HIGH SCHOOL 1-3	1,732	2,591
ELEMENTARY 8	1,818	2,268
ELEMENTARY UNDER 8	2,146	2,426
AGE 45-49		
COLLEGE 1-3	—	1,729
HIGH SCHOOL 4	1,690	2,045
HIGH SCHOOL 1-3	2,115	2,496
ELEMENTARY 8	1,976	2,769
ELEMENTARY UNDER 8	2,271	2,507

Legend: ▨ MARRIED ONCE-HUSBAND PRESENT ■ OTHER EVER MARRIED

CHILDREN EVER BORN PER 1,000 WOMEN (0, 400, 800, 1,200, 1,600, 2,000, 2,400, 2,800, 3,200)

Source: Derived from *1950 Census of Population*, Vol. IV, *Special Reports*, Chapter C, Fertility, tables 22 and 23.

Urban-rural residence.   An inverse relation of fertility to education existed in each type of residence.   However, the 1940–50 trend toward narrowing of differences in fertility by education was more pronounced in urban than in rural areas, especially at ages 25 to 39.   The conventional tendency for fertility rates to be lowest in urban areas, intermediate in rural-nonfarm areas, and highest in rural-farm areas held up with but few exceptions at specific educational levels.

Color.   In general, the tendency for cumulative fertility rates to vary inversely with educational attainment was found among nonwhites as well as whites (tables 77 and 78 and figure 68).   Because of the relatively low educational attainment of nonwhite women in rural areas, some of the educational groups contained too few women for the computation of fertility rates for nonwhites in rural areas for 1950.   Within the urban areas where complete ranges of rates for nonwhites by education were available, the relative spread of fertility rates by education was about the same for nonwhites as for whites.

Among urban ever-married women 30 years of age and over, the age-specific cumulative fertility rates were rather consistently and substantially higher for whites than for nonwhites of similar age and educational attainment.   This can be accounted for almost entirely by the very high percentage of childlessness among nonwhite urban ever-married women. When the analysis is restricted to mothers, the fertility rates tend to be higher for nonwhites than for whites of similar age and education.

The relatively high percentage of childlessness among urban nonwhite ever-married women 30 years old and over in 1950 was striking.   At ages 35 to 39 the proportion of childless women was about twice as high among nonwhites as among whites of similar education.   Among urban ever-married women with not more than 8 years of schooling the proportion of childlessness was 17 percent for whites and 35 percent for nonwhites. Among women of "college: 4 years or more" status the corresponding figures were 22 percent for whites and 50 percent for nonwhites.

The relatively high percentage of childlessness among urban nonwhite ever-married women was found at all ages above 25 in the 1940 Census. A similar situation existed to some extent in 1910, but the 1910 Census data for urban nonwhite married women showed a high fertility by modern standards and a low percentage of childlessness.[5]   That a change has emerged since 1940 is apparent from the 1950 data for the young married women.   Among urban ever-married women under 25 years of age, the cumulative fertility rates are consistently higher for nonwhites than for whites of similar educational attainment.   At these ages the percentages of childless women are lower for nonwhites than for whites at most of the educational levels.

---

[5] *1940 Census of Population, Differential Fertility, 1940 and 1910,* Fertility for States and Large Cities, tables 3 and 4.

TABLE **77.**—PERCENT CHILDLESS, NUMBER OF CHILDREN EVER BORN PER 1,000 WOMEN, AND NUMBER OF CHILDREN EVER BORN PER 1,000 MOTHERS, FOR EVER-MARRIED NONWHITE WOMEN 15 TO 49 YEARS OLD, BY AGE AND YEARS OF SCHOOL COMPLETED: 1950 AND 1940

[Data for nonwhite women in 1950 and Negro women in 1940. Percent or rate not shown where there are fewer than 4,000 women in 1950 or 3,000 in 1940]

Age and years of school completed	Percent childless			Children ever born per 1,000 women			Children ever born per 1,000 mothers		
	1950	1940	Percent change, 1940 to 1950	1950	1940	Percent change, 1940 to 1950	1950	1940	Percent change, 1940 to 1950
15 TO 19 YEARS OLD									
College: 4 yrs. or more..	...	...	...	...	...	...	...	...	...
1 to 3 years....	...	...	...	...	...	...	...	...	...
High school: 4 years.........	50.4	55.9	-9.8	551	505	9.1	1,110	...	...
1 to 3 years....	37.4	44.0	-15.0	912	731	24.8	1,457	1,304	11.7
None or elementary..........	36.7	39.9	-8.0	977	828	18.0	1,543	1,378	12.0
20 TO 24 YEARS OLD									
College: 4 yrs. or more..	54.5	...	...	588	...	...	1,294	...	...
1 to 3 years....	38.3	56.4	-32.1	913	654	39.6	1,480	...	...
High school: 4 years.........	31.3	45.5	-31.2	1,124	890	26.3	1,636	1,633	0.2
1 to 3 years....	27.5	36.2	-24.0	1,455	1,184	22.9	2,005	1,855	8.1
None or elementary..........	26.5	33.0	-19.7	1,711	1,409	21.4	2,327	2,104	10.6
25 TO 29 YEARS OLD									
College: 4 yrs. or more..	44.4	61.1	-27.3	905	611	48.1	1,629	...	...
1 to 3 years....	34.4	51.2	-32.8	1,204	926	30.0	1,837	1,897	-3.2
High school: 4 years.........	36.0	42.4	-15.1	1,361	1,154	17.9	2,127	2,004	6.1
1 to 3 years....	28.2	34.8	-19.0	1,938	1,622	19.5	2,700	2,490	8.4
None or elementary..........	25.7	29.2	-12.0	2,279	2,017	13.0	3,068	2,849	7.7
30 TO 34 YEARS OLD									
College: 4 yrs. or more..	41.2	53.9	-23.6	1,119	858	30.4	1,904	...	...
1 to 3 years....	40.6	45.0	-9.8	1,372	1,277	7.4	2,310	2,323	-0.6
High school: 4 years.........	35.0	43.5	-19.5	1,580	1,425	10.9	2,429	2,521	-3.6
1 to 3 years....	31.0	33.0	-6.1	2,148	1,912	12.3	3,114	2,853	9.1
None or elementary..........	27.2	26.1	4.2	2,598	2,513	3.4	3,569	3,401	4.9
35 TO 39 YEARS OLD									
College: 4 yrs. or more..	48.7	50.3	-3.2	1,109	1,041	6.5	2,162	...	...
1 to 3 years....	45.6	39.0	16.9	1,426	1,636	-12.8	2,624	2,682	-2.2
High school: 4 years.........	39.8	35.3	12.7	1,640	1,788	-8.3	2,726	2,766	-1.4
1 to 3 years....	31.4	32.2	-2.5	2,187	2,138	2.3	3,187	3,155	1.0
None or elementary..........	29.0	25.0	16.0	2,812	2,923	-3.8	3,963	3,899	1.6
40 TO 44 YEARS OLD									
College: 4 yrs. or more..	49.0	45.9	6.8	1,327	1,358	-2.3	2,603	...	...
1 to 3 years....	39.8	36.1	10.2	1,627	1,906	-14.6	2,704	2,980	-9.3
High school: 4 years.........	36.2	31.7	14.2	1,820	2,204	-17.4	2,852	3,225	-11.6
1 to 3 years....	31.2	28.5	9.5	2,409	2,532	-4.9	3,499	3,541	-1.2
None or elementary..........	27.2	22.4	21.4	2,912	3,248	-10.3	3,999	4,185	-4.4
45 TO 49 YEARS OLD									
College: 4 yrs. or more..	48.9	...	...	1,243	...	...	...	...	...
1 to 3 years....	44.1	33.8	30.5	1,942	2,009	-3.3	3,472	3,036	14.4
High school: 4 years.........	35.0	31.0	12.9	1,976	2,227	-11.3	3,039	3,228	-5.9
1 to 3 years....	28.5	25.2	13.1	2,521	2,812	-10.3	3,526	3,758	-6.2
None or elementary..........	26.6	20.7	28.5	2,964	3,478	-14.8	4,035	4,387	-8.0

Source: *1950 Census of Population*, Vol. IV, *Special Reports*, Part 5, Chapter C, Fertility, table 22; *1940 Census of Population, Differential Fertility, 1940 and 1910*, Women by Number of Children Ever Born, table 50.

Among both whites and nonwhites the relatively high proportion of childlessness among women who finished college is partly a reflection of a late age at marriage as compared with that for women of lower educational attainment.

TABLE **78.**—Percent Childless, Number of Children Ever Born per 1,000 Women, and Number of Children Ever Born per 1,000 Mothers, for Ever-Married Nonwhite Women 15 to 49 Years Old, by Age and Years of School Completed, Urban and Rural: 1950

[Percent or rate not shown where there are fewer than 4,000 women]

Age and years of school completed	Percent childless			Children ever born per 1,000 women			Children ever born per 1,000 mothers		
	Urban	Rural non-farm	Rural farm	Urban	Rural non-farm	Rural farm	Urban	Rural non-farm	Rural farm
15 TO 19 YEARS OLD									
College: 4 yrs. or more..	...	...	...	...	...	...	...	...	...
1 to 3 years....	...	...	...	...	...	...	...	...	...
High school: 4 years........	47.0	...	...	584	...	...	1,101	...	...
1 to 3 years....	37.4	36.7	38.4	924	896	866	1,475	1,415	1,406
None or elementary..........	37.8	33.5	37.8	958	1,045	948	1,540	1,572	1,523
20 TO 24 YEARS OLD									
College: 4 yrs. or more..	54.5	...	...	581	...	...	...	...	...
1 to 3 years....	38.3	...	...	927	...	...	1,504	...	...
High school: 4 years........	33.0	21.6	19.9	1,090	1,399	1,194	1,629	1,784	...
1 to 3 years....	28.9	23.1	23.6	1,417	1,537	1,606	1,992	1,998	2,102
None or elementary..........	32.4	21.6	18.1	1,480	1,851	2,078	2,190	2,362	2,538
25 TO 29 YEARS OLD									
College: 4 yrs. or more..	46.0	...	...	854	...	...	1,582	...	...
1 to 3 years....	35.9	...	...	1,165	...	...	1,818	...	...
High school: 4 years........	37.5	20.3	24.8	1,308	1,853	1,857	2,092	2,325	...
1 to 3 years....	31.0	17.8	16.0	1,798	2,328	2,753	2,606	2,831	3,278
None or elementary..........	30.9	20.2	16.3	1,863	2,656	3,103	2,695	3,330	3,708
30 TO 34 YEARS OLD									
College: 4 yrs. or more..	41.1	...	...	1,071	...	...	1,818	...	...
1 to 3 years....	41.6	...	...	1,335	...	...	2,288	...	...
High school: 4 years........	36.6	...	...	1,462	...	...	2,307	...	...
1 to 3 years....	33.5	19.9	17.0	1,955	2,830	3,465	2,940	3,533	4,175
None or elementary..........	33.2	21.7	13.6	1,960	3,104	4,107	2,936	3,963	4,754
35 TO 39 YEARS OLD									
College: 4 yrs. or more..	49.8	...	...	1,046	...	...	2,082	...	...
1 to 3 years....	47.6	...	...	1,263	...	...	2,411	...	...
High school: 4 years........	41.5	...	...	1,494	...	...	2,552	...	...
1 to 3 years....	34.2	21.8	13.4	1,864	2,877	4,648	2,834	3,680	5,368
None or elementary..........	35.2	23.0	15.0	2,080	3,448	4,552	3,210	4,476	5,353
40 TO 44 YEARS OLD									
College: 4 yrs. or more..	48.1	...	...	1,173	...	...	2,259	...	...
1 to 3 years....	41.5	...	...	1,370	...	...	2,342	...	...
High school: 4 years........	38.2	...	...	1,645	...	...	2,662	...	...
1 to 3 years....	33.7	22.6	12.9	2,129	3,145	4,636	3,213	4,065	5,322
None or elementary..........	31.7	24.1	15.1	2,196	3,432	4,819	3,213	4,524	5,674
45 TO 49 YEARS OLD									
College: 4 yrs. or more..	49.7	...	...	1,239	...	...	...	...	...
1 to 3 years....	48.4	...	...	1,901	...	...	3,685	...	...
High school: 4 years........	35.7	...	...	1,852	...	...	2,880	...	...
1 to 3 years....	29.4	...	...	2,274	...	...	3,220	...	...
None or elementary..........	30.6	23.9	14.5	2,335	3,256	4,941	3,364	4,277	5,781

Source: Derived from *1950 Census of Population*, Vol. IV, *Special Reports*, Part 5, Chapter C, Fertility, table 22.

In the rural-nonfarm areas the cumulative fertility rates for nonwhites tended to surpass those for whites of similar age and educational level in 1950. The chief exceptions were for older women of little education. Thus, among ever-married women of "none or elementary" schooling, the cumulative fertility rates were 3,211 and 3,448, respectively, for whites

FIGURE **68.**—NUMBER OF CHILDREN EVER BORN PER 1,000 EVER-MARRIED WOMEN 15 TO 49
YEARS OLD, BY COLOR, AGE, AND YEARS OF SCHOOL COMPLETED, FOR URBAN AREAS: 1950

[Rate not shown where there are fewer than 4,000 women]

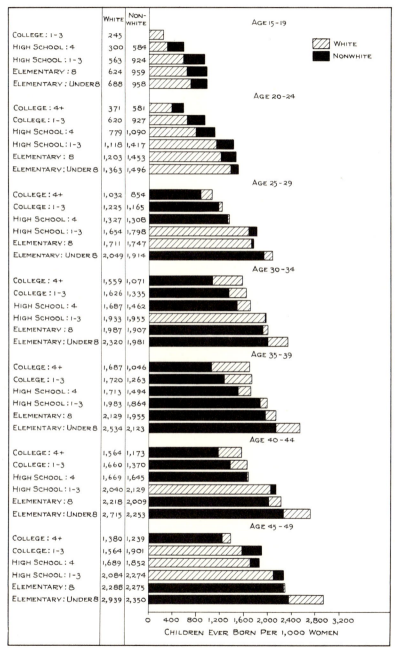

Source: *1950 Census of Population*, Vol. IV, *Special Reports*, Part 5, Chapter C, Fertility, tables 20 and 22.

and nonwhites 35 to 39 years old; 3,325 and 3,432 for those 40 to 44 years old, and 3,420 and 3,256 for those 45 to 49 years old. In these same groups the proportions of childless women were about twice as high among nonwhites as among whites. Except at youngest ages, 15 to 19, the proportion of childless women tended to be higher for nonwhites than for whites even if the whites exhibited lower fertility rates.

As already indicated, fertility is conspicuously high in the rural-farm population and especially among the nonwhite rural-farm population. This situation persists at specific educational levels. It is true that with the sampling scheme utilized, and with the extreme concentration of rural-farm nonwhite women in the lower educational groups, the fertility data ·by education for the nonwhites in rural-farm areas are very limited. No data are presented for nonwhites of college status at any age. At ages 45 to 49 no data are presented for women above the elementary school level.

Within rural-farm populations the cumulative fertility rates for nonwhites consistently surpassed those for whites of similar age and educational level in 1950. At ages 45 to 49 the average number of live births per ever-married woman of "none or elementary" status was 4.1 for whites and 4.9 for nonwhites. At ages 35 and over, the proportions of childless women usually were higher for nonwhites than for whites of similar age and education. Among women 15 to 19 years old, however, the proportions of childlessness tended to be lower for nonwhites than for whites of comparable age and education. This reflected the marked reduction in childlessness among the Negro marriages during the past decade. The section that follows gives a more detailed treatment of the distributions of women by number of children ever born.

Figure 69 shows age-specific fertility rates in 1940 by education, standardized and not standardized for duration of marriage. This type of standardization reduced the spread of the rates only slightly.

The differentials in fertility according to color may be briefly summarized thus:

Within urban areas the cumulative fertility rates for ever-married women under 25 years old in 1950 were consistently higher for nonwhites than for whites at each educational level. At older ages the reverse tended to be true; the cumulative fertility rates were lower for the nonwhites than for the whites. Within the rural-nonfarm areas the cumulative fertility rates for the nonwhites consistently surpassed those of the whites at each educational level of ever-married women under 35 years old. At older ages the reverse was true in only about half the age groups. Within the rural-farm areas the fertility rates for nonwhites were consistently higher than those for whites of similar age and educational attainment. Thus, the data again illustrate the principle of successively more rurality being associated with successively higher fertility of nonwhites relative to that of whites. It should be noted, however, that relative to whites, the Negroes exhibited high increases in fertility during 1940 to 1950. In 1940, the marital fertility ratios were rather uniformly lower for nonwhites than for whites. In

1950, this situation was still found among urban women 25 years of age and over. However, among urban women under 25 the increase in fertility was larger for the nonwhites than for the whites at all educational levels. One factor may be the improvement of social hygiene. The reduction in venereal diseases through the development of quick cures and the campaigns against "the shadow on the land" may be partially responsible for the increase in fertility of urban Negroes. Another factor may be an increasing stability of nonwhite marriages in urban areas.

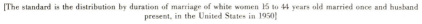

FIGURE **69.**—STANDARDIZED AND UNSTANDARDIZED NUMBER OF CHILDREN EVER BORN PER 1,000 WHITE WOMEN 15 TO 44 YEARS OLD MARRIED ONCE AND HUSBAND PRESENT, BY AGE AND YEARS OF SCHOOL COMPLETED BY WOMAN: 1950

[The standard is the distribution by duration of marriage of white women 15 to 44 years old married once and husband present, in the United States in 1950]

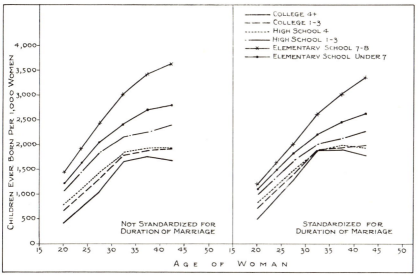

Source: Derived from *1950 Census of Population*, Series PC-14, No. 22, pp. 6–10.

G. Distribution of women by number of children ever born

Figure 70 presents 1940–50 comparisons of the distributions of urban white women of specified age by number of children ever born.

Among ever-married urban white women 25 to 29 years old, a conspicuous change during the 1940–50 decade was the reduction in the differentials in the proportions of childlessness. The proportion of women still childless by ages 25 to 29 declined at each educational level, but the magnitude of the decline decreased with lowering of educational status. Thus, among college graduates 25 to 29 years old, those who had not borne a child constituted 54 percent in 1940 and 34 percent in 1950. For women of elementary school education or less, the comparable figures were 24 percent for 1940 and 18 percent for 1950.

FIGURE **70.**—PERCENT DISTRIBUTION BY NUMBER OF CHILDREN EVER BORN, FOR EVER-MAR-
RIED WHITE WOMEN IN SPECIFIED AGE GROUPS, BY YEARS OF SCHOOL COMPLETED, FOR
URBAN AREAS: 1950 AND 1940

[Data for white women in 1950 and native white women in 1940]

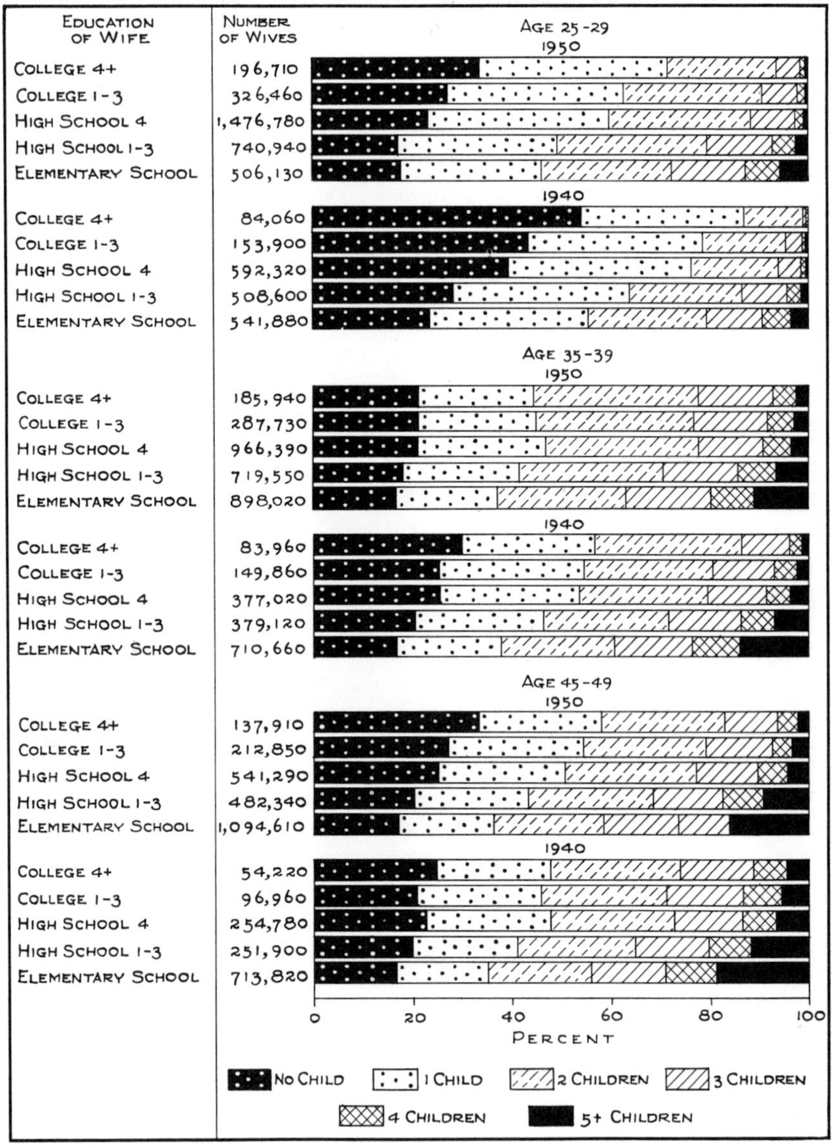

Note: Based on data in table 79.

In contrast, among urban white ever-married women 45 to 49 years
old and reporting 4 or more years of college, the percentage of childlessness was lower in 1940 than in 1950 (25 and 33 percent). Among those
of "none or elementary" status, the childless comprised approximately 17
percent in both 1940 and 1950.

Much of the lower rate of completed fertility of college women in 1950 than in 1940 stemmed from declines in the importance of the large family. Among urban white ever-married women 45 to 49 years old who had completed college the proportions with four or more children were 11 percent in 1940 and 7 percent in 1950. For women whose education was restricted to elementary school the comparable figures were 29 and 27 percent (tables 79–82, figures 70–72).

TABLE **79.**—PERCENT DISTRIBUTION BY NUMBER OF CHILDREN EVER BORN, FOR EVER-MARRIED WHITE WOMEN IN SPECIFIED AGE GROUPS, BY YEARS OF SCHOOL COMPLETED, FOR URBAN AREAS: 1950 AND 1940

[Data for white women in 1950 and native white women in 1940]

Year, age, and years of school completed	Number of women	Percent with specified number of children ever born						Children ever born	
		None	1	2	3	4	5 or more	Per 1,000 women	Per 1,000 mothers
25 TO 29 YEARS OLD									
1950									
College: 4 years or more..	196,710	34.0	37.6	22.1	4.8	1.1	0.3	1,032	1,565
1 to 3 years.....	326,460	27.5	35.3	28.1	7.2	1.4	0.6	1,225	1,690
High school: 4 years.........	1,476,780	23.7	35.9	28.9	8.9	1.8	0.8	1,327	1,739
1 to 3 years.....	740,940	17.2	32.3	30.1	13.4	4.7	2.4	1,654	1,997
None or elementary...........	506,130	18.0	28.1	26.2	14.9	7.1	5.6	1,867	2,278
1940									
College: 4 years or more..	84,060	54.4	32.8	10.9	1.5	0.2	0.1	607	1,332
1 to 3 years.....	153,900	43.5	35.0	16.8	3.7	0.7	0.3	846	1,497
High school: 4 years.........	592,320	39.5	36.7	17.7	4.6	1.2	0.5	930	1,537
1 to 3 years.....	508,600	28.8	35.1	22.6	8.8	3.2	1.6	1,279	1,798
None or elementary...........	541,880	23.9	31.5	23.9	11.6	5.3	3.9	1,572	2,065
35 TO 39 YEARS OLD									
1950									
College: 4 years or more..	185,940	21.5	22.8	33.3	15.4	4.5	2.5	1,687	2,149
1 to 3 years.....	287,730	21.4	23.5	31.7	15.2	5.3	2.9	1,720	2,189
High school: 4 years.........	966,390	21.4	25.5	30.3	13.7	5.6	3.6	1,713	2,178
1 to 3 years.....	719,550	18.1	23.6	28.7	15.4	7.8	6.5	1,983	2,420
None or elementary...........	898,020	16.8	20.2	25.9	17.1	8.9	11.0	2,306	2,773
1940									
College: 4 years or more..	83,960	29.9	27.0	29.4	9.8	2.7	1.2	1,328	1,895
1 to 3 years.....	149,860	25.3	29.3	26.1	12.3	4.6	2.3	1,502	2,011
High school: 4 years.........	377,020	25.6	28.2	25.6	12.0	4.8	3.8	1,579	2,123
1 to 3 years.....	379,120	20.6	26.0	24.7	14.9	6.8	7.1	1,903	2,396
None or elementary...........	710,660	17.0	21.0	22.7	15.6	9.7	13.9	2,406	2,899
45 TO 49 YEARS OLD									
1950									
College: 4 years or more..	137,910	33.3	24.7	25.0	10.3	4.5	2.3	1,380	2,067
1 to 3 years.....	212,850	27.2	27.3	24.6	13.2	4.0	3.7	1,564	2,149
High school: 4 years.........	541,290	25.1	25.5	26.5	12.4	5.7	4.7	1,689	2,255
1 to 3 years.....	482,340	20.2	23.0	25.4	14.0	8.0	9.4	2,084	2,612
None or elementary...........	1,094,610	17.1	19.0	22.1	15.3	10.2	16.3	2,601	3,137
1940									
College: 4 years or more..	54,220	24.6	22.8	26.4	14.8	6.6	4.8	1,755	2,329
1 to 3 years.....	96,960	20.9	24.7	25.4	15.8	7.5	5.6	1,865	2,358
High school: 4 years.........	254,780	22.8	24.5	25.2	13.9	6.9	6.7	1,845	2,390
1 to 3 years.....	251,900	19.9	21.2	23.7	14.8	8.5	11.9	2,230	2,785
None or elementary...........	713,820	16.6	18.5	20.6	15.2	10.0	19.0	2,751	3,300

Source: Derived from *1950 Census of Population*, Vol. IV, *Special Reports*, Part 5, Chapter C, Fertility, table 20; *1940 Census of Population, Differential Fertility, 1940 and 1910*, Women by Number of Children Ever Born, table 47.

Table 80.—Percent Distribution by Number of Children Ever Born, for Ever-Married White Women in Specified Age Groups, by Years of School Completed, for Rural-Nonfarm Areas: 1950 and 1940

[Data for white women in 1950 and native white women in 1940]

Year, age, and years of school completed	Number of women	Percent with specified number of children ever born						Children ever born	
		None	1	2	3	4	5 or more	Per 1,000 women	Per 1,000 mothers
25 TO 29 YEARS OLD									
1950									
College: 4 years or more..	41,310	32.0	37.0	23.7	5.5	1.2	0.5	1,095	1,610
1 to 3 years.....	84,030	23.0	34.7	30.2	8.9	2.4	0.8	1,368	1,776
High school: 4 years..........	395,910	18.0	31.9	32.9	12.4	3.6	1.3	1,565	1,907
1 to 3 years.....	252,030	12.4	25.0	30.4	19.0	7.6	5.5	2,058	2,350
None or elementary............	277,770	12.3	21.1	25.2	19.7	10.8	10.9	2,363	2,696
1940									
College: 4 years or more..	25,320	47.1	37.3	13.7	1.6	0.2	0.2	716	1,353
1 to 3 years.....	58,960	35.8	38.7	19.7	4.0	1.4	0.4	982	1,528
High school: 4 years..........	200,920	27.5	35.7	24.2	8.7	2.6	1.3	1,279	1,764
1 to 3 years.....	182,440	18.6	29.8	26.9	14.6	6.2	3.9	1,742	2,140
None or elementary............	279,000	15.0	23.6	23.8	17.1	11.0	9.5	2,198	2,586
35 TO 39 YEARS OLD									
1950									
College: 4 years or more..	46,350	19.5	28.4	32.0	13.7	3.7	2.8	1,637	2,034
1 to 3 years.....	78,720	17.9	20.4	32.7	17.6	6.9	4.5	1,948	2,372
High school: 4 years..........	233,010	17.3	21.3	29.4	17.4	7.8	6.9	2,065	2,497
1 to 3 years.....	199,080	14.4	20.1	25.8	16.6	10.7	12.3	2,432	2,841
None or elementary............	340,830	12.3	14.6	19.1	15.5	13.2	25.3	3,211	3,664
1940									
College: 4 years or more..	28,160	28.4	26.4	28.8	11.6	3.2	1.6	1,412	1,972
1 to 3 years.....	57,500	19.6	26.5	28.6	14.3	6.3	4.8	1,800	2,239
High school: 4 years..........	110,520	20.1	25.2	26.1	15.7	7.1	5.9	1,887	2,360
1 to 3 years.....	133,580	13.6	21.1	24.1	16.1	10.9	14.1	2,504	2,897
None or elementary............	307,580	11.2	15.6	18.4	15.4	12.3	27.2	3,271	3,682
45 TO 49 YEARS OLD									
1950									
College: 4 years or more..	29,010	31.9	22.5	23.7	10.9	8.3	2.8	1,538	2,256
1 to 3 years.....	59,100	22.9	22.8	27.7	13.7	6.6	6.2	1,828	2,373
High school: 4 years..........	107,820	23.7	20.9	24.0	14.1	8.0	9.3	2,034	2,664
1 to 3 years.....	119,400	19.1	19.3	22.8	16.0	9.6	13.3	2,428	3,000
None or elementary............	338,100	13.8	14.2	17.9	14.5	11.6	28.0	3,420	3,966
1940									
College: 4 years or more..	14,800	23.8	19.3	25.0	15.4	9.6	6.9	1,950	2,559
1 to 3 years.....	32,240	19.7	21.3	24.3	14.3	9.8	10.6	2,167	2,698
High school: 4 years..........	64,160	17.7	21.9	24.5	16.1	8.3	11.4	2,261	2,748
1 to 3 years.....	84,860	14.6	18.0	19.9	15.6	10.5	21.4	2,845	3,330
None or elementary............	275,500	11.2	13.9	16.2	14.7	12.2	31.7	3,641	4,101

Source: Same as table 79.

As expected, for both 1940 and 1950 as one proceeds from urban to rural-nonfarm to rural-farm areas, one witnesses successively lower proportions of childlessness and successively higher proportions of families reporting four or more live births. Among ever-married white women 45 to 49 years old and living in rural-farm areas, the proportion of childlessness in 1940 ranged from 19 percent for "college: 4 years or more" women to 8 percent for the women of "none or elementary" school status.

TABLE **81.**—PERCENT DISTRIBUTION BY NUMBER OF CHILDREN EVER BORN, FOR EVER-MARRIED WHITE WOMEN IN SPECIFIED AGE GROUPS, BY YEARS OF SCHOOL COMPLETED, FOR RURAL-FARM AREAS: 1950 AND 1940

[Data for white women in 1950 and native white women in 1940]

Year, age, and years of school completed	Number of women	Percent with specified number of children ever born						Children ever born	
		None	1	2	3	4	5 or more	Per 1,000 women	Per 1,000 mothers
25 TO 29 YEARS OLD									
1950									
College: 4 years or more..	10,800	32.2	26.7	25.6	11.7	1.4	2.5	1,316	1,941
1 to 3 years.....	33,810	15.9	35.7	32.5	11.9	2.0	2.1	1,557	1,851
High school: 4 years.........	172,140	14.3	27.3	34.0	15.7	6.0	2.8	1,832	2,137
1 to 3 years.....	115,800	11.6	21.0	27.5	22.6	11.7	5.6	2,220	2,512
None or elementary...........	198,510	10.2	18.2	25.6	19.9	12.9	13.2	2,574	2,866
1940									
College: 4 years or more..	5,780	45.3	32.5	16.6	4.8	0.7	...	830	1,519
1 to 3 years.....	31,460	26.4	37.8	24.3	7.7	2.2	1.7	1,281	1,741
High school: 4 years.........	114,000	20.4	33.4	27.0	12.9	4.2	2.2	1,554	1,951
1 to 3 years.....	126,520	12.6	25.9	29.0	18.1	8.9	5.6	2,054	2,348
None or elementary...........	281,220	11.4	21.1	25.0	19.2	12.2	11.1	2,402	2,710
35 TO 39 YEARS OLD									
1950									
College: 4 years or more..	15,030	21.8	20.8	26.9	16.2	9.4	5.0	1,936	2,475
1 to 3 years.....	40,440	13.1	18.9	27.5	22.3	9.9	8.3	2,306	2,655
High school: 4 years.........	131,070	13.5	17.3	24.7	21.6	10.6	12.4	2,491	2,879
1 to 3 years.....	130,080	9.7	16.2	21.8	19.1	14.4	18.7	2,917	3,232
None or elementary...........	286,650	9.5	11.5	16.2	16.3	13.4	33.1	3,710	4,098
1940									
College: 4 years or more..	8,560	25.0	21.0	26.6	15.0	7.2	5.1	1,797	2,396
1 to 3 years.....	36,680	18.6	21.3	24.9	16.9	10.2	8.0	2,121	2,607
High school: 4 years.........	64,800	13.2	19.5	23.6	18.8	11.1	13.8	2,517	2,900
1 to 3 years.....	99,580	9.7	15.4	19.6	17.5	13.3	24.4	3,158	3,498
None or elementary...........	356,480	7.1	11.1	15.6	15.5	13.4	37.3	3,959	4,262
45 TO 49 YEARS OLD									
1950									
College: 4 years or more..	13,410	27.1	23.0	22.6	14.8	5.6	7.0	1,809	2,480
1 to 3 years.....	39,240	21.2	17.7	24.0	16.6	10.0	10.5	2,230	2,829
High school: 4 years.........	58,500	16.1	17.6	22.9	17.5	10.4	15.6	2,606	3,106
1 to 3 years.....	85,800	14.2	12.0	19.8	17.6	12.0	24.4	3,257	3,797
None or elementary...........	311,550	10.4	10.8	14.7	14.2	12.2	37.6	4,088	4,562
1940									
College: 4 years or more..	6,600	19.4	22.1	24.2	13.3	10.0	10.9	2,189	2,716
1 to 3 years.....	22,740	16.2	14.6	20.0	16.8	13.0	19.4	2,790	3,329
High school: 4 years.........	40,860	13.8	16.1	22.5	18.0	12.0	17.7	2,790	3,235
1 to 3 years.....	77,300	10.8	13.1	17.7	15.9	11.4	31.0	3,573	4,006
None or elementary...........	383,300	7.5	10.2	13.6	13.1	12.5	43.0	4,451	4,799

Source: Same as table 79.

In 1950, the proportion of childless women was about 27 percent for women of "college: 4 years or more" status and 10 percent for the women of "none or elementary" status. For reasons previously indicated, the percent distributions for 1940 tended to understate the proportions of childless women. This tended to reduce the observed 1940–50 decreases in childlessness for younger women and to enhance the 1940–50 increases in childlessness for older women. In 1940, the proportion of rural-farm ever-married white women with four or more children was about 21 percent for the women of "college: 4 years or more" status and 56 percent for the women of "none or elementary" status. In 1950, the respective proportions were 13 percent and 50 percent.

TABLE **82.**—Percent Distribution by Number of Children Ever Born, for Ever-Married Nonwhite Women in Specified Age Groups, by Years of School Completed: 1950 and 1940

[Data for nonwhite women in 1950 and Negro women in 1940. Percent or rate not shown where there are fewer than 3,000 women in 1940]

Year, age, and years of school completed	Number of women	Percent with specified number of children ever born						Children ever born	
		None	1	2	3	4	5 or more	Per 1,000 women	Per 1,000 mothers
25 TO 29 YEARS OLD									
1950									
College: 4 years or more..	16,620	44.4	33.6	16.2	2.7	1.3	1.9	905	1,629
1 to 3 years.....	23,880	34.4	31.8	21.4	7.2	3.6	1.7	1,204	1,837
High school: 4 years..........	102,840	36.0	26.2	19.3	9.9	5.3	3.4	1,361	2,127
1 to 3 years.....	143,220	28.2	21.3	18.5	12.1	9.8	10.2	1,938	2,700
None or elementary............	302,670	25.7	19.4	16.0	12.6	9.8	16.5	2,279	3,068
1940									
College: 4 years or more..	3,860	61.1	22.3	10.9	5.7	...	...	611	...
1 to 3 years.....	10,040	51.2	23.9	14.7	4.8	3.2	2.2	926	1,897
High school: 4 years..........	30,740	42.4	25.6	17.4	7.6	4.4	2.6	1,154	2,004
1 to 3 years.....	71,980	34.8	21.6	17.9	10.9	7.4	7.5	1,622	2,490
None or elementary............	296,220	29.2	21.0	15.8	11.7	9.4	12.9	2,017	2,849
35 TO 39 YEARS OLD									
1950									
College: 4 years or more..	13,920	48.7	20.3	17.5	7.1	2.2	4.3	1,109	2,162
1 to 3 years.....	21,030	45.6	20.4	12.7	8.3	5.1	7.8	1,426	2,624
High school: 4 years..........	55,410	39.8	20.7	13.0	10.0	7.4	9.1	1,640	2,726
1 to 3 years.....	96,150	31.4	19.9	16.3	9.4	7.3	15.8	2,187	3,187
None or elementary............	378,300	29.0	17.7	12.3	8.9	7.0	25.1	2,812	3,963
1940									
College: 4 years or more..	3,860	50.3	20.7	16.6	8.8	...	3.6	1,041	...
1 to 3 years.....	8,260	39.0	18.6	17.2	10.7	6.1	8.5	1,636	2,682
High school: 4 years..........	19,300	35.3	21.3	16.9	7.7	7.7	11.1	1,788	2,766
1 to 3 years.....	44,140	32.2	20.9	14.9	10.6	5.8	15.6	2,138	3,155
None or elementary............	327,160	25.0	17.4	14.1	10.2	7.9	25.4	2,923	3,899
45 TO 49 YEARS OLD									
1950									
College: 4 years or more..	6,930	48.9	14.7	20.8	8.2	2.6	4.7	1,243	...
1 to 3 years.....	10,620	44.1	14.7	15.8	6.5	4.8	14.1	1,942	3,472
High school: 4 years..........	25,050	35.0	20.7	13.1	12.2	6.0	13.0	1,976	3,039
1 to 3 years.....	44,730	28.5	21.7	13.1	11.1	6.6	19.0	2,521	3,526
None or elementary............	327,990	26.6	17.5	13.6	10.2	7.6	24.5	2,964	4,035
1940									
College: 4 years or more..	2,560	...	...	...	...	...	...	...	...
1 to 3 years.....	5,320	33.8	20.7	16.2	9.8	4.1	15.5	2,009	3,036
High school: 4 years..........	9,800	31.0	18.6	16.3	8.8	8.6	16.7	2,227	3,228
1 to 3 years.....	20,180	25.2	17.9	14.3	12.4	6.8	23.4	2,812	3,758
None or elementary............	235,600	20.7	14.1	13.8	11.3	9.2	30.9	3,478	4,387

Source: Derived from *1950 Census of Population*, Vol. IV, *Special Reports*, Part 5, Chapter C, Fertility, table 22; *1940 Census of Population, Differential Fertility, 1940 and 1910*, Women by Number of Children Ever Born, table 48.

FIGURE **71.**—PERCENT DISTRIBUTION BY NUMBER OF CHILDREN EVER BORN, FOR EVER-MAR-
RIED WHITE WOMEN IN SPECIFIED AGE GROUPS, BY YEARS OF SCHOOL COMPLETED, FOR
RURAL-NONFARM AREAS: 1950 AND 1940

[Data for white women in 1950 and native white women in 1940]

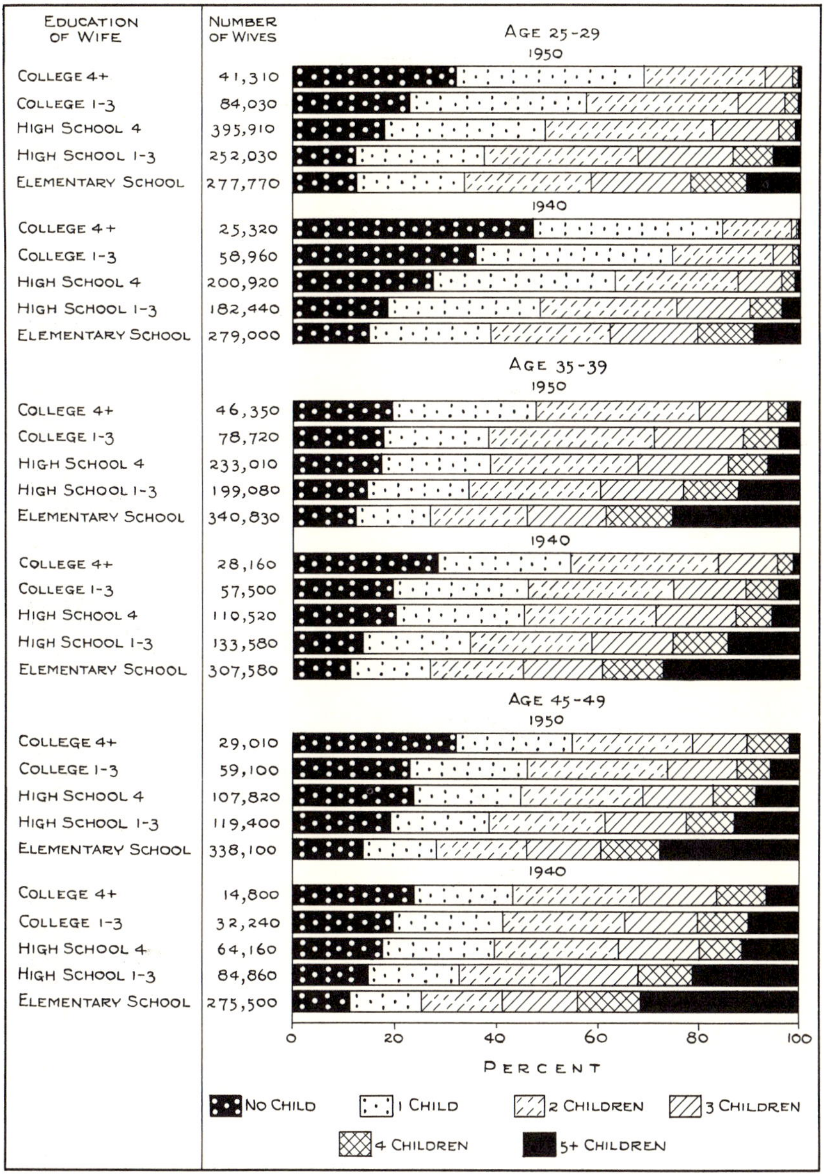

Note: Based on data in table 80.

FIGURE **72.**—PERCENT DISTRIBUTION BY NUMBER OF CHILDREN EVER BORN, FOR EVER-MARRIED WHITE WOMEN IN SPECIFIED AGE GROUPS, BY YEARS OF SCHOOL COMPLETED, FOR RURAL-FARM AREAS: 1950 AND 1940

[Data for white women in 1950 and native white women in 1940]

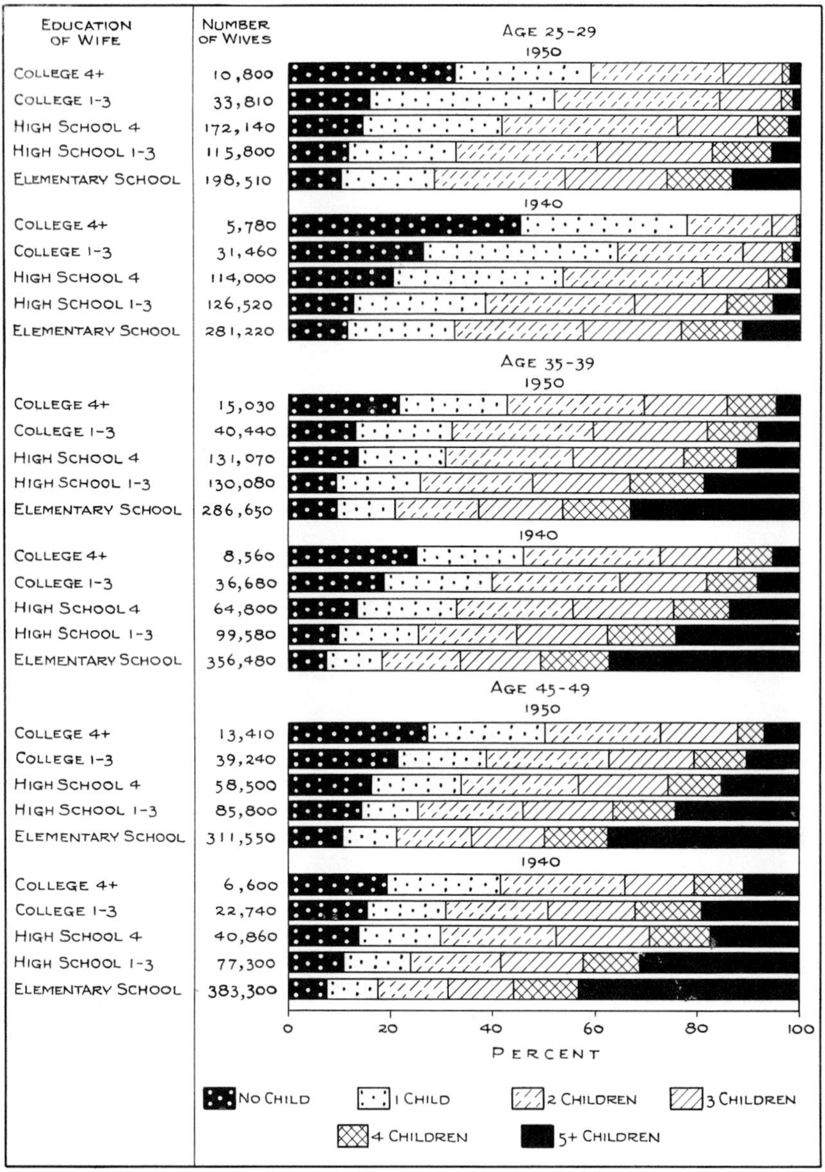

EDUCATION OF WIFE	NUMBER OF WIVES
AGE 25-29 1950	
COLLEGE 4+	10,800
COLLEGE 1-3	33,810
HIGH SCHOOL 4	172,140
HIGH SCHOOL 1-3	115,800
ELEMENTARY SCHOOL	198,510
1940	
COLLEGE 4+	5,780
COLLEGE 1-3	31,460
HIGH SCHOOL 4	114,000
HIGH SCHOOL 1-3	126,520
ELEMENTARY SCHOOL	281,220
AGE 35-39 1950	
COLLEGE 4+	15,030
COLLEGE 1-3	40,440
HIGH SCHOOL 4	131,070
HIGH SCHOOL 1-3	130,080
ELEMENTARY SCHOOL	286,650
1940	
COLLEGE 4+	8,560
COLLEGE 1-3	36,680
HIGH SCHOOL 4	64,800
HIGH SCHOOL 1-3	99,580
ELEMENTARY SCHOOL	356,480
AGE 45-49 1950	
COLLEGE 4+	13,410
COLLEGE 1-3	39,240
HIGH SCHOOL 4	58,500
HIGH SCHOOL 1-3	85,800
ELEMENTARY SCHOOL	311,550
1940	
COLLEGE 4+	6,600
COLLEGE 1-3	22,740
HIGH SCHOOL 4	40,860
HIGH SCHOOL 1-3	77,300
ELEMENTARY SCHOOL	383,300

PERCENT (0, 20, 40, 60, 80, 100)

Legend: No Child | 1 Child | 2 Children | 3 Children | 4 Children | 5+ Children

Note: Based on data in table 81.

Comparisons by color in distributions by number of children ever born. As already noted, childlessness tended to be higher among nonwhites than among whites in urban areas in 1950. The higher rate of childlessness among nonwhites tended to be somewhat more pronounced at the two extremes than at middle educational levels (cf. tables 78 and 79). Thus, among urban ever-married women 45 to 49 years old, the proportion of childlessness at the "college: 4 years or more" level was about one-third for whites and one-half for nonwhites. At the "none or elementary" level, the proportions were 17 percent for the whites and 31 percent for the nonwhites. However, at the "high school: 4 years" level, the proportions childless were 25 percent for the whites and 36 percent for the nonwhites.

Among urban ever-married women 25 to 29 years old who had finished college, the proportions of childlessness were 34 percent for the whites and 46 percent for the nonwhites. Among women of this age whose schooling was restricted to elementary grades, the percentages with no children were 18 for whites and 31 for nonwhites. The comparable percentages for women who finished high school were 24 for whites and 38 for nonwhites.

That the percentages of childless women for both whites and nonwhites are directly associated with educational attainment reflects a direct relation of education to age at marriage and also to voluntary family limitation. The excess proportions of childless women of nonwhites over whites at lowest educational levels in urban areas may arise in part from a high proportion of sterility from venereal infection.

As before, the distributions reveal the conspicuously high fertility of the nonwhites in rural-farm areas. Thus, among rural-farm nonwhite women 45 to 49 years old and of "none or elementary" status, only 14 percent were childless and nearly half, 49 percent, had five or more children. Among whites, the corresponding percentages were 10 and 38.

H. Fertility ratios by educational attainment, 1940 and 1950

As previously indicated, fertility ratios (numbers of own children under 5 years old per 1,000 women of given age) have certain weaknesses and strengths as measures of fertility. As for weaknesses, they are affected by mortality, separate residence of children and mother, and timing of births. Quantitative information on the first two items is given in Appendix A.

As for strength, the fertility ratio represents current fertility, or, more accurately, fertility during the preceding 5 years.

In figure 73, fertility ratios are presented by urban-rural residence and educational attainment for native white women 15 to 49 years old in 1940 and for white women in 1950. The ratios are standardized for age. It is clear that whereas rather well-marked inverse relations of fertility ratios to educational attainment existed in 1940 (insofar as averages are concerned) these differentials had virtually disappeared by 1950. Figure 74 presents standardized ratios for nonwhites in 1940 and 1950.

The above statement of a virtual eradication of differentials by 1950 relates to the average situation for the complete childbearing age range. There were marked differences by age in the level of the fertility ratio, in the magnitude of the increase during 1940 to 1950, and in the pattern of variation in fertility ratios by educational attainment.

FIGURE **73.**—STANDARDIZED NUMBER OF OWN CHILDREN UNDER 5 YEARS OLD PER 1,000 EVER-MARRIED WHITE WOMEN 15 TO 49 YEARS OLD, BY YEARS OF SCHOOL COMPLETED, URBAN AND RURAL: 1940 AND 1950

[Data for white women in 1950 and native white women in 1940. The standard is the distribution by age of all ever-married women 15 to 49 years old in the United States in 1950]

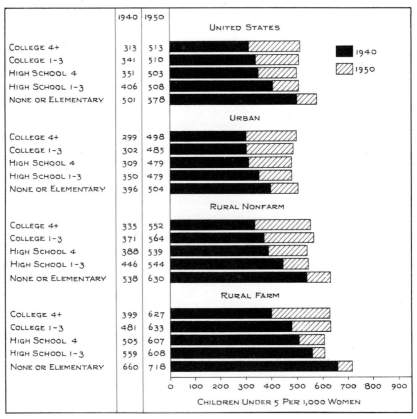

Source: Derived from age-specific ratios in table 83 and from standard distribution computed from *1950 Census of Population*, Vol. IV, *Special Reports*, Part 5, Chapter C, Fertility, table 1.

As already stated, the magnitude of the cumulative fertility rate (total number of children ever born) naturally increases with age. The fertility ratio, however, relating as it does to number of own children under 5 years old, reaches a peak at some point *before* the end of the childbearing period. The ratio is characteristically very low at the end of the child-bearing ages.

FIGURE **74.**—STANDARDIZED NUMBER OF OWN CHILDREN UNDER 5 YEARS OLD PER 1,000 EVER-MARRIED NONWHITE WOMEN 15 TO 49 YEARS OLD, BY YEARS OF SCHOOL COMPLETED: 1950 AND 1940

[Data for nonwhite women in 1950 and Negro women in 1940. The standard is the distribution by age of all ever-married women 15 to 49 years old in the United States in 1950]

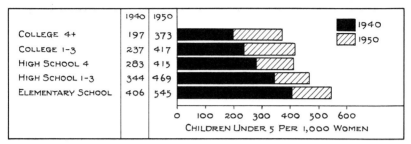

	1940	1950
COLLEGE 4+	197	373
COLLEGE 1-3	237	417
HIGH SCHOOL 4	283	415
HIGH SCHOOL 1-3	344	469
ELEMENTARY SCHOOL	406	545

Source: Derived from age-specific fertility ratios in table 83 and from standard distribution computed from *1950 Census of Population*, Vol. IV, *Special Reports*, Part 5, Chapter C, Fertility, table 1.

There are marked differences by educational status in the age at which the peak fertility ratio is reached (table 83 and figure 75). Thus, among ever-married white women in each type of residence and in both 1940 and 1950, the peak was consistently reached at ages 20 to 24 for women of "none or elementary" and "high school: 1 to 3 years" status. It was consistently reached at ages 25 to 29 for women of "high school: 4 years" and "college: 1 to 3 years" status. It was reached at ages 30 to 34 for women of "college: 4 years or more" status in urban and rural-nonfarm areas. The ever-married rural-farm women of "college: 4 years or more" status exhibited the highest fertility ratio at ages 25 to 29 instead of 30 to 34 and provided the only exception to the patterns described above for white women.

Among the nonwhites in urban areas, the fertility ratio for college graduates reached a peak at ages 30 to 34 in 1940 and 1950. The highest fertility ratios among nonwhites in other educational groups in both urban and rural-nonfarm areas were at ages 20 to 24. Within rural-nonfarm areas the peak fertility ratios of nonwhites came at ages 20 to 24 for the women with only elementary schooling and at ages 25 to 29 for women completing 1 to 3 years and 4 years of high school.

The ages at which the highest fertility ratios occurred in various educational classes were closely related to the whole pattern of variations in fertility ratios by age and educational attainment. As may be noted in figure 75, the urban whites in 1950 had a very sharp and virtually complete change from an inverse to a direct relation of education to fertility ratios as the women passed from age 20–24 to age 30–34. The age group 25 to 29 was pivotal in that the fertility ratios for all educational groups were much the same.

Whereas, the transition from inverse to direct relation of fertility ratios to educational attainment was especially pronounced among the urban whites in the 1950 Census, it was also present to some extent in the 1940 data (figure 76) for urban whites and in other types of residence for both 1940 and 1950. The fertility ratios varied less by education among non-whites than among whites. Also, except in urban areas, the nonwhites were still largely concentrated in the lower educational groups.

TABLE **83.**—NUMBER OF OWN CHILDREN UNDER 5 YEARS OLD PER 1,000 EVER-MARRIED WOMEN 15 TO 44 YEARS OLD, BY AGE, COLOR, AND YEARS OF SCHOOL COMPLETED, URBAN AND RURAL: 1950 AND 1940

[Rate not shown where there are fewer than 4,000 women in 1950 or 3,000 in 1940]

Age and years of school completed	1950								1940				
	White				Nonwhite				Native white				Negro, total
	United States	Urban	Rural nonfarm	Rural farm	United States	Urban	Rural nonfarm	Rural farm	United States	Urban	Rural nonfarm	Rural farm	
15 TO 19 YEARS OLD													
College: 4 yrs. or more	239	...	...	...	...	...	...	...	...	...	...	...	...
1 to 3 years	193	178	...	...	...	...	...	...	130	128	...	...	...
High school: 4 years	291	275	322	306	501	527	...	...	249	231	284	251	366
1 to 3 years	542	522	586	533	771	761	807	781	457	431	523	433	577
None or elementary	621	568	694	619	819	796	870	809	561	502	604	576	579
20 TO 24 YEARS OLD													
College: 4 yrs. or more	375	337	520	622	503	521	...	...	227	205	290	...	...
1 to 3 years	623	573	776	744	797	812	...	...	403	353	475	551	383
High school: 4 years	777	713	887	976	853	...	1,231	1,033	565	490	658	738	602
1 to 3 years	998	927	1,116	1,142	1,026	980	1,136	1,193	818	726	926	983	736
None or elementary	1,089	969	1,207	1,228	1,064	869	1,178	1,380	941	797	1,016	1,070	755
25 TO 29 YEARS OLD													
College: 4 yrs. or more	868	856	894	986	565	565	...	...	484	467	520	565	323
1 to 3 years	923	889	973	1,129	656	584	...	...	613	556	648	810	469
High school: 4 years	920	879	985	1,124	701	664	1,010	1,088	649	570	730	908	442
1 to 3 years	885	842	943	1,029	738	652	962	1,262	686	603	745	929	552
None or elementary	972	870	1,014	1,175	835	649	960	1,245	813	675	876	1,017	606
30 TO 34 YEARS OLD													
College: 4 yrs. or more	882	861	950	948	562	575	...	...	569	555	593	635	241
1 to 3 years	775	755	776	938	484	465	...	...	532	481	549	702	289
High school: 4 years	672	662	677	749	447	406	...	...	469	428	493	656	282
1 to 3 years	581	562	588	693	457	381	671	1,042	462	400	501	648	344
None or elementary	663	589	710	809	594	414	760	1,001	571	445	616	796	434
35 TO 39 YEARS OLD													
College: 4 yrs. or more	534	527	515	689	265	249	...	...	352	339	362	447	95
1 to 3 years	452	431	500	513	298	264	...	...	297	255	320	430	99
High school: 4 years	395	380	417	463	290	257	...	...	253	224	261	411	196
1 to 3 years	340	321	353	428	313	254	388	828	274	215	305	453	215
None or elementary	424	345	487	595	409	270	529	741	373	258	399	580	325
40 TO 44 YEARS OLD													
College: 4 yrs. or more	224	216	224	299	155	138	...	...	125	115	125	195	60
1 to 3 years	171	152	180	261	136	98	...	...	119	93	112	238	94
High school: 4 years	158	146	174	225	84	67	...	...	102	79	116	212	124
1 to 3 years	158	138	177	247	172	127	312	497	124	94	120	231	118
None or elementary	205	153	238	340	202	114	244	452	193	119	207	328	175

Source: *1950 Census of Population,* Vol. IV, *Special Reports,* Part 5, Chapter C, Fertility, tables 44 and 45; *1940 Census of Population, Differential Fertility, 1940 and 1910,* Women by Number of Children Under 5 Years Old, tables 25 and 26.

Probably the important factors underlying the shift with age from an inverse to a direct relation of fertility ratios to educational attainment were the related ones of (1) the direct relation of education to age at marriage and (2) the probably greater tendency to attempt longer spacing of children among the women of high than of low educational attainment.

Figures 77, 78, and 79 point up the 1940–50 changes in age-specific rates by education. Among the whites in each type of residence, the excess of the 1950 over the 1940 fertility ratio was especially large among the women with college training.

FIGURE 75.—NUMBER OF OWN CHILDREN UNDER 5 YEARS OLD PER 1,000 EVER-MARRIED WHITE WOMEN 15 TO 49 YEARS OLD, BY AGE AND YEARS OF SCHOOL COMPLETED, URBAN AND RURAL: 1950 AND 1940

[Data for white women in 1950 and native white women in 1940]

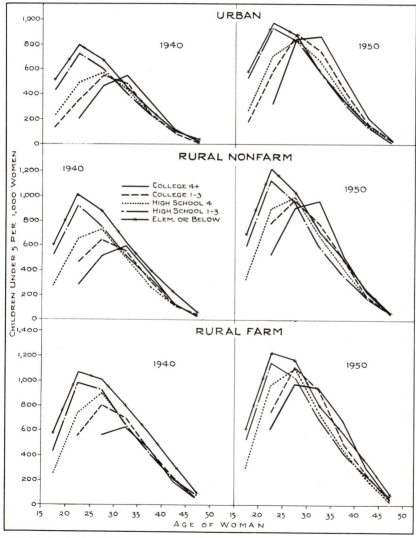

Note: Based on data in table 83.

FIGURE **76.**—NUMBER OF OWN CHILDREN UNDER 5 YEARS OLD PER 1,000 EVER-MARRIED
WHITE WOMEN 15 TO 49 YEARS OLD, BY AGE AND YEARS OF SCHOOL COMPLETED, FOR
URBAN AREAS: 1950 AND 1940

[Data for white women in 1950 and native white women in 1940]

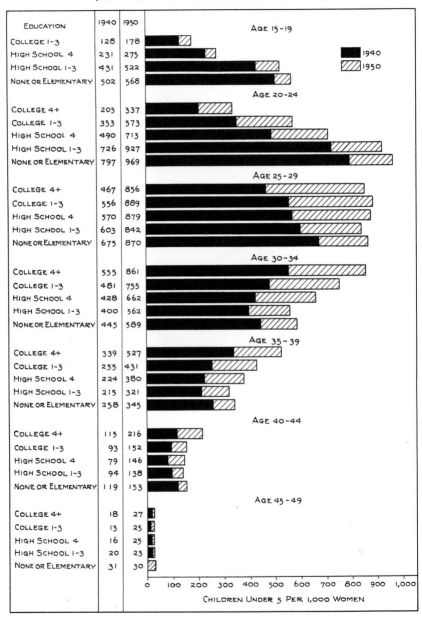

Note: Based on data in table 83.

FIGURE **77.**—COMPARISON OF THE AGE-SPECIFIC FERTILITY RATIOS OF WHITE WOMEN IN 1950 WITH THOSE OF NATIVE WHITE WOMEN IN 1940, FOR EVER-MARRIED WOMEN 15 TO 49 YEARS OLD, BY YEARS OF SCHOOL COMPLETED, FOR URBAN AREAS

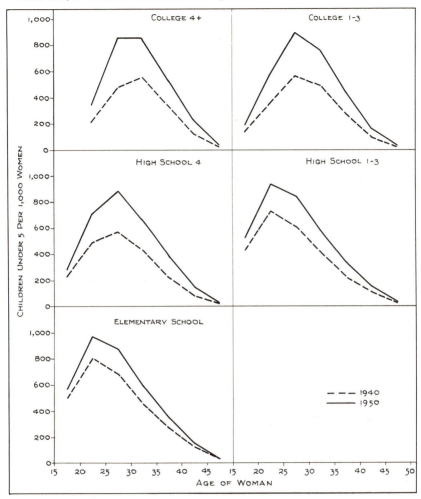

Note: Based on data in table 83.

I. Fertility ratios by education of the husband and wife

One of the Census Bureau's reports presented fertility ratios as of 1940 by educational attainment of the wife and husband jointly considered.[6] These ratios are given for native white women, married once and husband present, by age and urban-rural status. Table 84 presents the data for three age groups: 20 to 24, 25 to 29, and 30 to 34.

---

[6] *1940 Census of Population, Differential Fertility, 1940 and 1910,* Women by Number of Children Under 5 Years Old, table 30.

FIGURE **78.**—COMPARISON OF THE AGE-SPECIFIC FERTILITY RATIOS OF WHITE WOMEN IN 1950 WITH THOSE OF NATIVE WHITE WOMEN IN 1940, FOR EVER-MARRIED WOMEN 15 TO 49 YEARS OLD, BY YEARS OF SCHOOL COMPLETED, FOR RURAL-NONFARM AREAS

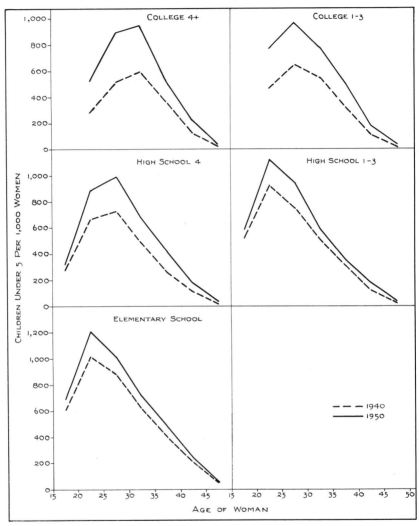

Note: Based on data in table 83.

Several points may be noted. In the first place, it is apparent that the relation of fertility ratios to educational attainment was of much the same pattern and order of magnitude for husbands and wives considered separately. This may have arisen partly from assortive mating in that wives and husbands tended to be of the same broad educational class. It will be noted, for instance, that the cases of college men marrying women of under-fifth-grade status, were too few to afford a reliable rate.

FIGURE **79.**—COMPARISON OF THE AGE-SPECIFIC FERTILITY RATIOS OF WHITE WOMEN IN 1950
WITH THOSE OF NATIVE WHITE WOMEN IN 1940, FOR EVER-MARRIED WOMEN 15 TO 49 YEARS
OLD, BY YEARS OF SCHOOL COMPLETED, FOR RURAL-FARM AREAS

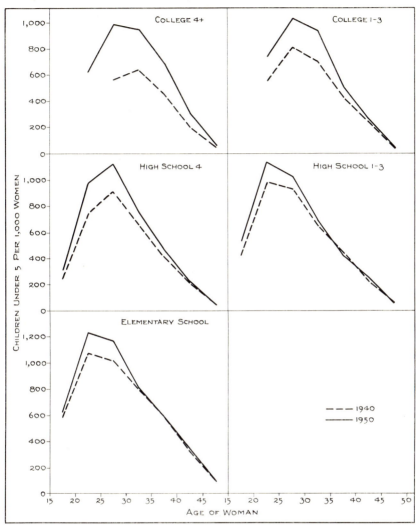

Note: Based on data in table 83.

When the educational attainment of one spouse is held constant, the
inverse relation of fertility ratios to educational attainment of the other
spouse is reduced but not eliminated. Under these conditions the per-
sistence of the relationship of fertility to education of the wife appears to
be a little stronger than to education of the husband.

The cross-classified materials afford several types of evidence of a
somewhat closer relation of fertility ratios to education of the wife than to

education of the husband. In about two-thirds of the possible comparisons in table 84 the range of variation in fertility by education of the wife,
with education of the husband held constant, was wider than that by education of the husband, with education of the wife held constant. To illustrate, among urban native white married women 20 to 24 years old whose
husbands had completed 7 or 8 years of elementary school, the fertility
ratios extended from 316 for wives of college status to 1,006 for wives
who had under 5 years of schooling. This is a range of 690 points. In
contrast, among women of this age who themselves were of seventh-to-
eighth-grade status, the fertility ratios extended from 595 for those whose
husbands were of college status to 961 for those whose husbands had
under 5 years of schooling. This is a range of only 366 points. In most
of the comparisons of this type the differences are much smaller, but about
two out of three cases show the range to be wider for wives than for
husbands.

TABLE **84.**—NUMBER OF OWN CHILDREN UNDER 5 YEARS OLD PER 1,000 NATIVE WHITE
WOMEN OF SPECIFIED AGE, MARRIED ONCE AND HUSBAND PRESENT, BY YEARS OF SCHOOL
COMPLETED BY WIFE AND HUSBAND, FOR URBAN AREAS: 1940

[Ratio not shown where there are fewer than 3,000 women]

| Age and years of school completed by wife | Years of school completed by husband | | | | | |
| | College | High school | | Grade school | | |
	1 year or more	4 years	1 to 3 years	7 and 8 years	5 and 6 years	Less than 5 years
20 TO 24 YEARS OLD						
College: 1 year or more	303	370	414	316	...	...
High school: 4 years	440	474	565	633	672	409
1 to 3 years	588	666	770	838	1,002	811
Elementary: 7 and 8 years	595	665	782	842	984	961
5 and 6 years	...	...	719	942	975	1,063
Less than 5 years	...	...	...	1,006	...	985
25 TO 29 YEARS OLD						
College: 1 year or more	554	553	589	624	...	...
High school: 4 years	568	590	639	681	702	674
1 to 3 years	632	603	643	697	774	693
Elementary: 7 and 8 years	680	702	724	709	790	759
5 and 6 years	...	...	816	802	817	943
Less than 5 years	...	...	...	705	900	835
30 TO 34 YEARS OLD						
College: 1 year or more	604	478	515	491	...	...
High school: 4 years	521	451	471	469	500	350
1 to 3 years	466	437	456	446	489	450
Elementary: 7 and 8 years	441	483	466	473	515	518
5 and 6 years	...	...	522	548	549	602
Less than 5 years	...	...	...	534	605	681

Source: *1940 Census of Population, Differential Fertility, 1940 and 1910*, Women by Number of Children Under 5
Years Old, table 30.

Table 85 presents something of a summary approach to the question of
whether the fertility ratios of the couple tend to vary more by education
of the wife or by education of the husband. First, the fertility ratios and
relative range of these ratios are shown by education of the wife considered

separately. Next, they are shown by education of the wife with education of the husband held constant. Similarly, in the next panel, the fertility ratios and the relative variations of these ratios are shown by education of the husband considered separately. Next, the ratios are shown by education of the husband with education of the wife held constant. The process is illustrated in figure 80 for the 25 to 29 age group of urban whites.

TABLE **85.**—Fertility Ratios and Their Relative Variations by Education of the Wife and Husband, Unstandardized and Standardized for Years of School Completed by the Spouse, for Native White Women 20 to 34 Years Old Married Once and Husband Present, by Age of Women, for Urban Areas: 1940

Years of school completed	20 to 24 years old		25 to 29 years old		30 to 34 years old	
	Fertility ratio	Relative varia- tion	Fertility ratio	Relative varia- tion	Fertility ratio	Relative varia- tion
Total (base ratio)...........	650	100	651	100	490	100
EDUCATION OF WIFE, UNSTANDARDIZED						
College: 1 year or more........	329	51	560	86	559	114
High school: 4 years...............	512	79	611	94	475	97
1 to 3 years..........	766	118	656	101	452	92
Elementary: 7 and 8 years.........	818	126	720	111	478	98
5 and 6 years.........	935	144	816	125	552	113
Less than 5 years.....	983	151	842	129	658	134
EDUCATION OF WIFE, STANDARDIZED[1]						
College: 1 year or more........	358	55	580	89	510	104
High school: 4 years...............	539	83	630	97	472	96
1 to 3 years..........	743	114	654	100	453	92
Elementary: 7 and 8 years.........	751	116	711	109	472	96
5 and 6 years.........	844	130	759	117	520	106
Less than 5 years.....	704	108	626	96	537	110
EDUCATION OF HUSBAND, UNSTANDARDIZED						
College: 1 year or more........	406	62	572	88	552	113
High school: 4 years...............	530	82	598	92	457	93
1 to 3 years..........	694	107	658	101	469	96
Elementary: 7 and 8 years.........	800	123	703	108	471	96
5 and 6 years.........	955	147	788	121	521	106
Less than 5 years.....	885	136	782	120	556	113
EDUCATION OF HUSBAND, STANDARDIZED[2]						
College: 1 year or more........	513	79	613	94	494	101
High school: 4 years...............	572	88	612	94	463	94
1 to 3 years..........	662	102	658	101	478	98
Elementary: 7 and 8 years.........	722	111	688	106	473	97
5 and 6 years.........	842	130	742	114	499	102
Less than 5 years.....	650	100	687	106	440	90

[1] The standard is the distribution by education of husbands of native white women of given age in urban areas in 1940.
[2] The standard is the distribution by education of native white wives of given age in urban areas in 1940.

Source: Derived from *1940 Census of Population, Differential Fertility, 1940 and 1910,* Women by Number of Children Under 5 Years Old, table 30.

In general, the results suggest that standardizing for education of the wife may have a little more leveling effect on fertility rates by education of the husband than does the reverse process. However, the difference is small. Furthermore, as shown by the figures below, the zero order coefficients of correlation between number of children under 5 and education of the wife are almost precisely the same as those between number of children under 5 and education of the husband for the ages indicated:

	Age of wife	Education of wife	Education of husband
20 to 24		−.23	−.22
25 to 29		−.12	−.13
30 to 34		−.05	−.06

FIGURE 80.—RELATIVE SPREAD OF FERTILITY RATIOS BY YEARS OF SCHOOL COMPLETED BY WOMAN AND HUSBAND, UNSTANDARDIZED AND STANDARDIZED FOR EDUCATION OF THE SPOUSE, FOR NATIVE WHITE WOMEN 25 TO 29 YEARS OLD MARRIED ONCE AND HUSBAND PRESENT, FOR URBAN AREAS: 1940

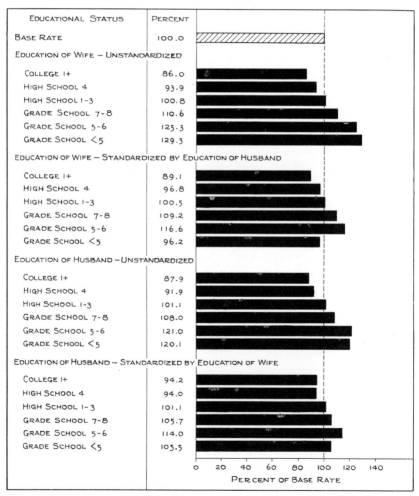

Note: Based on data in table 85.

J. Fertility ratios in 1940 according to jointly considered major occupational group of the husband and educational attainment of the wife

One of the special reports on differential fertility, 1910 and 1940, contains ratios of children under 5 per 1,000 native white women married once and husband present according to major occupation group of the husband and education of the wife.   In the original report the data are presented according to age of the wife.   In table 86 they are shown for three age groups of urban whites.

TABLE **86.**—NUMBER OF OWN CHILDREN UNDER 5 YEARS OLD PER 1,000 NATIVE WHITE WOMEN 20 TO 34 YEARS OLD MARRIED ONCE AND HUSBAND PRESENT, BY AGE AND YEARS OF SCHOOL COMPLETED BY WOMAN AND MAJOR OCCUPATION GROUP OF HUSBAND, FOR URBAN AREAS: 1940

[Ratio not shown where there are fewer than 3,000 women]

Age and years of school completed	Professional, techn'l, and kindred workers	Managers, officials, and proprietors, exc. farm	Clerical, sales, and kindred workers	Craftsmen, foremen, and kindred workers	Operatives and kindred workers	Service workers, incl. private household	Laborers, except farm and mine
20 TO 24 YEARS OLD							
College: 1 year or more...	267	381	313	387	436	...	...
High school: 4 years..........	396	451	443	542	573	511	648
1 to 3 years.....	673	678	659	760	768	684	933
Elementary: 7 and 8 years....	...	705	690	810	795	739	954
5 and 6 years....	...	...	...	915	876	...	1,051
Less than 5 yrs..	...	...	...	...	940	...	1,156
25 TO 29 YEARS OLD							
College: 1 year or more...	549	622	531	616	553	505	636
High school: 4 years..........	567	593	556	637	668	596	771
1 to 3 years.....	610	611	583	673	670	645	767
Elementary: 7 and 8 years....	669	654	631	732	714	644	826
5 and 6 years....	...	...	768	769	789	627	928
Less than 5 yrs..	...	...	...	658	726	...	962
30 TO 34 YEARS OLD							
College: 1 year or more...	632	573	524	515	451	456	696
High school: 4 years..........	521	465	458	497	467	416	514
1 to 3 years.....	492	396	434	448	452	450	578
Elementary: 7 and 8 years....	483	465	432	462	472	443	587
5 and 6 years....	...	518	529	536	504	496	706
Less than 5 yrs..	...	...	541	552	593	...	753

Source: *1940 Census of Population, Differential Fertility, 1940 and 1910,* Women by Number of Children Under 5 Years Old, table 32.

The chief point of interest in the data relates to the nature of the variations in fertility ratios (*a*) by education of the wife among wives of professional men and (*b*) by occupation group of the husband among women of college status.   In each instance the relation of the fertility ratios to the factor that is allowed to vary is inverse and rather strong at ages 20 to 24, mixed and slight at ages 25 to 29, and direct and strong at ages 30 to 34.   At later ages the highest fertility ratio tends to be that for the class of topmost socio-economic status (wives of professional men or wives with a year or more of college).

More specifically, among wives of college status, fertility ratios were inversely related to major occupation group of husbands at ages (of wife) 20 to 24; they were directly related at ages 30 to 34. Similarly, among wives of professional men, the fertility ratios were inversely related to educational attainment of wives 20 to 24 years old; they were directly related to educational attainment of wives 30 to 34 years old.

When the analysis is restricted to wives of unskilled nonfarm laborers, the fertility ratios tend to be inversely related to educational attainment of the wife at all ages. In like manner, when the analysis is restricted to wives of lowest educational attainment "elementary school: less than 5 years," the fertility ratios are inversely related to major occupation group of the husband at all ages.

When the controlled factor is a class of intermediate status, the fertility ratios tend to be inversely related to the criterion of socio-economic status that is allowed to vary. This relationship tends to be strong at young ages. At older ages it is manifested mainly by the relatively low fertility levels of the wives of professional men and wives with a year or more of college and by the rather high fertility levels of the wives of unskilled laborers and wives below fifth-grade status.

These data indicate no substantial difference between education of the wife and occupation group of the husband with respect to bearing on fertility ratio.

K. Proportionate contribution of children by women of various educational classes

In view of the relatively high increases during 1940–1950 in marriage and fertility rates of women with "high school: 4 years" or more education, the question may be asked whether these women are still contributing less than their quota of births. Table 87 and figure 81 are designed to shed light on such questions. In table 87 the proportionate importance of high school graduates among ever-married women of given age, residence, and color is shown in the columns indicated as "women." Thus, in the United States as a whole in 1950, about 56.7 percent of the white women 25 to 29 years old had completed at least 4 years of high school. These women may be assigned a quota of 56.7 percent of the total children ever born to all white women 25 to 29 years of age in 1950. The actual proportion of children ever born to these women, however, was 47.4 percent. Hence they contributed slightly less than their quota of total births. However, they contributed 56.4 percent of all the children under 5 years old reported by white women 25 to 29 years old in 1950.

Figure 81 presents for three age groups of whites the complete distributions of the women by educational attainment for comparison with distributions of their children ever born, and their children under 5 years old.

TABLE **87.**—Percent of High School Graduates Among Ever-Married Women 15 to 49 Years Old and Percent of Children Ever Born and of Own Children Under 5 Years Old with Mothers Who Are High School Graduates, by Color and Age of Woman, Urban and Rural: 1950

[Data include women who have completed 1 year or more of college]

Area and age of woman	White			Nonwhite		
	Women	Children ever born	Children under 5	Women	Children ever born	Children under 5
UNITED STATES						
15 to 19 years	27.3	15.8	15.6	8.9	5.4	5.7
20 to 24 years	53.9	41.8	45.2	23.4	16.7	20.0
25 to 29 years	56.7	47.4	56.4	24.4	16.0	21.3
30 to 34 years	50.9	43.9	54.2	19.3	12.4	16.7
35 to 39 years	43.5	35.7	45.7	16.0	9.6	12.3
40 to 44 years	38.9	29.9	36.6	13.0	8.0	7.8
45 to 49 years	33.1	23.2	25.5	10.3	6.8	6.3
URBAN						
15 to 19 years	31.1	18.4	18.2	12.5	8.0	8.8
20 to 24 years	58.3	46.2	49.5	29.8	23.3	27.6
25 to 29 years	61.7	54.2	62.3	30.3	22.6	30.1
30 to 34 years	55.3	50.4	60.1	24.0	18.3	25.5
35 to 39 years	47.1	41.4	52.2	20.3	14.8	19.8
40 to 44 years	42.3	34.8	44.0	16.1	11.5	12.8
45 to 49 years	36.1	27.2	33.7	13.0	10.2	10.5
RURAL NONFARM						
15 to 19 years	22.8	12.9	12.9	7.0	2.4	2.5
20 to 24 years	47.4	36.7	39.8	12.4	9.4	11.9
25 to 29 years	49.6	39.9	49.5	10.5	6.9	10.2
30 to 34 years	44.9	37.1	47.3	10.0	6.3	7.6
35 to 39 years	39.9	31.0	40.4	7.9	5.3	7.2
40 to 44 years	35.8	26.1	32.0	7.1	5.8	8.1
45 to 49 years	29.9	20.5	23.0	4.9	3.2	4.1
RURAL FARM						
15 to 19 years	22.9	13.2	13.5	2.2	1.8	2.1
20 to 24 years	43.6	34.2	38.0	7.5	4.3	5.4
25 to 29 years	40.8	33.2	40.7	7.7	4.6	6.7
30 to 34 years	36.7	30.3	37.3	4.8	3.5	5.0
35 to 39 years	30.9	23.7	28.9	3.6	2.9	3.6
40 to 44 years	27.2	19.4	22.4	4.7	2.8	2.1
45 to 49 years	21.8	14.5	13.8	2.7	1.8	1.7

Source: Derived from *1950 Census of Population*, Vol. IV, *Special Reports*, Part 5, Chapter C, Fertility, tables 20, 22, 44, and 45.

In the data available, the various groups of women having a full high school education or any college training contributed fewer children ever born than would be expected on the basis of the proportion of women. Correspondingly, groups with any lower level of education contributed more children than would be expected on the basis of proportionate importance of the educational class considered.

In 1950, among urban white ever-married women 25 to 29 years old, 38 percent of the women had less than a 4-year high school education but they contributed 46 percent of the births to that age group. Among the women 35 to 39 years old, 53 percent failed to finish 4 years of high school but contributed 59 percent of the births. At ages 45 to 49, those with less than 4 years of high school formed 64 percent of the women of this age group but contributed 73 percent of the births.

FIGURE **81.**—PERCENT DISTRIBUTION OF WOMEN, CHILDREN EVER BORN, AND OWN CHILDREN UNDER 5 YEARS OLD BY YEARS OF SCHOOL COMPLETED BY THE WOMEN, FOR EVER-MARRIED WHITE WOMEN OF SPECIFIED AGE, URBAN AND RURAL: 1950

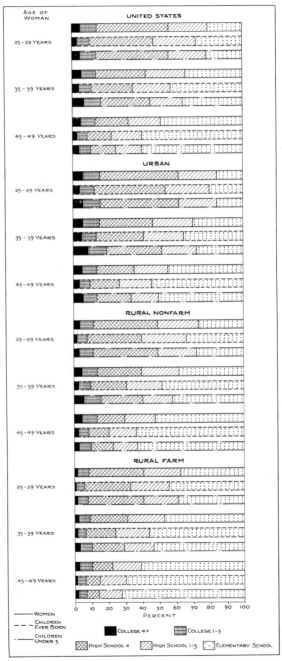

Note: Part of the legend has reference to the border of the bar, and indicates that the sets of distributions relate respectively to women, children ever born, and children under 5.

Source: Derived from *1950 Census of Population*, Vol. IV, *Special Reports*, Part 5, Chapter C, Fertility, tables 20 and 44.

A disproportionate number of children born to women failing to complete high school is also found in the rural areas. Thus, among rural-farm ever-married white women 45 to 49 years old, 78 percent reported an education status below "high school: 4 years" but contributed 86 percent of the live births to this age group.

Among the urban nonwhites the disproportionate number of live births to those of lower education follows about the some pattern as that for whites. Within the rural-nonfarm and especially within the rural-farm areas the tendency for the nonwhite women to be concentrated in the low educational classes leaves little room for any substantial variation between the educational classes with respect to proportionate contribution of children.

L. Parity progression ratios by educational attainment

The concept of the parity progression ratios is described briefly in Chapter 5 and in more detail in Chapter 9. Stated briefly, it indicates the extent to which women of a given age have in the past progressed from one parity to the next.

From the distributions of women by number of children ever born one is able to derive (a) the number of women ever having been of parity N, and (b) number of women ever having been of parity N + 1. Obviously, only the women who ever attained parity N were ever at immediate risk of attaining parity N + 1. The parity progression ratio is the proportion of women of parity N progressing to parity N + 1.[7] Thus 0-to-1 parity progression ratios are the proportions of zero-parity women that progressed to one-parity status by having a child; the 1-to-2 ratios are the proportions of one-parity women that progressed to two-parity status, etc.

Parity progression ratios are shown for 1940 and 1950 in table 88 for urban white ever-married women by age and educational attainment. The 0-to-1, 1-to-2, and 2-to-3 parity progression ratios for women under 40 years old tended to be rather consistently higher in 1950 than in 1940 among women of given age and educational attainment. The 1950 excesses were especially marked among women of college attainment.

Among women 40 to 49 years old the 1950 parity progression ratios tended to be lower than those of 1940. This is consistent with the 1940–50 trend of cumulative fertility rates among women of these ages and it means, among other things, that the recent baby boom had relatively little impact on women of virtually completed fertility.

Of special interest is the fact that among women who had had three children, the proportion who had had a fourth child tended to be a little

---

[7] The computation of the parity progression ratios is described in more detail in Chapters 5 and 9. To illustrate briefly, among 350,400 urban white ever-married women 20 to 24 years old and of "none or elementary" status, 93,810 reported that they had never borne a child, 256,590 had borne one or more, and 127,860 had borne two or more. All of these were "at risk" of a first birth at some time. Those ever bearing one child represent 73.2 percent of those at risk: $(256,590 \div 350,400 \times 100)$. Those ever bearing two children represent 49.8 percent of those at risk: $(127,860 \div 256,590)$, table 88.

lower in 1950 than in 1940 for women of all ages and at all educational levels except that of college graduates. The fact that the 3-to-4 and 4-to-5 parity progression ratios tended to be a little lower in 1950 than in 1940 would not seem to augur well for any substantial future increase in the proportion of families with four or more children. It should be remembered, however, that if the 3-to-4 ratios remain virtually the same, some increase in the proportion of four-child families might accrue from increases in proportions of women at risk of the fourth birth. It should also be remembered that changes in parity progression ratios by certain ages reflect changes in the spacing of children as well as changes in the size of completed families.

TABLE **88.**—PARITY PROGRESSION RATIOS—PERCENT OF WOMEN EVER OF GIVEN PARITY (N) WHO EVER PROGRESSED TO THE NEXT PARITY (N + 1), FOR EVER-MARRIED WHITE WOMEN 20 TO 49 YEARS OLD, BY AGE AND YEARS OF SCHOOL COMPLETED, FOR URBAN AREAS: 1950 AND 1940

[Data for white women in 1950 and native white women in 1940. Ratio not shown where there are fewer than 4,000 women in 1950 or 3,000 in 1940]

Age and years of school completed	0 to 1 parity		1 to 2 parity		2 to 3 parity		3 to 4 parity		4 to 5 parity	
	1950	1940	1950	1940	1950	1940	1950	1940	1950	1940
COLLEGE										
4 Years or More										
20 to 24 years old.........	31.2	23.5	16.1	13.1	13.2	...	...	...	...	...
25 to 29 years old.........	66.0	45.6	43.0	28.0	22.2	14.7	23.5	...	...	...
30 to 34 years old.........	80.7	64.9	63.6	48.5	32.5	23.7	25.2	24.2	26.3	...
35 to 39 years old.........	78.5	70.1	70.9	61.4	40.2	31.7	31.0	28.4	35.6	...
40 to 44 years old.........	73.1	73.9	67.9	64.6	40.8	42.6	35.6	32.9	34.2	38.3
45 to 49 years old.........	66.7	75.4	63.0	69.8	40.5	49.8	39.6	43.7	33.9	41.9
1 to 3 Years										
20 to 24 years old.........	48.3	35.6	24.7	16.8	13.0	15.8	...	...	...	...
25 to 29 years old.........	72.5	56.5	51.3	38.1	24.5	22.1	20.8	21.1	28.2	...
30 to 34 years old.........	81.1	68.9	66.0	52.5	36.8	28.2	27.8	26.7	29.1	24.6
35 to 39 years old.........	78.6	74.7	70.1	60.7	42.4	42.4	35.1	35.9	35.8	33.4
40 to 44 years old.........	76.8	78.0	67.2	65.7	41.6	46.0	38.4	41.5	39.8	40.1
45 to 49 years old.........	72.8	79.1	62.4	68.7	45.9	53.3	36.6	45.5	48.1	42.7
HIGH SCHOOL										
4 Years										
20 to 24 years old.........	57.8	46.9	29.7	23.4	15.0	18.8	11.8	22.9	...	...
25 to 29 years old.........	76.3	60.5	52.9	39.4	28.5	25.9	22.4	26.3	28.4	28.5
30 to 34 years old.........	81.6	69.7	66.7	54.2	38.3	36.1	33.1	34.9	32.0	35.0
35 to 39 years old.........	78.6	74.4	67.5	62.1	43.0	44.6	40.2	41.6	39.2	44.4
40 to 44 years old.........	76.4	77.0	65.7	68.1	45.1	49.4	44.7	47.4	44.4	44.7
45 to 49 years old.........	74.9	77.2	65.9	68.2	46.2	52.2	45.7	49.4	45.4	49.2
1 to 3 Years										
20 to 24 years old.........	71.6	63.0	42.3	37.1	25.4	25.1	21.0	22.5	25.6	27.9
25 to 29 years old.........	82.8	71.2	61.1	50.7	40.4	37.5	34.6	34.9	33.9	33.1
30 to 34 years old.........	84.0	76.8	70.4	61.7	47.4	46.3	43.1	45.4	40.4	43.4
35 to 39 years old.........	81.9	79.4	71.2	67.3	50.9	53.7	48.1	48.2	45.4	51.0
40 to 44 years old.........	81.3	81.6	70.3	70.7	53.6	57.0	51.3	53.9	49.4	55.5
45 to 49 years old.........	79.8	80.1	71.2	73.6	55.3	59.8	55.4	58.0	54.0	58.4
NONE OR ELEMENTARY										
20 to 24 years old.........	73.2	67.7	49.8	44.4	34.6	34.7	28.7	29.9	32.2	26.9
25 to 29 years old.........	82.0	76.1	65.7	58.6	51.4	46.5	46.1	44.3	44.0	42.4
30 to 34 years old.........	83.9	80.7	72.7	69.0	55.7	56.8	50.8	55.1	49.0	55.0
35 to 39 years old.........	83.2	83.0	75.7	74.7	58.8	63.3	53.7	60.2	55.2	58.8
40 to 44 years old.........	82.6	84.2	75.8	76.8	62.4	65.6	59.3	64.5	58.6	62.3
45 to 49 years old.........	82.9	83.4	77.1	77.8	65.4	68.3	63.4	65.6	61.6	65.4

Source: Derived from *1950 Census of Population*, Vol. IV, *Special Reports*, Part 5, Chapter C, Fertility, table 20; *1940 Census of Population, Differential Fertility, 1940 and 1910*, Women by Number of Children Ever Born, table 47.

Three charts, figures 82, 83, and 84, bring out the different types of relationships in the 1950 data. Separate panels are used for the various age groups in figure 82. The inverse relation of fertility to educational attainment is found to persist when the fertility relates to specific orders of birth among women ever at risk for such birth orders. At ages 20 to 24, the inverse relation is sharp and consistent for all birth orders considered. The differentials are especially wide with respect to rate of first births at ages 20 to 24. Thus, whereas some 73 percent of the urban white ever-married women of "none or elementary" status had borne at least one child at the time of the Census, only 31 percent of the comparable "college: 4 years or more" women had done so. It should be emphasized, however, that the comparison of college graduates with others 20 to 24 years old is accompanied by a definite bias. Few college graduates receive their B.A. degrees before age 21, and many receive it at age 22. Since there are intervals of varying duration between graduation and marriage, one would expect most of the married women in the 20-to-24 age group who are college graduates to be 23 and 24 years old, whereas the women of less education would not be expected to exhibit this type of concentration. This bias disappears in older age groups. However, as already noted in figure 69, the lack of control over duration of marriage accounts for some of the inverse relation of cumulative fertility rates to educational attainment at all ages. The strength of this type of bias is reduced in parity progression ratios since these relate to women of given age who were ever at risk of having a birth of a given order.

At each age, parity progression ratios tend to be lowest for the college graduates and highest for the women of elementary school status. The women of intermediate education tend to exhibit parity progression ratios consistent with the principle of inverse relation of fertility to education.

There are several reservations to the above, however. After age 30, the progression ratios for zero- and first-parity women are much the same at all educational levels. Most people appear to want one or two children regardless of educational status. The variations by education emerge in strong fashion insofar as the 2-to-3, 3-to-4, and 4-to-5 parity progression ratios are concerned. These again are consistent with the principle of inverse relation of fertility to education.

It was noted previously that at ages 30 to 34, 35 to 39, and 40 to 44 the numbers of children under 5 per 1,000 women were *directly* related to the educational attainment of the woman whereas the numbers of children ever born were *inversely* associated with educational attainment. Since the parity progression ratios tend to confirm the inverse relation that was found in the cumulative fertility rates, it seems likely that the direct relation exhibited by the fertility ratios largely reflects the later age at which the women of high educational attainment tend to begin their families.

Among second parity women of given age, progression ratios were lowest for the college graduates in 1950. In the 35-to-39 age group, the full

FIGURE **82.**—PARITY PROGRESSION RATIOS—PERCENT OF WOMEN EVER OF GIVEN PARITY
(N) WHO EVER PROGRESSED TO THE NEXT PARITY (N + 1), FOR EVER-MARRIED WHITE
WOMEN 20 TO 49 YEARS OLD, BY AGE AND YEARS OF SCHOOL COMPLETED, FOR URBAN
AREAS: 1950

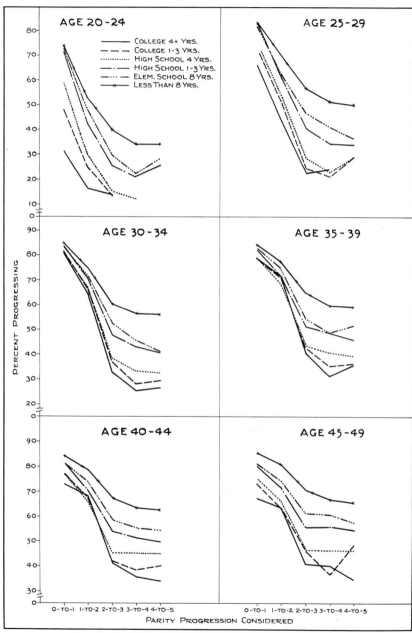

Note: Based on data in table 88.

spread of the ratios by educational class was quite large, ranging from 40 for the "college: 4 years or more" group to 59 for the "none or elementary" group.

Figure 83 points up the relation of age and education to the different orders of birth. Within the two elementary school groups represented, the 0-to-1 ratios level off at 80 to 85 per 100 after ages 25 to 29. At these educational levels, most of those who have first births do so by ages 30 to 34. Some tendency is also found for the 1-to-2 ratios to level off after ages 30 to 34 or 35 to 39. For higher orders of birth the parity progression ratios tend to increase with age. Of course, birth probabilities relating to births during one year would be expected to *decrease* with age. This type of decrease is found in the birth probabilities presented by Whelpton in *Cohort Fertility*.[8] The parity progression ratios in the present materials tend to *increase* with age to age 44, because the opportunity to have a birth of given order increases with age. Increases at ages above 44 also occur but these mainly reflect the secular declines in size of completed family.

Among women of college status, the 0-to-1 progression ratios reach a peak at ages 30 to 34 and then become smaller with age. The 1-to-2 ratios reach a peak at ages 35 to 39 and then decline with age. This again reflects the upsurge in fertility of young women of college attainment.

Figure 84 shows differences by education in the age pattern of parity progression ratios. This again points up the "leveling-off" of the 0-to-1 ratios after ages 25 to 29 for the three lowest educational classes represented. It also points up the general tendency for the ratios of the college graduates to fall in lowest position. Exceptions are the ratios for second births among college graduates 35 years old and over.

The 1940–50 differences in parity progression ratios observed for urban areas, in table 88, tend also to be found for rural-nonfarm and rural-farm areas (tables 89 and 90). An important qualification, however, is that the 1940–50 changes in parity progression ratios tend to be less marked in rural-nonfarm and rural-farm areas than in urban areas.

The parity progression ratios for the nonwhites (table 91) resembled those for whites with respect to pattern of variation by age, education, and residence in 1950. The 0-to-1 and 1-to-2 ratios tended to be higher for whites than for nonwhites among women 25 years old and over in urban and rural-nonfarm areas and of comparable age and education. Within rural-farm areas, only the 0-to-1 ratios for whites tended to exceed those for nonwhites. The 1-to-2 ratios were much the same by color and those for higher parities tended to be larger for nonwhites than for whites.

---

[8] P. K. Whelpton, *Cohort Fertility: Native White Women in the United States*, Princeton University Press, Princeton, 1954, pp. 71–80 and 327–347.

FIGURE **83.**—PARITY PROGRESSION RATIOS—PERCENT OF WOMEN EVER OF GIVEN PARITY (N)
WHO EVER PROGRESSED TO THE NEXT PARITY (N + 1), FOR EVER-MARRIED WHITE WOMEN
20 TO 49 YEARS OLD, BY YEARS OF SCHOOL COMPLETED AND AGE, FOR URBAN AREAS: 1950

[Numbers above curves refer to parity progression]

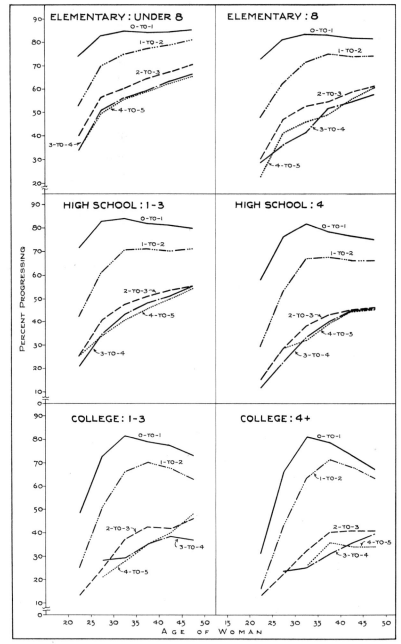

Note: Based on data in table 88.

Figure **84.**—Percent of Women Ever of Given Parity (N) Who Ever Progressed to the Next Parity (N + 1), for Ever-Married White Women 20 to 49 Years Old, by Age, and Years of School Completed, for Urban Areas: 1950

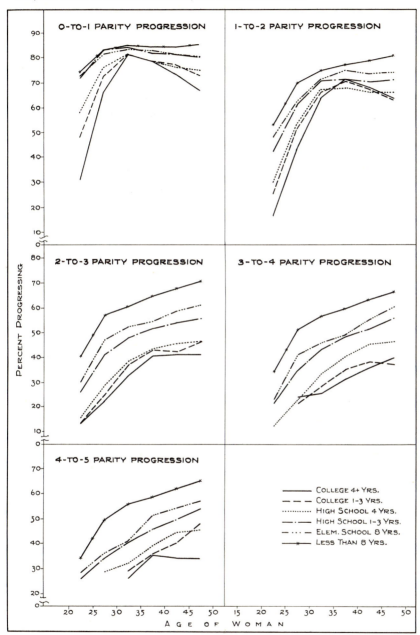

Note: Based on data in table 88.

TABLE **89.**—PARITY PROGRESSION RATIOS—PERCENT OF WOMEN EVER OF GIVEN PARITY (N) WHO EVER PROGRESSED TO THE NEXT PARITY (N + 1), FOR EVER-MARRIED WHITE WOMEN 20 TO 49 YEARS OLD, BY AGE AND YEARS OF SCHOOL COMPLETED, FOR RURAL-NONFARM AREAS: 1950 AND 1940

[Data for white women in 1950 and native white women in 1940. Ratio not shown where there are fewer than 4,000 women in 1950 or 3,000 in 1940]

Age and years of school completed	0 to 1 parity		1 to 2 parity		2 to 3 parity		3 to 4 parity		4 to 5 parity	
	1950	1940	1950	1940	1950	1940	1950	1940	1950	1940
COLLEGE										
4 Years or More										
20 to 24 years old........	48.1	28.7	25.4	...	...	...	...	...	...	...
25 to 29 years old........	68.0	52.9	45.6	29.6	23.4	...	...	...	...	...
30 to 34 years old........	82.2	67.3	64.8	50.7	43.1	28.7	25.6	...	...	...
35 to 39 years old........	80.5	71.6	64.7	63.1	38.5	36.2	31.9	29.1	...	...
40 to 44 years old........	75.1	75.0	66.5	62.8	46.9	51.1	45.0	45.1	35.0	...
45 to 49 years old........	68.1	76.2	66.9	74.6	48.1	56.1	50.5	51.7	...	...
1 to 3 Years										
20 to 24 years old........	62.3	45.8	31.0	20.2	14.6	...	...	...	...	...
25 to 29 years old........	77.0	64.2	55.0	39.8	28.8	22.8	27.0	...	...	...
30 to 34 years old........	84.9	75.7	70.7	57.9	43.5	38.3	35.0	31.7	26.2	...
35 to 39 years old........	82.1	80.4	75.2	67.1	47.0	47.0	39.2	43.5	39.8	43.2
40 to 44 years old........	77.9	80.2	72.5	68.5	52.3	52.0	49.9	51.7	45.5	44.8
45 to 49 years old........	77.1	80.3	70.4	73.4	48.9	58.9	48.3	58.8	48.4	52.0
HIGH SCHOOL										
4 Years										
20 to 24 years old........	67.6	58.6	37.6	29.7	16.5	20.2	12.3	25.7	...	...
25 to 29 years old........	82.0	72.5	61.1	50.7	34.4	34.3	28.2	31.0	26.1	32.6
30 to 34 years old........	86.1	76.8	71.7	61.7	46.3	45.5	42.0	42.4	37.3	41.5
35 to 39 years old........	82.7	79.9	74.3	68.5	52.1	52.3	45.8	45.3	47.0	45.3
40 to 44 years old........	78.5	82.6	71.4	70.4	55.7	58.3	52.7	51.3	48.4	50.1
45 to 49 years old........	76.3	82.3	72.7	73.4	56.7	59.4	55.1	55.0	53.6	58.0
1 to 3 Years										
20 to 24 years old........	80.2	76.4	50.4	44.9	27.9	29.1	25.9	24.9	24.4	18.4
25 to 29 years old........	87.6	81.4	71.5	63.4	51.4	47.9	41.1	40.9	42.3	39.0
30 to 34 years old........	88.5	85.0	76.0	71.7	59.7	57.4	51.2	52.4	50.1	49.2
35 to 39 years old........	85.6	86.4	76.6	75.5	60.6	63.1	58.1	60.8	53.5	56.4
40 to 44 years old........	83.6	85.5	77.3	77.4	66.7	67.1	63.0	61.3	56.8	60.4
45 to 49 years old........	80.9	85.4	76.2	78.9	63.1	70.5	58.9	67.1	58.2	67.1
NONE OR ELEMENTARY										
20 to 24 years old........	80.9	78.5	60.7	55.0	39.2	38.9	33.5	31.9	28.4	22.7
25 to 29 years old........	87.7	85.0	75.9	72.2	52.5	61.2	52.5	54.5	50.1	46.4
30 to 34 years old........	88.5	87.9	81.2	80.2	69.0	70.0	64.3	64.9	62.5	61.1
35 to 39 years old........	87.7	88.8	83.4	82.5	73.9	74.9	71.4	71.9	65.7	68.9
40 to 44 years old........	87.0	89.1	82.4	83.8	73.9	77.0	72.9	74.0	69.2	72.1
45 to 49 years old........	86.2	88.8	83.5	84.3	75.2	78.3	73.2	74.9	70.7	72.2

Source: Same as table 88.

M. Reproduction rates by educational attainment

Period gross and net reproduction rates by educational attainment and residence are presented in figure 85. The method of computation was described in a preceding chapter. Briefly stated, the rates are based upon the 1950 Census data concerning own children under 5 years old per 1,000 women of given ages. The conversion to reproduction rates included adjustments for mortality of women and children, for absence of some children from home at the time of the census, and for an undercount of young children. This was done in order to make the data theoretically equivalent to number of births and women during the preceding 5 years.

TABLE **90.**—PARITY PROGRESSION RATIOS—PERCENT OF WOMEN EVER OF GIVEN PARITY (N) WHO EVER PROGRESSED TO THE NEXT PARITY (N + 1), FOR EVER-MARRIED WHITE WOMEN 20 TO 49 YEARS OLD, BY AGE AND YEARS OF SCHOOL COMPLETED, FOR RURAL-FARM AREAS: 1950 AND 1940

[Data for white women in 1950 and native white women in 1940. Ratio not shown where there are fewer than 4,000 women in 1950 or 3,000 in 1940]

Age and years of school completed	0 to 1 parity		1 to 2 parity		2 to 3 parity		3 to 4 parity		4 to 5 parity	
	1950	1940	1950	1940	1950	1940	1950	1940	1950	1940
COLLEGE										
4 Years or More										
20 to 24 years old........	53.8	...	...	...	...	...	...	...	...	...
25 to 29 years old........	67.8	54.7	60.7	...	37.8	...	...	...	...	...
30 to 34 years old........	83.1	72.0	78.4	59.2	41.3	39.8	...	...	...	...
35 to 39 years old........	78.2	75.0	73.5	72.0	53.1	50.6	47.1	...	...	...
40 to 44 years old........	72.8	75.9	70.9	76.1	48.0	56.7	45.5	...	...	...
45 to 49 years old........	72.9	80.6	68.4	72.6	54.7	...	...	...	...	...
1 to 3 Years										
20 to 24 years old........	57.7	52.5	30.3	29.1	...	...	...	...	...	...
25 to 29 years old........	84.1	73.6	57.6	48.7	33.0	32.1	25.6	...	38.9	...
30 to 34 years old........	87.4	79.6	76.3	67.4	49.9	50.0	41.8	40.4	45.7	45.7
35 to 39 years old........	86.9	81.4	78.2	73.8	59.5	58.5	45.0	51.9	45.7	44.0
40 to 44 years old........	83.0	86.2	80.4	80.5	60.8	66.6	58.3	65.5	54.4	57.4
45 to 49 years old........	78.8	83.8	77.5	82.6	60.7	71.2	55.3	65.9	51.1	59.9
HIGH SCHOOL										
4 Years										
20 to 24 years old........	70.5	64.7	39.1	33.4	24.9	21.3	15.1	21.4	...	...
25 to 29 years old........	85.7	79.6	68.2	58.1	41.8	41.7	35.7	33.2	31.6	34.0
30 to 34 years old........	88.8	85.9	79.1	72.9	55.8	55.1	47.4	49.6	42.8	46.2
35 to 39 years old........	86.5	86.8	80.0	77.6	64.3	64.9	51.5	57.0	54.0	55.4
40 to 44 years old........	84.4	86.9	79.1	79.1	62.2	68.1	60.2	66.8	56.1	61.2
45 to 49 years old........	83.9	86.2	79.0	81.3	65.4	67.9	79.7	62.3	60.0	59.6
1 to 3 Years										
20 to 24 years old........	79.2	78.3	55.7	47.1	32.5	31.6	25.1	25.0	...	...
25 to 29 years old........	88.4	87.4	76.2	70.4	59.2	52.9	43.4	44.3	32.3	38.7
30 to 34 years old........	91.5	89.7	81.6	79.2	66.2	66.7	57.8	60.1	51.5	54.1
35 to 39 years old........	90.3	90.3	82.0	82.9	70.5	73.8	63.4	68.3	56.5	64.8
40 to 44 years old........	87.6	90.6	84.2	85.3	71.0	77.1	69.8	69.6	66.2	68.4
45 to 49 years old........	85.8	89.2	86.1	85.3	73.1	76.7	67.5	72.7	67.0	73.1
NONE OR ELEMENTARY										
20 to 24 years old........	81.8	81.6	60.3	56.0	40.9	40.0	32.7	29.4	25.7	26.9
25 to 29 years old........	89.8	88.6	79.8	76.2	64.3	63.0	56.7	54.8	50.6	47.6
30 to 34 years old........	90.8	92.2	85.2	84.7	73.5	75.7	65.1	69.8	61.1	63.9
35 to 39 years old........	90.5	92.9	87.3	88.1	79.5	81.0	74.0	76.6	71.1	73.6
40 to 44 years old........	90.2	93.0	87.6	89.1	80.6	82.8	76.0	79.8	73.7	76.5
45 to 49 years old........	89.6	92.5	87.9	88.9	81.3	83.4	77.8	80.9	75.5	77.4

Source: Same as table 88.

The computed gross and net reproduction rates for the whites in the country as a whole during 1945 to 1950 were 1,411 and 1,340, respectively.[9] By residence, the gross reproduction rates per 1,000 white women were: urban—1,221, rural nonfarm—1,724, and rural farm—1,988. Of particular relevance here, however, are the levels and differentials in reproduction rates by education. Contrary to the situation in 1935–40 when women (all races) who finished college had a net reproduction rate 48

---

[9] A check on the reproduction rates computed from census data on children under 5 is available from a series of gross and net reproduction rates based upon annually registered births (with adjustment for underregistration), recently released by the National Office of Vital Statistics. It will be

percent below replacement requirements, whites exceeded this requirement by 9 percent in 1945–50. In 1935–40, fertility was 33 percent below replacement requirements for women with 1 to 3 years of college training and 26 percent below for those with 4 years of high school. It was hardly at replacement requirement even for those with 1 to 3 years of high school.[10] In 1945–50, in contrast, the fertility was *above* replacement requirement by 18 percent for the white women with 1 to 3 years of college training, by 28 percent for those with 4 years of high school, and by 39 percent for those with 1 to 3 years of high school. It should be emphasized that net reproduction rates simply express the *potentiality* for increase through births that is implicit in the age-specific fertility and mortality rates. They should not be interpreted as having any relation to the actual size of the educational groups in the future.

As expected, for given educational classes the reproduction rates were lowest for women in the urban areas, in intermediate position for women in rural-nonfarm areas, and highest for women in rural-farm areas. Clearly, although part of the total urban-rural differential in fertility may accrue from differences in composition by educational attainment, this is not the complete explanation.

That the differences between gross and net reproduction rates were fairly constant by education arises simply from the fact that the adjustment factors for mortality were the same by education within a given residence group. Mortality data by education were not available. Hence, the adjustment factors differed by residence and color but not by education.

The relative spread of the net reproduction rates by educational attainment of the white women was approximately the same within each type of community. The net reproduction rate for women with less than 8 years of elementary school was higher than that for the college graduates by 35 percent in urban areas, 38 percent in rural-nonfarm areas, and 33 percent

---

noted from the figures given below that the averages of the five reproduction rates for whites based upon annual births for 1945–49 are practically identical with those computed from the 1950 Census data regarding children under 5 years of age:

Year	Gross reproduction rate	Net reproduction rate
1949	1,461	1,396
1948	1,468	1,401
1947	1,568	1,492
1946	1,406	1,331
1945	1,175	1,106
Straight average (annual rates)	1,416	1,345
Based on children under 5	1,411	1,340

Source: Annual data from National Office of Vital Statistics, "Births by Age of Mother, Race, and Birth Order, United States, 1953," *Vital Statistics—Special Reports*, Vol. 42, No. 13, p. 294.

[10] U. S. Bureau of the Census, *Current Population Reports*, Series P-20, No. 18, p. 6.

TABLE 91.—PARITY PROGRESSION RATIOS—PERCENT OF WOMEN EVER OF GIVEN PARITY (N) WHO EVER PROGRESSED TO THE NEXT PARITY (N + 1), FOR EVER-MARRIED NONWHITE WOMEN 20 TO 49 YEARS OLD, BY AGE AND YEARS OF SCHOOL COMPLETED, URBAN AND RURAL: 1950

[Ratio not shown where there are fewer than 4,000 women]

Age and years of school completed	0 to 1 parity			1 to 2 parity			2 to 3 parity			3 to 4 parity			4 to 5 parity		
	Urban	Rural nonfarm	Rural farm	Urban	Rural nonfarm	Rural farm	Urban	Rural nonfarm	Rural farm	Urban	Rural nonfarm	Rural farm	Urban	Rural nonfarm	Rural farm
College, 4 years or more:															
20 to 24 years old	45.5	...	...	...	...	...	...	...	...	...	...	...	...	...	...
25 to 29 years old	54.0	...	...	40.5	...	...	25.0	...	...	...	...	...	...	...	...
30 to 34 years old	58.9	...	...	50.0	...	...	37.8	...	...	...	...	...	...	...	...
35 to 39 years old	50.2	...	...	60.4	...	...	52.8	...	...	...	...	...	...	...	...
40 to 44 years old	51.9	...	...	59.5	...	...	59.2	...	...	...	...	...	...	...	...
45 to 49 years old	50.3	...	...	...	...	...	61.9	...	...	...	...	...	...	...	...
College, 1 to 3 years:															
20 to 24 years old	61.7	...	...	38.8	...	...	...	...	...	...	...	...	...	...	...
25 to 29 years old	64.1	...	...	50.0	...	...	...	...	...	...	...	...	...	...	...
30 to 34 years old	58.4	...	...	61.9	...	...	...	...	...	...	...	...	...	...	...
35 to 39 years old	52.4	...	...	59.6	...	...	...	...	...	...	...	...	...	...	...
40 to 44 years old	58.5	...	...	59.0	...	...	...	...	...	...	...	...	...	...	...
45 to 49 years old	51.6	...	...	75.3	...	...	...	...	...	...	...	...	...	...	...
High school, 4 years:															
20 to 24 years old	67.0	78.4	...	43.2	57.0	...	31.9	...	...	32.3	...	...	...	...	...
25 to 29 years old	62.5	79.7	...	57.8	65.0	...	47.8	...	...	45.9	...	...	...	...	...
30 to 34 years old	63.4	...	...	63.4	...	...	53.0	...	...	48.1	...	...	37.6	...	...
35 to 39 years old	58.5	...	...	63.4	...	...	64.0	...	...	58.3	...	...	58.4	...	...
40 to 44 years old	61.8	...	...	63.0	...	...	55.9	...	...	64.5	...	...	50.2	...	...
45 to 49 years old	64.3	...	...	67.0	...	...	69.7	...	...	57.5	...	...	71.4	...	...
High school, 1 to 3 years:															
20 to 24 years old	71.1	76.9	76.4	60.7	62.0	62.8	41.6	40.5	50.8	35.6	37.8	...	32.5	...	...
25 to 29 years old	69.0	82.2	84.0	68.3	75.0	79.4	61.2	68.1	72.0	61.8	53.9	...	48.6	...	...
30 to 34 years old	66.5	80.1	83.0	67.5	75.6	86.2	67.1	77.9	80.6	68.9	71.1	74.9	64.1	...	...
35 to 39 years old	65.8	78.2	86.6	68.4	75.0	87.2	61.2	76.7	89.8	66.5	78.3	76.5	63.1	...	60.6
40 to 44 years old	66.3	77.4	87.1	65.4	80.1	82.4	72.5	74.5	...	65.9	...	84.7	73.3	...	...
45 to 49 years old	70.6	...	...	65.1	...	...	72.8	...	...	65.8	...	...	71.8	...	82.0
None or elementary:															
20 to 24 years old	67.6	78.4	81.9	62.4	69.5	72.4	52.6	53.6	61.4	46.7	45.0	50.2	37.7	49.1	41.3
25 to 29 years old	69.1	79.8	83.7	68.0	78.2	83.7	64.7	74.5	79.8	63.1	68.5	73.5	55.4	66.8	69.5
30 to 34 years old	66.8	78.3	86.4	66.7	81.6	85.6	66.9	78.6	84.4	66.0	78.1	84.2	67.6	74.5	81.9
35 to 39 years old	64.8	77.0	85.0	69.0	78.8	86.9	69.2	82.8	87.2	71.9	81.5	85.9	72.1	79.7	84.5
40 to 44 years old	68.3	75.9	84.9	66.9	80.9	87.4	67.5	78.4	88.2	70.5	78.6	85.4	70.4	79.4	85.4
45 to 49 years old	69.4	76.1	85.5	70.6	80.5	88.9	70.1	78.1	86.9	70.6	77.1	84.7	69.8	76.1	86.8

Source: *1950 Census of Population*, Vol. IV, *Special Reports*, Part 5, Chapter C, Fertility, table 22.

in rural-farm areas. For the United States as a whole, the net reproduction rate was 52 percent higher for the women of under eighth-grade status than for the college graduates. This wider discrepancy for the country as a whole reflected the urban-rural differences in reproduction and education.

FIGURE 85.—GROSS AND NET REPRODUCTION RATES, 1945 TO 1950, FOR WHITE WOMEN BY YEARS OF SCHOOL COMPLETED, URBAN AND RURAL

[Rates derived from data on women by age and number of own children under 5 years old]

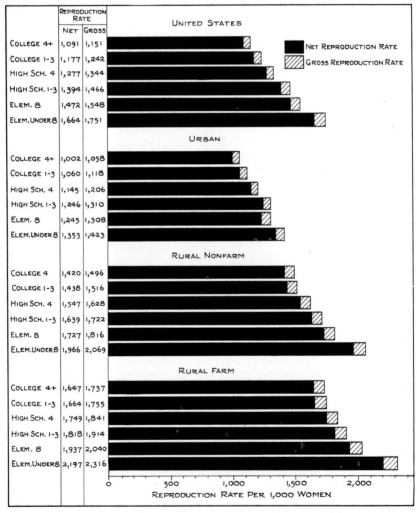

Source: Derived from *1950 Census of Population*, Vol. IV, *Special Reports*, Part 5, Chapter C, Fertility, table 44, with allowance for children not living with their mothers (Appendix A), and using United States life tables for years from 1945 to 1950.

N. Indices of the trend of fertility differentials by educational attainment, 1940–50

As with occupation in the previous chapter, two methods have been used for a more precise indication of 1940–50 trends in differentials in fertility by education. These methods are (a) the average of the percentage deviations of the cumulative fertility rates of the various educational classes from the base rate for the total group, and (b) the relative spread of the cumulative fertility rates by educational attainment obtained by expressing the rate of each educational class as a percentage of the base rate.

Indices of average percent deviation from base rates. Table 92 presents for each age group the average of the percentage deviations of the cumulative fertility rates of the various educational groups from the base rate for the age group. These data are shown for 1940 and 1950 for all white women and ever-married white women of given age and residence.

TABLE 92.—MEASURE OF AVERAGE INTERCLASS DIFFERENCES IN CUMULATIVE FERTILITY RATES BY YEARS OF SCHOOL COMPLETED, FOR WHITE WOMEN 15 TO 49 YEARS OLD, BY AGE AND MARITAL STATUS, URBAN AND RURAL: 1950 AND 1940

[Data for white women in 1950 and native white women in 1940. Measure not shown where there are fewer than 4,000 women in 1950 or 3,000 in 1940. An operational definition of the measure is as follows: First, for each area, age group, and marital status group represented fertility rates for each of five educational groups was listed for 1950 and 1940. Second, "base rates" or standardized average rates for the five educational classes combined were computed. (The rates for 1940 were standardized to the 1950 distribution of women for ever-married women by educational attainment.) Third, for each census year, the percent difference (regardless of direction) of the fertility rate for each of the five educational groups from the base rate was computed. Fourth, the simple averages of these five percentage differences were obtained and these are the figures given in the table]

Area and age	Total women		Ever-married women	
	1950	1940	1950	1940
URBAN				
15 to 19 years..........................	42.9	59.5	30.5	31.1
20 to 24 years..........................	50.1	64.5	33.3	39.2
25 to 29 years..........................	24.4	39.4	19.2	28.4
30 to 34 years..........................	14.9	29.7	11.3	21.8
35 to 39 years..........................	15.8	26.0	11.6	19.1
40 to 44 years..........................	20.1	24.5	16.0	18.4
45 to 49 years..........................	25.8	24.2	22.2	18.0
RURAL NONFARM				
15 to 19 years..........................	38.1	57.4	...	...
20 to 24 years..........................	41.0	63.9	28.2	38.3
25 to 29 years..........................	27.0	42.2	24.4	32.7
30 to 34 years..........................	19.2	33.6	17.6	27.8
35 to 39 years..........................	21.7	29.7	21.0	25.5
40 to 44 years..........................	24.0	27.9	22.9	25.1
45 to 49 years..........................	29.5	25.8	27.8	23.0
RURAL FARM				
15 to 19 years..........................	41.1	63.2	...	...
20 to 24 years..........................	38.6	64.3	27.8	27.1
25 to 29 years..........................	23.5	41.0	20.9	28.9
30 to 34 years..........................	17.8	30.6	16.2	24.8
35 to 39 years..........................	21.1	29.4	19.7	24.4
40 to 44 years..........................	24.0	24.5	22.8	21.6
45 to 49 years..........................	26.0	24.7	25.5	22.7

Source: Derived from *1950 Census of Population*, Vol. IV, *Special Reports*, Part 5, Chapter C, Fertility, table 20; *1940 Census of Population, Differential Fertility, 1940 and 1910*, Women by Number of Children Ever Born, table 49.

There are several points of interest in table 92. In the first place, the data point up the contractions of class differences in fertility as measured for 1940 and 1950. The indices of average deviation were characteristically lower in 1950 than in 1940 for all age groups except 45 to 49. The only exceptions were at ages 45 to 49 for each type of residence and 40 to 44 for ever-married women in rural-farm areas. The 1940–50 reductions in the indices were especially marked at ages 25 to 39. It is well to remember that the contraction of class differences in fertility during 1940 to 1950 occurred in the context of increasing fertility. One might think that general increases in fertility would have provided room for larger class differences in fertility. As already indicated, however, the 1940–50 increases in fertility tended to be most pronounced among the classes that previously had been characterized by lowest fertility.

A second point to note regarding table 92 is that the indices of deviation were consistently higher for women of all marital classes than for ever-married women. As previously stated, the group variations in general fertility reflected group differences in proportions married as well as group differences in marital fertility.

Thirdly, in 1940, the indices of deviation were inversely related to age. For 1950, they were highest at ages 20 to 24 and lowest at ages 30 to 34. These relationships held for general and marital cumulative fertility rates, and, with certain exceptions, for each type of residence. The inverse relation may have arisen to some extent simply from the fact that cumulative fertility rates themselves increased with age. A small deviation from a relatively low base rate might easily have been a high percent deviation. A substantial absolute deviation from the completed fertility rate at ages 45 to 49 might easily have been a low percent deviation. It is recognized that to some extent the generally higher fertility rates for 1950 than for 1940 helped to account for the lower indices for 1950 than for 1940. The fact that the fertility rates at ages 45 to 49 were a little higher in 1940 than in 1950 may account for the slightly higher average deviations in 1950 than in 1940 at these ages. On the other hand, the basic fertility data themselves and the data regarding percent increases in fertility during 1940 to 1950 give overwhelming evidence of a narrowing of differences in fertility by educational attainment at ages 20 to 39.

There was not much difference by type of residence in the magnitude of the average percent deviations of the various educational classes in 1940 or 1950. The most systematic difference observed was a slightly higher average in rural-nonfarm areas than in urban areas or rural-farm areas at ages 25 to 49. There was not much difference by residence in the 1940–50 decline in indices of average deviation.

A high average percent deviation from the base rate could have arisen from wide unsystematic variations of the education subgroups with respect to fertility or it could have arisen from a wide relative spread of the fertility rates along systematic lines such as an inverse or a direct relationship.

The relative spread of the fertility rates by education of the woman is given in table 93 for all white women and ever-married white women in 1940 and 1950, by age and residence of the women. These again attest to a narrowing of the fertility differentials by education, particularly among women 20 to 34 years old. For example, in 1940 among urban native white women 25 to 29 years old, the fertility rate for the college graduates was 37 percent of (or 63 percent below) the base rate for the total age group. The fertility rate for the "none or elementary" group was 153 percent of (or 53 percent above) the base rate. The difference between these extremes is 116 percentage points. In 1950, the corresponding range was from 58 percent to 128 percent of the base rate; a difference of only 70 percentage points. Again the 1940–50 contrasts were not so wide when they were related to relative spread of marital fertility rates. However, they were still quite striking. Thus, among urban white ever-married women 25 to 29 years old in 1940, the fertility rate for college graduates was 54 percent of (or 46 percent below) the base rate, and that for the women of elementary education was 141 percent of (or 41 percent above) the base rate. The difference between these extremes is 87 percentage points. In 1950, the comparable range is represented by 69 and 125, a total range of 56 percentage points. (See figures 86–88.)

Trends in differentials in fertility among the nonwhites. As already indicated, a precise determination of 1940–50 trends in fertility differentials by education among the nonwhites in this country is made difficult by the lack of published data for 1940 by urban-rural residence. It is well known that educational attainment tends to be lower in rural than in urban areas. Thus, when the data are not broken down by urban-rural residence, the results concerning variations in fertility by educational attainment may reflect urban-rural differentials to some extent and this may partly vitiate the analysis of 1940–50 trends. Despite the above limitations, it is of interest to examine the available materials. In general, the indices of average deviation tended to be lower in 1950 than in 1940 for women at ages under 35. At older ages the indices were a little higher in 1950 than in 1940. The indices for Negroes in the total United States in 1940 tended to be about as high as those for rural-nonfarm whites in the same year. The indices for the nonwhites in the United States in 1950 tended to be higher than those for rural-nonfarm whites except at ages 45 to 49.

The relative spread of cumulative fertility rates by educational attainment of the Negroes in 1940 and the nonwhites in 1950 also points up the reduction of differentials in fertility by educational attainment. Among Negro women of all marital classes and 25 to 29 years old in 1940, the fertility rates for the "college: 4 years or more" and "none or elementary" groups were respectively 21 and 126 percent of the base rates. In 1950,

TABLE 93.—RELATIVE VARIATION OF CUMULATIVE FERTILITY RATES BY YEARS OF SCHOOL COMPLETED BY WHITE WOMEN 15 TO 49 YEARS OLD, BY AGE AND MARITAL STATUS, URBAN AND RURAL: 1950 AND 1940

[Data for white women in 1950 and native white women in 1940. See table 66 for an analogous definition of relative spread of rates in terms of occupation; the standard is the distribution by years of school completed for white women of given age and marital status in the United States in 1950. Relative variation not shown where there are fewer than 4,000 women in 1950 or 3,000 in 1940]

Age and years of school completed	Total women						Ever-married women					
	Urban		Rural nonfarm		Rural farm		Urban		Rural nonfarm		Rural farm	
	1950	1940	1950	1940	1950	1940	1950	1940	1950	1940	1950	1940
15 TO 19 YEARS OLD												
Base rate	79	39	128	75	90	55	518	518	592	611	565	597
Relative variation, total (base rate)	100	100	100	100	100	100	100	100	100	100	100	100
College: 4 years or more	124	...	...	...	...	...	...	...	...	...	...	...
1 to 3 years	20	23	32	8	23	18	47	53	...	...	...	...
High school: 4 years	66	56	83	65	107	66	58	59	59	65	61	68
1 to 3 years	91	81	89	84	77	73	109	107	106	106	106	100
None or elementary	168	198	156	187	162	210	126	128	129	125	128	128
20 TO 24 YEARS OLD												
Base rate	617	332	903	583	888	550	940	772	1,178	1,015	1,231	1,119
Relative variation, total (base rate)	100	100	100	100	100	100	100	100	100	100	100	100
College: 4 years or more	27	18	35	13	39	14	39	37	53	38	57	...
1 to 3 years	42	33	55	29	51	23	66	56	73	57	64	64
High school: 4 years	80	67	85	71	89	73	83	79	83	79	86	83
1 to 3 years	143	156	133	157	135	156	119	122	116	122	116	117
None or elementary	157	184	146	176	136	175	136	146	135	143	130	137
25 TO 29 YEARS OLD												
Base rate	1,271	790	1,653	1,250	1,828	1,396	1,489	1,118	1,800	1,518	2,022	1,781
Relative variation, total (base rate)	100	100	100	100	100	100	100	100	100	100	100	100
College: 4 years or more	58	37	53	30	56	25	69	54	61	47	65	47
1 to 3 years	78	69	74	56	76	58	82	76	76	65	77	72
High school: 4 years	89	77	88	82	92	85	89	83	87	84	91	87
1 to 3 years	118	127	119	126	115	129	111	114	114	115	110	115
None or elementary	128	153	131	153	127	144	125	141	131	145	127	135

30 TO 34 YEARS OLD

Base rate	1,654	1,250	2,143	1,791	2,420	2,163	1,848	1,545	2,274	2,016	2,592	2,488
Relative variation, total (base rate)	100	100	100	100	100	100	100	100	100	100	100	100
College: 4 years or more	74	53	68	44	69	41	84	69	74	57	74	56
1 to 3 years	86	72	81	67	81	68	88	77	82	72	82	72
High school: 4 years	91	79	88	79	90	86	91	83	87	80	90	86
1 to 3 years	109	112	107	113	109	112	105	106	104	108	106	107
None or elementary	117	140	126	144	120	135	115	132	126	140	121	132

35 TO 39 YEARS OLD

Base rate	1,787	1,617	2,356	2,230	2,787	2,773	1,973	1,910	2,500	2,459	2,951	3,073
Relative variation, total (base rate)	100	100	100	100	100	100	100	100	100	100	100	100
College: 4 years or more	72	53	60	47	59	44	86	70	65	57	66	58
1 to 3 years	85	74	77	70	78	65	87	79	78	73	78	69
High school: 4 years	86	79	83	76	85	82	87	83	83	77	84	82
1 to 3 years	104	103	100	105	101	106	101	100	97	102	99	103
None or elementary	119	133	129	136	126	132	117	126	128	133	126	129

40 TO 44 YEARS OLD

Base rate	1,866	1,862	2,466	2,507	3,021	3,236	2,053	2,169	2,628	2,750	3,190	3,504
Relative variation, total (base rate)	100	100	100	100	100	100	100	100	100	100	100	100
College: 4 years or more	64	53	57	49	50	47	76	70	63	60	55	58
1 to 3 years	79	74	73	68	76	77	81	79	74	70	77	78
High school: 4 years	81	79	78	76	81	82	83	82	77	77	80	80
1 to 3 years	103	100	100	100	101	102	99	98	98	97	99	99
None or elementary	122	127	127	132	126	126	119	121	127	129	125	124

45 TO 49 YEARS OLD

Base rate	1,978	2,039	2,555	2,737	3,180	3,444	2,178	2,353	2,735	3,014	3,372	3,703
Relative variation, total (base rate)	100	100	100	100	100	100	100	100	100	100	100	100
College: 4 years or more	51	55	48	55	50	51	63	75	56	65	54	59
1 to 3 years	69	73	66	68	67	72	72	79	67	72	66	75
High school: 4 years	76	76	75	74	78	76	78	78	74	75	77	75
1 to 3 years	98	97	91	97	98	99	96	95	89	94	97	96
None or elementary	123	122	127	124	123	122	119	117	125	121	121	120

Source: Same as table 92.

FIGURE **86.**—Relative Spread of Cumulative Fertility Rates by Years of School Completed by White Women 15 to 49 Years Old, by Age and Marital Status, for Urban
Areas: 1950 and 1940

[Data for white women in 1950 and native white women in 1940. See source table for definition of relative spread of rates]

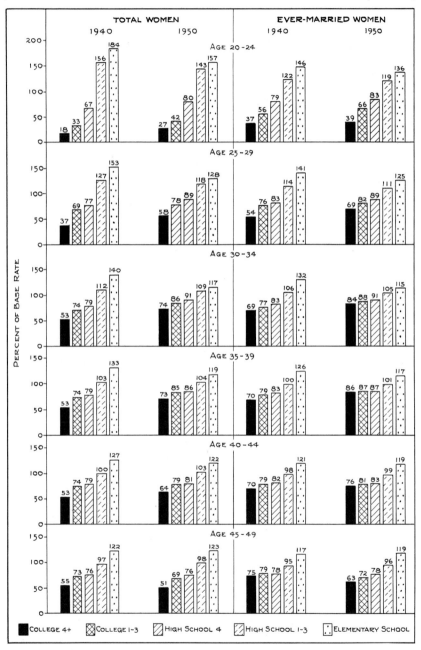

Note: Based on data in table 93.

FIGURE **87.**—RELATIVE SPREAD OF CUMULATIVE FERTILITY RATES BY YEARS OF SCHOOL COM-
PLETED BY WHITE WOMEN 15 TO 49 YEARS OLD, BY AGE AND MARITAL STATUS, FOR RURAL-
NONFARM AREAS: 1950 AND 1940

[Data for white women in 1950 and native white women in 1940. See source table for definition of relative spread of rates]

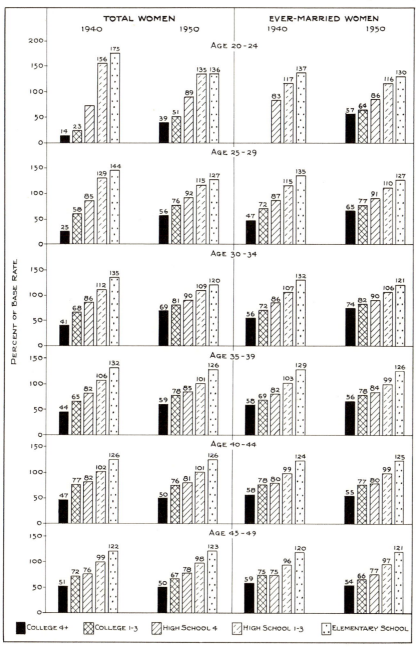

Note: Based on data in table 93.

FIGURE **88.**—RELATIVE SPREAD OF CUMULATIVE FERTILITY RATES BY YEARS OF SCHOOL COM-
PLETED BY WHITE WOMEN 15 TO 49 YEARS OLD, BY AGE AND MARITAL STATUS, FOR RURAL-
FARM AREAS: 1950 AND 1940

[Data for white women in 1950 and native white women in 1940. See source table for definition of relative spread of rates]

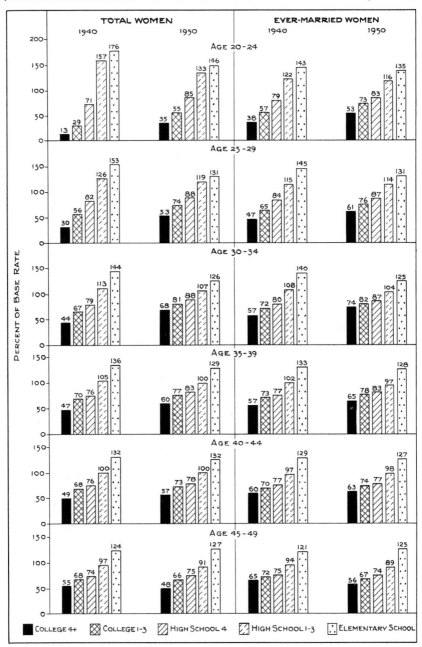

Note: Based on data in table 93.

the corresponding figures for nonwhites were 37 and 119. This is a substantial narrowing of the range. When the analysis is restricted to ever-married women of the same age, the corresponding figures were 36 and 119 for 1940 and 46 and 117 for 1950.

In general, for both whites and nonwhites, the increases in fertility that occurred during 1940 to 1950 were such as to bring a narrowing of the differentials in fertility by education of the woman.

C H A P T E R   7

ADDITIONAL SOCIO-ECONOMIC FACTORS
IN RELATION TO FERTILITY

With data from various sources it is possible to consider briefly the relation of cumulative fertility rates and fertility ratios to certain socio-economic characteristics besides occupational and educational status. The 1950 Census provides data on fertility in relation to labor force status of women. Data are available from the 1940 Census concerning the relation of fertility to monthly rental value of the dwelling unit. Several reports based upon the Current Population Survey have included analyses of fertility ratios and cumulative fertility rates in relation to income of the husband and family income as well as to occupation, education, and rental value of the home.[1] Finally, there are some data from studies conducted by individuals and private agencies concerning the relation of fertility to religion, degree of practice and success of family limitation, and certain psychological characteristics.

A. Labor force status of women in relation to fertility

As used in the 1950 Census, the *labor force* includes all persons 14 years old and over classified as employed or unemployed by census definition and also members of the Armed Forces (Appendix A).

Our present concern is with the labor force status of women. As expected, the percentage of the women in the labor force varies sharply with marital status, residence, age, and color. In 1950, approximately one-third (32 percent) of all white women 15 to 49 years old, were in the labor force. The proportion was slightly over half (53 percent) for the single women and approximately one-fourth (26 percent) for the ever-married women. The proportion in the labor force was 22 percent for the "married once and husband present" group and 42 percent for the "other ever married" group (table 94).

---

[1] Rental and value of home data were collected from a sample of households in 1950 but this sample differed from the fertility sample, so the data could not be used in the fertility tabulations.

Likewise the 1950 Census also collected some data on income for a sample of people. However, sampling design was such that no analysis of children ever born to married women by income of the husband or by total family income is possible. In short, husbands, wives, and household heads were not jointly in the samples for which additional questions were asked.

TABLE **94.**—PERCENT OF WOMEN 15 TO 49 YEARS OLD IN THE LABOR FORCE, BY AGE, COLOR, AND MARITAL STATUS, URBAN AND RURAL: 1950

Age and marital status	White				Nonwhite			
	United States	Urban	Rural nonfarm	Rural farm	United States	Urban	Rural nonfarm	Rural farm
ALL MARITAL CLASSES								
Total, 15 to 49 years..	32.4	37.1	25.8	17.4	40.8	47.0	32.3	23.7
15 to 19 years............	27.1	32.5	21.2	15.0	20.9	22.4	18.1	19.7
20 to 24 years............	42.8	49.2	30.8	24.0	38.9	44.3	29.6	25.5
25 to 29 years............	30.6	35.2	22.8	16.0	42.7	48.0	33.5	24.4
30 to 34 years............	28.2	31.9	22.6	16.3	46.6	53.0	35.7	24.3
35 to 39 years............	31.2	35.2	26.5	16.9	47.8	54.6	39.5	23.8
40 to 44 years............	33.9	38.1	29.5	18.0	47.6	53.7	39.6	27.5
45 to 49 years............	32.5	36.5	29.0	16.9	45.2	51.1	39.0	24.2
SINGLE								
Total, 15 to 49 years..	53.0	60.9	39.1	26.9	40.1	46.9	32.0	26.6
15 to 19 years............	28.1	33.2	22.5	15.9	20.9	21.8	19.1	20.3
20 to 24 years............	75.5	78.7	69.1	56.3	56.8	63.6	46.3	39.0
25 to 29 years............	81.7	86.9	65.7	51.2	66.2	71.9	55.9	43.3
30 to 34 years............	79.0	85.3	59.5	46.8	67.9	73.4	55.4	42.9
35 to 39 years............	77.0	83.6	57.5	42.7	67.7	75.4	49.1	42.7
40 to 44 years............	76.2	82.9	55.4	43.0	63.2	70.1	46.7	43.5
45 to 49 years............	73.4	79.9	54.9	37.9	58.8	68.2	39.4	27.5
EVER MARRIED								
Total, 15 to 49 years..	26.2	29.5	22.6	14.6	41.1	47.0	32.4	22.4
15 to 19 years............	22.0	28.3	16.7	10.5	20.8	24.7	15.0	17.2
20 to 24 years............	27.6	32.6	20.7	12.1	30.7	35.5	22.8	18.8
25 to 29 years............	23.0	26.0	19.1	12.5	38.8	43.8	30.0	21.5
30 to 34 years............	23.1	25.5	20.4	14.3	44.6	51.0	34.0	23.0
35 to 39 years............	27.0	29.9	24.6	15.5	46.4	53.0	38.7	22.9
40 to 44 years............	30.0	33.2	27.7	16.7	46.6	52.7	39.1	26.9
45 to 49 years............	28.8	31.9	27.2	15.9	44.5	50.2	39.0	24.1
MARRIED ONCE, HUSBAND PRESENT								
Total, 15 to 49 years..	22.2	24.7	20.3	13.4	32.0	37.6	25.4	18.2
15 to 19 years............	20.2	26.0	15.6	9.7	16.1	19.2	11.3	13.9
20 to 24 years............	25.6	30.3	19.3	12.3	24.3	28.4	17.4	16.1
25 to 29 years............	20.0	22.4	17.3	11.3	31.6	36.3	24.4	17.9
30 to 34 years............	19.3	20.7	18.6	13.3	37.1	43.7	28.1	19.2
35 to 39 years............	22.5	24.3	22.2	14.6	36.3	42.6	32.0	18.8
40 to 44 years............	25.0	27.2	24.8	15.5	36.1	41.9	33.4	20.7
45 to 49 years............	23.1	25.0	24.0	14.3	34.0	40.4	30.5	19.0
OTHER EVER MARRIED								
Total, 15 to 49 years..	41.9	47.1	32.1	21.8	52.8	57.6	43.2	31.9
15 to 19 years............	33.3	40.8	25.6	15.8	33.9	37.4	28.9	27.7
20 to 24 years............	40.2	46.4	29.8	11.9	44.5	49.2	36.7	26.6
25 to 29 years............	38.2	43.2	28.3	20.8	50.8	55.1	41.3	30.4
30 to 34 years............	39.7	45.1	28.3	21.2	55.0	59.7	43.5	32.6
35 to 39 years............	43.4	48.6	33.6	21.2	57.6	63.1	46.6	31.8
40 to 44 years............	45.2	50.1	36.4	23.5	56.1	60.6	45.4	37.5
45 to 49 years............	43.7	48.2	35.3	23.3	52.1	56.1	45.5	32.3

Source: Derived from *1950 Census of Population*, Vol. IV, *Special Reports*, Part 5, Chapter C, Fertility, tables 46 and 47.

By residence, the proportions in the labor force among white women 15 to 49 years old were approximately 37 percent for the urban areas, 26 for the rural-nonfarm areas, and 17 for the rural-farm areas. Among the nonwhites the comparable proportions were 47, 32, and 24.

Among all white women regardless of marital status the percentage in the labor force in 1950 was highest (43 percent) at ages 20 to 24. At these ages many of the women had completed their schooling but had not yet married. About 27 percent were in the labor force at ages 15 to 19, 31 at ages 25 to 29, and 34 at ages 40 to 44.

The relation of age to labor force varied somewhat by marital status. Among the single white women in the United States the proportion in the labor force was only about one-fourth (28 percent) at ages 15 to 19; many of those not in the labor force at this age were students. The proportion in the labor force jumped to 76 percent for ages 20 to 24 and to 82 percent for ages 25 to 29. It stayed at 73 to 80 percent throughout ages 30 to 49.

Among all ever-married white women in the United States, the proportion in the labor force in 1950 was about 22 percent at ages 15 to 19. It was 28 percent at ages 20 to 24. It fell to 23 percent at ages 25 to 29 and then increased gradually with increasing age and reached 30 percent at ages 40 to 44. The low point at ages 25 to 29 coincides with the presence of a maximum number of children of preschool age.

Among the ever-married childless white women 15 to 19 years old, approximately 31 percent were in the labor force in 1950. This proportion was slightly higher than that for single women of this age. At later ages, the proportions in the labor force were much lower for the ever-married childless women than for the single women. However, the proportions of the ever-married childless white women that were in the labor force in 1950 were about 50 percent or higher at ages 20 to 34 and 40 percent or higher at ages 35 to 44.

Fertility by labor force status. In table 95 and figure 89, age-specific rates of children ever born are shown for ever-married white women, by residence and labor force status. Within each type of residence, the cumulative fertility rates are found to be considerably lower for women in the labor force than for those not in the labor force. The gap between these types of rates would be larger in data relating to all women regardless of marital status than in those shown for ever-married women, because many infertile single, widowed, and divorced women are in the labor force.

The foregoing statements apply to the nonwhites as well as to the whites. However, within the rural-farm areas the fertility differential by labor force status is somewhat less pronounced among the nonwhites than among the whites (table 95).

Percent childless. The percentage of women who are childless is in most cases much higher among women in the labor force than among those who are not in the labor force. This holds true within each type of residence and at each age group of the childbearing span. As also indicated, however, there are certain differences in the patterns of the relationships of childlessness to labor force status (figure 90).

In general, the excess of childlessness among women in the labor force over that of women not in the labor force is greatest in the urban areas and smallest in the rural-farm areas. Although the present data afford no evidence on the subject, it seems possible that the employment opportunities for women in rural-farm areas may interfere less with household activities than is the case in urban and rural-nonfarm areas. It is also likely that by virtue of higher fertility and by virtue of a greater tendency to take parents and relatives into the household, the presence of children per se does not tend to tie the mother to the home as much in rural-farm areas as in other areas.

TABLE 95.—NUMBER OF CHILDREN EVER BORN PER 1,000 EVER-MARRIED WOMEN 15 TO 49 YEARS OLD, BY AGE, COLOR, AND LABOR FORCE STATUS, URBAN AND RURAL: 1950

[Rate not shown where there are fewer than 4,000 women]

Area and age	White			Nonwhite		
	All women	Labor force	Not in labor force	All women	Labor force	Not in labor force
UNITED STATES						
15 to 19 years......................	548	249	632	1,222	1,168	1,227
20 to 24 years......................	1,028	462	1,244	1,548	1,394	1,568
25 to 29 years......................	1,620	919	1,829	2,025	1,751	2,063
30 to 34 years......................	2,034	1,377	2,232	2,437	2,136	2,489
35 to 39 years......................	2,218	1,651	2,428	2,715	2,419	2,783
40 to 44 years......................	2,329	1,765	2,571	2,923	2,506	3,040
45 to 49 years......................	2,456	1,956	2,658	3,088	2,718	3,187
URBAN						
15 to 19 years......................	502	223	611	1,188	1,125	1,195
20 to 24 years......................	910	407	1,154	1,463	1,340	1,481
25 to 29 years......................	1,454	824	1,675	1,867	1,661	1,898
30 to 34 years......................	1,821	1,225	2,024	2,229	2,006	2,268
35 to 39 years......................	1,943	1,491	2,136	2,426	2,259	2,468
40 to 44 years......................	2,022	1,604	2,230	2,582	2,321	2,663
45 to 49 years......................	2,141	1,782	2,309	2,735	2,516	2,798
RURAL NONFARM						
15 to 19 years......................	612	287	677	1,256	1,262	1,256
20 to 24 years......................	1,218	597	1,380	1,640	1,450	1,661
25 to 29 years......................	1,857	1,085	2,038	2,218	1,804	2,272
30 to 34 years......................	2,325	1,648	2,498	2,673	2,195	2,762
35 to 39 years......................	2,543	1,944	2,738	2,997	2,555	3,104
40 to 44 years......................	2,661	2,066	2,889	3,249	2,742	3,398
45 to 49 years......................	2,776	2,264	2,967	3,389	2,953	3,513
RURAL FARM						
15 to 19 years......................	589	376	615	1,256	...	1,259
20 to 24 years......................	1,320	866	1,383	1,744	1,629	1,754
25 to 29 years......................	2,167	1,630	2,243	2,488	2,261	2,512
30 to 34 years......................	2,732	2,228	2,816	3,067	2,800	3,103
35 to 39 years......................	3,137	2,526	3,250	3,546	3,135	3,611
40 to 44 years......................	3,403	2,660	3,553	3,900	3,280	4,005
45 to 49 years......................	3,582	2,981	3,695	4,111	3,586	4,194

Source: *1950 Census of Population*, Vol. IV, *Special Reports*, Part 5, Chapter C, Fertility, tables 24 and 26.

In interpreting the age patterns of the proportions of childlessness by labor force status it is important to remember that the term "childless," as used here, means that the woman *never* had a live birth. The considerably higher proportion of childlessness among women in the labor force than among those not in the labor force, reflects both selective and determinative relationships. It seems probable that the selective factors are more important than the determinative influences insofar as young women are concerned. That is, the labor force tends to *select* childless women rather than to influence women to remain childless. Although the proportion of childlessness is much higher among the women in the labor force than among those not in the labor force, the proportion declines sharply with age, just as it does among women not in the labor force. In other words, among women in the labor force as well as among those not in the labor force, with the advance of age there are *increasing* proportions of women who have borne one child or more.

FIGURE **89.**—NUMBER OF CHILDREN EVER BORN PER 1,000 EVER-MARRIED WHITE WOMEN 15 TO 49 YEARS OLD, BY AGE AND LABOR FORCE STATUS, URBAN AND RURAL: 1950

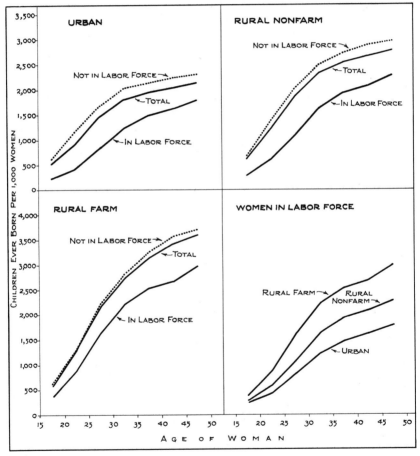

Note: Based on data in table 95.

After age 35 the gap between the proportion of childless women in the labor force and those not in the labor force tends to become smaller, because (1) the proportion of childlessness after this age is too small to allow wide internal variations, and (2) mothers sometimes enter the labor force after their children are old enough to take care of themselves while the mother is at work; probably in some cases the older children care for the younger ones and thus enable the mother to enter or re-enter the labor force.

FIGURE 90.—PERCENT CHILDLESS AMONG EVER-MARRIED WHITE WOMEN 15 TO 49 YEARS OLD, BY AGE AND LABOR FORCE STATUS, URBAN AND RURAL: 1950

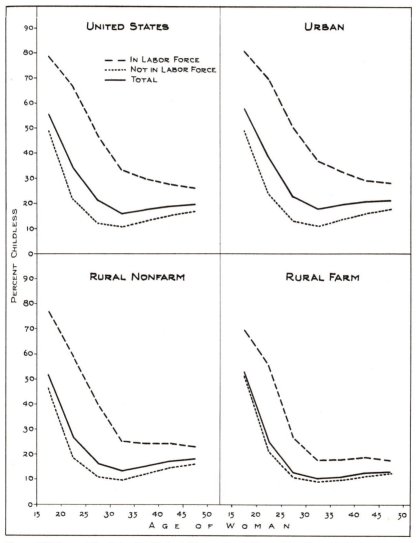

Source: *1950 Census of Population*, Vol. IV, *Special Reports*, Part 5, Chapter C, Fertility, table 24.

The data by color point up the fact that at young ages the proportion of childlessness among the nonwhite women falls below that of the whites within all three types of communities. At young ages the fertility rates of the nonwhites surpass those of the whites even in the urban areas. This held true for women in the labor force as well as for those not in the labor force.

Finally, attention may be called to the slight rise in the proportion of childlessness with advancing age after age 35, among women not in the labor force. This simply reflects a corresponding situation for all women regardless of labor force status. Although women 45 to 49 years old showed a higher average fertility than those 35 to 39 in 1950, they also exhibited somewhat higher proportions of childlessness. The lower proportions of childlessness among women 35 to 39 in 1950 than among those 40 to 44 are consequences of the baby boom during 1940 to 1950.

Fertility ratios and labor force status. As may be expected, the extent to which there are own children under 5 years old is more pertinent to labor force status of the married woman than is the number of children ever born. The crucial difference, of course, is that after children reach the age when they do not require the mother's close supervision they cease to interfere with the mother's entrance into the labor force.

As an illustration, among urban white ever-married women 30 to 34 years old reporting at least one child ever born, 19 percent were in the labor force in 1950. Among urban white ever-married women 30 to 34 years old reporting the presence of at least one child under 5 years old in the household in 1950, only 11 percent were in the labor force. However, the proportion in the labor force among women reporting *no live birth* was 54 percent; among those reporting *no children under 5,* the proportion in the labor force was 40 percent.

The comparison can also be given in terms of proportions of childless women and proportions of those with no children under 5. (See figure 91.) Thus, among urban ever-married white women 30 to 34 years old in the labor force in 1950, about 37 percent were childless (figure 90), but nearly 80 percent were without children under 5 (figure 91). Among the corresponding women who were not in the labor force in 1950, about 11 percent were childless, and 41 percent were without children under 5.

Figures 92 and 93 present data for white and nonwhite ever-married women, respectively, on the number of own children under 5, by labor force status, age, and urban-rural residence. As in the case of cumulative fertility rates, the difference between fertility ratios of women in and not in the labor force would tend to be greater for the ratios based upon all women regardless of marital status than for those shown by the charts which are limited to ever-married women. As previously stated, this results from the fact that many of the single, widowed, and divorced women are in the labor force.

Also as before, the contrast between the fertility ratios for the women in and not in the labor force tends to be greater in the urban areas than in the rural-farm areas.

FIGURE **91.**—PERCENT WITH NO OWN CHILDREN UNDER 5 YEARS OLD, FOR EVER-MARRIED WHITE WOMEN 15 TO 49 YEARS OLD, BY AGE AND LABOR FORCE STATUS, URBAN AND RURAL: 1950

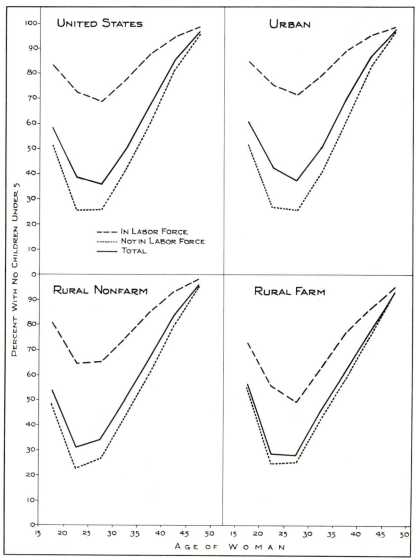

Source: *1950 Census of Population,* Vol. IV, *Special Reports,* Part 5, Chapter C, Fertility, table 46.

If the figures 92 and 93 were superimposed on one another, it would be seen that there is not much difference by color in the relationship of labor force status to fertility ratios. In urban areas, the fertility ratios for whites tend to surpass those for nonwhites except at youngest ages (under 25) and this holds regardless of labor force status. However, allowance for an undercount of young children and for children not living with their

Figure **92.**—Number of Own Children under 5 Years Old per 1,000 Ever-Married White Women 15 to 49 Years Old, by Age and Labor Force Status, Urban and Rural: 1950

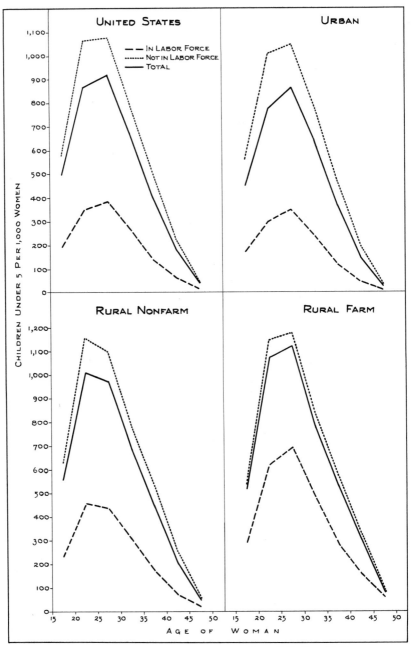

Source: *1950 Census of Population*, Vol. IV, *Special Reports*, Part 5, Chapter C, Fertility, table 46.

FIGURE **93.**—NUMBER OF OWN CHILDREN UNDER 5 YEARS OLD PER 1,000 EVER-MARRIED NONWHITE WOMEN 15 TO 49 YEARS OLD, BY AGE AND LABOR FORCE STATUS, URBAN AND RURAL: 1950

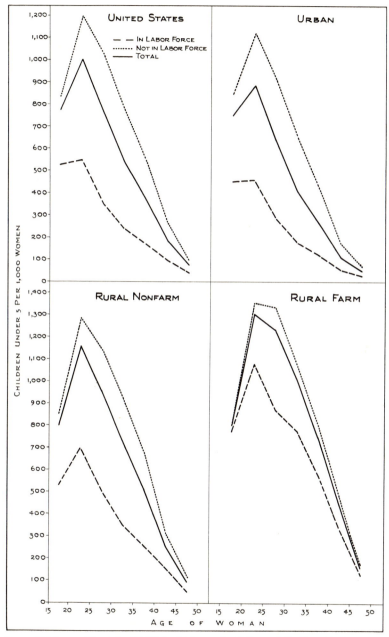

Source: *1950 Census of Population*, Vol. IV, *Special Reports*, Part 5, Chapter C, Fertility, table 47.

mothers might reverse the relative ranking by color. Within the rural-nonfarm and rural-farm areas the fertility ratios for nonwhite women are higher than those for white women regardless of labor force status and this holds rather consistently at successive ages and for each type of marital status considered.

Finally, to summarize the section on fertility ratios, we may quote from the census report on fertility:

> Women in the labor force at a given point in time generally have fewer young children than women not in the labor force. . . . If a woman has a baby she is likely to give up a job or not to look for a job, as the case may be. In the last decade or so, however, a life pattern seems to be developing among many married women in which they work until the arrival of the first baby, temporarily withdraw from the labor force while their children are young, and then return to the labor force after their children are old enough to require little care. Even in terms of children ever born, young women who happen to be in the labor force are less fertile than those who happen not to be in the labor force; but it is possible that the two groups will not differ very much in the size of their completed families. . . . Since labor force status is not a fixed characteristic throughout adult life, the status of women at the end of the childbearing period does not tell us very much about their status during this period. Furthermore, the present pattern of childbearing, child care, and gainful employment mentioned above may be too recent to have had much effect on women over 45 in 1950. Nevertheless, the present data should shed some additional light on the interrelationships between fertility and the employment of women and hence on the most dynamic part of the labor supply.[2]

B. Rental value of the dwelling unit

Figure 94 presents some results from 1940 Census data on the average number of children ever born per 1,000 ever-married native white women 45 to 49 years old, by monthly rental value of the dwelling unit (actual rent of rented homes and 1/100 of value of owned homes) and by region and urban-rural residence. Rent and value of home data were collected from a sample of households in the 1950 Census, but this sample differed from the fertility sample and the data could not be used in the special fertility tabulations on which this monograph is based.

It will be noted that within each region and urban or rural area the fertility rates in 1940 tend to vary inversely with rental value of the home. However, this relationship did not usually extend into the upper rental value levels. There was a leveling-off of the fertility rate above the $50-per-month level. Below this level the inverse relation was rather sharp and consistent, especially when it is considered that the rental value levels of adjacent classes differed by only $10 per month. The interclass differentials and the total range of variations in fertility by monthly rental value of the dwelling unit tended to be smallest in the urban Northeast.

Figure 95, based upon Current Population Survey data collected in April 1947, presents the number of own children under 5 per 1,000 women 15

---

[2] *1950 Census of Population*, Vol. IV, *Special Reports*, Part 5, Chapter C, Fertility, p. 11.

to 49 years old, married and husband present, by monthly rent paid for the home. The fertility ratios are standardized for age and they relate to renters of homes in urban and rural-nonfarm areas.[3] The inverse relation of fertility ratios to amount of rent extends throughout all rental classes, but the topmost rental class is only "$50 or more," and it should also be noted that the data relate to "civilian population" regardless of color or nativity.

FIGURE **94.**—AVERAGE NUMBER OF CHILDREN EVER BORN PER EVER-MARRIED NATIVE WHITE WOMAN 45 TO 49 YEARS OLD, BY MONTHLY RENTAL VALUE OF THE HOME, FOR REGIONS, URBAN AND RURAL: 1940

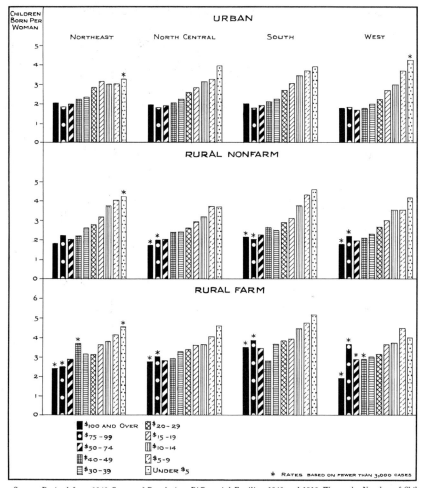

Source: Derived from *1940 Census of Population, Differential Fertility, 1940 and 1910*, Women by Number of Children Ever Born, table 122.

[3] U. S. Bureau of the Census, *Current Population Reports*, Series P–20, No. 18, p. 17.

FIGURE **95.**—STANDARDIZED NUMBER OF OWN CHILDREN UNDER 5 YEARS OLD PER 1,000 WOMEN 15 TO 49 YEARS OLD MARRIED AND HUSBAND PRESENT, LIVING IN RENTED HOMES, BY MONTHLY RENT OF HOME, FOR URBAN AND RURAL-NONFARM AREAS: CIVILIAN POPULATION, APRIL 1947

[The standard is the distribution by age of all civilian married women, husband present, in April 1947]

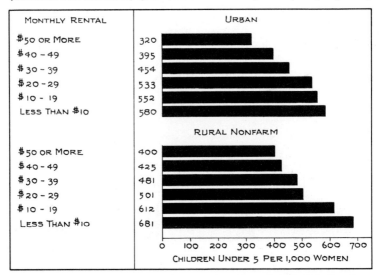

Source: Derived from U. S. Bureau of the Census, *Current Population Reports*, Series P–20, No. 18, p. 17.

There are certain selective factors in the previously mentioned leveling-off of the fertility rates at upper rental value levels. Couples with many children tend to need a large house and some may fall into the upper rental value groups for this reason. Nevertheless, the failure of the inverse relation of fertility to socio-economic status to extend consistently into the upper echelons of socio-economic status has been observed when use is made of other criteria of status such as income.

C. Income

Data from various privately sponsored surveys, such as the Indianapolis Study (briefly described in Chapter 7), generally have shown a strong inverse relation between income and total number of children ever born. Data collected in a Current Population Survey in 1949 indicated a sharp inverse relation of number of own children under 5 *per 1,000 married women 15 to 49 years old* to *total money income of the family in 1948.*[4] (See figure 96.) However, data collected in a Current Population Survey in 1952 indicated no corresponding inverse relation of number of own children under 5 *per 1,000 married men 20 to 59 years old in April 1952* to *total money income of the man in 1951.* (See figure 97.) Concerning these data, the Census Bureau's report states:

---

[4] U. S. Bureau of the Census, *Current Population Reports*, Series P–20, No. 27, p. 10.

In past studies, high fertility has been associated with low economic status and low fertility with high economic status. The present study shows no such simple relationship. . . . Instead, the figures on current fertility by money income of the husband fluctuate irregularly from one income class to another. It seems fair to conclude that children are not now found in relatively great numbers among fathers who are especially hard-pressed to support them.[5]

It is not possible to give an adequate explanation of the differences between figures 96 and 97 but several pertinent points may be mentioned. In the first place, because of relatively small numbers the Current Population Survey data on differential fertility are not always presented separately by residence and color. Thus, both figures 96 and 97 relate to all races. Furthermore, figure 96 relates to urban and rural areas combined. One might suppose that the proportion of rural people increases with lowering of "money income" and that this helps to account for the inverse relation in figure 96 and its absence in figure 97, which relates to urban and rural nonfarm areas. However, the figure 97 data are also given in the source for the country as a whole and these again exhibit no variations by income.

FIGURE **96.**—STANDARDIZED NUMBER OF OWN CHILDREN UNDER 5 YEARS OLD IN APRIL 1949 PER 1,000 WOMEN 15 TO 49 YEARS OLD MARRIED AND HUSBAND PRESENT, BY TOTAL MONEY INCOME OF THE FAMILY IN 1948

[The standard is the distribution by age of all civilian married women, husband present, in April 1947]

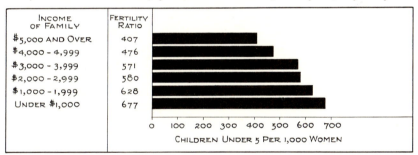

Source: Adapted from U. S. Bureau of the Census, *Current Population Reports*, Series P-20, No. 27, p. 10.

In the second place, figure 96 relates to *family income* and figure 97 to *husband's income*. A selective factor conducive to an inverse relation of *family income* to fertility is that gainfully employed wives help to increase the family income and they tend to be a select group with respect to low fertility and lack of children under 5 years old.

Finally, one may be tempted to lay the difference between figures 96 and 97 to the fact that in the former the dependent variable is that of children under 5 to women 15 to 49 years old and in the latter it is children under 5 to men 20 to 59 years old. It is true that the childbearing ages are not so precisely delineated for men as for women. However,

---

[5] U. S. Bureau of the Census, *Current Population Reports*, Series P–20, No. 46, p. 5.

data collected in the same 1952 survey and relating to children ever born per 1,000 married women of given age, by income of husband, suggest the importance of residence and age in patterns of differential fertility by income.

FIGURE **97.**—STANDARDIZED NUMBER OF OWN CHILDREN UNDER 5 YEARS OLD PER 1,000 MEN 20 TO 59 YEARS OLD MARRIED AND WIFE PRESENT IN APRIL 1952, BY TOTAL MONEY INCOME OF THE MAN IN 1951, FOR URBAN AND RURAL-NONFARM AREAS

[The standard is the distribution by age of married men, wife present, in the United States in April 1952]

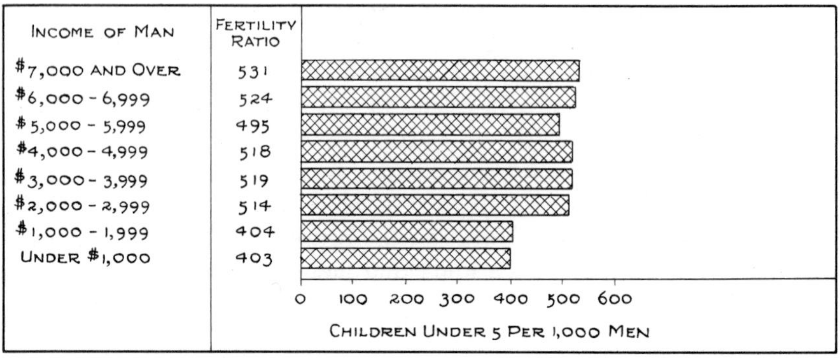

INCOME OF MAN	FERTILITY RATIO
$7,000 AND OVER	531
$6,000 - 6,999	524
$5,000 - 5,999	495
$4,000 - 4,999	518
$3,000 - 3,999	519
$2,000 - 2,999	514
$1,000 - 1,999	404
UNDER $1,000	403

CHILDREN UNDER 5 PER 1,000 MEN

Source: Adapted from U. S. Bureau of the Census, *Current Population Reports*, Series P-20, No. 46, p. 22.

The 1952 data on children ever born in relation to money income of the man are shown in figure 98. As noted, these are expressed in terms of number of children ever born per 1,000 married women 15 to 44 years old and 45 years old and over. The rates for women 15 to 44 years old are standardized for age. The fertility rates for women 15 to 44 are indicated by the shaded portions of the bars; those for women 45 and over are indicated by the total lengths of the bars. The top section of the chart is for the total United States and the lower part is for the urban and rural-nonfarm areas combined.

It will be noted that the data for the married women 45 years of age and over, in both the total United States and in the urban or nonfarm areas, sharply exhibit the traditional inverse relation of fertility to income of the husband. The data for the younger women, in contrast, do not exhibit any such inverse relationship. True, the data for the women 15 to 44 in the sample for the United States as a whole exhibit a direct relationship at the upper end of the income scale and an inverse relationship at the lower end of the income scale. The inverse relationship may reflect the influence of differential proportions of rural people in the sample. Among the urban and rural-nonfarm women (lower section of figure 98) there is little difference in fertility by income of the husband. "Only among married women 45 years old and over do the new data show the traditional pattern of higher fertility in groups of low economic status than in groups of high economic status. Among women 15 to 44 years old, standardized for age, fertility was quite similar at different income levels."[6]

[6] *Ibid.*, p. 3.

FIGURE 98.—NUMBER OF CHILDREN EVER BORN PER 1,000 WOMEN MARRIED AND HUSBAND PRESENT IN APRIL 1952, STANDARDIZED FOR WOMEN 15 TO 44 YEARS OLD AND UNSTANDARDIZED FOR WOMEN 45 YEARS OLD AND OVER, BY TOTAL MONEY INCOME OF HUSBAND IN 1951

[The standard is the distribution by age of married women, husband present, in the United States in April 1952]

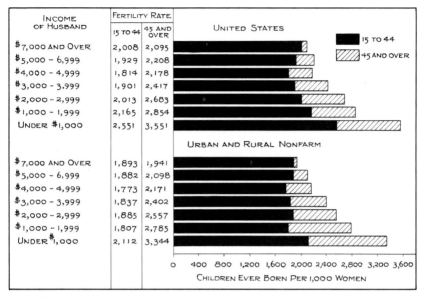

INCOME OF HUSBAND	FERTILITY RATE		UNITED STATES
	15 TO 44	45 AND OVER	
$7,000 AND OVER	2,008	2,095	
$5,000 – 6,999	1,929	2,208	
$4,000 – 4,999	1,814	2,178	
$3,000 – 3,999	1,901	2,417	
$2,000 – 2,999	2,013	2,683	
$1,000 – 1,999	2,165	2,854	
UNDER $1,000	2,551	3,551	

URBAN AND RURAL NONFARM

$7,000 AND OVER	1,893	1,941	
$5,000 – 6,999	1,882	2,098	
$4,000 – 4,999	1,773	2,171	
$3,000 – 3,999	1,837	2,402	
$2,000 – 2,999	1,885	2,557	
$1,000 – 1,999	1,807	2,785	
UNDER $1,000	2,112	3,344	

CHILDREN EVER BORN PER 1,000 WOMEN

Source: Adapted from U. S. Bureau of the Census, *Current Population Reports*, Series P-20, No. 46, p. 13.

Although the 1949 data are in accord with the traditional inverse relation of fertility to income, they are also subject to certain biases to which the 1952 data are not. As already indicated, the lack of restriction by urban-rural status would tend to yield an inverse relation of fertility to income. Also the factor of gainfully employed wives would tend to enhance the inverse relation of fertility to total *family* income but would presumably have little relevance to the relation of fertility to income of the *husband*. Neither the 1949 nor the 1952 Current Population Survey materials are specific with reference to color. In each case the sample is too small to provide this and other desirable refinements of the data.

D. Fertility of farm operators by family income in 1949

In a recent report, *Characteristics of Farm-Operator Households by Number of Young Children*, one table based upon 1950 Census data gives the number of children under 5 years old per 1,000 ever-married women 15 to 49 years old in farm-operator households, according to total family income in 1949.[7] The ratios were standardized for age. As indicated in figure 99, the data for the United States and those for the South yielded a

[7] Calvin L. Beale, *Characteristics of Farm-Operator Households by Number of Young Children*, U. S. Department of Agriculture, Agricultural Marketing Service, Washington, June 1956, p. 21. The children under 5 data utilized in this report are those from a sample of the returns of households enumerated in both the 1950 Census of Agriculture and the 1950 Census of Population.

picture of inverse relation of fertility ratio to income. The sample from the North and West (not shown) was too small to yield reliable rates for all income classes. The existing data for the farm-operator families in the North and West suggest little in the way of differential current fertility by income. Since the data were not restricted by color, and since nonwhites formed about one-fourth of the southern farm-operator households, but only 1 percent of those in the North and West, it seems likely that the presence of nonwhites contributes to the inverse relation of fertility to income in the South, and hence in the country as a whole. In this connection, the following statement is made in another section of the report:

> When farms are classified by economic class based on the total value of the products sold, a rather consistent inverse relation between class of farm and the fertility of farm-operator households is evident, especially when fertility ratios are standardized for age. . . . The lowest ratio among commercial farms, 432 per 1,000 women, was found among farms selling over $10,000 worth of products in 1949 (Classes I and II). The ratios were higher among women on smaller-scale farms, rising to a maximum of 580 on the least productive commercial farms (Class VI—farms selling goods worth $250 to $1,199 and having little or no income from nonfarm sources).[8]

Another table indicates that the proportion of nonwhites extended from only 4.7 percent of the Classes I and II farms to 41.5 percent of the Class VI farms in the South.[9]

FIGURE **99.**—STANDARDIZED NUMBER OF CHILDREN UNDER 5 YEARS OLD PER 1,000 EVER-MARRIED WOMEN 15 TO 49 YEARS OLD IN FARM-OPERATOR HOUSEHOLDS, BY TOTAL FAMILY INCOME IN 1949, FOR THE UNITED STATES AND THE SOUTH: 1950

[The standard is the distribution by age of ever-married women in farm-operator households in the United States in 1950]

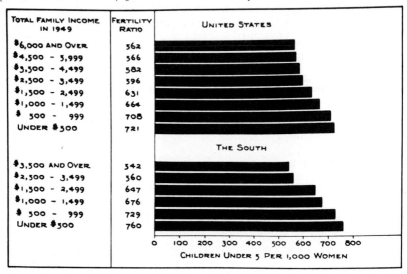

Source: Adapted from U. S. Department of Agriculture, Agricultural Marketing Service, *Farm Population—Characteristics of Farm-Operator Households by Number of Young Children*, 1956, p. 21.

---

[8] *Ibid.*, pp. 2–3.
[9] *Ibid.*, p. 3.

E. Religion

In a world setting religion is one of the complex of factors accounting for international differences in fertility. Some religions place higher values on the large family than do others. Some of those that place high value on the large family also have explicit injunctions against family limitation or certain forms of it. Students of demographic problems in the so-called underdeveloped areas have frequently emphasized the role of religion in perpetuating the large-family system.

High fertility is generally characteristic of the Mohammedans, Hindus, Confucianists, and Buddhists. Since most of these people live in underdeveloped areas under conditions of poverty and agrarianism, it is difficult to know how much of the high fertility can be attributed to religion per se. Some of these religions do place high value on the large family and on sons. There are uncertainties and differences of opinion regarding the degree to which they explicitly prohibit family limitation. It is probable that none of them forbids contraception by "artificial" means so unequivocally as does the Catholic Church.

Although some 38 countries, including Canada and Mexico, ask about religion in their regular censuses, the United States has never done so. Some State censuses have asked a question on religion, and Rhode Island, in the 1905 State Census, tabulated data on religion of women in association with number of children ever born. The United States has conducted several censuses of religious bodies, but these do not provide any means for relating religious affiliation with other characteristics of individuals. It was noted in Chapter 4 that some large cities in the United States had very low rates of children ever born in 1940 and also a largely Roman Catholic population.

Again, however, it is possible to draw upon the results of special studies for a brief summary of the relation of religion to family size in this country. At the time of this writing, more precise information on this topic was not available from the March 1957 Current Population Survey.

The Household Survey of the Indianapolis Study clearly indicated highest fertility rates for "Both Catholic" couples and lowest rates for the "Both Jewish" couples. The "Both Protestant" couples were of intermediate status with respect to fertility. In quantitative terms, the fertility rate standardized for age was about 25 percent higher for Catholic than for Protestant unions. It was about 18 percent lower for Jewish than for Protestant unions. Interestingly, the fertility rate for the Protestant-Catholic mixed marriages was about 10 percent lower than that for the Protestant couples.[10] This was found to be associated with relatively late age at marriage and relatively high proportions of childlessness among the Protestant-Catholic mixed marriages.

---

[10] P. K. Whelpton and C. V. Kiser (Editors), *Social and Psychological Factors Affecting Fertility*, Vol. 1, *The Household Survey in Indianapolis*, The Milbank Memorial Fund, New York, 1946, pp. 6–8.

The higher fertility of the Catholic than of the Protestant unions in Indianapolis cannot be explained on the basis of lower economic status or by the factor of higher proportions of foreign born. The comparisons cited above relate to *native white* Catholics and Protestants. The average economic status as determined by rental value of the home actually was a little higher for the Catholics than for the Protestants in the Indianapolis Study.

Kirk estimated that the crude birth rate for Catholics in the United States in 1953 was 35.0 per 1,000.[11] This estimate was based upon tabulations of infant baptisms and population from the 1954 edition of the *Official Catholic Directory*. The crude birth rate for the United States as a whole in that year was 25.0. The derived birth rate for non-Catholics based upon Kirk's figures for births and populations was 22.6. The comparison may also be pointed up by saying that in 1953, according to Kirk's figures, the Catholics comprised 19.5 percent of the population of the United States and contributed 27.3 percent of the births.

The Mormons have long been noted for their high fertility. In this case the factor of religion operates within the context of prosperous agriculture. However, it should also be noted that in *Who's Who in America* even the Mormons, presumably mainly urban, have relatively high fertility in comparison with others in *Who's Who*. In their study of men listed in the 1926–27 edition of *Who's Who in America,* Huntington and Whitney found the following average number of children among men reporting the specified religious affiliations and reporting number of children: Jews—2.6, Congregationalists—2.7, Baptists—3.1, Lutherans—3.3, Roman Catholics —3.3, and Mormons—5.3.[12]

The Hutterites have been described by Eaton and Mayer as a population which "is reproducing itself close to the theoretical maximum level of human fertility."[13] They number about 8,700 and they live in 93 colonies in South Dakota, North Dakota, Montana, Alberta, and Manitoba.

The Hutterites share certain religious beliefs with the Amish and Dunkers in Pennsylvania. An important difference is the greater degree of communal living among the Hutterites. They live in colonies under systems of communal ownership. The colonies generally contain about fifteen families. Each colony has a farmstead on which all work. Meals for the whole colony are prepared by different women in rotation and are served in a common dining room. There are communal provisions not only for schools but also for attending the children while the adults are at work.

---

[11] Dudley Kirk, "Recent Trends of Catholic Fertility in the United States," *Current Research in Human Fertility*. The Milbank Memorial Fund, New York, 1955, p. 101. Note: It seems possible that the inclusion of births to mixed marriages may tend to inflate the birth rate computed for Catholics. A counter bias may arise from any tendency to count as Catholic population persons whose names are on the Parish records, but whose migration to another area or death may not have been reported.

[12] Ellsworth Huntington and Leon F. Whitney, *The Builders of America*, Morrow, New York, p. 342.

[13] Joseph W. Eaton and Albert J. Mayer, "Man's Capacity to Reproduce: The Demography of a Unique Population," The Free Press, Glencoe, Illinois, 1954, pp. 1–2.

According to data procured by Eaton and Mayer for about 80 percent of the Hutterite population, the annual crude birth rate for the group for the period 1946 to 1950 was 45.9 per 1,000.[14] "Between 1880 and 1950 the sect has increased 19 times, from 443 to 8,542 persons. This growth has largely been the result of natural increase."[15] The cited work by Eaton and Mayer is a by-product of a study of the mental health of the Hutterites.[16]

F. Family planning in relation to fertility differentials by socio-economic status

The Indianapolis Study of Social and Psychological Factors Affecting Fertility threw some important light on the interrelations of fecundity status, socio-economic status, fertility-planning status, and fertility. In the first place, it may be noted that a basic separation was made between the "relatively sterile" and "relatively fecund" couples. This division was made on an arbitrary basis.[17]

Under the definitions used, 1,444 of the couples in the Indianapolis Study adjusted sample were classified as "relatively fecund" and 533 as "relatively sterile." The proportion classified as "relatively sterile" did not appear to vary by socio-economic status in any systematic manner. Also, the actual fertility of the "relatively sterile" couples did not appear to be systematically associated with socio-economic status.[18]

One of the most stable findings in the Indianapolis Study was the relation of socio-economic status to fertility-planning status and to fertility of the "relatively fecund" couples. Several criteria of socio-economic status were used separately and in combination. These included average annual earnings of the husband since marriage, husband's longest occupation since marriage, education of the wife and husband, rental value of the dwelling unit, net worth, Chapin's social status scale, purchase price of car, and a summary index of socio-economic status based on all of the criteria mentioned above. In general, the proportion of families classi-

---

[14] *Ibid.*, p. 15.

[15] *Ibid.*, p. 1.

[16] Joseph W. Eaton and Robert J. Weil, *Culture and Mental Disorders*, The Free Press, Glencoe, Illinois, 1955, p. 212.

[17] "Couples with three or fewer live births were classified as 'relatively fecund' unless they knew or had good reasons for believing that conception was physiologically impossible during a period of at least 24 or 36 consecutive months since marriage (24 for never-pregnant women, 36 for others). Failure to conceive when contraception was not practiced 'always' or 'usually' during periods of the above durations was considered good reason for such belief. Couples not classified as relatively 'fecund' were considered 'relatively sterile.' "

P. K. Whelpton and C. V. Kiser (Editors), *Social and Psychological Factors Affecting Fertility*, Vol. II, *The Intensive Study: Purpose, Scope, Methods, and Partial Results*, The Milbank Memorial Fund, New York, 1950, pp. 370–371.

[18] There was a partially inverse relation of "fecundity status" to score on Chapin's Social Status Scale, but this may have been partially selective since one component of the scale was neatness of the living room. The task of keeping a living room neat is in the nature of the case made somewhat more difficult by the presence of children.

282   THE FERTILITY OF AMERICAN WOMEN

fied as "planned families" was directly related to socio-economic status regardless of criteria of status used.[19]

This direct relation of fertility-planning status to socio-economic condition accounted for the generally inverse relation of fertility to socio-economic status. One of the most publicized findings of the Indianapolis Study, however, is the *direct* relation of fertility to socio-economic status within the "number and spacing planned" group. This is illustrated in figure 100 in which fertility rates are presented by husband's average annual earnings since marriage and fertility-planning status. It will be noted that although the fertility rates within the "number and spacing planned" group are low, the internal variations are in the pattern of a direct relation of fertility to amount of income.

Some further insight into this situation is afforded by the Indianapolis Study data on economic security. Within the "number and spacing planned" group, fertility rates increased with strength of "feeling of economic security." There is the strong suggestion that when the factor of successful planning of family size is as effectively controlled as it is within the "number and spacing planned" group, subjective factors like economic security emerge as important determinants of family size.

Finally, it should be emphasized that the Indianapolis Study relates to an era of low fertility. Since its inception, the United States has experienced the wartime and postwar increases in cumulative fertility rates that were documented by the 1950 Census data and the Current Population Surveys. Two private studies that are currently under way are concerned with the extent of family limitation practices and fertility desires in relation to social, economic, and psychological factors. One of these is a study of fertility and fertility expectations among a national cross section of nearly 3,000 white married women 18 to 39 years of age and a small number of single women 18 to 24 years old.[20] The other is a partially longitudinal study of the factors affecting the future fertility of two-child families.[21] It is by supplementing the census type of data with special studies that we may hope to increase our knowledge of the trends and determinants of family formation and family size.

---

[19] The "planned families" consisted of two groups as defined in the Indianapolis Study. These were the "number and spacing planned" and the "number planned" couples. The "number and spacing planned" couples were those who had no pregnancies that were not planned by stopping contraception in order to conceive. They were either "never pregnant" couples who had successfully avoided conception by contraception since marriage or couples who had planned all their pregnancies by stopping contraception in order to conceive. The "number planned" couples were those who planned the *last* pregnancy by stopping contraception in order to conceive but who had had one or more previous pregnancies under other circumstances.

[20] P. K. Whelpton, "A Study of the 'Expected' Completed Fertility of a National Sample of White Women," *Current Research in Human Fertility*, The Milbank Memorial Fund, New York, 1955, pp. 106–114.

[21] C. V. Kiser, E. G. Mishler, C. F. Westoff, and R. G. Potter, Jr., "Development of Plans for a Social Psychological Study of the Future Fertility of Two-Child Families," *Population Studies*, Vol. 10, July 1956, pp. 43–52.

FIGURE **100.**—NUMBER OF CHILDREN EVER BORN PER 100 COUPLES, BY FERTILITY-PLANNING STATUS AND HUSBAND'S AVERAGE ANNUAL EARNINGS SINCE MARRIAGE, FOR INDIANAPOLIS, INDIANA: 1941

[Data for native white Protestant couples whose marriages were contracted during 1927-29 and were unbroken at time of interview in 1941, wife under 30 and husband under 40 at marriage, couple resided in large city most of time since marriage, and both husband and wife completed at least grammar school]

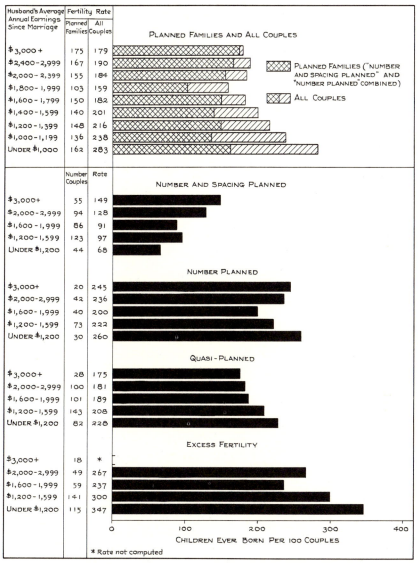

Source: P. K. Whelpton and Clyde V. Kiser (Editors), *Social and Psychological Factors Affecting Fertility*, Vol. Two, Milbank Memorial Fund, New York, 1950, p. 395.

C H A P T E R   8

MARRIAGE AND FERTILITY[1]

A. Marriage, widowhood, and divorce

Legitimacy of marriage and births. In the United States marriages are licensed by the State and performed either by the clergy or by lay officials. Some consensual or informal "marriages" do occur, perhaps particularly among small groups of Negroes of the lower class, Spanish-Americans, Puerto Ricans, and Indians.

On the basis of national vital statistics for 1950, it would seem that at least 4 percent of the births in that year were illegitimate. This includes an estimate of illegitimate births in the thirteen States in which the birth record includes no question about legitimacy. Allowing for some misreporting of legitimacy in other States, the true number of illegitimate births may be upward of 200,000 per year, or 6 percent of the total births for the country. It is probable that most of the mothers rearing an illegitimate child are reported in the census as married, widowed, or divorced; perhaps many of these women married after the birth of the child. In 1940, only 13,400, or 0.1 percent, of the single native white women 15 to 49 years and only 16,040, or 1.5 percent, of the single Negro women of this age, were identifiable as mothers of children under 5 years old.

Distribution of population by marital status. Figure 101 shows the distribution of the population by age, sex, and marital status in 1950. As expected, most women of childbearing age, 15 to 44 years, were married. The proportion of women who were married increased rapidly after the age of 17 or 18 years, and it may be inferred that many of the women married within the narrow age range of 18 to 24 years. Men tended to marry over a wider age range.

Trends in percentage of women who have married. Trends in the percentage of women of childbearing age who have ever married are shown in table 96. The proportion ever married increased slightly between 1900 and 1930, decreased between 1930 and 1940, and increased greatly between 1940 and 1950 among women in age groups under 30

---

[1] A further and more complete discussion of marriage and family building patterns appear in another census monograph: Paul C. Glick, *American Families*, John Wiley and Sons, New York, 1957.

years.   Little change occurred at ages over 30 years between 1900 and
1940, and small increases occurred between 1940 and 1950.   The effect
of the economic depression of the 1930's is evident in the slightly lower
percentages of those ever married among young women in 1940 than in
1930.   Estimates from the Current Population Survey indicate that the
proportion ever married may have increased between 1950 and 1955
among the women of each age group shown in the table.   Most of the increases were within the range of possible sampling variability, however.

FIGURE **101.**—MARITAL STATUS OF PERSONS 14 TO 74 YEARS OLD, BY SINGLE YEARS OF AGE
AND SEX: 1950

[Data smoothed]

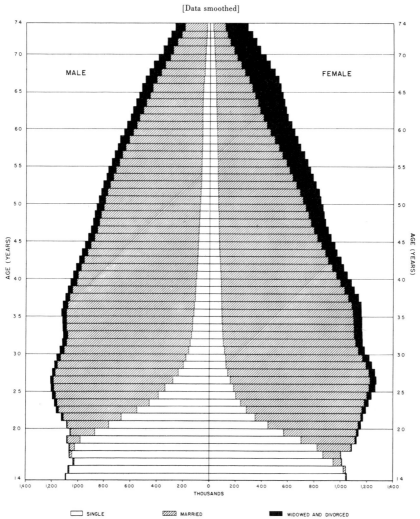

Source: *1950 Census of Population,* Vol. IV, *Special Reports,* Part 2, Chapter D, Marital Status, p. 2.

The increases between 1910 and 1950 in the percentage of young women who had ever married reflected relatively more first marriages at young ages. Successive groups of women were tending to marry at a younger age, as will be explained later. This trend toward a younger average age at first marriage existed on a cohort basis but not necessarily on the basis of the average age of brides as reported in marriage registration data. Monahan has shown for a few States that there has been a long-time *upward* trend in the average age of brides in annual marriage registration data when no account is taken of the population at risk of a marriage.[2] The trend reflects the general aging of the population since 1800 and the increased proportion of women in the older ages rather than the experience of cohorts of women. Some exceptions to the trend toward a younger average age at first marriage on a successive cohort basis may be noted in data for 1930 and 1940 (table 96). As explained in Chapter 9, sections B and C, the cohorts who reached the most marriageable ages during the early part of the decade of the 1930's had lower marriage rates then other cohorts at similar ages before 1930 and after 1940.

Decennial census data and current population survey data on women classified by age and marital status may be used for rough estimates of the median age at first marriage on a cohort basis. (A special type of cohort is involved here as will be explained.) Estimates of this type are presented in the last column of table 96. The median is computed as follows: First, an assumption is made as to the approximate proportion of women who will ever marry during their lifetimes. It is convenient to use as an assumption the proportion of women ever married among those 55 to 59 years old or among women of some similar advanced group for the United States as a whole, for the same census or survey for which the estimate is being made. Among women 55 to 59 years old, the percent ever married has varied from about 90 percent in 1890 to 93 percent in 1954. The halfway point will then be from 45 to 46.5 percent. Second, data for women by single years of age (in censuses) or by 5-year age groups (in sample surveys) are mathematically interpolated (as by Sprague's formula) to find that age at which the percentage of women who have ever married is exactly at the halfway point of the anticipated lifetime percentage. This age is the median age at first marriage. About half of the eventual total marriages for this cohort of young persons have already occurred, many within the 3 years prior to the survey date, and about half will occur in future years, many within the 3 years following the survey date. This is a real cohort of persons journeying through life but the group was born at the same instant in time rather than in a calendar year, and hence it is a very narrow or special kind of cohort.

---

[2] Thomas P. Monahan, *The Pattern of Age at Marriage in the United States*, Vol. I, Stephenson-Brothers, Philadelphia, 1951, pp. 161, 172, 176.

The median age at first marriage, computed as explained above, declined from 22.0 years for the cohort at the halfway mark in 1890 to 21.2 years for the corresponding cohort in 1920, rose to 21.5 in 1940, and then fell sharply to 20.2 in 1950, 1952, and 1954.

TABLE 96.—PERCENT EVER MARRIED AMONG WOMEN 15 TO 54 YEARS OLD, BY AGE AT SURVEY DATE AND ESTIMATED MEDIAN AGE AT FIRST MARRIAGE: 1890 TO 1955

Year	Age at survey date (year)[1]						Estimated median age at first marriage[2]
	15 to 19	20 to 24	25 to 29	30 to 34	35 to 44	45 to 54	
1955............................	17.3	70.9	88.4	92.9	93.1	93.2	20.2
1954............................	15.8	69.3	89.0	91.3	93.1	92.7	20.3
1952............................	17.1	70.4	87.7	91.2	92.3	92.1	20.2
1950............................	17.1	67.7	86.7	90.7	91.7	92.2	20.2
1948............................	16.9	66.9	88.2		91.3	92.0	20.4
1946............................	12.2	60.8	85.6		91.4	[3]92.8	[4]
1944............................	13.9	59.2	85.0		89.5	[3]92.6	[4]
1940............................	11.9	52.8	77.2	85.3	89.6	91.3	21.5
1930............................	13.2	54.0	78.3	86.8	90.0	90.9	21.3
1920............................	13.0	54.4	77.0	85.1	88.6	90.4	21.2
1910............................	12.1	51.7	75.1	83.9	88.6	91.5	21.6
1900............................	11.3	48.4	72.5	83.4	88.9	92.2	21.9
1890............................	9.7	48.2	74.6	84.8	90.1	92.9	22.0
Percent change:							
1940 to 1955.............	45.4	34.3	14.5	8.9	3.9	2.1	...
1900 to 1940.............	5.3	9.1	6.5	2.3	0.8	-1.0	...

[1] Age at last birthday, 1900 to 1955; age at nearest birthday, 1890.
[2] Age at survey date at which the percent ever married among women is half of the expected lifetime percent; data for women 45 to 64 years old used as approximation to the lifetime percent.
[3] Women 45 to 64 years old.
[4] Not computed.

Source: U. S. Bureau of the Census, *Current Population Reports*, Series P-20, Nos. 44, 56, and 62; *Population*, Series P-S, No. 16; *1950 Census of Population*, Vol. II, *Characteristics of the Population*, Part 1, U. S. Summary, table 102; unpublished tabulation detail from the Current Population Survey for April 1948, and unpublished population estimates for elimination of females age 14 from data for some years.

Detailed marital status in relation to number of own children under 5 years old. Census data on women classified by marital status and by number of own children under 5 years old in the household provide some indication of variations in current fertility by detailed marital status of women (table 97). The marital status, of course, is that at the census date and may differ from that at the time any infant was born.

In Chapter 4, it was noted that with age-specific marital status as in 1950, white women could expect to spend about two-thirds of the child-bearing ages in a married-and-husband-present status. The comparable proportion for nonwhite women was about half of the childbearing ages. As may be noted from table 97, most of the "married and husband present" women are in first marriages, but an appreciable number are in re-marriages. Among whites, the women in remarriages in 1950 had about as many children under 5 years old per 1,000 women as the women in first marriages, on a standardized-for-age basis. Among nonwhites, a change from a first-marriage status meant a sharp drop in current fertility.

Women in 1950 who were separated from their husbands had many more children under 5 years old per 1,000 women than those who were divorced. The two groups were thus quite different with respect to recent fertility. This may in small degree reflect the fact that the separated women had been parted from their spouses for a shorter time (median of 4.1 years for women 15–59) than the divorced woman (4.6 years). Perhaps some of the separated women were more fertile than the divorced women for reasons relating to an economically and educationally disadvantaged status. The separations include some desertions, which are often termed the poor man's divorce. Among the white women 15 to 44 years old in 1950, there were nearly two divorced women for each separated woman. Among the nonwhites there were nearly four separated women for each divorced woman.

TABLE **97.**—STANDARDIZED AND UNSTANDARDIZED NUMBER OF OWN CHILDREN UNDER 5 YEARS OLD FOR WOMEN 15 TO 49 YEARS OLD, BY DETAILED MARITAL STATUS AND COLOR: 1950

[The standard is the distribution by age of white women of all marital classes combined]

Marital status of woman	White			Nonwhite		
	Number of women	Children under 5 per 1,000 women		Number of women	Children under 5 per 1,000 women	
		Unstand-ardized	Stand-ardized		Unstand-ardized	Stand-ardized
Total........................	34,473,570	404	404	4,275,000	396	390
Single...........................	7,934,640	...	...	990,030	...	...
Married..........................	25,036,650	548	551	2,923,620	558	571
Husband present.................	24,160,230	555	559	2,393,730	603	616
Married once..................	21,205,500	571	564	1,853,730	671	648
Married more than once.........	2,954,730	444	534	540,000	369	476
Husband absent.................	876,420	341	345	529,890	356	369
Separated.....................	461,880	339	371	416,970	346	378
Other.........................	414,540	344	329	112,920	395	352
Widowed..........................	682,530	115	288	236,130	154	281
Divorced.........................	819,750	173	230	125,220	206	230

Source: Derived from *1950 Census of Population*, Vol. IV, *Special Reports*, Part 5, Chapter C, Fertility, tables 42 and 43.

Reproduction loss from variations in marital status. For women 45 to 49 years old, and hence of completed fertility, it is possible to assess, very roughly, the reproduction losses arising from the failure of some women to marry and from the breakup of marriages. It is necessary to assume that the women in the other marital classes would have had about the same fertility as the women in unbroken first marriages had they been in that category. Such an assumption is not strictly justified. One can express the fertility of the women in various marital classes as a proportion of the fertility for women in unbroken first marriages. The results are presented in table 98.

In 1950, the average number of children ever born for all white women 45 to 49 years old, regardless of marital status, was 89.1 percent of the average for the women married once and husband present. This implies a net reproduction loss to all white women 45 to 49 years old of 10.9 percent from the lower fertility of women in other than unbroken first marriages. Among nonwhites, the net loss was much greater, about 18.1 percent. The smallest net loss, 5.4 percent, occurred among whites in rural-farm areas but this may have been spurious if there was any heavy net migration of relatively infertile single, widowed, and divorced women from farm to nonfarm areas.

TABLE **98.**—NUMBER OF CHILDREN EVER BORN PER 1,000 WOMEN 45 TO 49 YEARS OLD, BY DETAILED MARITAL STATUS AND COLOR, URBAN AND RURAL: 1950 AND 1940

[Rate not shown where there are fewer than 4,000 women]

Subject	White		Urban, 1950	Rural nonfarm, 1950	Rural farm, 1950	Nonwhite	
	United States						
	1950	1940[1]				1950	1940[2]
PERCENT DISTRIBUTION OF WOMEN							
Total	100.0	100.0	100.0	100.0	100.0	100.0	100.0
Single	8.4	9.8	9.6	6.4	4.7	5.0	5.2
Married	81.3	78.0	78.7	84.4	90.9	72.9	67.7
Husband present	78.5	74.6	75.7	80.9	89.8	60.6	57.9
Married once	66.2	65.8	63.5	67.2	78.7	39.9	42.6
Married more than once	12.3	8.8	12.1	13.7	11.0	20.7	15.3
Husband absent	2.9	3.3	3.0	3.5	1.1	12.3	9.8
Separated	1.7	(3)	1.9	1.6	0.5	10.1	(3)
Other	1.2	(3)	1.2	1.9	0.6	2.2	(3)
Widowed	7.0	9.5	7.7	6.8	3.8	18.5	24.7
Divorced	3.3	2.7	4.0	2.4	0.7	3.6	2.4
CHILDREN EVER BORN PER 1,000 WOMEN							
Total, unstandardized	2,251	2,602	1,936	2,598	3,414	2,663	3,138
Single	...	...	...	...	...	...	...
Married	2,482	2,967	2,154	2,773	3,591	2,846	3,483
Husband present	2,487	2,981	2,154	2,772	3,595	2,960	3,612
Married once	2,525	3,024	2,191	2,796	3,608	3,250	3,833
Married more than once	2,282	2,658	1,960	2,654	3,499	2,398	3,009
Husband absent	2,345	2,641	2,152	2,787	3,253	2,290	2,684
Separated	2,491	(3)	2,311	3,180	...	2,262	(3)
Other	2,146	(3)	1,892	2,452	...	2,420	(3)
Widowed	2,464	2,817	2,229	3,028	3,587	2,802	3,043
Divorced	1,801	1,919	1,727	2,156	...	1,916	2,369
Total, standardized for[4]—							
Marital status of women	2,251	2,666	1,967	2,544	3,242	2,773	3,277
Percent of unstandardized rate	100.0	102.5	101.6	97.9	95.0	104.1	104.4
Fertility of each marital status	2,251	2,222	2,214	2,301	2,370	2,299	2,306
Percent of unstandardized rate	100.0	85.4	114.4	88.6	64.4	86.3	73.5
CHILDREN EVER BORN, RELATIVE TO AVERAGE FOR WOMEN MARRIED ONCE, HUSBAND PRESENT							
Total	89.1	86.0	88.4	92.9	94.6	81.9	81.9
Single	...	...	...	...	...	...	...
Married	98.3	98.1	98.3	99.2	99.5	87.6	90.9
Husband present	98.5	98.6	98.3	99.1	99.6	91.1	94.2
Married once	100.0	100.0	100.0	100.0	100.0	100.0	100.0
Married more than once	90.4	87.9	89.5	94.9	97.0	73.8	78.5
Husband absent	92.9	87.3	98.2	99.7	90.2	70.5	70.0
Separated	98.7	(3)	105.5	113.7	...	69.6	(3)
Other	85.0	(3)	86.4	87.7	...	74.5	(3)
Widowed	97.6	93.2	101.7	108.3	99.4	86.2	79.4
Divorced	71.3	63.5	78.8	77.1	...	59.0	61.8

[1] Native white; unknown times married distributed.
[2] Negro; unknown times married distributed.
[3] Not available.
[4] The distribution (by marital status or fertility) of white women in the United States in 1950 is the standard.

Source: Derived from *1950 Census of Population*, Vol. IV, *Special Reports*, Part 5, Chapter C, Fertility, tables 16 and 17; *1940 Census of Population, Differential Fertility, 1940 and 1910*, Women by Number of Children Ever Born, tables 17 and 18, and unpublished tabulation detail.

White women 45 to 49 years old in remarriages, nationally, were 90.4 percent as fertile as those in first marriages, but nonwhite women of this age in remarriages were only 73.8 percent as fertile. Single women were not asked about children ever born and were presumed to be childless. The next least fertile marital class was that of the divorced women, among whites and nonwhites alike. Among whites, but not nonwhites, the separated women and the widowed women were almost as fertile as those still in first marriages. In fact, they were more fertile than the women in unbroken marriages in urban and rural-nonfarm areas. In part, this probably represented different social and economic backgrounds among the women whose marriages were broken as compared with the women in unbroken unions and of identical age. In part it probably stemmed from out-migration of some fertile women from rural-farm areas after they had lost their husbands. Other data indicate that the women still in unbroken first marriages at the time of the census were married at slightly older ages, on the average, than the women no longer in first marriages. For example, in 1940, among women 45 to 64 years old, the median age at first marriage reported by women married once and husband present was 22.1 years, and among other ever-married women of this age it was 20.8 years, a difference of 1.3 years.[3] The women who married young had a longer period of risk of divorce or widowhood than the women who married more recently, at an older age.

Although there were marked variations by color and residence in the distribution of women by detailed marital status, an experimental standardization for marital status eliminated only a very small part of the large differences in fertility. Differences in the fertility of women in unbroken first marriages were a much more important source of total fertility variation than were intergroup differences in the proportion of women who were married once and husband present.

Age at first marriage. A direct question on age at first marriage was asked of all women in 1940 who had ever been married. Some of the results are shown in table 99. In 1950, women were asked the number of years in their present marital status rather than the age at first marriage.

The median age at first marriage was 22.1 years among native white women 45 to 49 years old, married once and husband present, in 1940. About 73 percent of the women were married before the age of 24, and 92 percent were married before the age of 30. A marriage age of 30 may provide plenty of time for most women to have three children if they want that many and if the spouses are in average physical condition. The median age at marriage was oldest in cities of 250,000 or more, declined with size of place, and was youngest in rural-farm areas.

Nationally, less than 4 percent of the native white women who married

---

[3] U. S. Bureau of the Census, *Population—Special Reports*, Series P–45, No. 7, table 5.

before the age of 18 were childless by age 45 to 49 years in 1940. Perhaps some of the very young marriages occurred because of a premarital conception. Among the native white women married once and husband present who were 20 and 21 years old at marriage and who were 45 to 49 years old in 1940, only 6.1 percent in rural-farm areas were childless as compared with 14.7 percent in cities of 250,000 or more. The variation in percent childless probably reflects differences in family limitation practices rather than any greater physiological inability of urban women to have children.

TABLE **99.**—AGE AT MARRIAGE, PERCENT CHILDLESS, AND NUMBER OF CHILDREN EVER BORN PER 1,000 WOMEN 45 TO 49 YEARS OLD MARRIED ONCE AND HUSBAND PRESENT, FOR NATIVE WHITE WOMEN, URBAN (BY SIZE OF PLACE) AND RURAL, AND FOR NEGRO WOMEN: 1940

[Rate and percent not shown where there are fewer than 3,000 women]

Subject	United States	Native white					Rural nonfarm	Rural farm	Negro, total
		Total	Urban						
			Cities of 250,000 or more	Places of 25,000 to 250,000	Places of 2,500 to 25,000				
PERCENT DISTRIBUTION OF WOMEN BY AGE AT MARRIAGE									
Total.....................	100.0	100.0	100.0	100.0	100.0	100.0	100.0	100.0
Under 18 years..................	8.4	6.2	5.3	6.6	7.0	10.4	11.5	19.3
18 and 19 years................	18.4	15.7	14.2	15.9	17.4	19.7	23.3	23.4
20 and 21 years................	22.5	21.5	21.1	21.4	22.0	22.8	24.4	24.0
22 to 24 years.................	24.0	25.8	25.9	26.4	24.9	22.9	20.9	15.9
25 and 26 years...............	11.0	12.4	13.1	12.2	12.0	9.8	8.5	7.6
27 to 29 years.................	7.7	9.1	9.9	9.0	8.2	7.0	5.3	3.4
30 to 34 years.................	5.1	6.0	6.9	5.5	5.6	4.7	3.4	4.0
35 to 39 years.................	1.8	2.0	2.4	1.7	1.8	1.7	1.4	} 2.5
40 years and over..............	1.1	1.2	1.2	1.2	1.1	1.0	1.2	
Median age...............years..	22.1	22.8	23.1	22.7	22.4	21.7	21.2	20.6
PERCENT CHILDLESS BY AGE AT MARRIAGE									
Total.....................	14.9	18.2	22.6	22.0	15.1	13.6	8.8	22.5
Under 18 years..................	3.6	4.6	5.8	4.9	2.9	3.4	2.4	9.6
18 and 19 years................	6.1	7.3	8.9	6.6	6.5	5.9	4.3	14.8
20 and 21 years................	10.3	12.6	14.7	12.4	10.1	8.8	6.9	22.6
22 to 24 years.................	13.5	15.4	17.6	15.2	12.8	13.8	8.3	27.5
25 and 26 years...............	19.8	22.1	25.9	20.8	18.7	19.4	12.4	37.4
27 to 29 years.................	25.0	27.5	30.1	27.4	23.5	22.7	18.2	40.7
30 to 34 years.................	36.2	40.1	45.6	37.2	35.2	33.2	24.0	44.7
35 to 39 years.................	63.4	68.4	70.4	67.0	67.0	65.0	45.8	...
40 years and over..............	84.6	90.8	92.2	89.0	...	83.4	70.9	...
CHILDREN EVER BORN PER 1,000 WOMEN BY AGE AT MARRIAGE									
Total.....................	3,022	2,449	2,326	3,065	2,733	3,196	4,136	3,835
Under 18 years..................	5,128	4,292	3,835	4,284	4,763	5,073	6,159	5,443
18 and 19 years................	4,009	3,345	3,062	3,286	3,732	4,094	4,933	4,554
20 and 21 years................	3,223	2,682	2,501	2,682	2,917	3,391	4,138	3,500
22 to 24 years.................	2,736	2,355	2,187	2,378	2,553	2,804	3,706	3,305
25 and 26 years...............	2,201	1,927	1,798	1,976	2,043	2,287	3,003	3,200
27 to 29 years.................	1,876	1,686	1,590	1,710	1,800	1,956	2,506	2,181
30 to 34 years.................	1,322	1,135	1,008	1,252	1,179	1,353	2,032	1,516
35 to 39 years.................	595	497	468	478	573	532	973	...
40 years and over..............	342	180	167	145	...	281	762	...

Source: Derived from *1940 Census of Population, Differential Fertility, 1940 and 1910,* Women by Number of Children Ever Born, tables 23 and 24.

Negro women married at ages under 20 in much larger proportions than the native white women. The higher fertility of nonwhites than of whites in 1940 was not simply a result of an earlier age at marriage, however. This is apparent when comparisons are made for specific ages at marriage. The Negroes had a higher incidence of childlessness than whites among women married at each age, and they also had more children per mother.

The large percentage of childless women among Negroes who married before 18 suggested that in this group early marriages resulted from following a traditional way of life rather than from premarital pregnancies.

It may be noted that the average number of children ever born had a strong inverse relation to the age at marriage of native white and Negro women 45 to 49 years old in 1940.

Women who married late accounted for about a fourth of childless marriages. In 1940, only 8 percent of the native white women 45 to 49 years old, married once and husband present, reported a marriage age of 30 years or more. Almost half, 49 percent, of the late marriages were childless, and these accounted for 26 percent of the total number of childless women 45 to 49 years old in unbroken marriages.

More precise information on the importance of age at marriage for fertility is given by the data for 1950 in table 100. These data are partly controlled for duration of marriage. The women married at least 10 years were married long enough to have had several children, if they had wanted and could have had them. The percentage with one or two children ever born is remarkably consistent among women married at different ages over age 18, except among nonwhites in rural-farm areas. In this sense, perhaps couples do tend to want one or two children in fairly constant proportions. However, there was no consistency in the percentage of women who were childless, or in the percentage who had three children or more.

Very large differences in percent childless exist in nonfarm and farm areas, especially among nonwhites.

Duration of marriage. Table 101 shows the fundamental stability of the median duration of marriage for women in unbroken first marriages in 1910, 1945, and 1950. It is evident that once the age of 30 was passed, beyond which point relatively few first marriages occurred, the median duration of marriage could be roughly estimated by subtracting 21 from the current age of women. However, the true median duration of marriage usually increases by slightly less than 5.0 years from one 5-year age group to another.

Small absolute increases occurred in the median duration of marriage among women under 35 years old in 1950, as compared with women of similar age in 1940. Decreases in the median duration of marriage occurred among the women 35 to 44 years old. The women 15 to 29 years old gained about half a year in the median duration of marriage; they should carry this advantage with them through life.

TABLE **100.**—PERCENT DISTRIBUTION BY NUMBER OF CHILDREN EVER BORN, BY AGE AT MAR-
RIAGE, FOR WOMEN 15 TO 59 YEARS OLD MARRIED ONCE AND HUSBAND PRESENT, MARRIED
10 YEARS OR MORE, BY COLOR, FOR FARM AND NONFARM AREAS: 1950

Farm residence and age at marriage[1]	Total				Nonwhite			
	Number of women	Percent with specified number of children ever born			Number of women	Percent with specified number of children ever born		
		None	1 and 2	3 or more		None	1 and 2	3 or more
URBAN AND RURAL NONFARM								
Married 10 years or more..	14,042,000	15.0	45.6	39.3	869,000	26.3	30.1	43.6
14 to 17 years old...........	2,049,000	7.0	36.8	56.2	222,000	16.1	28.9	55.1
18 and 19 years...............	2,709,000	8.2	44.2	47.7	168,000	17.9	31.6	50.4
20 and 21 years...............	2,900,000	11.7	46.7	41.5	155,000	26.2	27.6	46.1
22 to 24 years................	3,199,000	15.2	49.9	34.9	149,000	28.3	33.3	38.4
25 to 29 years................	2,306,000	23.6	49.9	26.5	112,000	42.5	30.1	27.4
30 to 59 years................	879,000	42.4	40.5	17.1	63,000	51.0	29.0	19.9
Median age.............years..	21.0	23.6	21.3	20.0	20.0	22.0	20.1	19.1
RURAL FARM								
Married 10 years or more..	2,774,000	9.8	30.7	59.5	260,000	10.1	16.2	73.7
14 to 17 years old...........	564,000	4.7	22.5	72.8	79,000	5.4	14.2	80.4
18 and 19 years...............	621,000	6.3	29.1	64.6	56,000	7.7	13.7	78.6
20 and 21 years...............	577,000	8.1	32.4	59.5	43,000	9.1	16.6	74.4
22 to 24 years................	535,000	10.5	35.0	54.5	41,000	12.6	17.0	70.4
25 to 29 years................	341,000	17.2	35.7	47.1	27,000	18.0	21.1	60.9
30 to 59 years................	136,000	33.4	35.8	30.8	15,000	25.3	25.3	49.3
Median age.............years..	20.1	22.7	20.7	19.6	19.3	21.8	20.0	19.0

[1] Difference between age at census and years married.

Source: Derived from *1950 Census of Population*, Vol. IV, *Special Reports*, Part 2, Chapter E, Duration of Current Marital Status, table 4.

TABLE **101.**—MEDIAN YEARS MARRIED, FOR WHITE WOMEN 15 TO 49 YEARS OLD MARRIED
ONCE AND HUSBAND PRESENT, BY AGE: 1950, 1940, AND 1910

Age at census	White, 1950	Native white	
		1940	1910
15 to 19 years.............................	1.6	1.2	([1])
20 to 24 years.............................	3.4	3.0	3.5
25 to 29 years.............................	6.8	6.2	6.8
30 to 34 years.............................	11.1	10.9	11.0
35 to 39 years.............................	15.5	15.8	15.8
40 to 44 years.............................	20.1	20.7	20.9
45 to 49 years.............................	([1])	25.2	25.9

[1] Not available.

Source: Derived from *1950 Census of Population*, Vol. IV, *Special Reports*, Part 5, Chapter C, Fertility, table 50; *1940 Census of Population, Differential Fertility, 1940 and 1910*, Fertility by Duration of Marriage, tables 5 and 7, and unpublished tabulation detail.

The 1950 and 1910 median durations of marriage were almost identical for women in each 5-year age group under 35, and the 1950 medians were slightly less than the 1910 medians for women 35 to 44 years old. The women 35 to 44 years old in 1950 had a lower median duration of marriage than the women of this age in 1910, because some of the women of this age in 1950 had postponed marriage in the economic depression of the 1930's. Many women in this age range married during the 1940's when the employment of married women was becoming more widely accepted. The women under 35 years old in 1950 were not so much affected by the depression as those under 35 years old in 1940. It is possible that the 1910 and 1950 data on duration are not strictly comparable; the 1910 data were slightly overstated if there was any tendency to give the nearest whole year of duration rather than completed years.

Some comparisons of data on children ever born are possible for women in 1950 and 1940 by age at census and duration of marriage (table 102). The comparisons should be made with caution, because some rather extensive adjustments were made. Duration of marriage was asked directly in 1950 and was derived in 1940 by subtraction of single years of age at marriage from single years of age at census. This subtraction resulted in estimates of 2-year ranges that were centered at the exact duration 1.0, 2.0, 3.0, etc., whereas the 1950 Census data were for conventional 1-year intervals, centered at 1.5, 2.5, etc. The 1940 data were adjusted by taking a two-point moving average of the rates of children ever born by duration of marriage so as to shift the data one-half year to put midpoints on a comparable basis with the conventional data for 1950, although the comparison cannot be exact. Also, an allowance was made for the 1940 rates being slightly too high because of a limitation of data to women reporting on children ever born, times married, and age at first marriage (see Appendix A). The women not reporting on children ever born had relatively fewer young children in the household and, hence, presumably were less fertile than the women who reported. The 1940 rates in table 102 had been reduced by 3 percent to allow somewhat for the bias. The 1950 data needed no such treatment because the published data already included estimates of children, times married, and duration of marriage for women with no report on these subjects.

As stated above, the data in table 102 have been subjected to rather extreme adjustments. However, they suggest that rates of children ever born for women of combined childbearing ages 15 to 44 years decreased slightly between 1940 and 1950, among white women married 1 and 2 years, increased among those married 3 to 14 years, and decreased among those married 15 years or more. The largest percent increase was only 12 and the data for 1950 involved women who married 4 years earlier at a time when millions of veterans of World War II had recently been discharged from the Armed Forces. Thus, when duration of marriage but not age is controlled, no very startling increases are noted for women in the first few years after marriage for 1950 as compared with 1940. In Chapter 9, cohort fertility tables show that first birth rates for ever-married women aged 15 to 19 and 20 to 24 were higher on January 1, 1955, than on January 1, 1950, and exceeded by larger amounts the rates for January 1, 1945. This may have been due in part to a decrease in the average length of the interval from marriage to first birth, but it may have resulted entirely from an increase in the duration of marriage among the ever-married women in each age group.

The women 15 to 19 years old and 20 to 24 years old in 1950 had fewer children ever born by the end of each year of marriage than

TABLE **102.**—NUMBER OF CHILDREN EVER BORN PER 1,000 WOMEN BY DURATION OF MARRIAGE, FOR WHITE WOMEN 15 TO 49 YEARS OLD MARRIED ONCE AND HUSBAND PRESENT, BY AGE: 1950 AND 1940

[Data for white women in 1950 and native white in 1940]

Age at census and years married	Number of women, 1950	Children ever born per 1,000 women		
		1950	1940, adjusted[1]	Percent change
Total, 15 to 44 years old.........	18,535,110	1,846	...	...
Married--				
Less than 1 year......................	693,480	130	([2])	([2])
1 year................................	679,950	430	433	-0.7
2 years...............................	1,118,040	679	686	-1.0
3 years...............................	1,287,960	973	894	8.8
4 years...............................	1,199,010	1,209	1,077	12.3
5 years...............................	940,740	1,371	1,256	9.2
6 years...............................	791,370	1,565	1,450	7.9
7 years...............................	853,650	1,695	1,618	4.8
8 years...............................	1,006,440	1,770	1,749	1.2
9 years...............................	892,680	1,964	1,964	...
10 to 14 years........................	3,957,060	2,198	2,175	1.1
15 to 19 years........................	2,783,490	2,534	2,758	-8.1
20 years or more......................	2,331,240	3,046	([3])	([3])
15 to 19 years old...................	675,660	546	...	...
Married--				
Less than 1 year......................	235,980	97	([2])	([2])
1 year................................	170,340	465	618	-24.8
2 years...............................	161,070	795	1,061	-25.1
3 years or more.......................	108,270	1,281	([3])	([3])
20 to 24 years old...................	3,082,170	1,018	...	...
Married--				
Less than 1 year......................	306,990	91	([2])	([2])
1 year................................	346,710	412	431	-4.4
2 years...............................	607,410	669	754	-11.3
3 years...............................	656,250	1,030	1,060	-2.8
4 years...............................	492,870	1,336	1,350	-1.0
5 years...............................	288,240	1,577	1,645	-4.1
6 years...............................	169,440	1,839	1,959	-6.1
7 years...............................	104,910	1,969	2,251	-12.5
8 years...............................	64,260	2,230	2,540	-12.2
9 years...............................	24,630	2,499	2,696	-7.3
10 years or more......................	20,460	2,403	([3])	([3])
25 to 29 years old...................	4,091,520	1,632	...	...
Married--				
Less than 1 year......................	90,960	162	([2])	([2])
1 year................................	109,860	444	343	29.4
2 years...............................	242,910	642	562	14.2
3 years...............................	382,230	920	762	20.7
4 years...............................	467,340	1,172	977	20.0
5 years...............................	421,350	1,362	1,211	12.5
6 years...............................	399,720	1,618	1,484	9.0
7 years...............................	453,060	1,800	1,754	2.6
8 years...............................	489,600	1,941	1,984	-2.2
9 years...............................	370,650	2,181	2,328	-6.3
10 years or more......................	663,840	2,653	([3])	([3])
30 to 34 years old...................	3,910,860	2,085	...	...
Married--				
Less than 1 year......................	33,360	311	([2])	([2])
1 year................................	30,840	358	406	-11.8
2 years...............................	67,920	687	568	21.0
3 years...............................	111,120	861	637	35.2
4 years...............................	142,020	1,037	787	31.8
5 years...............................	148,440	1,245	958	30.0
6 years...............................	150,900	1,358	1,145	18.6
7 years...............................	205,380	1,564	1,322	18.3
8 years...............................	314,880	1,642	1,492	10.1
9 years...............................	346,650	1,892	1,892	...
10 to 14 years........................	1,796,970	2,345	2,316	1.3
15 years or more......................	562,380	3,102	([3])	([3])

See footnotes at end of table.

TABLE **102.**—NUMBER OF CHILDREN EVER BORN PER 1,000 WOMEN BY DURATION OF MARRIAGE, FOR WHITE WOMEN 15 TO 49 YEARS OLD MARRIED ONCE AND HUSBAND PRESENT, BY AGE: 1950 AND 1940—Cont.

Age at census and years married	Number of women, 1950	Children ever born per 1,000 women		
		1950	1940, adjusted[1]	Percent change
35 to 39 years old..................	3,629,790	2,284	...	...
Married--				
Less than 1 year.......................	16,410	456	([2])	([2])
1 year.................................	13,950	512	269	90.3
2 years................................	25,740	571	375	52.3
3 years................................	44,220	630	531	18.6
4 years................................	51,960	872	663	31.5
5 years................................	53,100	955	761	25.5
6 years................................	51,270	1,135	941	20.6
7 years................................	66,630	1,244	1,060	17.4
8 years................................	104,190	1,323	1,203	10.0
9 years................................	115,620	1,608	1,536	4.7
10 to 14 years.........................	1,118,640	1,931	1,846	4.6
15 to 19 years.........................	1,440,450	2,594	2,849	-9.0
20 years or more.......................	527,610	3,369	([3])	([3])
40 to 44 years old..................	3,145,110	2,410	...	...
Married--				
Less than 1 year.......................	9,780	671	([2])	([2])
1 year.................................	8,250	409	136	200.7
2 years................................	12,990	628	235	167.2
3 years................................	17,460	702	361	94.5
4 years................................	19,470	671	432	55.3
5 years................................	23,370	653	529	23.4
6 years................................	20,040	831	660	25.9
7 years................................	23,670	866	738	17.3
8 years................................	33,510	977	825	18.4
9 years................................	35,130	1,169	1,151	1.6
10 to 14 years.........................	376,140	1,532	1,454	5.4
15 to 19 years.........................	793,200	2,055	2,256	-8.9
20 years or more.......................	1,772,100	2,937	([3])	([3])

[1] The original 1940 Census data on marriage duration were derived by subtraction of age at marriage from age at census and the original rates excluded the relatively infertile women with no report on children ever born. For comparability with data from the 1950 Census, which had a direct question on duration of marriage, it was necessary to shift the derived 1940 Census marriage durations upward by one-half year by interpolation; and to match an inclusion of estimates of children for women in 1950 when they did not report on children ever born, it was necessary to reduce the 1940 Census rates by 3 percent.

[2] Derived data not reliable.

[3] Data not available.

Source: Derived from *1950 Census of Population*, Vol. IV, *Special Reports*, Part 5, Chapter C, Fertility, table 18; *1940 Census of Population, Differential Fertility, 1940 and 1910*, Fertility by Duration of Marriage, table 5, and unpublished tabulation detail.

their predecessors had in 1940. In these particular group comparisons there was no indication that the young women were tending to have a first baby earlier after the marriage than had been customary; rather, it appeared that the very young women in 1950 limited their childbearing more severely than did young women in 1940. At ages over 25 years the situation was very different. The women of these mature ages who had been married only a few years had more children in 1950 than the corresponding women in 1940, as though the women in 1950 were more inclined to make up for their late start on marriage and in raising a family. However, relatively few of the women married at an advanced age.

The 1950 Census data were not tabulated by single years of duration of marriage beyond 9 years. The 1940 Census data were tabulated in additional single years and yield some findings which may be of general applicability (tables 103 and 104 and figure 102).

TABLE **103.**—VARIATION IN COMPLETED FERTILITY BY DURATION OF MARRIAGE, FOR NATIVE WHITE WOMEN 45 TO 49 YEARS OLD MARRIED ONCE AND HUSBAND PRESENT: 1940

Years married[1]	Number of women	Percent with specified number of children ever born					Children ever born per 1,000 women	Average number of children born per 1,000 women per year of married life
		None	1	2	3	4 or more		
Total..............	1,790,000	14.9	16.6	20.3	15.1	33.1	3,022	121
34 and over..........	5,000	1.9	5.0	4.3	10.5	78.3	6,261	179
33 years..............	13,000	4.0	8.7	8.7	8.4	70.1	5,670	172
32 years..............	28,000	3.1	7.9	14.3	11.9	62.9	5,254	164
31 years..............	57,000	4.5	9.1	13.4	14.4	58.6	4,715	152
30 years..............	90,000	6.0	10.8	14.6	15.6	53.0	4,435	148
29 years..............	124,000	7.1	12.1	17.5	15.1	48.1	3,932	136
28 years..............	149,000	7.6	13.3	19.2	15.5	44.4	3,737	133
27 years..............	170,000	9.7	14.1	20.2	16.0	40.1	3,458	128
26 years..............	165,000	9.0	16.2	20.6	17.8	36.4	3,261	125
25 years..............	165,000	11.9	16.4	22.2	16.8	32.6	2,976	119
24 years..............	143,000	12.2	17.3	23.8	17.0	29.6	2,810	117
23 years..............	125,000	16.4	18.2	23.9	16.2	25.4	2,522	110
22 years..............	97,000	17.7	19.0	23.6	16.8	22.9	2,386	108
21 years..............	74,000	18.8	19.9	24.0	14.9	22.4	2,295	109
20 years..............	81,000	21.9	22.4	25.1	14.6	15.9	2,017	101
19 years..............	45,000	24.0	25.2	23.2	12.4	15.2	1,834	97
18 years..............	35,000	29.5	22.6	22.0	13.3	12.6	1,707	95
17 years..............	30,000	29.1	25.8	21.7	12.1	11.3	1,631	96
16 years..............	22,000	32.4	28.1	20.0	10.7	8.7	1,416	89
15 years..............	19,000	36.9	28.3	19.5	9.4	5.9	1,250	83
14 years..............	12,000	44.0	23.3	19.8	6.1	6.7	1,130	81
13 years..............	10,000	45.1	29.0	15.6	5.6	4.7	999	77
12 years..............	8,000	53.3	27.5	13.2	4.2	1.7	738	62
11 years..............	7,000	59.2	23.3	7.4	5.8	4.2	754	69
10 years..............	8,000	64.3	22.9	9.3	2.8	0.8	530	53
9 years..............	4,000	59.1	22.1	12.7	3.9	2.2	702	78
8 years..............	3,000	81.0	14.6	2.5	0.6	1.3	278	35
7 years..............	3,000	82.2	8.6	5.9	2.0	1.3	316	45
6 years..............	3,000	85.7	11.1	2.4	0.8	...	183	31
Other[2]..............	95,000	28.8	15.7	17.6	12.2	25.6	2,435	...

[1] Difference between age at first marriage and age at census.
[2] Less than 6 years, and age at marriage not reported.
Source: Derived from the 1950 Census of Population, unpublished tabulation detail.

TABLE **104.**—VARIATION IN COMPLETED FERTILITY BY DURATION OF MARRIAGE, FOR NEGRO WOMEN 45 TO 49 YEARS OLD MARRIED ONCE AND HUSBAND PRESENT: 1940

Years married[1]	Number of women	Percent with specified number of children ever born					Children ever born per 1,000 women	Average number of children born per 1,000 women per year of married life
		None	1	2	3	4 or more		
Total..............	128,000	22.5	10.9	10.9	10.2	45.7	3,835	142
33 years and over......	5,000	13.8	10.3	8.5	9.8	57.6	5,339	157
32 years..............	4,000	8.7	11.7	11.7	9.7	58.2	5,613	175
31 years..............	7,000	6.8	12.0	12.3	6.5	62.3	5,065	163
30 years..............	11,000	13.6	8.2	7.5	10.4	60.3	5,063	169
29 years..............	12,000	16.0	9.3	9.0	13.2	52.4	4,349	150
28 years..............	15,000	15.0	11.4	13.4	11.4	48.7	4,154	148
27 years..............	11,000	19.7	7.3	8.9	12.0	52.1	4,226	157
26 years..............	11,000	23.8	8.7	8.8	11.2	47.5	3,831	147
25 years..............	11,000	25.3	11.8	11.6	11.8	39.5	3,324	133
24 years..............	7,000	24.3	12.3	17.0	10.2	36.3	3,193	133
23 years..............	6,000	33.9	9.5	11.5	9.2	35.9	3,008	131
22 years..............	4,000	30.0	13.8	13.8	9.4	33.0	2,694	122
21 years..............	3,000	31.6	13.8	11.8	7.2	35.5	2,515	120
20 years..............	4,000	39.8	17.6	13.6	5.7	23.3	2,172	109
Other[2]..............	18,000	41.0	13.4	10.1	7.0	28.5	2,386	...

[1] Difference between age at first marriage and age at census.
[2] Less than 20 years, and age at marriage not reported.
Source: Derived from the 1950 Census of Population, unpublished tabulation detail.

FIGURE **102.**—NUMBER OF CHILDREN EVER BORN PER 1,000 NATIVE WHITE WOMEN 45 TO 49
YEARS OLD MARRIED ONCE AND HUSBAND PRESENT, BY DURATION OF MARRIAGE, URBAN AND
RURAL: 1940

[Dotted free-hand curve shown where fewer than 3,000 women. Duration of marriage derived by subtraction of age at
marriage from age at census]

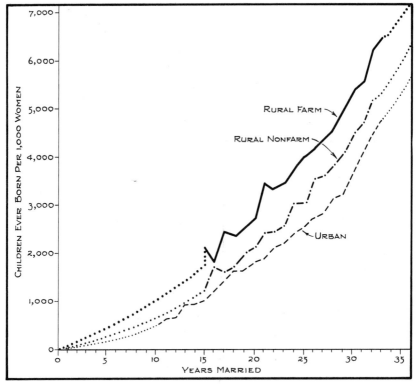

Source: Unpublished tabulation detail from the 1940 Census of Population.

The longer the women 45 to 49 years old in 1940 had been married,
or the earlier the marriage, the greater was the average number of children ever born per year of married life. Perhaps the women who married
late had births early after the marriage in an effort to compensate for their
late start in having children, but women in the group shown did not attain as large an average number of children per year of married life as the
women who married early.

*Recently widowed and divorced women by age and children
ever born.* The census ordinarily records as widowed or divorced only
those women who have not remarried, without regard for the length of
time the women have been widowed or divorced. Some information on
children ever born was tabulated for recently divorced women in 1950,
for the first time, and published in a report on duration of current marital
status. Some of the data are presented in tables 105 and 106, along with
cumulative data for total widowed or divorced women. For purposes of
further comparison, some data for married women are given in table 107.

TABLE **105.**—Percent Distribution by Number of Children Ever Born, for Women 15 to 59 Years Old Widowed Less than 2 Years, by Age at Widowhood, and for All Widowed Women 15 to 59 Years Old by Age at Census: 1950

[Percent not shown where there are fewer than 4,000 women]

Age	Number of women	Percent with specified number of children ever born		
		None	1 and 2	3 or more
Widowed less than 2 years, by age at widowhood[1]............................	283,000	22.2	39.2	38.5
14 to 19 years old..........................	3,000	...	...	...
20 to 24 years old..........................	11,000	32.1	49.3	18.6
25 to 29 years old..........................	14,000	21.9	46.9	31.2
30 to 34 years old..........................	19,000	26.2	46.0	27.8
35 to 39 years old..........................	28,000	19.9	42.6	37.5
40 to 44 years old..........................	36,000	23.0	40.4	36.6
45 to 59 years old..........................	172,000	21.2	36.0	42.8
Median age at widowhood..............years..	47.7	46.6	46.3	49.7
Total widowed, by age at census.......	2,163,000	19.9	40.3	39.8
15 to 19 years old..........................	4,000	29.9	62.4	7.7
20 to 24 years old..........................	25,000	30.3	54.0	15.7
25 to 29 years old..........................	54,000	22.3	54.5	23.2
30 to 34 years old..........................	91,000	24.2	48.2	27.6
35 to 39 years old..........................	151,000	24.8	43.5	31.7
40 to 44 years old..........................	229,000	22.6	42.7	34.7
45 to 59 years old..........................	1,609,000	18.6	38.4	43.0

[1] Difference between age at census and years widowed.

Source: Derived from *1950 Census of Population*, Vol. IV, *Special Reports*, Part 2, Chapter E, Duration of Current Marital Status, table 28, and Part 5, Chapter C, Fertility, tables 16 and 17.

The recently widowed or divorced women had higher fertility than the total widowed or divorced women. This reflected the perhaps obvious fact that the women who were widowed or divorced some time ago could not have been married so long, on the average, as the women of the same age who recently became widowed or divorced.

TABLE **106.**—Percent Distribution by Number of Children Ever Born, for Women 15 to 59 Years Old by Age at Divorce, and for All Divorced Women 15 to 59 Years Old by Age at Census: 1950

Age	Number of women	Percent with specified number of children ever born		
		None	1 and 2	3 or more
Divorced less than 2 years, by age at divorce[1]............................	263,000	32.7	49.1	18.2
14 to 19 years old..........................	17,000	52.8	46.0	1.2
20 to 24 years old..........................	57,000	38.1	55.2	6.7
25 to 29 years old..........................	52,000	32.1	53.7	14.2
30 to 34 years old..........................	36,000	31.0	50.6	18.4
35 to 39 years old..........................	32,000	28.4	44.2	27.4
40 to 44 years old..........................	31,000	27.8	46.5	25.6
45 to 59 years old..........................	37,000	25.4	39.7	34.9
Median age at divorce...............years..	30.2	28.2	29.0	37.8
Total divorced, by age at census......	1,154,000	31.6	48.2	20.3
15 to 19 years old..........................	18,000	53.8	43.7	2.6
20 to 24 years old..........................	97,000	39.9	54.6	5.5
25 to 29 years old..........................	159,000	32.3	55.0	12.7
30 to 34 years old..........................	167,000	32.8	51.7	15.5
35 to 39 years old..........................	178,000	33.2	46.0	20.8
40 to 44 years old..........................	177,000	30.0	48.2	21.9
45 to 59 years old..........................	358,000	27.3	43.0	29.7

[1] Difference between age at census and years divorced.

Source: Derived from *1950 Census of Population*, Vol. IV, *Special Reports*, Part 2, Chapter E, Duration of Current Marital Status, table 23, and Part 5, Chapter C, Fertility, tables 16 and 17.

TABLE **107.**—PERCENT DISTRIBUTION BY NUMBER OF CHILDREN EVER BORN, FOR MARRIED
WOMEN 15 TO 59 YEARS OLD, BY AGE: 1950

Age	Number of women	Percent with specified number of children ever born		
		None	1 and 2	3 or more
Total, 15 to 59 years...............	33,563,000	21.4	48.1	30.5
15 to 19 years...........................	904,000	52.8	45.4	1.8
20 to 24 years...........................	3,938,000	33.2	58.0	8.8
25 to 29 years...........................	5,283,000	20.8	57.8	21.5
30 to 34 years...........................	5,097,000	16.7	52.0	31.3
35 to 39 years...........................	4,872,000	18.4	46.4	35.2
40 to 44 years...........................	4,261,000	19.5	44.1	36.4
45 to 59 years...........................	9,209,000	18.7	39.1	42.2

Source: Derived from *1950 Census of Population*, Vol. IV, *Special Reports*, Part 5, Chapter C, Fertility, tables 16 and 17.

The recently widowed women, especially the young widows, were slightly more fertile than the married women of similar age as may be seen in a comparison of tables 105 and 107. This comparison may reflect higher mortality among the husbands of some economically and educationally disadvantaged women who while married have above average fertility, or it may reflect some misreporting of marital status by women with an illegitimate child.

The recently divorced women had much smaller rates of children ever born than the married women of similar age. This may indicate the relevance of the adage that children help to preserve the marriage. Yet, more than two-thirds of the divorced women had borne at least one child. Divorces occur at all ages, but among women, about half appear to occur by the age of 30 years.

B. Spacing of children

Table 108 presents data from the Current Population Survey for April 1954 on the spacing of children under 4 years old. The spacing shown is the difference in age between the youngest child under 4 years old and the next older child of any age or between the number of years the mother has been married and the age of an only child under 4 years old. The marriage duration itself is the difference between the mother's age at marriage and her age in April 1954. The data shown are limited to those for women who have all their children ever born living with them. Perhaps the women who were excluded from the data because some children were absent had different child-spacing patterns than the women who were included. The excluded women were a small minority of the mothers of children under 4 years old, however. (By the time this monograph is published, some information on child spacing should be available in a report that is currently in preparation by the National Office of Vital Statistics.)

The spacing intervals shown in tables 108, 109, and 110 do not have a conventional meaning, because they were derived by subtraction of whole years of age from one another. In all three tables, the spacing intervals *between children* came by a single subtraction of the age of a younger child from the age of the woman's next older one. Except for the interval "less than 1 year," the results tend to be the rough equivalent of yearly spacings that are *centered on the listed values.* For example, the interval "1 year" as shown in the tables is the rough equivalent of a range from 0.50 years to 1.49 years at a full weight. (The true range in this case is from 0.01 years to 1.99 years, but the various combinations of detailed spacing that are possible from two single years of age are such that spacings near the center of the range occur many times as often as spacings near the extreme limits.) Similarly, the interval "2 years" is the rough equivalent of a range from 1.50 years to 2.49 years, and higher intervals may be interpreted in an analogous way. In tables 108 and 109, the spacing interval *between marriage of the woman and the birth of the first child* came by a double subtraction process that used the age at first marriage reported by the woman, her age in April 1954, and the age of her first child. Except for the intervals under 2 years, the results tend to be the rough equivalent of yearly spacings that *end on the listed values.* For example, the interval "2 years" as shown in the tables is the rough equivalent of a range from 1.00 years to 1.99 years at a full weight. In table 110, data from the 1950 Census are used and information on the duration of the woman's marriage was directly available, so that only a single subtraction, of the age of the first child from the mother's marriage duration, was needed to get the spacing of the first child. In table 110 the spacing of the first child may be interpreted in the same way as the spacing between children.

The data based on subtractions of two ages from one another are actually a series of overlapping 2-year intervals, but only the midpoint reflects a full 365 days of spacing experience; the number of days experience declines as one goes from the midpoint to either end of the 2-year range and becomes zero at the extreme limits. The whole 2-year range with variable days of experience is equal in weight to 1 year with 365 days of experience. The intervals based on double subtractions of two ages and a calendar year of marriage are actually a series of overlapping 3-year intervals, each of which is equal in total weight to 1 year with 365 days of experience.

It appears from table 108 that among the mothers of children under 4 years old in 1954 the median spacing from marriage to the first birth was about 1.5 years. The second child was born at a median spacing of 2.6 years from the birth of the first child. The spacing between the second and third child was about the same as that between the second and the first child, but the fourth and higher orders had a much narrower spacing. The data in table 108 for women with six or more children ever born suggest that in the absence of effective family limitation women in general might have successive children at an average (median) spacing of 2.0 years or less. It appears from the table that very few women have a birth either in the first year of marriage or in the first year following a prior

birth. The first year of marriage ("married less than 1 year") or the age
at marriage may not be accurately reported by some women who wish to
avoid any hint that the oldest child may have been conceived before marriage. Christensen noted in his data on matched marriage and birth
records for one county in Indiana that 43 percent of first births occurred
less than 1 year after marriage.[4] The mean spacing is usually a little longer
than the median spacing.

TABLE **108.**—SPACING OF CHILDREN BORN IN PERIOD APRIL 1950 TO 1954, FOR MOTHERS
MARRIED ONCE, HUSBAND AND ALL CHILDREN EVER BORN LIVING IN THE HOUSEHOLD: APRIL
1954

Spacing interval since prior event[1]	Total	Order of birth: Mother's—					
		First child	Second child	Third child	Fourth child	Fifth child	Sixth or more
Number of births....thousands..	10,244	3,425	3,160	1,995	907	386	371
Percent.....................	100.0	100.0	100.0	100.0	100.0	100.0	100.0
Less than 1 year.................	2.8	5.5	0.5	1.6	3.1	4.4	0.5
1 year..........................	23.4	27.0	20.5	20.5	24.1	29.3	24.0
2 years.........................	29.4	32.8	26.4	25.3	28.8	29.5	46.9
3 years.........................	16.9	11.8	21.1	19.7	17.2	12.7	15.1
4 years.........................	10.1	6.7	13.0	11.9	10.5	11.4	5.9
5 and 6 years...................	10.7	8.3	12.5	12.9	11.2	9.1	6.5
7 to 9 years....................	4.2	4.3	4.1	5.2	4.1	3.6	1.1
10 years or more................	2.5	3.6	1.9	3.0	1.0	...	...
Median spacing............years..	2.1	1.5	2.6	2.6	2.3	2.1	2.0

[1] Interval between the birth of successive children or between the marriage of woman and birth of her first child. See
text for explanation of unconventional nature of intervals shown.

Source: Derived from U. S. Bureau of the Census, Current Population Survey, April 1954, special tabulation made for
National Office of Vital Statistics.

It appears from table 102 that the bulk of second and later births occur
within 3 years of a prior birth. Hence, most of the women who have not
given birth to a child for 5 or 6 years probably have completed their
childbearing.

The data in table 108 are for children born in the period from April
1950 to April 1954, without regard for the age of the mother and eventual
size of completed family. The spacing pattern is not the same among
women with completed families and women whose families have not been
completed, as may be seen from a comparison of tables 108 and 109.

Table 109, also from the April 1954 survey, shows the spacing of the
woman's last child, regardless of how long ago it was born, and therefore
permits a study of data for women near the end of the childbearing ages
separate from those who are not near the end of the childbearing ages.
The table also differs from table 108 in that the unit of measurement is
the woman, not the child. Hence table 109 provides some data for childless women, by years since the marriage. As in table 108, all spacing intervals are derived by subtraction of ages.

[4] Harold T. Christensen and Olive P. Bowden, "Studies in Child Spacing: II. The Time-Interval
Between Marriage of Parents and Birth of Their First Child, Tippecanoe County, Indiana," *Social
Forces*, Vol. 31, No. 4, May 1953, p. 346.

TABLE 109.—YEARS MARRIED FOR CHILDLESS WOMEN AND SPACING OF THE MOST RECENT CHILD FOR MOTHERS 15 TO 44 YEARS OLD MARRIED ONCE, 0 TO 4 CHILDREN EVER BORN, HUSBAND AND ALL CHILDREN PRESENT IN THE HOUSEHOLD, BY AGE OF WOMAN: APRIL 1954

[Percent not shown where there are fewer than 200,000 women]

Age of woman in 1954 and spacing[1]	No children ever born	1 child	2 children	3 children	4 children
15 to 19 years old............	296,000	277,000	35,000	5,000	...
Spacing, percent....................	100.0	100.0	...	...	...
Less than 1 year...................	37.2	15.2	...	...	...
1 year.............................	46.3	57.8	...	...	...
2 years............................	11.8	23.8	...	...	...
3 years or more....................	4.7	3.2	...	...	...
Median spacing................years..	0.8	0.8	...	...	...
20 to 24 years old............	728,000	1,081,000	742,000	233,000	54,000
Spacing, percent....................	100.0	100.0	100.0	100.0	...
Less than 1 year...................	19.9	7.9	1.3	3.9	...
1 year.............................	29.3	29.4	41.1	42.9	...
2 years............................	19.8	42.0	32.2	37.3	...
3 years............................	14.7	12.0	16.6	11.6	...
4 years............................	7.4	5.6	6.2	2.1	...
5 and 6 years......................	6.9	2.4	2.6	2.1	...
7 years or more....................	2.1	0.6	...	...	...
Median spacing................years..	1.5	1.3	1.7	1.6	...
25 to 29 years old............	702,000	960,000	1,144,000	690,000	278,000
Spacing, percent....................	100.0	100.0	100.0	100.0	100.0
Less than 1 year...................	7.4	4.7	1.2	2.2	4.7
1 year.............................	13.5	19.1	13.5	21.7	24.8
2 years............................	9.1	23.6	31.0	30.0	36.7
3 years............................	11.8	17.9	24.2	22.2	18.7
4 years............................	11.8	11.9	14.1	13.8	9.4
5 and 6 years......................	22.8	15.3	13.4	8.7	5.8
7 to 9 years.......................	18.5	6.7	2.6	0.7	...
10 years or more...................	5.0	0.8	...	0.7	...
Median spacing................years..	4.2	2.1	2.7	2.4	2.1
30 to 34 years old............	565,000	762,000	1,377,000	789,000	266,000
Spacing, percent....................	100.0	100.0	100.0	100.0	100.0
Less than 1 year...................	0.9	5.3	0.1	1.8	1.9
1 year.............................	3.4	17.5	13.6	12.7	19.5
2 years............................	2.8	18.1	23.0	22.3	26.7
3 years............................	3.9	15.4	18.8	25.1	17.3
4 years............................	8.3	11.8	17.0	15.5	13.9
5 and 6 years......................	12.0	17.7	18.5	16.2	16.2
7 to 9 years.......................	28.0	9.8	7.0	5.8	4.5
10 years or more...................	40.7	4.5	1.9	0.6	...
Median spacing................years..	8.5	2.6	3.2	3.0	2.6
35 to 44 years old............	1,097,000	1,132,000	1,863,000	948,000	410,000
Spacing, percent....................	100.0	100.0	100.0	100.0	100.0
Less than 1 year...................	1.7	4.3	0.6	3.0	2.7
1 year.............................	1.3	14.0	8.1	9.5	13.4
2 years............................	2.5	17.0	18.0	16.0	24.9
3 years............................	2.6	10.6	18.5	16.8	19.3
4 years............................	1.7	8.4	15.6	14.0	12.2
5 and 6 years......................	3.9	16.3	19.3	23.5	16.3
7 to 9 years.......................	10.6	12.7	14.3	10.5	9.3
10 years or more...................	75.8	16.8	5.7	6.6	2.0
Median spacing................years..	10+	3.5	3.8	3.8	3.0

[1] Years since marriage, for childless women; years between marriage and birth of child, for women with 1 child ever born; years between birth of first child and birth of second child, for women with 2 children ever born; years between birth of second child and birth of third child, for women with 3 children ever born; years between birth of third child and birth of fourth child, for women with 4 children ever born. See text for explanation of unconventional nature of intervals shown.

Source: Derived from U. S. Bureau of the Census, Current Population Survey, April 1954.

It appears that although the median spacing between all marriages and first births was about 1.5 years (table 108) the spacing of first births among first parity women 35 to 44 years old at the time of the survey (table 109)—hence not so likely to have more—was 3.5 years. The median spacing of second births among the two-child women 35 to 44 years old at the time of the survey was nearly as long, 3.8 years. The women 15 to 19 years old and 20 to 24 years old had a very short first-child spacing.

An indication of variations in spacing of all children ever born is possible from data from a 1-percent sample of 1950 Census data for women married once, 38 years old, married 18 years, one to four children ever born, husband and all children present in the household (table 110). As noted from the table, the average interval between marriage and the first child was greatest for the women who later had no more children and least for women who had several more children. Similarly, the spacing of higher orders of children was least for those women who had still more children.

TABLE 110.—SPACING OF ALL CHILDREN EVER BORN, FOR WOMEN 38 YEARS OLD MARRIED AT AGE 20, 1 TO 5 CHILDREN EVER BORN, FIRST HUSBAND AND ALL CHILDREN PRESENT IN THE HOUSEHOLD: 1950

[Data based on special 1-percent sample of women. Median and percent not shown where there are fewer than 10,000 women]

Order of birth and spacing[1]	Total	Women with--			
		1 child ever born by 1950	2 children ever born	3 children ever born	4 and 5 children ever born
FIRST BIRTH (Spacing since marriage)					
Number of women......................	52,300	12,400	18,700	11,900	9,300
Percent...........................	100.0	100.0	100.0	100.0	...
Less than 1 year......................	3.8	2.4	3.2	3.4	...
1 year...............................	30.2	20.2	28.3	33.6	...
2 years..............................	25.0	14.5	26.2	31.1	...
3 years..............................	9.9	7.3	10.2	12.6	...
4 years..............................	4.6	4.8	4.3	5.9	...
5 to 9 years.........................	18.2	27.4	21.9	11.8	...
10 to 18 years.......................	8.2	23.4	5.9	1.7	...
Median spacing..................years..	2.1	4.6	2.2	1.9	...
SECOND BIRTH (Spacing since first birth)					
Number of women......................	39,700	...	18,800	11,600	9,300
Percent...........................	100.0	...	100.0	100.0	...
Less than 1 year......................	0.8	...	0.5	...	...
1 year...............................	11.6	...	6.4	15.5	...
2 years..............................	17.9	...	14.9	13.8	...
3 years..............................	19.6	...	19.1	18.1	...
4 years..............................	18.9	...	16.5	23.3	...
5 to 9 years.........................	22.9	...	27.1	25.9	...
10 to 18 years.......................	8.3	...	15.4	3.4	...
Median spacing..................years..	3.5	...	4.0	3.6	...
THIRD TO FIFTH BIRTH (Spacing since prior birth)					
Number of women......................	33,700	...	...	11,700	22,000
Percent...........................	100.0	...	...	100.0	100.0
Less than 1 year......................	1.8	...	...	4.3	0.5
1 year...............................	8.9	...	...	7.7	9.5
2 years..............................	27.9	...	...	15.4	34.5
3 years..............................	13.6	...	...	11.1	15.0
4 years..............................	13.6	...	...	12.8	14.1
5 to 9 years.........................	28.8	...	...	39.3	23.2
10 to 18 years.......................	5.3	...	...	9.4	3.2
Median spacing..................years..	3.3	...	...	4.4	2.9

[1] Years between marriage and birth of first child and between births of successive children. See text for explanation of unconventional nature of intervals shown.

Source: Derived from the 1950 Census of Population, special hand count of machine listings of a subsample of C cards for women with all children present in the household.

CHAPTER 9

THE FERTILITY OF COHORTS OF NATIVE
WHITE WOMEN

A. What is meant by cohort fertility

Attention will be focused in this chapter on the reproductive history of certain groups of women as they live through the childbearing period. These groups will be compared with respect to their lifetime fertility and also with respect to their fertility up to and during younger ages. Two of the measures of fertility which will be used are very similar to two which have been used in preceding chapters, namely, cumulative birth rates up to various ages and distributions of women by the number of children they have borne. Here, however, we shall not be restricted to rates and distributions based on data collected in decennial censuses or in the Census Bureau's Current Population Surveys, which are available only for 1910, 1940, 1950, 1952, and 1954. Instead, we shall consider those derived from annual numbers of births for each year since 1910 and related census data.

The groups of women to be considered are those born in successive years, and will be referred to as birth cohorts. For example, the girls born during the twelve months centering on January 1, 1900, make up the birth cohort of 1900, those born during the twelve months centering on January 1, 1901, make up the birth cohort of 1901, etc. Most of these girl babies grew up and had one or more babies themselves. The consideration of the various relationships between the number of the original girl babies (or their survivors at a given age) and the number of babies they bear is the essence of cohort fertility analysis. For some countries it is possible to classify women by the year in which they marry and to study the fertility of marriage cohorts. For the United States, however, the information needed to measure and analyze fertility year by year is available for birth cohorts but not for marriage cohorts. From the standpoint of collecting data on the number of marriages by age, race, and marital status of bride and on the number of births by duration of marriage, the United States has been a backward country. Since only birth cohorts can be considered in this chapter, the term "birth cohort" will be shortened to "cohort" in most places.

The chief advantage of fertility rates for real cohorts is that they show changes in the number of children actually borne per woman—information which is not yielded by annual birth rates as traditionally used. This information is important because long-run population growth is influenced primarily by changes in the lifetime births per woman, and short-run growth by changes in the age at which women bear their first child, their second child, etc. The effects of these two variables on annual fertility are so closely intermingled that there have been wide differences of opinion as to the extent to which the large changes in annual birth rates and numbers of births in recent decades have been due to long-term changes in the size of completed families and to differences in timing (for example, the postponement of marriage and childbearing during the great depression of the 1930's, and the reduction in age at marriage and at the starting of families after World War II). Up to 1945 (or thereabouts) the large decrease in fertility rates from the 1920's to the 1930's was commonly interpreted as being merely the continuation of the long-time downward trend in the average number of children per family. We know now, however, that the low birth rates of the 1930's were, to an important degree, caused by the postponement of marriages and births to later years. To be sure, many of the women who were bearing children in the 1930's had smaller families than the women belonging to preceding generations, but the decline in average family size was substantially less than the annual fertility rates of the period seemed to suggest.

In the United States today we are faced with a set of circumstances which differs greatly from that of the 1930's, but precautions must still be observed if a repetition of error in the interpretation of current fertility trends is to be avoided. Now the appropriate questions are: (a) To what extent is the size of completed families increasing and (b) how much of the high level of fertility since the end of World War II arises from the fact that women nowadays are marrying and having babies at younger ages than did the women of earlier generations? These questions, as well as others relating to past trends in fertility, will be discussed in this chapter after a brief review of the concepts and measures employed in cohort analysis.

How cohort fertility is measured. Nearly all the basic data used in computing cohort fertility tables are provided by the National Office of Vital Statistics and the Bureau of the Census. The National Office of Vital Statistics has published tables for each year since 1917 which show the number of births occurring in the expanding Birth Registration Area, classified by color, nativity and age of mother, and order of birth of child. It has also prepared tables on the completeness of birth registration in years since 1935. Each decennial census shows the number of women by color, nativity, age, and marital status, and those of 1910, 1940, and 1950 provide data on ever-married women by number of children ever born. Similar information for a sample of the population comes from the Current Population Survey for certain years.

The procedures followed in preparing cohort fertility tables are explained in some detail in Appendix B, and the validity of the results is also discussed. Only summary statements will be made here. Because the basic data are biased in varying degree, or are incomplete, it was necessary to adjust them and to make estimates to fill the gaps. In general, the adjustments and estimates are small for recent years and larger for earlier years. The next step was to compute annual birth rates by order of birth for each cohort in each year from 1917 to 1954, and for some cohorts in years from 1910 to 1916. The rates for 1950 are shown in table 111. These rates are very similar to the conventional central age-specific rates by birth order, being based on the annual numbers of births to native white women by age of mother and order of birth of child, and the midyear numbers of native white women by cohort. Ages 14 and 49 were taken as the youngest and oldest ages at which women could bear children, and the very small numbers of births reported at ages below 14 or above 49 were treated as occurring at these ages.[1] The next step was to bring together the central rates for each cohort at different ages and in different years. The results for the cohorts of 1931, 1906, and 1881 are shown in table 112.

Adding the appropriate annual rates gave the cumulative rates desired for the cohorts of 1896 to 1940. For example, the sum of the central rates for the cohort of 1931 in 1945, 1946, and each subsequent year through 1954 is the cumulative birth rate by age 24 (by 1955) and represents the number of babies borne by each 1,000 women in the 1931 cohort who live to exact age 24, which they reach (on an average) at midnight of December 31, 1954. (See table 113.) Similarly, successive sums of the annual rates for the cohort of 1906 in each year from 1920 through 1954 are cumulative rates up to each age from 16 (reached on January 1, 1922) to 49 (reached on January 1, 1955). For the cohorts from 1894 back to 1871, cumulative birth rates by 1910 were based chiefly on the 1910 Census data. Rates by subsequent years were obtained by adding the annual rates mentioned above to the rates by 1910 and by making minor adjustments.

Although a precise evaluation of the accuracy of the cumulative rates for the women in each cohort is not possible, the tests which have been made indicate that the latest rates for all births to most of the recent cohorts probably are within 2 percent of the true values and that few of the rates for other cohorts diverge by more than 5 percent. Rates for all births probably are slightly more accurate than those for births by order, because positive errors for certain orders may be offset by negative errors for others. First birth rates probably are slightly too large, and those for other orders slightly too small, because some of the women who have an illegitimate first birth wish to conceal this event when their first *legitimate* birth occurs and report it, too, as a first birth. Aside from this bias, it is probable that larger allowances for possible errors should be

---

[1] Ages 14 and 49 were chosen as limits for cohort fertility tables before the preparation of this monograph was begun. Ages 15 and 44 are used as limits in other chapters.

made for the higher order births than those of lower order. The absolute size of the errors is of primary importance when the rates are being interpreted in terms of population growth. In contrast, when the rates are used primarily for comparing cohorts and determining trends, as in this chapter, the relative accuracy of the rates for different cohorts is more important than the size of the absolute errors. Whereas the rates for earlier cohorts and years may not be quite as close to the true values as those for later cohorts and years, there is now no way of determining whether the errors are all plus, all minus, or shift from one to the other. It appears, however, that the computed rates come sufficiently close to the true values so that they can be used with a high degree of confidence both in considering population growth and in comparing the fertility of cohorts and determining fertility trends.

TABLE 111.—BIRTHS BY ORDER OF BIRTH PER 1,000 NATIVE WHITE WOMEN, BY AGE AND COHORT: 1950

[These are central rates based on the number of registered births, adjusted for underregistration, and the number of women on July 1, 1950, as estimated from the 1950 Census after adjusting for incomplete enumeration and misstatement of age, and for deaths between the census date and July 1. For a more detailed explanation, see Appendix B]

Current age	Cohort	All births	Order or birth							
			First	Second	Third	Fourth	Fifth	Sixth	Seventh	Eighth and higher
14[1] ....1936..		1.8	1.8	...	...	...	...	...	...	...
15 ....1935..		7.9	7.4	0.5	(2)	(2)	...	...	...	...
16 ....1934..		27.4	24.9	2.3	0.2	(2)	...	...	...	...
17 ....1933..		59.9	50.5	8.6	0.7	0.1	...	...	...	...
18 ....1932..		101.1	76.5	21.5	2.8	0.3	...	...	...	...
19 ....1931..		143.0	96.1	38.7	7.3	0.9	...	...	...	...
20 ....1930..		169.9	97.6	55.0	14.3	2.4	0.5	0.1	(2)	(2)
21 ....1929..		185.8	92.6	65.7	21.8	4.8	0.8	0.1	(2)	(2)
22 ....1928..		193.0	84.3	71.5	27.6	7.4	1.7	0.4	0.1	(2)
23 ....1927..		196.5	74.8	74.4	32.5	10.7	3.0	0.8	0.2	0.1
24 ....1926..		191.6	63.8	73.2	35.2	13.2	4.3	1.3	0.4	0.2
25 ....1925..		186.2	54.3	71.5	36.6	15.0	5.7	2.1	0.7	0.3
26 ....1924..		174.8	45.0	66.0	36.5	15.9	6.9	2.9	1.1	0.5
27 ....1923..		161.8	36.7	60.0	35.9	16.1	7.4	3.4	1.5	0.8
28 ....1922..		154.2	30.8	54.7	35.6	17.2	8.2	4.2	2.1	1.4
29 ....1921..		140.2	24.8	47.1	33.5	17.0	8.5	4.8	2.6	1.9
30 ....1920..		130.5	21.5	41.1	31.6	16.9	8.7	5.0	2.9	2.8
31 ....1919..		110.0	17.0	33.3	26.8	14.6	7.9	4.6	2.8	3.0
32 ....1918..		99.9	13.9	27.9	24.5	14.2	7.7	4.8	3.0	3.9
33 ....1917..		86.2	11.1	22.4	20.7	12.9	7.2	4.6	3.0	4.3
34 ....1916..		77.7	9.7	18.5	18.0	12.1	7.0	4.5	3.0	4.9
35 ....1915..		67.3	8.1	15.0	15.0	10.4	6.3	4.1	3.0	5.4
36 ....1914..		58.5	6.8	12.0	12.4	8.9	5.8	4.0	2.8	5.8
37 ....1913..		49.7	5.5	9.3	10.0	7.6	5.0	3.5	2.6	6.2
38 ....1912..		43.1	4.4	7.6	7.9	6.2	4.5	3.3	2.5	6.7
39 ....1911..		34.3	3.5	5.5	6.0	4.8	3.5	2.6	2.1	6.3
40 ....1910..		25.8	2.5	3.7	4.0	3.5	2.7	2.0	1.7	5.7
41 ....1909..		16.8	1.5	2.2	2.4	2.1	1.8	1.4	1.2	4.2
42 ....1908..		13.7	1.1	1.5	1.8	1.7	1.5	1.1	0.9	4.1
43 ....1907..		8.3	0.6	0.9	0.9	0.9	0.8	0.7	0.6	2.9
44 ....1906..		4.5	0.4	0.4	0.4	0.4	0.4	0.4	0.3	1.8
45 ....1905..		2.7	0.2	0.2	0.2	0.3	0.3	0.2	0.2	1.1
46 ....1904..		1.3	0.1	0.1	0.1	0.1	0.1	0.1	0.1	0.6
47 ....1903..		0.4	(2)	(2)	(2)	0.1	(2)	(2)	(2)	0.3
48 ....1902..		0.1	(2)	(2)	(2)	(2)	(2)	(2)	(2)	0.1
49[1] ....1901..		0.1	(2)	(2)	(2)	(2)	(2)	(2)	(2)	0.1

[1] Ages 14 and 49 are the first and last for which rates are computed. Births reported as occurring to women younger than 14 or older than 49 are combined with births reported for women of these ages.

[2] 0.05 or less.

Source: Scripps Foundation for Research in Population Problems.

TABLE **112.**—ANNUAL BIRTH RATES, BY AGE AND ORDER, FOR SELECTED COHORTS OF NATIVE WHITE WOMEN

[These are central rates like those in table 111. The calculations were carried to one decimal place; each figure was rounded independently]

Current age	Year	All births	Order of birth							
			First	Second	Third	Fourth	Fifth	Sixth	Seventh	Eighth and higher
Cohort of 1931										
14[1]	1945	1	1	···	···	···	···	···	···	···
15	1946	4	4	(2)	(2)	(2)	···	···	···	···
16	1947	23	22	1	(2)	(2)	···	···	···	···
17	1948	59	52	7	(2)	(2)	···	···	···	···
18	1949	103	79	21	2	(2)	···	···	···	···
19	1950	143	96	39	7	1	···	···	···	···
20	1951	184	108	56	16	3	1	(2)	(2)	(2)
21	1952	208	102	72	26	6	1	(2)	(2)	(2)
22	1953	220	90	81	35	11	3	(2)	(2)	(2)
23	1954	234	80	86	45	17	5	1	(2)	(2)
Cohort of 1906										
14[1]	1920	3	3	(2)	···	···	···	···	···	···
15	1921	4	4	(2)	···	···	···	···	···	···
16	1922	17	17	1	(2)	···	···	···	···	···
17	1923	43	38	5	(2)	(2)	···	···	···	···
18	1924	86	70	14	2	(2)	···	···	···	···
19	1925	118	83	29	5	1	···	···	···	···
20	1926	126	73	40	11	2	(2)	(2)	(2)	···
21	1927	140	70	46	18	4	1	(2)	(2)	(2)
22	1928	141	62	46	23	8	2	(2)	(2)	(2)
23	1929	140	54	44	27	11	3	1	(2)	(2)
24	1930	142	48	42	28	15	6	2	(2)	(2)
25	1931	131	40	38	26	16	7	3	1	(2)
26	1932	121	33	33	24	16	9	4	1	1
27	1933	108	26	29	21	15	9	5	2	1
28	1934	111	24	28	21	16	11	6	3	2
29	1935	98	20	24	18	14	10	7	3	2
30	1936	94	18	22	17	13	10	7	4	3
31	1937	79	15	18	14	10	8	6	4	4
32	1938	79	13	17	13	10	8	7	5	6
33	1939	68	11	14	12	9	7	5	4	6
34	1940	63	9	12	10	8	6	5	4	8
35	1941	57	8	11	9	7	6	5	4	8
36	1942	53	7	9	8	7	5	4	4	8
37	1943	50	6	9	8	6	5	4	3	8
38	1944	46	5	7	7	6	5	4	3	10
39	1945	37	4	5	6	5	4	3	3	8
40	1946	28	3	4	4	3	3	2	2	7
41	1947	19	2	3	2	2	2	2	1	5
42	1948	14	1	2	2	2	1	1	1	5
43	1949	8	1	1	1	1	1	1	1	3
44	1950	4	(2)	(2)	(2)	(2)	(2)	(2)	(2)	2
45	1951	3	(2)	(2)	(2)	(2)	(2)	(2)	(2)	1
46	1952	1	(2)	(2)	(2)	(2)	(2)	(2)	(2)	1
47	1953	(2)	(2)	(2)	(2)	(2)	(2)	(2)	(2)	(2)
48	1954	(2)	(2)	(2)	(2)	(2)	(2)	(2)	(2)	(2)
Cohort of 1881										
36	1917	92	5	8	11	11	12	12	11	22
37	1918	78	4	6	8	9	10	10	9	22
38	1919	79	4	5	7	8	9	10	10	26
39	1920	63	2	4	5	6	8	7	7	24
40	1921	54	2	3	4	5	6	5	6	23
41	1922	33	1	2	2	3	3	3	4	15
42	1923	30	1	1	2	2	3	3	3	15
43	1924	21	(2)	1	1	1	2	2	2	12
44	1925	12	(2)	(2)	(2)	1	1	1	1	8
45	1926	8	(2)	(2)	(2)	(2)	1	1	1	5
46	1927	4	(2)	(2)	(2)	(2)	(2)	1	1	2
47	1928	2	(2)	(2)	(2)	(2)	(2)	(2)	1	1
48	1929	1	(2)	(2)	(2)	(2)	(2)	(2)	(2)	1
49[1]	1930	1	(2)	(2)	(2)	(2)	(2)	(2)	(2)	1

[1] See footnote 1, table 111.

[2] 0.5 or less.

Source: Scripps Foundation for Research in Population Problems.

THE FERTILITY OF AMERICAN WOMEN

TABLE **113.**—CUMULATIVE BIRTH RATES, BY AGE AND ORDER, FOR SELECTED COHORTS OF NATIVE WHITE WOMEN

[The cumulative rates up to the beginning of age x for the cohorts of 1931 and 1906 are obtained by adding annual rates like those in table 111 for ages younger than x. Those for the cohort of 1881 are obtained by (a) estimating the cumulative rates by age 50 from data in the 1910 and 1940 Censuses and rates for the cohorts of 1901 and later years, and (b) subtracting the rates in table 112 at ages x and older. These rates are preliminary estimates, subject to minor change. See also table 111, footnote 1. The calculations were carried to one decimal place; each figure was rounded independently]

Up to the beginning of--		All births	Order of birth							
Age	Year		First	Second	Third	Fourth	Fifth	Sixth	Seventh	Eighth and higher
Cohort of 1931										
15.............1946..		1	1	...	...	...	...	...	...	...
16.............1947..		6	6	(^{1})	...	...	...	...	...	...
17.............1948..		29	27	2	(^{1})	...	...	...	...	...
18.............1949..		88	79	8	1	...	...	...	...	...
19.............1950..		190	158	29	3	(^{1})	...	...	...	...
20.............1951..		334	254	68	10	1	...	...	...	...
21.............1952..		517	362	124	26	4	1	(^{1})	(^{1})	...
22.............1953..		726	464	196	52	10	2	(^{1})	(^{1})	...
23.............1954..		945	554	277	87	21	5	1	(^{1})	(^{1})
24.............1955..		1,180	634	363	132	38	10	2	(^{1})	(^{1})
Cohort of 1906										
15.............1921..		3	3	...	...	...	...	...	...	...
16.............1922..		7	6	(^{1})	...	...	...	...	...	...
17.............1923..		24	23	1	...	...	...	...	...	...
18.............1924..		67	61	6	(^{1})	...	...	...	...	...
19.............1925..		153	131	20	2	(^{1})	...	...	...	...
20.............1926..		271	214	49	7	1	...	...	...	...
21.............1927..		398	287	89	18	3	(^{1})	(^{1})	...	...
22.............1928..		537	357	136	36	7	1	(^{1})	(^{1})	...
23.............1929..		679	419	182	59	15	3	1	(^{1})	(^{1})
24.............1930..		819	472	226	86	26	6	2	(^{1})	(^{1})
25.............1931..		961	521	268	114	42	12	3	1	(^{1})
26.............1932..		1,092	561	306	139	58	20	6	2	1
27.............1933..		1,213	593	340	164	74	29	10	3	1
28.............1934..		1,321	619	368	185	90	38	14	5	2
29.............1935..		1,432	644	396	206	105	49	21	7	4
30.............1936..		1,530	664	420	224	119	59	27	11	6
31.............1937..		1,624	682	441	241	132	69	34	15	10
32.............1938..		1,702	697	459	254	142	77	40	19	14
33.............1939..		1,781	711	476	268	152	85	47	24	20
34.............1940..		1,849	721	490	279	161	91	52	28	26
35.............1941..		1,912	730	503	290	169	98	57	32	33
36.............1942..		1,969	739	514	299	176	103	62	36	41
37.............1943..		2,022	746	523	307	182	108	66	40	49
38.............1944..		2,071	752	532	315	189	113	70	43	58
39.............1945..		2,117	757	539	322	195	118	74	46	67
40.............1946..		2,154	760	544	328	199	122	77	48	75
41.............1947..		2,182	763	548	332	203	124	80	50	82
42.............1948..		2,201	765	550	334	205	126	81	52	87
43.............1949..		2,216	766	552	336	207	128	82	53	92
44.............1950..		2,224	767	553	337	208	128	83	54	95
45.............1951..		2,229	767	553	337	208	129	83	54	97
46.............1952..		2,231	768	553	338	208	129	84	54	98
47.............1953..		2,232	768	553	338	208	129	84	54	98
48.............1954..		2,233	768	553	338	208	129	84	54	99
49.............1955..		2,233	768	553	338	208	129	84	54	99

^{1} 0.5 or less.

TABLE **113.**—CUMULATIVE BIRTH RATES, BY AGE AND ORDER, FOR SELECTED COHORTS OF
NATIVE WHITE WOMEN—Cont.

Up to the beginning of--		All births	Order of birth							
Age	Year		First	Second	Third	Fourth	Fifth	Sixth	Seventh	Eighth and higher
			Cohort of 1881							
36..............1917..		2,692	802	616	442	308	200	137	84	103
37..............1918..		2,784	807	624	453	319	212	149	95	125
38..............1919..		2,862	811	630	461	328	222	159	104	147
39..............1920..		2,941	815	635	468	336	231	169	114	173
40..............1921..		3,004	817	639	473	342	239	176	121	197
41..............1922..		3,058	819	642	477	347	245	181	127	220
42..............1923..		3,091	820	644	479	350	248	184	131	235
43..............1924..		3,121	821	645	481	352	251	187	134	250
44..............1925..		3,142	821	646	482	353	253	189	136	262
45..............1926..		3,154	821	646	482	354	254	190	137	270
46..............1927..		3,162	821	646	482	354	255	191	138	275
47..............1928..		3,166	821	646	482	354	255	192	139	277
48..............1929..		3,168	821	646	482	354	255	192	140	278
49..............1930..		3,169	821	646	482	354	255	192	140	279
50..............1931..		3,170	821	646	482	354	255	192	140	280

Source: Table 112.

Although tables for all women are most useful in some phases of fertility analysis, tables for ever-married women are needed for certain other purposes. In order to obtain them one should have accurate annual information about the number of first marriages by color or race, nativity, and age of bride, so that annual and cumulative marriage rates could be computed for the women in each cohort in the same way as cumulative birth rates. Unfortunately, the United States has lagged far behind many Western nations in collecting and tabulating annual data on marriages by characteristics of bride and groom, comparable to those which are provided for persons born or deceased. A beginning has been made in recent years,[2] but in order to determine what has taken place over a longer period, it is necessary to utilize other data. The results of marriage questions asked in some censuses and surveys are helpful but do not provide information for enough years. Thus, information on years married was obtained in 1910, 1948, and 1950; information on the age of women at first marriage was obtained in 1940 and in 1954; and information on the calendar year of marriage was obtained in 1953. Except in 1910, the data were obtained on a sample basis. Fortunately, one can easily compute reliable cumulative marriage rates for cohorts up to 1910, 1920, 1930, 1940, and 1950 from census data on marital status. Estimates for cumulative marriage rates up to 1915, 1925, 1935, and 1945, which are believed to be quite close to the true values, have been made by using these data, comparable data from the 1955 Current Population Survey, the annual numbers of marriages reported by the National Office of Vital Statistics, and the cumulative first birth rates of all women in cohort

[2] The National Office of Vital Statistics has published several detailed tables on marriages in each year since 1948, based on reports from a varying number of States. A Federal Marriage Registration Area consisting of 29 States, 4 Territories, and 1 city was established January 1, 1957. The National Office of Vital Statistics hopes that the remaining States will qualify within a few years.

tables.   The procedure which was followed is explained in Appendix B, section 3.

Since the cumulative marriage rate by age x is on a "per 1,000" basis, moving the decimal point three places to the left gives the proportion of ever-married women on a unit basis at age x.   Dividing the cumulative birth rates of all women of each age by the corresponding proportion married gives the cumulative birth rates for ever-married women.[3]   Although the results are believed to be highly reliable for 1955 and recent census years, and very close to the true values for other years, a slightly lower rating must be given to the figures showing the rise of the cumulative marriage rate and cumulative birth rates of ever-married women as cohorts live through a 5-year age interval.   For example, if the marriage rate of 476 for the cohorts of 1916–20 by ages 20–24 (obtained from the 1940 Census) is correct, but the estimated rate of 810 for these cohorts by ages 25–29 (by 1945) is too low by 1 percent (the correct figure is 818), the rise in the rate during the age interval is 342 instead of 334 and the understatement of the rise amounts to 2.4 percent.

The distribution by parity (number of children borne) of all the women (or of the ever-married women) in each cohort living to age x is useful information in fertility analysis and can be computed easily from the cumulative rates in cohort tables for births of successive orders.   For example, subtracting the cumulative second birth rate by age 20 from the cumulative first birth rate by that age for all women in the cohort of 1906 (214 minus 49 in table 113) and dividing by ten gives 16.5—the percentage of one-parity women in the cohort at exact age 20.   Similar subtractions give percentages for successively higher parities.   The percentage for zero parity is obtained for all women by subtracting the first birth rate from 1,000 and dividing by ten; it is 78.6 for the cohort of 1906 at exact age 20.   Parity distributions for ever-married women can be computed in a similar manner but with an additional step, namely, dividing by the proportion of ever-married women at the age in question.   The results are comparable with the parity distributions obtained from the census data on the number of children ever born.[4]

Another measure which is helpful in cohort analysis is the parity progression ratio.   As was indicated in Chapters 5 and 6 this ratio shows

---

[3] Because births are not tabulated by marital status of mother, it is necessary to assume that all women bearing a child by age x have been married by that age.   This assumption does not bias appreciably the cumulative rates by the older childbearing ages, because almost all of the women who have borne a child while single have married by these ages.   In contrast, rates at the youngest ages (15 and 16) are inflated substantially.   (See Appendix B, section 4.)

[4] The procedure here is the reverse of that followed with the census data on number of children ever born.   There the women are classified by the number of births each has had, the groups are counted, and percentage distributions by parity are computed directly.   The cumulative rate for all births is obtained by adding the reported numbers of children ever born to women of age x and dividing by the number of these women.   Cumulative rates for births of N order to women up to age x are secured later by adding the number of women of age x who are of N and each higher parity and dividing by the total number of women of age x.   The sum of the rates for births of each order is the same as the rate for all births mentioned above.

what proportion of the women of a given age who have reached parity N have moved on to parity N + 1 by bearing a child of order N + 1. Such ratios are computed conveniently for women of age x in a given cohort by dividing the cumulative rate for births of order N + 1 by the cumulative rate for births of order N. This is a type of cumulative parity-specific rate, since the births of order N + 1 up to age x are related to the women exposed to the risk of having such a birth, namely, the women who reached parity N prior to age x. Both parity distributions and parity progression ratios will be used in later sections of this chapter.

Still another useful measure available from cohort fertility tables is the age-parity-specific birth rate, which relates (a) the number of births of order N in year y to women aged x in the cohort of $y-x$ and (b) the number of women of cohort $y - x$ who were of parity N + 1 in year y. These rates were mentioned briefly in Chapter 3 but will not be utilized here.

Advantages of the cohort approach.   The cohort approach has certain definite advantages in fertility analysis.   One is that it provides an accurate and convenient way of measuring the extent to which the women of a given generation are replacing themselves and contributing to population growth.   The desirability of comparing the numbers of people in successive generations has long been recognized.   Previously, however, efforts centered on another way of using annual fertility rates, namely, putting together the rates for successive ages in a given period (commonly 1 to 5 years) in order to describe the lifetime experience of a hypothetical cohort of women.[5]   Gross reproduction rates, net reproduction rates, and intrinsic (or "true") rates of natural increase were obtained in this way.

The concepts involved have considerable theoretical value.   Furthermore, the rates obtained for the hypothetical cohorts of the base period are useful in comparisons of various groups of people, for each such rate shows in a single figure what a given set of age-specific birth and death rates would mean in terms of population growth *if that set of rates should continue for 50 to 100 years or more.*[6]   Their disadvantage is that they do not represent an actual situation, since no population has exactly the same set of age-specific birth and death rates for 10 years, let alone 50 or 100. As measures of the contribution of one real generation to the next, they are best suited for use with populations which have had stable sex-age-specific birth and death rates for several years and are likely to continue to have the same set of rates in the future, and are least suited for use with populations which have had, or are likely to have, important changes in these annual rates.   Unfortunately, very few (if any) of the countries col-

---

[5] The procedure was patterned after that commonly used in computing period life tables, that is, life tables based on mortality in 1 year or in a somewhat longer period (frequently 2 or 3 years).

[6] The number of years of unchanged age-specific birth and death rates which an actual population must have after a base year in order for its reproduction rates to reach the values for a hypothetical cohort of the base year varies with the age and sex composition of the population and the type of reproduction rate.   Fifty years of unchanged age-specific rates are commonly required for the net reproduction rate, and at least 100 years for the intrinsic rate of natural increase.   The gross reproduction rate is more theoretical, since it assumes that no women die during the reproductive ages.

lecting the basic data needed for net reproduction rates or intrinsic rates of natural increase fall in the former group. Substantial fluctuations in annual death rates are common in the countries which are less developed economically, and substantial changes in birth rates are common in the countries which are more developed.[7]

Gross reproduction rates for actual cohorts can be computed easily by multiplying each lifetime cumulative birth rate by the proportion of the babies that were female. Little use will be made of them here because the same intercohort comparisons can be made from lifetime cumulative rates, and comparing these rates with 2,058 serves the same purpose as comparing gross reproduction rates with 1,000.[8] Net reproduction rates can be computed for a few actual cohorts by utilizing cohort life tables in addition to cohort fertility tables and considering only the female births to the women of the first generation. Life tables for additional cohorts are needed before net rates can be used to advantage.

Cohort fertility rates are especially useful in measuring the extent to which changes have taken place in the "timing" of births, for example, in the average age at which women have their first baby, their second, etc. Major shifts of this nature are a relatively recent development in human history. Even today they are negligible in underdeveloped countries with large segments of the world's population, where year after year most young people marry at a given age which is fixed by local custom, and children arrive thereafter at fairly regular intervals which are governed largely by physiological factors. In contrast, in the United States and other countries where a large majority of fecund married couples try to plan the number and spacing of their children and achieve at least partial success, important changes have taken place not only in the age at which people marry but also in the length of the intervals between marriage and the first birth and between successive births. As will be shown in more detail in sections C and D of this chapter, these changes can cause wide fluctuations in annual birth rates even though the average number of children borne per woman living through the childbearing period remains constant. Cohort fertility tables are of much help in trying to "unscramble" the mixed influence of variations in the timing of births, and of increases or decreases in the size of completed family.

The cumulative rates for actual cohorts, together with the additions to these rates during various age intervals, are decidedly helpful in forming opinions regarding trends in fertility and population growth—the subject of Chapter 10. One reason is that, as just mentioned, they facilitate taking into account the changes in the timing of the births which may have occurred already or which may occur in the future. Other reasons are especially pertinent when preparing population projections for a period of

---

[7] The gross or net reproduction rate or the intrinsic rate of natural increase, as ordinarily computed, may imply impossible results for births of certain orders in periods when large fluctuations occur in annual rates. This is illustrated and discussed in section E.

[8] During recent years there have been approximately 1,000 girl babies among 2,058 of both sexes.

10 years or longer. The likelihood of making unreasonable assumptions about changes in the size of completed families is smaller if the cohort approach is utilized than if consideration is restricted to annual rates and their past trends. This was especially true in 1958, when the high annual birth rates since the end of World War II gave most observers an exaggerated impression of the increase which is to be expected in the average number of children borne per woman living to age 50. Moreover, when projections of the future course of fertility are made with the cohort approach, they can utilize the information which is beginning to be collected about the number of additional children expected by the couples that are currently able to have children.

Although the advantages of specific birth rates have long been recognized and rates which are specific for race (or nativity), sex, and age have been used commonly for many years, it was not until the cohort tables were developed that rates which are specific for order of birth and parity of woman could be computed for many years. The reason is that although information on the number of women of each parity was available from the 1910, 1940, and 1950 Censuses, it was difficult to prepare sufficiently reliable estimates of the number of women by parity by age for the various race and nativity groups in intercensal years. Age-parity-specific birth rates are especially useful in measuring changes in fertility from year to year and analyzing their relation to changes in conditions influencing annual fertility, because they take into account the previous childbearing experience of the women of each reproductive age.[9] The availability of these rates should facilitate making substantial additions to our knowledge regarding the relationships between the year-to-year changes in fertility and those in economic conditions and other factors. This does not mean that such rates as first births per 1,000 women aged 20 to 24 should be discarded; on the contrary, they are valuable and are available for many populations for which age-parity-specific rates cannot be obtained.[10] What it does mean is that age-parity-specific rates permit more detailed and accurate analyses of certain interrelationships than do the less specific rates.

Cohort fertility tables have one limitation in common with other indices of fertility, namely, they can measure past events but not those yet to come. Thus, the lifetime fertility of women in the cohorts of 1931–35, who were

---

[9] To illustrate what is involved, let us consider two populations, A and B, having in a given year the same number of married women of each age (each married the same number of years) and the same number of first births to married women of each age. The first impression may be that the fertility rate of these two groups of women must be the same in that year with respect to first births. Suppose, however, that the number of first births during the preceding 1 to 3 years was large in group A and small in B. It follows that by the year in question, group A had fewer zero-parity married women of each age than group B. Since the only women who can have a first birth in a given year are those who have not had one previously, a picture which is more useful in some ways is given when, age by age, the number of first births is related to the number of zero-parity women rather than to the total number of women. At the age used in this example, population A has higher age-parity-specific rates for first births than population B.

[10] Such rates are not order-specific rates, because all women are used in the denominator regardless of whether they already have had a birth of this order or one of the preceding order.

aged 20–24 at the beginning of 1955 and had more than half of the reproductive period ahead of them, will not be known exactly until after
1980 because it depends so much on their annual fertility during 1957 to
1980, which is not yet known.   While this limitation of cohort tables cannot be completely overcome, it can be reduced somewhat by estimating
fertility during the latter part of the reproductive period on the basis of
the previous experience of earlier cohorts.   For example, one could be
fairly certain in 1956 that the cumulative rate of the cohorts of 1911–15,
which was 2,224 by ages 40–44 on January 1, 1955, would rise to between 2,250 and 2,280 by ages 50–54 on January 1, 1965.   Similarly, it
is quite probable that the cumulative rate of the cohorts of 1916–20,
which was 2,278 by ages 35–39 on January 1, 1955, will be between
2,400 and 2,600 by ages 50–54 on January 1, 1970.

**The similarity of measures of fertility from cohort tables and
from census data.**   The cumulative birth rates and distributions of
women by parity, which are provided by the cohort fertility tables and are
discussed in this chapter, are very similar to, but not exactly the same as,
those which are provided by the census data on number of children ever
born per 1,000 women and are presented in other chapters.   From a
conceptual standpoint, the main difference is that the number of children
ever born per 1,000 women living to a given age as reported in the census
reflects the experience of these living women and no others, but as derived
from the cohort tables it is influenced slightly by the experience of the
women in the cohort who die before reaching the age being considered.
The implications of this difference are discussed in Appendix B, section 2.
Fortunately, it has little if any numerical effect on the rates and parity
distributions.

On the whole, the cumulative fertility rates from these cohort fertility
tables appear somewhat lower at the younger childbearing ages, and very
slightly higher at the older ages, than the cumulative rates from census data
which are presented in other chapters.   The main reason for the discrepancy at the younger ages is the difference in the age groupings that are
used; a very minor reason is the difference in the time periods.   Both may
be illustrated by considering the cumulative rate for all births to women
in the age group labeled 15–19 as of 1950.   The rates from the census
series are based on the children born prior to April 1, 1950, to women
who, on that date, had passed exact age 15 but had not attained exact age
20, and whose median age was approximately 17.5.   In contrast, the rates
from the cohort tables which are used here for women aged 15 to 19 in
1950 are the average of the rates for five cohorts, whose women on January 1, 1950, on a life table basis were at exact ages 15, 16, 17, 18, and
19, and had a median age of approximately 17.   Stated differently, the
rates from census data exclude the small number of births to women aged
14.50 to 14.99 but include the large number of births to women aged
19.50 to 19.99; the reverse is true for the cohort rates in this chapter.   The

difference in the dates (January 1 and April 1, 1950) in this example tends to make the census rates at ages 15–19 very slightly larger than those from the cohort tables because of the upward trend of fertility after World War II.

By making appropriate weighted averages of rates for different cohorts it is possible to obtain rates which correspond almost exactly to the census-based rates with respect to age and date. When this is done (as in Appendix B, section 4) one finds that those from the cohort tables usually exceed the others by small amounts. There are two factors which tend to cause such differences: (a) The adjustments for the incomplete registration of births are larger than those for the incomplete enumeration of women (except in recent years), and (b) the cohort tables are based on all births, whereas the census rates are restricted to births to women reported as having married (because the census enumerators were instructed not to ask about births to women reported as single). On the other hand, the rates from the 1940 Census have an upward bias compared with those from cohort tables, because the former are based on the ever-married women for whom the number of children ever born was reported and exclude the ever-married women for whom no report was made. The Bureau of the Census has evidence that these excluded women had been less fertile than the others.[11]

In most cases the relative excess of the rates from cohort tables is slightly larger for first births at younger ages than at older ages, and for first births than higher order births at any age. This excess is probably due in part to a slight bias in the reported order of registered births which was mentioned earlier, namely, the reporting of two first births by some of the women whose first birth is illegitimate. Readers who wish a a more detailed discussion of these problems are referred to Appendix B, sections 1 and 4.

The differences between rates derived from census data and cohort tables have little effect on the discussion in this chapter but should be kept in mind if comparisons are made between the rates cited in this chapter and those cited in other chapters.

Limitation to native white women in groups of cohorts. This chapter is limited to the fertility of cohorts of native white women; nothing will be said about foreign-born white women, all white women, non-white women, or all women. Cohort fertility tables were prepared first for native white women partly because more accurate data are available for these women than for others. The census enumeration of women and the registration of births are more nearly complete, and the reporting of age in both cases is more accurate, for white women than for nonwhite women. Differences in these respects between native white and foreign-born white women probably are quite small (or even negligible),

---

[11] *1940 Census of Population, Differential Fertility 1940 and 1910,* Women by Number of Children Ever Born, p. 409.

but estimates of the number of women by age in intercensal years can be made more accurately for the native than for the foreign-born group because the number moving into or out of the United States year by year is substantially smaller numerically, and much smaller proportionally, for the former than for the latter.

The other main reason for restricting the chapter to native white women is that they have been a more homogeneous group with respect to fertility during past decades than have all white women or all women. Both of the latter groups include the foreign-born women, who were much more numerous in the first quarter of this century than now, and whose birth rates at that time were substantially larger than those of native white women. During more recent decades the number of foreign-born women of reproductive age has decreased both absolutely and relatively, and the country of origin has changed—in both cases in part as a result of the immigration legislation developed after World War I. The reduction in quantity has lessened the relative influence of the fertility of foreign-born white women and lowered the birth rates of all white women and all women. In addition, the quota system has reduced the movement from the high fertility countries of southern and eastern Europe, and aging has depressed the birth rates of the women who arrived before World War I. Because of these changes the decrease in annual birth rates from 1910 to 1935 was substantially larger for all women, and for all white women, than for native white women. In considering fertility trends, therefore, it is helpful to concentrate on the experience of native white women—a much more homogeneous group than the other two mentioned and now including a large majority (85 percent) of all women of childbearing age.

In most cases cohorts will be considered in groups of five, for example, the cohorts of 1901–05, rather than singly. This is done in part to increase the accuracy of the comparisons, because it is probable that the minor discrepancies in one direction which may exist in the figures for one cohort will be partially or fully balanced by those in the opposite direction for one or more of the other cohorts in the group. The main reason, however, is to reduce the number of comparisons.

In presenting rates and distributions for groups of cohorts it is desirable to deal either with the same ages for all of the cohorts in a given group (in which case the calendar years when the age is reached will differ) or with the same calendar years (in which case the ages reached by the cohorts in a group will differ). For example, the first plan would show the cumulative birth rate of the cohorts of 1921–25 up to age 30—or to 1951–55—that is, the average of the rate for the cohort of 1921 by 1951, the cohort of 1922 by 1952, and so on, up to the cohort of 1925 by 1955. In contrast, the second plan would show the cumulative birth rate of the cohorts of 1921–25 up to 1955—or to ages 30–34—that is, the average of the rate for the 1925 cohort by age 30, the 1924 cohort by age 31, and so on, back to the 1921 cohort by age 34. Because there have been such large variations in annual fertility during recent decades it seems preferable to use the second plan in order to deal with the same calendar years for all cohorts in a group and let age vary within a 5-year range.

B. Are families becoming larger?

In discussing this question it is very helpful to consider various age groups of women separately, because of the striking differences between developments by younger and older ages.

More childbearing by younger women. Much has been said and written about the upsurge of annual birth rates and numbers of births during the first 2 years after the end of World War II, and the high levels maintained during 1948 to 1956. It is not surprising, therefore, to see that the cumulative birth rate of native white women by ages 15–19 is much higher for recent groups of cohorts than for any of the earlier groups that we know about. This rate is fairly uniform among the cohorts of 1891–95 to 1926–30, the largest being 51 per 1,000 for the 1906–10 group and the smallest, 41 for the 1916–20 group. From 1945 to 1955, however, it jumped about 75 percent. In the cohorts of 1926–30 there were approximately 44 births per 1,000 women up to ages 15–19 (by 1945); 5 years later the comparable figure for the cohorts of 1931–35 was 67, and 10 years later (on January 1, 1955) it was 77 for the cohorts of 1936–40. (See the top deck of table 114.) Nearly all the births by these ages are first births; consequently, the recent increase of the rate for first births has been about as large as that for all births. The rate for second births, which is small, has more than doubled.

The magnitude of the postwar "baby boom" is also reflected strikingly by the cumulative birth rate up to ages 20–24. Among the women in the cohorts of 1886–90, who reached these ages on January 1, 1910, there had been approximately 568 births per 1,000 women. Among subsequent cohorts this rate declined somewhat irregularly to a low of about 454 for the cohorts of 1911–15 (by 1935) and remained at about the same figure for the cohorts of 1916–20 (by 1940). Then, after rising to 520 for the cohorts of 1921–25 (by 1945), it shot up to a record-breaking 789 for the cohorts of 1931–35 (by 1955). This figure is about 220 points or 39 percent larger than that of the earliest group which can be considered here (cohorts of 1886–90). If the cumulative rate up to ages 20–24 were available for each prior cohort as far back as 1800, it is possible that some would exceed 789, but there is no assurance that this would be the case.

Changes in the cumulative rates for first, second, and third births by ages 20–24 have been similar in direction to those for all births, but on somewhat different scales. By far the largest numerical change is the rise in the first birth rate from a low of 300 for the 1911–15 cohorts to 479 for the 1931–35 group. Much larger on a percentage basis, however, is the jump of the cumulative rate for third births from 29 for the cohorts of 1916–20 to 67 for those of 1931–35—up 130 percent in 15 years! Changes for second births are intermediate in size.

TABLE **114.**—CUMULATIVE BIRTH RATES, BY ORDER OF BIRTH, UP TO SELECTED EXACT AGES AND DATES, FOR GROUPS OF COHORTS OF NATIVE WHITE WOMEN

[These cumulative rates are averages of rates like those in table 113. The rates for the cohorts of 1896–1900 and earlier are preliminary estimates, subject to minor changes. See table 113, headnote]

Cohorts of--	Jan. 1 of--	All births	First	Second	Third	Fourth	Fifth	Sixth	Seventh	Eighth and higher
						Order of birth				
Exact ages 15 to 19[1]										
1936-40	1955..	77	65	11	1	([2])	...	...	...	...
1931-35	1950..	67	57	9	1	([2])	...	...	...	...
1926-30	1945..	44	39	5	1	([2])	...	...	...	...
1921-25	1940..	44	39	5	([2])	([2])	...	...	...	...
1916-20	1935..	41	36	4	([2])	([2])	...	...	...	...
1911-15	1930..	49	43	5	([2])	([2])	...	...	...	...
1906-10	1925..	51	45	5	([2])	([2])	...	...	...	...
1901-05	1920..	43	38	5	([2])	([2])	...	...	...	...
1896-1900	1915..	49	43	5	([2])	([2])	...	...	...	...
1891-95	1910..	50	44	6	([2])	([2])	...	...	...	...
Exact ages 20 to 24[1]										
1931-35	1955..	789	479	222	67	17	4	1	([2])	([2])
1926-30	1950..	636	427	159	39	9	2	([2])	([2])	([2])
1921-25	1945..	520	348	125	36	9	2	([2])	([2])	([2])
1916-20	1940..	453	308	108	29	7	1	([2])	([2])	([2])
1911-15	1935..	454	300	112	32	8	2	([2])	([2])	([2])
1906-10	1930..	526	340	133	40	10	2	1	([2])	([2])
1901-05	1925..	560	358	144	44	11	2	1	([2])	([2])
1896-1900	1920..	533	339	138	44	10	2	([2])	([2])	([2])
1891-95	1915..	557	349	146	48	12	2	([2])	([2])	([2])
1886-90	1910..	568	349	151	50	14	3	([2])	([2])	([2])
Exact ages 25 to 29[1]										
1926-30	1955..	1,642	757	519	233	87	30	10	3	2
1921-25	1950..	1,389	715	415	163	60	22	8	3	1
1916-20	1945..	1,188	621	337	140	57	22	8	3	1
1911-15	1940..	1,064	555	293	127	55	22	8	3	1
1906-10	1935..	1,149	567	320	151	69	28	10	3	2
1901-05	1930..	1,275	604	357	178	83	34	13	4	2
1896-1900	1925..	1,331	618	373	191	91	37	14	5	2
1891-95	1920..	1,335	619	372	194	91	37	15	5	2
1886-90	1915..	1,417	629	389	220	109	46	17	5	2
1881-85	1910..	1,453	632	394	228	119	52	19	6	3
Exact ages 30 to 34[1]										
1921-25	1955..	2,126	845	648	346	158	69	32	15	12
1916-20	1950..	1,857	789	554	274	126	60	29	14	11
1911-15	1945..	1,638	715	462	230	115	59	30	15	12
1906-10	1940..	1,639	689	445	238	129	69	37	18	14
1901-05	1935..	1,795	704	478	277	159	88	48	23	17
1896-1900	1930..	1,938	724	510	310	183	105	57	29	20
1891-95	1925..	2,016	742	521	326	198	113	62	31	23
1886-90	1920..	2,076	747	533	340	209	118	68	35	26
1881-85	1915..	2,175	757	544	362	230	136	76	40	30
1876-80	1910..	2,282	759	545	380	256	163	95	48	36
Exact ages 35 to 39[1]										
1916-20	1955..	2,278	839	653	376	195	99	53	29	35
1911-15	1950..	2,046	782	567	316	168	91	53	30	38
1906-10	1945..	1,987	748	524	299	172	100	61	36	46
1901-05	1940..	2,112	745	533	327	201	123	78	47	58
1896-1900	1935..	2,300	760	563	366	234	149	97	60	71
1891-95	1930..	2,448	780	581	393	260	168	111	69	86
1886-90	1925..	2,567	791	597	414	280	184	125	79	98
1881-85	1920..	2,707	802	615	438	305	204	140	90	112
1876-80	1915..	2,873	809	630	464	335	235	162	103	135
1871-75	1910..	3,051	812	632	486	367	270	192	125	167

See footnotes at end of table.

TABLE **114.**—CUMULATIVE BIRTH RATES, BY ORDER OF BIRTH, UP TO SELECTED EXACT AGES AND DATES, FOR GROUPS OF COHORTS OF NATIVE WHITE WOMEN—Cont.

Cohorts of--	Jan. 1 of--	All births	Order of birth							
			First	Second	Third	Fourth	Fifth	Sixth	Seventh	Eighth and higher
			Exact ages 40 to 44[1]							
1911-15...........1955..		2,224	799	597	350	196	111	66	40	64
1906-10...........1950..		2,174	770	557	331	196	118	75	47	79
1901-05...........1945..		2,274	761	554	348	219	140	93	60	100
1896-1900.........1940..		2,473	770	579	384	254	168	115	76	125
1891-95...........1935..		2,656	791	597	414	283	191	133	91	156
1886-90...........1930..		2,828	803	616	440	309	213	154	106	186
1881-85...........1925..		3,010	816	636	467	337	238	174	123	218
1876-80...........1920..		3,206	824	654	494	367	265	199	144	260
1871-75...........1915..		3,424	828	662	521	399	300	231	171	312
			Exact ages 45 to 49[1]							
1906-10...........1955..		2,209	773	561	335	200	122	78	50	89
1901-05...........1950..		2,313	764	557	352	223	143	96	63	114
1896-1900.........1945..		2,510	772	581	387	257	172	119	81	143
1891-95...........1940..		2,703	792	599	417	286	195	138	96	180
1886-90...........1935..		2,887	805	618	443	313	218	159	113	217
1881-85...........1930..		3,084	817	639	471	342	244	182	131	258
1876-80...........1925..		3,292	826	657	498	372	273	207	153	307
1871-75...........1920..		3,515	830	666	526	405	308	239	181	360
			Exact ages 50 to 54[1]							
1901-05...........1955..		2,315	764	557	352	224	144	96	63	115
1896-1900.........1950..		2,512	772	581	387	257	172	119	81	144
1891-95...........1945..		2,705	792	599	417	286	195	138	96	182
1886-90...........1940..		2,891	805	618	443	313	218	160	113	221
1881-85...........1935..		3,088	817	639	471	342	244	182	132	261
1876-80...........1930..		3,299	826	657	498	372	273	207	153	312
1871-75...........1925..		3,521	830	666	526	405	308	240	181	365

[1] The year in which these ages were reached is given in the second column from the left. For example, the cohorts of 1936-40 reached ages 15 to 19 at the beginning of 1955, i.e., on Jan. 1, 1955, the average age of the women in the cohort of 1940 was exactly 15 years; for those in the cohort of 1939 it was exactly 16 years, etc.

[2] 0.5 or less.

Source: Scripps Foundation for Research in Population Problems.

The upsurge since 1945 in the cumulative rates for first, second, and third births by ages 20–24 followed a wartime recovery from the low points reached during the great depression of the 1930's. The first birth rate by ages 20–24 was fairly steady from the cohorts of 1886–90 (by 1910) to those of 1906–10 (by 1930), slumped about 10 percent in the next two groups, and returned to the former level for the women of 1921–25 (by 1945). Rates for second and third births by ages 20–24 had a steeper downward trend and a smaller recovery by 1945. Thus, the second birth rate decreased from 151 for the cohorts of 1886–90 (by 1910) to 108 for those of 1916–20 (by 1940)—down 28 percent—and only about 40 percent of this loss was regained by the cohorts of 1921–25 (by 1945). Among the same cohorts, the third birth rate dropped more rapidly—down 42 percent—and only about one-third of the loss was regained by 1945.[12]

It is clear that the number of children borne by younger women was de-

---

[12] These changes are shown graphically in figures 104 to 106 on pages 332 to 334.

creasing slowly from cohort to cohort up to the depression, that it went up somewhat during World War II, and that it has climbed abruptly in the postwar period. The postwar increase is commonly interpreted as evidence that families are rapidly becoming much larger. Little attention is given to the fact that major changes can take place in the ages at which women bear their children without affecting the number they eventually have. Because this possibility is not well understood, it is desirable to illustrate how it can come about.

The problem involved can be explained easily by using an example from another field—military training. Let us suppose that a nation has 1,000,000 young men reaching age 17 each year, that each of them must have 2 years of military training (none being excused), and that no deaths occur at ages 17–21.[13] If the men are drafted on January 1 after their eighteenth birthday, there will at all times be 2,000,000 in training, that is, two age classes (or cohorts) of 1,000,000 each. Next, let us suppose it is decided that the men should be drafted on January 1 after their nineteenth birthday rather than their eighteenth. This change will cause the number in training to drop to 1,000,000 for 2 years, because no new cohort is drafted in the year that the change is made and no cohort is completing training during the next year. By the third year, however, the trainees will be back to the 2,000,000 mark and remain there. (See table 115.)

TABLE 115.—EFFECT OF CERTAIN CHANGES IN AGE AT DRAFTING ON NUMBER OF MEN CURRENTLY RECEIVING MILITARY TRAINING IN A POPULATION WITH 1,000,000 MEN REACHING AGE 17 EVERY YEAR AND TWO YEARS OF TRAINING REQUIRED

[The example is described more fully in the text. The small letters identify birth cohorts of men. Each cohort must appear twice in the table (once for each year of training) except cohort "a" (which receives its first year of training in the year preceding Y_1) and cohort "n" (which receives its second year of training in the year following Y_{12})]

| Age of current trainees on July 1[1] | Number of trainees (in millions) in each year from Y_1 to Y_{12} if men are drafted on January 1 after their--[1] | | | | | | | | | | | |
| | Eighteenth birthday | | | Nineteenth birthday | | | | | Seventeenth birthday | | | |
	Y_1	Y_2	Y_3	Y_4	Y_5	Y_6	Y_7	Y_8	Y_9	Y_{10}	Y_{11}	Y_{12}
17 to 18 years....	...	...	...	...	...	...	...	...	1k	1L	1m	1n
18 to 19 years....	1b	1c	1d	...	...	...	...	...	1j	1k	1L	1m
19 to 20 years....	1a	1b	1c	1d	1e	1f	1g	1h	1i	1j	...	...
20 to 21 years....	...	...	...	...	1e	1f	1g	1h	1i	...	...
Total...........	2	2	2	1	1	2	2	2	4	4	2	2

[1] These are the intervals between the exact ages listed. They apply to any other day of the year as well as to July 1.

Finally, suppose that the older age for training proves unsatisfactory, and it is decided to try drafting at age 17. In the year that the change from 19 to 17 is made, three cohorts will be drafted instead of one; hence, in this year, and in the following year as well, there will be 4,000,000

[13] The first and last of these assumptions approximate actual conditions in the United States, since about 1,100,000 males reached age 17 in 1956, and taking into account current death rates, only about 7,000 of them will die before reaching age 21.

men receiving military training instead of 2,000,000. A year later, however, the number will drop back to 2,000,000, where it will remain. Note that the annual number of trainees in this example falls from 2,000,000 to 1,000,000, returns to 2,000,000, jumps to 4,000,000, and once again returns to 2,000,000, with no change in the number of men in the different age classes (or cohorts) or in the number of years of training which each man receives. These abrupt fluctuations reflect only the changes in the timing of the training—in the age at which it occurs.

The principles involved in this illustration apply equally to marriage and childbearing in the United States, but are not so easy to see. This is partly because of the lack of adequate data on first marriages by age of bride, but mainly because women are not "drafted" for marriage at given ages as are men for military service, and because the potential childbearing period of most women is more than 20 years long, whereas military training usually lasts less than 2 years. In order to see how these principles have affected fertility, let us look first at the available data regarding past changes in age at marriage.

From 1910 (or earlier) to about 1925, there was a slight upward trend in the proportion of women marrying at younger ages. Specifically, the cumulative marriage rate by ages 15–19 rose from 82 for the cohorts of 1891–95 (by 1910) to 93 for those of 1906–10 (by 1925), and the rate by ages 20–24 rose from 449 for the 1886–90 group (by 1910) to 490 for that of 1901–05 (by 1925). (See the left-hand column of table 116.) After reaching a peak in about 1925, the propensity to marry younger declined slightly during the remainder of the decade. Then, with the business slump of 1929 and the early 1930's, came a tendency to postpone marriage. By 1935 the cumulative rate by ages 15–19 (cohorts of 1916–20) was less than the 1910 figure, and the rate by ages 20–24 (cohorts of 1911–15) was almost as low as in 1915. (The latter occurred in spite of the fact that the cohorts of 1911–15 ranked second from the top by ages 15–19.) Another reversal in trend took place in 1935 or thereabouts, a small increase in the proportion married by ages 15–19 and 20–24 going on between 1935 and 1940, and a somewhat larger increase during the World War II period. With demobilization, G.I. benefits, and postwar prosperity, younger women flocked to the altar in unprecedented numbers during 1945 to 1954. By January 1, 1955, approximately 120 of each 1,000 women aged 15–19 (cohorts of 1936–40) had married, and nearly 660 of each 1,000 aged 20–24 (cohorts of 1931–35). Each of these cumulative rates is over one-third larger than the high prewar mark. It should be noted, however, that the rate by ages 15–19 declined from 128 for the cohorts of 1931–35 (by 1950) to 120 for those of 1936–40 (by 1955).

The extent to which intercohort changes in cumulative marriage rates by younger ages reflect changes in the average age at marriage depends in part on whether changes are taking place in the proportion of women

TABLE **116.**—CUMULATIVE MARRIAGE RATE, AND CUMULATIVE BIRTH RATES BY ORDER OF BIRTH, UP TO SELECTED AGES AND DATES, FOR EVER-MARRIED WOMEN IN GROUPS OF NATIVE WHITE COHORTS

Cohorts of--	Jan. 1 of--	Cumulative marriage rate[1]	Order of birth								
			All births[2]	First	Second	Third	Fourth	Fifth	Sixth	Seventh	Eighth and higher
Exact ages 15 to 19											
1936–40	1955..	120	642	542	92	8	...	...	...	...	...
1931–35	1950..	128	523	445	70	8	...	...	...	...	...
1926–30	1945..	89	505	438	56	11	...	...	...	...	...
1921–25	1940..	85	518	459	59	...	...	...	...	...	...
1916–20	1935..	81	494	445	49	...	...	...	...	...	...
1911–15	1930..	91	528	473	55	...	...	...	...	...	...
1906–10	1925..	93	538	484	54	...	...	...	...	...	...
1901–05	1920..	89	483	427	56	...	...	...	...	...	...
1896–1900	1915..	86	558	500	58	...	...	...	...	...	...
1891–95	1910..	82	610	537	73	...	...	...	...	...	...
Exact ages 20 to 24											
1931–35	1955..	658	1,201	728	337	102	26	6	2	...	...
1926–30	1950..	635	1,000	672	250	61	14	3	...	...	...
1921–25	1945..	562	925	619	222	64	16	4	...	...	...
1916–20	1940..	476	952	647	227	61	15	2	...	...	...
1911–15	1935..	467	972	642	240	69	17	4	...	...	...
1906–10	1930..	483	1,089	704	275	83	21	4	2	...	...
1901–05	1925..	490	1,143	731	294	90	22	4	2	...	...
1896–1900	1920..	473	1,127	717	292	93	21	4	...	...	...
1891–95	1915..	464	1,200	752	315	103	26	4	...	...	...
1886–90	1910..	449	1,262	777	336	111	31	7	...	...	...
Exact ages 25 to 29											
1926–30	1955..	873	1,879	867	595	267	100	34	11	3	2
1921–25	1950..	860	1,613	831	483	190	70	26	9	3	1
1916–20	1945..	810	1,468	767	416	173	70	27	10	4	1
1911–15	1940..	753	1,413	737	389	169	73	29	11	4	1
1906–10	1935..	742	1,550	764	431	204	93	38	13	4	3
1901–05	1930..	755	1,689	800	473	236	110	45	17	5	3
1896–1900	1925..	749	1,777	825	498	255	121	49	19	7	3
1891–95	1920..	728	1,834	850	511	266	125	51	21	7	3
1886–90	1915..	720	1,969	874	540	306	151	64	24	7	3
1881–85	1910..	712	2,040	888	553	320	167	73	27	8	4
Exact ages 30 to 34											
1921–25	1955..	924	2,300	915	701	374	171	75	35	16	13
1916–20	1950..	906	2,049	871	612	302	139	66	32	15	12
1911–15	1945..	870	1,882	822	531	264	132	68	34	17	14
1906–10	1940..	844	1,942	816	527	282	153	82	44	21	17
1901–05	1935..	844	2,124	834	566	328	188	104	57	27	20
1896–1900	1930..	852	2,275	850	599	364	215	123	67	34	23
1891–95	1925..	845	2,386	878	617	386	234	134	73	37	27
1886–90	1920..	827	2,510	903	645	411	253	143	82	42	31
1881–85	1915..	827	2,629	915	658	438	278	164	92	48	36
1876–80	1910..	818	2,790	928	666	465	313	199	116	59	44
Exact ages 35 to 39											
1916–20	1955..	931	2,447	901	701	404	209	106	57	31	38
1911–15	1950..	916	2,232	854	619	345	183	99	58	33	41
1906–10	1945..	894	2,220	837	586	334	192	112	68	40	51
1901–05	1940..	883	2,392	844	604	370	228	139	88	53	66
1896–1900	1935..	880	2,614	864	640	416	266	169	110	68	81
1891–95	1930..	882	2,776	884	659	446	295	190	126	78	98
1886–90	1925..	874	2,938	905	683	474	320	211	143	90	112
1881–85	1920..	863	3,135	929	713	508	353	236	162	104	130
1876–80	1915..	859	3,345	942	733	540	390	274	189	120	157
1871–75	1910..	860	3,547	944	735	565	427	314	223	145	194

See footnotes at end of table.

TABLE **116.**—Cumulative Marriage Rate, and Cumulative Birth Rates by Order of Birth, Up to Selected Ages and Dates, for Ever-Married Women in Groups of Native White Cohorts—Cont.

Cohorts of--	Jan. 1 of--	Cumulative marriage rate[1]	Order of birth								
			All births[2]	First	Second	Third	Fourth	Fifth	Sixth	Seventh	Eighth and higher
			Exact ages 40 to 44								
1911-15..........1955..		931	2,388	858	641	376	211	119	71	43	69
1906-10..........1950..		916	2,372	841	608	361	214	129	82	51	86
1901-05..........1945..		892	2,550	853	621	390	246	157	104	67	112
1896-1900........1940..		895	2,761	860	647	429	284	188	128	85	140
1891-95..........1935..		893	2,976	886	669	464	317	214	149	102	175
1886-90..........1930..		890	3,175	902	692	494	347	239	173	119	209
1881-85..........1925..		884	3,403	923	719	528	381	269	197	139	247
1876-80..........1920..		877	3,656	940	746	563	418	302	227	164	296
1871-75..........1915..		874	3,917	947	757	596	457	343	264	196	357
			Exact ages 45 to 49								
1906-10..........1955..		928	2,380	833	605	361	216	131	84	54	96
1901-05..........1950..		918	2,519	832	607	383	243	156	105	69	124
1896-1900........1945..		908	2,765	850	640	426	283	189	131	89	157
1891-95..........1940..		902	2,996	878	664	462	317	216	153	106	200
1886-90..........1935..		895	3,224	899	690	495	350	244	178	126	242
1881-85..........1930..		895	3,445	913	714	526	382	273	203	146	288
1876-80..........1925..		889	3,703	929	739	560	418	307	233	172	345
1871-75..........1920..		885	3,973	938	753	594	458	348	270	205	407
			Exact ages 50 to 54								
1901-05..........1955..		930	2,491	822	599	379	241	155	103	68	124
1896-1900........1950..		920	2,732	839	632	421	279	187	129	88	157
1891-95..........1945..		908	2,979	872	660	459	315	215	152	106	200
1886-90..........1940..		899	3,215	895	687	493	348	242	178	126	246
1881-85..........1935..		899	3,434	909	711	524	380	271	202	147	290
1876-80..........1930..		895	3,685	923	734	556	416	305	231	171	349
1871-75..........1925..		893	3,944	929	746	589	454	345	269	203	409

[1] The cumulative marriage rates for 1955, 1950, and earlier census years are based on data from the Current Population Survey and the decennial censuses. Those for other years are preliminary estimates of the Scripps Foundation.

[2] The birth rates for ever-married women are obtained by dividing the rates for all women in table 114 by the cumulative marriage rate of this table. No rate is shown here if the rate in table 114 is 0.5 or less.

Source: Scripps Foundation for Research in Population Problems.

marrying by older ages. For example, if the cumulative rates by each age were 10 percent higher for one cohort than for another, this difference alone would not affect the average age at marriage. In contrast, if the relative excess in the rate were larger for younger women than for older women, the average age at marriage would be lower. For an actual example, let us compare the cohorts of 1931–35 with those of 1906–10. We find that the cumulative marriage rate of the later group exceeds that of the earlier group by about 38 percent at ages 15–19 and 36 percent at ages 20–24, and that the rate of the 1906–10 cohorts by ages 45–49 is 928. We do not know as yet what the rate of the later cohorts will be by ages 45–49, but we do know that it cannot be as much as 1,000 and therefore cannot exceed 928 by as much as 7.7 percent. Since the excess at ages 45–49 must be so much smaller than those at ages 15–19 and 20–24, we can be sure that the larger cumulative marriage rates of recent cohorts by younger ages signify that an important reduction in average age at marriage has taken place.

FIGURE **103.**—CUMULATIVE FIRST MARRIAGE RATE FOR COHORTS OF NATIVE WHITE WOMEN

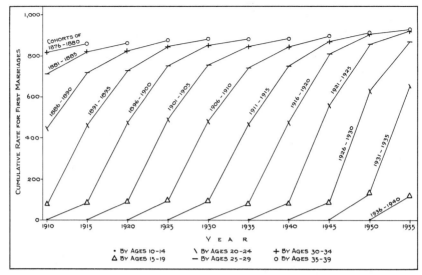

Note: Based on data in table 116.

The aforementioned changes in marriage rates of younger women have caused birth rates at these ages to appear quite different for wives than for all women.[14] For example, the birth rate for all women by ages 15–19 was 41 for the cohorts of 1916–20 (by 1935) and 77 for those of 1936–40 (by 1955); the later group exceeded the earlier by 88 percent. In contrast, the rates for wives were 494 and 642, respectively, and the later cohorts exceeded the earlier by only 30 percent. (Compare tables 114 and 116.) A similar situation is found at ages 20–24. Here the cumulative birth rate of the 1931–35 cohorts (by 1955) is larger than that of the 1911–15 cohorts (by 1935) by 74 percent when based on all women but by only 24 percent when based on wives. It is clear, therefore, that the higher fertility rates of younger women during recent years reflect primarily more marriages at younger ages. More definite proof will be presented in section E. (See also the data on trends in fertility by marital status for young age groups of women, presented in Chapters 3, 5, 6, and 8.)

Have the variations in the proportion of women marrying while young been accompanied by variations in the proportion of young married women bearing a child, and in the length of the interval between marriage and the beginning of childbearing? Theoretically, it would be expected that the conditions which lead single women to postpone marriage would lead married couples to postpone their first child or even to remain childless, and that those which encourage women to marry younger would en-

---

[14] Here and later, for the sake of brevity, "wives" will be used occasionally as synonymous with "ever married women."

courage wives to have at least one child and to start their families soon after marriage. How closely fact accords with theory in these cases cannot be determined precisely, because the birth records of the United States, unlike those of many Western countries, do not contain information on date of marriage. As mentioned in Chapter 8, some indirect information on trends in the time elapsing between marriage and first birth has been derived from 1940 and 1950 Census data on women by duration of marriage by number of children ever born (table 102) and some derived spacing intervals are presented from data in the April 1954 Current Population Survey on women by their current age, their age at marriage, and the ages of their children (table 108). A note of caution is needed regarding the interpretation of differences between the average length of interval from marriage to first birth for young wives in one group of cohorts on one date and for wives of the same ages in another group of cohorts on another date. Conclusions should not be drawn without taking into account the extent to which these first births represent all the first births that will eventually occur to the women in the two groups of cohorts. For example, the average interval between marriage and first birth may be *shorter* for the first births *at each age* to women in one group of cohorts than to those in another group, but *longer* for *all* first births. This apparent paradox will occur if there are substantial differences between the groups in the proportion of the first babies that are borne at the earlier and later childbearing ages, because the average interval is relatively short for the first births at the earlier ages as compared with those at the later ages. Substantial differences between groups of cohorts in the proportion of the first births which come at younger ages have occurred in the past and may be expected to occur in the future. For example, a comparison of the time from marriage to the first births by ages 20–24 for the cohorts of 1916–20 (by 1940) and the cohorts of 1926–30 (by 1950) may show a *shorter* average interval for the earlier group. In contrast, comparisons based on all first births (which cannot be made precisely until the 1970's) very probably will show a *longer* average interval for all first births to women in the earlier groups because of the much larger proportion of these births which took place at the older ages.[15]

---

[15] According to census data, the proportion of native white women who had a first birth by ages 20–24 was about 32.5 percent for the cohorts of 1916–20 (by July 1, 1940) and about 44.6 percent for the cohorts of 1926–30 (by July 1, 1950). Unpublished data from the 1955 study "Growth of American Families" indicate that the average interval from marriage to first birth is about 17 months for the white wives in the cohorts of 1926–30 who had a first birth by ages 20–24 and about 35 months for all the women in the cohorts of 1916–20 who will ever have a first birth.

Let us assume that 85 percent of the women living to age 50 in the cohorts of 1916–20 and 1926–30 will have a first birth (83.9 percent of those in the cohorts of 1916–20 actually had a first birth by ages 35–39). This means that the proportion who will have a first birth after ages 20–24 will be about 52.5 for the cohorts of 1916–20 and 40.4 for those of 1926–30. (To simplify this illustration, no allowance is made for deaths of women during the childbearing ages.) Let us assume also that the average interval between marriage and first birth was 16 months for the women in the cohorts of 1916–20 who had a first birth by ages 20–24, i.e., it was one month *shorter* for the earlier group of cohorts

Other clues as to the direction and amount of change may be obtained from the cumulative marriage rates and cumulative first birth rates of ever-married women in the cohort tables. The principle involved is the same as that discussed above in connection with the relation between changes in cumulative marriage rates and in average age at marriage. Specifically, if the cumulative rate for first births to young wives rises from cohort to cohort and if no change occurs in the lifetime first birth rate, or in the cumulative marriage rate by various ages, first births are coming earlier in married life. Conversely, if the lifetime first birth rate and the cumulative marriage rate by various ages are stable but the cumulative first birth rate of young wives is decreasing, first births are being postponed longer after marriage. Problems of interpretation arise when there are changes from cohort to cohort not only in the cumulative first birth rate of young wives but also in the lifetime first birth rate of wives or in the cumulative marriage rate by various ages, or when the cohorts are still so recent that an important proportion of the first marriages and

---

than for the later group. We can now compute for the cohorts of 1916–20 the average length of the interval from marriage to first birth for the women having their first birth after ages 20–24 under the conditions described; it is 46.8 months.

Finally, let us assume that for women whose first birth occurs after ages 20–24 the average length of the interval from marriage to first birth is *shorter* for the cohorts of 1916–20 (as was the case with births before ages 20–24) and is 49 months for the cohorts of 1926–30.

When all first births are considered together, the average interval under the conditions described is 35 months for the 1916–20 cohorts and 32.2 months for the 1926–30 group, i.e., it is *longer* for the earlier group instead of shorter. This could be true because a much larger proportion of all the first births has occurred before ages 20–24 (when the interval is relatively short) in the cohorts of 1926–30 than in those of 1916–20.

The data are summarized below:

	Cohorts of—	
	1916–20	1926–30
1. Percent of women married by ages 20–24[a]	51.5	67.6
2. Percent of married women having a first birth by ages 20–24[a]	63.2	66.0
3. Percent of all women having a first birth by ages 20–24 (line 1 times line 2)	32.5	44.6
4. Percent of all women who will have a first birth by age 50[b]	85.0	85.0
5. Percent of all women who will have a first birth after ages 20–24 (line 4 minus line 3)	52.5	40.4
6. Average number of months from marriage to—		
a. First births before ages 20–24	16[c]	17[d]
b. First births after ages 20–24	46.8[e]	49[c]
c. All first births	35[d]	32.2[e]

[a] From *1940 Census of Population, Differential Fertility, 1940 and 1910*, Women by Number of Children Ever Born, p. 7; *1950 Census of Population*, Vol. IV, *Special Reports*, Part 5, Chapter C, Fertility, p. 19. The 1940 data are for the native white women reporting. The 1950 data are for all white women (97.7 percent of whom were native white). The percentages for women aged 20–24 on the census date (April 1) are assumed to apply also to women aged 20–24 on the following July 1.

[b] This estimate probably is slightly too low, in view of the fact that approximately 83.9 percent of the native white women in the 1916–20 cohorts had borne a child by ages 35–39 (by 1955) according to cohort fertility tables.

[c] Assumptions of the writer (Whelpton) for illustrative purposes.

[d] Based on unpublished data from the study "Growth of American Families."

[e] Computed from the other data in this column.

first births have not yet occurred. It is for these reasons that such qualifying words as "apparently," "probably," and "may have been" are used so frequently in the next six paragraphs.

There apparently have been important changes in the rapidity with which wives start childbearing after marriage. Among ever-married women aged 15–19 in 1920 there may have been a marked tendency to postpone the first child during 1915 to 1919, since the cumulative first birth rate dropped from about 500 for the cohorts of 1896–1900 (by 1915) to 427 for the cohorts of 1901–05 (by 1920). A smaller decline (from 752 to 717) is found by ages 20–24. In contrast, conditions during the postwar period of 1920–24 apparently encouraged the early starting of families, the two rates in question being higher in 1925 than in 1920. During 1925 to 1945, as a whole, the trend was in the opposite direction, the cumulative first birth rate for wives by ages 15–19 decreasing from 484 to 438, and the rate by ages 20–24 falling from 731 to 619. The period was not uniform, however, during 1935 to 1939, while economic conditions were improving, there apparently was a tendency for the first child to come sooner after marriage whereas during the World War years of 1940–1944 the net tendency was one of delay. The latter conclusion is contrary to what seems to be thought generally about events during World War II and might not be supported if adequate direct data were available on changes in the length of the interval from marriage to first birth. All that can now be said with confidence is that relatively more young women were wives in early 1945 than in early 1940 or 1935, but that fewer of the younger wives had become mothers by early 1945 than by early 1940 or 1935.

Since 1945 the situation has changed greatly, with the first birth rate of ever-married women jumping from 438 to 542 by ages 15–19, and from 619 to 728 by ages 20–24. (See table 116.) The 1955 rate of 542 by ages 15–19 is the highest on record, and the rate of 728 by ages 20–24 exceeds that for most years since 1915. Here is striking statistical support for the common observation that more young wives have started their families quickly since the end of World War II. That this presages a continuation of the decrease in the proportion who never have a child is probable but cannot be stated with assurance, because childlessness depends in part on the first birth rate at ages older than 24.

Another question of interest is: Has the recent tendency for more young wives to have a first child relatively soon after marriage been matched by a similar tendency for more of them to have a second and third child with less delay than formerly? The answer to this question depends largely on how it is interpreted. If it refers to the time between marriage and second birth or between marriage and third birth, the recent large increases in the cumulative rates for second and third births to young wives are relevant. For example, the second birth rate of wives by ages 15–19 is 92 for the cohorts of 1936–40 and 70 for those of 1931–35, compared with rates between 49 and 59 for the groups from 1926–30 as far back as

1896–1900. Likewise, the second birth rate by ages 20–24 of wives in the cohorts of 1931–35 (337) is well above the rates of the seven prior groups (between 222 and 294). A similar statement holds for third births by these ages, the rate of 102 for the 1931–35 cohorts exceeding those of the 4 prior groups by a large margin (48 to 67 percent) and those of the 3 still earlier groups by a smaller margin (10 to 23 percent). The increases in these rates point strongly to a reduction in the length of the intervals from marriage to second or third births. It is possible, however, that their influence will be partially balanced, or more than balanced, by future increases in rates for second and third births at older ages. Only time will tell. Now we are certain merely that a higher proportion of young wives in the cohorts of 1931 to 1940 are having second and third babies relatively quickly after marriage than was the case among the 30 to 40 preceding cohorts.

The other interpretation of the question asked above is: Has the second child tended to come more quickly after the first, the third more quickly after the second, etc.? Information which is relevant here is furnished by the parity progression ratios, which are discussed in section D but will be utilized briefly here. They show that, among the women aged 15–19 or 20–24 who have borne their first child, the proportion who have also had a second child is higher among recent cohorts than among those of preceding years. At ages 15–19 the percentages are 16 and 15, respectively, for the cohorts of 1936–40 and 1931–35, compared with between 11 and 13 for the groups from 1926–30 back to 1896–1900 (table 121). At ages 20–24 the percentage is 46 for the cohorts of 1931–35 compared with between 35 and 43 for earlier groups. Changes in the proportion of the young women with two children who have gone on to have a third are smaller and show a less definite trend.

Here, as before, it is obvious that if, among the wives who have a first birth by given ages, there is a large rise in the proportion who also have a second birth by these ages, the change probably means that on the whole the second is coming more quickly after the first. Again, however, it is necessary to withold final judgment. Although we know that more young wives than formerly are having their second child relatively soon after their first, and their third relatively soon after their second, we cannot be certain of the extent to which this reflects a reduction in the *average* length of these intervals until at least another 10 years have passed and we have more data on the changes that are occurring in the lifetime rates for second and third births to the cohorts in question.

What has been said above suggests that the intercohort rise in the fertility of the younger wives from 1935 to 1945 and 1955 came about because more of them had children, rather than because those with children had larger families. This will be discussed more adequately in section E. If it is true that most of the postwar baby boom to date can be accounted for by the facts that more women are marrying at the younger ages and more young wives are having their first and second children quickly, questions arise as to the effect which these changes are likely to have on annual birth rates and on the average size of completed families during coming years. These questions will be considered in Chapter 10.

The past decrease in the lifetime fertility of middle-aged women. In striking contrast to the postwar upsurge in childbearing at younger ages is the large reduction in the average number of births per woman living to the end of the reproductive period. This began over a century ago and only now is about to end. The magnitude of the reduction is shown clearly in figure 104 and in the lower decks of table 114. Among the native white women in the cohorts of 1871–75 (who reached ages 50–54 on January 1, 1925), there were slightly more than 3,500 births per 1,000 women. This rate decreased steadily among subsequent cohorts and for those of 1901–05 (by 1955) was only about 2,300; the drop in 30 years was approximately 34 percent. The women in the cohorts of 1906–10 will not reach ages 50–54 until 1960, but so few will bear children after ages 45–49 that their completed fertility is certain to be only a few points above 2,200, and 37 percent below that of the 1871–75 group. If women in the cohorts of years prior to 1870 could be brought into the comparison the decrease undoubtedly would be much larger.

Because gross reproduction rates have been computed for many hypothetical cohorts during short periods (usually 1 to 5 years) it is of interest to obtain them for actual cohorts. This can be done easily by dividing the completed fertility rates by 2.058—the average ratio of total white births to female white births in recent decades. The results (on a per 1,000 basis) are shown in the accompanying table:

Cohorts of—	Gross reproduction rate	Cohorts of—	Gross reproduction rate
1906–10	1,074	1886–90	1,405
1901–05	1,125	1881–85	1,500
1896–1900	1,221	1876–80	1,603
1891–95	1,314	1871–75	1,711

The rate of 1,074 for the 1906–10 *cohorts* is about the same as the rates of 1,080 and 1,060 for white women in the 1930–35 and 1935–40 *periods* (shown in Chapter 3, table 14), and the rate of 1,711 for the 1871–75 *cohorts* is about the same as that of 1,740 for the 1905–10 *period.*

Net reproduction rates can be computed for the cohorts of 1900 and later which have reached (or will soon reach) the end of the reproductive period, but can only be estimated roughly for earlier cohorts until more is known about age-specific birth and death rates in years before 1900. The net reproduction rate of the cohorts of 1901–05 is 905—well below replacement—and that of the cohorts of 1906–10 is 874—still further below replacement. Both of these rates are significantly smaller than the smallest *period* rates for white women in Chapter 3, table 14, namely, 970 for 1930–35 and 960 for 1935–40.

FIGURE **104.**—CUMULATIVE RATE FOR ALL BIRTHS FOR COHORTS OF NATIVE WHITE WOMEN

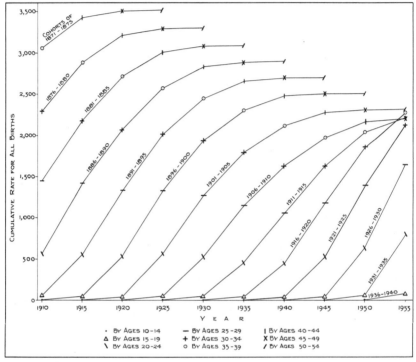

Note: Based on data in table 114.

The difference between the gross and net reproduction rates is 200 for the 1906–10 cohorts and 220 for the 1901–05 group. It is almost certain that the women in the cohorts of 1896–1900 did not quite replace themselves, for their gross rate is 1,221. Since the gross rate for the cohorts of 1891–95 is 1,314, the net rate probably is somewhat above the replacement figure. Among the earlier cohorts shown in the foregoing table, the margin probably becomes successively larger. As will be brought out in the next section, the gross and net reproduction rates will almost certainly rise from the cohorts of 1906–10 to those of 1916–20 (and probably later), but the exact amount of the increase will depend on future developments. The net rate of the cohorts of 1911–15 is sure to be below replacement, because the gross rate will be about 1,100. Since the gross rate of the 1916–20 cohorts probably will be between 1,170 and 1,260, the net rate may be above replacement. Altogether there probably are 20 cohorts of native white women—those of 1898 to 1917—that will not contribute to population growth.

FIGURE **105.**—CUMULATIVE FIRST BIRTH RATE FOR COHORTS OF NATIVE WHITE WOMEN

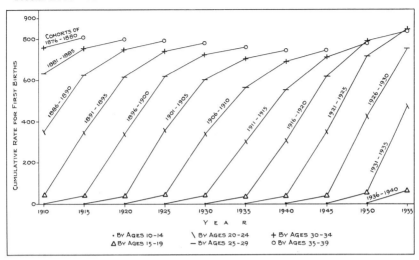

Note: Based on data in table 114.

The great shrinkage in completed fertility from the cohorts of 1871–75 to those of 1906–10 has come about almost entirely because fewer married couples have many children, rather than because fewer women marry, or more married women are childless or bear only one child. Major proof of this statement may be found by looking at the changes from cohort to cohort in rates for births of different orders by ages 50–54. Although decreases have occurred for each order, they are quite small for first births and successively larger for subsequent births. In the native white cohorts of 1871–75 there were 830 first births per 1,000 women who lived to ages 50–54 (to 1925). In subsequent cohorts there was a gradual decline to 764 for the cohorts of 1901–05 (by 1955)—the low mark for the groups under consideration, but a reduction of only 66 points or 8 percent. At the same time the rate for second births by ages 50–54 decreased from 666 to 557—a reduction of 109 points or 16 percent, which is substantially larger than that for first births.

At the other extreme, the rate for eighth and higher order births by ages 50–54 already has plummeted much further, both absolutely and relatively; from 365 for the cohorts of 1871–75 (by 1925) it dropped to 115 for those of 1901–05 (by 1955)—a fall of 68 percent. Moreover, it has not yet reached bottom, as can be seen by looking at the rates of the cohorts of 1906–10 and 1911–15 by ages 45–49 and 40–44, respectively. It now appears highly probable that the rate for eighth and higher order births by ages 50–54 will be about 90 for the 1906–10 group (by 1960) and in the upper 70's or lower 80's for the 1911–15 cohorts (by 1965). The latter will represent a drop of about 285 points or 80 percent from the rate of 1871–75 cohorts.

FIGURE **106.**—CUMULATIVE SECOND BIRTH RATE FOR COHORTS OF NATIVE WHITE WOMEN

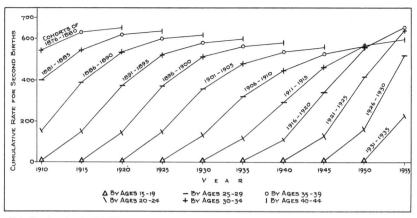

Note: Based on data in table 114.

The patterns of change in rates for third to seventh births are intermediate between those described above for second births and for eighth and higher order births. The low mark for third births is almost certain to be set by the cohorts of 1906–10, that for fourth and fifth births by this group or the 1911–15 cohorts, and that for sixth and seventh births by the latter group or the one after it. The numerical declines in the rates for third to seventh births will amount, respectively, to approximately 191, 205, 190, 165, and 135 points. The relative declines will be approximately 36, 51, 60, 70, and 75 percent, respectively.

FIGURE **107.**—CUMULATIVE RATES FOR THIRD AND FOURTH BIRTHS FOR COHORTS OF NATIVE WHITE WOMEN

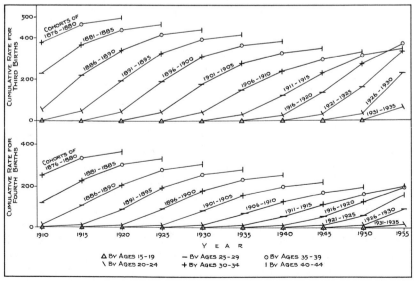

Note: Based on data in table 114.

FIGURE **108.**—CUMULATIVE RATES FOR FIFTH AND SIXTH BIRTHS (COMBINED) AND FOR SEVENTH AND HIGHER ORDER BIRTHS (COMBINED) FOR COHORTS OF NATIVE WHITE WOMEN

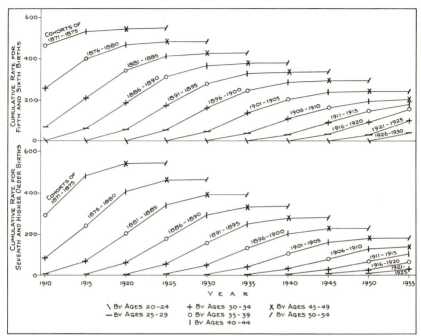

Note: Based on data in table 114.

A high proportion (over 88 percent) of women marry before the end of the childbearing period, and the variations in the proportion of married women are small from one cohort to another. In consequence, the behavior of cumulative birth rates for ever-married women has been much like that of the rates for all women at the middle ages, in contrast to the differences at the young ages. The cumulative marriage rate by ages 45–49 rose slowly from about 885 for the cohorts of 1871–75 to 928 for those of 1906–1910 (a gain of less than 5 percent), hence the downward trend of the lifetime fertility rate for ever-married women was only a little more rapid than that of the rate for all women. For example, the decreases from the cohorts of 1871–75 to those of 1906–10 in cumulative birth rates by ages 45–49 for all women and for ever-married women are, respectively, 37 and 40 percent for all births, 7 and 11 percent for first births, and 75 and 76 percent for eighth and higher order births. In both cases the declines for second to seventh births are intermediate in size between those for first and eighth births and are only slightly smaller for all women than for wives.

The extent to which the dwindling number of large families has contributed to the shrinkage of average family size may be observed more clearly if the reduction in the rate for all births to ever-married women is distributed by birth order. The average number of babies borne by

1,000 ever-married women living to ages 45–49 fell from about 3,973 for the cohorts of 1871–75 to 2,380 for those of 1906–10, a drop of nearly 1,600. Only about 16 percent of this decline occurred because fewer couples had a first or second birth, compared with about 29 percent, because fewer had seven or more children. Similarly, the decreases in first, second, and third births (combined) account for about 30 percent of the total reduction, whereas those for fourth and subsequent births add up to 70 percent of the total.

Intercohort changes in childbearing by intermediate ages. The apparent contradiction between a trend toward larger families among young women and a trend toward smaller families among middle-aged women can be explained easily by referring to what has happened by intermediate ages. The most noteworthy fact is that the long-time reduction in lifetime fertility is almost certain to end with the cohorts of 1906–10 and to be reversed by later cohorts. In the 1906–10 group there were about 2,174 births per 1,000 women living to ages 40–44 (in 1950); the corresponding figure for the cohorts of 1911–15 (in 1955) is 2,224— larger by 50 points, or 2 percent. (See table 114 and figure 104.) In past decades this rate has risen only about 50 points (or 2 percent) after ages 40–44, hence the lead of the more recent group is almost certain to be maintained with little change to the end of the childbearing period.

That the lifetime fertility of the women of 1916–20 will be still higher than that of the women of 1911–15 is indicated fairly clearly by their cumulative birth rates by ages 35–39, where the more recent group exceeds the earlier group by about 230 points or 11 percent. Because only 10 to 15 percent of the babies borne by women in still earlier cohorts came after ages 35–39, it is most unlikely that the completed fertility of the 1916–20 cohorts will fail to exceed that of the three preceding groups. The gross reproduction rate is likely to rise from 1,074 for the 1906–10 cohorts to about 1,200 for the 1916–20 group, and the net reproduction rate to rise from 874 to about 1,000.

When we look at the cumulative birth rates by ages 30–34 and 25–29 we find not only rising rates among recent cohorts but also a widening of the differences between successive groups. For example, the cohorts which reached ages 35–39 at the beginning of 1955 had a rate 11 percent larger than the preceding group, but the cohorts which reached ages 30–34 at that time had a lead of 14 percent, and those which reached ages 25–29 had a lead of over 18 percent. A comparison between the rates of the latest cohorts to reach given ages and the previous low marks for these ages shows an even greater tendency for the margin to widen at successively younger ages. Thus, at ages 35–39 the rate of the 1916–20 cohorts (2,278 by 1955) is nearly 15 percent above the lowest rate (1,987 for the 1906–10 group by 1945), but at ages 25–29 the rate of the 1926–30 cohorts (1,642 by 1955) is 54 percent above the lowest rate (1,064 for the 1911–15 group by 1940).

Increases in marriage rates have contributed in varying degree to the changes mentioned above. The cumulative rate by ages 40–44 rose gradually from about 874 for the cohorts of 1871–75 (by 1910) to 931 for the 1911–15 group (by 1955). (See table 116 and figure 103.) This tended in a small way to counterbalance the decline in the fertility of married women from the cohorts of 1871–75 to 1906–10 and to add to the rise from the latter group to the following one. A similar statement holds true for ages 35–39.

At ages 30–34 and 25–29 the tendency to marry younger becomes apparent. The cumulative marriage rate by ages 30–34 rose from 818 for the cohorts of 1876–80 (by 1910) to 845 for those of 1891–95 (by 1925), remained close to this figure for the next three groups, and then went up somewhat faster to 924 for the cohorts of 1921–25 (by 1955). This almost equals the highest mark attained by any earlier group by ages 45–49. A somewhat greater change is found at ages 25–29. Here the cumulative rate increased from 712 for the cohorts of 1881–85 (by 1910) to 749 for those of 1896–1900 (by 1925), was about the same for the next three groups, and climbed to 873 for the cohorts of 1926–30 (by 1955). This is a larger relative rise than can occur at ages 45–49 and supports the previous statement that the average age at marriage is declining among recent cohorts.

The decrease from 1910 to 1940 or 1945 in cumulative fertility rates by ages 30–34 and 25–29 is larger for rates based on ever-married women than for those based on all women, as would be expected in view of the tendency for more women to marry before these ages. Thus, the decline in the cumulative rate for all births by ages 30–34 from the cohorts of 1876–80 to those of 1911–15 amounts to about 28 percent when the base is all women but to 33 percent when the base is ever-married women. (See tables 114 and 116.) Similarly, the percentage declines in the two rates by ages 25–29 from the cohorts of 1881–85 to the 1911–15 group are 27 and 31, respectively. In contrast, but again as would be expected, the rise in cumulative birth rates from 1940 or 1945 to 1955 is smaller when the base is ever-married women than when it is all women. The respective percentage gains by ages 30–34 are about 22 and 30, and by ages 25–29 about 33 and 54. Here, as with the younger women discussed above, it is clear that the marriage of more young women has contributed substantially to the postwar baby boom.

Intercohort trends of the cumulative rate for first births to ever-married women by the intermediate childbearing ages under consideration here have been as a rule in the same direction as trends of the rate for all births, but less rapidly down or up. (See table 116.) In consequence, the changes in the cumulative birth rates per mother have been relatively smaller than those per ever-married woman. Thus, the fall of the rate by ages 35–39 from the cohorts of 1871–75 (by 1910) to those of 1906–10 (by 1945) was over 37 percent for ever-married women but only 29 percent for mothers. Likewise, the recent rise amounted to 10 percent for ever-married women but to barely 2 percent for mothers. (Compare tables 116 and 117.)

A similar situation, but one with larger numerical differences, is found in the rates by ages 25–29. Here the drop from the cohorts of 1881–85 (by 1910) to those of 1911–15 (by 1940) is 31 percent for ever-married women and 17 percent for mothers, and the subsequent recovery amounts to 33 percent and 13 percent. Again it is evident that the postwar upsurge in annual birth rates and numbers of births owes much more to an increase in the proportion of married women bearing children than to an increase in size of family among the women who have children.

Changes in the relative ranking of cohorts as age rises. Although there has been some tendency for the group of cohorts having the lowest cumulative rates by one age to have the lowest rates by other ages, important exceptions can be seen. Thus, the cohorts of 1916–20 had significantly lower rates up to ages 15–19 than any other group on record here, were practically tied with the cohorts of 1911–15 for last place at ages 20–24, but by ages 35–39 had raised their fertility so much that it was not only substantially above that of the 1911–15 group, but also exceeded that of the cohorts of 1906–10 and 1901–05. (See tables 114 and 118.) In other words, as will be brought out in section E, the birth rates of the 1916–20 cohorts during ages 20–24 through 34–38 were well above those of the other groups just mentioned. The fact that these cohorts lived through this age interval during 1940–54 is highly significant in this connection.

The picture for births of specific orders varies somewhat from that for all orders. The similarity is greatest for first and second births, the cohorts of 1916–20 ranking lowest at ages 15–19, lowest or second from the bottom at ages 20–24, and then climbing to the top of the array and setting a new record by ages 35–39. For subsequent births the rise in standing is not so marked. The 1916–20 cohorts had the lowest third birth rate by ages 20–24, ranked ninth at ages 25–29, but rose only to sixth place by ages 35–39. It is possible, but by no means certain, that they will have a higher rank by ages 40–44 (by 1960). Gains in relative standing are successively smaller for births of higher orders. The group is at the bottom of the list for sixth and subsequent births at all ages reached by 1955 and is very unlikely to overtake preceding cohorts. It will outrank later groups unless there is a reversal of the past tendency for an increasing proportion of couples to avoid having more than five children. Finally, it is important to note that the cumulative fertility rate of the 1916–20 cohorts caught up with, and then passed, the rates of the two preceding groups chiefly because of more first, second, and third births, and in spite of fewer sixth and higher order births.

Shifts in the relative standing of the cohorts of 1906–10 are in the opposite direction. This group had a cumulative rate for all births by ages

TABLE 117.—CUMULATIVE BIRTH RATES UP TO SELECTED AGES AND DATES, FOR MOTHERS IN GROUPS OF NATIVE WHITE COHORTS

[These rates are obtained from table 114 by dividing each rate for all births by the corresponding rate for first births. The year by which the rate is reached is shown in parentheses to the right of the rate]

Cohorts of—	Exact age							
	15 to 19 years	20 to 24 years	25 to 29 years	30 to 34 years	35 to 39 years	40 to 44 years	45 to 49 years	50 to 54 years
1936–40	1,185 (1955)	...	...	...	...	...	...	...
1931–35	1,175 (1950)	1,647 (1955)	...	...	...	...	...	...
1926–30	1,128 (1945)	1,489 (1950)	2,169 (1955)	...	...	...	...	...
1921–25	1,128 (1940)	1,494 (1945)	1,943 (1950)	2,515 (1955)	...	...	...	...
1916–20	1,139 (1935)	1,471 (1940)	1,913 (1945)	2,354 (1950)	2,715 (1955)	...	...	...
1911–15	1,140 (1930)	1,513 (1935)	1,917 (1940)	2,291 (1945)	2,616 (1950)	2,783 (1955)	...	...
1906–10	1,133 (1925)	1,545 (1930)	2,026 (1935)	2,380 (1940)	2,656 (1945)	2,823 (1950)	2,858 (1955)	...
1901–05	1,132 (1920)	1,564 (1925)	2,111 (1930)	2,550 (1935)	2,835 (1940)	2,988 (1945)	3,027 (1950)	3,030 (1955)
1896–1900	1,140 (1915)	1,572 (1920)	2,154 (1925)	2,677 (1930)	3,026 (1935)	3,212 (1940)	3,251 (1945)	3,254 (1950)
1891–95	1,136 (1910)	1,596 (1915)	2,157 (1920)	2,717 (1925)	3,138 (1930)	3,358 (1935)	3,413 (1940)	3,415 (1945)
1886–90	...	1,628 (1910)	2,253 (1915)	2,779 (1920)	3,245 (1925)	3,522 (1930)	3,586 (1935)	3,591 (1940)
1881–85	...	...	2,299 (1910)	2,873 (1915)	3,375 (1920)	3,689 (1925)	3,775 (1930)	3,780 (1935)
1876–80	...	...	...	3,007 (1910)	3,551 (1915)	3,891 (1920)	3,985 (1925)	3,994 (1930)
1871–75	...	...	...	...	3,757 (1910)	4,135 (1915)	4,235 (1920)	4,242 (1925)

Source: Table 114.

15–19 (reached in 1925) which exceeded that of any preceding group, probably due in part to demobilization after World War I and to urban prosperity during 1920 to 1924. (See tables 114 and 118.) The rate by ages 20–24 was somewhat below those of earlier groups, but still substantially above those of the cohorts of 1911–15 and 1916–20. On reaching 20–24, however, the 1906–10 cohorts were hit by the depression of the 1930's; their rate for all births rose so slowly during the 1930's that by ages 30–34 (reached in 1940) the group was almost tied for lowest rank. Since then it has had an undisputed claim on last place at ages 35–39 and older, and seems destined to continue to do so for several years to come. A similar situation is found for first and second births.

TABLE 118.—RANKING OF GROUPS OF COHORTS WITH RESPECT TO CUMULATIVE RATES BY SUCCESSIVE AGES

[The top number of each column refers to 1955, the second number to 1950, and (finally) the bottom number to 1910. 1955 and 1910 are the latest and earliest years for which data are available]

Cohorts	Exact age							
	15 to 19 years	20 to 24 years	25 to 29 years	30 to 34 years	35 to 39 years	40 to 44 years	45 to 49 years	50 to 54 years
1936–40	1	...	...	...	...	...	...	...
1931–35	2	1	...	...	...	...	...	...
1926–30	7–8	2	1	...	...	...	...	...
1921–25	7–8	8	4	2	...	...	...	...
1916–20	10	10	8	7	7	...	...	...
1911–15	5–6	9	10	10	9	9	...	...
1906–10	3	7	9	9	10	10	10	...
1901–05	9	4	7	8	8	8	9	10
1896–1900	5–6	6	6	6	6	7	8	9
1891–95	4	5	5	5	5	6	7	8
1886–90	...	3	3	4	4	5	6	7
1881–85	...	...	2	3	3	4	5	6
1876–80	...	...	...	1	2	3	4	5
1871–75	...	...	...	...	1	2	3	4
1866–70	...	...	...	...	...	1	2	3
1861–65	...	...	...	...	...	...	1	2
1856–60	...	...	...	...	...	...	...	1

Source: Table 114 and census data.

C. Changes in the distribution of women by number of children borne

This section will deal with changes from cohort to cohort in the proportion of women who have not borne a child, or who have borne one, two, or other numbers of children. These proportions are similar in meaning to those based on census counts of children ever born (discussed in other chapters) and are computed easily from the cumulative birth rates presented in tables 114 and 116. Because parity distribution represents the size of the differences between cumulative rates for births of successive orders, this section does not lead to conclusions about past or expected future trends in fertility which differ from those in section B. The situation is viewed from another angle, however, hence what follows complements the preceding discussion. With parity distributions, as with cumulative birth rates, the differences between earlier and later groups of cohorts at younger ages are quite unlike those at older ages; consequently, the various age groups will be considered separately.

More young women with one or two children. The outstanding change from early to recent cohorts in the parity distribution of all women at ages 20–24 is the shift of large numbers of these women from the childless to the one- or two-child categories. This would be expected, of course, from the new records for cumulative rates for first and second births by ages 20–24 which have been set by recent cohorts. The proportion of women who had not borne a child by ages 20–24 was fairly stable (about 65 percent) for the cohorts of 1886–90 to 1906–10, jumped to about 70 percent for the next two groups, and then dropped rapidly to 52 percent for the 1931–35 cohorts in 1955. (See the second deck of table 119 and figure 109.) The increase was due to a postponement of births, and took place in spite of a tendency for more women to marry by these ages. The larger decline which followed reflects partly the fact that more women are marrying and starting their families at younger ages and partly the desire of more women to have children instead of remaining permanently childless.

FIGURE **109.**—PERCENT DISTRIBUTION BY PARITY AT AGES 20–24 FOR COHORTS OF NATIVE WHITE WOMEN

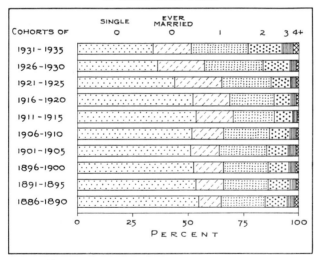

Note: Based on data in table 119.

It is not possible now to be sure which of these two factors has been the more important in bringing the change. The answer will depend on how the difference between the lifetime first birth rates of the 1911–15 and 1931–35 cohorts compares with the difference of 179 between their rates by ages 20–24. At one extreme, if the lifetime rate of the later group is the same as that of the earlier group (that is, about 803) the dif-

TABLE **119.**—PERCENT DISTRIBUTION BY PARITY AT SELECTED AGES AND DATES, FOR GROUPS
OF COHORTS OF NATIVE WHITE WOMEN

[Based on the cumulative rates in table 114. For example, the percent of women in the cohorts of 1936–40 who were
of zero parity at ages 15 to 19 may be obtained by subtracting the cumulative first birth rate from 1,000 and dividing
by 10. Similarly, the percent of women who were of one parity is one-tenth of the difference between the cumulative
rates for first and second births. The percentages for the cohorts of 1896–1900 and earlier are based in part on
estimates and are subject to minor change]

Cohorts of--	Jan. 1 of--	Total	Parity							
			Zero	One	Two	Three	Four	Five	Six	Seven and higher
Exact ages 15 to 19										
1936–40	1955	100.0	93.5	5.4	1.0	0.1	[1]	...	...	...
1931–35	1950	100.0	94.3	4.9	0.8	0.1	[1]	...	...	...
1926–30	1945	100.0	96.1	3.3	0.5	0.1	[1]	...	...	...
1921–25	1940	100.0	96.1	3.4	0.4	[1]	[1]	...	...	...
1916–20	1935	100.0	96.4	3.2	0.4	[1]	[1]	...	...	...
1911–15	1930	100.0	95.7	3.8	0.5	[1]	[1]	...	...	...
1906–10	1925	100.0	95.5	4.0	0.5	[1]	[1]	...	...	...
1901–05	1920	100.0	96.2	3.4	0.4	[1]	[1]	...	...	...
1896–1900	1915	100.0	95.7	3.8	0.5	[1]	[1]	...	...	...
1891–95	1910	100.0	95.6	3.8	0.6	[1]	[1]	...	...	...
Exact ages 20 to 24										
1931–35	1955	100.0	52.1	25.7	15.5	5.0	1.3	0.3	0.1	[1]
1926–30	1950	100.0	57.3	26.7	12.0	3.0	0.7	0.2	[1]	[1]
1921–25	1945	100.0	65.2	22.3	9.0	2.7	0.7	0.2	[1]	[1]
1916–20	1940	100.0	69.2	20.0	7.9	2.2	0.5	0.1	[1]	[1]
1911–15	1935	100.0	70.0	18.8	7.9	2.4	0.6	0.2	[1]	[1]
1906–10	1930	100.0	66.0	20.8	9.3	3.0	0.8	0.1	0.1	[1]
1901–05	1925	100.0	64.2	21.5	9.9	3.4	0.9	0.1	0.1	[1]
1896–1900	1920	100.0	66.1	20.1	9.4	3.4	0.8	0.2	[1]	[1]
1891–95	1915	100.0	65.1	20.3	9.8	3.6	1.0	0.2	[1]	[1]
1886–90	1910	100.0	65.1	19.8	10.1	3.6	1.1	0.3	[1]	[1]
Exact ages 25 to 29										
1926–30	1955	100.0	24.3	23.8	28.6	14.6	5.7	2.0	0.7	0.3
1921–25	1950	100.0	28.5	30.0	25.2	10.3	3.8	1.4	0.5	0.3
1916–20	1945	100.0	37.9	28.3	19.8	8.3	3.5	1.4	0.5	0.3
1911–15	1940	100.0	44.5	26.2	16.5	7.2	3.3	1.4	0.5	0.3
1906–10	1935	100.0	43.3	24.7	16.9	8.3	4.1	1.7	0.7	0.3
1901–05	1930	100.0	39.6	24.7	17.8	9.5	4.9	2.2	0.8	0.4
1896–1900	1925	100.0	38.2	24.5	18.1	10.1	5.3	2.4	0.8	0.5
1891–95	1920	100.0	38.1	24.7	17.8	10.3	5.4	2.2	1.0	0.5
1886–90	1915	100.0	37.1	24.0	16.9	11.1	6.3	2.9	1.2	0.5
1881–85	1910	100.0	36.8	23.8	16.6	10.9	6.7	3.3	1.3	0.6
Exact ages 30 to 34										
1921–25	1955	100.0	15.5	19.7	30.2	18.9	8.8	3.7	1.7	1.5
1916–20	1950	100.0	21.1	23.6	28.0	14.8	6.7	3.1	1.5	1.4
1911–15	1945	100.0	28.5	25.3	23.2	11.5	5.6	2.8	1.6	1.5
1906–10	1940	100.0	31.1	24.3	20.7	10.9	6.0	3.3	1.9	1.8
1901–05	1935	100.0	29.6	22.6	20.2	11.8	7.0	4.0	2.5	2.3
1896–1900	1930	100.0	27.6	21.4	20.0	12.7	7.9	4.7	2.9	2.9
1891–95	1925	100.0	25.8	22.1	19.5	12.8	8.5	5.1	3.1	3.1
1886–90	1920	100.0	25.3	21.4	19.3	13.2	9.0	5.0	3.3	3.5
1881–85	1915	100.0	24.3	21.3	18.2	13.2	9.4	6.0	3.6	4.0
1876–80	1910	100.0	24.1	21.4	16.5	12.4	9.3	6.8	4.7	4.8
Exact ages 35 to 39										
1916–20	1955	100.0	16.1	18.6	27.6	18.2	9.6	4.6	2.4	2.9
1911–15	1950	100.0	21.8	21.5	25.1	14.8	7.7	3.9	2.2	3.0
1906–10	1945	100.0	25.2	22.4	22.5	12.7	7.1	3.9	2.5	3.6
1901–05	1940	100.0	25.5	21.2	20.6	12.6	7.7	4.5	3.1	4.7
1896–1900	1935	100.0	24.0	19.6	19.7	13.2	8.5	5.2	3.7	6.0
1891–95	1930	100.0	22.0	20.0	18.8	13.3	9.3	5.7	4.2	6.9
1886–90	1925	100.0	20.9	19.4	18.3	13.3	9.6	5.9	4.6	7.9
1881–85	1920	100.0	19.8	18.7	17.7	13.3	10.1	6.4	4.9	9.0
1876–80	1915	100.0	19.1	17.9	16.6	12.9	10.0	7.3	5.9	10.3
1871–75	1910	100.0	18.8	18.0	14.6	11.9	9.7	7.8	6.7	12.5

[1] 0.05 or less.

TABLE **119.**—PERCENT DISTRIBUTION BY PARITY AT SELECTED AGES AND DATES, FOR GROUPS OF COHORTS OF NATIVE WHITE WOMEN—Cont.

Cohorts of--	Jan. 1 of--	Total	Parity							
			Zero	One	Two	Three	Four	Five	Six	Seven and higher
			Exact ages 40 to 44							
1911-15...........1955..		100.0	20.1	20.2	24.7	15.4	8.5	4.4	2.6	4.0
1906-10...........1950..		100.0	23.0	21.3	22.6	13.5	7.8	4.3	2.8	4.7
1901-05...........1945..		100.0	23.9	20.7	20.6	12.9	8.0	4.7	3.3	6.0
1896-1900........1940..		100.0	23.0	19.1	19.5	13.0	8.6	5.3	3.9	7.6
1891-95...........1935..		100.0	20.8	19.4	18.3	13.1	9.2	5.7	4.2	9.1
1886-90...........1930..		100.0	19.7	18.7	17.6	13.1	9.5	6.0	4.7	10.6
1881-85...........1925..		100.0	18.4	17.9	17.0	13.0	9.9	6.4	5.1	12.3
1876-80...........1920..		100.0	17.6	17.0	16.0	12.7	10.2	6.6	5.5	14.4
1871-75...........1915..		100.0	17.2	16.6	14.1	12.2	9.9	6.9	6.0	17.1
			Exact ages 45 to 49							
1906-10...........1955..		100.0	22.7	21.2	22.6	13.5	7.9	4.4	2.8	5.0
1901-05...........1950..		100.0	23.6	20.6	20.5	12.9	8.0	4.7	3.3	6.3
1896-1900........1945..		100.0	22.8	19.1	19.4	12.9	8.6	5.3	3.8	8.1
1891-95...........1940..		100.0	20.8	19.3	18.2	13.1	9.1	5.7	4.2	9.6
1886-90...........1935..		100.0	19.5	18.6	17.5	13.0	9.5	5.9	4.6	11.3
1881-85...........1930..		100.0	18.3	17.8	16.8	12.9	9.8	6.3	5.0	13.1
1876-80...........1925..		100.0	17.4	16.9	15.9	12.6	9.9	6.6	5.4	15.3
1871-75...........1920..		100.0	17.0	16.4	14.0	12.1	9.7	6.9	5.8	18.1

Source: Table 114.

ference of 179 in the rates by ages 20–24 would all be ascribed to the starting of childbearing at younger ages by the women of 1931–35. At the other extreme, if the lifetime rate of the later group should exceed that of the other group by 179 or more (that is, should reach 982), all of the difference by ages 20–24 could be ascribed to fewer couples remaining childless permanently. Similarly, a lifetime rate of 893 (803 plus half of 179) would indicate that each of the two factors had approximately the same weight. In this connection it is helpful to note that the highest rate recorded for the entire United States is 830 for the cohorts of 1871–75, and that a rate as high as 893 seems unlikely. It now appears, therefore, that the much smaller proportion of childless women among those aged 20–24 in the cohorts of 1931–35 than in the 1911–15 group will eventually prove to be due in greater degree to a reduction in the age at which the first child is borne than to a decrease in permanent childlessness.

The proportion of women aged 20–24 who were of first parity (that is, had borne one child but not two) was fairly stationary from the cohorts of 1886–90 to 1916–20 (between 18.8 and 21.5 percent) but rose significantly to 26.7 percent for the cohorts of 1926–30 (by 1950). Since then there has been a slight decline. The relative numbers of women of second and third parity decreased consistently from the cohorts of 1886–90 to those of 1916–20, but since then have more than doubled and have broken previous records. So few fourth or higher order births occur by these ages that the changes in the proportion of women of fourth and higher parity are of negligible importance.

Intercohort changes in the parity distribution of women aged 20–24 have been quite different in certain ways for ever-married women than for all women, chiefly because of changes in the proportion of women who married. The differences are most striking for zero parity, which is the residual group for wives but includes most single women. Among wives aged 20–24 the percent childless rose by more than one-half from the cohorts of 1886–90 (in 1910) to those of 1911–15 (in 1935), but the rise for all women was less than one-thirteenth. (See tables 119 and 120.) In contrast, the drop of the proportion at zero parity from the cohorts of 1911–15 (in 1935) to those of 1931–35 (in 1955) was close to one-fourth for both groups.

No reference was made above to the parity distribution of all women aged 15–19, because approximately 90 percent of them are single and have not borne a child. Among those that have married by 15–19, roughly half have started their families. The percentage has fluctuated irregularly between a low of 42.7 (cohorts of 1901–05 in 1920) and a high of 54.2 (cohorts of 1936–40 in 1955). The most rapid change in 5 years is the recent jump from 44.5 percent for the cohorts of 1931–35 to 54.2 for the next group.

Relatively few of the wives aged 15 to 19 are shown as having reached second parity, the computed percentages varying between 5 and 9. It should be remembered, however, that these figures are subject to considerable error (chiefly because of the desire to conceal a child born out of wedlock) and may be somewhat too low. One-child rather than two-child families are customary among the married women of these ages, between 35 and 50 percent of them being in the one-parity group. One of the most rapid changes in this proportion is the rise from 37.5 percent for the cohorts of 1931–35 (by 1950) to 45.0 percent for those of 1936–40 (by 1955).

Fewer middle-aged women with several children. Among successive cohorts of women reaching the end of the childbearing period there have been the large shifts from higher to lower parities which would be expected to accompany the much larger reductions in rates for higher order births than for lower order births which were discussed in section B. Women at seventh or higher parity were barely one-fourth as numerous relatively at ages 40–44 or 45–49 in the cohorts of 1911–15 or 1906–10 (by 1955) as in those of 1871–75 (by 1915 or 1920). (See the last two decks of table 119, and figure 110.) The proportion of women at six parity dropped by over one-half, while reductions of about one-third occurred at fifth parity. Third parity provides the pivot, the proportion of these women remaining relatively unchanged. By far the largest increase is found at second parity, where the percentage for ages 40–44 has jumped by about three-fourths (from 14.1 for the cohorts of 1871–75 to 24.7 for those of 1911–15). Increases at zero parity and first parity are decidedly smaller—between one-fourth and one-sixth as large as at second parity.

TABLE **120.**—PERCENT OF WOMEN EVER MARRIED AND PERCENT DISTRIBUTION BY PARITY OF EVER-MARRIED WOMEN AT SELECTED AGES AND DATES, FOR GROUPS OF NATIVE WHITE COHORTS

Cohorts of--	Jan. 1 of--	Percent ever married	Percent of all ever-married women, by parity							
			Total	Zero	One	Two	Three	Four	Five	Six	Seven and higher

					Exact ages 15 to 19						
1936-40	1955	12.0	100.0	45.8	45.0	8.4	0.8	...	...	...	...
1931-35	1950	12.8	100.0	55.5	37.5	6.2	0.8	...	...	...	...
1926-30	1945	8.9	100.0	56.2	38.2	4.5	1.1	...	...	...	...
1921-25	1940	8.5	100.0	54.1	40.0	5.9	...	...	...	...	...
1916-20	1935	8.1	100.0	55.5	39.6	4.9	...	...	...	...	...
1911-15	1930	9.1	100.0	52.7	41.8	5.5	...	...	...	...	...
1906-10	1925	9.3	100.0	51.6	43.0	5.4	...	...	...	...	...
1901-05	1920	8.9	100.0	57.3	37.1	5.6	...	...	...	...	...
1896-1900	1915	8.6	100.0	50.0	44.2	5.8	...	...	...	...	...
1891-95	1910	8.2	100.0	46.3	46.4	7.3	...	...	...	...	...

					Exact ages 20 to 24						
1931-35	1955	65.8	100.0	27.2	39.1	23.5	7.6	2.0	0.4	0.2	...
1926-30	1950	63.5	100.0	32.8	42.2	18.9	4.7	1.1	0.3	...	...
1921-25	1945	56.2	100.0	38.1	39.7	15.8	4.8	1.2	0.4	...	...
1916-20	1940	47.6	100.0	35.3	42.0	16.6	4.6	1.3	0.2	...	...
1911-15	1935	46.7	100.0	35.8	40.2	17.1	5.2	1.3	0.4	...	...
1906-10	1930	48.3	100.0	29.6	42.9	19.2	6.2	1.7	0.2	0.2	...
1901-05	1925	49.0	100.0	26.9	43.7	20.4	6.8	1.8	0.2	0.2	...
1896-1900	1920	47.3	100.0	28.3	42.5	19.9	7.2	1.7	0.4	...	...
1891-95	1915	46.4	100.0	24.8	43.7	21.2	7.7	2.2	0.4	...	...
1886-90	1910	44.9	100.0	22.3	44.1	22.5	8.0	2.4	0.7	...	...

					Exact ages 25 to 29						
1926-30	1955	87.3	100.0	13.3	27.2	32.8	16.7	6.6	2.3	0.8	0.3
1921-25	1950	86.0	100.0	16.9	34.8	29.3	12.0	4.4	1.7	0.6	0.3
1916-20	1945	81.0	100.0	23.3	35.1	24.3	10.3	4.3	1.7	0.6	0.4
1911-15	1940	75.3	100.0	26.3	34.8	22.0	9.6	4.4	1.8	0.7	0.4
1906-10	1935	74.2	100.0	23.6	33.3	22.7	11.1	5.5	2.5	0.9	0.4
1901-05	1930	75.5	100.0	20.0	32.7	23.7	12.6	6.5	2.8	1.2	0.5
1896-1900	1925	74.9	100.0	17.5	32.7	24.3	13.4	7.2	3.0	1.2	0.7
1891-95	1920	72.8	100.0	15.0	33.9	24.5	14.1	7.4	3.0	1.4	0.7
1886-90	1915	72.0	100.0	12.6	33.4	23.4	15.5	8.7	4.0	1.7	0.7
1881-85	1910	71.2	100.0	11.2	33.5	23.3	15.3	9.4	4.6	1.9	0.8

					Exact ages 30 to 34						
1921-25	1955	92.4	100.0	8.5	21.4	32.7	20.3	9.6	4.0	1.9	1.6
1916-20	1950	90.6	100.0	12.9	25.9	31.0	16.3	7.3	3.4	1.7	1.5
1911-15	1945	87.0	100.0	17.8	29.1	26.7	13.2	6.4	3.4	1.7	1.7
1906-10	1940	84.4	100.0	18.4	28.9	24.5	12.9	7.1	3.8	2.3	2.1
1901-05	1935	84.4	100.0	16.6	26.8	23.8	14.0	8.4	4.7	3.0	2.7
1896-1900	1930	85.2	100.0	15.0	25.1	23.5	14.9	9.2	5.6	3.3	3.4
1891-95	1925	84.5	100.0	12.2	26.1	23.1	15.2	10.0	6.1	3.6	3.7
1886-90	1920	82.7	100.0	9.7	25.8	23.4	15.8	11.0	6.1	4.0	4.2
1881-85	1915	82.7	100.0	8.5	25.7	22.0	16.0	11.4	7.2	4.4	4.8
1876-80	1910	81.8	100.0	7.2	26.2	20.1	15.2	11.4	8.3	5.7	5.9

					Exact ages 35 to 39						
1916-20	1955	93.1	100.0	9.9	20.0	29.7	19.5	10.3	4.9	2.6	3.1
1911-15	1950	91.6	100.0	14.6	23.5	27.4	16.2	8.4	4.1	2.5	3.3
1906-10	1945	89.4	100.0	16.3	25.1	25.2	14.2	8.0	4.4	2.8	4.0
1901-05	1940	88.3	100.0	15.6	24.0	23.4	14.2	8.9	5.1	3.5	5.3
1896-1900	1935	88.0	100.0	13.6	22.4	22.4	15.0	9.7	5.9	4.2	6.8
1891-95	1930	88.2	100.0	11.6	22.5	21.3	15.1	10.5	6.4	4.8	7.8
1886-90	1925	87.4	100.0	9.5	22.2	20.9	15.4	10.9	6.8	5.3	9.0
1881-85	1920	86.3	100.0	7.1	21.6	20.5	15.5	11.7	7.4	5.8	10.4
1876-80	1915	85.9	100.0	5.8	20.9	19.3	15.0	11.6	8.5	6.9	12.0
1871-75	1910	86.0	100.0	5.6	20.9	17.0	13.8	11.3	9.1	7.8	14.5

TABLE **120.**—PERCENT OF WOMEN EVER MARRIED AND PERCENT DISTRIBUTION BY PARITY OF EVER-MARRIED WOMEN AT SELECTED AGES AND DATES, FOR GROUPS OF NATIVE WHITE COHORTS—Cont.

Cohorts of—	Jan. 1 of—	Percent ever mar- ried	Percent of all ever-married women, by parity								
			Total	Zero	One	Two	Three	Four	Five	Six	Seven and higher
					Exact ages 40 to 44						
1911–15............1955..		93.1	100.0	14.2	21.7	26.5	16.5	9.2	4.8	2.8	4.3
1906–10............1950..		91.6	100.0	15.9	23.3	24.7	14.7	8.5	4.7	3.1	5.1
1901–05............1945..		89.2	100.0	14.7	23.2	23.1	14.4	8.9	5.3	3.7	6.7
1896–1900..........1940..		89.5	100.0	14.0	21.3	21.8	14.5	9.6	6.0	4.3	8.5
1891–95............1935..		89.3	100.0	11.4	21.7	20.5	14.7	10.3	6.5	4.7	10.2
1886–90............1930..		89.0	100.0	9.8	21.0	19.8	14.7	10.8	6.6	5.4	11.9
1881–85............1925..		88.4	100.0	7.7	20.4	19.1	14.7	11.2	7.2	5.8	13.9
1876–80............1920..		87.7	100.0	6.0	19.4	18.3	14.5	11.6	7.5	6.3	16.4
1871–75............1915..		87.4	100.0	5.3	19.0	16.1	13.9	11.4	7.9	6.8	19.6
					Exact ages 45 to 49						
1906–10............1955..		92.8	100.0	16.7	22.8	24.4	14.5	8.5	4.7	3.0	5.4
1901–05............1950..		91.8	100.0	16.8	22.5	22.4	14.0	8.7	5.1	3.6	6.9
1896–1900..........1945..		90.8	100.0	15.0	21.0	21.4	14.3	9.4	5.8	4.2	8.9
1891–95............1940..		90.2	100.0	12.2	21.4	20.2	14.5	10.1	6.3	4.7	10.6
1886–90............1935..		89.2	100.0	10.1	20.9	19.5	14.5	10.6	6.6	5.2	12.6
1881–85............1930..		89.5	100.0	8.7	19.9	18.8	14.4	10.9	7.0	5.7	14.6
1876–80............1925..		88.9	100.0	7.1	19.0	17.9	14.2	11.1	7.4	6.1	17.2
1871–75............1920..		88.5	100.0	6.2	18.5	15.9	13.6	11.0	7.8	6.5	20.5

Source: Table 116.

A broader comparison may be made by considering the changes in the approximate position of the median at ages 40–44 and 45–49. In the cohorts of 1871–75 the zero-, one-, and two-parity women together make up almost half the total. In contrast, in the cohorts of 1906–10 nearly half the women are in the zero- and one-parity groups alone, and the inclusion of two-parity women would raise the fraction to approximately two-thirds. That trend has been reversed, however, for the proportion of zero- and one-parity women at ages 40–44 is smaller in the 1911–15 cohorts (by 1955) than in those of 1906–10 (by 1950).

Because approximately nine out of ten women marry before reaching age 50, the parity distributions of all women and of ever-married women are much alike at the older reproductive ages, even though they differ widely at the younger ages. At ages 40–44 and 45–49 the proportion in the first, second, and each higher parity group is slightly larger (7 to 14 percent) among ever-married women than among all women, but the changes from cohort to cohort have been about the same in both cases. The chief difference in intercohort trends is found in the zero-parity group, which contains only about one-third to two-thirds as many of the ever-married women as of all women. As was brought out in section B, the changes in cumulative rates from cohort to cohort among women living to middle age have been downward for first births and upward for marriages. The net result is a much larger increase in the zero-parity group among ever-married women than all women. For example, the percentage of all women aged 45 to 49 who had not borne a child was about 1.3 times as large for the cohorts of 1906–10 (by 1955) as for those of 1871–75 (by 1920), but for the ever-married women it was more than 2.7 times as large. (Compare tables 119 and 120.)

FIGURE 110.—PERCENT DISTRIBUTION BY PARITY AT AGES 45–49 FOR COHORTS OF NATIVE WHITE WOMEN

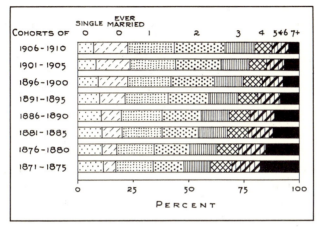

Note: Based on data in table 119.

Most of this important increase in childlessness among married women of completed fertility appears to have been voluntary, judging from the relevant information which is available. Some of the evidence comes from a few studies of selected groups of married couples, in which questions were asked about the number of children wanted, the type and regularity of contraceptive practices (including "rhythm") used, physiological conditions which might reduce the likelihood of conception, and the incidence of miscarriages and other types of pregnancy wastage. For example, in a study which covered nearly 90 percent of the native white Protestant husbands and wives living in Indianapolis in 1941 who had been married 12 to 14 years and had completed at least the eighth grade, there were 382 couples (19.3 percent of the group) that had not had a child. It was obvious that some of them regretted being childless, and that a few of the couples with one or more children had tried unsuccessfully to keep from having any. But since it was impossible to have the childless couples examined medically and given various clinical tests, it was impossible to determine precisely (a) how many of them could have had a child but prevented pregnancy by practicing contraception effectively, and (b) how many of them thought that their contraceptive efforts had prevented pregnancy while in fact these efforts had not been efficient and their childlessness was really due to sterility. It appears, however, that between one-third and one-half of the 382 childless couples (between 6 and 10 percent of the 1,977 couples covered) were childless from choice, and that between one-half and two-thirds of the childless couples (between 9.5 and 13.5 percent of all couples) were childless because of physiological impairments.[16]   In short, this and other studies show that both choice and sterility have been important causes of childlessness.

If the only changes in the proportion of all women or of ever-married women who are childless were substantial increases, it would be as reasonable (or perhaps more reasonable) to ascribe the change to more sterility due to various causes (for example, less vitamin E in the diet, rising nervous strain of urban living, etc.), as to an increase in the proportion of couples that do not want a child and are able to prevent conception.   In fact, however, the proportion of the women aged 45 to 49 who have married but have not borne a child, which rose from about 6 percent in the cohorts of 1871–75 to nearly 17 percent in those of 1901–05, will fall rapidly in the future.   This is shown conclusively by the cohorts of 1921–25, since 92.4 percent of these women had married by ages 30–34 (by 1955) but only 8.5 percent of those who had married had not borne a child.   (The proportion of ever-married women will almost certainly be a little higher at older ages, and the proportion of childless women probably will be a little lower.)   Moreover, there is evidence that opinions regarding certain aspects of marriage and family-building have changed in one direction for some years and in the opposite direction later.   These aspects include the age at which women marry, the length of the interval between marriage and the first child, and the number of children in the family.   It is much more probable that there have also been substantial increases and decreases in a related matter—the proportion of couples desiring to be childless—than that such changes have occurred in the physiological ability of couples to have the first child.

Mixed trends in family size by intermediate ages.   The situation at ages between 20–24 and 40–44 may be described in general as reflecting a gradual shift from one to the other of the two extremes discussed above.   At ages 30–34 (as at ages 45–49) the effect of the relatively large decreases in cumulative rates for higher order births is clearly evident. The proportion of women at sixth, seventh, or higher parity is about two-thirds lower for the cohorts of 1921–25 than for those of 1876–80, whereas the proportion at fifth parity is down by almost one-half.   (See figure 111 and the fourth deck of table 119.)   At all times, however, the number of women reaching fifth or higher parity by ages 30–34 has been comparatively small.   Much more important numerically are the changes in the zero-parity group, which rose from 24.1 percent for the cohorts of 1876–80 (by 1910) to 31.1 percent for those of 1906–10 (by 1940) and then tumbled to 15.5 percent (by 1955) for women born in 1921–25.

---

[16] P. K. Whelpton and Clyde V. Kiser (Editors), *Social and Psychological Factors Affecting Fertility*, Vol. II, *The Intensive Study: Purpose, Scope, Methods, and Partial Results*, Milbank Memorial Fund, New York, 1950, p. 336.

Differences between the earliest and latest cohorts on record are relatively small for the proportion of women at first parity and fourth parity, but among intervening cohorts the changes are substantial—a rise and decline for first parity and a decrease and recovery for fourth parity.

FIGURE 111.—PERCENT DISTRIBUTION BY PARITY AT AGES 30–34 FOR COHORTS
OF NATIVE WHITE WOMEN

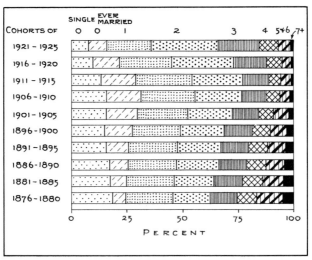

Note: Based on data in table 119.

By far the largest shifts are at second parity. The percentage of the women aged 30–34 who were in this group went up gradually from 16.5 for the cohorts of 1876–80 (by 1910) to 23.2 for those of 1911–15 (by 1945) and then jumped to 30.2 (by 1955) for the women of 1921–25. At third parity—the only other parity with relatively more women in the latest cohorts than the earliest—little change occurred among the cohorts of 1911–15 and earlier, the lowest percentage being 10.9 and the highest 13.2. The big jump is that of the cohorts of 1921–25 in which 18.9 percent of the women aged 30–34 were at third parity by 1955.

In the cohorts of 1876–80 to those of 1911–15, zero-parity women were more numerous than women of any other parity at ages 30–34. In the last two groups of cohorts to reach these ages, however, two-parity women ranked first. Three-parity women, who were substantially outnumbered by those in each of the lower parities in the cohorts of 1916–20 and earlier, climbed almost to second place in the cohorts of 1921–25.

The upward trend in the proportion of women who marry before ages 30–34 has made the intercohort changes in the parity distribution of ever-married women somewhat larger than those for all women. (Compare tables 119 and 120.) But at these ages, as at the 40's, the main difference is in the zero-parity group. Among all women the proportion with no birth by ages 30–34 rose by about one-fourth from the cohorts of 1876–80 (by 1910) to those of 1906–10 (by 1940), but among ever-married women it more than doubled. In both cases, however, the relative size of the childless group was more than cut in half from the cohorts of 1906–10 (by 1940) to those of 1921–25 (by 1950).

The intercohort changes in parity distribution at certain ages are quite different from those at other ages in part because the same cohorts are not being considered in all cases. The principle is illustrated by table 118, but may be made more specific here. For example, we know now that the 1931–35 cohorts, which reached ages 20–24 on January 1, 1955, had relatively few zero-parity women and relatively many first, second, and third parity women at these ages compared with earlier groups. Not until after 1980, however, can we be certain as to how the parity distribution of the 1931–35 cohorts will compare with that of prior groups at ages 45–49. It now appears likely that then, as now, the 1931–35 contingent will have relatively fewer zero-parity women and more first- and fourth-parity women than the preceding groups, thus reversing the trend shown to date in the bottom deck of table 119. But it is also quite likely that by then a new situation will be developing among subsequent cohorts, so that intercohort changes by younger ages will continue to differ from those by older ages.

Broadly speaking, the past trend toward fewer women with at least four children and more women with none, one, or two seems to be giving way to a new trend toward more families with three or four children and fewer with no child or only one, while the proportion with two children remains relatively stable. There are even some indications of a rise in the proportion of five-child families, but it is too early to say whether this will be significant. Old-fashioned large families with eight or more children have become relatively rare, and most probably will continue so. But no longer is there likely to be a net shift from large to very small; instead, a concentration in the two- or three-child group is indicated.

D. Changes in the tendency to bear the "next" child

The changes which have been taking place in the fertility of successive cohorts may be understood still better if they are considered from a third point of view, namely, that of parity progression ratios. The ratios used here show the number of women who bore a child of order N + 1 per 100 women reaching parity N by a given age.

Differences between the ratios for lower and higher parities. Because the parity progression ratio has not been a widely used measure of fertility, it is desirable to observe first how the ratios for a given parity compare in size with those for other parities. Among younger women there is an important drop in the size of the ratio as parity rises. For example, the 0-to-1-parity ratio of wives at ages 20–24 varies between 62 and 78 among the cohorts of 1886–90 to 1931–35 and the 1-to-2-parity ratio between 35 and 46; for each group of cohorts the latter is one-half to two-thirds as large as the former. (See the second deck of table 121.) The change becomes smaller as parity rises, nevertheless the progression ratio for third parity is at least 11 percent below that for second parity for all groups of cohorts, and is 28 percent smaller for the cohorts of 1896–1900.

The tendency among young wives for the ratio to decline as parity rises stems chiefly from the fact that at least nine months commonly elapse between marriage and the first birth, and at least twelve months between successive births (except in the case of twins and triplets). Many of the wives aged 20–24 on a given date have been married long enough to have borne one child, but fewer have had time for a second child, and still fewer for a third or fourth. This time factor loses importance as women become older and probably has little influence compared with others above ages 30–34.

The progression ratio for each parity becomes larger as age rises, but approaches an upper asymptote at a decreasing rate. For example, the 0-to-1 ratio climbs from a range of 44 to 54 at ages 15–19 to between 74 and 89 at ages 25–29, reaches a peak between 82 and 94 at ages 30–34 or 35–39, and then declines slightly in some cases. The reversal in trend reflects the fact that the women who do not marry until the late 30's or the early 40's are less likely to have a child than those who marry at younger ages. The 1-to-2-parity ratio changes in a somewhat similar manner as age rises, but has its largest increase 5 years later (from ages 15–19 to 20–24 instead of by 15–19) and does not climb so high. For a time the increases are larger numerically but smaller relatively for first and second parities than for the middle parities, consequently, the numerical difference between these parities widens somewhat while the relative difference narrows. Thus, at ages 20–24, the third-parity ratio averages 15 points or 38 percent smaller than the first, but at ages 30–34 the difference is 14 points, or 19 percent. Subsequently, both the numerical and relative differences tend to become smaller; for the ratios in question they are 7 points and 9 percent at ages 45–49. In other words, the tendency for the progression ratio to decrease as parity rises from 1 to 3 is continued as women live to middle age, but the size of the differential becomes much smaller as age rises.

Progression ratios for fourth parity are not significant until after ages 20–24, nor for sixth parity until after 25–29, because too few births of these orders occur by these ages. At ages 30–34 the proportion of women who had had an additional birth was successively smaller formerly as the number already borne rose above one. (See cohorts of 1876–80 to 1906–10 in the fourth deck of table 121.) In more recent cohorts, however, these differences have tended to disappear among women with three to six births.

TABLE **121.**—PARITY PROGRESSION RATIOS: NUMBER OF WOMEN WHO HAVE MOVED FROM PARITY N TO PARITY N + 1 PER 100 WHO HAVE REACHED PARITY N BY SELECTED AGES AND DATES, FOR GROUPS OF COHORTS OF NATIVE WHITE WOMEN

[Based on cumulative birth rates like those in table 114. For example, the ratio for progression from parity one to parity two for the cohorts of 1936-40 at ages 15 to 19 is obtained by dividing the cumulative rate for second births by ages 15 to 19 in table 114 by the rate for first births and multiplying by 100 (i.e., 10.64 ÷ 64.82 × 100 = 16.4). The ratios for the cohorts of 1896-1900 and earlier are preliminary estimates, subject to minor changes. The computations were carried to more decimal places than are shown; each figure was rounded independently]

Cohorts of--	Jan. 1 of--	Parity progression						
		Zero to one	One to two	Two to three	Three to four	Four to five	Five to six	Six to seven
		Exact ages 15 to 19						
1936–40	1955	54	16	11	...	...	...	...
1931–35	1950	45	15	9	...	...	...	...
1926–30	1945	44	13	11	...	...	...	...
1921–25	1940	46	12	9	...	...	...	...
1916–20	1935	44	11	7	...	...	...	...
1911–15	1930	47	12	9	...	...	...	...
1906–10	1925	48	12	8	...	...	...	...
1901–05	1920	43	12	9	...	...	...	...
1896–1900	1915	50	12	8	...	...	...	...
1891–95	1910	54	14	...	...	...	...	...
		Exact ages 20 to 24						
1931–35	1955	73	46	30	25	...	...	...
1926–30	1950	67	37	25	22	...	...	...
1921–25	1945	62	36	28	25	...	...	...
1916–20	1940	65	35	27	24	...	...	...
1911–15	1935	64	37	29	25	...	...	...
1906–10	1930	70	39	30	25	...	...	...
1901–05	1925	73	40	31	24	...	...	...
1896–1900	1920	72	41	32	23	...	...	...
1891–95	1915	75	42	33	25	...	...	...
1886–90	1910	78	43	33	28	...	...	...
		Exact ages 25 to 29						
1926–30	1955	87	69	45	37	35	33	...
1921–25	1950	83	58	39	37	37	37	...
1916–20	1945	77	54	41	41	39	36	...
1911–15	1940	74	53	44	43	40	37	...
1906–10	1935	76	56	47	45	40	37	...
1901–05	1930	80	59	50	47	41	37	...
1896–1900	1925	83	60	51	47	41	37	...
1891–95	1920	85	60	52	47	41	40	...
1886–90	1915	87	62	57	50	42	37	...
1881–85	1910	89	62	58	52	44	37	...
		Exact ages 30 to 34						
1921–25	1955	91	77	53	45	44	46	46
1916–20	1950	87	70	49	46	47	49	48
1911–15	1945	82	65	50	50	51	52	48
1906–10	1940	82	65	53	54	54	53	48
1901–05	1935	83	68	58	57	56	55	48
1896–1900	1930	85	70	61	59	57	55	50
1891–95	1925	88	70	63	61	57	55	50
1886–90	1920	90	71	64	61	57	58	51
1881–85	1915	92	72	67	64	59	56	53
1876–80	1910	93	72	70	67	64	58	51
		Exact ages 35 to 39						
1916–20	1955	90	78	58	52	51	53	55
1911–15	1950	85	73	56	53	54	58	58
1906–10	1945	84	70	57	57	58	61	59
1901–05	1940	84	71	61	61	62	63	60
1896–1900	1935	86	74	65	64	64	65	61
1891–95	1930	88	74	68	66	64	66	62
1886–90	1925	91	75	69	68	66	68	63
1881–85	1920	93	77	71	70	67	68	65
1876–80	1915	94	78	74	72	70	69	64
1871–75	1910	94	78	77	76	74	71	65

TABLE **121.**—Parity Progression Ratios: Number of Women Who Have Moved from Parity N to Parity N + 1 per 100 Who Have Reached Parity N by Selected Ages and Dates, for Groups of Cohorts of Native White Women—Cont.

Cohorts of--	Jan. 1 of--	Parity progression						
		Zero to one	One to two	Two to three	Three to four	Four to five	Five to six	Six to seven
		Exact ages 40 to 44						
1911-15...............1955..		86	75	59	56	57	60	61
1906-10...............1950..		84	72	59	59	60	63	63
1901-05...............1945..		85	73	63	63	64	67	64
1896-1900............1940..		86	75	66	66	66	68	66
1891-95...............1935..		89	76	69	68	67	70	68
1886-90...............1930..		90	77	71	70	69	72	69
1881-85...............1925..		92	78	73	72	71	73	71
1876-80...............1920..		94	79	76	74	72	75	72
1871-75...............1915..		95	80	79	77	75	77	74
		Exact ages 45 to 49						
1906-10...............1955..		83	73	60	60	61	64	64
1901-05...............1950..		83	73	63	63	64	67	65
1896-1900............1945..		85	75	67	67	67	69	68
1891-95...............1940..		88	76	70	69	68	71	70
1886-90...............1935..		89	77	72	71	70	73	71
1881-85...............1930..		91	78	74	73	71	74	72
1876-80...............1925..		93	80	76	75	73	76	74
1871-75...............1920..		94	80	79	77	76	78	76

Source: Table 114.

Later in the reproductive period there is a tendency among recent cohorts for the middle parity ratios to be the smallest, and for the higher parity ratios to be successively larger. This is true on the whole for third to fifth parity women aged 35–39 and 40–44 in the cohorts of 1901–05 and later. (See the lower decks of table 121.) Women who have borne six children are an exception, however, the 6-to-7 progression ratios having been slightly smaller than the 5-to-6. Among earlier cohorts (1871–75 to 1886–90) and at older ages (45–49), the tendency to have still another baby has been about the same for women who have borne two, three, four, five, or six.

Changes between cohorts in progression ratios by various ages. Patterns of intercohort change in parity progression ratios have differed widely with age. There has been a tendency for the ratios for parities 0, 1, and 2 at ages 20–24 to follow a U-shaped trend, declining from the 1886–90 cohorts to those of 1916–20 or 1921–25, and then rising to the 1931–35 group. (See table 121.) The recent rise of the 1-to-2 ratio (from 35 to 46) is somewhat larger than the previous decline (from 43 to 35), but the reverse is true for the other ratios. These changes show in another way the increase in the number of childless wives and the decrease in the number of children per mother which went on among earlier cohorts at the younger ages. Among more recent cohorts the rapid rise of the progression ratios for lower parities reflects the increase in the proportion of wives who have their first two children at younger ages. Whether the small increases from the 1926–30 to 1931–35 cohorts in the ratios from second to third and third to fourth parities mark the beginning of a trend toward more third and fourth babies soon after marriage remains to be seen.

Nearly all the progression ratios at the older childbearing ages (40–44 and 45–49) show a downward trend. At ages 40–44 the smallest decline is that of the 1-to-2 ratio, which went from 80 for the cohorts of 1871–75 to 72 for those of 1906–10, and then rose to 75 for the 1911–15 group—the latest to reach these ages. Similar changes on a slightly larger scale occurred in the 0-to-1 ratio. The largest reduction is that of the 3-to-4 ratio, which fell uninterruptedly from 77 for the 1871–75 cohorts (by 1915) to 56 for the 1911–15 group (by 1955)—a cut of nearly 25 percent. The 2-to-3 and 4-to-5 ratios dropped almost as rapidly, but the 5-to-6 and 6-to-7 ratios had smaller declines. These changes agree, of course, with those of cumulative birth rates which were shown in section B, where the decrease is smallest for first births and successively larger for subsequent births. But they bring out in sharper focus the fact that the tendency to stop having children reached a maximum after the third child in the cohorts of 1911–15, instead of after the fourth or sixth as was the case for earlier cohorts.

With parity progression ratios, as with the other measures of fertility, the picture at ages from 25–29 to 35–39 is along a continuum between ages 20–24 and 40–44. The intercohort trend of the 0-to-1 ratio is U-shaped at ages 25–29 and 30–34, similar to that at ages 20–24, but the recent rise is noticeably smaller at ages 35–39 as it approaches the age 40–44 situation. Statements of the same type can be made for the 1-to-2 and 2-to-3 parity ratios. In contrast, the 3-to-4 ratio, which shows a slight upturn at ages 20–24, has merely stopped declining at ages 25–29 and slackened its decrease at older ages. Ratios for higher parities also show reductions in the rate of decline. All this is in line with the long-time tendency to avoid large families and the more recent tendency to avoid being childless or to have only one child, which were brought out in sections B and C.

It is interesting to consider the reasons why the 1950 and 1955 parity progression ratios by ages 40–44 and 45–49 are smaller for the middle parities than for the lower and higher parities, and how the relationships may change in the future. The three main reasons why ever-married women of these ages have not had an additional child are:

(1) The marriage has been broken by death of husband, or by separation or divorce, and remarriage has not occurred.

(2) The wife and/or husband has become sterile.

(3) Contraception (including rhythm) has been practiced diligently (or abortion has been performed), because another child was not wanted.[17]

---

[17] Miscarriages or stillbirths may have been as important a reason for not having an additional child as marriage broken by death of the husband or by separation or divorce, where remarriage has not occured.

It seems probable that in recent years all three factors have operated to make the 1-to-2 parity progression ratio smaller than the 0-to-1, and the 2-to-3 ratio smaller than the 1-to-2. It also seems probable that the first two factors have tended to make subsequent ratios successively smaller. If this is true, the small increase from the 3-to-4 ratio to the 6-to-7 ratio would have occurred because the influence of the first two factors was more than balanced by a *decrease* in the proportion of effective users of contraception as parity rises above four.

That there has been such a decrease is indicated by one of the special studies which have been made. Among the Indianapolis couples mentioned previously it was found that about two-thirds of those classified as "relatively fecund" used some means of contraception (including rhythm) before the first pregnancy, about two-thirds of the remainder began to do so after the end of the first pregnancy, and a few more became users after the second or third.[18] In contrast, most of the remaining "relatively fecund" couples made no effort to control childbearing. Because some of the couples were completely successful with their contraceptive practices and nearly all others were partially successful, and because relatively few of the "relatively fecund" couples wanted three children and still fewer wanted four or more, it follows that most of the third and higher order conceptions were "accidents" or occurred among couples who did not practice contraception. Furthermore, because there was a tendency for the "relatively fecund" couples to become more careful after one or two "accidents," the proportion of births which were "accidental" declined after the fourth, and the proportion which occurred to non-users of contraception increased. In other words, it appears that as parity rises above 4: (*a*) couples who try to postpone or prevent conception become relatively less numerous because fewer want yet another child and fewer have "accidents," and (*b*) the couples who *do not* attempt prevention become relatively more numerous because the other couples are less likely to have an additional child. This would explain the increase in the parity progression ratios under consideration.

The second question—how the relationships of parity progression ratios are likely to change in the future—is more speculative, but there is a basis for some observations. Since the more recent cohorts now have larger 0-to-1 and 1-to-2 ratios than the preceding group (or groups) of cohorts by the younger ages (20–24 and 25–29), it seems highly probable that they will continue to do so through the remainder of the reproductive period. This will mean a reversal of past trends. What will happen to the ratios for higher parities will depend mainly on the changes that occur in the proportion of couples wanting three or more children, in the proportion that try to prevent unwanted pregnancies, and in the success of their efforts.[19]

---

[18] P. K. Whelpton and Clyde V. Kiser, *op. cit., pp. 212–214.*

[19] Definite information about a national sample of the population would be of great help in answering these questions and will soon be provided by the study—"Growth of American Families"—which

E. Fertility and marriage during 5-year time periods and age intervals

In sections B, C, and D attention was focused on the fertility of groups of women as they live through the reproductive period, and on the differences between these groups with respect to cumulative birth rates, parity distributions, and parity progression ratios by various ages.   In this section attention will be centered on fertility *within* 5-year time periods and age intervals, as measured by the additions to cumulative birth rates and marriage rates in cohort tables.   The "additions" are a type of age-specific period rate.   The easiest way to obtain them is to subtract the cumulative rates up to a given age period in table 114 from those up to the next older age period, but they can also be obtained by adding and averaging the annual rates for individual cohorts (like those which are shown in table 112 for cohorts of 1881, 1906, and 1931).   These rates are similar conceptually to the census-based ratios of own children under 5 years of age to women by 5-year age groups (which were discussed in the other chapters) but are larger numerically because the ratios do not include the children born during the 5 years preceding a census but dying before the census date.[20]

The composite picture for all ages.   Period rates from cohort fertility tables, like the conventional annual rates and ratios of children to women (in Chapter 3) show that current fertility was unusually high during the first half of the 1950's.   When the 1950–54 birth rates of different cohorts at different ages are combined to provide a composite picture,[21] the total for this period exceeds that for the other periods since 1910–14.   Additions to cumulative birth rates in 1950–54 total 3,176 per 1,000 women in the childbearing ages, which practically equals the 1910–14 number and is more than half again as large as the low mark reached in the last half of the 1930's.   (See table 122 and figure 112.)   This number means that if age-specific birth rates were to continue as they were in 1950–54, each 1,000 women living to the end of the reproductive period would bear 3,176 children—almost as many as the actual number borne by women in the cohorts of 1876–80.

---

is being conducted by P. K. Whelpton, Scripps Foundation for Research in Population Problems, Miami University, and Ronald Freedman, Department of Sociology, University of Michigan.   The first book *Family Planning, Sterility, and Population Growth* is scheduled for publication by The McGraw-Hill Book Company early in 1959.

[20] The additions to the cumulative rates are the same conceptually as the age-specific rates shown in Chapter 3, table 13, but differ with respect to the ages and years which are grouped together.   For example, the rate of 722 shown in table 122 for ages 15–19 through 19–23 in 1950–54 is the sum of the central rates for ages 15 through 19 in 1950, 16 through 20 in 1951, and so on to 19 through 23 in 1954.   This type of grouping is usually confined to cohort tables.

[21] The procedure parallels that followed in computing a female gross reproduction rate, except that the age-specific birth rates are based on total births rather than female births.

TABLE **122.**—ADDITIONS TO CUMULATIVE MARRIAGE RATES AND TO CUMULATIVE BIRTH RATES, BY ORDER OF BIRTH, DURING SELECTED AGE PERIODS AND YEARS, FOR GROUPS OF COHORTS OF NATIVE WHITE WOMEN

[These rates may be obtained by adding and averaging appropriate annual rates like those in tables 111 and 112, or by deducting the cumulative rates for a given age period in table 114 from those for the next older age period. The computations were carried to more decimal places than are shown; each figure was rounded independently]

Cohorts of--	Years	Marriage rate	Order of birth								
			All births	First	Second	Third	Fourth	Fifth	Sixth	Seventh	Eighth and higher
Exact ages 14 to 48
1906-40........1950-54..		1,016	3,176	1,017	951	585	292	141	76	42	71
1901-35........1945-49..		1,174	2,829	1,073	811	424	212	115	68	44	84
1896-1930......1940-44..		1,095	2,377	898	626	334	184	110	72	49	103
1891-1925......1935-39..		935	2,093	740	487	281	180	121	88	63	133
1886-1920......1930-34..		853	2,220	668	490	321	220	154	115	82	169
1881-1915......1925-29..		919	2,613	742	563	390	271	190	140	101	210
1876-1910......1920-24..		975	2,928	826	616	429	309	222	162	117	248
1871-1905......1915-19..		920	2,920	784	607	420	302	215	175	136	281
1866-1901......1910-14..		928	3,189	822	652	477	336	240	188	144	329

Exact ages 14 to 48

Cohorts of-- / Years	Marriage rate	All births	First	Second	Third	Fourth	Fifth	Sixth	Seventh	Eighth and higher
Exact ages 10-14 to 14-18[1]										
1936-40........1950-54..	120	77	65	11	1	(2)	...	...	...	...
1931-35........1945-49..	128	67	57	9	1	(2)	...	...	...	...
1926-30........1940-44..	89	44	39	5	1	(2)	...	...	...	...
1921-25........1935-39..	85	44	39	5	(2)	(2)	...	...	...	...
1916-20........1930-34..	81	41	36	4	(2)	(2)	...	...	...	...
1911-15........1925-29..	91	49	43	5	(2)	(2)	...	...	...	...
1906-10........1920-24..	93	51	45	5	(2)	(2)	...	...	...	...
1901-05........1915-19..	89	43	38	5	(2)	(2)	...	...	...	...
1896-1900......1910-14..	86	49	43	5	(2)	(2)	...	...	...	...
Exact ages 15-19 to 19-23[1]										
1931-35........1950-54..	530	722	422	214	66	17	4	1	(2)	(2)
1926-30........1945-49..	546	592	388	154	39	9	2	(2)	(2)	(2)
1921-25........1940-44..	477	476	309	120	35	9	2	(2)	(2)	(2)
1916-20........1935-39..	395	413	272	104	28	7	1	(2)	(2)	(2)
1911-15........1930-34..	376	405	257	106	32	8	2	(2)	(2)	(2)
1906-10........1925-29..	390	475	295	127	40	10	2	1	(2)	(2)
1901-05........1920-24..	401	517	320	139	43	11	2	1	(2)	(2)
1896-1900......1915-19..	387	484	296	133	43	10	2	(2)	(2)	(2)
1891-95........1910-14..	382	507	305	140	48	12	2	(2)	(2)	(2)
Exact ages 20-24 to 24-28[1]										
1926-30........1950-54..	238	1,006	331	360	194	78	28	10	3	1
1921-25........1945-49..	298	869	367	290	128	52	20	8	3	1
1916-20........1940-44..	334	735	313	230	111	50	20	8	2	1
1911-15........1935-39..	286	610	255	181	95	47	20	8	2	1
1906-10........1930-34..	259	623	226	187	111	59	25	10	3	2
1901-05........1925-29..	265	715	245	213	134	73	32	12	4	2
1896-1900......1920-24..	276	798	278	235	148	81	36	14	5	2
1891-95........1915-19..	264	778	270	220	146	79	35	15	5	2
1886-90........1910-14..	271	849	280	238	170	95	43	16	5	2
Exact ages 25-29 to 29-33[1]										
1921-25........1950-54..	64	737	130	233	183	97	47	24	12	10
1916-20........1945-49..	96	668	169	216	134	70	38	21	11	10
1911-15........1940-44..	117	575	160	170	103	60	37	22	12	10
1906-10........1935-39..	102	490	122	125	87	61	42	27	15	12
1901-05........1930-34..	89	520	101	121	98	75	54	36	19	15
1896-1900......1925-29..	103	607	106	137	119	93	67	43	23	18
1891-95........1920-24..	117	681	123	149	132	107	76	47	26	21
1886-90........1915-19..	107	659	118	144	120	100	72	51	30	24
1881-85........1910-14..	115	722	125	150	134	111	84	57	28	33

See footnotes at end of table.

TABLE **122.**—ADDITIONS TO CUMULATIVE MARRIAGE RATES AND TO CUMULATIVE BIRTH RATES, BY ORDER OF BIRTH, DURING SELECTED AGE PERIODS AND YEARS, FOR GROUPS OF COHORTS OF NATIVE WHITE WOMEN—Cont.

Cohorts of--	Years	Marriage rate	Order of birth								
			All births	First	Second	Third	Fourth	Fifth	Sixth	Seventh	Eighth and higher
Exact ages 30-34 to 34-38[1]										
1916-20........1950-54..		25	421	49	99	102	68	39	24	15	24
1911-15........1945-49..		46	408	67	105	86	53	33	22	16	26
1906-10........1940-44..		50	348	60	79	61	43	31	24	18	32
1901-05........1935-39..		39	317	40	54	50	42	35	30	24	41
1896-1900.....1930-34..		28	363	36	53	56	51	45	40	31	51
1891-95........1925-29..		37	432	39	60	67	62	54	48	38	63
1886-90........1920-24..		47	491	44	64	73	72	66	57	44	72
1881-85........1915-19..		36	532	45	71	76	75	68	64	50	82
1876-80........1910-14..		41	591	50	85	84	79	72	67	55	99
Exact ages 35-39 to 39-43[1]										
1911-15........1950-54..		15	178	17	30	34	28	19	14	10	26
1906-10........1945-49..		22	186	22	33	32	24	18	14	11	33
1901-05........1940-44..		9	162	16	21	21	19	16	15	13	42
1896-1900.....1935-39..		15	172	11	16	18	20	19	18	17	54
1891-95........1930-34..		11	209	11	17	21	23	23	23	22	70
1886-90........1925-29..		16	261	13	19	26	28	29	29	28	88
1881-85........1920-24..		21	303	14	21	28	32	34	35	33	106
1876-80........1915-19..		18	333	15	24	30	32	30	37	41	125
1871-75........1910-14..		14	373	16	30	35	32	30	39	46	145
Exact ages 40-44 to 44-48[1]										
1906-10........1950-54..		12	35	3	4	5	4	4	3	2	10
1901-05........1945-49..		26	39	3	4	4	4	4	3	3	14
1896-1900.....1940-44..		13	37	1	1	2	3	4	3	4	18
1891-95........1935-39..		9	47	1	2	3	3	4	5	5	25
1886-90........1930-34..		5	59	1	2	3	4	5	6	7	31
1881-85........1925-29..		11	74	1	2	4	5	6	7	8	39
1876-80........1920-24..		12	87	2	3	5	6	8	8	9	47
1871-75........1915-19..		11	91	2	4	5	6	8	8	10	48
1866-70........1910-14..		11	98	3	4	6	7	9	9	10	50

[1] To illustrate the meaning of these age intervals, the average age of the cohorts of 1931-35 on Jan. 1, 1950, was 15-19, i.e., it was 15 for the cohort of 1935, 16 for that of 1934, etc. Between that date and Dec. 31, 1954, when these cohorts, respectively, had reached the end of ages 19-23, the average cumulative birth rate of the group had risen by 722 points. This is the difference between the rates for these cohorts at ages 15-19 and 20-24, as shown in table 114.
[2] 0.05 or less.

Source: Table 114 for birth rates and table 116 for marriage rates.

Although fertility during 1945–49 was much higher than during any period from 1930–34 to 1940–44, it was well below 1950–54. This reflects the fact that birth rates were relatively low in 1945, and that the demobilization of the Armed Forces after the end of World War II could not have much influence on childbearing until 1946. Hypothetical lifetime fertility rates based on the 4-year period 1946–49 are closer to those for 1950–54. The widespread impression that fertility rose during World War II finds support in the cohort tables, for a hypothetical cohort with the age-specific birth rates of 1940–44 would have 2,377 births per 1,000 women living to age 50 compared with 2,093 for a hypothetical cohort living under the conditions of 1935–39. Nevertheless, this increase of 284 is less than two-thirds as large as the increase of 452 from 1940–44 to 1945–49.

FIGURE **112.**—COMPLETED BIRTH RATES, BY ORDER OF BIRTH, FOR HYPOTHETICAL COHORTS OF NATIVE WHITE WOMEN HAVING CURRENT FERTILITY RATES OF FIVE-YEAR PERIODS FROM 1910–14 TO 1950–54

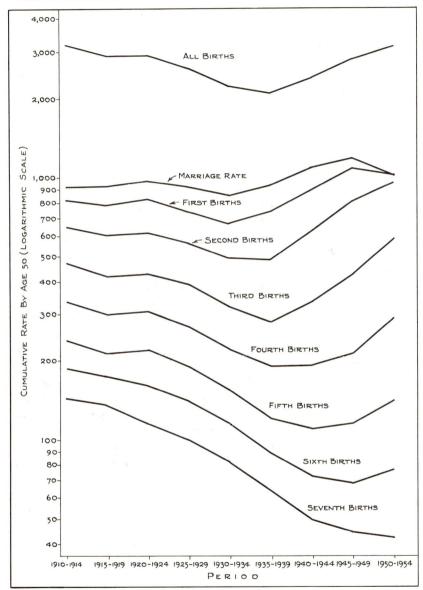

Note: Based on data in table 122.

Although some indices of business conditions show that the depression hit the national economy harder in 1930–34 than 1935–39, its impact on current fertility apparently was greater during the later of these two periods, for the additions to cumulative birth rates amounted to 2,093 in 1935–39 compared with 2,220 in 1930–34.   Before the depression there had been a marked downward trend, which reduced this rate by about 18 percent from 1910–14 to 1925–29.   An additional decrease of 15 percent occurred from 1925–29 to 1930–34.   World War I apparently caused a minor interruption in the decline from one 5-year period to another, the rate for 1920–24 being slightly larger than that for 1915–19.   Had there been no such war it is probable that the difference between these periods would have been larger, and in the opposite direction.   Nevertheless, there is little doubt but that the events associated with World War I had a much smaller impact on current fertility than those associated with World War II.

Marriages and first births at all ages.   An examination of the differences in marriage rates and in birth rates by order of birth helps one to understand the significance of the changes in total fertility from one period to another.   Here, as with the rates for all births, the equivalent of the conventional gross reproduction rate procedure, which is to add annual rates by single years of age, has been followed.   This procedure gives results for marriages and first births during recent periods which are impossible for actual cohorts.   For example, in a hypothetical cohort having at successive ages the age-specific first marriage rates of 1945–49, there would be 1,174 *first* marriages among each 1,000 women living to age 50. Similarly, in a hypothetical cohort having at successive ages the age-specific first birth rates of 1945–49, there would be 1,073 *first* births per 1,000 women.   It is obvious that 1,000 women in an actual cohort cannot have more than 1,000 first marriages, nor more than 1,000 first births,[22] and that the actual numbers will be smaller than 1,000 because of spinsterhood and sterility.   But while such figures cannot be interpreted as representing the possible experience of actual cohorts, they do provide trustworthy indices to use in comparing the tendency to marry or to have first births in the different 5-year periods under consideration.[23]

As mentioned in section A, the cumulative first marriage rates for intercensal years depend on estimates in greater degree than the rates for births; hence the additions to the marriage rates during 5-year periods must be interpreted with somewhat more caution than the additions to birth rates.   It is clear, however, that first marriage rates for all women aged 14 through

---

[22] One of each pair of twins is always listed as born after the other, even though in some Caesarean deliveries the interval is very short.

[23] The correct procedure for obtaining results which would be possible for actual cohorts requires the use of age-specific rates for women at risk, that is, rates computed by relating first marriages to never-married women, first births to zero-parity women, second births to one-parity women, etc.   For a more complete discussion of this problem see P. K. Whelpton, "Reproduction Rates Adjusted for Age, Parity, Fecundity, and Marriage," *Journal of the American Statistical Association*, December 1946, Vol. 41, pp. 501–503.

49 were unusually low during the first half of the 1930's, and unusually high during the 15-year period 1940 to 1954. The computed rate of 853 per 1,000 women during 1930–34 is 66 points, or 7 percent, below the previous low rate, while that of 1945–49 is 199 points, or 20 percent, above the highest rate prior to World War II. (See table 122 and figure 112.)

World War I, unlike World War II, seems to have had little current impact on the tendency of single women to become brides by age 50, the cumulative marriage rate under conditions of 1915–19 being about the same as that for 1910–14, whereas there was a 17-percent rise from 1935–39 to 1940–44. The difference probably reflects in important degree the influence of the great depression, which led to the postponement of many thousands of marriages during the 1930's, a high proportion of which were performed in the 1940's. The rise in the marriage rate after World War I was nearly as large as that after World War II—approximately 6 percent and 7 percent, respectively—in spite of the decidedly higher rates during the later war. This reflects the marked tendency for more women to marry young in the cohorts of 1926 to 1935 than in prior cohorts.

Changes in marriage rates from one period to another would be expected to influence, with a slight lag, the rates for first births; consequently, it is not surprising that a strong relationship is shown in table 122. Not only do the largest and the smallest rates for first births come in the same 5-year periods as those for first marriages, but the direction of change from one period to another is the same in each case.

Second and subsequent births at all ages. When rates for successively higher order births are examined, two facts are shown clearly. One is that the lag between the changes in marriage rates and those in birth rates increases as birth order rises, and the other is that the dwindling number of large families had a great impact on total fertility. The latter is brought out by the pattern of differences between the 1950–54 and the 1910–14 additions to cumulative rates for births of successively higher orders. Those for the later period exceed the others by 24 percent for first births, 46 percent for second births, and 23 percent for third births, but fall below in increasing degree for fourth and later births until, for eighth and higher order births, the 1950–54 figure is barely one-fifth as large as that of 1910–14. (These diverging rates of change are pictured accurately by the semi-logarithmic scale used in figure 112.) Furthermore, while the direction of change of the rate for first births from one 5-year period to another is up four times and down four times, among subsequent birth orders the downward movements gradually replace the upward movements until all are downward for seventh births, and for eighth and higher order births.

Rates for second, third, and fourth births changed in the same direction as marriage rates from one 5-year period to another during 1910–14 to

1930–34, but not in the same degree. The increase from 1915–19 to 1920–24 was much smaller for each of these birth rates than for the marriage rate, but all four rates had similar decreases from 1925–29 to 1930–34. More significant, however, are the differentials after 1930–34. Although the marriage rate and the first birth rate were about 10 percent higher during 1935–39 than 1930–34, the second birth rate was slightly lower, and the rates for third and fourth births were down by 12 percent and 18 percent, respectively. And whereas the large rise in the marriage rate and first birth rate occurred from 1930–34 to 1945–49 (followed by a small decline to 1950–54), the rates for second, third, and fourth births made their big gains from 1935–39 to 1950–54.

The examination of composite rates for single years in Chapter 3 pinpoints more exactly the later turning points of trends as birth order rises. The general picture shown by the 5-year rates is clear, however, for the trough associated with the depression is in 1930–34 for marriages and first births, in 1930–39 for second births, in 1935–39 for third births, in 1935–44 for fourth births, in 1940–44 for fifth births, in 1945–49 for sixth births, and in 1950–54 for seventh births. Stated differently, when the periods are ranked with respect to rates for the various birth orders, as in table 123, we see a strong tendency for the rankings to be similar along diagonals with an upward slope from left to right. This is especially true for the lowest rank (9) which is on the fifth line (1930–34) for the marriage rate but rises to the top line (1950–54) for eighth and higher order births. It is manifested in a different way for the high rankings, the 1's, 2's, and 3's being highly concentrated in triangles at the upper left and lower right.

TABLE **123.**—RANKING OF FIVE-YEAR PERIODS WITH RESPECT TO SIZE OF ADDITIONS TO
CUMULATIVE RATES FOR MARRIAGE AND FOR BIRTHS OF SPECIFIED ORDER

Period	Marriage	Order of birth							
		First	Second	Third	Fourth	Fifth	Sixth	Seventh	Eighth and higher
1950–54.....................	3	2	1	1	4	6	7	9	9
1945–49.....................	1	1	2	4	7	8	9	8	8
1940–44.....................	2	3	4	7	8	9	8	7	7
1935–39.....................	5	8	9	9	9	7	6	6	6
1930–34.....................	9	9	8	8	6	5	5	5	5
1925–29.....................	8	7	7	6	5	4	4	4	4
1920–24.....................	4	4	5	3	2	2	3	3	3
1915–19.....................	7	6	6	5	3	3	2	2	2
1910–14.....................	6	5	3	2	1	1	1	1	1

Source: Table 122.

If, as is highly probable, a similar relationship occurs in the future with respect to the peaks associated with the end of World War II, the marriage and first birth rates (which established records in 1945–49) will decline until 1960–64 or later, the second birth rate will recede from its high mark of 1950–54, the third birth rate will start declining after 1955–59, and the fourth and fifth birth rates will reach their peaks in 1955–59 and then start down. The probable trends for higher birth orders are not so clear, because they are influenced in increasing degree by the desire to avoid large families. It now seems probable that births of these orders will continue to include less than 6 percent of all births as they did in 1950–54, and that the long-time trend will be slightly downward. It is possible that there may be a temporary rise in the 1960's, but if so, it probably will be small. A safe conclusion is that sixth and higher order births will not be important numerically during the next few decades at least.

Differences between time periods with respect to marriage and fertility rates during age intervals. Clues regarding the relative standing of different time periods with respect to birth rates during age intervals are given in the preceding section by the remarks about the pattern of rates by birth order. First births tend to come early in the reproductive period, eighth and subsequent births to come late, and births of intermediate orders to be interspersed in between; hence, what was said above about marriage and fertility rates by order of birth applies fairly well to rates by age intervals. The pattern is not as clear, however, with age as with birth order. Thus, the tendency for rankings 9 and 8 to apply to later time periods as age rises is not as marked (see table 124) as is the tendency for these ratings to move up as birth order rises (see table 123). On the other hand, it is the recent cohorts which have the two top ratings for the younger ages as they do for marriage rates and first and second birth rates, and the early cohorts which have top ratings at the older ages as they do for rates for the higher order births.

TABLE **124.**—RANKING OF FIVE-YEAR PERIODS WITH RESPECT TO SIZE OF ADDITIONS TO CUMULATIVE RATES FOR TOTAL BIRTHS DURING FIVE-YEAR AGE INTERVALS

Period	All ages	Age interval (exact ages)					
		10–14 to 14–18	15–19 to 19–23	20–24 to 24–28	25–29 to 29–33	30–34 to 34–38	35–39 to 39–43
1950–54	2	1	1	1	1	5	7
1945–49	5	2	2	2	4	6	6
1940–44	7	6–7	6	6	7	8	9
1935–39	9	6–7	8	9	9	9	8
1930–34	8	9	9	8	8	7	5
1925–29	6	4–5	7	7	6	4	4
1920–24	3	3	3	4	3	3	3
1915–19	4	8	5	5	5	2	2
1910–14	1	4–5	4	3	2	1	1

Source: Table 122.

The age intervals refer to five successive cohorts of women who live from exact ages x, x + 1, . . . x + 4 on a given date to the end of ages x + 4, x + 5 . . . x + 8 on a date five years later, e.g., from exact ages 10–14 to the end of ages 14–18.

Wide divergence in the standing of a 5-year period with respect to rates during different age intervals is found in some cases. For example, 1950–54 ranks first at the four youngest age intervals, and fifth and seventh in the next two, while 1910–14 ranks fourth and fifth at the two

FIGURE **113.**—ADDITIONS TO CUMULATIVE RATES FOR ALL BIRTHS, BY FIVE-YEAR AGE GROUPS, FOR COHORTS OF NATIVE WHITE WOMEN DURING FIVE-YEAR PERIODS FROM 1910–14 TO 1950–54

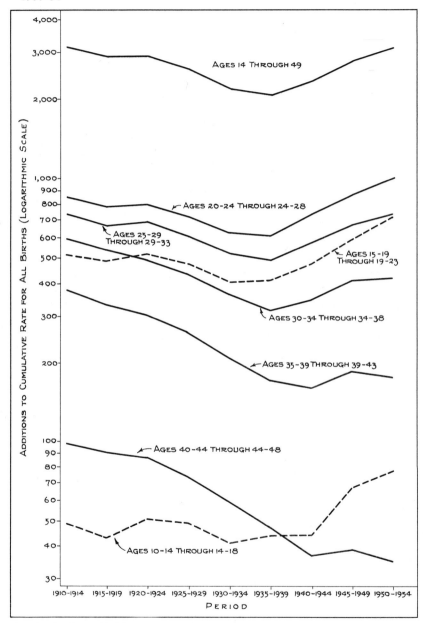

Note: Based on data in table 122.

youngest age intervals but rises to the top of the list at ages 35–39 and 40–44. (See table 124 and figure 113.) In contrast, the low ranking of 1930–34, 1935–39, and 1940–44 with respect to rates for all ages combined (mentioned above) emerges from relatively low rankings at each age. This is especially true for the 1935–39 period, which is at the bottom of the "all ages" list, is last at three of the six age intervals shown in table 124, and never rises above a tie for sixth place (at ages 10–14 to 15–19). The 1930–34 period also ranks consistently low at each age interval.

The "sources" of the much higher fertility during 1945–54 than 1930–39. That there has been a great upsurge in numbers of births and in the birth rate in the United States since the end of World War II is widely known. The average annual number of births could not increase from 2,437,400 during 1930–39 to 3,678,300 during 1945–54— up 50 percent—without attracting much attention. What is not widely known is how the change has come about. The popular explanation seems to be that families are becoming larger. Much less is said regarding the effect of younger marriage, the starting of families more quickly after marriage, and the larger size of the population. Since the future trend of fertility and of population growth (to be discussed in the next chapter) will be influenced to a major degree by the events of recent years, it is important that these events be interpreted correctly. Marriage rates and birth rates from cohort tables are helpful in this connection.

No attempt will be made in this section to deal with the basic factors which effect decisions as to whether and when to marry, how many children to have, and when to have each of them. Instead, attention will be confined to four variables: (a) the number of women grouped by childbearing age, (b) the cumulative marriage rate per 1,000 women, (c) the cumulative first birth rate per 1,000 ever-married women, and (d) the cumulative rate for all births per 1,000 mothers. The three rates measure, respectively, the effect of differences in decisions as to whether and when single women marry, brides have a first child, and mothers have additional children. When the changes in these rates are combined, they account for the change in the rate for all births to all women of reproductive age.[24] Combining them with the change in the number of women accounts for all of the change in the number of births. Although numbers of births to all women were mentioned in the preceding paragraph, the following discussion (like the rest of this chapter) is restricted to births to native white women.

---

[24] The combined effect of these three rates may be illustrated by referring to the cumulative rates of the cohorts of 1931–35 by ages 20–24. If the cumulative first marriage rate (658 in table 116) is multiplied by the cumulative first birth rate of ever-married women (728 in table 116), and the product is multiplied by the cumulative rate of all births to mothers (1,647 in table 117), the result is the cumulative rate for all births to all women (789 in table 114). The same principle applies to the additions to these rates from one age to another.

The procedure followed is a simple one. It consists of (a) estimating the number of babies that would have been born during 1945–54 if one of the four variables had been as it actually was during 1945–54 and the other three had remained as they were during 1930–39, and (b) comparing the resulting number of births with the actual number during 1930–39. The difference is a "first estimate" of the increase in births due to the change in the variable in question. Repeating the process for each of the other three factors gives "first estimates" of their contribution to the postwar baby boom. Because there are wide differences between certain ages (and cohorts) in the behavior of these variables and in the number of women involved, it is necessary to consider each group of ages and cohorts separately.[25]

The computations are shown in detail in appendix table B–6 but may be illustrated here by referring to the experience from exact ages 20–24 to exact ages 30–34 of the cohorts of 1906–10 (whose women were aged 20–24 on January 1, 1930), and the cohorts of 1921–25 (whose women were aged 20–24 on January 1, 1945). The earlier group of women bore about 5,043,000 babies in the 1930's and the later group about 8,293,000 during 1945–54, an increase of 3,250,000 or 64.4 percent. There were 4,527,000 women aged 25–29 in the earlier group on January 1, 1935, and 5,163,000 in the later group on January 1, 1950. If the only difference between the two groups had been this increase in the number of women (that is, if the three rates mentioned above had remained unchanged), the later group would have had 5,754,000 births during 1945–54, an increase of 711,000 or 14.1 percent over 1930–39. (See table 125, columns G and H.)

The second of the four variables—the cumulative marriage rate—is 483 for the 1906–10 cohorts by ages 20–24 (by 1930) and 844 by ages 30–34 (by 1940); for the 1921–25 cohorts the corresponding figures are 562 (by 1945) and 924 (by 1955). (See table 116.) If we assume that the later group had been the same as the earlier except for its higher cumulative marriage rates, it would have had 5,355,000 births in 1945–54, a gain of 312,000 or 6.2 percent over the 1930–39 figure for the age interval. (See table 125, columns I and J.) Next, the cumulative first birth rate per 1,000 ever-married women by ages 20–24 and 30–34 is 704 and 816 for the cohorts of 1906–10 (by 1930 and 1940) and 619 and 915 for those of 1921–25 (by 1945 and 1955). (See table 116.) Had this been the only change, the increase of the number of births would have been 1,186,000, or 23.5 percent. (See table 125, columns K and L.)

Finally, the number of births per 1,000 mothers by ages 20–24 and 30–34 is 1,545 and 2,380 for the cohorts of 1906–10 (by 1930 and 1940) and 1,494 and 2,515 for the 1921–25 group (by 1945 and 1955).

---

[25] For a more detailed explanation of the procedure see Appendix B, section 5. Considering ages and cohorts singly rather than in groups of five would not improve the results sufficiently to justify the additional work involved.

(See table 117.)   This change alone would have raised the number of births by 498,000, or 9.9 percent.   (See table 125, columns M and N.) It is clear, therefore, that as far as this age interval is concerned the much larger number of births in 1945–54 than in 1930–39 is due primarily to causes which led more married women to have first births, with the larger size of the cohort in second place (but much less important), and more marriages and more births per mother having still less effect.

TABLE 125.—CONTRIBUTION TO THE LARGER NUMBERS OF BIRTHS TO NATIVE WHITE WOMEN DURING 1945–54 THAN 1930–39 FROM (A) LARGER NUMBERS OF WOMEN, (B) HIGHER MARRIAGE RATES FOR ALL WOMEN, (C) HIGHER FIRST BIRTH RATES FOR EVER-MARRIED WOMEN, AND (D) HIGHER RATES FOR ALL BIRTHS TO MOTHERS

Age interval (exact ages)	Cohorts living through age interval during--		Number of births (thousands)			
	1930–39 (A)	1945–54 (B)	1930–39 (C)	1945–54 (D)	Increase (E)	Percent increase (F)
5–9 to 14–18...................	1921–25	1936–40	243	358	115	47.2
10–14 to 19–23.................	1916–20	1931–35	2,404	4,049	1,645	68.4
15–19 to 24–28.................	1911–15	1926–30	5,108	8,639	3,531	69.1
20–24 to 29–33.................	1906–10	1921–25	5,043	8,293	3,250	64.4
25–29 to 34–38.................	1901–05	1916–20	3,276	5,278	2,002	61.1
30–34 to 39–43.................	1896–1900	1911–15	1,900	2,545	644	33.9
35–39 to 44–48.................	1891–95	1906–10	837	829	-8	-1.0
40–44 to 49–53.................	1886–90	1901–05	181	141	-39	-21.6
Total.....................			18,992	30,132	11,139	58.7

Age interval (exact ages)	Increase in births due to--									
	Larger numbers of women		Higher marriage rates per 1,000 women		Higher first birth rates per 1,000 ever-married women		Higher rates for all births per 1,000 mothers		Interaction of these four factors	
	Number (thousands) (G)	Percent (H)	Number (thousands) (I)	Percent (J)	Number (thousands) (K)	Percent (L)	Number (thousands) (M)	Percent (N)	Number (thousands) (O)[1]	Percent (P)
5–9 to 14–18........	-39	-15.9	105	43.2	44	18.2	11	4.5	-7	-2.7
10–14 to 19–23......	-79	-3.3	918	38.2	302	12.6	292	12.1	212	8.8
15–19 to 24–28......	388	7.6	856	16.7	966	18.9	700	13.7	621	12.2
20–24 to 29–33......	711	14.1	312	6.2	1,186	23.5	498	9.9	543	10.8
25–29 to 34–38......	783	23.9	86	2.6	759	23.2	117	3.6	256	7.8
30–34 to 39–43......	418	22.0	207	10.9	207	10.9	-178	-9.4	-9	-0.5
35–39 to 44–48......	119	14.2	147	17.6	-26	-3.1	-209	-25.0	-39	-4.6
40–44 to 49–53......	33	18.5	261	144.6	-228	-126.2	-72	-40.0	-34	-18.6
Total..........	2,334	12.3	2,892	15.2	3,211	16.9	1,158	6.1	1,544	8.1

[1] O = E − G − I − K − M.
Source: Appendix table B-6.
The age intervals refer to five successive cohorts of women who live from exact ages x, x + 1, . . . x + 4 on a given date to the end of ages x + 9, x + 10 . . . x + 13 on a date ten years later, e.g., from exact ages 5–9 to the end of ages 14–18.

Before examining the other age intervals, let us compare the sum of the four separate hypothetical increases, which is 2,707,000, and the total increase of 3,250,000. The difference of 543,000 is the result of the interaction of the four factors when they vary at the same time, and accounts for 10.8 percent of the additional births during this age interval in 1945–54 than in 1930–39. If the increases shown for each variable operating singly are raised proportionally so that their sum equals the total increase, the results may be called "second estimates" of the influence of each variable.

The effect of each of the four factors varies widely from one age interval to another, three of them causing decreases as well as increases, and all causing large changes as well as small. (See figure 114.) At the two younger age intervals there were fewer women in 1945–54 than in 1930–39, which tends to reduce the number of births. This is more than offset, however, by the much stronger effect of the larger numbers of women aged 15 to 44 in 1945 than in 1930. In fact at age intervals 25–29 through 34–38 and 30–34 through 39–43, population growth contributed more than any one of the other three factors to the excess of births during 1945–54 compared with 1930–39. For all ages combined, it is third in importance, accounting for about one-fourth of the total change. (See table 126.) This means that the changes in the other three factors, namely, the increases in rates for marriages of single women, first births of wives, and second, third, etc., births of mothers, together account for three-fourths of the larger number of births during 1945–54 than 1930–39, and for almost all of the gain in crude birth rate.

TABLE 126.—INCREASE IN BIRTHS TO NATIVE WHITE WOMEN, 1930–39 TO 1945–54, ASCRIBABLE TO EACH OF FOUR VARIABLES

Variables	Showing interaction separately		Distributing interaction proportionally	
	Number (thousands)	Percent	Number (thousands)	Percent
Larger numbers of women.......................	2,334	21.0	2,710	24.3
Higher cumulative rates for:				
Marriages per 1,000 women..................	2,892	26.0	3,357	30.1
First births per 1,000 ever-married women...	3,211	28.8	3,728	33.5
All births per 1,000 mothers................	1,158	10.4	1,344	12.1
Interaction.................................	1,544	13.9	...	...
Total.......................................	11,139	100.0	11,139	100.0

Source: Table 125.

The rise in cumulative marriage rates contributed about 30 percent of the increase in the number of births from 1930–39 to 1945–54, a somewhat larger proportion than population growth but not quite as much as the higher cumulative first birth rates of married women. The greater tendency to marry is especially significant for younger women, adding more than 900,000 births (or nearly two-thirds of the total gain) at the age interval 10–14 through 19–23, and contributing heavily at the age interval 15–19 through 24–28. Its influence diminishes rapidly by the age interval 25–29 through 34–38, but is more important at the next older interval.[26] In other words the major change in the marriage pattern is a

[26] The large increase in births at age interval 40–44 through 49–53 which is shown in table 125 as due to higher marriage rates is less valid than the other parts of this table. The reason is that the relatively large increase of the cumulative marriage rate of the cohorts of 1901–05 from 892 by ages 40–44 to 930 by ages 50–54 was accompanied by a relatively large decline in the cumulative rate for first births to ever-married women (from 853 to 822). This would be expected, because most of the women whose first marriage takes place after their fortieth birthday do not bear a child. Among the 1886–90 cohorts at these ages, the increase in the marriage rate was small (890 to 899) as was the decrease of the first birth rate to ever-married women (from 902 to 895). It is highly unlikely that

FIGURE **114.**—CHANGES FROM 1930–39 TO 1945–54 IN NUMBERS OF BIRTHS TO NATIVE
WHITE WOMEN, BY AGE, DISTRIBUTED BY EFFECT OF CHANGES IN FOUR VARIABLES

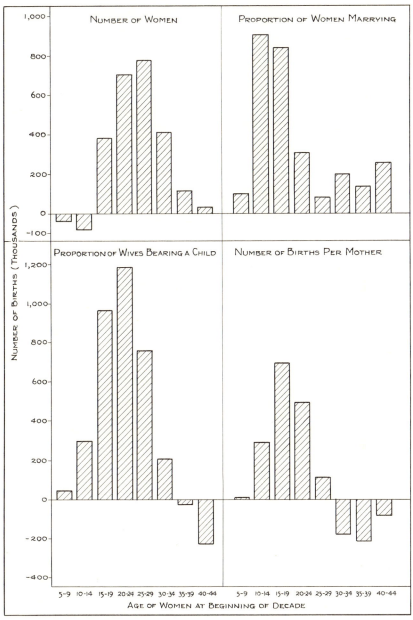

Note: Based on data in table 125.

the large increase between ages 40–44 and 50–54 in the marriage rate of the later cohorts and the
small decrease at these ages in the first birth rate of the earlier cohorts could have occurred together,
or that a large decrease in the first birth rate would have occurred at these ages with a small increase
in the marriage rate.   These are the only combinations of assumptions which appear highly improbable in the example in question.

reduction in the age at marriage, with only a small increase in the proportion of women marrying by middle age. Nevertheless, this is the only one of the four factors which brought about a larger number of births in every age interval.

The third factor—more first births per 1,000 ever-married women— has a slightly greater impact than any of the other three variables under consideration, accounting for about one-third of the postwar upsurge in the number of births.   (See table 126 and figure 115.)   Its contribution increases rapidly to a peak at the age interval 20–24 through 29–33, where it accounts for over 40 percent of the extra births, and then decreases even more rapidly.   Here, too, the difference in the timing pattern is highly significant, for more than half of the larger additions to the cumulative first birth rates of wives during 1945–54 than 1930–39 comes from the tendency to have the first child at younger ages during the more recent period.   This statement does not deny the decrease in the proportion of wives who never bear a child, but ranks the effect of that decrease definitely below the other change.

FIGURE **115.**—PROPORTION OF NET INCREASE FROM 1930–39 TO 1945–54 IN NUMBER OF BIRTHS TO NATIVE WHITE WOMEN THAT IS ASCRIBABLE TO CHANGES IN EACH OF FOUR VARIABLES

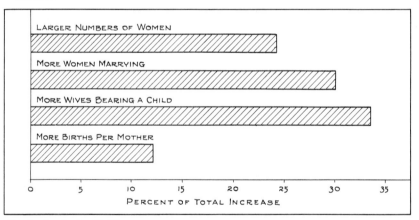

Note: Based on data in table 126.

The fourth variable—more children per woman with children—is by far the least important on the whole, explaining only about 12 percent of the extra births during 1945–54.   Its greatest influence is at the age interval 15–19 through 24–28 (adding about 840,000 births including its share of interaction), but even here it ranks considerably below higher marriage rates and higher first birth rates.   Moreover, at age intervals 30–34 through 39–43 and older, the lower rates for children per mother in the later cohorts lead to sizable reductions—rather than increases—in the number of births.

The foregoing discussion gives added support to earlier statements regarding the importance of changes in age at marriage and at the birth of the first child in connection with the major changes in annual numbers of births and crude birth rates during the last 30 years. The postwar "baby boom" has not occurred mainly because families are larger, if family size is measured by the number of children *per married woman having children,* as has been done above. If the yardstick of family size is children *per married woman,* the conclusion is somewhat different, because there has been a large increase in the proportion of wives who have had a first birth, especially among those in the younger ages. As has been pointed out, however, this results chiefly from younger marriage and the starting of childbearing more quickly after marriage, and only in minor degree from a decrease in the proportion of wives who never have any children.

If fewer wives remain childless, this in itself will certainly tend to raise the average number of births per married woman. Younger marriage would certainly have the same effect in many countries where effective family planning is not widespread. Opinions differ as to whether it will have much impact in the United States, where a large majority of married couples are able to prevent pregnancy after having as many babies as they desire. The major unknown seems to be: Will marriage at younger ages in itself lead couples to want more children? Strange as it may seem, practically no information is available on this topic. It is well known, of course, that women who marry younger have more children than those who marry older. But it is equally well known that those who marry younger differ from the others with respect to education, occupation and income of father and husband, and other socio-economic characteristics. Moreover, there is evidence of personality differences. Is the difference in number of children due to the difference in age at marriage or to the other differences? Here is where facts are lacking and should be obtained.

CHAPTER   1 0

THE OUTLOOK FOR BIRTHS

A. Birth assumptions in population projections

Projections of population numbers to future dates have been made by many people in many ways. Very often the projection is on a simple basis such as, "If the present rate of population increase should continue, the population in the year _____ will be _____." Sometimes different rates of increase are assumed and computations made for each, as was done by DeBow in the Compendium of the 1850 Census. Mathematical methods have been used in large variety, such as linear or parabolic extrapolation, geometric or exponential progression, and projections of fitted curves, such as the logistic. Methods have also been used that take explicit account of the components of population change (births, deaths, and net migration). Some methods go further and take explicit account of the factors that affect the components of population growth. A relatively recent development is the projections of births by cohorts of women, made by the Scripps Foundation for Research in Population Problems.

The components of population change are always involved, at least implicitly, whether or not the makers of the population projections consciously take them into account. The projections may seem reasonable on the basis of the facts used and unreasonable on the basis of direct consideration of the outlook for the components of population change. The methods may be descriptive of what happened before but there may be an indication in other data of some impending change that should be taken into account. In particular, it appears that in the future, fertility will be the main component of population change in the United States, and that many projections of population are in effect indirect and sometimes unreasoned assumptions as to the future course of fertility.

Mortality probably will be a less important source of variation than fertility in future population growth in the United States because mortality in recent years has been so low that not even an improbable complete elimination of deaths of females before the end of the reproductive period could greatly augment the supply of future parents. For example, according to United States life tables for 1953, about 95 percent of white female infants and 88 percent of nonwhite female infants would live to age 40. (Babies born in 1953 and subsequent years will of course be subject to different, probably lower, death rates as they pass through life.) Changes in mortality that do not increase the number of potential parents may result in a population attaining a certain size a few years earlier than it would have otherwise, but the death rates at postreproductive ages have no cumulative effect on population growth from generation to generation.

The general outlook is for further reductions in mortality at most ages because of the increasing knowledge of healthful diet and living practices by the general population, better medical care, extensive medical research, a more than adequate food supply, and a generally rising standard of living.

A 50-percent reduction in death rates at every age would increase the expectation of life for newborn infants of both sexes, all races combined, by only about 4 years. It is quite likely that research into cancer and heart disease and other degenerative ailments will prolong life and raise the average age at death somewhat, although the illustrative 50-percent cut in total death rates at each age used above may be on the optimistic side. In fact, it is possible that at some advanced ages the death rates will actually increase as a consequence of more weakened survivors at these ages who once would have died sooner.

Domestic migration is a very important factor in population change on a local basis but not on a national basis. Present restrictions on immigration are such that the annual net immigration from abroad has tended to be less than 0.2 percent of the present national population. A large change in this percentage is regarded as unlikely in the near future in view of the present attitudes of the American people toward large-scale immigration.

The birth projections are the main source of uncertainty for national population projections. Different assumptions of trends in fertility result in population projections that differ by several million within a few years time.

B. Short-run birth projections based on age-specific birth rates

The Bureau of the Census has occasionally made illustrative projections of population on the basis of assumed trends in age-specific birth and death rates. The Bureau used the age-specific birth rates in the accompanying table for population projections published in October 1955 (with the birth results shown in table 127 and figure 116):

Annual births per 1,000 women

Age of woman	Extrapolated 1954–55 rates	Estimated 1950–53 average	Approximate "prewar" level (1939–40)
15 to 19 years[1]	87.5	87.9	61.2
20 to 24 years	232.5	213.4	152.3
25 to 29 years	195.0	176.0	135.4
30 to 34 years	122.2	109.5	81.1
35 to 39 years	60.2	56.2	38.8
40 to 44 years[2]	16.5	17.1	11.4

[1] Rates include births to females under 15 years old.

[2] Rates include births to females over 44 years old.

Source: U. S. Bureau of the Census, *Current Population Reports*, Series P–25, No. 123, by Meyer Zitter, p. 4.

The combinations used for population projections are spelled out in figure 116. They will be discussed briefly.

A wide variation existed between the schedule of the age-specific birth rates for 1954–55 and that of "prewar" 1939–40. This was a prima facie basis for supposing that a similar range of variation (in reverse) was possible for the coming few years. The Bureau did not allow for an increase in age-specific birth rates beyond the 1954–55 level because this was regarded as unlikely. The constant 1954–55 level used for Series AA involved an implicit assumption that the increase in age-specific birth rates had about run its course. The central Series A and B estimates were based on the assumption that a slight decrease would occur soon. The Series C assumed a return to the "prewar" fertility levels of 1939–40. It must be emphasized that these schedules of birth rates and the trends assumed were selected simply for purposes of illustration, and that the short-run rather than long-run possibilities were taken as major considerations because the projections are revised at frequent intervals.

TABLE 127.—PROJECTED BIRTHS AND BIRTH RATES, 1955 TO 1975, AND ACTUAL RATES, 1950 TO 1955

[See figure 116 for explanation of Series AA, A, B, and C. Rates based on population including Armed Forces abroad]

Period	Births (millions)				Average annual rate per 1,000 of the midperiod population			
	Series AA	Series A	Series B	Series C	Series AA	Series A	Series B	Series C
July 1950 to 1955	19.6	19.6	19.6	19.6	24.8	24.8	24.8	24.8
July 1955 to 1960	20.6	19.1	19.1	17.7	24.0	22.3	22.3	20.7
July 1960 to 1965	21.7	20.1	20.1	17.4	23.3	21.8	21.8	19.2
July 1965 to 1970	24.4	22.7	21.0	18.3	24.2	23.0	21.4	19.2
July 1970 to 1975	28.2	25.9	20.5	19.4	25.7	24.3	19.7	19.3

Source: Adapted from U. S. Bureau of the Census, *Current Population Reports*, Series P-25, No. 123, "Revised Projections of the Population of the United States, by Age and Sex: 1960 to 1975," by Meyer Zitter, table D; National Office of Vital Statisics, *Vital Statistics of the United States*, annual volumes, 1950 to 1954, and provisional data for 1955.

The birth rates used may be evaluated for long-range reasonableness in terms of the implications for the eventual size of families (even though the projections did not take this factor directly into account). One may add the age-specific birth rates for 5-year age groups and multiply the sum by 5 in order to estimate the number of children that would be born to a group of 1,000 women by the end of the childbearing period if the group were subject to the specific birth rates at each age and if none of the group died before age 45. On this basis, the schedule for 1954–55 implies that the women of all marital classes would bear an average of 3.6 children, about as many as Whelpton found for the native white cohorts of 1871–75. Corresponding averages for 1950–53 and 1939–40 are 3.3 and 2.4, respectively. Are these averages reasonable?

It was noted previously that if the women 25 to 29 years old in 1952 were about 55 percent through childbearing, they would eventually complete the childbearing ages with an average of 2.8 children. If many of the women in this group were only having children earlier than usual, the 55 percent is too low, and the 2.8 average is too high. With the 2.8 average as a standard of comparison, it appears that the age-specific birth rates for 1954–55 and 1950–53 and their implied averages of 3.6 and 3.3 are much too high to continue indefinitely. Further evidence of "abnormality" in the age-specific birth rates appears when they are subdivided by order of birth (see Chapter 9, section E). An eventual return to lower age-specific birth rates, or at least to lower first birth rates is to be expected. Perhaps 1965 is too remote a date for this process to begin, as assumed in Series B.

FIGURE 116.—ACTUAL AND PROJECTED AVERAGE ANNUAL NUMBER OF BIRTHS PER 1,000 POPULATION: 1910 TO 1975

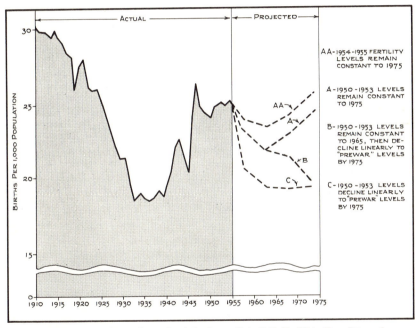

Source: U. S. Bureau of the Census, *Current Population Reports*, Series P-25, No. 123, by Meyer Zitter, p. 5.

The Series AA and A estimates assumed that age-specific birth rates would not change in the future. The trends in projected births for these series therefore reflected the effect of changing numbers of women by age. However, this effect is not the same when different schedules of birth rates are used. Series AA and Series A differ in that AA shows no dip whereas A shows a dip in the total number of births in the next few years. In all four series, AA, A, B, and C, it appeared that the birth rates per 1,000 population will decline between 1955 and 1965 and then rise again. There will be more women of childbearing age in the coming few years and yet a temporary dip in the level of the crude birth rate. Subtraction of the births in Series C from those in Series AA yields a variation amounting to about 22.1 million births for the whole period from 1955 to 1975, a variation amounting to about a tenth of the 1975 population (207 to 228 million). The figures are limited in meaning because of the arbitrary nature of the different series and do not indicate the full range of variation that is possible.

C. Birth projections by cohorts

A partial discussion of the outlook for fertility on a cohort basis has already been given in various places in the monograph, notably in Chapter 9. (See also the several crude projections made in Chapters 3, 4, and 8 on the basis of data for white and nonwhite women 25 to 29 years old in 1950, 1952, and 1954 and assumptions that the women had completed from 50 to 60 percent of their childbearing.) As stated in Chapter 9, the cumulative rates for actual cohorts of native white women are decidedly helpful in forming opinions regarding trends in fertility and in trying to distinguish between the mixed influences of variations in the timing of births and of increases or decreases in the average size of completed families. The likelihood of making unreasonable assumptions about changes in the size of completed families is smaller if the cohort approach is used than if consideration is restricted to annual rates and their past trends. Moreover, when projections of the future course of fertility are made with the cohort approach, the projections can utilize the information which is beginning to be collected by the Scripps Foundation of Miami University and the Survey Research Center of the University of Michigan about the additional number of children expected by a national probability sample of about 3,000 white married women 18 to 39 years old living with their husbands. This new study is entitled "Growth of American Families."[1] (It is necessary to allow for future variations in the proportion of women who have no husbands or are separated, and to allow for sampling variability. In addition, the study should be repeated to show how the expectations of couples are modified by different types of actual future events.)

It was also stated in Chapter 9 that one can now be fairly certain that the cumulative fertility of the native white women in the cohorts of 1911–15 will be between 2,250 and 2,280 births per 1,000 women by ages 50 to 54 on January 1, 1965. Similarly, it is quite probable that the cumulative rates of the cohorts of 1916–20 will be between 2,400 and 2,600 by ages 50 to 54 on January 1, 1970. One can determine these future values quite well, because the women already had completed most of their childbearing by January 1, 1955, at which time actual vital statistics gave way to projections of births to future years on a cohort basis. According to computations based on the projections, the cohort of 1911–15 had com-

---

[1] P. K. Whelpton and Ronald Freedman, "A Study of the Growth of American Families," *American Journal of Sociology*, Vol. LXI, No. 6, May 1956, pp. 595–601.

pleted 98 to 99 percent of its childbearing on January 1, 1955, when it was 40 to 44 years old, and the cohort of 1916–20 had completed 88 to 95 percent of its childbearing when it was 35 to 39 years old. There is no doubt that the average size of completed families will increase between these successive cohorts of native white women. Furthermore, in an analysis of data for young cohorts of native white women it was noted that "broadly speaking, the past trend toward fewer women with at least four children and more women with none, one, or two seems to be giving way to a new trend toward more families with three or four children and fewer with no children or only one, while the proportion with two children remains relatively stable."

On the basis of a preliminary analysis of the findings from the study, "Growth of American Families," Whelpton noted in May 1956 that a good medium estimate of future change in the rate for completed fertility is a rise from approximately 2,300 births per 1,000 women living to age 50 for the cohorts of 1906–10 to 2,900 for the cohorts of 1926–30 and later years.[2] It appears from this preliminary analysis that the rise is unlikely to stop below a rate of 2,700 for the cohorts of 1921–25 or to fall below 2,500 or rise above 3,300 for subsequent cohorts. These probable lower and upper limits are about 14 percent above and below the medium figure of 2,900. (The medium figure of 2,900 implies that there will be about 1,440 daughters per 1,000 women, or an increase of 44 percent in the next generation if no allowance is made for the relatively few deaths of the daughters before they reach the childbearing ages in their turn. This large increase fits only the specific cohorts, however, not necessarily the total population.)

The number of births that occur in the total population at any given time depend on the joint contribution of many cohorts of women and on the contributions of nonwhites (11percent of the women of childbearing age in 1950) as well as of whites (89 percent). For projections of population to future dates, it is necessary to predict the "timing" of births as well as the total number the women will have in their lifetimes. To some extent, the earlier childbearing by some cohorts in the post-World War II years means that there will be fewer births to these women in later years. With allowance for nonwhites as well as whites, for different cohorts of women, for variations in the timing of births, and for the total number of children per woman as expected from "Growth of American Families," Whelpton estimated in May 1956 that there would be between 64 million and 96 million births during 1955–1975, with a medium estimate of 80 million births. The medium estimate was slightly below the Bureau's B series mentioned earlier, the high estimate was 1 million below the Bureau's AA series, and the low estimate was 9 million below the Bureau's C series.

[2] P. K. Whelpton, "Census Projections: Some Areas of Doubt," *Conference Board Business Record*, Vol. XIII, No. 8, August 1956.

The general conclusion reached by Whelpton was that any one of the Bureau's series of rough estimates gave a reasonable figure for the 1975 population, but that as a group the Bureau's series exaggerated growth during 1955–1975 and the population in 1975.

D. The outlook for fertility differentials

It seems likely to the authors that the long-range trend will be toward continued narrowing of group differences in fertility. The differences between rural and urban areas with respect to style of life are being lessened by reduction in the relative size of the farm population, by improvements in highways and means of transportation, and by television, radio, and movies.   The previous sharp lines of demarcation at the edges of cities have become blurred by the rise of the suburbs and more recently by the large movement of people to new homes in the open country.   In a real sense the city has gone to the country to live, and the country has gone to the city to work, and both have undergone marked changes.   Selective factors alone probably will continue to account for appreciable urban-rural differences in fertility, but, in general, the outlook is for reduction in the magnitude of these differentials.

During the past 30 years there has been a marked trend toward elimination of differentials by nativity in the fertility of white women of European stock.   That trend has practically run its course and there is now little difference by nativity in the fertility of urban whites of European extraction. Relatively few foreign-born whites from Europe live in rural areas.   The whites with Spanish surnames in this country are characterized by relatively high fertility. The published census data on fertility of these groups afford no internal comparison by nativity.

The outlook is for continued convergence in the fertility rates by color. In 1940, the southern rural-farm Negroes were characterized by conspicuously high fertility, and the urban Negroes were characterized by low fertility rates and high proportions of childlessness.   Various modernizing influences and the efforts to make information about family limitation available to southern rural-farm areas probably will serve to reduce the fertility of both whites and nonwhites in these areas substantially, but eventually will narrow the gap between these groups by reducing the excess fertility of the nonwhites in rural-farm areas.   Correspondingly, the opposite type of differential fertility by color within urban areas also appears to be diminishing.   In 1940, because of the high prevalence of childlessness, the average number of children per ever-married woman was lower among nonwhites than whites in urban areas.   This past condition is still reflected in the 1950 data for women of recently completed fertility.   However, during 1940 to 1950 there were marked reductions in childlessness among young nonwhite married women in urban areas and in 1950 the average number of children ever born was frequently higher among nonwhite than white ever-married women under 25 years of age.

With respect to fertility differentials by socio-economic status it seems likely that the long-range trend will be toward reduction of the inverse relation. Some rather striking decreases of differentials in cumulative fertility rates by education of the woman and by occupation of the husband were noted for the *younger women* during the 1940–50 decade. These were explained as reflecting a rebound in the fertility rates of certain classes that were characterized by very low fertility rates in 1940. Since a repetition of the 1940–50 *increases* in fertility probably will not occur during 1950 to 1960, marked reductions in fertility differentials on a par with those occurring in 1940 to 1950 are not to be expected. Furthermore, it is emphasized that among ever-married women of nearly completed fertility (40 to 44 and 45 to 49 years of age), the differentials in fertility appear to be of about the same strength in 1950 as in 1940. Actually, the indices of average deviation of the fertility rates by education among ever-married white women of these ages were a little larger in 1950 than in 1940. Yet the trend toward convergence exhibited by the younger women appears likely to continue because class lines themselves are becoming less conspicuous.

Finally, it should be mentioned that since increasing proportions of the families are exercising some degree of planning with respect to size of family and are using more effective means of control, there may be more and larger short-term fluctuations in the birth rate. It therefore becomes increasingly important to understand the manner in which current and completed fertility rates are interrelated with social and economic conditions and with changes in those conditions.

CHAPTER 11

SUMMARY

A. A long view

Early high fertility. From the time of the first settlements to about 1820, the fertility of the American people was among the world's highest. Contemporary writers attributed this situation to the ease with which land could be acquired by individuals and with which large families could be supported. The women of completed fertility had an average of about eight children. Perhaps two-thirds of the children survived to age 20, according to life tables of fair reliability. Despite the formerly high infant mortality, there were about three times as many persons under 16 years old per white household in the United States in 1790 as in 1950. The fertility in early times was so high that computations indicate it must have created a largely native population at an early date and much of the annual population growth in the Colonial period must have been from natural increase rather than directly from a given year's net immigration. Thus, in the area that later formed the United States, the population may have been predominantly native as early as 1660.[1]

Although fertility was high in early times, it varied in different population groups. It was determined from a series of Colonial censuses that throughout the eighteenth century the ratio of children under 16 years old to white women 16 years old and over was much less in the largely urban population of New York County than in the largely rural population of the balance of the Colony of New York. In 1751, Benjamin Franklin cited some of the reasons for a lower fertility in urban areas than in rural areas. Ratios of young children to women in 1800 were highest in the newer areas of settlement and lowest in the longer settled areas.

Nineteenth century declines in fertility. Ratios of children under 5 years old to white women 20 to 44 years old, computed from decennial censuses, suggest that the national birth rate declined after 1810. The adjusted ratio fell from 1,358 children under 5 years old per 1,000 women 20 to 44 years old in 1810 to 1,085 by 1840, 780 by 1880, 604 by 1920, and 419 by 1940. Subsequently it increased to 587 by 1950. The bulk

---

[1] Indians on reservations were not enumerated in censuses until 1890. Prior to 1890, the population count in Colonial and Federal censuses included white persons, free colored, and slaves, but excluded Indians not taxed.

of the decline thus occurred before 1880, perhaps much of it before there had been very large reductions in infant mortality. Declines in ratios of young children to white women occurred in all parts of the country by 1820, not only in the longer settled areas but also in the newer frontier areas. Evidence such as newspaper advertisements (between 1820 and 1873) of contraceptives and abortifacients, pamphlets and circulars on birth control, and printed sermons by clergymen disturbed by the small families of native women as compared with the large ones of foreign-born women indicate that the decline involved family limitation.

It was noted that in much of the period from 1810 to 1940 the country was largely rural and it was demonstrated that declines in rural fertility accounted for more than half the national decline in ratios of young children to white women between 1810 and 1940. The proportion of the population residing in urban areas did not increase much until after 1840.

Negroes appear to have had a history of fairly high fertility prior to 1890. Data from the 1910 Census indicate that nonwhite women 70 to 74 years old had an average of 6.6 children ever born as compared with 4.4 children for native white women. Nonwhite women 70 to 74 years old in rural-farm areas of the South had averages of 7 to 9 children.

The twentieth century. Because increases in the number of women of childbearing age more than offset the effect of a declining birth rate per woman, the annual number of births increased elevenfold between 1800 (about 280,000) and 1921 (about 3.1 million). Subsequently the number decreased to 2.3 million in 1933, in the first lengthy decline in absolute numbers of births this country had experienced. These numbers were partly estimated because the Birth Registration Area did not attain nation-wide coverage until 1933. The number of births increased slowly, in ir-regular fashion, to 2.6 million in 1940, while the birth rate fluctuated from 18 to 19 per 1,000 population in the period 1933 to 1940. The an-nual number of births increased sharply after 1940, to 3.1 million in 1943, dipped to 2.9 million in the last year of World War II (1945), and rose to a new high after 1945, setting new records of 3.4 million births in 1946, 3.8 million in 1947, 4.1 million in 1954 and 1955, and 4.2 million in 1956. Between 1946 and 1956 the birth rate fluctuated around a level of about 25 per 1,000 population.

By color, the birth rate fluctuated around a level of about 24 for whites and 34 for nonwhites after 1946; these rates for each race were about as large as the corresponding rates in 1925.

Much of the recovery in the birth rate after 1933 or after 1940 involved young women and first to third births, and there was a continua-tion of an underlying trend for relatively fewer women to have large families. In the 1930's, for the first time in the Nation's history, the balance of age schedules of birth and death rates was a little below that needed for permanent maintenance of a population through births. The age schedules of birth rates were unduly lowered at all ages by the effect of the economic depression of the 1930's, and no real cohort of women was subject to these particular rates on a lifetime basis.

Between 1910 and 1950, the average number of children ever born to white women 45 to 49 years old at the census date declined from 4.1 to 2.3 and that for nonwhite women declined from 5.9 to 2.7. The averages just cited were for women of all marital classes including single (assumed to be childless). Between 1910 and 1950 the percentage of ever-married women 45 to 49 years old who had never borne a child more than doubled among whites and tripled among nonwhites. The major changes, however, involved reductions in the proportion of ever-married women who had four or more children and increases in the proportion of women with two, one, none, and three children ever born. In 1954, only about 20.5 percent of the ever-married women 40 to 44 years old, all races, had four or more children ever born as compared with 21.7 percent in 1950, 21.9 percent in 1940, and 52.7 percent in 1910. Some younger cohorts of women may reach age 45 to 49 years in future years with little further reduction or even a small increase in the percentage with four or more children. These younger cohorts may reach age 45 to 49 years with larger average family sizes than some of their predecessors, however, because more of these younger women may have two and three children and fewer may have none or one child. Thus, it was noted that the women (all marital classes) who were 25 to 29 years old in 1954 may complete the childbearing ages with an average of about 2.8 children ever born if they were about 55 percent through childbearing in 1954. This average of 2.8 children would represent a substantial increase in lifetime fertility as compared with that of some predecessor groups of women. Census data for 1940 to 1954 show larger percentage increases in rates of children ever born for young women of all marital classes than for ever-married women— proof that earlier marriages were a partial factor in the increase.

B. Residence, nativity, and ethnic groups

In the early part of the nineteenth century ratios of children under 5 years old to women 20 to 44 years old tended to be least in the longer settled parts of the United States and largest in the newer parts. The ratios tended to converge over the years. The South became the most fertile region by a process of slower decline in fertility than occurred in other regions after the War Between the States. In 1940 the fertility ratios were temporarily below the level needed for permanent replacement of the population in all but the three southern divisions and the Mountain Division. A large upsurge occurred in the ratios by 1950 in the divisions in which the ratios were lowest, and smaller increases occurred in the three southern divisions and the Mountain Division.

By States, among white women 70 to 74 years old in 1910, the average number of children ever born varied from 3.3 in Maine to 7.4 in Utah. Because of an influx of quite fertile foreign-born white women, some States had higher fertility in urban areas than in rural-farm areas. The average number of children ever born to white women 45 to 49 years old in 1950 was below that needed for replacement of population in 24 States and in the District of Columbia, and varied from 1.48 in the District of Columbia and 1.79 in New York to 3.12 in New Mexico and Utah and 3.19 in Arkansas. It was concluded, from data for women 25 to 29 years old in 1950 and from assumptions as to the percentage of lifetime fertility completed, that the prospects were bright for substantial increases in completed fertility of the oncoming cohort of women as compared with that of women 45 to 49 years old in 1950. Several States and the District of Columbia would still have average numbers of children per woman that were below replacement needs; these were all areas of extensive in-migration of women in search of employment, and these largely unmarried and childless in-migrants may have depressed the average fertility somewhat. Nonwhite women were noted to have had more children on the average than the white women in most States, although nonwhites in the urban parts of States had average numbers of children ever born that were below population replacement needs.

Data on children ever born for women classified by region of residence and region of woman's birth indicate that both the place of residence and the place of woman's birth had some influence on the childbearing of women. The migrants generally had an average number of children that was intermediate between that of nonmigrant women in the region of residence and that of nonmigrant women in the region of origin.

Net reproduction rates for counties in 1945–50 and 1935–40 indicated that annual fertility increased greatly in all parts of the country, including such places as the Appalachian area where there already was a pattern of early marriage and very high fertility. This increase in the Appalachian area's rate indicated perhaps that something more than early marriage or a desire to have more children was involved. However, the county reproduction rates increased most where they originally were lowest.

In 1940, the white women 45 to 49 years old in cities of 250,000 inhabitants or more had an average of only 1.8 children ever born, and even those in the smallest urban group shown (2,500 to 25,000) had an average (2.4 children) that was a little below replacement needs for this cohort. Some data were presented for individual large cities to show that fertility variations were not just a function of the size of the city. Variations in fertility were examined for central cities and the remainder of several large metropolitan areas. Some neighborhood variation in fertility within a large city (Chicago) were studied to show that fertility tended to be relatively high in slum areas.

In 1950, the foreign-born white women 20 to 44 years old had fewer children ever born per woman than the native women had at these ages. The lesser fertility of the foreign-born white women arose in part from their concentration in urban areas where fertility normally was lower than in rural areas and in part from the effect of immigration quotas that were somewhat selective of relatively infertile women from countries of northern and western Europe. The lesser fertility of the foreign-born women than of the native women in 1950 represented a drastic change from conditions in 1910 when the foreign born generally had large families. In 1910 about 20 percent of the white women 15 to 44 years old in the United States were foreign born as compared with less than 5 percent in 1950.

The fertility of Negroes as compared with that of whites has been discussed in many places in this monograph and will not be discussed further at this point. No data were tabulated specifically for Indians, but data for other races in rural areas may serve as a rough approximation to the fertility of Indians. The Indians comprised 75 percent of the other races group in 1950 and another 8 percent were part Indian. The women of other races 45 to 59 years old in 1950 had an average of 4.6 children ever born as compared with 5.6 children in 1910 among women 45 to 74 years old.

The women of Spanish surname in five southwestern States, many of whom were of Mexican origin or descent, had ratios of children under 5 years old per 1,000 women 15 to 49 years old that were nearly as large as those for Indians and for Negroes in rural-farm areas, although many of the women of Spanish surname lived in urban areas. They had higher ratios than the white women in rural-farm areas of Utah, which State contains many Mormons according to annual reports of the National Council of Churches.

C. Socio-economic status in relation to fertility

The trends and differentials in fertility by socio-economic status are matters of interest to many students of social science. Two important criteria of socio-economic status, major occupation group of the husband and number of years of school completed by the wife, were related to number of children ever born to the wife and to number of own children under 5 years old in the fertility tabulations for 1950. Since fairly comparable data on fertility by occupation of the husband were available from the 1910 and 1940 Censuses, these were used for an analysis of trends and differentials in fertility by major occupation group of the husband since 1910. Census data on fertility in relation to education of the woman were available from the 1940 Census; thus the 1940–50 changes in fertility by educational attainment of the woman were studied.

Occupation. The rates of children ever born, or "cumulative fertility rates" for all occupational groups were lower in 1940 than in 1910. The percent reductions over this period were fairly uniform by occupational class. In contrast, the 1940–50 period was marked by important increases in fertility among women under 40 years of age and the magnitude of the percent increase differed rather systematically by occupation group of the husband. In general terms, the percent increase in cumulative fertility rates tended to be largest for occupation groups characterized by lowest fertility in 1940 and smallest for occupation groups characterized by highest fertility in 1940. Thus, among urban white women 25 to 29 years of age "married once and husband present," the 1940–50 increase in the cumulative fertility rate ranged from 53 percent for wives of professional men to 19 percent for the wives of "laborers, except farm." Among women of virtually completed fertility, those 40 to 44 and 45 to 49 years old, the cumulative fertility rates were lower in 1950 than in 1940 for virtually all the occupation groups. The lower fertility of the women age 40 to 49 reflects the long-standing decline in the proportionate importance of large families.

When the 1940–50 comparisons relate to "fertility ratios," or ratios of own children under 5 years old to women of a given age, the 1940–50 percent increases tend to be highest for the professional class, and the increases persist among women 40 to 44 and 45 to 49 years of age. Thus, even the women nearing the end of the childbearing period exhibited some increases in *current fertility* during the 1940–50 decade but these increases were not sufficient to counteract the decrease in cumulative fertility that had already occurred.

The 1940–50 increases in average number of children ever born among women under 40 years of age existed in rural-nonfarm and rural-farm areas as well as in urban areas. However, the magnitude of the percent increases in fertility tended to decline with increasing rurality of the residence. This is consistent with the principle of relatively greatest rebound in the lowest cumulative fertility rates.

Although the relative increases in cumulative fertility rates during 1940 to 1950 tended to be largest for wives of professional men and smallest for wives of unskilled laborers, the former group still had the lowest fertility levels at most of the ages represented.

In more general terms, whereas the order and relative spread of cumulative fertility rates by occupation group were much the same in 1940 as in 1910, there was a marked narrowing of the occupational differentials during the 1940–50 decade. As an illustration, among urban white women 25 to 29 years of age "married once and husband present" the average deviation of the cumulative fertility rates of seven nonagricultural occupational groups from the mean rate for all women of that age who were wives of nonagricultural workers was 18 percent for 1910, 16 percent for 1940, and 10 percent for 1950. However, the various occupation groups remained in about the same order with respect to fertility in 1950 as in 1940 and 1910. Except for the lower fertility of the wives of clerical workers than of wives of proprietors, the cumulative fertility rates tended to be inversely related to occupational class as conventionally ranked.

The occupational differentials in fertility among the nonwhites tend to be like those exhibited by the whites. It should be emphasized, however, that because of their predominantly rural heritage, and because of their relative lack of education, training, and occupational opportunity, the non-whites are much more heavily concentrated in the agricultural and laboring classes than are the whites. During the 1940–50 decade there was a marked reduction in the proportion of farmers and farm laborers among the nonwhites but the chief compensating gain was in the category of operatives. The proportion with white-collar occupations among husbands of urban women 35 to 39 years of age in 1950 was about one-third for the whites, but less than one-tenth for the nonwhites.

After age 25, the percents childless tend to be higher among nonwhites than among whites of similar age and occupational class, especially in urban and rural-nonfarm areas. However, the extent of this excess of childlessness among the nonwhites has decreased considerably since 1940. Among urban women under 30 the cumulative fertility rates of nonwhites were higher than those of whites in the same groupings by occupation of the husband. Among older urban women, and especially among older urban wives of unskilled laborers, the cumulative fertility rates tended to be higher among the whites than nonwhites. Among the whites the 1950 fertility *ratios* (based on children under 5 years old) rather universally exceeded those for 1940. Indeed, they frequently exceeded those for 1910. The excesses of the 1950 ratios over those for 1910 were especially marked among urban white wives 20 to 34 years old whose husbands were in the white-collar occupations. In 1950 the inverse relation of fertility ratios to occupational status of the husband was rather strong for urban white women 20 to 24 years old. The range of variation in the fertility ratios by occupation group of the husband was narrow at older ages.

Among the nonwhite women under 30 years old, the fertility ratios for 1950 not only exceeded those for 1940, they consistently exceeded those for 1910 within all occupational groups. A higher ratio for 1950 than for 1910 was not uncommon at older ages. As among the whites, the inverse relation of the 1950 fertility ratios by occupational status of the nonwhites was fairly strong at young ages.

Education. In major respects the trends and differentials in fertility by education of the woman are similar to those by occupation of the husband. Thus, the 1940–50 percent increases in cumulative fertility rates tended to be largest among the women who finished college and smallest among those of "none or elementary" status. As a result there has been a substantial narrowing of the fertility differentials by education since 1940. Thus, among urban white ever-married women 25 to 29 years of age, the average deviation of the cumulative fertility rate of the five educational classes from the mean for the total age group was 28 percent in 1940 and 19 percent in 1950.

The extent to which the upper educational classes have participated in the baby boom is pointed up by the fact that among urban white ever-married women, 30 to 39 years of age, there was a *direct* relation of fertility ratios to educational attainment. At these same ages the cumulative fertility rates were *inversely* related to educational attainment of the wife. Whereas the fertility ratios have the advantage of reflecting current fertility rather than total past fertility, they have the disadvantage of being affected heavily by the timing of births. The high fertility ratios in 1950 for women who graduated from college during 1925 to 1935 reflected a current "making up" for a previous delay of marriage and of starting a family.

Since number of years of school completed is applicable equally to single and married women, it was possible to compute percentages of women ever married, percentages of women married once and husband present, and general cumulative fertility rates (which include single women) as well as marital cumulative fertility rates, by educational attainment. These data point up the relatively high increases in the proportions of ever-married women as well as the relatively large increases in marital fertility during 1940 to 1950 among college-trained women under 40 years of age. The 1940–50 percent increases in the general fertility rates of college graduates were especially striking. Despite the trends described, however, there was still in 1950 an inverse relation between proportion ever married and educational attainment among women of given age. Among the ever-married women themselves, there was a *direct relation* of educational attainment to proportion classified as married once and husband present.

The 0-to-1, 1-to-2, 2-to-3 parity progression ratios for 1950 tended to exceed those for 1940 among women under 40 years of age and of given educational attainment. These 1940–50 increases were particularly marked for women reporting some college attendance. The parity progression ratios tended to be *lower* in 1950 than in 1940 for women 40 to 49 years of age and for births of fourth or higher order. With some slight exception for the college graduates, the ratio of three-parity women progressing to fourth parity by given ages tended to be lower in 1950 than in 1940. This at first glance would seem to rule out a substantial future increase in the proportion of large families. It must be remembered, however, that with substantially larger 2-to-3 parity progression ratios for 1950 than for 1940 the base of three-parity women was proportionately larger in 1950 than in 1940. This would provide an increase in the proportion of four-parity couples even if the parity progression ratio from third to fourth parity were the same in 1950 as in 1940. Furthermore, the young cohorts exhibiting high parity progression ratios for 1950 may continue to exhibit them as they grow older or as they reach higher parity status.

Period gross and net reproduction rates were computed from data relating to children under 5 years old. The method included allowances for deceased children and for children not enumerated in the homes of their parents in 1940 or 1950. The 1935–40 net reproduction rate was a little below replacement requirements for women who had completed 1 to

3 years of high school. It was definitely above replacement requirements only for the women failing to report as much as 1 year of high school. The deficit became greater at higher educational levels. It was 26 percent below for high school graduates, 33 percent below for women completing 1 to 3 years of college, and 48 percent below for the college graduates. In 1945 to 1950, in contrast, even the college graduates were reproducing at a rate 9 percent above the requirements for permanent replacement of the population through births. The excess of births over replacement requirements was 18 percent for the women reporting 1 to 3 years of college training, 28 percent for the high school graduates, and 39 percent for those completing 1 to 3 years of high school. It is again emphasized, however, that the differentials in reproduction rates have little relation to the actual rates of growth for the groups discussed.

Approximately 32 percent of the white women and 41 percent of the nonwhite women 15 to 49 years old were in the labor force in 1950. Among the women classified as "married once and husband present" the proportions in the labor force were 22 percent for whites and 32 percent for nonwhites. The fertility rates and ratios were considerably lower for women in the labor force than for those not in it. The percentages with no children ever born and particularly the percentages with no living children under 5 years old were higher for women in the labor force than for those not in the labor force. Doubtless these differences are due mainly to selective rather than determinative factors.

Various studies have indicated that the relation of fertility to other measures of socio-economic status, such as income and rental value of the home, is much the same as that to occupation and education. The census materials have been supplemented by various studies which have provided evidence of the important role of contraception in differential fertility. Efforts to ascertain some of the social and psychological correlates of family limitation and size of family were made in the Indianapolis Study and are being continued in two current private studies.

D. Marriage and child-spacing

In the United States an estimated 94 percent of the annual births in 1950 were legitimate. The percentage of women who had ever been married changed little at any given age between 1900 and 1930, and decreased slightly between 1930 and 1940. In contrast, the percentage of ever married increased sharply among the women under 30 years old after 1940. For example, among the women 20 to 24 years old, the percent ever married rose from 52.7 percent in 1940 to 67.7 percent in 1950 and 70.9 percent in 1955. It was figured that the women 21.9 years old in 1900, 21.3 in 1930, 21.5 in 1940, and 20.2 in 1950 and 1955 had completed exactly half their eventual lifetime proportion of ever marrying.

About 62 percent of the white women 15 to 49 years old in 1950 were married and living with their first husbands as compared with 43 percent of the nonwhite women. (About 77 percent of the white and nonwhite women 15 to 49 years old had ever been married.) The non-white women in remarriages had far fewer children under 5 years old on the average than those in first marriages, whereas among white women the fertility ratios were about equal for women in first marriages and remarriages.

The white women of all marital classes 45 to 49 years old in 1940 had a rate of children ever born that was 89 percent of the average for white women of this age in first marriages. This percentage indicates, roughly, the reproductive loss that arises from the failure of some women to marry and the lower fertility of the women whose first marriages were broken or interrupted before age 45 to 49 years. Of course the unmarried, re-married, widowed, divorced, or separated women might have had a dif-ferent degree of ability to conceive that would have prevented them from having as many (or as few) children as the women in unbroken marriages if they had been in that status.

White women 20 to 24 years old, married once and husband present, had been married for a somewhat longer time in 1950 (median of 3.4 years) than the corresponding group of native white women in 1940 (median of 2.9 years). The longer marriage duration in 1950 reflected the effect of an earlier average age at marriage. The longer marriage duration was, of course, a factor in the 1940–50 increase in the average number of children ever born to women 20 to 24 years old. The earlier marriage, however, did not necessarily mean that the women in 1950 bore children sooner after their marriage than the women in 1940. When com-parisons of children ever born were made for white women married identical lengths of time in 1940 and 1950, it was found that the women 15 to 19 years old and 20 to 24 years old in 1950 had fewer children ever born by the end of each year of marriage than their predecessors had in 1940, whereas among the women 25 to 44 years old there was a pattern of more children in the first few years after marriage by 1950 than by 1940.

Data from the Current Population Survey indicated that there was a median spacing interval of 1.5 years between the marriage of the mother and the birth of the first child, for women whose first children were born in a 4-year period ending in April 1954. There was a median spacing interval of 2.6 years between the birth of a first child and the birth of the second child, for women whose second children were born in April 1950 to 1954.

Data from the 1950 Census on child-spacing for women 38 years old provided a rough indication of the spacing of the "last" child, as few women have births after age 38. It was found that the women who had only one child or only two children had much longer average spacing in-tervals than were noted before for women of all childbearing ages who bore children in April 1950 to 1954.

E. The fertility of cohorts of native white women

The cohort approach is helpful in a consideration of fertility trends, because it relates to actual groups of women (born in different years) as they proceed through life. Cumulative rates for births of each order up to each age can be computed for the cohort of 1895 and each later year by adding the central age-specific rates for each cohort in successive years. (These central rates are based on (a) numbers of registered births adjusted for incomplete registration and estimated numbers of births in States not in the registration area, and (b) numbers of women enumerated in the census, adjusted for incomplete enumeration and misstatements of age.) Rates for each cohort from 1870 to 1895 up to the age reached in 1910 and each later year can be computed by using the foregoing annual rates and the cumulative rates up to 1910 provided by census data on women by number of children ever born. Dividing the rates for all women by the proportion of women who have married gives the rates for ever-married women. Distributions by parity (number of children ever born) and parity progression ratios can be computed from the cumulative birth rates.

The cohort rates for native white women show a general downward trend prior to 1940 in childbearing by younger women, and then a rapid rise to a record breaking high by 1955. For example, the cumulative rate by ages 20–24 was 568 in 1910 (cohorts of 1886–90), 453 in 1940 (cohorts of 1916–20), and 789 in 1955 (cohorts of 1931–35). On a percentage basis, the earlier decrease and the recent increase were smallest for first births and successively larger for births of higher orders. Younger marriages contributed greatly to the increase, the proportion of the women aged 20–24 who had ever been married rising from about 48 percent for the cohorts of 1916–20 in 1940 to 66 percent for the 1931–35 cohorts in 1955. Relatively more of the ever-married women had two or three children by ages 20–24; relatively fewer had no child.

In contrast to the foregoing trends at the younger ages, the decline in lifetime fertility which began over a century ago continued uninterruptedly to 1955. The cumulative birth rate per 1,000 women living to ages 45 –49 was only 2,209 for the cohorts of 1906–10 (by 1955) compared with about 3,515 for the cohorts of 1871–75 (by 1920). The absolute decrease was largest for the rates for third, fourth, and fifth births (close to 200 points in each case), but the relative decrease rose from 7 percent for first births to 75 percent for births of eighth and higher orders. There was a small increase in the proportion of women marrying by ages 45– 49. Among those who married there was a marked decrease in the proportion that had borne four or more children and a marked increase in the proportion that had borne none, one, or two.

A glance at rates by intermediate ages shows that the long-time downward trend of the lifetime fertility rate is about to end. Thus, women in the cohorts of 1911–15 had a rate of 2,224 by ages 40–44, which is somewhat larger than the final rate (by ages 50–54) of about 2,212 for the cohorts of 1906–10. Similarly, the rate by ages 35–39 was 2,278 for the cohorts of 1916–20 (by 1955), which is well above that of 2,046 for the 1911–15 cohorts by the same ages. A still larger lead of the most recent group over the preceding is found at ages 30–34, where the cumulative rate is 2,126 for the cohorts of 1921–25, compared with 1,857 for those of 1916–20 and 1,638 for the 1911–15 group. It is almost certain that the rankings of these groups will be the same at age 50 as at the ages mentioned, but the size of the differentials undoubtedly will change somewhat.

The reversal of the long-time downward trend owes the most so far to a rise in the rate for second births but reflects in important degree more first, third, and fourth births. Whether there will be significant increases in fifth and higher order births remains to be seen. Up to 1956 the substantial rise in the popularity of two-, three-, and four-child families had occurred mainly at the expense of those with no child or only one.

The age-specific fertility rates of actual cohorts in a given period may be combined so as to represent the experience of a hypothetical group of cohorts always living under the conditions of the period, by following procedures like those for computing conventional gross or net reproduction rates. Hypothetical lifetime fertility dropped rapidly from 3,189 births per 1,000 women living to the end of the childbearing ages under conditions of 1910–14 to 2,093 for conditions of 1935–39 and then rose even more rapidly to 3,176 for 1950–54. The pattern of change varies widely from one birth order to another. The lifetime first birth rate is the most stable; as birth order rises the earlier decline becomes larger and lasts longer, and the subsequent recovery becomes smaller; finally, the rate for eighth and higher order births falls steadily from about 329 during 1910–1914 to 71 during 1950–1954.

The large size of the postwar baby boom is illustrated by the jump of the number of births to native white women from about 19 million during 1930 to 1939 to over 30 million during 1945 to 1954. Approximately 24 percent of this increase would have occurred if marriage and birth rates had remained unchanged, because of the larger numbers of women at most of the childbearing ages during 1945 to 1954 than during 1930 to 1939. A slightly larger proportion (about 30 percent) of the increase may be credited to the marked tendency of more women to marry at the younger ages, helped in minor degree by a small decrease in the proportion not marrying at all.

The most important factor—accounting for about 34 percent of the extra births in 1945 to 1954—is the larger proportion of married women having a first birth at the younger ages. A minor part of this change represents a decrease in the proportion of wives who never bear a child; the major part is merely the earlier bearing of first children that would have come in 1955 and later years under the timing pattern of 1930–39.

The least important of these four factors (accounting for only about 12 percent of the total gain) is the increase in the average number of births per woman bearing one or more children.

F. The outlook for fertility

In countries where death rates are low and migration to and from the country is not an important factor, variations in fertility are likely to be the major cause of variations in future population size and composition. It has not been possible thus far to pin down the expected variation in fertility to a narrow range, because various components affecting fertility are very changeable. Methods which project fertility rates on the basis of cohort experience may yield better results than have been heretofore possible, and studies like "Growth of American Families," on the intentions of married couples, may provide an improved basis of short-run projections of fertility. At the moment, it seems possible that the white women 25 to 29 years old on January 1 of 1955 may complete the childbearing period with an average of 2.5 to 3.3 children ever born as compared with an average of 2.3 among the cohort of 1906–10 by age 50.

There may be between 64 million and 96 million births during 1955 to 1975, with a medium estimate of 80 million births, according to projections by Whelpton. The Bureau of the Census estimated that the population may contain from 207 to 228 million persons in 1975; according to Whelpton's projections these figures are reasonable but so are estimates as large as 243 million and as small as 193 million. Business conditions, the international situation, and attitudes toward family size will no doubt have much influence on fertility and population growth.

Social and economic differentials in fertility are likely to narrow in the future but not to disappear entirely. Some new patterns of relationship are also possible.

BIBLIOGRAPHY

Books

1. Beard, C. A., and M. R. Beard, *The Beard's Basic History of the United States*, Doubleday, Doran and Company, New York, 1944.
2. Blodget, S., *Economica, A Statistical Manual for the United States of America*, Washington, 1806.
3. Bossard, J. H. S., *The Large Family System*, University of Pennsylvania Press, Philadelphia, 1956.
4. Carr-Saunders, A. M., *World Population*, Clarendon Press, Oxford, 1936.
5. Dandekar, V. M., and K. Dandekar, *Survey of Fertility and Mortality in Poona District*, Publication No. 27, Gokhale Institute of Politics and Economics, Poona (India), 1953.
6. De Beaujour, Chevalier F., *Sketch of the United States of North America*, several printing firms, London, 1814.
7. Dinkel, R. M., "Regional, Rural-Urban, and Occupational Fertility Trends, 1910–1940," doctoral dissertation, University of North Carolina, 1950.
8. Duncan, O. D., and A. J. Reiss, Jr., *Social Characteristics of Urban and Rural Communities, 1950*, Census Monograph Series, John Wiley and Sons, New York, 1956.
9. Eaton, J. W., and A. J. Mayer, *Man's Capacity to Reproduce: The Demography of a Unique Population*, The Free Press, Glencoe, Illinois, 1954.
10. Eaton, J. W., and R. J. Weil, *Culture and Mental Disorders*, The Free Press, Glencoe, Illinois, 1955.
11. Glick, P. C., *American Families*, Census Monograph Series, John Wiley and Sons, New York, 1957.
12. Hatt, P. K., *Backgrounds of Human Fertility in Puerto Rico*, Princeton University Press, Princeton, 1952.
13. Hauser, P. M., and E. Kitagawa, Editors, *Local Community Fact Book for Chicago, 1950*, Chicago Community Inventory, University of Chicago, Chicago, 1953.
14. Himes, N. E., *Medical History of Contraception*, The Williams and Wilkins Company, Baltimore, 1936.
15. Hogben, L. (Editor), *Political Arithmetic*, Allen and Unwin, London, 1938.
16. Huntington, E., and L. F. Whitney, *The Builders of America*, William Morrow and Company, New York, 1927.
17. Hutchinson, E. P., *Immigrants and Their Children, 1850–1950*, Census Monograph Series, John Wiley and Sons, New York, 1956.
18. Innes, J. W., *Class Fertility Trends in England and Wales, 1876–1934*, Princeton University Press, Princeton, 1938.
19. Kiser, C. V., *Group Differences in Urban Fertility*, The Williams and Wilkins Company, Baltimore, 1942.
20. Kuczynski, R. R., *The Measurement of Population Growth, Methods and Result*, Oxford University Press, New York, 1936; *The Balance of Births and Deaths*, Vol. I, "Western and Northern Europe," The Macmillan Company, New York, 1928, and Vol. II, "Eastern and Southern Europe," The Brookings Institution, Washington, 1931.
21. Lorimer, F., et al., *Foundations of American Population Policy*, Harper and Brothers, New York, 1940.
22. Lorimer, F., and F. Osborn, *Dynamics of Population. Social and Biological Significance of Changing Birth Rates in the United States*, The Macmillan Company, New York, 1934.
23. Mair, G. F. (Editor), *Studies in Population, Proceedings of the Annual Meeting of the Population Association of America at Princeton, New Jersey, May 1949*, Princeton University Press, Princeton, 1949.
24. Miller, J. C., *Origins of the American Revolution*, Little, Brown and Company, Boston, 1943.

25. Monahan, T. P., *The Pattern of Age at Marriage in the United States*, Vols. I and II, Stephenson-Brothers, Philadelphia, 1951.
26. National Committee on Maternal Health, *The Abortion Problem*, The Williams and Wilkins Company, Baltimore, 1944.
27. Odum, H. W., *Southern Regions of the United States*, University of North Carolina Press, Chapel Hill, 1936.
28. Pearl, R., *The Natural History of Population*, Oxford University Press, New York, 1939.
29. Sheldon, H. D., *Older Population of the United States at the Mid-Century*, Census Monograph Series, John Wiley and Sons, New York (in press).
30. Spiegelman, M., *Introduction to Demography*, Society of Actuaries, Chicago, 1955.
31. Stix, R. K., and F. W. Notestein, *Controlled Fertility: An Evaluation of Clinical Service*, The Williams and Wilkins Company, Baltimore, 1940.
32. Süssmilch, J. P., *Die göttliche Ordnung in den Veränderungen des menschilichen Geschlechts, aus der Geburt, dem Tode und der Fortpflanzung desselben erwiesen*, Berlin, 1741; 6th edition by C. J. Baumann, 1798.
33. Taeuber, C., and I. B. Taeuber, *The Changing Population of the United States*, Census Monograph Series, John Wiley and Sons, New York, 1958.
34. Thompson, W., *Population and Peace in the Pacific*, University of Chicago Press, Chicago, 1946; *Population Problems* (Fourth Edition), McGraw-Hill Book Company, New York, 1953.
35. Thompson, W., and P. K. Whelpton, *Population Trends in the United States*, McGraw-Hill Book Company, New York, 1933.
36. Vance, R. B., *All These People. The Nation's Human Resources in the South*, University of North Carolina Press, Chapel Hill, 1945.
37. Whelpton, P. K., *Cohort Fertility: Native White Women in the United States*, Princeton University Press, Princeton, 1954.
38. Whelpton, P. K., and C. V. Kiser (Editors), *Social and Psychological Factors Affecting Fertility*, Milbank Memorial Fund, New York: Vol. I, The Household Survey in Indianapolis (1946); Vol. II, The Intensive Study: Purpose, Scope, Methods, and Partial Results (1950); Vol. III, Further Reports on Hypotheses in the Indianapolis Study (1952); Vol. IV, Further Reports on Hypotheses and Other Data in the Indianapolis Study (1954); Vol. V (planned).
39. Williamson, G. F., *Saints and Strangers*, Reynal and Hitchcock, New York, 1945.

Articles and pamphlets

1. Alfred Politz Research, Inc., "Planned vs. Unplanned Births, Sex Preference of First Child," *Sociological Studies*, Report 1, New York, 1956.
2. Allen, N., "Lessons on Population Suggested by Grecian and Roman History," *Congregational Quarterly*, October 1871 (on inadequate fertility in New England, contraception and abortion).
3. Bash, W. H., "Differential Fertility in Madison County, New York, 1865," *Milbank Memorial Fund Quarterly*, Vol. XXXIII, No. 2, April 1955.
4. Berent, J., "Relationship Between Family Sizes of Two Successive Generations," *Milbank Memorial Fund Quarterly*, Vol. XXXI, No. 1, January 1953.
5. Burt, C., "Intelligence and Fertility—The Effect of the Differential Birth Rate on Inborn Mental Characteristics," *Occasional Papers on Eugenics*, No. 2, The Eugenics Society, Cassell and Company, London, 1952.
6. Chandrasekaran, C., "Fertility Survey in Mysore State, India," *Current Research in Human Fertility*, Milbank Memorial Fund, New York, 1955.
7. Christensen, H. T., and O. P. Bowden, "Studies in Child Spacing: II. The Time Interval Between Marriage of Parents and Birth of Their First Child, Tippecanoe County, Indiana," *Social Forces*, Vol. 31, No. 4, May 1953.
8. Coale, A. J., "The Population of the United States in 1950, Classified by Age, Sex, and Color—A Revision of Census Figures," *Journal of the American Statistical Association*, Vol. 50, No. 269, March 1955.
9. Colombo, B., "Preliminary Analysis of Recent Demographic Trends in Italy," *Population Index*, Vol. 18, No. 4, October 1952.
10. Crum, F. S., "The Statistical Work of Süssmilch," *Quarterly Publications of the American Statistical Association*, Vol. VII, New Series No. 55, September 1901.
11. Davis, J. S., "The Population Upsurge in the United States," *War-Peace Pamphlets, No. 12*, Food Research Institute, December 1949.
12. Davis, K., "Human Fertility in India," *American Journal of Sociology*, Vol. LII, No. 3, November 1946.

13. Dinkel, R. M., "Occupation and Fertility in the United States," *American Sociological Review*, Vol. 17, No. 2, April 1952.
14. Dorn, H. F., "Pitfalls in Population Forecasts and Projections," *Journal of the American Statistical Association*, Vol. 45, No. 251, September 1950.
15. Dorn, H. F., and A. J. McDowell, "The Relationship of Fertility and Longevity," *American Sociological Review*, Vol. 4, No. 2, April 1939.
16. Dublin, L. I., and A. J. Lotka, "On the True Rate of Natural Increase of a Population," *Journal of the American Statistical Association*, Vol. 20, New Series No. 150, September 1925.
17. Duncan, O. D., "Is the Intelligence of the Population Declining?" *American Sociological Review*, Vol. 17, No. 4, August 1952.
18. Eaton, J. W., and A. J. Mayer, "The Social Biology of a Very High Fertility Among the Hutterites —The Demography of a Unique Population," *Human Biology*, Vol. 25, No. 3, September 1953.
19. Edin, K. A., "Fertility in Marriage and Infantile Mortality in the Different Social Classes in Stockholm from 1919–1922," *Proceedings of the World Population Conference*, Edward Arnold and Company, London, 1927.
20. Foote, N., "Changes in American Marriage Patterns and the Role of Women," *Eugenics Quarterly*, Vol. I, December 1954.
21. Franklin, B., "Observations Concerning the Increase of Mankind, The Peopling of Countries, etc.," *The Magazine of History, With Notes and Quotes*, Extra Number, No. 63, 1755.
22. Frazier, E., "The Impact of Urban Civilization Upon Negro Family Life," *American Sociological Review*, Vol. 2, October 1937.
23. Freeman, B. C., "Fertility and Longevity in Married Women Dying After the End of the Reproductive Period," *Human Biology*, Vol. 7, No. 3, September 1935.
24. Galbraith, V. L., and D. S. Thomas, "Birth Rates and the Interwar Business Cycles," *Journal of the American Statistical Association*, Vol. 36, No. 216, December 1941.
25. Grabill, W. H., "A Method for Calculating Gross and Net Reproduction Rates from Census Data," M. A. Thesis, American University, Washington, 1942; "Attrition Life Tables for the Single Population," *Journal of the American Statistical Association*, Vol. 40, No. 231, September 1945; "Effect of Wartime Marriage Boom," *Domestic Commerce*, Vol. 33, No. 1, January 1945.
26. Guttmacher, A. F., "Selective Pregnancy," *Human Fertility*, Vol. 6, No. 2, April 1941.
27. Hajnal, J., "Age at Marriage and Proportions Marrying," *Population Studies*, Vol. VII, No. 1, 1950.
28. Hauser, P. M., and E. M. Kitagawa, "Demographic Glimpses into Burma, 1952," a paper in *The Interrelations of Demographic, Economic, and Social Problems in Selected Underdeveloped Areas*, Milbank Memorial Fund, New York, 1954.
29. Henripen, J., "La fécondité des ménages canadiens au début du XVIIIe siécle," *Population*, Vol. 9, No. 1, January-March 1954.
30. Henry, L., "Notes et documents, Intervalles entre naissances," *Population*, Vol. 9, No. 4, October-December 1954.
31. Hope II, J., "The Employment of Negroes in the United States by Major Occupation Group and Industry," *Journal of Negro Education*, Vol. XXII, No. 3, Summer 1951.
32. Innes, J. W., "Class Birth Rates in England and Wales, 1921–1931," *The Milbank Memorial Fund Quarterly*, Vol. XIX, No. 1, January 1941.
33. Jaffe, A. J., "Differential Fertility in the White Population in Early America," *Journal of Heredity*, Vol. 31, No. 1, September 1940; "Population Growth and Fertility Trends in the United States," *Journal of Heredity*, Vol. 32, No. 12, December 1941.
34. Karmel, P. H., "An Analysis of the Sources and Magnitudes of Inconsistencies between Male and Female Net Reproduction Rates in Actual Populations," *Population Studies*, Vol. 2, No. 2, September 1948.
35. Kirk, D., "Problems of Collection and Comparability of International Statistics," *Problems of Collection and Comparability of International Statistics*, Milbank Memorial Fund, New York, 1949; "Recent Trends of Catholic Fertility in the United States," *Current Research in Human Fertility*, The Milbank Memorial Fund, New York, 1955.
36. Kiser, C. V., "Changes in Fertility by Socio-Economic Status During 1940–1950," *Milbank Memorial Fund Quarterly*, Vol. XXXIII, No. 4, October 1955; "Fertility of Social Classes in Various Types of Communities in the East North Central States in 1900," *Journal of the American Statistical Association*, Vol. 27, No. 180, December 1932; "Trends in the Fertility of Social Classes from 1900 to 1910," *Human Biology*, Vol. 5, No. 2, May 1933.
37. Kiser, C. V., E. G. Mishler, C. F. Westoff, and R. G. Potter, Jr., "Development of Plans for a Social Psychological Study of the Future Fertility of Two-Child Families," *Population Studies*, Vol. 10, July 1956.

38. Koya, Y., "A Study of Induced Abortion in Japan and Its Significance," *Milbank Memorial Fund Quarterly*, Vol. XXXII, No. 3, July 1954.
39. Kuczynski, R. R., "The Registration Laws in the Colonies of Massachusetts Bay and New Plymouth," *Quarterly Publications of the American Statistical Association*, Vol. VII, New Series No. 51, September 1900.
40. Lampe, P. H. J., "A Study of Human Fertility in the British Caribbean Territories," Guardian Commercial Printery, Port-of-Spain, 1951. (Reprinted from *Caribbean Economic Review.)*
41. Leslie, G. R., H. T. Christensen, and G. L. Pearman, "Studies in Child Spacing: IV. The Time-Interval Separating All Children In Completed Families of Purdue University Graduates," *Social Forces*, Vol. 34, No. 1, October 1955 (contains references to other studies of spacing).
42. Lotka, A. J., "The Size of American Families in the Eighteenth Century," *Journal of the American Statistical Association*, Vol. 22, 1927.
43. Maxwell, J., "Intelligence, Fertility and the Future: A Report on the 1947 Scottish Mental Survey," *Eugenics Quarterly*, Vol. 1, No. 4, December 1954.
44. Notestein, F. W., "Class Differences in Fertility," *The Annals of the American Academy of Political and Social Science*, Vol. 188, November 1936; "Differential Fertility in the East North Central States," *Milbank Memorial Fund Quarterly*, Vol. XVI, No. 2, April 1938; "The Decrease in Size of Families from 1890 to 1910," *Milbank Memorial Fund Quarterly*, Vol. 9, 1931.
45. Ogburn, W. F. (with the assistance of C. Tibbetts), "The Family and Its Functions," *Recent Social Trends in the United States*, Vol. 1, McGraw-Hill Book Company, New York, 1933.
46. Pringle, H. F., "What do the Women of America Think About Birth Control?" *Ladies Home Journal*, March 1938.
47. Roberts, G. W., "Some Aspects of Mating and Fertility in the West Indies," *Population Studies*, Vol. VIII, No. 3, March 1955.
48. Roeber, W. F., and R. M. Marshall, "An American Remarriage Table," *Proceedings of the Casualty Actuarial Society*, Vol. 19, May 1953.
49. Sallume, X., and F. W. Notestein, "Trends in the Size of Families Completed Prior to 1910 in Various Social Classes," *The American Journal of Sociology*, Vol. 38, No. 3, November 1932.
50. Sharpe, F., and A. J. Lotka, *"A Problem in Age Distribution,"* *Philosophical Magazine*, Vol. 21, April 1911.
51. Shryock, H. S., Jr., "Accuracy of Population Projections for the United States," *Estadística*, Vol. XII, December 1954.
52. Siegel, J. S., and C. H. Hamilton, "Some Considerations in the Use of the Residual Method of Estimating Net Migration," *Journal of the American Statistical Association*, Vol. 47, No. 259, September 1952.
53. Sontheimer, M., "Abortion in America Today," *Woman's Home Companion*, October 1955, p. 44.
54. Spengler, J. J., "The Fecundity of Native White and Foreign-Born White Women in New England," *Brookings Institution Pamphlet Series*, Vol. II, No. 1, June 30, 1930.
55. Stolmitz, G. J., and N. B. Ryder, "Recent Discussion of the Net Reproduction Rate," *Population Index*, Vol. 15, No. 2, April 1949.
56. Sydenstricker, E., and F. W. Notestein, "Differential Fertility According to Social Class: A Study of 69,620 Native White Married Women Under 45 Years of Age Based upon United States Census Returns of 1910," *Journal of the American Statistical Association*, Vol. 25, No. 169, March 1930.
57. Taeuber, I. B., "Literature on Future Population, 1943–1948," *Population Index*, Vol. 15, No. 1, January 1949.
58. Taeuber, I. B., and C. C. Pan, "Micronesian Islands under United States Trusteeship: Demographic Paradox," *Population Index*, Vol. 16, No. 2, April 1950.
59. Taylor, W., "Cohort Analysis of Fertility in England and Wales, 1939–50," *British Journal of Social Medicine*, Vol. 6, No. 4, October 1952.
60. Thompson, W. S. (assisted by N. E. Jackson and R. O. Lang), *Average Number of Children per Woman in Butler County, Ohio, A Study in Differential Fertility*, U. S. Department of Commerce with Cooperation of Scripps Foundation for Research in Population Problems, Edward Brothers, Inc., Ann Arbor, 1941.
61. Tietze, C., and W. H. Grabill, "Differential Fertility by Duration of Marriage," *Eugenics Quarterly*, Vol. 4, No. 1, March 1957.
62. Tietze, C., and P. Lauriat, "Age at Marriage by Educational Attainment," *Population Studies*, Vol. 9, No. 2, November 1955.
63. Tietze, C., and S. Lewit, "Patterns of Family Limitation in a Rural Negro Community," *American Sociological Review*, Vol. 18, No. 5, October 1953.

64. Valien, P. and A. P. Fitzgerald, "Attitudes of the Negro Mother Toward Birth Control," *American Journal of Sociology*, Vol. LV, No. 3, November 1949.
65. Vincent, P., "La famille normale," *Population*, Vol. 5, No. 2, April-June 1950.
66. Walker, F. A., "Restriction of Immigration," *Atlantic Monthly*, Vol. 77, 1896.
67. Westoff, C. F., "Differential Fertility in the United States: 1900 to 1952," *American Sociological Review*, Vol. 19, No. 5, October 1954.
68. Westoff, C. F., E. G. Mishler, and E. L. Kelly, "Preferences in Size of Family and Eventual Fertility Twenty Years After," *The American Journal of Sociology*, Vol. LXII, No. 5, March 1957, pp. 491–497.
69. Whelpton, P. K., "A Study of the 'Expected' Completed Fertility of a National Sample of White Women," *Current Research in Human Fertility*, The Milbank Memorial Fund, New York, 1955; "Census Projections: Some Areas of Doubt," *Conference Board Business Record*, Vol. XIII, No. 8, August 1956; "Future Fertility of American Women," *Eugenics Quarterly*, Vol. I, March 1954; "Reproduction Rates Adjusted for Age, Parity, Fecundity, and Marriage," *Journal of the American Statistical Association*, Vol. 41, No. 236, December 1946.
70. Whelpton, P. K., and R. Freedman, "A Study of the Growth of American Families," *American Journal of Sociology*, Vol. LXI, No. 6, May 1956.
71. Whelpton, P. K., and C. V. Kiser, "The Comparative Influence on Fertility of Contraception and Impairments of Fertility," *Milbank Memorial Fund Quarterly*, Vol. XXVI, No. 2, April 1948, pp. 182–232.
72. Wicksell, S. D., "Nuptiality, Fertility, and Reproductivity," *Skandinavisk Aktuarietidskrift*, Vol. 14, No. 3, 1931.
73. Wiehl, D. G., "A Summary of Data on Reported Incidence of Abortion," *Milbank Memorial Fund Quarterly*, Vol. XVI, No. 1, 1938.
74. Woofter, T. H., "Completed Generation Reproduction Rates," *Human Biology*, Vol. 19, No. 3, September 1947.
75. "World Population in Transition," *Annals of the American Academy of Political and Social Science*, Vol. 237, January 1945.

Public Documents

1. Canada, Dominion Bureau of Statistics, Charles, E., *The Changing Size of the Family in Canada*, Census Monograph No. 1, Eighth Census of Canada, Edmond Cloutier, Ottawa, 1948.
2. City of Boston, Shattuck, L., et al., *Report to the City Council Appointed to Obtain the Census of Boston for the Year 1845*, John H. Eastburn, Boston, 1846.
3. Commonwealth of Massachusetts, *The Census of Massachusetts: 1885*, Vol. I, *Population and Social Statistics*, Part 2, Wright and Potter Printing Co., State Printers, Boston, 1888 (contains data on children ever born); *The Census of Massachusetts: 1875*, Vol. I, *Population and Social Statistics*, Albert J. Wright, State Printer, Boston, 1876 (contains data on children ever born).
4. Institut National d'Etudes Demographiques, Bourgeois-Pichat, J., *Mesure de la fécondité des populations*, Travaux et Documents, Cahier No. 12, Presses Universitaires de France, Paris, 1950; Henry, L., *Fécondité des mariages, Nouvelle méthode de mesure*, Travaux et Documents, Cahier No. 16, Presses Universitaires de France, Paris, 1953.
5. Institut National de la Statistique et des Etudes Economiques, Direction de la Statistique Générale, *Résultats statistiques du recensement général de la population*, Vol. IV, *Familles*, (effectué 1 Mars 1946), Imprimerie Nationale, Paris, 1950.
6. State of Rhode Island and Providence Plantations, *Twenty-First Annual Report of the Commissioner of Industrial Statistics, Made to the General Assembly at Its January Session, 1908*, E. F. Freeman Co., State Printers, Providence, 1908 (contains data on children ever born from State Census, 1905).
7. Statistique Générale de la France, Depoid, P., *Reproduction nette en Europe depuis l'origine des statistiques de l'état civil*, Études Démographiques No. 1, Paris, 1941.
8. United Kingdom, General Register Office, *Census of England and Wales, 1911*, Vol. XIII, *Fertility of Marriage*, Parts 1 and 2, His Majesty's Stationery Office, London, 1917 (Part 1) and 1923 (Part 2).
9. United Kingdom, Royal Commission in Population, *Report*, His Majesty's Stationery Office, London, 1949; Glass, D. V., and E. Grebenik, *The Trend and Pattern of Fertility in Great Britain: A Report on the Family Census of 1946*, Parts I and II, Papers of the Royal Commission on Population, Vol. 6, Her Majesty's Stationery Office, London, 1954.

10. United Nations, Department of Economic Affairs, *Handbook of Population Census Methods*, New York, 1954; Department of Social Affairs and Department of Economic Affairs, *Demographic Yearbook* (annual volume); Educational, Scientific, and Cultural Organization, and International Union for the Scientific Study of Population, Lorimer, F., et al., *Culture and Human Fertility: A Study of the Relation of Cultural Conditions to Fertility in Non-Industrial and Transitional Societies*, Paris, 1954; Population Division, *Population Growth and the Standard of Living in Underdeveloped Countries*, Population Studies No. 20, New York, October 1954; Population Division, *The Determinants and Consequences of Population Trends*, New York, 1953; Population Division, *Fertility Data in Population Censuses*, Population Studies No. 6, Lake Success, 1939; World Health Organization, Regional Office for S.E. Asia, *Final Report on Pilot Studies in Family Planning*, Vols. I and II, New Delhi, 1954.

11. United States, National Resources Committee, *The Problems of a Changing Population*, Government Printing Office, Washington, 1938.

12. U. S. Congress, Immigration Commission, *Reports of the Immigration Commission*, Vol. 28, *Occupations of the First and Second Generations of Immigrants in the United States—Fecundity of Immigrant Women* (Senate Document No. 282, 61st Congress, 2nd Session), Government Printing Office, Washington, 1911. (Contains data on children ever born for native white and foreign-born white women in several cities and counties from 1900 Census.)

13. U. S. Department of Agriculture, Agricultural Marketing Service, Beale, C. L., *Characteristics of Farm-Operator Households by Number of Young Children*, Washington, June 1956.

14. U. S. Department of Commerce, Bureau of the Census, Glover, J. W., *United States Life Tables, 1890, 1901, 1910, and 1901–10*, Government Printing Office, Washington, 1921.

   Jaffe, A. J., *Handbook of Statistical Methods for Demographers*, Government Printing Office, Washington, 1951.

   Thompson, W. S., *Ratios of Children to Women, 1920*, Census Monograph XI, Government Printing Office, Washington, 1931.

   Whelpton, P. K., assisted by H. T. Eldridge and J. S. Siegel, *Forecasts of the Population of the United States, 1945–1975*, Government Printing Office, Washington, 1947.

   Historical Statistics of the United States, 1789–1945, Government Printing Office, Washington, 1949.

   Statistical Abstract of the United States (annual volumes)

   1940 Census of Population:
   Vol. II, *Characteristics of the Population*, Parts 1–7. Vol. IV, *Characteristics by Age*, Parts 1–4. *Differential Fertility, 1940 and 1910*, "Fertility for States and Large Cities," "Standardized Fertility Rates and Reproduction Rates," "Women by Number of Children Under 5 years Old," "Women by Number of Children Ever Born," "Fertility by Duration of Marriage."

   Procedural Studies of the 1950 Censuses:
   No. 1, Infant Enumeration Study; No. 2, The 1950 Censuses—How They were Taken.

   1950 Census of Population:
   Vol. I, *Number of Inhabitants;* Vol. II, *Characteristics of the Population*, Parts 1–54; Vol. IV, *Special Reports;* Part 2 (Chapter D, Marital Status; Chapter E, Duration of Current Marital Status); Part 3 (Chapter B, Nonwhite Population by Race; Chapter C, Persons of Spanish Surname);
   Series PC–14: No. 21, "Fertility by Social and Economic Status for Puerto Rico: 1950," June 24, 1954; No. 22, "Fertility by Duration of Marriage: 1950," September 7, 1956.

   Population—Special Reports:
   Series P–45, No. 7, "Age at First Marriage," May 28, 1945.
   Series P–S, No. 16, "Marital Status of the Civilian Population and of Heads of Families: June 1946," February 10, 1947.

   Current Population Reports, Series P–20:
   No. 18, "Fertility: April 1947," June 30, 1948.
   No. 27, "Marital Fertility: April 1949," February 3, 1950.
   No. 29, "Estimated Net Reproduction Rates for the White Population, by Counties: April, 1935, to April, 1940," March 24, 1950.
   No. 44, "Marital Status and Household Characteristics: April 1952," September 6, 1953.
   No. 46, "Fertility of the Population: April 1952," December 31, 1953.
   No. 56, "Marital Status and Family Status: April 1954," March 18, 1955.
   No. 62, "Marital Status and Family Status: April 1955," October 31, 1955.
   No. 65, "Fertility of the Population: April 1954," March 28, 1954.

Current Population Reports, Series P–25:

No. 98, "Estimates of the Population of the United States and of the Components of Change, by Age, Color, and Sex: 1940 to 1950," August 13, 1954.

No. 106, "Estimates of the Civilian Population of States by Broad Age Groups: July 1, 1953," December 6, 1954.

No. 121, "Estimates of the Population of the United States, by Age, Color, and Sex: July 1, 1950 to 1955," September 27, 1955.

No. 114, "Estimates of the Population of the United States, by Age, Color, and Sex: 1900 to 1940," April 27, 1955.

No. 123, "Revised Projections of the Population of the United States, by Age and Sex: 1960 to 1975," October 20, 1955.

No. 146, "Estimates of the Population of the United States, by Age, Color, and Sex: July 1, 1950 to 1956," November 12, 1956.

15. U. S. Department of Commerce and Labor, Census Office, *Supplemental Analysis, Twelfth Census, 1900*, Special Reports of the Census Office, Government Printing Office, Washington, 1906; Rossiter, W. S., *A Century of Population Growth, From the First Census to the Twelfth, 1790–1900*, Government Printing Office, Washington, 1909.

16. U. S. Department of Health, Education, and Welfare, National Office of Vital Statistics, *Vital Statistics of the United States* (annual volumes); *Monthly Vital Statistics Report* (preliminary data from telegraphic reports),

Vital Statistics—Special Reports:

Vol. 33, No. 8, Whelpton, P. K., "Births and Birth Rates in the Entire United States: 1909–1948," September 29, 1950.

Vol. 33, No. 11, United States National Committee on Vital and Health Statistics, "Statistics Needed Concerning Fertility," February 25, 1952.

Vol. 39, No. 8, United States National Committee on Vital and Health Statistics, "Progress in Development of Fertility Statistics and Population Estimates," May 14, 1956.

Vol. 42, No. 13, "Births by Age of Mother, Race, and Birth Order, United States, 1953," December 21, 1955.

Vol. 44, No. 8, "Births by Age of Mother, Race, and Birth Order, United States, 1954," July 24, 1956.

17. U. S. Department of Interior, Census Office, DeBow, J. D., *Statistical View of the United States. . . . being a Compendium of the Seventh Census . . .* (1850), A. O. P. Nicholson, Public Printer, Washington, 1854.

A P P E N D I X   A

DEFINITION OF TERMS, EXPLANATIONS, AND QUALITY OF DATA

Children ever born.   The decennial census data for 1940 and 1950 and the current population survey data for 1952 and 1954 were based on answers to a single question on number of children ever born, which was accompanied by a specific caution that stillbirths were not to be included.   The meaning of the phrase "children ever born" is clear to most people, but the enumerator was instructed that the count should not include adopted children, stepchildren, or other children not born to the woman; on the other hand, the count was to include children born before and during the present marriage, children who had died, and any other children born to the woman but no longer in the household as well as those still present.   A check box was provided for answers of "none" in 1950, 1952, and 1954, after experience in the 1940 Census indicated that some enumerators made no entry on the schedule rather than enter a "0" for women who had borne no children, despite specific instruction on this point.   Two questions were asked in 1910: "Mother of how many children?" and "Number now living?"   The enumerator in 1910 was instructed not to count stillbirths but this caution did not appear in the question wording or on the schedule itself, and it may not always have been passed on to the person answering the question.

An indication of the quality of reporting on children ever born is available from comparisons of 665,758 pairs of matched 1950 Census "Infant Cards" for infants born in the first three months of 1950 and the birth registration records for these same infants.   If the birth registration record entries of order of live birth are assumed to be accurate, then there was a net undercount of only 1.7 percent in the census entries of total children ever born to white mothers and of 7.6 percent in the entries for nonwhite mothers (table A–1).   In Canada, a similar comparison was made of records involving children under 1 year old at the time of the 1941 Census and a net difference of 0.1 percent was found.[1]   The reporting of children ever born may be of better quality for the women who have had a recent

---

[1] E. Charles, *The Changing Size of the Family in Canada*, Census Monograph No. 1, Eighth Census of Canada, 1941, p. 274.

birth than for the women who have not had a recent birth.   Another basis of measuring "errors" in the matched records assumes, not always correctly, that the larger count of children ever born is the right one when a difference exists.   On this basis, there was an undercount in census data on children ever born for recent mothers of about 1 percent in Canada and of 3.9 percent for whites and 14.6 percent for nonwhites in the United States.   In the United States, exact agreement of the two records occurred for 93.9 percent of whites and 78.3 percent of nonwhites.

TABLE A-1.—COMPARISON OF ENTRIES ON CENSUS INFANT CARD AND ON NATIONAL OFFICE OF VITAL STATISTICS BIRTH RECORD AS TO ORDER OF LIVE BIRTH, FOR CHILDREN BORN IN THE FIRST 3 MONTHS OF 1950, BY COLOR, URBAN AND RURAL: 1950

[Data exclude illegitimate births; births with order of live birth not reported on one or both records; births of twins, triplets, or quadruplets; and births with insufficient detail on record to establish a match, or which have only one record.   Urban-rural residence according to old definition]

Area and color of woman	Total records compared	Census records lower than NOVS records						Records identical	
		Total		3 or more children lower	2 children lower	1 child lower		Number	Percent of total records
		Number	Percent of total records (a)						
United States........	665,758	33,832	5.1	2,845	4,814	26,173		613,562	92.2
White.....................	591,289	22,944	3.9	1,667	3,005	18,272		555,224	93.9
Nonwhite..................	74,469	10,888	14.6	1,178	1,809	7,901		58,338	78.3
Urban..................	376,321	14,725	3.9	1,023	1,962	11,740		353,002	93.8
White.....................	334,931	10,600	3.2	663	1,288	8,649		318,117	95.0
Nonwhite..................	41,390	4,125	10.0	360	674	3,091		34,885	84.3
Rural nonfarm..........	177,162	9,157	5.2	810	1,269	7,078		162,959	92.0
White.....................	163,051	6,825	4.2	540	883	5,402		152,246	93.4
Nonwhite..................	14,111	2,332	16.5	270	386	1,676		10,713	75.9
Rural farm.............	112,275	9,950	8.9	1,012	1,583	7,355		97,601	86.9
White.....................	93,307	5,519	5.9	464	834	4,221		84,861	90.9
Nonwhite..................	18,968	4,431	23.4	548	749	3,134		12,740	67.2

Area and color of woman	Census records higher than NOVS records					Net percentage census records lower than NOVS records (a) - (b)
	Total		1 child higher	2 children higher	3 or more children higher	
	Number	Percent of total records (b)				
United States........	18,364	2.8	13,700	2,667	1,997	2.3
White.....................	13,121	2.2	10,169	1,765	1,187	1.7
Nonwhite..................	5,243	7.0	3,531	902	810	7.6
Urban..................	8,594	2.3	6,667	1,208	719	1.6
White.....................	6,214	1.9	4,990	819	405	1.3
Nonwhite..................	2,380	5.8	1,677	389	314	4.2
Rural nonfarm..........	5,046	2.8	3,781	732	533	2.4
White.....................	3,980	2.4	3,050	554	376	1.8
Nonwhite..................	1,066	7.6	731	178	157	8.9
Rural farm.............	4,724	4.2	3,252	727	745	4.7
White.....................	2,927	3.1	2,129	392	406	2.8
Nonwhite..................	1,797	9.5	1,123	335	339	13.9

Source: *1950 Census of Population,* Vol. IV, *Special Reports,* Part 5, Chapter C, Fertility, table A-3.

An overcount of children ever born may occur almost as easily as an undercount, but an overcount may be less frequent than an undercount. An overcount may arise from an inclusion, intentional or unintentional, of an adopted child, a stepchild, or a fetal death, or from an incorrect statement by a person supplying information for someone else. An undercount may occur from a reporting only of births to a current marriage, especially if an illegitimate child was not kept by the mother, or if some dead or absent children were overlooked. Perhaps it happens sometimes that an infant who died shortly after birth is reported as a fetal death to avoid expensive funeral requirements and is thereafter counted differently by the family and the physician. However, this is speculation. Neither the enumerator who fills out census records nor the doctor or other person who fills out the birth records necessarily attempts to obtain a precise answer to all parts of the respective records, especially when additional questions might be needed to be sure. Yet, it is probable that the bulk of the reports on children ever born are complete and accurate, at least for whites.

Rates of children ever born for women near or past the end of the childbearing ages in one census can be compared with the rate in the next census for the surviving women at older ages. This perhaps is more an indication of comparability than of quality, because both censuses may have a small bias in a similar direction. In 1940, the white women 45 to 49 years old had an average of about 2,704 children ever born per 1,000 women, including estimates of children for women who made no report. This compares with a rate of 2,689 children per 1,000 white women 55 to 59 years old in 1950. Among nonwhites, the corresponding rates were 3,120 in 1940 and 3,214 in 1950. In 1950, women of all races, 45 to 49 years old, had an average of 2,292 children ever born per 1,000 women, compared with an average of 2,249 children per 1,000 women 47 to 51 years old in the April 1952 Current Population Survey and with 2,437 children per 1,000 women 49 to 53 years old in the April 1954 Current Population Survey. The differences among these three rates are wthin the bounds of sampling variability, which are much wider in the Current Population Survey than in the 1950 Census data. Nothing in the data cited indicates that there is much loss in the proportion of children ever born reported as women age, as long as too old an age is not used. In contrast, the native white women 40 to 44 years old in 1910 had an average of 3,542 children ever born per 1,000 women, and were not quite through childbearing, whereas in 1940 the surviving native white women 70 to 74 years old had an average of about 3,200 children per 1,000 women. The rate may have been lower in 1940 because of underreporting of children by the aged survivors, but there is also a possibility that the wording of the question in the 1910 Census inadvertently picked up some stillbirths, adoptions, and stepchildren. The women 70 to 74 years old in 1940 were less than half as numerous as those living 30 years earlier at age 40 to 44, and differential mortality between women with many children and women with few probably had some effect.[2] For additional data on quality, see the comparisons of census data with cohort data in Appendix B.

In any comparison or use of census data on children ever born, not only errors of reporting but also failures to report should be considered. If the nonreports were sufficiently few or if they were random in nature, they would not be a source of appreciable bias in fertility rates limited to reporting women.   There is evidence that as a group the women who did not report on children ever born were less fertile than the women who did report.   The evidence consists of the relative numbers of children present in the household.   Perhaps more of the women with few or no children were away shopping, visiting, or working at the time the enumerator called as compared with the women with many children, and the enumerator may have obtained information from a neighbor for some of the women who were not at home, after several unsuccessful "call backs."   It is known from an inspection of the population schedules for 1940 and 1950 that many of the nonreports were traceable to the relatively few enumerators who made no entries of children ever born for any of the women in their enumeration district and thus apparently did not ask the question; nonreports from this cause would tend to be random in nature rather than selective of women with few children.   About 9.0 percent of the ever-married women 15 to 59 years old in 1950 and 12.6 percent of those 15 to 74 years old in 1940 had no report on children ever born.   The percentage of nonreports was less than 1.0 in the Current Population Surveys of April 1952 and April 1954.   The published 1950 Census data include estimates of children ever born when no report was made, the estimates were based on the number of children in the household and allowances were made for some absent or dead children.   This was done in an effort to reduce bias from nonreports.   Some of the data shown for 1940 have been revised to include such an allowance and were taken from the 1950 Census report on fertility, as noted in source notes to tables, but most of the 1940 Census figures used in this monograph were taken from the 1940 reports and are therefore limited to women who reported on children ever born.   The figures in table A–2 show the essentially small changes in the fertility rates for 1950 and 1940 that occurred when they were adjusted to include estimates of children for women with no report.

---

[2] A priori there would appear to be somewhat counter trends in differential mortality by number of children. Since both fertility and mortality rates are inversely related to socio-economic status one would expect the mortality rates among women 40 to 70 years of age to be higher among women with many children than among those with few children. On the other hand, there is the possibility that among women of completed fertility and of the same broad socio-economic class mortality rates may be to a slight extent inversely related to number of offspring. The two chief studies of this (cited below) yielded somewhat different types of results. See Harold F. Dorn and Arthur J. McDowell, "The Relationship of Fertility and Longevity," *American Sociological Review*, Vol. 4, No. 2, April 1939, pp. 234–246; Bettie C. Freeman, "Fertility and Longevity in Married Women Dying After the End of the Reproductive Period," *Human Biology*, September 1935, pp. 392–418.

TABLE **A-2.**—EFFECT ON FERTILITY RATES OF INCLUDING AN ESTIMATE OF CHILDREN EVER BORN FOR WOMEN WHO MADE NO REPORT, FOR WOMEN 15 TO 59 YEARS OLD, BY AGE AND MARITAL STATUS: 1950 AND 1940

Year and age of woman	Children ever born per 1,000 women			Children ever born per 1,000 women ever married		
	All reporting women[1] (a)	Including estimate for women not reporting (b)	Percent (a) ÷ (b)	Reporting women ever married (c)	Including estimate for women not reporting (d)	Percent (c) ÷ (d)
1950						
15 to 19 years...............	96	105	91.4	622	604	103.8
20 to 24 years...............	726	738	98.4	1,102	1,082	101.8
25 to 29 years...............	1,430	1,436	99.6	1,668	1,654	100.8
30 to 34 years...............	1,865	1,871	99.7	2,070	2,059	100.5
35 to 39 years...............	2,051	2,061	99.5	2,253	2,247	100.3
40 to 44 years...............	2,165	2,170	99.8	2,377	2,364	100.5
45 to 49 years...............	2,266	2,292	98.9	2,483	2,492	99.6
50 to 54 years...............	2,486	2,497	99.6	2,714	2,706	100.3
55 to 59 years...............	2,723	2,728	99.8	2,973	2,954	100.6
1940						
15 to 19 years...............	61	68	89.7	640	572	111.9
20 to 24 years...............	505	522	96.7	1,037	987	105.1
25 to 29 years...............	1,129	1,132	99.7	1,508	1,463	103.1
30 to 34 years...............	1,678	1,678	100.0	2,002	1,964	101.9
35 to 39 years...............	2,156	2,145	100.5	2,461	2,414	101.9
40 to 44 years...............	2,501	2,490	100.4	2,801	2,754	101.7
45 to 49 years...............	2,758	2,740	100.7	3,052	2,998	101.8
50 to 54 years...............	2,891	2,870	100.7	3,205	3,146	101.9
55 to 59 years...............	3,038	3,014	100.8	3,367	3,301	102.0

[1] Single women included; assumed to be childless.

Source: Derived from *1950 Census of Population*, Vol. IV, *Special Reports*, Part 5, Chapter C, Fertility, pp. 17, 23, and 25; *1940 Census of Population, Differential Fertility, 1940 and 1910*, Fertility for States and Large Cities, p. 13.

Childless women. Childless women are defined as those who have never borne a child.

Children under 5 years old. Two types of data on children under 5 years old are shown in this monograph: all enumerated persons under 5 years old and own children under 5 years old. The former are from tables showing the population classified by age and sex, and they are usually from the full census data rather than from a sample. The latter, shown only in reports on fertility, are based on a classification of women by number of own children (sons and daughters) enumerated in the woman's household. The classification was made by an inspection of the population schedule entries for each member of the woman's household, with special attention to information on relationship of each person to the head of the household, surnames, ages, and the order of listing (enumerators were instructed to list persons in parent-child groups wherever such existed). The classification of women by number of own children permits a tabulation of fertility data by detailed age, marital status, and other characteristics of the woman and her family that cannot otherwise be obtained from the census data. Comparisons of data for different groups should be made with awareness of the variable extent to which young children live with their mothers and of the differential completeness of the count of young children, differential mortality, etc. These matters are discussed in some detail below.

The extent to which the number of own children under 5 years old in the household is less than the number of all enumerated children under 5 years old is easily determined from a comparison of the two types of data (table A–3). The difference between the numbers largely reflects children not living with their mothers. Few of these children are orphans. The absent mothers were still living in most cases, according to computations from life tables. The difference also reflects the very few young children who were not classified as own children because they lived with mothers younger or older than the age range of 15 to 49 years used in the fertility tabulations, and there were a few children who because of insufficient information could not be classified as the son or daugther of a specific woman. An example of the difficult coding problems rarely encountered is a household comprised of an aged woman, several married or unmarried adult daughters, and several grandchildren, all with different surnames and all listed in other than a mother-child sequence. Also, no effort was made to count own children of single women except in 1940, but it seems likely that most women living with an illegitimate child were reported in the census as married, widowed, or divorced, rather than as single. The 1940 effort was not a rewarding one. Only 13,400 women, or 0.1 percent of all single native white women 15 to 49 years old, and only 16,040 women, or 1.5 percent of all single Negro women 15 to 49 years old, were found to be mothers of children under 5 years old. Most of the relatively few adopted children and stepchildren were not identifiable as such and were counted as own children even when an effort was made to limit the count to the woman's own progeny, as in 1910, 1940, and 1950. (For convenience, all adopted children and stepchildren were included in fertility tabulations based on the Current Population Survey.)

TABLE **A–3.**—Comparison of Number of Own Children with Total Number of Children Under 5 Years Old in the Census, by Color, Urban and Rural: 1950

Area and color	Total children under 5	Own children under 5	
		Number	Percent of total
White..........................	14,184,504	13,928,910	98.2
Urban....................................	8,667,561	8,546,070	98.6
Rural nonfarm...........................	3,398,079	3,291,810	96.9
Rural farm.............................	2,118,864	2,091,030	98.7
Nonwhite..........................	1,979,067	1,693,800	85.6
Urban....................................	1,105,158	951,840	86.1
Rural nonfarm...........................	373,103	319,530	85.6
Rural farm.............................	500,806	422,430	84.3

Source: *1950 Census of Population*, Vol. II, *Characteristics of the Population*, Part 1, U. S. Summary, table 38, and Vol. IV, *Special Reports*, Part 5, Chapter C, Fertility, table 34.

TABLE **A–4.**—Percent Own Children Are of All Children Under 5 Years Old (Including Allowance for Census Undercount), by Color, Urban and Rural, 1950, 1940, and 1910, with Region of Residence for Whites in 1940 and 1910

Year, color, and region of residence	Total	Urban	Rural nonfarm	Rural farm
1950				
White......................................	94.3	97.2	90.5	89.0
Nonwhite...................................	77.3	77.0	80.7	75.4
1940				
White......................................	90.9	93.1	92.0	86.0
Northeast.............................	90.0	91.1	89.8	80.2
North Central........................	92.6	94.9	92.1	88.6
South................................	89.9	94.2	92.8	85.5
West.................................	91.0	92.7	92.3	84.7
Nonwhite...................................	74.9	78.3	77.3	70.8
1910				
White......................................	90.9	94.6	92.5	85.1
Northeast.............................	93.1	93.8	92.7	92.6
North Central........................	91.6	95.5	91.4	87.6
South................................	88.2	94.8	93.0	84.5
West.................................	91.5	94.6	94.0	85.5
Nonwhite...................................	73.2	78.1	77.2	70.0

Source: Data for whites in 1950 derived from tables A–3 and A–8. Data for nonwhites in 1950 derived from various reports of the Bureau of the Census and the National Office of Vital Statistics. Data for 1940 and 1910 derived from *1940 Census of Population, Differential Fertility, 1940 and 1910,* Standardized Fertility Rates and Reproduction Rates, Appendixes A and B.

Table A–4 presents measures of the combined effect of the census undercount of young children and of children not classified as own children. The percentages shown for region totals and United States totals in 1950 and 1940 are based on the number of children under 5 years old expected from (corrected) statistics of births, deaths, and net migration. Those for 1910 are based on the number of children under 5 years old expected from the number of persons enumerated in 1930 at age 20 to 24 years plus an allowance for deaths and net migration in the previous 20 years. (The source report did not use 1920 Census data for persons 10 to 14 years old because the 1920 Census was regarded as relatively inaccurate.) The percentages for urban-rural areas are based on a variety of techniques and the percentages for 1950 are only roughly comparable with those for 1940 and 1910. The color differentials provide a strong argument for tabulating data on fertility separately by color or else for whites only in preference to the total population in the interest of accuracy.

Undercounting of young children. Young children, particularly those under 2 years old, are characteristically underrepresented in population census returns. Many users of the data have assumed that the undercount arises chiefly from a failure to enumerate young children. Actually, as explained later, there are strong indications that a substantial part of the undercount probably comes from misstatements of age, especially from a tendency to report the age of a few children in terms of an approaching birthday. Misstatements occur at all ages but they may largely compensate one another at ages over 1 year. The undercount appears to be smallest in censuses which ask a question on date of birth, as in Japan in

1950, France in 1936, and the United States in 1900. Regardless of the cause, a measure of the net undercount from all sources of error usually is wanted.

In the United States, the undercount of young children in the census has been measured in various ways. Several methods are now described:

a. The number of children counted in the census has been compared with the number expected from statistics of births, deaths, and net migration. The accuracy of this method depends on the accuracy of the vital statistics and migration data. Some (small) error may exist in the correction of birth and death statistics for underregistration, in the manipulation of published death statistics to separate them into proper parts for specific birth cohorts, and in data on migration obtained from census counts of children under 5 years old by State or country of birth. It should be kept in mind that a full correction for the undercount of young children will result in slightly too-high ratios of young children to women if there is an uncorrected undercount of women. Estimates made by method *a* are shown in table A–5 for children under 5 years old in 1950 and in 1940 and for children up to age 14 in table A–6. Perhaps the data for children 2 years old and over are roughly indicative of the completeness of the census enumeration of adults as well as of the children 2 to 14 years old. Method *a* was used as early as 1906 by the Census Office to evaluate the completeness of the count of young children in Massachusetts, Connecticut, and Rhode Island.[3] It may be of much older origin.

b. The number of children under 5 years old counted in one census has been compared with the number counted at age 10 to 14 years in the next decennial census. This method assumes that the count of the children in the age group 10 to 14 years old is relatively complete and that the deaths and the net in- or out-migration in the preceding 10 years can be determined. Normally, the completeness of the count of children 10 to 14 years old is assumed, not tested. (Table A–6 indicates that the count of children 10 to 14 years old in 1950 was about 98.2 percent complete by method *a.*) It might be said that method *b* yields a measure for children under 5 years old that is in approximate proportion to the completeness of the count at all older ages. The mortality allowance for the age cohort between censuses usually is small and is not a source of much error. According to United States life tables for whites, only about 1 percent of the children under 5 years old in 1940 would have died before ages 10 to 14 in 1950. (The corresponding percent from life tables for whites in 1901–09, a period of high mortality by modern standards, is only 5.9 percent.) The problem of measuring net migration can be largely avoided on a national basis by limiting the computations to native whites and Negroes. (This is also true for method *a.*) Crude estimates of net migration can be made

[3] U. S. Bureau of the Census, *Special Reports of the Census Office, Supplementary Analysis and Derivative Tables, Twelfth Census, 1900*, pp. 139–143.

TABLE A–5.—PERCENT DIFFERENCE BETWEEN THE EXPECTED AND THE ENUMERATED NUMBER OF CHILDREN UNDER 5 YEARS OLD, BY COLOR, BY STATES: 1950 AND 1940

[Unless otherwise noted, differences represent excess of expected over enumerated population expressed as percentage of the expected population. Expected population computed from statistics of births, deaths, and net migration]

State	1950			1940	
	All classes	White	Nonwhite[1]	White	Nonwhite
United States..................	4.7	4.0	9.7	6.4	15.2
New England:					
Maine.........................	3.3	3.6	...	6.9	...
New Hampshire.................	2.0	2.1	...	4.7	...
Vermont.......................	4.9	5.0	...	6.3	...
Massachusetts.................	1.3	1.2	...	5.4	...
Rhode Island..................	2.4	2.2	...	6.3	...
Connecticut...................	4.8	5.0	...	6.0	...
Middle Atlantic:					
New York......................	4.0	3.6	8.5	6.8	13.9
New Jersey....................	6.0	5.5	11.3	8.8	14.4
Pennsylvania..................	3.7	3.5	5.7	7.4	16.3
East North Central:					
Ohio..........................	3.7	3.5	6.6	5.8	11.4
Indiana.......................	4.2	4.0	8.4	5.0	7.9
Illinois......................	5.3	4.6	12.4	6.3	15.4
Michigan......................	3.8	3.6	6.1	5.3	9.3
Wisconsin.....................	2.6	2.7	...	4.3	...
West North Central:					
Minnesota.....................	2.1	2.2	...	2.5	...
Iowa..........................	0.8	0.8	...	2.4	...
Missouri......................	2.8	2.2	8.8	5.4	12.9
North Dakota..................	[2]0.2	([3])	...	3.1	...
South Dakota..................	2.4	2.2	...	2.0	...
Nebraska......................	2.7	2.6	...	2.0	...
Kansas........................	4.6	4.8	...	3.2	...
South Atlantic:					
Delaware......................	2.1	0.5	...	6.1	13.0
Maryland[4]...................	3.7	2.3	9.8	8.3	18.0
District of Columbia[4].......	5.8	2.6	9.9	4.7	14.8
Virginia[4]...................	4.1	2.3	9.5	8.3	14.5
West Virginia.................	5.4	5.4	5.2	12.8	19.0
North Carolina................	5.5	4.0	8.8	9.1	17.7
South Carolina................	8.9	6.3	11.9	6.8	20.1
Georgia.......................	8.4	6.0	12.5	8.5	20.0
Florida.......................	4.0	1.8	10.2	9.7	13.4
East South Central:					
Kentucky......................	6.5	6.8	0.8	6.7	10.5
Tennessee.....................	5.6	4.5	10.6	7.2	10.5
Alabama.......................	7.2	6.2	9.0	8.4	14.5
Mississippi...................	6.3	2.9	9.1	6.2	16.4
West South Central:					
Arkansas......................	8.8	6.2	15.6	6.2	19.6
Louisiana.....................	7.2	5.4	10.0	5.4	13.1
Oklahoma......................	5.8	4.1	18.1	3.2	10.4
Texas.........................	8.0	7.4	11.4	7.9	11.9
Mountain:					
Montana.......................	3.8	3.7	...	5.5	...
Idaho.........................	4.6	4.6	...	4.3	...
Wyoming.......................	5.1	4.9	...	7.2	...
Colorado......................	4.6	4.6	...	5.2	...
New Mexico....................	8.3	7.2	...	12.1	...
Arizona.......................	5.2	4.5	8.9	7.4	...
Utah..........................	0.8	1.1	...	2.6	...
Nevada........................	0.4	0.7	...	9.4	...
Pacific:					
Washington....................	1.5	1.4	...	4.2	...
Oregon........................	1.9	2.1	...	3.9	...
California....................	4.8	4.6	7.3	7.7	15.0

[1] Percent not shown where population under 5 years old is less than 10,000.
[2] Figure represents excess of enumerated over expected population.
[3] Less than 0.1 percent.
[4] Figures shown are based on estimates for District of Columbia, Maryland, and Virginia combined.

Source: U. S. Bureau of the Census, *Current Population Reports*, Series P–25, No. 106, pp. 11 and 12.

on a State basis by several methods, all of which are subject to some error.[4] The technique of measuring the completeness of the count of children under 5 years old in one census by comparisons with the number 10 to 14 years old in the next census has been in use for about 100 years.   Some estimates by method *b* are shown for native whites and Negroes in table A–7. The results for Negroes in censuses before 1930 fluctuate considerably, probably in large part from variation in the quality of the census data at ages 10–14 years.   An unusually large undercount at age 10–14 in one census may result in an overestimate of the completeness of the count at ages under 5 years in the earlier census.   The results for native whites also exhibit some instability but this is far less marked than in the data for Negroes.

Some of the fluctuations shown in table A–7 can be traced to specific enumeration problems.   With the institution of a separate line on the enumeration schedule for each person, the 1850 Census was the first in which the age of each individual was listed separately rather than tallied in predesignated age groups as in earlier censuses.   Some enumerators began the age count with 1 year according to the Compendium of the Seventh Census, so the 1850 Census may have had more misstatements of age of infants than usual.   The 1870 Census was adversely affected by unsettled conditions in the South; a low count at the benchmark age 10–14 in 1870 caused at least a part of the quite high percent completeness estimated for the count of children under 5 in 1860.   The 1890 Census contained a question on age at nearest birthday, rather than at last birthday, with the result that a larger than usual proportion of children almost 5 years old was reported as 5 years old.   The 1900 Census asked a check question on date of birth and had a smaller than usual proportion of ages misreported in terms of a next birthday.   In 1920 the census was less complete than usual at all ages, partly because of enumerator-recruitment problems.   An undecount at age 10–14 in 1920 explains part of the high percentage of completeness estimated for the count of Negroes under 5 years old in 1910.   The percentage of 94.3 for native whites under

---

[4] One method of measuring migration on a State basis is to "age" the number of persons 5 to 9 years old in one census to age 15–19 in the following decennial census, with the aid of a life table.   It is assumed that the difference between the expected survivors and the enumerated number largely reflects net migration.   The individual State estimates may be adjusted to add to zero when summed for a national total, to take care of any minor error in the life table survival rate or other source of small bias.   A further assumption is then made that the population 10 to 14 years old migrated at the same rate and in the same direction (in or out of the State) as the population 15 to 19 years old, and the migration of the younger group is figured accordingly.   A modification of the last assumption may be needed for some population groups, such as Negroes, in which many children leave home at an early age.   These migration computations assume that there is no appreciable undercount of population at ages over 5 years and that the foreign born are not involved or are negligible in proportion.   For a fuller discussion of the general method, see Jacob S. Siegel and C. Horace Hamilton, "Some Considerations in the Use of the Residual Method of Estimating Net Migration," *Journal of the American Statistical Association*, September 1952, pp. 475–500.   Other methods of measuring migration make use of symptomatic materials, such as trends in school enrollment, and may or may not yield better results than the method discussed by way of illustration.

5 years old in 1940 in table A–7 corresponds to one of about 93.6 percent for whites in table A–5; the percentage of 90.9 for Negroes in 1940
corresponds to one of 84.8 in table A–5. Perhaps the difference between
the corresponding estimates in the two tables largely reflects an undercount of persons 10 to 14 years old in 1950. Such an undercount was
noted in table A–6.

TABLE **A–6.**—COMPARISON OF CENSUS COUNT OF CHILDREN UNDER 15 YEARS OLD WITH
NUMBER EXPECTED FROM STATISTICS OF BIRTHS, DEATHS, AND NET MIGRATION, BY AGE: 1950

[In thousands]

Age	Census count	Expected number on April 1, 1950	Difference	Difference as percent of expected number
Under 5 years.............................	16,164	16,966	802	4.7
Under 1 year.............................	3,147	3,537	390	11.0
1 year.............................	3,264	3,512	248	7.1
2 years.............................	3,513	3,604	91	2.5
3 years.............................	3,561	3,600	39	1.1
4 years.............................	2,679	2,714	35	1.3
5 to 9 years.............................	13,200	13,697	497	3.6
10 to 14 years.............................	11,119	11,318	199	1.8

Source: U. S. Bureau of the Census, *Procedural Studies of the 1950 Censuses*, No. 1, *Infant Enumeration Study: 1950*, p. 12; *Current Population Reports*, Series P–25, No. 106, p. 11.

 c. In some censuses it was noted that the number of children in the first
2 years of age was much less than the numbers at ages 2, 3, and 4, although fragmentary birth statistics pointed to rapidly increasing annual
numbers of births. Thus, the existence of an undercount of infants was
"obvious" from data on population by single years of age in some censuses
taken in a time of rapid population growth. Such an undercount was
noted as early as 1850, when the first tabulations of population by single
years of age were made for the United States. A 1900 Census report
compared the age distributions to show the existence of an undercount at
ages under 1 year and 1 year in a number of countries.[5] It noted that the
apparent undercount was much less in countries where there was a question on date of birth than in other countries where only a question on age
was asked. It set forth the theory that much of the undercount came from
misstatements of age or from a tendency to report ages of some infants in
terms of an approaching birthday. It explained an even larger undercount
at age 1 year than at age under 1 year on the theory that the baby was the
least likely person the family would overlook, and that the age group 1
year therefore gained less by misstatements of age from the age group
under 1 year than it contributed to the age group 2 years. Method *c* can
be used for quantitative estimates if one assumes that the count of children
3 and 4 years old is relatively complete and if an expected distribution of
children by age can be obtained. Only a *relative* distribution by age is
needed. Thus, birth statistics may be too low by the same proportion in

[5] Cf. the 1900 Census report cited under method *a.*

each year of some past period and yet correctly indicate that there should be about 120 children under 3 years old per 100 children aged 3 and 4; in such a case, it is proper to multiply the census numbers of children aged 3 and 4 by 1.20 to get the expected "complete" number of children at ages under 3.   Vital statistics for a representative small area might yield an acceptable relative distribution for a national estimate.   If deaths and migration are thought to be fairly small in relation to the births, it may be sufficient to use birth data alone to approximate the expected distribution of young children by age.   If the results are not as accurate as those obtained by method *a*, they may nonetheless be useful for preliminary estimates of the count in the urban, rural-nonfarm, and rural-farm parts of a State, and they can be adjusted by a prorating process to agree with the more precise State total values obtained by method *a*.   Table A–8 presents some estimates by method *c* for white children by regions, urban and rural, in 1950, with and without an adjustment to regional total values from method *a*.   No death or migration statistics were used in method *c*.

TABLE A–7.—ESTIMATED PERCENT OF NATIVE WHITE AND NEGRO CHILDREN UNDER 5 YEARS OLD COUNTED IN CENSUSES, RELATIVE TO THE NUMBER COUNTED AT AGE 10 TO 14 YEARS IN THE NEXT DECENNIAL CENSUS PLUS ALLOWANCE FOR DEATHS: 1850 TO 1940

Census year[1]	Native white	Negro	Census year[1]	Native white	Negro
1940	94.3	90.9	1890	90.3	82.6
1930	96.4	89.5	1880	93.8	92.8
1920	95.2	87.4	1870	88.4	81.6
1910	97.2	94.2	1860	92.0	95.9
1900	98.0	91.7	1850	90.2	86.0

[1] Year children under 5 years old were enumerated.

Source: Derived from various reports on population of the Bureau of the Census and from various life tables.

TABLE A–8.—ESTIMATED PERCENT COMPLETENESS OF CENSUS COUNT OF WHITE CHILDREN UNDER 5 YEARS OLD, BY REGIONS, BY TWO METHODS: 1950

[See text for explanation of methods]

Region	Method (a), total	Method (c), unadjusted				Method (c), prorated to agree with region totals by method (a)		
		Total	Urban	Rural nonfarm	Rural farm	Urban	Rural nonfarm	Rural farm
United States	96.0	95.1	97.7	92.4	89.5	98.6	93.3	90.3
Northeast	96.4	95.1	97.2	90.1	85.1	98.5	91.3	86.3
North Central	96.5	95.3	98.0	92.6	90.1	99.2	93.8	91.2
South	95.0	95.2	98.1	94.6	90.6	97.9	94.4	90.4
West	96.1	94.3	97.4	89.7	85.9	99.3	91.4	87.5

Source: Derived from various reports of the Bureau of the Census and of the National Office of Vital Statistics.

d.   The previous methods indicate that a shortage exists in the census count but they do not indicate how it came about.   A case-by-case check has rarely been made to determine the extent to which young children actually are missed in censuses and why they are missed.   In this method,

a representative list of children is used as a basis, such as a set of birth
records, and the census records are searched to see if the children have
been enumerated.   Canada made such a check, on a small scale, in connection with its 1941 Census.[6]   A similar study was made in the United
States, using birth records for nearly 800,000 infants born in the first three
months of 1950.[7]   In a case-by-case check of the birth records, plus a mail
inquiry of families to find changes of address, adoptions, etc., it was found
that only about 3.6 percent of the infants were not enumerated at some
age in the United States 1950 Census.   This figure of only 3.6 percent
contrasts sharply with the finding from method a that the count of all
young children under 1 year old was 11.0 percent short of the "true"
number.   Both the 3.6 percent and the 11.0 percent may be correct and
consistent if there was a considerable tendency to report children almost
a year old as 1 year old.   The infants born in the first three months of
1950 were for the most part not more than 3 or 4 months old at the time
of the census interview, and a finding that only 1.6 percent of them were
reported as a year old or more in the census probably understates the extent of age misstatements for the older infants.   A very small part of the
undercount of young children in 1950 arose from enumeration policies.
To meet legal requirements, the enumerators were instructed not to count
any infants born after April 1, 1950.   The Infant Card program indirectly
enforced this policy because the field offices were instructed to check the
number of Infant Cards turned in and any population schedule entries for
infants born after April 1, 1950, were to be cancelled.   The enumerators
were instructed to obtain age as of the time of interview, not as of April 1.
The resulting loss to the count of infants was kept low by a short enumeration period.   The enumeration was about two-thirds complete by mid-
April and nine-tenths complete by the end of the month.[8]

The Infant Enumeration Study showed that only about 5 percent of the
missed infants were "forgotten" by the family itself.   In about 82 percent
of the cases of missed infants, the parents also were missed.   Some of the
families were missed because they moved during the enumeration period,
some were temporarily away from home during the enumeration period
and the enumerator failed to call back or obtain information from a

---

[6] In a case-by-case check of 4,228 birth records of infants who should have been under 1 year old in
1941 against census records, it was found that only 45 infants or 1.1 percent were not enumerated in
the census at any age.   (The data are exclusive of known deaths.)   In another phase of the check, it
was found that according to 4,884 matched birth and census records for infants born less than a year
before the census date, 334 infants, or 6.8 percent, were reported in the census at age 1 year or more.
The loss to the older ages was partly offset by gains from 76 infants born after the census date who should
not have been enumerated, and from 9 infants whose birth records indicated that they actually were at
least a year old.   Hence, the Canadian experience showed that misstatements of age were more common than an actual missing of children.
[7] *Procedural Studies of the 1950 Censuses*, No. 1, *Infant Enumeration Study: 1950.*
[8] *1950 Census of Population*, Vol. I, *Number of Inhabitants*, p. IX.

neighbor, and some were families who lived in obscure places that the enumerator failed to find, such as quarters over a garage and in basements.

A Post-Enumeration Survey (PES) was made in 1950 to evaluate as nearly as possible the accuracy of the results of the Census. The PES was basically a careful re-enumeration of a small sample of the population. Many devices were used to make the procedure as accurate as possible. Thus, well-trained and carefully tested enumerators were used. The questions asked were of a probing type, to catch any uncertainty or misunderstanding. Efforts were made to interview each person individually rather than a landlady or other respondent. The results of the PES were compared on a case-by-case basis with the original enumeration records for each person. There was also a coverage check in the PES, in an effort to determine whether any households or people were missed or were incorrectly included in the original census enumeration. According to the PES results, there was a minimum net underenumeration of about 1.4 percent of the population, for all ages combined. This figure of 1.4 percent was believed to be a minimum one because some small groups, such as transients, could not be checked. The PES results did not yield any indication of a sizeable undercount of children under 5 years old, but in this respect it was subject to considerable sampling variability. The PES found little variability in the completeness of the count of the population by age groups. It is possible that despite the elaborate precautions some respondents tended to give the same incorrect answer both in the original census enumeration and in the re-enumeration.

Urban and rural residence. Most of the data shown in this monograph for urban and rural areas in 1950 and in subsequent years are by the 1950 Census rules of classification. In a few tables data are shown for 1950 by the old (1940 Census) definition, as noted in headnotes. The data for 1940 and prior years are invariably shown by the 1940 Census rules of classification.

According to the definition that was adopted for use in the 1950 Census, the urban population comprises all persons living in (a) places of 2,500 inhabitants or more incorporated as cities, boroughs, and villages, (b) incorporated towns of 2,500 inhabitants or more, except in New England, New York, and Wisconsin, where "towns" are simply minor subdivisions of counties, (c) the densely settled urban fringe, including both incorporated and unincorporated areas, around cities of 50,000 or more, and (d) unincorporated places of 2,500 inhabitants or more outside of any urban fringe. The remaining population is classified as rural. According to the definition used for 1940 and earlier years, and in a few tables for 1950 by the old definition as noted in headnotes, the urban population comprises all persons living in *incorporated* places of 2,500 or more and a few areas (usually minor civil divisions) classified as urban under special rules relating to population size and density. The effect of the change in definition on the 1950 Census fertility data is discussed in Chapter 4.

Farm and nonfarm population. The farm population for 1950, as for 1940, includes all persons living on farms without regard to occupation. In determining farm and nonfarm residence in 1950 and subsequent years, persons on "farms" who were paying cash rent for their house and yard only were classified as nonfarm residents; furthermore, persons in institutions, summer camps, and tourist courts were classified as nonfarm residents. Farm residence could be identified in 1910 only for the members of the household of the person responsible for the operation of the farm but it is estimated that less than 10 percent of all farm households in 1910 contained no one responsible for the operation of the farm.

Urbanized areas, size of place, and metropolitan districts. In some tables the urban population in 1950 and in 1952 is classified as living in urbanized areas or in urban places outside urbanized areas. According to the definition used in the 1950 Census and in the April 1952 Current Population Survey, the population in urbanized areas comprises all persons living in (*a*) cities of 50,000 inhabitants or more in 1940 or according to a special census taken between 1940 and 1950 and (*b*) the densely settled urban fringe, including both incorporated and unincorporated areas, surrounding these cities. Residents of urbanized areas were classified according to the size of the entire area rather than by the size of the place in which they lived. The remaining urban population was classified according to the size of the urban places not in the urbanized areas. In some tables for 1940, data are presented for metropolitan districts. A metropolitan district was set up for use in the 1940 Census of Population in connection with each city of 50,000 or more, two or more such cities sometimes being in one district. The general plan was to include, in addition to the central city or cities, all adjacent and contiguous minor civil divisions or incorporated places having a population density of 150 or more per square mile.

Age. The age classification in census and Current Population Survey data is based on the age of the person at the last birthday. Exceptions may be noted for the colonial censuses and the Federal Censuses of 1790 to 1840, in which the age concept was not defined, and for 1890 when the question called for age at *nearest* birthday.

Color, race, and nativity. The term "color" refers to the division of the population into two groups, white and nonwhite. The nonwhite group includes Negroes, Indians, Chinese, Japanese, and other nonwhite races. Persons of Mexican birth or ancestry who are not definitely Indian or of other nonwhite race are classified as white. In the classification by nativity, a person born in the United States or in any of its territories or possessions is counted as native. Likewise counted as native is the small group of persons who, although born in a foreign country or at sea, were American citizens by birth because their parents were American citizens. All other persons are counted as foreign born.

Many of the materials for 1940 and 1910 in this monograph relate to native white and Negro women whereas those for 1950 generally relate to total white and total nonwhite women, in accordance with the data available. The data for each color group in 1950 are quite comparable with the more restricted groups in 1940 and 1910 in that almost all (96 percent) of the white women 15 to 44 years old in 1950 were native and almost all (96 percent) of the nonwhite women 15 to 44 years old in 1950 were Negro.

Spanish surname.   In the 1950 Census, data relating to persons of Spanish-American and Mexican origin were obtained by the identification of white persons of Spanish surnames on the schedules as a part of the general coding operation.   The identification was built around a list of some 6,000 Spanish surnames compiled by the Immigration and Naturalization Service.   Although Spanish surnames are not completely efficient indicators of Spanish-American descent, the classification as judged in terms of the results appears to have been adequate.

Country of birth of foreign-born white women, and mother tongue.   Statistics for white women born in certain foreign countries are shown for 1940 and 1910.   In the 1940 Census, the question referred to the political boundaries as they were on January 1, 1937.   The classification of the 1910 population, while not referring to the political boundaries of a given date, largely represented the countries as they existed in 1910, with the exception of Poland which was not then a political entity but which was nonetheless reported by many immigrants as their country of birth.   The 1910 figures for "Poland" in this report also include those who reported Polish mother tongue but gave Germany, Austria-Hungary, and Russia as their country of birth.   Although the 1940 and 1910 figures for a given country or group of countries do not always pertain to the same political boundaries, they should be sufficiently comparable to permit an analysis of changes between 1910 and 1940 in the fertility of immigrants living in the United States.   Mother tongue, shown for some of the women, is defined, for 1940, as the language spoken in the home in earliest childhood.   For 1910, mother tongue is the language customarily spoken in the homes of the immigrants before immigration.

Marital status.   Most of the data in this report are shown for women of all marital classes (including single), ever-married women (married, widowed, separated, or divorced), and women married once and husband present.   Detailed marital status is shown in a few tables.   The marital status classification refers to the status at the time of enumeration.   Persons classified as "married" comprise, therefore, both those who have been married only once and those who have remarried after having been widowed or divorced.   Persons reported as separated or in common-law marriages are classified as married.   Those reported as never married or with annulled marriages are classified as single.   Since it is probable that some divorced persons are reported as single, married, or widowed, the census returns doubtless understate somewhat the actual number of divorced persons who have not remarried.

The category "married" is further divided into "married, spouse present," and "married, spouse absent." A person is classified as "married, spouse present," if the person's husband or wife was reported as a member of the household in which the person was enumerated even though the husband or wife may have been temporarily away on business or vacation, visiting, in a hospital, etc., at the time of enumeration.

Persons reported as separated are included in the group designated as "married, spouse absent." Separated persons are married persons permanently or temporarily living apart from their spouse because of marital discord. Other married persons with spouse absent include persons in the Armed Forces or employed and living at a considerable distance from their homes and other persons whose place of residence was not the same as that of their spouse.

The classification of married women by number of times married is based on replies to a question on whether she has been married more than once. In 1950, an appropriate entry was assigned by a prorating process when this question was not answered but in 1940 and 1910 the data for women married once were shown only for those women who answered the question.

Duration of marriage, age at marriage, and years in present marital status. In the 1940 Census the women who were married or had ever been married were asked their age at first marriage. Some information on the duration of marriage was obtained for women still in first marriages by subtraction of the age at marriage from the age of the woman in 1940. For example, women married at age 18 and who were 19 years old at census were credited with a duration of one year. Actually women in this example could have married at age 18.9 years and been 19.0 years old at the census date or they could have been 18.0 years old at marriage and 19.9 years old at the census date so that the subtracted result of 1 year had upper and lower limits of 1 day to almost 2 years. The same principle applies to other ages. For the purpose of computing medians, it is assumed that in effect the subtracted results are the practical equivalent of 1-year ranges centered at 1.0 years, 2.0 years, etc. In 1910 married women were asked the number of years they had been in the present marriage. In 1950 the married women were asked the number of years they had been in the present marriage, separated women were asked the number of years they had been separated, widowed women were asked the number of years they had been widowed, and divorced women were asked the number of years they had been divorced. The answers were in terms of whole years centered at 1.5 years, 2.5 years, etc., and thus were not strictly comparable with the subtracted results on duration for 1940, but in some tables this was allowed for by shifting the 1940 data upward one-half year by interpolation, to put the midpoints at comparable places with the data for 1950.

Years of school completed. The data on years of school completed represent the highest full grade of school completed in the regular school system—public, private, or parochical school, either day or night, full time or part time—that is, those schools where enrollment may lead to an elementary or high school diploma, or to a college, university, or professional school degree.

Employed. In data for 1950 and 1952, employed persons comprise those who during the survey week were either (a) "at work"—those who did any civilian work for pay or profit or worked without pay for fifteen hours or more on a family farm or business or (b) "with a job but not at work"—those who did not work and were not looking for work but had a civilian job or business from which they were temporarily absent because of vacation, illness, industrial dispute, bad weather, or layoff with definite instructions to return to work within 30 days of layoff. Also included are persons who had new jobs to which they were scheduled to report within 30 days. In 1940, the employed persons were not limited to civilians and persons who were on public emergency work (relief) were classified as unemployed.

Unemployed. In 1950 and 1952, unemployed persons include those who did not work at all during the survey week and who were looking for work. Also included as unemployed are persons who would have been looking for work except that (a) they were temporarily ill, (b) they expected to return to a job from which they had been laid off for an indefinite period, or (c) they believed no work was available in their line of work or in the community. In data for 1940, unemployed persons also include persons on public emergency work (relief).

Labor force. Persons are classified as in the labor force if they were employed as civilians, unemployed, or in the Armed Forces during the survey week.

Occupation. The occupation categories shown for 1950 and 1952 are major groups in the classification system used in the 1950 Census of Population and those shown for 1940 and 1910 are based on the similar classification system used in the 1940 Census of Population. It is believed that the changes do not affect seriously any conclusions which may be drawn from the data although the classifications before and after 1950 are not exactly comparable. The data shown for 1952 and 1950 relate to the occupation during the survey week of husbands who were in the experienced civilian labor force and refer to the job held during the calendar week preceding the enumerator's visit or, if the person was unemployed, to the last job held. Husbands with two or more jobs were classified according to the job in which they worked the greatest number of hours during the survey week. The occupation of husband data shown for 1940 vary in coverage according to whether the data involve women by own children under 5 years old or by children ever born. Thus, data involving own children under 5 years old were tabulated in 1940 for husbands without regard to employment status and involved the present occupation of husbands who were employed, the last occupation of husbands who were seeking work, and the kind of work being done by husbands on public emergency work (relief). The 1940 data involving children ever born were tabulated by occupation of husband only for husbands who were employed on other than public emergency work. The 1910 Census data on occupation were tabulated for husbands who were "gainful workers," and represented the usual occupation in which the husband earned money or a money equivalent, or assisted in the production of marketable goods, regardless of the employment status at the time of the census.

Money income. The total money income from all sources is shown for husbands in 1951, for families in 1948, and for farm-operator families in 1949. This is the total amount of (*a*) money wages or salary received in the given year, (*b*) the net amount of money received from self-employment in the given year, and (*c*) the amount of money received from other sources in the given year, such as interest, dividends, veteran's allowances, pensions, or rents. The term "family" refers to all members of the household who were related to the woman by blood, marriage, or adoption.

Tenure of home. Women are classified as living in an owned home if the dwelling unit in which the woman lived was owned with or without a mortgage, by her husband or a member of her family who was living in the dwelling unit or temporarily absent from it. Other women were classified as living in rented homes.

Monthly rent. The rent shown for rented homes in 1949 is that actually paid for the dwelling unit by the occupant household. If, however, no monthly rent was paid, as in the case of a doctor, minister, teacher, or tenant who received the use of the house as part of his wages, the monthly rent was based on the rent paid for similar dwelling units in the neighborhood. The monthly rental value shown for 1940 is a combination of the monthly rent actually paid for rented homes and one percent of the value of owner-occupied homes. The 1940 data are shown only for women in private households who were related to the head of the household.

Sampling and sampling variability. The source notes to the tables indicate which tables were based on census fertility reports. The census fertility reports are based on Sample C of the 1950 and 1940 Censuses, Sample W of the 1910 Census, and on the Current Population Survey. The samples varied in size for different areas at each date. The average size, nationally, was 8.9 percent in 1910, 3.3 percent in 1940, 2.4 percent in 1950, and about 0.05 percent in the Current Population Survey. The sample in the censuses consisted of every nth line on the population schedules and in each census yielded about one million observations. The sample in the Current Population Survey consisted of 20,000 to 30,000 households in 68 to 230 sampling areas (counties or parts thereof).

The sampling variability of a fertility rate depends on the size of the base, the distribution of women by each number of children, and any correlation of observations. (Correlation exists in the Current Population Survey; it comes from a "clustering" of observations, or a selection of several women from a single "sample area"; the people within a given small area tend to have similar characteristics.) Consequently, the standard errors of the fertility rates cannot be expressed in simple tables. However, a few examples serve to indicate the order of magnitude of most standard errors of the rates. In 1950, there were 1,804 children ever born per 1,000 ever-married white women 30 to 34 years old, in the United States. The standard error of this rate was 9. The chances are 2 out of 3 that the rate of 1,804 from Sample C differs by less than 9 from the rate that a complete census would show. The chances are about 19 out of 20 that the rate differs by less than twice the standard error from what a complete census would show. The larger 1940 and 1910 Census samples are subject to less error than the 1950 sample. In 1954, there were an estimated 2,051 children ever born per 1,000 women 30 to 34 years old including single women. The sampling error of the rate of 2,051 from the Current Population Survey is approximately 25. Most other Current Population Surveys have slightly larger variability than the example cited.

Further details on the nature of the surveys and on variability can be found in the census reports on fertility.

A P P E N D I X   B

PROCEDURES FOR CONSTRUCTING AND USING
COHORT FERTILITY TABLES IN CHAPTER 9,
AND EVALUATION OF RESULTS

The data on the fertility of cohorts of native white women which are used in Chapter 9 of this monograph are taken from the more comprehensive tables for native white women and for all women which are being prepared by the Scripps Foundation for Research in Population Problems, Miami University, and are scheduled for publication in late 1958 or in 1959. A more comprehensive description of procedures and evaluation of results will accompany the detailed tables. Portions of these materials are presented here in somewhat condensed form.

1. Computing central birth rates for all women in native white cohorts

As was stated in Chapter 9, a cohort of native white women in the fertility tables in question is defined as beginning with the girl babies who are born in the United States during a year from July 1 to June 30, inclusive, and as consisting thereafter of the survivors of these babies. Accordingly, on July 1 of subsequent calendar year y the members of the cohort of July-June year y-x are between exact ages x and $x + 1$ and their average age is approximately $x + \frac{1}{2}$ (for example, the women in the cohort of 1930 are between exact ages 20 and 21 on July 1, 1950, and their average age is about 20.5). In order to compute precisely the central birth rates in calendar year y for cohort y-x it is necessary to know (a) the number of women aged x to $x + 1$ on July 1 of year y, and (b) the number of births to these women during year y. Since exact numbers are not available, estimates must be used.

Annual numbers of women. The number of women in each cohort, that is, the number aged x to $x + 1$ on July 1 of each calendar year, was estimated in part from the numbers of women in 5-year age groups according to the Censuses of 1920 to 1950. First, the census data were adjusted in minor degree to allow for underenumeration and misstatement of age. The adjustment factors were developed by Dr. Norman B. Ryder while he was on the staff of the Scripps Foundation and took into account the work of Dr. Ansley J. Coale[1] and that of members of the staff of the Bureau of the Census. The factors by which the census numbers of women were multiplied are shown in table B–1. Second, the adjusted estimates by 5-year age groups were shifted from the census date to July 1 of each census year. Third, for the cohorts of 1875 to 1910, the estimates for 5-year age groups (i.e., for five cohorts) were subdivided into single years of age (single cohorts) by osculatory interpolation. Fourth, estimates for the cohorts of 1875 to 1910 on July 1 of 1917 to 1919 were prepared by working backwards from the 1920 estimates with the use of life-table survival rates.

TABLE **B–1.**—MULTIPLIERS USED TO ADJUST ENUMERATED NUMBERS OF NATIVE WHITE FEMALES IN FIVE-YEAR AGE GROUPS FOR UNDERENUMERATION AND MISSTATEMENTS OF AGE

Current age	1950	1940	1930	1920
Under 5 years	1.047	1.067	1.061	1.073
5 to 9 years	1.017	1.030	1.030	1.045
10 to 14 years	1.011	1.021	1.023	1.043
15 to 19 years	1.015	1.028	1.027	1.044
20 to 24 years	1.010	1.027	1.016	1.029
25 to 29 years	1.014	1.029	1.026	1.042
30 to 34 years	1.020	1.040	1.045	1.055
35 to 39 years	1.005	1.020	1.018	1.034
40 to 44 years	1.026	1.039	1.038	1.055
45 to 49 years	1.037	1.052	1.051	1.067
50 to 54 years	1.027	1.039	1.038	1.055

Source: Scripps Foundation for Research in Population Problems. Prepared by Dr. Norman B. Ryder.

Another set of estimates for the cohorts of 1911 and each later year was based on the number of births (corrected for underregistration) during July 1, 1910, through June 30, 1911, during July 1, 1911, through June 30, 1912, etc.[2] First, these numbers of births were multiplied by life-table survival rates to obtain estimates for July 1, 1920, 1930, 1940, and 1950. Second, very slight downward adjustments were made which brought the results for 5-year age periods into approximate agreement with the estimates obtained by the procedure described above. (A very slight reduction is needed to allow for the small net out-migration which occurred.)

The number of women in each cohort on July 1 of each intercensal year between 1920 and 1950 was estimated by straight-line interpolation between the population on July 1 of the census years. This procedure

---

[1] Ansley J. Coale, "The Population of the United States in 1950 Classified by Age, Sex, and Color—A Revision of Census Figures," *Journal of the American Statistical Association*, Volume 50, No. 269, March 1955, pp. 16–54.

[2] The numbers of births were obtained from worksheets used in the preparation of births corrected for underregistration shown in P. K. Whelpton, "Births and Birth Rates in the Entire United States, 1909 to 1948," National Office of Vital Statistics, *Vital Statistics—Special Reports*, Vol. 33, No. 8, September 29, 1950.

seemed most satisfactory in view of the inadequate information about the number and age of the women moving across the boundaries of continental United States. Furthermore, at the ages in question the number of deaths in each cohort tends to be about the same in each year of a decade, because the *decrease* of age-specific death rates from one calendar year to the next tends to balance the *increase* of these rates from one year of age to the next. The number of women in each cohort on July 1 of each year after 1950 or from 1917 to 1919 was computed by applying life table survival values to the estimated population on July 1, 1950, and July 1, 1920, respectively.

Allocating births to birth cohorts of mothers. Registered births are classified by age of mother but not by birth cohort of mother, hence it is necessary to estimate the latter classification from the former. This presents certain methodological difficulties because the women aged x to $x + 1$ when they bear a child in calendar year y belong to different cohorts. Let us consider, for example, the births in 1950 to women who at the time of delivery had reached their twentieth birthday but not their twenty-first. Some of these births occurred very early on January 1, 1950, to women who were born at a later hour on January 1, 1929 (so were almost 21) and others occurred late on December 31, 1950, to women who were born at an earlier hour on December 31, 1930 (so had just reached age 20). In other words, the women in question were themselves born during the 2 years from January 1, 1929, to December 31, 1930. If we assume that the births in 1929 and 1930 were evenly distributed within these 2 years and that births in 1950 to women aged 20 at delivery were evenly distributed within 1950, and if we define cohorts on the basis of birth during years from July 1 through June 30, we find that the 1950 births to 20-year-old women were distributed as follows: (*a*) 12.5 percent occurred to women who were born in the first half of 1929 and belong to the 1929 cohort, (*b*) 75 percent occurred to women who were born in the year from July 1, 1929, through June 30, 1930, and belong to the 1930 cohort, and (*c*) 12.5 percent occurred to women who were born in the last half of 1930 and belong to the 1931 cohort. Similarly, we find that 12.5 percent of the births to the 1930 cohort during age 20 occurred in 1949, 75 percent occurred in 1950, and 12.5 percent occurred in 1951.

A strict application of the cohort principle would require the apportioning of the births in each year in accordance with these percentages, which are commonly called separation factors. For example, the central birth rate of the 1930 cohort during age 20 would be computed by using in the numerator 12.5, 75.0, and 12.5 percent, respectively, of the births in 1949, 1950, and 1951 to women aged 20 at delivery. This would partially "scramble" the births during calendar years, and lessen the preciseness of calendar year comparisons based on cohort tables.

An alternative procedure is to adjust the denominator of the rate fraction to agree with the numerator. This would be done by using as the number of women in cohort y-x who are of current age x on July 1 of year y, 12.5 percent, 75.0 percent, and 12.5 percent, respectively, of the women of current ages x-1, x, and $x + 1$ on that date. The resulting rates are slightly less specific for individual cohorts, and slightly more specific for calendar years, than those yielded by the other procedure. Because of the great emphasis given to rates for calendar years in prior studies of fertility, and the continuing interest in comparing one year with another, the latter procedure was considered to be preferable and was adopted. When the rates for five cohorts during 5 years are averaged as is done in this report, the differences between the results for the two procedures are negligible.

The foregoing percentages may not be exact, but they were used because there are no adequate data to show precisely how they should be modified. At the young childbearing ages a weight of 12.5 percent usually is too small for the earliest cohort in each set of three and too large for the latest. The reverse is true at the old childbearing ages. It is probable, however, that the differences between 12.5 percent and the correct figure are relatively small in most cases. Furthermore, it is practically certain that the use of these weights instead of the correct weights does not bias appreciably the comparisons between rates for different cohorts or rates for different years.

Adjustments for annual numbers of births. The numerators of the birth rate fractions were based on the annual numbers of registered births as reported by the National Office of Vital Statistics, increased to allow for births in nonregistration States prior to 1933 and for the incomplete registration of births in each year. The number of births in each nonregistration State during the year preceding the Censuses of 1920 and 1930 was estimated by assuming that the ratio of births in that year to the census count of children under 1 was the same in a nonregistration State as in a registration State with similar socio-economic characteristics. The number of births in each nonregistration State in each other year was estimated by assuming that the year-to-year changes in birth rates in a given State were comparable to those in a similar registration State.[3]

The numbers of registered births of each order in each year since 1935 were increased to allow for incomplete registration by means of the new percentages prepared by the National Office of Vital Statistics. The percentages for 1950 represent essentially the proportions of the babies under three months of age enumerated in the 1950 Census whose births were found to have been registered and are for births of various orders to white and nonwhite women in 5-year age groups. Those for all white births (shown for 1950 in table B–2) were used for births to native white

---

[3] For a detailed explanation the reader is referred to "Births and Birth Rates in the Entire United States, 1909–1948," *Vital Statistics—Special Reports*, Vol. 33, No. 8, September 29, 1950, or to Pascal K. Whelpton, *Cohort Fertility: Native White Women in the United States*, Princeton University Press, Princeton, 1954, pp. 400–427.

mothers.   The original 1940 proportions were not obtained by order, but
estimates by order were made later by applying in prior years the 1950
pattern of relationships between the correction factors by order for each
age group.   Proportions for years between 1940 and 1950 were estimated
by assuming straight line trends by age and order for completeness of registration of births occurring in certain institutions (mostly hospitals) and
births occurring elsewhere.   Proportions for 1935 to 1939 were estimated
from the 1940 figures by allowing for changes in the percentage of births
occurring in hospitals and elsewhere.[4]   Proportions for years before 1935
were estimated by the writer (Whelpton), following a procedure similar to
that described in "Births and Birth Rates in the Entire United States,
1909–1948," *Vital Statistics—Special Reports,* Vol. 33, No. 8, pp. 146–
157.   The estimated percentages of all the white births that were registered
in each year are shown in table B–3.

TABLE **B–2.**—PERCENT OF WHITE BIRTHS REGISTERED, BY AGE OF MOTHER AND ORDER OF
BIRTH OF CHILD, ACCORDING TO THE 1950 TEST

Current age	Total	Order of birth						
		First	Second	Third	Fourth	Fifth	Sixth and seventh	Eighth and higher
Total....................	98.6	99.3	99.1	98.8	98.0	97.0	95.6	93.9
Under 15 years..............	94.6	94.2	100.0	100.0	100.0	...	...	...
15 to 19 years..............	98.3	98.7	97.4	96.8	98.1	83.3	100.0	...
20 to 24 years..............	98.8	99.5	98.8	97.9	96.1	94.5	93.0	90.6
25 to 29 years..............	98.8	99.6	99.5	98.9	97.7	96.2	94.4	94.2
30 to 34 years..............	98.7	99.4	99.6	99.4	98.6	97.6	95.5	93.3
35 to 39 years..............	98.0	99.2	99.4	99.2	98.8	97.6	96.3	93.9
40 to 44 years..............	97.5	99.0	99.3	99.4	99.1	97.9	97.1	94.6
45 years and over..........	93.8	99.0	96.7	95.2	95.8	93.0	94.0	93.2

Source: National Office of Vital Statistics, *Vital Statistics of the United States, 1950,* Vol. I, p. 127.

Rapid progress has been made in improving the completeness of birth
registration, the 1950 test showing that 98.6 percent of the white births
were registered, compared with 94.0 percent in the 1940 test and estimates of 91.5 percent in 1930 and 90.6 percent in 1920.   It is probable
that these percentages are slightly too large (and that the corrected numbers of births are slightly too small) because the births of infants *not*
enumerated in the census (and hence not included in the tests) are less
likely to be recorded than the births of enumerated infants.
   The new adjustment factors show that the proportion registered is highest
for first births and successively lower for births of subsequent orders.
Their use improves significantly the estimated numbers of births of each
order, because the previous factors were specific by age but not by birth
order.[5]   It is probable, however, that there is still a slight bias in the

[4] For a description of the derivation of these factors the reader is referred to *Vital Statistics of the United States, 1950,* Vol. I, Chapter 6.

[5] For a discussion of this bias and of the difficulty of removing it, see Whelpton, *op, cit.,* pp. 31–39 and 435–461.

adjusted numbers of births by order, the numbers of lower order births being too large and the numbers of higher order births being too small. This is believed to occur because many of the women whose first birth is illegitimate try to conceal this fact, and report their first legitimate birth as a first birth instead of a second birth (or third, etc.). Such women also understate the order of their subsequent legitimate births.

TABLE **B-3.**—ESTIMATED PERCENT OF WHITE BIRTHS REGISTERED: 1910 TO 1954

Year	Per-cent	Year	Per-cent	Year	Per-cent
1954......................	99.1	1939......................	93.6	1924......................	90.9
1953......................	99.0	1938......................	93.4	1923......................	90.9
1952......................	99.0	1937......................	93.1	1922......................	90.8
1951......................	98.8	1936......................	92.8	1921......................	90.7
1950......................	98.6	1935......................	92.4	1920......................	90.6
1949......................	98.3	1934......................	92.2	1919......................	90.6
1948......................	98.1	1933......................	92.0	1918......................	90.5
1947......................	97.8	1932......................	91.8	1917......................	90.1
1946......................	97.4	1931......................	91.6	1916......................	92.0
1945......................	97.0	1930......................	91.5	1915......................	91.5
1944......................	96.5	1929......................	91.3	1914......................	91.0
1943......................	96.0	1928......................	91.2	1913......................	90.6
1942......................	95.5	1927......................	91.2	1912......................	90.1
1941......................	94.6	1926......................	91.1	1911......................	89.6
1940......................	94.0	1925......................	91.0	1910......................	89.1

Source: National Office of Vital Statistics, 1950 to 1935, *Vital Statistics of the United States, 1950,* Vol. I, p. 127; 1934 to 1910, "Births and Birth Rates in the Entire United States, 1909-1948," *Vital Statistics, Special Reports, Selected Studies,* Vol. 33, No. 8, September 29, 1950, p. 148.

The occurrence of stillbirths and infant deaths probably leads to some errors in the reporting of birth order. If a woman incorrectly includes a stillbirth when telling how many babies she has borne previously, the birth order is too high on the birth record. On the other hand, if a woman incorrectly excludes a baby that died after birth, the birth order is too low on the record.

Because of the lack of exact information regarding biases in reported birth order, no adjustment for such biases has been made. It is believed, however, that the rates for lower order births are slightly too large, and that those for higher order births are slightly too small.

2. The validity of obtaining cumulative birth rates for all women in a cohort by adding the central birth rates of successive years

Ideally, a cumulative birth rate for the women in a cohort who live to a specified age would be computed by adding the annual rates for *these women* during younger ages, rather than the rates for all the women living at each younger age. This is impossible when using annual numbers of births from vital statistics. The births in a given year can not be classified currently according to mother's age at death because nearly all of the mothers are still living. A classification might be made many years later but would not be worth the high cost. It is for this reason that annual birth rates were computed for each cohort based on the total number of women living at the midpoint of each year, and that cumulative rates were obtained by adding these annual rates.

When the cumulative birth rates of a cohort up to age x (that is, any age under 50—the end of the childbearing period) are obtained by adding the central rates for prior ages and years, it is assumed that the fertility at each age before death is not affected by age at death; for example, it is the same up to age 20 for the women in the cohort who die during age 21 as it is for those who live to age 50. (Note that this assumption is made for all women, and not for married women.) Even though the assumption may be contrary to fact, the error introduced is small for the cohorts under consideration because a large majority of the women who were alive at the youngest childbearing age did live to the end of the childbearing period or to 1955 (whichever came first). For example, in the cohort of 1896— the earliest for which a cohort life table has been computed—approximately 85 percent of the women reaching age 14 lived to age 50. For the cohort of 1920, whose women are now about 37 years old, it is almost certain that at least 90 percent of those who were alive at age 14 will live to age 50.

Whether there are significant differences in the fertility up to age at death between the women who die at age x, those who die between age x and 50, and those who live to 50 is a debatable question. On the one hand there is evidence of an inverse relation between economic status and mortality and also between economic status and the fertility of married women. This suggests, for example, that the number of children born per 1,000 married women by age 30 may be slightly smaller for those who live to age 50 than for those who die during age 30, hence the cumulative birth rate of the women in the cohort who actually live to age x is slightly *smaller* than the sum of the annual birth rates of all women in a cohort up to age x. On the other hand, there is evidence that mortality is higher and fertility lower among single, widowed, and divorced women (combined) than among currently married women at most ages under 50. Moreover, there are indications that healthy women not only are more likely than others to live to the end of the childbearing period, but also that they are more likely to marry and to bear more children subsequently. These two relationships would tend to make the cumulative rate of the women in the cohort who actually live to age x slightly *larger* than the sum of the annual birth rates of all women in a cohort, which is the opposite of the foregoing. It seems certain, therefore, that if fertility by age x is different for women who die shortly after reaching this age than for those who live longer, the differences are small.

It should be noted that each age-specific central birth rate for year y is obtained in the conventional manner, that is, by dividing the number of births during year y to women of current age x at delivery by the number of women in cohort y-x who were of current age x on July 1 of year y. For various reasons the sum of such central rates up to and including the rate of the cohort of year y-x during current age x in year y is referred to as the cumulative rate of the cohort of year y-x by exact age $x + 1$ which is reached on January 1 of year $y + 1$. This is equivalent to saying that the rate whose denominator is the number of women of current age x on July 1 of year y who live to December 31 of year y, and whose numerator is the number of births during year y to the women of current age x at de-livery who live to December 31 of year y, is the same as the conventional central rate defined above.

The size of the difference between the two rates depends on (a) the size of mortality rates and (b) the size of the difference between the birth rate per day lived during current age x of the women who die during this age and those who live to exact age $x + 1$. In fact, the two rates in question are practically identical, because both these factors are so small. In 1910 the mortality rate (q_x) of native white women of childbearing age varied between 2.58 per 1,000 at age 14 and 13.68 at age 49; by 1950 the cor-responding rates for all white women were 0.48 and 5.19. Equally pre-cise data are not available regarding the second factor. We do know that from age 15 to age 24 (or thereabouts) the birth rate per day lived in each age interval increases with the number of days lived in the age interval, that from about age 24 to age 49 the opposite is true, and that at most ages the differences are too small to affect appreciably the cumulative rates in question. Moreover, by the end of the childbearing period the biases in one direction at the younger ages tend to be canceled by those in the other direction at subsequent ages. It appears, therefore, that there are only negligible differences between the cumulative rates up to exact age x at the beginning of year y which were obtained by the procedure utilized and those which might have been obtained by a more elaborate procedure.

3. Estimating the cumulative marriage rates of cohorts

It should be possible to compute cumulative marriage rates for cohorts in the same way as cumulative birth rates, that is, by computing and add-ing annual central marriage rates. This procedure cannot be used for most cohorts because the Federal Marriage Registration Area was not organized until 1957. Data available for certain States provide a basis for national estimates of the number of first marriages by race and age of bride for a few recent years only. In consequence, substitute measures are required.

Highly accurate cumulative marriage rates for cohorts of native white women by January 1 of each census year from 1910 to 1950, comparable to the cumulative birth rates, were obtained quite easily from the census data on women by age by marital status. The first step was to convert from a current age to an exact age. For example, (a) adding the numbers of all women and of ever-married women aged 20, 21, 22, and 23, and half the numbers of those aged 19 and 24 on April 1, 1950, and (b) divid-ing the total for ever-married women by the total for all women, gave (c)

428 APPENDIX B

the estimated proportion ever married among those at exact ages 20–24
on the census date.

The second step was to estimate the proportion for January 1, 1950.
This was done by interpolation. Multiplying the resulting proportion by
1,000 gave the cumulative marriage rate by exact ages 20–24 (by January 1, 1950), that is, the rate for the cohorts of 1926–30. Because less
detail was available in the 1955 data from the Current Population Survey,
it was necessary to use a similar but less precise conversion procedure for
that year.

Estimates of cumulative marriage rates by 1915, 1925, 1935, and 1945
were desired also. The preparation of such estimates is part of a major
research project now being conducted by P. K. Whelpton and Arthur A.
Campbell at the Scripps Foundation for Research in Population Problems.
Only preliminary results are available for use here. The chief steps in
the planned procedure are as follows:

a. The number of native white women in any cohort who marry for the
first time between one census and the next can be estimated by deducting
the number of ever-married women in the cohort on the first of these dates
from the number on the second, and allowing for the influence of mortality. (So few native white women move across the boundaries of the
United States between one census and the next that it is safe to ignore this
movement.)

b. The number of first marriages for each cohort in each intercensal
period (from step *a*) can be distributed by single years by using as a guide
the distribution of first births eighteen months later. These estimates will
be biased, however, because of changes in the average number of months
between marriage and the first birth (for example, the longer intervals in
the 1930's than in the 1920's and the shorter intervals in 1945–54 than
in the preceding 10-year periods).

c. Adding these annual estimates in step *b* for all cohorts whose women
are between exact ages 14 and 50 in the year in question will give a series
of annual estimates of the number of first marriages of women aged 14 to
50. These estimates will be biased for the reason given in step *b*.

d. A more accurate series of annual estimates for women aged 14 to
50 can be made from the data which have been collected by certain States,
counties, and cities and summarized by the National Office of Vital
Statistics.

e. The estimates in step *d* can be used as a basis for redistributing those
in step *b*, so that the results obtained agree on a cohort basis with those in
step *a* and on an annual basis with those in step *d*.

The cumulative marriage rates from 1915, 1925, 1935, and 1945 presented in table 116 (and elsewhere) are preliminary, obtained by applying
this type of procedure to the first and last halves of each decade, rather
than to each year. It is believed, however, that the results of the more detailed study will differ in only minor degree from the preliminary figures.

4. Comparisons of cumulative birth rates from cohort tables and from census data on women by number of children ever born

Effect of adjustments in basic data which were made in computing the cohort tables. Small differences would be expected between cumulative birth rates from cohort fertility tables and those from the census tabulations of women by number of children born because the census data were adjusted only to the extent of estimating the number of births to ever-married women for whom this figure was not reported, whereas a preliminary step in computing the cohort tables was to increase the numbers of registered births so as to allow for those not registered, and to adjust the census data so as to allow for the women not counted and for biases in reporting age. A comparison of tables B–1 and B–3 shows that the allowance for births not registered is larger until recent years than that for women not enumerated in the census, hence the net effect of the adjustments is to increase the rates. It is possible that the adjustments are too large or too small in the numerator or the denominator, and that the cumulative rates from the cohort tables are biased accordingly. Because the evidence is not conclusive or easy to summarize, only an opinion can be presented here: (*a*) Both sets of adjustment factors are conservative, (*b*) if one set is more conservative than the other, it probably is that for incomplete enumeration, hence, the cohort tables may tend to exaggerate fertility slightly, and (*c*) the rates are more accurate than if no adjustments had been made.

Possible biases in the census data. The census data on children ever born are believed to be of relatively high quality, but there are three possible sources of bias which merit brief consideration. First, some of the ever-married women who are seen by a census enumerator undoubtedly report one or more stillborn babies, adopted children, or stepchildren that should not be counted, but it is probable that a slightly larger number fail to report one or more babies that were born alive but died in early infancy, or that were given up for adoption. The resulting net error is believed to be quite small, however. Second, the underreporting of babies born probably occurs on a larger scale for those ever-married women who are not seen by an enumerator and for whom the number of children ever born is reported by someone else. In such cases, some of the informants do not know about all children who have died or who are not living with the mother for other reasons. Third, no information was obtained regarding the number of children borne by some of the ever-married women.[6]

An analysis made by the Bureau of the Census in the early 1940's showed that the number of own children under 5 years old in the household per 1,000 ever-married women for whom information on children

---

[6] There was no report for 9.0 percent of ever-married women of all races in the 1950 Census, for 12.5 percent in the 1940 Census, and for 7.6 percent in the 1910 Census. The proportion not reporting in the Current Population Survey has been too small to influence the results appreciably (only 0.5 percent in 1954 and 1952).

ever born was not obtained in the 1940 Census was substantially smaller
at the younger ages than the corresponding number for the ever-married
women for whom the question was answered. (The ratio of the number of
own children under 5 years old per 1,000 of the nonreporting native
white women to the ratio of the reporting women was found to vary from
.490 at ages 15–19 to .849 at ages 40–44.)[7] In consequence, basing the
cumulative birth rate for ever-married women on the data for those reporting, or the rate for all women on the data for all single women and the reporting ever-married women, tends to exaggerate the rates very slightly as
is demonstrated in Appendix A. Although this procedure was followed by
the Bureau in the preparation of rates for the 1940 Census reports—many
of which are referred to in Chapters 2 to 8 of this monograph—the resulting bias is small because reports were obtained from 87.5 percent of the
eligible women, in 1940, and at a majority of ages the difference between
the fertility of the reporting and nonreporting women is small. In order
to avoid this type of bias in connection with the 1950 Census, the number of children ever born was estimated carefully for each ever-married
woman for whom this information was not obtained. (See Appendix A.)

In summary, one would expect that (a) in the 1950 Census the second
factor would make the cumulative birth rates based on the number of children ever born somewhat too low, and (b) in the 1940 Census the downward bias of the second factor would be partially balanced by the upward
bias of the third, which would bring the rates closer to the true values.

Differences in the treatment of births to single women.   The
cumulative rates based on the census data exclude births to women reported as single at the time of the census. These births are not restricted
to those of women who have never been married but include those from
marriages which have been annulled. (Some of the women whose marriages have been annulled have borne several children.[8])

Fortunately, excluding such births is not so serious as it might seem
at first glance, because (a) "common law marriages" may be reported to
enumerators as marriages (b) some of the single women who have borne
a child are reported to enumerators as having been married in order to
conceal the stigma of illegitimacy, and (c) ever-married women are asked
about *all* the children they have borne and not merely about their legitimate children.

In the cohort tables, births to single women are included, and are treated
as having occurred to ever-married women. This is contrary to fact, of
course, but the resulting error is small for births to native white women
except at the very early childbearing ages. No State classifies registered
births by marital status of mother, but several classify them by legitimacy.

---

[7] *1940 Census of Population, Differential Fertility, 1940 and 1910*, Women by Number of Children
Ever Born, p. 409.

[8] Such situations are most frequent in New York and California, where "annulment" is a common
way of terminating marriage.

It is estimated that if all States had done so in 1953, 1.7 percent of all white births and 10 percent of the 95,000 births to white women aged 15 to 17 would have been reported as illegitimate. The true proportion is larger, of course, because a substantial number of the births which actually are illegitimate are reported as legitimate. As age rises above 18 the relative number of illegitimate births drops rapidly. Furthermore, nearly all women who have births while single marry later and should be credited with their premarital births.

The net result of the foregoing is to make the cumulative birth rates by the younger ages somewhat larger in the cohort fertility tables than in those based on the census data.

Comparisons which are feasible. Comparisons between cumulative birth rates from cohort fertility tables and census data can be made advantageously for women aged 15 to 59 in 1950 and 15 to 54 in 1940. It is less worthwhile to make them for older women, partly because many of the older women began childbearing prior to 1915 (the year in which the Birth Registration Area was established); hence the 1910 Census data on children ever born were used to some extent in estimating their cumulative birth rates. The 1940 and 1950 Censuses give the cumulative birth rates by the census date (April 1) for women classified by *current* age on those dates, whereas the cohort tables give them by January 1, 1940 and 1950 for women classified by *exact* ages. The first step in making comparisons, therefore, is to convert the rates by the ages and dates of one series to those of the other. The procedure is simpler and the results more accurate if the cohort rates are converted to the census ages and dates.

The conversion procedure may be illustrated by referring to a specific group of ages and cohorts. If for all births and births of each order the cumulative rates of the cohort of 1926 by exact ages 24 and 25, the cohort of 1927 by exact ages 23 and 24, etc., up to the cohort of 1930 by exact ages 20 and 21 are averaged, the result may be taken as the cumulative rate of the cohorts of 1926–30 by current ages 20–24, reached on July 1, 1950. Repeating the process for the cohorts of 1925 through 1929 gives the rate by current ages 20–24 by July 1, 1949. Averaging these rates (the former having a weight of 3 and the latter a weight of 1) gives the rate by current ages 20–24 by April 1, 1950. These cohort and census rates are shown in table B–4, and the differences between them in table B–5.

The direction and size of the differences between the two sets of rates. As would be expected from the earlier description of the rates and their probable biases, a substantial majority of the cumulative birth rates from the cohort tables are slightly larger than those from the census data. On the whole, however, one is struck by the similarities rather than by the differences between the rates from the two sources. For all births, the cohort based rates exceed the others by absolute amounts which increase rapidly as age rises—from 8 at ages 15–19 to 117 at ages 55–59 in 1950,

TABLE **B-4.**—CUMULATIVE BIRTH RATES BY ORDER OF BIRTH FROM COHORT FERTILITY TABLES AND FROM CENSUS DATA ON NUMBER OF CHILDREN EVER BORN, FOR NATIVE WHITE WOMEN, BY AGE: 1950 AND 1940

[Six cohorts are referred to in each group (e.g., 1930–35, 1925–30, etc.) instead of five as in other tables of Appendix B and Chapter 9 because it was necessary to average the rates for six cohorts in order to obtain rates for the date and age groups used by the census. In averaging, the earliest cohort in each group was given a weight of 0.75, the latest cohort a weight of 0.25, and each intervening cohort a weight of 1]

Current age	Cohorts	All births	Order of birth							
			First	Second	Third	Fourth	Fifth	Sixth	Seventh	Eighth and higher
April 1, 1950: Cohort tables										
15–19.........1930–35..		100	83	15	2	(1)	...	...	...	...
20–24.........1925–30..		722	465	189	51	12	3	1	(1)	(1)
25–29.........1920–25..		1,463	732	441	179	68	26	10	4	2
30–34.........1915–20..		1,891	792	562	283	132	63	31	15	13
35–39.........1910–15..		2,067	783	570	320	172	94	55	32	41
40–44.........1905–10..		2,184	771	557	332	198	120	76	48	82
45–49.........1900–05..		2,322	762	558	354	225	145	98	64	116
50–54........1895–1900..		2,518	773	581	388	258	172	120	81	145
55–59.........1890–95..		2,714	793	600	418	287	196	140	97	184
April 1, 1950: Census data										
15–19.........1930–35..		91	75	14	2	(1)	(1)	...	...	...
20–24.........1925–30..		701	450	185	49	12	3	1	(1)	(1)
25–29.........1920–25..		1,417	697	426	176	67	27	12	5	7
30–34.........1915–20..		1,854	766	551	277	130	61	32	16	22
35–39.........1910–15..		2,036	755	562	316	171	94	55	32	50
40–44.........1905–10..		2,136	740	547	326	195	116	74	48	89
45–49.........1900–05..		2,244	732	547	345	217	137	91	61	114
50–54........1895–1900..		2,410	744	572	379	247	160	106	71	132
55–59.........1890–95..		2,597	750	591	406	276	184	129	89	172
April 1, 1940: Cohort tables										
15–19.........1920–25..		67	56	9	1	(1)	...	...	...	...
20–24.........1915–20..		515	339	127	37	10	2	1	(1)	(1)
25–29.........1910–15..		1,124	573	310	138	62	26	10	3	2
30–34.........1905–10..		1,686	697	456	247	135	74	40	20	17
35–39.........1900–05..		2,143	746	537	332	205	127	82	50	64
40–44........1895–1900..		2,486	772	580	386	256	170	116	77	129
45–49.........1890–95..		2,712	793	600	418	287	196	139	97	183
50–54.........1885–90..		2,900	805	620	444	314	220	161	114	222
April 1, 1940: Census data										
15–19.........1920–25..		54	44	8	1	(1)	(1)	...	...	...
20–24.........1915–20..		475	301	121	38	10	3	...	(1)	...
25–29.........1910–15..		1,090	542	305	139	61	26	...	4	...
30–34.........1905–10..		1,643	662	447	247	136	74	...	20	...
35–39.........1900–05..		2,107	718	531	334	205	128	...	49	...
40–44........1895–1900..		2,417	745	575	383	252	165	...	72	...
45–49.........1890–95..		2,602	751	592	413	281	191	...	88	...
50–54.........1885–90..		2,684	745	596	427	297	207	...	96	...

[1] 0.5 or less.

Source: Cohort-based rates are from Scripps Foundation for Research in Population Problems; census-based rates for all births are from *1940 Census of Population, Differential Fertility, 1940 and 1910*, Women by Number of Children Ever Born, p. 11, and from special tabulations of 1950 Census data purchased by the Scripps Foundation for Research in Population Problems with funds provided by the Population Council. Rates for births by order are computed from the number of women of specified parity shown on p. 7 of the 1940 report and in the special tabulations for 1950. No census-based rates are shown for sixth births or for eighth and higher order births in 1940 since the data needed for computing them were not tabulated by the Bureau of the Census.

and from 13 at ages 15–19 to 216 at ages 50–54 in 1940—and which are substantially larger for 1940 than for 1950. The relative excess, in contrast, is substantially larger at ages 15–19 than the older ages, and varies little (between 2 and 4 percent) from ages 25–29 to ages 45–49. Moreover, at these ages the 1950 and 1940 percentages are about equal in size, although at ages 15–19 and 20–24 the 1950 percentage is less than half as large as the 1940 figure.

In discussing the possible biases of the census based rates in the preceding subsection, it was stated that one would expect, a priori, that the excess of the cohort based rates would be smaller in 1940 than 1950, because the 1940 Census based rates were exaggerated through the omission of the ever-married women for whom the number of children ever borne was not reported. In fact, however, the excess is smaller for 1950 than for 1940. One explanation may be that there was less understating of past births in the 1950 Census than in that of 1940.

TABLE **B–5.**—EXCESS OF CUMULATIVE BIRTH RATES BY ORDER OF BIRTH, FROM COHORT FERTILITY TABLES OVER THOSE FROM CENSUS DATA ON NUMBER OF CHILDREN EVER BORN, FOR NATIVE WHITE WOMEN, BY AGE: 1950 AND 1940

Current age	Cohorts	All births	Order of birth							
			First	Second	Third	Fourth	Fifth	Sixth	Seventh	Eighth and higher
April 1, 1950: Numerical excess										
15–19	1930–35..	8	8	1	(1)	(1)	(1)	...	...	...
20–24	1925–30..	21	16	4	2	(1)	(1)	(1)	(1)	(1)
25–29	1920–25..	46	36	15	4	1	-1	-2	-2	-5
30–34	1915–20..	37	26	11	6	3	2	-1	-1	-9
35–39	1910–15..	31	28	8	3	1	(1)	(1)	(1)	-9
40–44	1905–10..	48	31	10	6	3	4	2	(1)	-8
45–49	1900–05..	78	30	10	9	8	8	7	3	2
50–54	1895–1900..	109	29	10	9	11	12	14	10	13
55–59	1890–95..	117	42	9	12	11	11	11	8	12
April 1, 1940: Numerical excess										
15–19	1920–25..	13	13	1	(1)	(1)	(1)	...	...	...
20–24	1915–20..	40	38	5	-1	-1	(1)	...	(1)	...
25–29	1910–15..	34	31	6	-1	(1)	(1)	...	(1)	...
30–34	1905–10..	43	35	9	(1)	(1)	-1	...	(1)	...
35–39	1900–05..	36	29	6	-2	(1)	(1)	...	(1)	...
40–44	1895–1900..	69	27	6	3	4	5	...	5	...
45–49	1890–95..	110	42	7	5	6	4	...	9	...
50–54	1885–90..	216	60	23	17	17	13	...	18	...
April 1, 1950: Percent excess										
15–19	1930–35..	9	11	8	(2)	(2)	(2)	...	...	...
20–24	1925–30..	3	3	2	4	3	(2)	(2)	(2)	(2)
25–29	1920–25..	3	5	4	2	1	-3	-15	(2)	(2)
30–34	1915–20..	2	3	2	2	2	3	-2	-8	-41
35–39	1910–15..	2	4	1	1	(1)	(1)	(1)	-1	-17
40–44	1905–10..	2	4	2	2	1	4	3	(1)	-8
45–49	1900–05..	3	4	2	2	4	6	8	5	2
50–54	1895–1900..	5	4	2	2	5	8	13	15	10
55–59	1890–95..	5	6	2	3	4	6	8	9	7
April 1, 1940: Percent excess										
15–19	1920–25..	24	29	(2)	(2)	(2)	(2)	...	...	...
20–24	1915–20..	8	12	4	-2	-6	(2)	...	(2)	...
25–29	1910–15..	3	6	2	-1	(1)	-1	...	(2)	...
30–34	1905–10..	3	5	2	(1)	(1)	-1	...	-1	...
35–39	1900–05..	2	4	1	-1	(1)	(1)	...	1	...
40–44	1895–1900..	3	4	1	1	2	3	...	7	...
45–49	1890–95..	4	6	1	1	2	2	...	11	...
50–54	1885–90..	8	8	4	4	6	6	...	19	...

[1] 0.5 or less.
[2] Base less than 10.

Source: Appendix table B–4.

Although for women aged 15–19 the excess of the rates from cohort tables over rates from census data is small numerically—8 points for all births and first births in 1950 and 13 points in 1940 (table B–5)—it is large on a percentage basis—9 and 11 percent for all births and first births in 1950 and 24 to 29 percent in 1940 (table B–5). The chief reason probably is the different treatment of illegitimate births, which constitute an important proportion of the births to very young women. Most of these illegitimate births are registered; in computing cohort fertility tables all registered births are included and an allowance is made for those not registered. In contrast, many of these illegitimate births are not reported in the census because the mothers are unmarried and the question about number of children ever born is not asked; the census data are not adjusted to allow for these children.

The absolute and relative excess of the cohort based rates tends to be largest for first births and to decrease as birth order rises. (The large percentage differences at some of the higher orders are based on small numbers of births or women and may not be reliable.) Much of this could result from the suspected tendency of a woman with an illegitimate first birth to conceal this fact and report her second birth as a first birth also.

It is of interest to compare the relative excess of the cohort based rates for a given group of cohorts as of 1940 and 1950:

	Percent excess of cohort-based birth rates over census-based rates	
Cohorts of—	1940	1950
1920–25	24	3
1915–20	8	2
1910–15	3	2
1905–10	3	2
1900–05	2	3
1895–1900	3	5
1890–95	4	5

For five of the seven groups which can be compared, the changes are slight—1 or 2 percentage points (cohorts of 1890–95 to 1910–15)—with 2 decreases and 3 increases. By far the largest change is from 24 to 3 for the 1920–25 group; the second largest is from 8 to 2 for the 1915–20 group. The women in the 1920–25 group were 15–19 years old in 1940 and 25–29 in 1950. The chief reason why their birth rate at ages 15–19 was 24 percent higher according to cohort tables than census data probably is the difference in the treatment of illegitimate births (mentioned above). As women live from ages 15–19 to 25–29 they have more than 20 times as many births as they had by ages 15–19, and the proportion of the additional births which are illegitimate drops greatly. In consequence, the more complete inclusion of illegitimate births in the cohort tables than in the census causes a very much smaller difference between the birth rates from these two sources by ages 25–29 than by ages 15–19. Most of the reduction in the excess of the rates from cohort tables for the 1915–20 group (from 8 percent by ages 20–24 in 1940 to 2 percent by ages 30–34 in 1950) probably can be explained in the same way.

In summary, the cumulative birth rates from census data and cohort fertility tables are in relatively close agreement, 49 of the 117 cells in the two lower decks of table B–5 having a difference of 2 or fewer percentage points, only 35 having a difference of more than 5, and only 12 having a difference of more than 10. Moreover, most of the major differences are to be expected on the basis of our knowledge about probable biases. These facts give one confidence in the general reliability of the rates from both sources. Some think that the census-based rates probably are not quite as close to the true values, on the whole, as are the cohort-based rates, because the former have not been adjusted (a) for a tendency for the number of children ever born to be underreported, or (b) for the omission of the children born to women reported as single on the census date. It is possible, of course, that the cohort-based rates have been overcorrected for the incomplete recording of births and/or undercorrected for the incomplete enumeration of women, and that most of the true values are not only between the census-based rates and the cohort-based rates but are closer to the former than the latter.

5. The "sources" of the much higher fertility during 1945–54 than 1930–39

The procedure followed in distributing the extra births is shown in detail in table B–6 and is described in the last section of Chapter 9, using as an example the interval between exact ages 20–24 and exact ages 30–34. The marriage and birth rates are taken from tables 114 and 116. A brief explanation of the other data required for the procedure—the numbers of women and of births in columns B, L, B1, and L1 of table B–6—is desirable here.

The computations could have been made for each cohort in each year of each decade rather than for groups of cohorts in each decade as a whole. The simpler method was chosen because the other would have increased the cost appreciably without a commensurate improvement in results.

If each year had been treated separately, the numbers of births in columns L and L1 would be the same as the corresponding numbers used in computing the annual rates (illustrated in Chapter 9, tables 111 and 112) except for the effect of dropping decimals. (Each annual birth rate was obtained by dividing the number of births by the number of women; hence, multiplying the number of women by the rate would give the number of births.) Actually, in dealing with each group of cohorts in each decade as a whole, the sum of the annual rates for the decade (which is the same as the cumulative rate by the end of the decade minus the rate by the beginning in columns K and K1) was multiplied by the population at the midpoint of the decade in columns B and B1 to obtain the number

TABLE B-6.—COMPUTATIONS TO MEASURE HOW MUCH OF THE LARGER NUMBER OF BIRTHS TO NATIVE WHITE WOMEN DURING 1945–54 THAN DURING 1930–39 IS DUE TO (a) LARGER NUMBERS OF WOMEN, (b) HIGHER FIRST MARRIAGE RATES, (c) HIGHER FIRST BIRTH RATES FOR EVER-MARRIED WOMEN, AND (d) HIGHER RATES FOR ALL BIRTHS TO MOTHERS

Actual conditions, Jan. 1, 1930, to Jan. 1, 1940

Exact ages at— Beginning of decade	End of decade	Cohorts (A)	Number of women on Jan. 1, 1935 (B)	First marriages per 1,000 women 1930 (C)	First marriages per 1,000 women 1940 (D)	First births per 1,000 ever-married women 1930 (E)	First births per 1,000 ever-married women 1940 (F)	All births per 1,000 mothers 1930 (G)	All births per 1,000 mothers 1940 (H)	All births per 1,000 women 1930 (I) (CxExG)	All births per 1,000 women 1940 (J) (DxFxH)	Additions to cumulative rates, 1930 to 1940 (K) (J-I)	Number of births in 1930–39 (L) (BxK)
5–9	15–19	1921–25	5,529,551	...	85	...	459	...	1,135	...	44	44	243,300
10–14	20–24	1916–20	5,306,432	...	476	...	647	...	1,471	...	453	453	2,403,814
15–19	25–29	1911–15	5,032,898	91	753	473	737	1,136	1,917	49	1,064	1,015	5,108,391
20–24	30–34	1906–10	4,526,605	483	844	704	816	1,545	2,380	525	1,639	1,114	5,042,638
25–29	35–39	1901–05	3,914,005	755	883	800	844	2,113	2,835	1,276	2,113	837	3,276,022
30–34	40–44	1896–1900	3,565,645	852	895	850	860	2,676	3,210	1,938	2,471	533	1,900,489
35–39	45–49	1891–95	3,270,415	882	902	884	878	3,136	3,411	2,445	2,701	256	837,226
40–44	50–54	1886–90	2,777,790	890	899	902	895	3,520	3,593	2,826	2,891	65	180,556
Total			33,923,341										18,992,436

Actual conditions, Jan. 1, 1945, to Jan. 1, 1955

Exact ages at— Beginning of decade	End of decade	Cohorts (A1)	Number of women on Jan. 1, 1935 (B1)	First marriages per 1,000 women 1945 (C1)	First marriages per 1,000 women 1955 (D1)	First births per 1,000 ever-married women 1945 (E1)	First births per 1,000 ever-married women 1955 (F1)	All births per 1,000 mothers 1945 (G1)	All births per 1,000 mothers 1955 (H1)	All births per 1,000 women 1945 (I1) (C1xE1xG1)	All births per 1,000 women 1955 (J1) (D1xF1xH1)	Additions to cumulative rates, 1945 to 1955 (K1) (J1-I1)	Number of births in 1945–54 (L1) (B1xK1)
5–9	15–19	1936–40	4,652,263	...	120	...	542	...	1,183	...	77	77	358,224
10–14	20–24	1931–35	5,132,020	...	658	...	728	...	1,648	...	789	789	4,049,164
15–19	25–29	1926–30	5,413,032	89	873	438	867	1,148	2,168	45	1,641	1,596	8,639,199
20–24	30–34	1921–25	5,163,461	562	924	619	915	1,494	2,515	520	2,126	1,606	8,292,518
25–29	35–39	1916–20	4,850,873	810	931	767	901	1,914	2,715	1,189	2,277	1,088	5,277,750
30–34	40–44	1911–15	4,349,745	870	931	822	858	2,291	2,783	1,638	2,223	585	2,544,601
35–39	45–49	1906–10	3,733,860	894	928	837	833	2,656	2,857	1,987	2,209	222	828,917
40–44	50–54	1901–05	3,290,455	892	930	853	822	2,989	3,031	2,274	2,317	43	141,490
Total			36,585,709										30,131,863

Hypothetical: 1930-39 conditions except--

Exact ages at-- Beginning of decade	End of decade	Increase in births, 1930-39 to 1945-54 Number (M) (Il-L)	Percent (N) (Ml-L)	Number of women as of Jan. 1, 1950 Number (P) (OxL)	Increase in births Percent (O) (100 B1/B -100)	Cumulative first marriage rate per 1,000 women as of 1945 and 1955 — Cumulative birth rate for all women 1930 (Q) (ClxExG)	1940 (R) (DlxFxH)	Addition in decade (S) (R-Q)	Number of births in 1930-39 (T) (BxS)	Increase in births Number (U) (T-L)	Percent (V) (Ul-L)	Cumulative first birth rate per 1,000 ever-married women as of 1945 and 1955 — Cumulative birth rate for all women 1930 (Q1) (CxElxG)	1940 (R1) (DxFlxH)	Addition in decade (S1) (R1-Q1)	Number of births in 1930-39 (T1) (BxS1)	Increase in births Number (U1) (T1-L)	Percent (V1) (Ul÷L)
5-9	15-19	114,924	47.2	-38,848	-15.9	...	63	63	348,362	105,062	43.2	...	52	52	287,537	44,237	18.2
10-14	20-24	1,645,350	68.4	-79,326	-3.3	...	626	626	3,321,826	918,012	38.2	...	510	510	2,706,280	302,466	12.6
15-19	25-29	3,530,808	69.1	388,238	7.6	48	1,233	1,185	5,963,984	855,593	16.7	45	1,252	1,207	6,074,708	966,317	18.9
20-24	30-34	3,249,880	64.4	711,012	14.1	611	1,794	1,183	5,354,974	312,336	6.2	462	1,838	1,376	6,228,608	1,185,970	23.5
25-29	35-39	2,001,728	61.1	782,969	23.9	1,369	2,228	859	3,362,130	86,108	2.6	1,224	2,255	1,031	4,035,339	759,317	23.2
30-34	40-44	644,112	33.9	418,108	22.0	1,979	2,570	591	2,107,296	206,807	10.9	1,874	2,465	591	2,107,296	206,807	10.9
35-39	45-49	-8,309	-1.0	118,886	14.2	2,478	2,779	301	984,395	147,169	17.6	2,315	2,563	248	811,063	-26,163	-3.1
40-44	50-54	-39,066	-21.6	33,403	18.5	2,832	2,991	159	441,669	261,113	144.6	2,672	2,655	-17	-47,222	-227,778	-126.2
Total		11,139,427		2,334,442					21,884,636	2,892,200					22,203,609	3,211,173	

Hypothetical: 1930-39 conditions except--

Exact ages at-- Beginning of decade	End of decade	Cumulative birth rate per 1,000 mothers as of 1945 and 1955 — Cumulative birth rate for all women 1930 (Q2) (CxExG1)	1940 (R2) (DxFxH1)	Addition in decade (S2) (R2-Q2)	Number of births in 1930-39 (T2) (BxS2)	Increase in births Number (U2) (T2-L)	Percent (V2) (U2÷L)	Sum of increases in number of births with four separate changes (W) (P+U+U1+U2)	Increase in births due to interaction Number (X) (M-W)	Percent (Y) (X÷L)
5-9	15-19	...	46	46	254,359	11,059	4.5	121,510	-6,586	-2.7
10-14	20-24	...	508	508	2,695,667	291,853	12.1	1,433,005	212,345	8.8
15-19	25-29	49	1,203	1,154	5,807,964	699,573	13.7	2,909,721	621,087	12.2
20-24	30-34	508	1,732	1,224	5,540,565	497,927	9.9	2,707,245	542,635	10.8
25-29	35-39	1,156	2,023	867	3,393,442	117,420	3.6	1,745,814	255,914	7.8
30-34	40-44	1,659	2,142	483	1,722,207	-178,282	-9.4	653,440	-9,328	-0.5
35-39	45-49	2,071	2,263	192	627,920	-209,306	-25.0	30,586	-38,895	-4.6
40-44	50-54	2,400	2,439	39	108,334	-72,222	-40.0	-5,484	-33,582	-18.6
Total					20,150,458	1,158,022		9,595,837	1,543,590	

Source: Columns B and B1, tables of Scripps Foundation; columns C, C1, D, D1, E, E1, F, and F1, table 116; and columns G, G1, H, and H1, computed from table 116. The rates in columns I, I1, J, and J1 agree with those in table 114 except for slight differences due to treatment of decimals.

of births in columns L and L1.   The total numbers of births thus obtained are 18,992,000 for 1930 to 1939 and 30,132,000 for 1945 to 1954, which are smaller by 0.24 and 1.59 percent than the original figures of 19,038,000 and 30,618,000.   The differences occurred primarily because the portion of the 10-year increase in rates which took place during the first half of the decade was given too little weight and the portion which took place during the second half was given too much weight.

The differences are too small to affect appreciably the results under discussion—the relative distribution among the 4 specified variables of the difference between the number of births during 1945 to 1954 and the number during 1930 to 1939.

INDEX

439

Illegitimate births, mothers with annulled marriages, 430
  prevalence of, 284, 431
  treatment of in census and cohort data, 430
Illegitimate children, in census data, 284, 405
  indication of by education, 188
Immigration, annual, 1790–1805, 7
  changing characteristics of, 318
  effect of on natives, 103–105
  effect on fertility ratios, 54, 74
  fertility of immigrants, 1900, 115
  foreigners not naturalized, 1820, 9
  hindered by King of England, 1
  in Colonial period, 8–9
  in period 1820–1950, 2
  of Irish to Massachusetts, 11
  proportion staying permanently, 2
  selectivity of, 105
  temporary addition to population, 9
  trend in, 1825–1914, 105
  vs. natural increase, 1910–1913, 2–3
  Walker theory, 103–105
Income, census procedures on, 262
  fertility ratios by, 274–278
  relation to children ever born, 274–276, 281–283
  selective of employed wives, 275–277
Indianapolis Study, fertility and socio-economic status, 281–283
  other findings from, 347–348, 355
Indians, age at marriage of, 112
  classification problems, 108–109
  education, 112
  fertility of, 109–112
  mixed stock, 110
  number before white men came, 1
Indices of fertility differentials, advantages of, 173
  average deviation by education, 253–255
  average deviation by occupation, 174–175
  by education, 175, 253–261
  by occupation of husband, 173–179
  computation of, 173–174
  occupation and education compared, 175
  relative variations, by education, 255–261
  relative variations, by occupation, 175–179
Infant Enumeration Study, 412–413
Innes, J. W., 116, 123, 180
Intelligence and fertility, 113
Intrinsic rate of natural increase, see Reproduction rates

Jaffe, A. J., 114, 180
Japanese, 110

Jefferson, T., 1, 6
Jews, fertility of, 279–280

Kennedy, J. C. G., 11
King, W. A., 114
Kirk, D., 280
Kiser, C. V., 23, 41, 114–115, 116, 123, 181–182, 279, 281–282, 348, 355

Laborers, see Occupation of husband
Labor force, defined, 262, 417
Labor force status of women, by age, 262–267
  changes in, 272
  color, 262–265
  cumulative fertility by, 264–266
  fertility ratios by, 268–272
  marital status by, 262–264
  selective of childless, 265–266, 272
  urban-rural by, 262–265
Lauriat, P., 186
Life tables, early American, 11
  England and Wales, 1838–54, 10
  Glover's (United States), 1901, 13
  see also Mortality
Lifetime fertility, see Children ever born, Cohort fertility
Literacy, asked before 1940, 183
Lotka, A. J., 37–38
Lutherans, fertility of, 280

McDowell, A. J., 403
Madison County, N. Y., data on children ever born, 116
Managers, see Occupation of husband
Marital status, annulments, 415, 430
  by color, urban-rural, 289
  common-law marriages, 430
  defined, 415–416
  distribution of population by, 284–285, 288–289
  effect of migration on, 100–103
  fertility by detailed, 287–290
  in Colonial times, 53
  labor force status by, 262–264
  percent ever married, by age and education, 184–189
  percent ever married, 1890–1955, 284–287
  presence of husband, 67–68, 87–88
  separation and divorce compared, 288
  spinsters in Colonial times, 53
  urban-rural by size of place, 87–88
Marriage, age at, see Age at first marriage
  among school teachers, 32
  and fertility, 284–304